INSIDERS' GUIDE® SERIES

INSIDERS' GUIDE® TO SAN DIEGO

FIFTH EDITION

MARIBETH MELLIN AND JANE ONSTOTT

INSIDERS' GUIDE®

GUILFORD, CONNECTICUT

AN IMPRINT OF THE GLOBE PEQUOT PRESS

The prices and rates in this guidebook were confirmed at press time. We recommend, however, that you call establishments before traveling to obtain current information.

INSIDERS' GUIDE®

Text design by LeAnna Weller Smith
Maps by XNR Productions, Inc. © Morris Book Publishing, LLC

ISSN: 1533-5224
ISBN-13: 978-0-7627-4191-5
ISBN-10: 0-7627-4191-0

Manufactured in the United States of America
Fifth Edition/First Printing

CONTENTS

Preface . . . xii
Acknowledgments . . . xiv
How to Use This Book . . . 1
Area Overview . . . 4
Getting Here, Getting Around . . . 15
History . . . 27
Hotels and Motels . . . 34
Bed-and-Breakfast Inns . . . 61
Spas and Resorts . . . 67
Vacation Rentals . . . 75
Restaurants . . . 79
Nightlife . . . 102
Shopping . . . 115
Attractions . . . 141
Kidstuff . . . 159
Balboa Park . . . 171
Annual Events . . . 183
The Arts . . . 202
Parks . . . 221
Recreation . . . 230
Beaches and Water Sports . . . 247
Golf . . . 268
Spectator Sports . . . 281
Day Trips . . . 291
South of the Border . . . 300
Relocation . . . 311
Education and Child Care . . . 332
Higher Education . . . 340

Health and Wellness 350
Retirement 359
Media 365
Worship 373
Index 379
About the Authors 397

Directory of Maps

San Diego County v
Central San Diego Region vi
Downtown San Diego vii
North County Coastal Region viii
North County Inland Region ix
East County Region x
South Bay Region xi

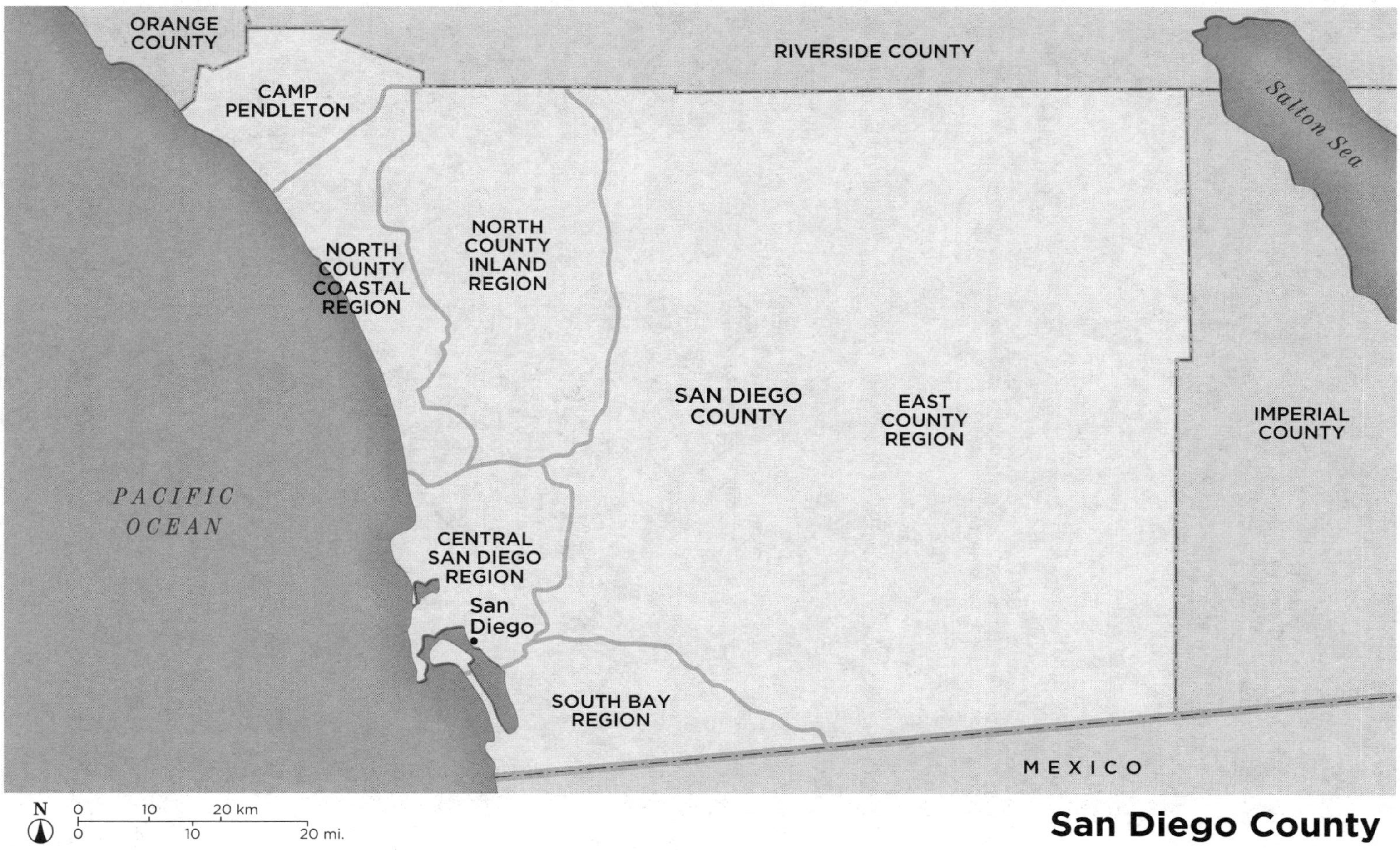

San Diego County

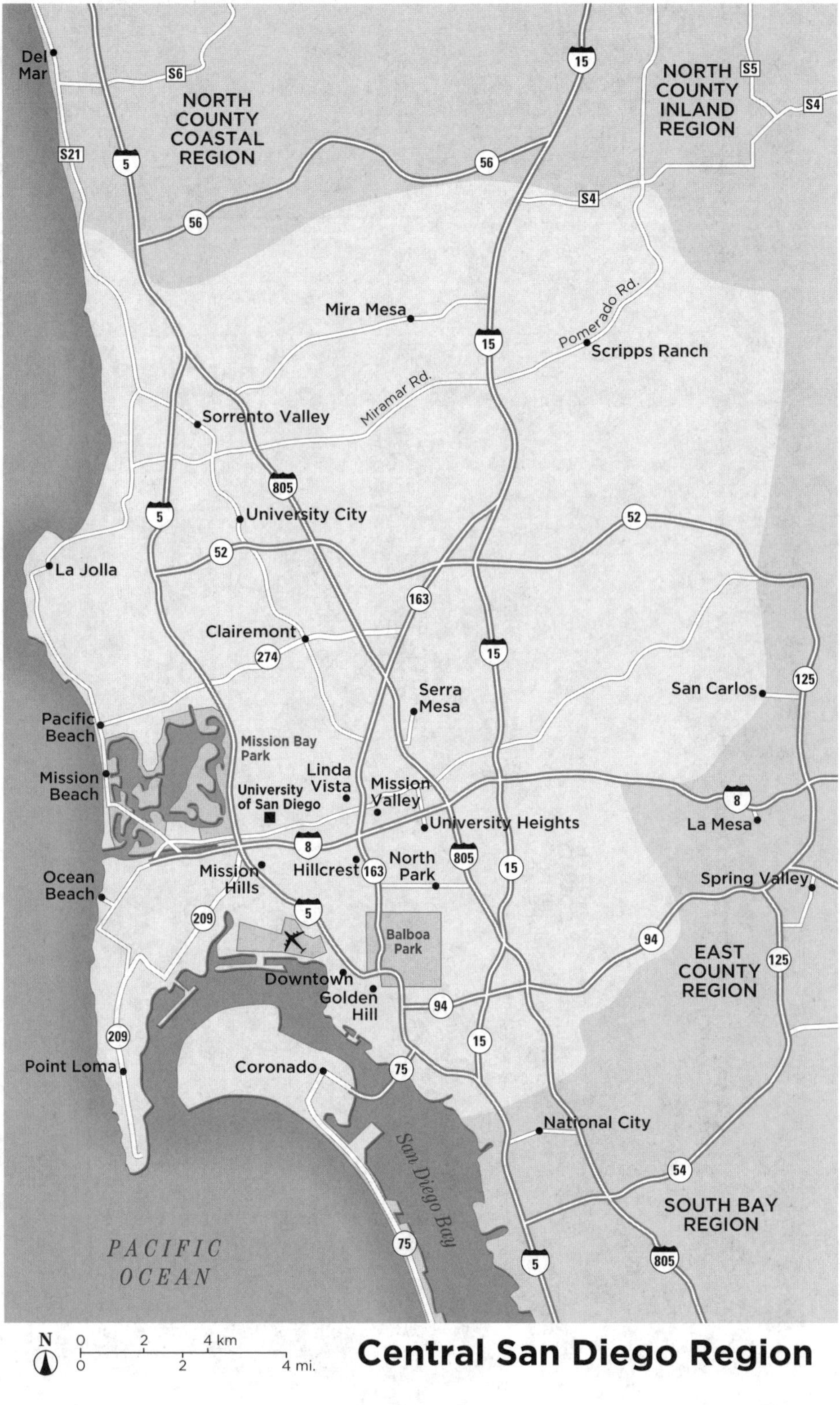
Del Mar
NORTH COUNTY COASTAL REGION
NORTH COUNTY INLAND REGION
S6
S5
S4
S21
5
15
56
Mira Mesa
Pomerado Rd.
Scripps Ranch
Miramar Rd.
Sorrento Valley
805
University City
52
La Jolla
163
Clairemont
274
Serra Mesa
San Carlos
125
Pacific Beach
Mission Bay Park
Mission Beach
Linda Vista
University of San Diego
Mission Valley
8
La Mesa
University Heights
Ocean Beach
Mission Hills
Hillcrest
North Park
Spring Valley
209
Balboa Park
94
EAST COUNTY REGION
Downtown
Golden Hill
Point Loma
Coronado
75
National City
San Diego Bay
54
SOUTH BAY REGION
PACIFIC OCEAN
N
0 2 4 km
0 2 4 mi.

Central San Diego Region

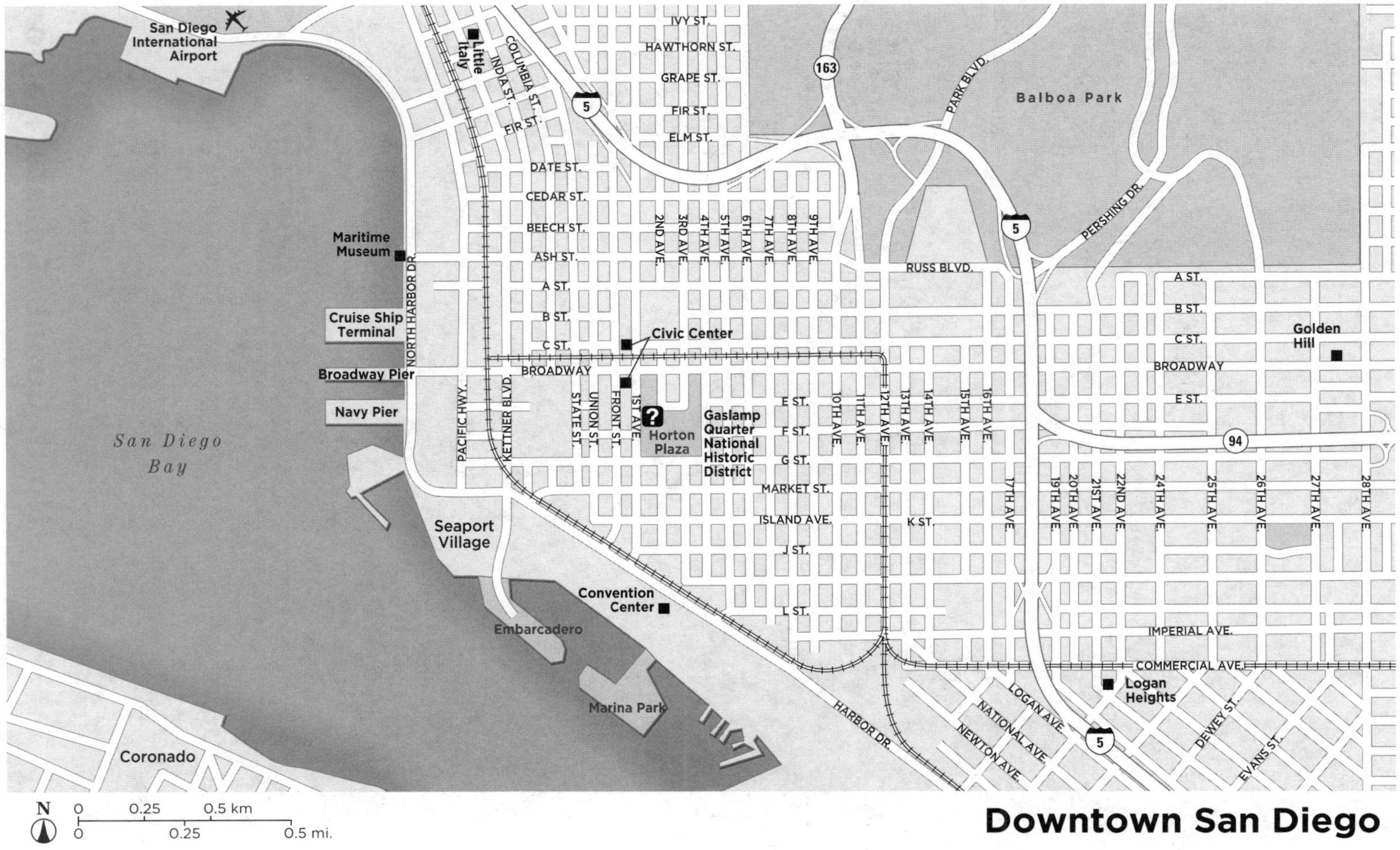

San Diego International Airport
Little Italy
COLUMBIA ST.
INDIA ST.
FIR ST.
IVY ST.
HAWTHORN ST.
GRAPE ST.
FIR ST.
ELM ST.
163
5
PARK BLVD.
Balboa Park
DATE ST.
CEDAR ST.
BEECH ST.
ASH ST.
A ST.
B ST.
C ST.
BROADWAY
2ND AVE.
3RD AVE.
4TH AVE.
5TH AVE.
6TH AVE.
7TH AVE.
8TH AVE.
9TH AVE.
RUSS BLVD.
PERSHING DR.
Maritime Museum
NORTH HARBOR DR.
Cruise Ship Terminal
Civic Center
Broadway Pier
Navy Pier
PACIFIC HWY.
KETTNER BLVD.
STATE ST.
UNION ST.
FRONT ST.
1ST AVE.
Horton Plaza
Gaslamp Quarter National Historic District
E ST.
F ST.
G ST.
MARKET ST.
ISLAND AVE.
J ST.
L ST.
10TH AVE.
11TH AVE.
12TH AVE.
13TH AVE.
14TH AVE.
15TH AVE.
16TH AVE.
K ST.
17TH AVE.
19TH AVE.
20TH AVE.
21ST AVE.
22ND AVE.
24TH AVE.
25TH AVE.
26TH AVE.
27TH AVE.
28TH AVE.
94
Golden Hill
IMPERIAL AVE.
COMMERCIAL AVE.
Logan Heights
LOGAN AVE.
NATIONAL AVE.
NEWTON AVE.
DEWEY ST.
EVANS ST.
HARBOR DR.
San Diego Bay
Seaport Village
Convention Center
Embarcadero
Marina Park
Coronado
N
0 0.25 0.5 km
0 0.25 0.5 mi.

Downtown San Diego

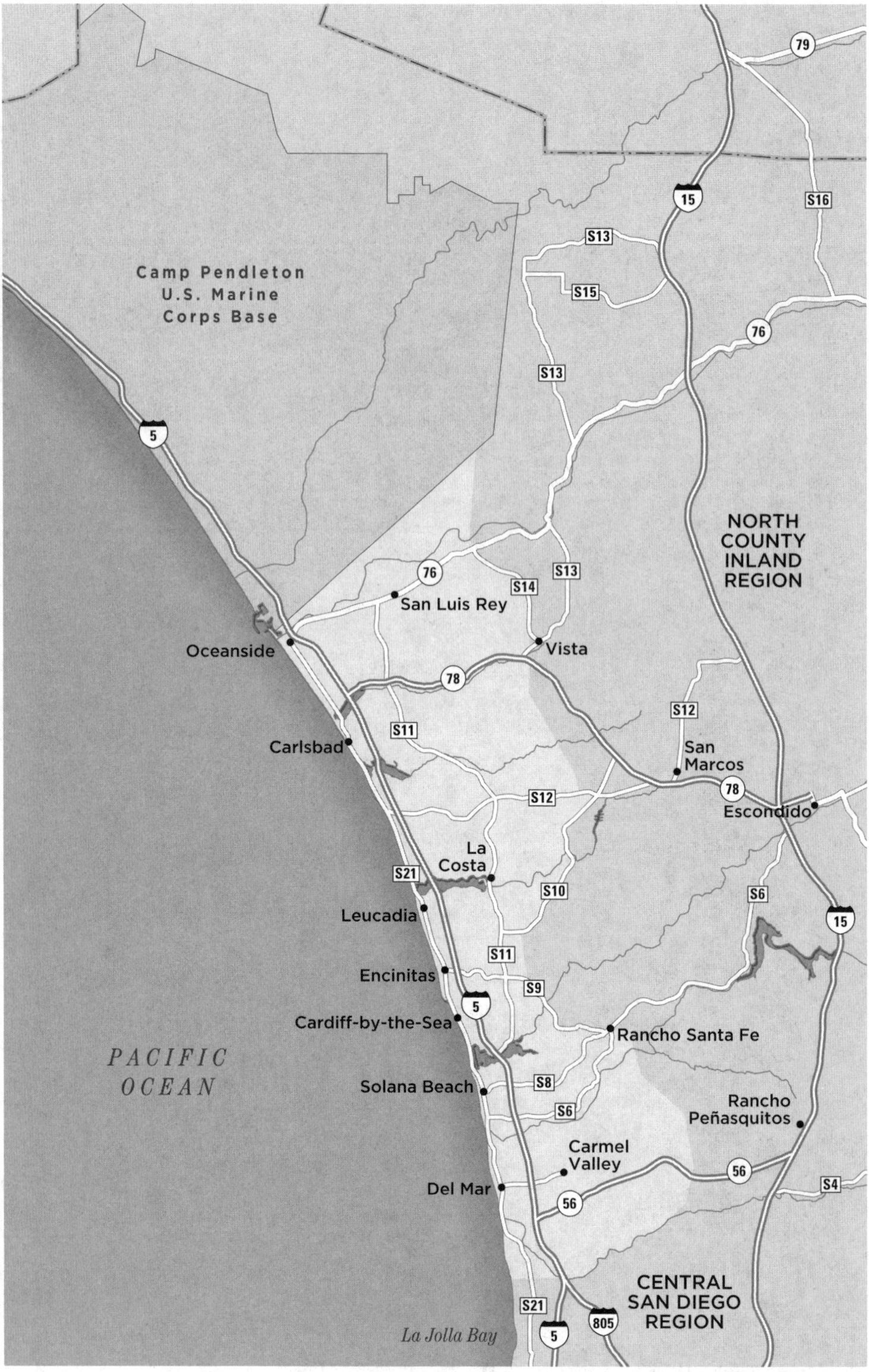
Camp Pendleton
U.S. Marine
Corps Base
NORTH
COUNTY
INLAND
REGION
San Luis Rey
Oceanside
Vista
Carlsbad
San
Marcos
Escondido
La
Costa
Leucadia
Encinitas
Cardiff-by-the-Sea
Rancho Santa Fe
PACIFIC
OCEAN
Solana Beach
Rancho
Peñasquitos
Carmel
Valley
Del Mar
CENTRAL
SAN DIEGO
REGION
La Jolla Bay
N
0 2 4 km
0 2 4 mi.

North County Coastal Region

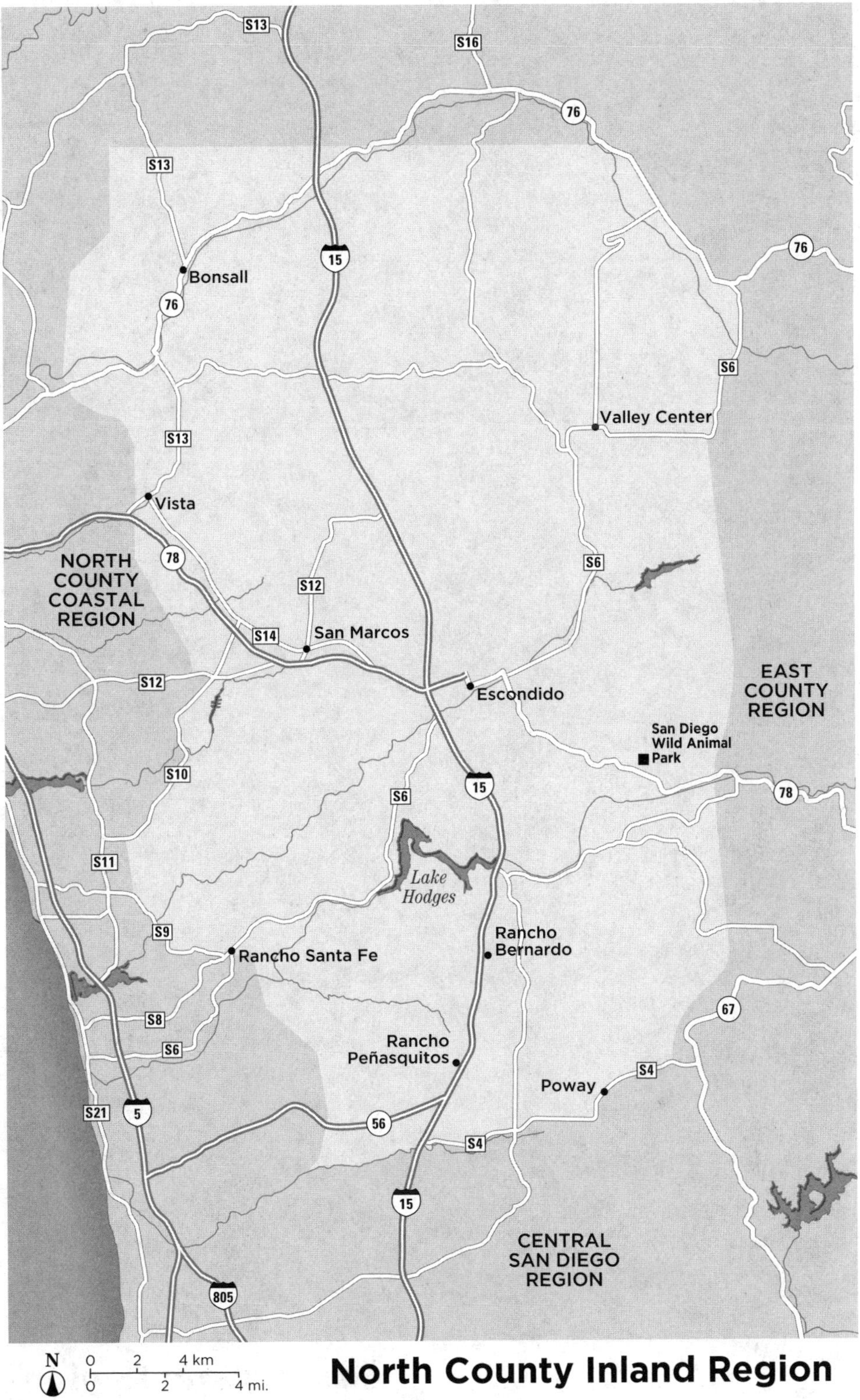

North County Inland Region

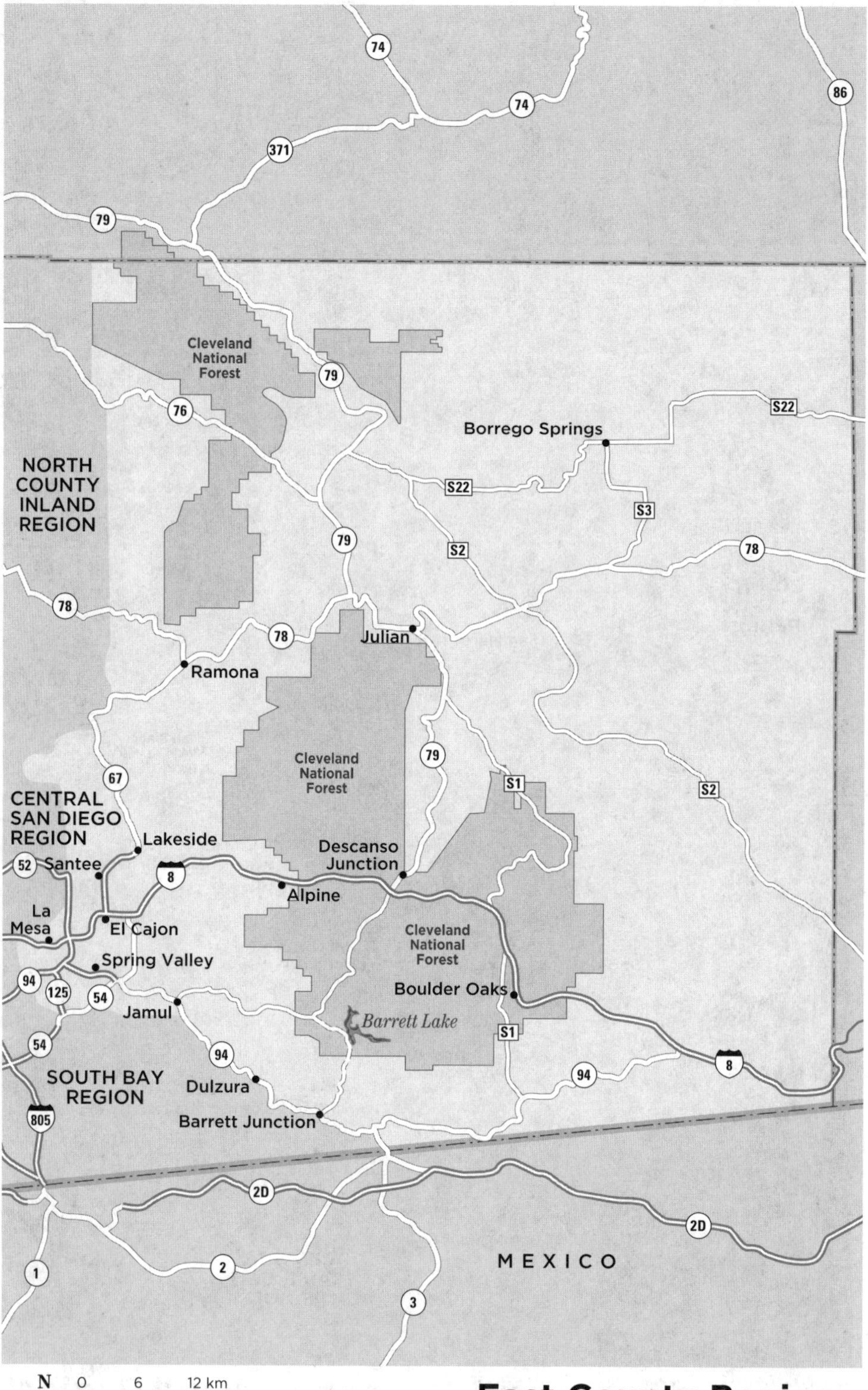

East County Region

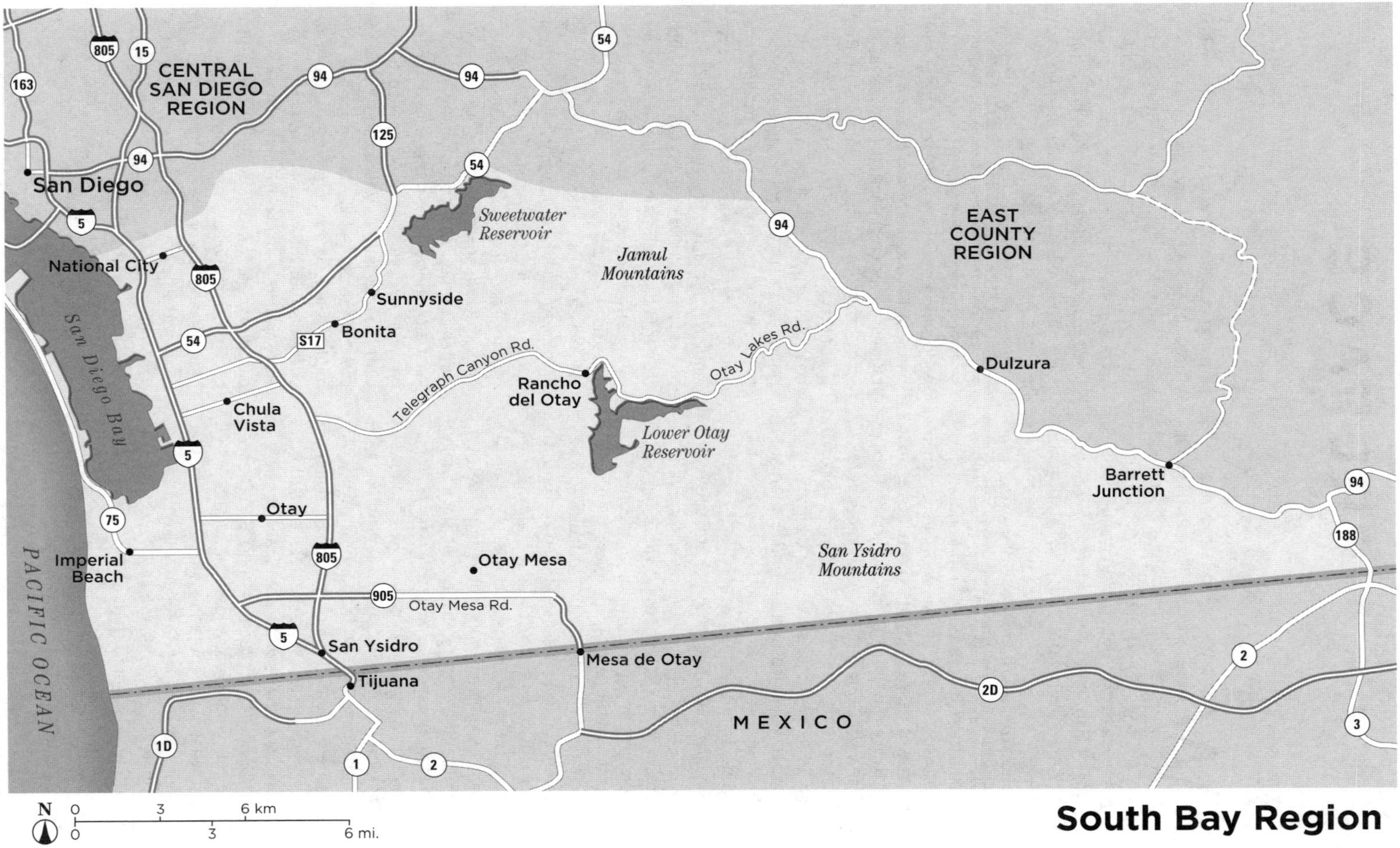

South Bay Region

PREFACE

Welcome to San Diego, aka America's finest cities. Haven't seen the word "cities" showing up in the glossy advertisements? That's because they're only talking about the city of San Diego. As Insiders know, San Diego is much more than one location or destination.

We're inviting you to explore all of the enticing locales that form San Diego County. Stretching south from Camp Pendleton to our international border with Mexico, this is one of the best places in America to visit or to live. On the west you'll find the Pacific Ocean, and lining its shores, interesting communities, each with its own flavor and style. To the east rise several beautiful mountain ranges, and beyond, the Anza-Borrego Desert—stark and eerie and flat—with a beauty all its own.

Like many first-time visitors, you might be a bit surprised by the diversity. Even those of us who live here have to remind ourselves to stray beyond our favorite, most familiar haunts to explore the myriad landscapes that make up our county. You can rough it on a weekend camping trip to unmarked tracts of desert or treat yourself like a queen at a high-end spa. Hang glide above the beach, spot native or migratory birds in the estuaries, or just lie back amid the tall grasses in a riparian forest. Gallop through the mountains on a well-fed horse or dine at a classic country eatery. There's just nothing like San Diego for diversity of scenery and choices of outdoor activities.

Here in San Diego we take recreation seriously. However, it's not all about sweat and sinew, blading and surfing. San Diego County also has boatloads of cultural activities. Our reputation is for being laid-back rather than high-energy like Los Angeles or cutting-edge like New York. But our easygoing spirit doesn't keep us from being ambitious. In San Diego you'll find biotech and telecommunications firms sharing economic indicator statistics with the military, tourism, and agriculture. Together with a substantial artistic community, these San Diego players contribute to one of the country's most eclectic lifestyles and cultures. And we work, play, study, and create under a cerulean blue sky in a perfect climate.

On any given day, San Diego offers a smorgasbord of possibilities. You might start your day with a sunrise walk along a wide sandy beach, with a stop at a surfer hangout for a kicked-back breakfast. Your biggest problem? Whether to order a spicy breakfast burrito or yogurt with fresh fruit and granola—not to mention which beautiful beach to walk on and at which patio restaurant to cool your heels. You might spend the day inspired by sunshine and the scent of sage in the lonely desert. And, not to put too fine a point on our diversity, you could end the evening with dinner in the mountains under a firmament of stars. If there's one thing San Diego does not lack, it's variety.

We can offer a choice of weather, too. For those folks who actually like to shovel snow (or at least play in it), San Diego County encompasses towns that experience the four seasons. That's right. Every winter our mountain communities get at least a dusting—if not more—of winter white. If you prefer wearing cool cotton clothing and sandals year-round, that's just the uniform some folks have adopted. You might have to dress up a bit for your boss or clients, but then it's back to the shorts and sandals. In general, clothing here is casual, except for the few occasions when grown-up clothes are required. Weddings, funerals, and the opera spring to mind, but even at the opera you'll see the range of tastes and fashion statements that mark San Diego as unique.

With so much to offer, it's no surprise that tourism is a mainstay of our economy. Visitors from the north and east flock here in winter to escape harsher climes. "Zonies" head for the sea during summer, when temperatures in their home state of Arizona soar to unbearable highs. But no matter where you're from, you'll not feel like an outsider. Although most don't like to admit it, relatively few San Diegans are natives themselves. Most of us weren't born here, truth be told, but selected the county as the place to live, go to school, or raise a family because we like it here.

So you're coming to San Diego, or you live here, and you want to explore. The Day Trips chapter offers great getaways, including sunny Palm Springs and Temecula's wine country. If you want to just relax, the Spas and Resorts chapter can direct you to a place where you can tune up your body and unburden your mind. And if you're bringing along your sweetie, the Bed-and-Breakfast Inns chapter can help you find the perfect romantic getaway.

Welcome to San Diego. It's a great place to visit and the best place to call home. But maybe we should just keep that to ourselves.

ACKNOWLEDGMENTS

We would like to thank Rhiannon Toth, Susan Humphrey, Elizabeth Ranta, San Diego North Convention and Visitors Bureau, Joe Timko, Junvi Ola, and everyone at the San Diego Convention and Visitors Bureau for their contributions to this book.

HOW TO USE THIS BOOK ?

Most visitors and residents think of San Diego in regions. San Diego County is so large (4,255 square miles) that it has to be broken down into more manageable areas. We refer to them as Central San Diego, North County Coastal, North County Inland, East County, and South Bay.

The actual city of San Diego includes the spectacular buildings and gorgeous harbor you may have seen if you arrived at San Diego International Airport, locally known as Lindbergh Field. For our purposes the Central San Diego area includes Downtown, the Gaslamp Quarter, Mission Hills, Hillcrest, several beach communities, Coronado, La Jolla, the Golden Triangle, and some inland communities. Some Insiders will bristle at the divisions. It's tough to slice a perfect pie. Our goal with the format was to make it easy for newcomers and tourists to get around.

To make it easier to locate what you want and need in San Diego County, we've broken the outer regions into the four smaller areas noted above. These are the labels Insiders use, so you'll see and hear these areas referred to in the newspaper, on television, and in conversations.

Think of the regions as making a half-circle around the core of our county. Out of the city proper we move north, up the coast using Interstate 5, to North County Coastal. This area includes the beach communities that touch or are close to the Pacific Ocean. Included are the communities of Rancho Santa Fe, Del Mar, Solana Beach, Cardiff, Encinitas (with its neighborhood region called Leucadia), La Costa, Carlsbad, and Oceanside.

East of the ocean is the region we called North County Inland. It includes the communities of Vista, San Marcos, Escondido, Fallbrook, Valley Center, Bonsall, Rancho Bernardo, Rancho Peñasquitos, and Poway.

The next region is East County. For our purposes it includes the cities of La Mesa, Lemon Grove, Spring Valley, El Cajon, Santee, Bonita, Lakeside, and Alpine. East County also embraces the mountain towns of Pine Valley, Ramona, and Julian and spreads farther to the desert area of Borrego Springs.

Completing the scene is the South Bay area. It includes Chula Vista, National City, Imperial Beach, and San Ysidro, the communities close to the border between the United States and Mexico. Because much of our region is bicultural, you'll find information and recommendations on activities, shopping, accommodations, and dining for Mexico in our chapter titled South of the Border.

When organizing the book we followed the outline of these natural regions. It made sense. There were exceptions, of course. Sometimes, such as in the chapter Higher Education, we've listed colleges and universities by category. Beaches and Water Sports and our Media chapters are also organized by categories.

Even if your family has been in California since the gold rush days, you'll enjoy reading the History chapter to get the full scope of San Diego. It will give you a feel for San Diego's terrain, our traditions, and our colorful and somewhat checkered past. In the Area Overview we bring you up to date on our industries, cultural activities, distinct population, role in the international marketplace, and close bonds with Mexico.

Annual events are listed with month-by-month notations. If you're visiting San Diego County in the summer, you may want to find out about the Carlsbad Spring Faire. If you're here during the December holidays, you won't want to miss Balboa Park December Nights. These events are just examples of the many possibilities we've listed.

You'll notice by looking at the table of contents that we've devoted separate chapters to Golf, Spas and Resorts, Retirement, and Balboa Park. These are "big ticket items" in our county and make us unique. In Balboa Park alone, you can find museums, plays, and concerts along with the world-famous San Diego Zoo and its treasure trove of botanical exhibits. As longtime residents of San Diego, we know that you can't devote just one afternoon to our Balboa Park. It deserves repeat visits.

To make this book really useful, we've cross-referenced places and events. We've tried to keep repetition to a minimum but have allowed some duplication of entries to save you the trouble of flipping back and forth. For example, a great picnic area might be mentioned in the Parks chapter and in the Kidstuff chapter. Each entry will probably be slightly different depending on its placement. For example, the entry in Kidstuff might include the fact that this is the site of Easter egg and candy hunts for youngsters. Check the index if you want to read everything on a particular site.

The book's regional divisions and cross-referenced entries should make it easy for you to find the closest bed-and-breakfast inn, Asian grocery store, Cinco de Mayo fiesta, or beach. Keep in mind that Insiders never blink at traveling across the county for dinner, to visit a theater, or to attend a festival or event. For instance, when snowflakes sprinkle Mount Laguna, San Diegans often take off to let the kids (of all ages) play in the snow. For those of us living on the coast, it's a fun drive that's well worth the time. Since we feel that all of San Diego is our backyard, distance isn't an obstacle. Don't make it one for you.

Our roads and highways are clearly marked and referred to locally by number. As an example you'll hear people say, "Take 5 to 78 and then 15." Translated that means to go north on I-5 to U.S. Highway 78, which begins in Carlsbad and takes travelers to the North County Inland area. After about 20 miles, US 78 easily merges with Interstate 15, and the signs are large and noticeable.

When navigating the county by car, we recommend buying a map. Most bookstores have them. Maps are also available at the Transit Store, 102 Broadway. The Transit Store is on the northeast corner of First Avenue and Broadway, and the phone numbers are (619) 234-1060 and (619) 233-3004 (for bus routes). They're open Monday through Friday 8:30 A.M. to 5:30 P.M., Saturday and Sunday noon to 4:00 P.M.

Parking isn't a big problem in the county, except at the beaches. However, if you're attending a well-publicized event, parade, or a Chargers football game, you could be in for a short hike. Remember, sneakers are acceptable here; comfortable clothes are the fashion choice for most San Diegans.

Throughout the book distances and times are given from the downtown area of San Diego, traveling on multilane freeways and highways, unless noted otherwise. Allow about 20 minutes to get from the downtown hotels to Del Mar. Rush hours and the occasional rainstorm always play a role in the time it takes to get anywhere. So if you're meeting friends after work in Solana Beach (North County Coastal) and it's stormy, give yourself extra time. Yes, there are traffic jams even in Paradise.

A few words on our area codes. It doesn't take a rocket scientist to notice that the region is booming. (Although we have plenty of scientists in the area.) With a recent influx of high-tech firms and high-tech folks, we finally stretched the limits of our area codes. As we go to press, we have four area codes for the county, so next to each telephone listing you'll find the area code along with the phone number. A fifth may be added soon.

Now for addresses. We provide street addresses, where available, to help you find your way around. Reading the Getting Here, Getting Around chapter will help you further, by identifying some of San Diego's major districts. Once you know those, you can take a shuttle from the airport to the Gaslamp Quarter, for example, by asking for it by name. No numbered address is needed, unless you want to go to a specific building in the area.

Throughout the chapters we've included Insiders' Tips (indicated by i) for quick insights. These are recommendations you won't find in tour books and are guaranteed to make your visit or move here more enjoyable or memorable. The Close-ups will let you meet the people and places that make the area exceptional.

We hope you'll make this book your own. We wrote it for you. You might want to keep it in your desk for daydreaming or trip-planning purposes. You could put it in your briefcase to study during your morning commute or your flight into Lindbergh Field. Or add it to the glove box of your car when you're maneuvering around San Diego.

Use highlighting pens, sticky notes, and corner folds on the pages to plan an itinerary, a weekend, a holiday adventure, or your future. You've already started to feel comfortable here because, at this very moment, all of San Diego is at your fingertips.

AREA OVERVIEW

When the Census of 2000 was completed, San Diego lost its ranking as the sixth-largest city in the United States. Phoenix took over that position, and San Diego became the nation's seventh-largest city. Guess what? That doesn't bother San Diegans a bit. It's not a sign that things have taken a turn for the worse. In fact, just the opposite is true. The economy is relatively strong, jobs are available, crime is less prevalent than in other large cities, and the weather is still balmy. All it means is that Phoenix is growing faster than San Diego and suffering from the drawbacks of rapid development.

San Diegans have always appreciated quality over quantity, and while all reports indicate continued population growth, city leaders prefer to be ready for it. Predictions are that the next 20 years will bring about a million newcomers to San Diego, and those already here are taking steps to ensure that the same quality of life they now enjoy will be preserved for generations to come.

In spite of the city's burgeoning reputation as a major player in international business, and in spite of the fact that it continues to grow on a dozen different levels, it still somehow preserves its low-key, laid-back image right alongside its more polished one.

REGIONS

Describing San Diego geographically can sometimes be a challenge. It's a city, but within that city are more than 100 separate, identifiable neighborhoods. It's also a county. And within San Diego County are 18 incorporated cities (including the city of San Diego) and many more unincorporated towns and communities. The county stretches south from the Orange County line all the way to the U.S.–Mexico border.

The rhythm of life is a little faster in downtown San Diego, which boasts hotels, restaurants, and nightlife. PHOTO: COURTESY OF BRET SHOAF

Its western boundary is the Pacific Ocean, and its eastern reaches include the Laguna Mountains and the Anza-Borrego Desert.

When locals try to describe where they live, they usually tack a few qualifiers onto the end of their description. Someone living in the tiny northern town of Jesmond Dene, for example, would say "I live in Jesmond Dene, a little town in North County, near Escondido." Or even if their hometown is within the city limits, it occasionally needs a bit more information to pinpoint its location. "I come from Nestor. It's in San Diego, in the South Bay." Even though residents of every locale within the boundaries of the county feel enormous pride for their neighborhood, sometimes it's just simpler to say we all live in San Diego.

To make things easier for you to understand, we've separated the county into five regions: Central San Diego, North County Coastal, North County Inland, East County, and the South Bay. The lines separating the regions are blurry in places, and some locals may disagree about which region, in fact, contains their neighborhood. But each region has different characteristics that give it a definable flavor all its own. As you travel around the county, you'll soon discover that San Diego is indeed a complex place. And we have little doubt that you'll like what you find.

As of 2004, the average commuter spends 26 minutes getting to work each day; however, many commuters deal with longer drives. Carpooling is encouraged; many freeways have diamond lanes for cars with two or more occupants. To avoid frustration (and road rage), allow extra time for heavy traffic.

Central San Diego

It would be easy to say that the city of San Diego is the center of all the action. That may have been true at one time, but not anymore. Everything that makes San Diego a great place to visit and an even greater place to live can be found in other regions. But Central San Diego is still the heart of the county, the metropolitan center where the largest concentration of people live. From the lazy, sun-soaked beaches to the no-nonsense high-tech companies in Sorrento Valley; from the nightlife of the Gaslamp Quarter to the bedroom communities nestled inland, Central San Diego has it all.

The rhythm of life is a little faster around downtown than in other regions of the county. A good number of the major businesses are located within the city limits. If you fly into Lindbergh Field, San Diego's international airport, you'll notice that you're almost downtown already. Of course, you probably figured that out while your plane was making its hair-raising descent through the maze of high-rises.

Central San Diego has several major business areas. Downtown has the convention center; dozens of hotels, restaurants, and nightspots; and a high concentration of banks and law firms. Mission Valley, running east from just shy of the coast, has two major shopping malls and several smaller shopping centers. It has also become a popular neighborhood for newcomers, with numerous condo and apartment complexes. And the hotels in Mission Valley are popular with travelers who are more concerned with convenience than scenery. The Golden Triangle, Sorrento Valley, and Rancho Bernardo are where the high-tech, biotech, and telecommunications firms congregate, along with a growing enclave in Carlsbad. The streets of Miramar and Mira Mesa are lined with furniture, appliance, and computer stores and warehouses.

The neighborhoods within the city limits are defined by several factors. Downtown and Hillcrest are urbane and trendy; Golden Hill and Bankers' Hill are experiencing a regentrification boom;

San Diego Vital Statistics

Mayor/governor: Mayor Jerry Sanders/Governor Arnold Schwarzenegger

Capital/major cities/outlying counties:
Sacramento/Los Angeles, San Francisco/Los Angeles County to the north, Riverside-San Bernardino County to the northeast, Imperial County to the east

Population: City: 1.3 million, county: 3.017 million

Area (sq. miles): City of San Diego: 320 sq. miles, County of San Diego: 4,621 sq. miles

Nickname/motto: America's Finest City

Average temperatures (high/low): July: 76/65, January: 65/48

Average rain/days of sunshine: Rain: 10.3 inches annually/sunny days per year: 249

Founded: 1850

Major universities: University of California, San Diego; San Diego State University; University of San Diego; California State University, San Marcos

Important date in history: September 28, 1542 (Cabrillo landed in San Diego Bay)

Major area private employers: Sharp HealthCare, Scripps Health, Kaiser Permanente San Diego

Famous sons and daughters: Baseball legend Ted Williams, actors Gregory Peck and Cliff Robertson, actress Annette Bening, Ted Geisel (Dr. Seuss)

State/city holidays: All national holidays; schools close for California Admission Day, September 9

Toll roads/major airports/major interstates:
San Diego-Coronado Bay Bridge (toll-free)

North Park and Normal Heights are mixed residential and business neighborhoods in the process of reinventing themselves. Ocean, Pacific, and Mission Beaches are just what you'd expect: casual beach communities where businesses post signs asking customers to wear shoes and shirts. Mission Valley, the Golden Triangle, and the College area, which are close to universities, tend to have lots of twenty-something residents. La Jolla is inhabited by an upscale population who can afford multimillion-dollar ocean-view homes. For purposes of this book, we have included all the neighborhoods south of Del Mar, north of Chula Vista, and west of La Mesa in the Central San Diego region. For detailed descriptions of the neighborhoods and cities within the entire San Diego County, check out our Relocation chapter.

North County Coastal

Stretching north from Del Mar to Oceanside, San Diego's North County Coastal region has some of the area's prettiest beaches, offbeat clubs and cafes, clusters of interior design businesses, and its own collection of emerging high-tech and manufacturing headquarters. In short, North County Coastal has just about everything Central San Diego has—even

San Diego International Airport (Lindbergh Field)
Interstates 5, 8, 15, and 805

Public transportation: Amtrak, Coaster, Trolley, Bus, Taxi

Military bases (in order from most personnel to fewest): Marine Corps Base Camp Pendleton, Oceanside; Naval Station, San Diego; Naval Air Station North Island, Coronado; Marine Corps Air Station, Miramar; Naval Amphibious Base, Coronado; Point Loma Naval Base; Naval Medical Center, San Diego; Marine Corps Recruit Depot San Diego; Space and Naval Weapons Systems Command (SPAWAR), San Diego; Naval Weapons Station, Fallbrook; Naval Outlying Landing Field, Imperial Beach

Driving laws: Seat belts–yes, car seats–yes, speed limit–65 mph, wipers/headlights–no, HOV lanes–2+ per vehicle

Alcohol laws: age 21; DUI Limit: .08; alcohol available in liquor stores, convenience stores, supermarkets, drug stores 7 days a week; bars open until 2:00 A.M.

Daily newspapers: *San Diego Union-Tribune, North County Times*

Sales tax: 7.75% on everything but most foods

Room tax/meal tax: Room tax is 10.5%/meal tax is same as sales tax, 7.75%

Chamber of commerce:

San Diego Regional Chamber of Commerce
402 West Broadway, San Diego
(619) 544-1300; www.sdchamber.org

Time/weather: (619) 853-1212/(858) 675-8706

its own airport. You can catch regular commuter flights to Los Angeles, Phoenix, or Las Vegas from Palomar Airport in Carlsbad.

Also in Carlsbad, behind the rainbow of flower fields visible from Interstate 5, is an explosion of new office complexes. Numerous businesses moving into San Diego have chosen Carlsbad as their base. This ever-growing business community has provided an economic shot in the arm to North County Coastal as well as the rest of the county.

Houses in beach communities such as Del Mar, Solana Beach, and Encinitas command some of the most spectacular views in California. A few miles inland, interspersed among thousands of eucalyptus trees, is the village of Rancho Santa Fe. Here you find sprawling estates, a gentrified country atmosphere, and some of the most expensive real estate in the United States.

Drive around North County Coastal for a few hours and you'll see why this region has grown so quickly in recent years. In the first place, there was land to develop. Housing developments have sprouted up all over canyons and fields, creating full-fledged communities with schools and businesses in Carmel Valley, Rancho Peñasquitos, La Costa, and other areas. Access to the coast makes it desirable, as does the abundance of new businesses.

It's just like Central San Diego—only newer, farther away from downtown, with more of a vacation attitude. Those differences give it its own special charm.

North County Inland

Continuing the circle of San Diego County, we come to North County Inland. Home to the cities of Vista, San Marcos, Escondido, and Poway, North County Inland also has smaller communities with such charming names as Harmony Grove and the Elfin Forest. These are not misnomers, either. Trees, chaparral, horses, and hiking trails are abundant, and life has a decidedly more rural flavor.

As more and more people gravitate to San Diego, many have found their way to North County Inland, where housing tends to be more affordable and traditional family neighborhoods are more common than in Central San Diego. Many residents commute to Central San Diego for work, preferring the more relaxed atmosphere of the northern region over the hustle and bustle of San Diego.

An emerging trend in North County Inland is to live, work, and play within the confines of the region. Many residents have moved or started their businesses close to home, avoiding the commute altogether and taking advantage of the quality of life in the northeastern reaches of the county.

The communities are a good mix of folks who have been around for a couple of generations and young families just starting out. Families are drawn to North County Inland for another reason, too: top-notch schools. Poway High School, for instance, has one of the highest percentages of graduates in the county who go on to college.

East County

Largest in terms of physical area, East County includes the suburban communities and cities just east of the San Diego city limits, the Laguna Mountains, the Cuyamaca Mountains, Palomar Mountain, and the desert city of Borrego Springs. East County is where you'll find the hottest temperatures during the summer months and the coldest in wintertime.

East County is even more rural than North County Inland. Many residents there share their neighborhoods with farm animals and country-western bars. And if you're looking for the ultimate cowboy hat or the perfect pair of boots, you're in the right place.

But don't let the casually rugged appearance of some of the inhabitants fool you. Hidden treasures of a most sophisticated nature abound in the region. The East County Performing Arts organization in El Cajon stages a variety of wonderfully entertaining productions every year. The annual Oktoberfest in La Mesa draws folks from all over the county. And the Palomar Observatory, in the mountains, is a magnet for international professional and amateur astronomers. Borrego Springs, located in the desert east of San Diego's mountains, is home to one of the most venerated resorts in the county, La Casa del Zorro (see our Hotels and Motels chapter for a detailed description).

East County has more than its share of pleasures. Give the residents credit for having figured out how to enjoy the best of both worlds. They have the serenity of the quiet life, but the lights of the big city are only a short drive away.

South Bay

At the southernmost end of the county, the South Bay has beautiful beaches and great neighborhoods. By now you've noticed that's not unique within the county. But South Bay does have something that no other region can claim: an international border. Only 20 minutes from downtown San Diego, the U.S.-Mexico border is the gateway to Baja California and a whole different set of experiences, which you'll find described in our South of the Border chapter.

Even locals are surprised to learn that within the entire county, South Bay's Chula Vista is one of the fastest growing population centers in the country. Chula Vista is also home to BF Goodrich Aerospace (formerly called Rohr Industries), an aircraft manufacturer.

As the county's population slowly spreads to outlying regions, the South Bay has not been ignored. As in North County Inland, many young neighborhoods, such as EastLake and Otay Ranch, are springing up to complement the older ones, including National City, Imperial Beach, and San Ysidro, and home prices are among the most affordable in the county.

Several attractions draw visitors and residents to South Bay. The Olympic Training Center is a hub for international athletes. The Coors Amphitheater, a 20,000-seat outdoor amphitheater, has become the most popular venue for the biggest concert stars. As with San Diego's other regions, the South Bay is constantly looking to the future and finding ways to make its little corner of paradise even better.

GOVERNMENT

Describing the structure of government is almost as confusing as describing the geography of San Diego, but if you remember the cities and the regions within the county, you'll have a pretty good idea of the various governments, which tend to follow those same separations. The city of San Diego has a mayor and an eight-member city council, which represents eight different areas within the city limits. The 17 other incorporated cities within the county also have mayors and city councils.

Representing the entire county is a board of supervisors, composed of five elected members who represent areas that generally correspond to the regional divisions we use here. Even those hardy souls who live in the most remote speck on the county map still have an elected official representing their interests.

To learn more about San Diego's politics and government, visit the city's Web site at www.sannet.gov, or check out the county's at www.co.san-diego.ca.us. For information on the county's many communities, go to www.sandiego-links.com.

DEMOGRAPHICS

To give you an idea of the geographic reach of San Diego, it lies in the southwest corner of California, 120 miles south of the city of Los Angeles. The city of San Diego encompasses an area of 320 square miles; add in the other four regions, and the area of the entire county jumps to 4,621 square miles. The population of the city is about 1.3 million, while the county's numbers remain around 3.017 million.

Like most other major cities in the United States, San Diego's "minority" population has increased significantly in recent years, especially because of its proximity to the U.S.-Mexico border. Estimates are that the county population will increase to 3.8 million by 2020, with a Hispanic composition of about 33 percent.

In addition to being the seventh-largest city in the country and the third-largest county in California, San Diego is the second-largest city in California, behind Los Angeles. Living in the shadow of that megalopolis to the north has been both a blessing and a curse. National newspapers and magazines tend to overlook San Diego in favor of Los Angeles. When something newsworthy happens in La Jolla or Rancho Santa Fe, it will often be referred to by the national press as "a community south of Los Angeles."

Even though locals bristle at that kind

Downtown San Diego is easy to explore. PHOTO: COURTESY OF BRETT SHOAF

of liberal manipulation of county lines, there's a certain quiet satisfaction in believing that their city still has an aura of secrecy about it. It's not that we mind sharing it with visitors, we just prefer to keep it as quiet as possible. No one wants to spoil a good thing.

INDUSTRY AND JOBS

Ask an Insider what the top industry is in San Diego and the likely response will be, with hardly a pause, "Tourism." Sometimes even Insiders can be wrong. Although tourism is a driving force in San Diego's economy, it's not number one. It's not even number two. San Diego's industries rank as follows: manufacturing, military defense, and then tourism followed by agriculture.

From the early days, manufacturing has been a leader in supporting the local economy. The types of goods produced have shifted in the past decade, however. The aerospace industry used to be the giant in town, and it still is strong. The local defense industry accounts for more than 18 percent of the county's gross domestic product and creates several billion dollars in contract work for local companies. And San Diego has shipyards large enough to build and repair the navy's huge ships. But other industries are coming to the forefront. San Diego's top three private-sector employers are all involved in computer software or telecommunications.

The biggest mover and shaker, Qualcomm, is San Diego's leading technology industry, employing 5,000 San Diegans. The homegrown software company has become a visible force in the local community. The football stadium even carries its name.

Life Science is an umbrella term for biotech companies and their medical device partners, the former producing mainly pharmaceuticals and the latter such things as pacemakers and prosthetics. San Diego is one of the nation's most important regions for biomedical companies, employing nearly 39,000 people. In 2005 the San Diego Regional Chamber of Commerce estimated the biotech impact on the local economy at $8.5 billion.

San Diego's next largest employers by sector are computer/electronics manufacturers, which employ 30,500 people, and the communications industry, employing more than 29,000 workers. All of these "sexy" (to use an industry term) corporations are highly sought after by communities as they are high-paying industries that attract top people; also relatively nonpolluting, they don't destroy forests or other natural resources.

Despite the high cost of living, these and other research and development companies have flocked to San Diego. This is thanks to (in addition to the weather and attractive lifestyle) the intellectual resources of our excellent research facilities, such as The Salk Institute and Scripps Research Institute, and of our many institutes of higher education. The San Diego Super Computer Center at University of California, San Diego (UCSD) has some of the fastest computers in the world—a valuable resource for research teams. More than a third of San Diego's 500-plus biomedical companies have their origins in local research institutions and universities. Many have launched international searches and are stuffing employment packages with perks to try to lure engineers, researchers, and technicians to San Diego.

Despite rising tension revolving around the issues of illegal immigration, San Diego and its neighbor to the south enjoy financial as well as cultural and historic ties. Vigorous trade between the two countries helps bolster the ever-growing maquiladora industry. Maquiladoras are companies with offices and manufacturing facilities both within Mexico and outside its borders, many in the United States.

The military remains a strong contributor to the economy, pumping nearly $13.4 billion annually into the local economy, with another $10.4 billion indirect fiscal impact. Tourism, even though it ranks third, will never be underappreciated. The number of overnight visitors in San Diego reached 26.7 million in 2004; they spent some $55 billion. Nearly 110,000 San Diegans work in fields directly related to the tourist industry, including lodging, food service, attractions, and transportation. A large proportion of the new jobs created in San Diego are in the service-producing industries and in wholesale and retail trade.

New communities rise up and highways appear with amazing frequency, and maps are quickly outdated. Be sure to get the most current edition of any map you purchase.

The construction industry continues strong. Its growth seems to be limited only by the amount of available land for new homes. With an annual growth rate of 8.4 percent between 2000 and 2005, and no end in sight, the demand for homes continues and the construction industry employs some 74,000 workers.

The median household income for San Diegans is $64,355. Many San Diegans work more than one job just to keep up with the high cost of living in this place many see as their personal paradise. Fortunately, unemployment is at its lowest rate in four decades, down to 3.8 precent in the year 2005. There are plenty of jobs to be had, and many exciting opportunities for training in cutting-edge fields.

COST OF LIVING

There's a price to be paid for living in a paradise where the weather's great, jobs are plentiful, and attitudes are casual. The cost of living in San Diego is undeniably higher than in many other cities, and the main reason is real estate. Real estate has traditionally been the barometer of the local economy, rising and falling with the fortune of the rest of the city. However, even at its lowest, real estate is rarely a bargain in California's southernmost cul-de-sac. Housing prices fluctuate, of course, but the median price of a detached, single-family house in March 2006 was $580,000 and climbing. San Diego ranks 245.1 in cost of living for housing compared to Raleigh, North Carolina at 80.4 and San Francisco at 304.8. (The national average is 100.)

CLOSE-UP

SANDAG Helps Make Sense of It All

Think about it: 18 incorporated cities exist within the county of San Diego. That's 18 mayors, city councils, and cities full of citizens fiercely protective of their quality of life within their geographic limits. Add another layer of government, the county board of supervisors, which is responsible for the 5 geographic regions that encompass all 18 cities. How in the world do they all get along?

The answer is SANDAG. Although the name conjures up pictures of some critter burrowing in the sand, SANDAG is actually a serious organization dedicated to facilitating the smooth flow of cooperation and understanding among the cities and regions of San Diego. Formally known as the San Diego Association of Governments, SANDAG is a forum for regional decision-making. Its goal is to build consensus among the various governments of San Diego County when it comes time to making decisions about strategic planning and allocation of resources.

Who runs SANDAG? That's where the brilliance of the association is most evident. The very people who oversee the cities and the county regions are the same people who make up SANDAG. Mayors, council members, and county supervisors from all 18 cities are the voting members of SANDAG's board of directors. Representatives from other agencies, including the U.S. Department of Defense (the military has long been influential in San Diego because of its strong physical presence), the San Diego Unified Port District, Caltrans (California Department of Transportation), and Tijuana/Baja California/Mexico serve as advisors.

Each month SANDAG meets to

Gasoline prices are higher than in other places, too. And since San Diegans tenaciously cling to their autos as the preferred mode of transportation, they pay for it.

But the good news is that bargains are always to be found. Inexpensive dining, off-price shopping, and discount entertainment opportunities are common. With judicious planning, a visit or even a permanent move to San Diego doesn't have to break the bank.

WEATHER

San Diego is famous for many things: the zoo, SeaWorld, Balboa Park, Dr. Seuss, and Scripps Institution of Oceanography, to name a few. But ask anyone what comes to mind when they think of San Diego, and more likely than not they'll say the weather. Let's face it—the average daytime temperature is 70 degrees, and most days are sunny. Humidity is usually low, even during the summer, and winter consider crucial issues including growth, transportation, environmental management, housing, open space, air quality, energy, fiscal management, economic development, and criminal justice. Sounds like a monumental task, but San Diego County's leaders understand that planning cannot be effective if done in a piecemeal manner. With everyone working together through SANDAG, the odds of making plans that enhance life for all San Diegans are greatly improved.

One of the appealing features of SANDAG is that the average citizen has access to the organization. Public forums are encouraged whenever an issue is about to be decided, whether that issue is recycling or traffic management. Citizens and special interest groups are actively involved in SANDAG's planning process. They serve on committees, attend workshops, and participate in public hearings.

Legally, SANDAG is a "joint powers agency," created in 1966 as the Comprehensive Planning Organization. It was renamed SANDAG in 1980. Each May SANDAG pools local, state, and federal funds and develops a budget to tackle its goals for the upcoming year.

The organization has accomplished plenty.

In 1975 SANDAG developed a comprehensive Regional Transportation Plan. In 1992 the association helped form a five-county rail coalition. Four years later SANDAG convinced Congress and the California state legislature to allocate funds for massive amounts of sand to replenish local beaches.

In keeping with its history, current plans are far-reaching. SANDAG is working on growth management in anticipation of the nearly million newcomers expected by the year 2020. It also is focusing on habitat conservation, criminal justice research, hazardous waste management, and traffic management.

It sounds like a lot. It is. But this is a coalition of leaders with the same goal: to improve the quality of life in San Diego. Keeping things running smoothly among 18 cities in the same county is a big job. SANDAG is up to the challenge.

temperatures rarely dip below 40 degrees at night. It doesn't get much more pleasant than that.

Yet vacationing Midwesterners can often be seen shivering in shorts and T-shirts near the beach on a summer day or at the zoo on an evening in spring. The key word to our climate is "mild." The absence of humidity, rain, snow, and sleet makes it the country's most livable climate, yet it's rarely as warm (especially in the summer at the beach) as outsiders expect it to be. The key to success is to layer your clothing, and to observe what locals are wearing. You'll note that some stalwart San Diegans refuse to give up their shorts even in winter, no matter how cold it gets.

Of course, if you travel to the far ends of the county, you can find some extremes. Desert temperatures in Borrego Springs soar above 100 degrees for much of the summer, and the mountains get cold enough to keep snow on the ground for at least a few days during the winter. But aside from a few heat waves during the summer

Weather in San Diego can be changeable. Those Pacific breezes aren't always balmy. Insiders layer clothing and keep a sweatshirt in the car, just in case it turns cool.

and cold snaps during the winter, it's extremely comfortable most of the time.

Rainfall averages 10 inches per year, except in the El Niño years, when anything can happen. The only other weather oddity is the occasional condition known as a Santa Ana. During a Santa Ana, hot and dry winds blow in from the desert, the temperature climbs into the high 80s or low 90s, and the humidity plunges to 10 percent or less. Most common during the late fall or early winter months, these winds usually last only a few days. Unfortunately, they exacerbate wildfires and wreak havoc on remote sections of highways.

EARTHQUAKES

Anyone who has endured an earthquake of any magnitude will confirm that they are nothing to be scoffed at. They are every bit as frightening as a tornado or a hurricane and can cause devastating damage. The good news is that the big ones are few and far between. Even though earthquakes are almost a daily occurrence in and around Southern California, most are too small to be noticed. The wise traveler or resident is prepared for any eventuality, though, and will have evacuation routes planned in advance, just as you would in case of fire.

The white pages of the local telephone book have comprehensive instructions and suggestions for earthquake safety. Knowing what to do ahead of time will lessen the scare factor of the occasional shaker.

CRIME AND PERSONAL SAFETY

We want your time in San Diego to be safe. This is a big city, and it has crime and safety issues like every other large city. It's always wise to keep in mind the same basic safety precautions you would take in your hometown or in any other major metropolitan city.

Whether sightseeing, dining, or shopping, it's a good idea to travel in groups. There's safety in numbers, and you will lessen the opportunity to be singled out as a target. Also, try to have a good idea of your current surroundings and where you're headed. The more confident you appear, the less vulnerable you are to unscrupulous strangers.

Now that you have an idea of what San Diego is all about, hop in your car or head for the trolley, and explore. You'll like what you find. And don't forget to bring your *Insiders' Guide.*

GETTING HERE, GETTING AROUND

San Diego is a destination city. In fact, it is sometimes referred to as the cul-de-sac of the Southwest, a distinction that rankles most locals, but ultimately they grudgingly agree. Few people come through San Diego on their way to someplace else, as they do with major hubs like Los Angeles, Chicago, or Dallas. Of course, Lindbergh Field is called San Diego International Airport, but unless you're headed to Mexico, leaving the country usually involves a stop in Los Angeles first. Once you're here, well, there's really no reason to go anyplace else aside from an occasional day trip. As you'll soon discover, that's not such a bad thing. The city has more than enough attractions and entertainment to amuse you for weeks. And if you're really determined to go someplace else when you leave San Diego, we'll get you there . . . eventually.

Another distinction San Diego has is the location of its primary airport, Lindbergh Field. It sits right smack in the middle of the city, not on the outskirts of town like most major airports. That means when you land, you're already here. You don't have to spend an hour or more finding your way into the city. Oh, and just a word about the landing. Because the airport is right next to downtown, your pilot will have to navigate some high-rises during final approach. But don't let that worry you—they've been doing it for years and they're used to it. Just wave to the office workers on the top floors as you fly by.

We've designed this chapter to help you find your way to San Diego and to get around once you're here. We've included all the traditional modes of transportation as well as a few that may surprise and delight you, such as pedicabs, water taxis, and ferries.

San Diego is an excellent home base, and there's so much to do here that there's really little reason to venture farther afield. But should you choose to venture north—to visit Disneyland and Knott's Berry Farm or Temecula's wine country or the old mission at San Juan Capistrano—we won't hold it against you. We'll be here to welcome you back at the end of the day or weekend.

GETTING HERE

By Air

San Diego International Airport/ Lindbergh Field
(619) 400-2400
www.san.org

Named for aviation pioneer Charles A. Lindbergh, whose famed *Spirit of St. Louis* was built in San Diego, San Diego International Airport carries his name as tribute to his epic solo flight across the Atlantic Ocean. Lindbergh Field opened in 1928, and although the airport has changed substantially over the years, it remains at its original location—sandwiched between Pacific Highway and Harbor Drive—and still has just one runway.

Approximately 17 million passengers travel through the airport annually on more than 600 daily flights. Terminal 1 has been in existence since 1967, with quite a bit of remodeling in the ensuing years, and Terminal 2 opened in 1979. The Commuter Terminal was added in 1996 and handles 25,000 passengers daily. A major expansion and renovation of Terminal 2 was completed in 1998.

Traffic is always heavy in front of the San Diego International Airport, and security is vigilant. Don't leave your car unattended, or it may be towed. Just north of the commuter terminal at 2701 Harbor Drive, there's a 50-space, 24-hour cell phone lot where drivers can await incoming passengers for up to an hour.

For the past 30 years or so, even while in the midst of remodeling, talk about the airport has mostly been, where should we move it? The drawbacks to having an airport in the middle of the city are many. The land the airport occupies is precious. Nearby residents constantly complain about airplane noise, and many consider the steep descent to pose a hazard with every landing. At press time, San Diegans are still waiting for a recommendation regarding a new airport site, a decision that will ultimately be left to voters to decide.

ARRIVALS

Terminal 1 and Terminal 2
3707 North Harbor Drive
Once you have deplaned, signs will direct you to the baggage-claim area as well as to ground transportation. If you've arrived at one of the far gates, it can be a bit of a hike, especially in Terminal 2, so muster up your extra energy and concentrate on the delights that await you. You'll have to take the escalator or elevator down to the baggage area, but once you're there, lighted signs will indicate which carousel will deliver your bags. Should your bags not arrive (this almost never happens in San Diego, but then, we believe hardly anything bad ever happens here), lost-baggage offices are conveniently located in the claim area, and agents will do their best to reunite you with your luggage.

Located adjacent to the baggage-claim area are rental car and hotel information boards with telephones that will connect you directly to your preferred agency or hotel for pickup, information, and reservations. As you leave the baggage area, you can proceed directly to the outside curb if you are taking the Metropolitan Transit Service bus called the Airport Flyer. The bus stop is curbside as you exit any of the three terminals, and the 10-minute Airport Flyer service will transport you to or from downtown, Amtrak, the Coaster, the Trolley, and other bus routes for a $2.25 fare.

If you've arrived at Terminal 1 or 2, you can cross the street at the light (or via the skybridge in inclement weather) and proceed to the transportation plaza or the parking lot. There you will find taxis, shuttles, and rental car transport.

Commuter Terminal
3225 North Harbor Drive
From destinations such as Los Angeles and Fresno, a half dozen commuter airlines arrive at one of the 10 gateways of the Commuter Terminal. (These are Alaska Commuter, American Eagle, Continental Express, Northwest AirLink, Skywest, Delta Connection, and United Express.) Smaller but just as efficient, the Commuter Terminal has much the same system as Terminals 1 and 2. The only difference is that ground transportation is available curbside as soon as you leave the baggage area. In addition to taxis, shuttles, and the Airport Flyer, a complimentary red airport shuttle bus transports passengers between the Commuter Terminal and Terminals 1 and 2. Pedestrians may not walk between the Commuter Terminal and Terminals 1 and 2, so make sure you know from which your flight departs before leaving for the airport, be it by taxi, shuttle, or in your own car.

Rental Car Agencies
Alamo (619) 297-0311, (800) 327-9633; www.alamo.com

Avis (619) 231-7171, (888) 897-8448; www.avis.com

Budget (800) 527-0700
Dollar (619) 234-3389, (800) 800-4000; www.dollar.com

Enterprise Rent-a-Car (619) 294-3313, (800) 736-8222; www.enterprise.com

Hertz (619) 220-5222, (800) 654-3131; www.hertz.com

National (619) 497-6777, (800) 227-7368

DEPARTURES

The most convenient way to reach the airport is to have a friend drive you, or take a cab, bus, or shuttle. Access to Lindbergh Field is from Interstate 5, either south or north. If you're traveling south, take the Sassafras Street exit, and follow the airport signs to Laurel Street, where you will turn right. Laurel Street feeds into North Harbor Drive, which takes you directly to the airport. From I-5 north, take the Hawthorn Street exit to North Harbor Drive and turn right. Signs will direct drivers to specific airlines at the three terminals.

Ticketing is downstairs at both the Commuter Terminal and Terminal 1, and upstairs in Terminal 2. A variety of shuttle services are available to transport you to the airport, as well as taxis and park-and-ride facilities. Be aware that on-site airport parking is limited; competition for the lot's 3,000 spaces can be fierce. Leave extra time for finding a spot, use off-site airport parking, or arrange another form of transportation. Airport parking rates are as follows:

0–½ hour	50 cents
½–1 hour	$1.00
1–2 hours	$3.00
2–3 hours	$5.00
3–4 hours	$7.00
4–5 hours	$10.00
5–6 hours	$13.00
6–7 hours	$16.00
7–24 hours	$18.00

Per day (or partial day) after 1st day $24.00

Killing time while waiting for a flight? Check out your favorite Web site at one of Lindbergh Field's Internet kiosks.

Private Airport Shuttles
Rates vary widely from company to company. Some charge a per-person rate, others a per-carload rate. Still others charge by the mile. Van or sedan service is available, depending on the company.

Airport Shuttle (619) 234-4403
Cloud 9 Shuttle (858) 505-4998, (800) 974-8853; www.cloud9shuttle.com

Coronado Livery (619) 435-6310

5 Star Shuttle (619) 294-3300; www.fivestarshuttle.com

Sea Breeze Shuttle (619) 297-7463; www.seabreezeshuttle.com

Xpress Shuttle (619) 222-5800, (800) 900-7433; www.xpressshuttle.com

Torrey Pines Transfer (858) 587-1409, (800) 761-2914; www.torreypinestrans.com

Many travelers take advantage of the numerous private park-and-ride facilities located near the airport. You can park your car in their secured lot, and they will shuttle you to and from the airport for a fee that is substantially less than the airport's parking fee. Fees range from $11 to $14 per day, depending whether you choose open-air or covered parking. Here are a few park-and-ride companies:

Aladdin Parking Garage (619) 696-7275
Laurel Travel Center (619) 233-0412
Park and Ride Co. (619) 295-2832
For long-term parking ($12 per day) leave your car at the SAN Park Harbor Lot at 3015 North Harbor Drive or the larger NTC Lot on the former Naval Training Center at 4157 North Harbor Drive. Both have airport shuttle service.

There are small county airports at Fallbrook, Ramona, and Borrego. For more information see the Web site at www.sdcounty.ca.gov/dpw/airports. There are unmanned East County airstrips at Jacumba and in the desert at Ocotillo and Agua Caliente; the latter is near the hot springs for which it is named.

REGIONAL AIRPORTS

The following airports located around the county are mostly private or small airports serving small planes and corporate aircraft. The exception is Palomar Airport in Carlsbad, which, in addition to its private aircraft facilities, has daily commercial flights to Los Angeles, Phoenix, and Las Vegas.

As the fees and availability change frequently, we recommend you contact the desired airport well in advance of your arrival to make arrangements for landing.

Brown Field Municipal Airport
1424 Continental Street, San Ysidro
(619) 424-0455
Owned and poorly operated by the city of San Diego, badly neglected Brown Field is located just north of the U.S.-Mexico border and has two runways, 8,000 and 3,000 feet long. The airport has three FBOs (Fixed Base Operators) for full-service maintenance and fuel. Amenities include a restaurant and bar, and rental car arrangements can be made at the airport.

Gillespie Field
1960 Joe Crosson Road, El Cajon
(619) 956-4800
www.sdcounty.ca.gov/dpw/airports
Operated by the county and located in East County, Gillespie Field has three runways, 5,300, 4,000, and 2,800 feet long. Fuel services and maintenance facilities are available. Inside the small terminal is a comfortable lounge with soft drink and snack vending machines, and there are two small restaurants. Rental cars are not located on-site, but Enterprise Rent-a-Car has an arrangement with Gillespie Field to pick up travelers and transport them to the agency, usually within 30 minutes.

Montgomery Field
3750 John J. Montgomery Drive
San Diego
(858) 573-1440
City-owned Montgomery Field has two parallel runways, 4,600 feet (with displaced threshold) and 3,400 feet long, and a cross runway of 3,400 feet. Located in the Kearney Mesa business district of San Diego, the airport has aircraft rentals and flight schools, full fueling services, as well as three FBOs for aircraft maintenance. Car rentals are available, and the Casa Machado restaurant and bar is situated overlooking the runway.

Oceanside Municipal Airport
480 Airport Road, Oceanside
(760) 435-5189
www.oceansideairport.org
Oceanside Airport has one runway, 2,700 feet in length. Self-service fueling is available. Inside the terminal is a small lounge complete with snack and coffee machines. Enterprise and Avis will deliver rental cars to this airport.

McClellan-Palomar Airport
2198 Palomar Airport Road, Carlsbad
(760) 431-4646
www.sdcounty.ca.gov/dwp/airports
Daily flights to and from Los Angeles International Airport and Phoenix Sky Harbor Airport are available from McClellan-Palomar on America West Express and United Express Airlines respectively. Most of the traffic at Palomar, however, is private aircraft. The single runway is 4,600 feet for landing and 5,000 feet for takeoff. Three FBOs provide full-service mainte-

nance and fueling. A restaurant is located on-site, and rental cars are available.

By Train

Amtrak
(800) USA-RAIL (872-7245) reservations
www.amtrak.com
Traveling by train is probably one of the more pleasant ways to reach San Diego, and train routes feed from every part of the country. Scenic rides down the coast of California are popular. For overland routes through the deserts to points east of San Diego, one must connect with trains in Los Angeles. Amtrak makes three stops in San Diego County: Oceanside, Solana Beach, and the Santa Fe Depot in downtown San Diego.

Taxi stands are prominent at all three stops, and bus service is available from all three, too. The San Diego Trolley, which serves parts of San Diego, also has a station at the Santa Fe Depot.

Checked baggage service is available at all stations. A $1.3 billion investment recently enhanced Southern California trains with improved windows and seats (the latter with laptop dataports), classier menus, new business-class coaches, and expanded storage facilities, including storage racks for surfboards and bicycles.

Reservations may be made in advance through any travel agent, at Amtrak stations, or by calling the 24-hour toll-free number listed above. Tickets can also be purchased the day of travel at Amtrak stations. Amtrak accepts cash and all major credit cards. Seniors age 62 and older receive a 15 percent discount. Animals are not permitted on trains unless they are certified guide or service animals accompanying passengers with disabilities, and Amtrak requires that you carry necessary documentation.

Dial 211 any time 24/7 for information about San Diego County's health, disaster services, or human services. A real human being can help with suggestions for learning of and contacting a variety of not-for-profit services. Discover drug treatment, hospice or elder care for a loved one, or where to do volunteer work in your community.

By Bus

Greyhound Bus
Fare and Schedule Information
(800) 231-2222
www.greyhound.com
If you're on a tight budget, Greyhound may be the perfect solution. In an effort to attract more customers, it seems that Greyhound always has some kind of special, such as two-for-one fares. Greyhound offers 40-percent-off fares for kids 11 years of age and younger. Babies younger than age 2 (one per paying adult) travel for free.

Greyhound has several stations throughout San Diego County, which we've listed below.

San Diego: 120 West Broadway
(619) 239-6737

El Cajon: 250 South Marshall Avenue
(619) 444-2591

San Ysidro: 799 East San Ysidro Boulevard
(619) 428-1194

Oceanside: 205 South Tremont Street
(760) 722-1587

Escondido: 700 West Valley Parkway
(760) 745-6522

By Car

To reach San Diego from Washington, Oregon, or northern California, take I-5 and keep your car pointed south; it'll lead you all the way into the city. If you're not in a hurry and would like a more scenic drive, California Highway 101, which begins in Eureka, California, is a nice alternative. It'll keep you close to the coast as you drive through such picturesque towns as Big Sur, Monterey, and San Luis Obispo. From points east, hook up with Interstate 15 in Nevada or Utah, or Interstate 8 in Arizona. Both freeways end up in San Diego. I-15 takes you through Las Vegas and the high desert in eastern California, and I-8 winds through the desert and the Laguna Mountains before entering San Diego.

GETTING AROUND

Now that you're here, let us show you how to move around the county. You have many options: auto, bus, taxi, trolley, train, and a few unusual modes, too. Take a map and your *Insiders' Guide* and go exploring.

By Car

ROADWAYS

California is known for its extensive freeway system, and San Diego has one of the best systems in the state. With a combination of interstate, state, and county highways, navigating the county is easy, except that traffic congestion is constantly worsening, especially during morning and afternoon commutes, when traffic on most freeways ranges from slow-and-go to stop-and-go. Weekdays avoid traveling from 6:00 to 9:00 A.M. and 2:30 to 7:00 P.M. when possible.

If you're in the exploring mood and happen to see one of San Diego's trademark blue-and-yellow signs with a big white seagull on it, follow it. That's the sign for a scenic drive, and there are many throughout the county, especially along the coast.

All interstate and state highways have emergency call boxes spaced every quarter mile or so. These provide direct connections to emergency services, such as police, ambulance, fire, and towing.

For free, current information on area traffic call (866) 500-0977 or log on to http://traffic.calit2.net.

U.S. Interstate Highways

Interstate 8

I-8 begins at the western edge of San Diego, at Sunset Cliffs Boulevard, and travels east through Mission Valley, East County, across the mountains and desert and into Arizona. It's the main east/west artery in the city. Every north/south interstate and state and county route intersects with I-8.

It has a tendency to bunch up between the East County and downtown during rush hours, the westbound lanes in the morning and the eastbound lanes in the afternoon. With more and more people commuting, and most using their own cars, traffic on I-8 at peak times is frustrating. Avoid it during these times, or practice the Zen of driving.

Interstate 5

I-5 begins at the U.S.-Mexico border and ends at the U.S.-Canada border. It meanders north along the coastal region of San Diego, offering some spectacular ocean views before veering inland once it passes the county line.

Its rush-hour bottlenecks are up and down the coast but especially in North County Coastal: during morning hours they happen in southbound lanes; the ones leading north back up in the afternoon. As North County continues to grow, even weekend traffic on I-5 can be slow, although a partial HOV (high-occupancy vehicle) lane speeds things up for families and carpoolers. I-5 is at press time being widened north of Genesee Avenue to Del Mar. An auxiliary lane from Via de la Valle to Lomas Santa Fe Road should be completed by summer of 2007.

Interstate 15

The second major north/south freeway is I-15. Its southern leg emerges from I-5 in National City, and it travels north through inland San Diego and North County, eventually leaving the county in Riverside.

Rush-hour slowdowns are in North County Inland, southbound in the morning and northbound in the afternoon. An auxiliary lane on I-15 from north of Friars Road to I-8 does help ease some major slowdowns at the merge between I-15 and I-8, and an 8-mile HOV eases congestion somewhat. The direction of the lanes is switched from south to north to accommodate morning and afternoon heavy traffic. Lanes are being added north of Mira Mesa Boulevard to Del Mar Heights Road.

Interstate 805

I-805 provides a much-needed north/south inland sweep between I-5 and I-15. It emerges from I-5 in San Ysidro, just north of the U.S.-Mexico border, and makes its way north through central San Diego, reconnecting with I-5 in Sorrento Valley at the infamous "merge." Traffic at the merge is always heavy, especially when North County residents make their way home during the afternoon commute.

California State Highways

All state highways have the familiar green sign with white numbers that designate them as California highways, but in truth, some are little more than surface streets or roadway extensions of highways that may or may not be completed one day. Here we will mention only those that qualify as true highways. If you're looking at a map and see the California State Highway designation and it hasn't been described here, keep in mind that it may well be a winding two-lane road through the mountains or a busy commercial street that you'd just as soon avoid.

California Highway 54

We'll start in the South Bay with CA 54. This is a fairly new freeway that travels east/west, connecting I-5 with I-805 and California Highway 94. It has been helpful in relieving a lot of traffic on South Bay surface streets and providing East County and South Bay residents a quicker and less-congested way to visit one another's communities.

Traffic reports will often refer to a backup at the "merge" or the "S curve." The merge refers to the area just north of La Jolla where I-5 and I-805 join to become one freeway going north; the S curve is the portion of I-5 that runs through downtown like an S.

California Highway 94

Moving north, you come to CA 94, another east/west freeway that connects I-5 and California Highway 125 before continuing east through Jamul and Dulzura in the southeast corner of the county. Also called the Martin Luther King Jr. Freeway, the portion west of I-8 is heavily traveled during commute hours, west in the morning and east in the afternoon. The highway eventually turns into a surface road that becomes a scenic back route through the foothills of East County, near the Mexican border.

California Highway 163

CA 163 (the downtown section is also known as the Cabrillo Freeway) has historic status in San Diego. It is a north/south freeway whose southern end is downtown. As it travels north, it winds through Balboa Park and is about as scenic a freeway as you'll ever see, surrounded by lush greenery and soaring old trees. If you drive it during rush hour, south in the morning and north in the afternoon, you'll have ample opportunity to enjoy its beauty. It continues north through Mission Valley and ultimately connects with I-15 near the Miramar Marine Corps Air Station.

California Highway 125

Now we're moving into East County, where

Like most Californians, San Diegans may rely heavily on their cars, but they also take advantage of the region's 700 miles of bikeways and bike paths.

you'll find CA 125. It is a north/south freeway connecting Highways 52, 8, 94, and 54. This short freeway provides a much-appreciated link between the four highways.

California Highway 67
CA 67, another north/south freeway, links Lakeside and Santee to Ramona, a slowed-down, laid-back community on the way to the mountain town of Julian. It's a journey back in time. Except for the El Cajon to Lakeside portion, it's a two-lane road most of the time.

California Highway 52
CA 52 has been called San Diego's godsend. It is an east/west freeway that intersects four major north/south freeways: I-5, I-805, CA 163, and I-15. Currently petering out in Santee, in the East County, it is scheduled to intersect with CA 67 in the next few years. It doesn't seem to suffer the same level of rush-hour traffic as San Diego's other freeways, and it has provided a much-needed link between the coast and East County.

California Highway 56
Located just south of Del Mar, four-lane CA 56 is a sorely needed east/west link between North County Coastal and North County Inland.

California Highway 78
This is the original major east/west artery connecting North County Coastal with North County Inland. CA 78 begins in Oceanside and travels east through Vista and San Marcos, before turning into a surface street in Escondido and continuing to Ramona. It, too, is heavily congested during rush hour—in both directions, both morning and afternoon.

San Diego County Routes
Identified by a white hexagonal sign with a black *S* followed by a number, county routes are exclusively surface streets and roads. Some are major business streets, others are scenic drives that meander through the back country. If you're looking to get somewhere fast, don't mistake a county route for a shortcut. The county route designation is mostly an indication of who is responsible for maintenance—in this case, the county rather than the city in which they are located.

TAXI SERVICE

San Diego has about as many taxi companies as it has animals in the zoo. Fees vary by company, but all are clearly posted on the inside and outside of the cab. If you're catching a taxi from the airport, they will be queued up in the transportation plaza outside the terminals.

Taxis usually gather around major hotels and are available on demand. If none are immediately available, your hotel doorman or receptionist will be happy to call one for you. Unfortunately, taxis aren't hailed from the street; they don't cruise for fares. If you're leaving a club or restaurant, ask the host or hostess to call a taxi for you.

Make sure the taxi driver resets the meter as soon as you depart. Most companies charge $1.80 to start the cab and $2.30 per mile.

Here are a few taxi companies:

American Cab (619) 234-1111
City Cab (858) 485-5544
North City Cab (619) 260-1003
San Diego Cab (619) 226-8294
Silver Cab (619) 280-5555
Yellow Cab (619) 234-6161

Public Transportation

Metropolitan Transit System
(619) 233-3004, (800) 226-6883
www.sdcommute.com

The Metropolitan Transit System (MTS) includes the bus system and the San Diego Trolley. Dating from 1886, the MTS began when the first streetcar made its way up Fifth Avenue from the downtown waterfront. San Diego was the second city in the nation to replace the horse with electric streetcars, but by 1945 all the streetcars had been replaced by buses.

The bus system covers 635 miles on 29 fixed routes and serves the cities of Chula Vista, Coronado, El Cajon, Imperial Beach, La Mesa, Lemon Grove, National City, Poway, San Diego, and Santee, as well as adjacent unincorporated sections of San Diego County. The system also connects with other regional systems, including the North County Transit District (which serves inland and coastal cities in the North County) and Direct Access to Regional Transit (DART). Residents of Paradise Hills, Mira Mesa, Rancho Bernardo, Scripps Ranch, and the midcity areas can call ahead to DART at (877) 841-DART for transport to the nearest bus stop.

All buses accommodate wheelchairs and are equipped to carry bicycles on racks mounted on the back. Local bus route fare is $1.75, and it's $2.25 for urban routes one way, and exact change is required. Children age 5 and younger ride free with any paying passenger, and discounts are available for seniors and disabled riders. Day Tripper passes provide unlimited access to all MTS buses and the trolley. They are available for one day ($5.00), two days ($9.00), three days ($12.00), or four days ($15.00). Monthly passes are also available (as well as half-monthly for the last two weeks of the month); all can be purchased at the Transit Store at 102 Broadway, San Diego, or at supermarkets and drug stores around the county. For locations and information call (800) 266-6883 or (619) 234-1060.

Transfers are free; they are good for two hours. Printed bus routes and schedules are available in many hotels and at the Transit Store.

To be completed some time in 2007, the SPRINTER light-rail system will connect Vista, Escondido, Oceanside, and San Marcos. Paralleling Route 78 for 22 miles, the line will have 15 stations and trains running on the half hour between approximately 5:00 A.M. and 9:00 P.M. daily.

North County Transit District Route Information
(800) 266-6883
www.gonctd.com

The North County Transit District (NCTD) serves all of North County, both coastal and inland. Connections to San Diego MTS buses are plentiful and easy, and many routes connect to Greyhound, the Coaster, and Amtrak at the Oceanside and Solana Beach Transit Centers.

Basic fares are $1.75 ($3.75 day pass) for adults and free for children age 5 and younger traveling with any fare-paying passenger. Seniors and the disabled (with NCTD photo ID card) pay 75 cents (day pass, $1.50). Transfers are free.

Coaster
(800) 262-7837

The Coaster operates regional rail service between Oceanside and San Diego. The blue, green, and white express train mainly serves commuters, but it's a good way to travel between San Diego and North County Coastal. Moving north from the Santa Fe Depot in downtown San Diego, it stops in Old Town, Sorrento Valley, Solana Beach, Encinitas, Carlsbad Poinsettia, Carlsbad Village, and Oceanside.

About a dozen round-trips are scheduled during weekdays, with extended service on Fridays, and a modified schedule is offered on Saturdays. Extra trains are added during special events such as the Street Scene in downtown San Diego or the annual Holiday Bowl at Qualcomm Stadium.

The North County Transit District (NCTD) offers a special bus that goes up and down Old Highway 101 during peak summer months. Participating merchants give discounts and gifts (from free toys to discounted dinner and acupuncture sessions) to riders with BREEZE day passes. The pass costs $3.75 a day or $54.00 a month, less for seniors.

Tickets are purchased from vending machines on the station platform before boarding the train, and the machines accept cash (dispensing a maximum of $10.00 in change), VISA, and MasterCard. Fares range from $3.75 one way to $5.25, depending on the distance you travel. All tickets must be validated before boarding the train by validating machines that are also located on the station platform.

Passengers must present a validated ticket to the conductor, ticket inspector, or police officer upon request. Coaster tickets provide a free transfer to all connecting San Diego MTS buses, trolleys, and NCTD buses within two hours from the time validated. Your Coaster ticket also provides a free transfer to the Airport Flyer, which departs for Lindbergh Field from the Santa Fe Depot in San Diego.

San Diego Trolley
(619) 233-3004
www.sdcommute.com

Part of the MTS, this light-rail system with bright red cars serves San Diego, East County, and the South Bay. Connections to the trolley from Amtrak and the Coaster are available at the San Diego Santa Fe Depot, and an additional connection from the Coaster is available at Old Town.

The trolley has three lines, the Blue, Green, and Orange Lines. The Blue Line is an S-shaped line that serves San Diego from Qualcomm Stadium west through Mission Valley and the Old Town Transit Center and south through downtown to the U.S.-Mexico border. The Orange Line makes a loop through downtown San Diego, serving the 12th and Imperial Transit Center as well as Seaport Village, the convention center, and the Gaslamp Quarter, then continues to the East County, to El Cajon. The Green Line connects the Old Town Transit Center with El Cajon and Santee in the East County, with stops at Mission de Alcala and San Diego State University.

Trolley tickets are purchased at vending machines located on the station platform and are priced according to the distance to be traveled. One-way fares range from $1.25 to $3.00, with senior and disabled-rider discounts available. Day Tripper passes give visitors one- to four-day unlimited access to the trolley and MTS buses for the same prices as listed under the MTS section. Passes can be purchased at trolley stations or at the Transit Store at 102 Broadway, San Diego. If you're using a prepaid pass, you must validate it before boarding the trolley. Validating machines are located on every trolley platform near the ticket vending machines.

Trolley tickets serve as transfers to MTS buses, with connections at most stations. Keep your tickets with you while on the trolley. They won't be collected as you board, but trolley officers periodically check to make sure all passengers have tickets.

San Diego–Coronado Bay Bridge

This graceful blue bridge soars across San Diego Bay and links downtown San Diego with the peaceful island enclave of Coronado. The views of both the San Diego skyline and Coronado are breathtaking from the top of the bridge. The bridge is quite high and narrow, and the trip across can be a little hair-raising. So if you're the driver, let your passengers describe the view to you. The toll was suspended in July 2002.

San Diego–Coronado Ferry
(619) 234-4111, (800) 44-CRUISE
www.sdhe.com

If you prefer a waterborne approach to Coronado, try taking the ferry across San Diego Bay. Ferrying passengers and bicycles only (no autos), it departs from the Broadway Pier at 1050 North Harbor Drive, San Diego, and docks at the Ferry Landing Marketplace on Coronado. It leaves San Diego every hour on the hour from 9:00 A.M. to 9:00 P.M. Sunday through Thursday, and until 10:00 P.M. Friday and Saturday. It leaves Coronado every hour on the half hour from 9:30 A.M. to 9:30 P.M. Sunday through Thursday, and until 10:30 P.M. Friday and Saturday. The fare is $3.00 per person, one way. If you're bringing your bike, the fare is $3.50.

San Diego Water Taxi
(619) 235-8294 (reservations)
(619) 234-4111 (information)
www.sdro.com

San Diego Water Taxi offers on-call boat transportation service along San Diego Bay for a $5.00 per person fare; it operates between 2:00 and 10:00 P.M. Monday through Thursday and 11:00 A.M. to 11:00 P.M. Friday and Saturday (often until midnight on weekends in summer). You can take in skyline scenery on your way to waterfront hotels, restaurants, and shopping centers. San Diego Water Taxi offers service to all points in San Diego Bay, including Shelter and Harbor Islands, Coronado, and downtown; there's a $20 minimum for service to Chula Vista and the South Bay.

Plan to drive a rental car to Mexico? Make sure the rental agency allows its cars to travel across the border. If you drive often in Mexico, a yearly policy saves time and money.

Crossing the Border

Some folks feel that no visit to San Diego would be complete without a trip across the border to Mexico. All the details of a visit to Tijuana and beyond are covered in our South of the Border chapter, but we'll give you a general idea of how best to approach it here.

These colorful murals at Chicano Park are painted on the cement support beams of the Coronado Bay Bridge. PHOTO: COURTESY OF BRETT SHOAF

If all you're planning is a shopping and dining expedition to Tijuana, the best way to get there is via the San Diego Trolley. The trolley ends right at the border, and you can walk across. Should you be driving, you can park in one of several lots on the U.S. side of the border and, again, walk across. Once you've passed through the border checkpoints, you can hail a Tijuana taxi to take you to the main shopping area or the restaurant of your choice. If you're just headed to the main tourist areas, walking is another option.

For more adventurous drivers, it's perfectly safe to venture south of the border. Just remember that the streets are not laid out quite as efficiently as they are north of the border, and it's easy to get lost. Also, be sure to purchase Mexican insurance from one of the many storefront insurance shops before you drive into Tijuana. If you were to have an accident, your Mexican insurance policy will make life much easier while dealing with the local authorities and keep you out of jail.

HISTORY

Although most San Diego schoolchildren above fourth grade know the name Juan Rodríguez Cabrillo, historians in general pay him scant attention. After all, he was just one of many who set out in the wake of Christopher Columbus, Hernán Cortés, and other explorers to chart new territory for Spain. When Cabrillo sailed with his two ships into San Diego Bay on September 28, 1542, he wasn't eager to spend much time exploring. Profit and glory lured him northward; Cabrillo's quest was to discover a northwest passage linking the Pacific and Atlantic Oceans. Still, he couldn't help admiring the natural attributes of the bay he had happened upon. Its south-facing opening, between the Point Loma peninsula and Coronado, made a U-turn and traveled southward between the mainland and a narrow stretch of land to the west. Cabrillo noted that the bay was well situated to withstand both violent storms and seafaring intruders.

THE FIRST SAN DIEGANS

Cabrillo's arrival on the eve of the feast day of St. Michael the Archangel inspired him to name his discovery San Miguel. He and his crew continued exploring to the north, but Cabrillo returned to San Miguel only to be buried. He died at sea that winter as a result of an infected wound.

As might be expected, native people had inhabited the area long before Cabrillo and his men arrived to admire the perfection of its port. As far back as 9000 B.C., Indians now known as the San Dieguito were settling in San Diego. They were descendants of Asians who had traversed the bridge of land that connected Asia and North America in prehistoric times, and of others who had traveled westward across North America, crossing the Sierra Nevada Mountains and moving down the coastal plains.

The Kumeyaay Indians joined the San Dieguito around 1000 B.C., and they lived in relative harmony until Cabrillo's arrival more than two millennia later. Although they greeted Cabrillo guardedly, they had little to fear—at least for the moment. Lacking gold and other resources that drove Spanish exploration at the time, the area was left for future generations to explore and conquer.

In 1602 Spanish explorer Sebastián Vizcaíno sailed into San Miguel during a voyage to inspect the west coast of New Spain. Fortunately for the resident Indians, Vizcaíno had no more interest in settling the territory than had Cabrillo. His only contribution was to rename the area San Diego, in honor of his flagship's patron saint, San Diego de Alcalá. Like Cabrillo, Vizcaíno quickly left to sail northward, and the Indians once again were left in peace.

RELUCTANT COLONIZATION

By the mid-1700s Spain's reluctance to colonize the Baja California peninsula and Alta (or Upper) California was overcome by the encroachment of Russian fur traders. Moving down from the Pacific Northwest and into California, they threatened to claim Spain's territories for themselves. Spain's previous lack of interest evaporated with the threat of losing the region to its competitors. Forts and adjacent missions from San Diego to San Francisco Bay would provide defensive settlements to repel foreign invaders and to populate the area with settlers loyal to Spain. Also, Spain sincerely wished to convert the "heathen" Indians, although this desire sprang from convenience as much as from true religious fervor.

Along with the Catalonian military governor Don Gaspar de Portolá, King Charles sent Father Junipero Serra, a Franciscan priest who would establish a string of missions throughout California. De Portolá and Serra began their quest in Loreto, Baja California, and finally arrived in San Diego in 1769. Although de Portolá quickly pressed on, Father Serra remained behind, dedicating the first of 21 missions in California on July 16, 1769. Located atop Presidio Hill, Misión San Diego de Alcalá overlooked the bay and the Pacific Ocean beyond.

As in mission settlements in northern Mexico and Baja California, the local Indians were conscripted for construction, farming, and other tasks. After several initial rebellions, they accepted the inevitability of their new life under the dominion of the mission fathers and the presidio's soldiers. However, they had no natural defenses against introduced European diseases such as smallpox and measles. By the year 1800 mission records show that more than half of the 16,000 converts during the previous 10 years had succumbed to disease. Many were buried in mass graves.

San Diego de Alcalá mission remained on Presidio Hill for only five years before it was moved to its current location in Mission Valley, on the banks of the San Diego River. A lack of arable land, fresh water, and a good-size population of potential indigenous converts prompted the move.

Despite its rocky start and scant resources, the mission was a success, with irrigated fields of wheat, vineyards, orchards of dates and fruit trees, and herds of cattle and sheep grazing in the arid countryside. Spain's claim to California was strengthened, and peace reigned until 1821, when Mexico achieved its independence from Spain. San Diego and its two missions were now under the authority of Mexico and would remain so until the end of the Mexican-American War.

Seeing the strategic value of San Diego's natural harbor, the United States was quick to wrest control of it from Mexico and met little physical resistance. By the time the war ended in 1847 and San Diego (along with the rest of California) officially became part of the United States three years later, the population was fewer than 1,000 people, most of them settled at the foot of Presidio Hill in the area now known as Old Town.

Initiated in 1857, the "Jackass Mail" brought correspondence and passengers 1,500 miles from San Antonio, Texas, to San Diego. Its name derives from the fact that a mule team brought coaches to the Colorado River; from there both people and parcels were packed in on the mules themselves. Interrupted by the Civil War, the Jackass Mail was replaced by the railroad.

THE BEGINNINGS OF A CITY

Although blessed with a mild climate and a beautiful port, San Diego didn't grow as quickly as you might think. By the end of the Civil War, the population had dwindled considerably because San Diego residents flocked to northern California to join the gold rush. What finally started San Diego on the path to becoming a city was the same commodity that fuels its economy today: real estate.

First-time visitors to San Diego will note the popularity of the name Horton, seen at the popular downtown shopping mall Horton Plaza, the stately Horton Grand Hotel, and tiny Horton Avenue.

Alonzo Erastus Horton was the city's official founding father, and he was among the first to recognize the value of real estate in San Diego. Unlike others before him, he wasted little time in capitalizing on it.

Horton was living in San Francisco when he attended a lecture on the ports of California. The discussion about the prospects of San Diego caught his interest, and within three days he was on a steamer to San Diego with dreams of building a great city. He pulled into San Diego Harbor on April 15, 1867, disembarking at what is now the foot of Market Street. Horton's first stop was Old Town, the original settlement nestled beneath the burned-out ruins of the old Presidio. Scarcely disguising his contempt for what he saw, he declared his intention to relocate the heart of the city to the area near the wharf. "I have been nearly all over the United States," Horton said, "and that is the prettiest place for a city I ever saw."

Horton's first land purchase was enviable even by 19th-century standards: 960 acres for $265, or about 27½ cents per acre. Horton swiftly began to develop the parcel, and within three years New Town had far outpaced Old Town with a population that had swelled to 2,301. The economy of the young city was precarious, however, because it was tied so closely to land speculation. From 1867 forward San Diego's economy would fluctuate between boom and bust as the price of real estate rose and fell.

IN SEARCH OF A RAILROAD

Adding to the uncertain land market was speculation about the arrival of a railroad. Three barriers kept stalling the prospects: the two natural barriers of the mountains to the east and the ocean to the west and the political barrier of the Mexican border to the south. Commerce-hungry San Diegans would not give up their dream, though, and whenever rumors spread that the railroad was finally coming, land prices would soar. Then when the bubble burst with the news that there would be no railroad, the real-estate market would plummet, followed by the population, and the city's economy would be left in shambles. In 1872 the news that San Diego would become the western terminus for the Texas & Pacific Railroad produced wild speculation. Residents and outsiders alike scraped together whatever money they could to buy property and build, build,

Old Town State Historic Park recreates life in the 1800s. PHOTO: COURTESY OF BRETT SHOAF

build. The population soared to 4,000. But when railroad plans fell through, the economy collapsed and the population dropped to less than half that number.

Alonzo Horton took a financial bath during the bust of the 1870s and was never again the same driving force in San Diego. His contribution to the city is well remembered, however, as is evidenced by the many visible tributes to him.

The railroad did finally make its way to San Diego in the mid-1880s. The Santa Fe–Atlantic & Pacific Railroad built its West Coast terminus in National City, just south of San Diego. The line went north and then east, through Barstow in central California. Once again the economy boomed, and the population grew to more than 35,000. New Town boasted 71 saloons, playing host to such notable visitors as Wyatt Earp, who lived in San Diego for a time and operated a handful of gambling casinos. Prostitutes were abundant, occupying 120 bawdy houses and nearly outnumbering the more traditional businesspeople. Hotels, restaurants, rooming houses, opium dens, and dance halls were bursting at the seams.

But true to San Diego's short history, bust was right around the corner. The Santa Fe–Atlantic & Pacific Railroad never became much more than a spur line. Most of the real rail traffic went north to Los Angeles, already a commercial rival. By 1889 San Diego had crashed again. The wharves and warehouses were empty, and half the city's population had disappeared—along with a good number of jobs. Those who had their fortunes tied up in real estate suffered greatly as the bottom dropped out of the land market. Once again, San Diego would have to reinvent itself.

SPRECKELS TO THE RESCUE

Whenever San Diego's fortunes looked especially bleak, a savior was inevitably waiting in the wings. As was Alonzo Horton, John D. Spreckels was captivated by the temperate climate of this city by the bay. Heir to the Spreckels sugar fortune, he liberally poured his family money into his adopted city and for the next 20 years laid claim to much of its assets. He owned the streetcar system, most of Coronado and North Island, the historic Hotel del Coronado (a million-dollar property even then), two of the three newspapers, the water company, the ferry system, and numerous businesses.

Spreckels's most prized holding was undoubtedly the Hotel del Coronado. A favorite getaway for the rich, famous, and notorious, it was also home to Tent City. In the summer of 1900, Spreckels erected a sea of tents on the beach just southeast of the hotel. There families could spend the summer in a casual but elegant fashion, literally living in a luxurious tent on the sand. Along with the square tents, Tent City featured a dance pavilion, shops, restaurants, regular entertainment, an indoor swimming pool, and a floating casino. The resort was so popular, it remained open every summer until 1938.

Despite the Hotel del Coronado's success and San Diego's obvious touristic appeal, city leaders held fast to the notion that San Diego's fortunes were inextricably linked to the railroad.

That coveted rail line, the San Diego & Arizona Railroad, finally became a reality in 1919. And it was Spreckels who guaranteed the financing.

Benjamin Harrison was the first U.S. president to visit San Diego, in 1891. He was treated to a reception at the Hotel del Coronado. Since then, presidents Nixon, Reagan, and Clinton have stayed there. Some say King Edward VIII of England met Wallace Simpson there. While this is most likely legend, the monarch did stay at the Hotel Del while still the Prince of Wales.

AN EXPOSITION AND A WAR

If early city leaders had one fault, it was their failure to recognize the value of San Diego's natural attributes: its climate and its deep-water harbor. No railroad and no piece of land would positively influence the city's future in the way those two features did.

To celebrate the opening of the Panama Canal, San Diego hosted an exposition from 1915 to 1916, which lured thousands of tourists. They marveled at the city's arid natural beauty and mild weather. And when they went home, they told their friends about this newfound paradise. They came back—in droves. Then, when Congress declared war on Germany in 1917, San Diego was remembered because of its strategic importance during the Spanish-American War. The army set up Camp Kearny, the navy took over North Island on Coronado, and the marines established their recruit depot just to the north and across the bay from the naval base. The military was here, and it never left. In that brief span, between 1915 and 1917, San Diego's future as both a tourist mecca and a military town was decided.

The Panama-California Exposition drew thousands of visitors from all over the country. Located in what is now the heart of the city—Balboa Park—the exposition gave birth to the park's most beautiful buildings. By the early 1920s Balboa Park had become the site for the world-famous San Diego Zoo. (Be sure to read all about the history of the zoo in our Balboa Park chapter.) Founded by Dr. Harry Wegeforth with animals left over from the exposition, it was funded in large part by Ellen Browning Scripps, also a major benefactress of the Scripps Institution of Oceanography in La Jolla.

In 1937, with funds advanced by the Works Progress Administration, actors Pat O'Brien and Bing Crosby cofounded the Del Mar Racetrack, a lure for locals and for bored Hollywood denizens. With attractions such as the racetrack, Balboa Park, and the Hotel del Coronado resort, as well as pristine beaches and the gambling houses just across the border in Tijuana, San Diego soon became impossible to resist. The Los Angeles film colony discovered the beauty and energy of its neighbor to the south and quickly made San Diego a regular day trip. Tourists from other parts of the country found a myriad of reasons to winter or summer here.

San Diego's leaders finally conceded that maybe there was life beyond the railroad. Real estate speculation proved to be a hard habit to break, though. It remains the sport of choice for many San Diegans even today.

THE AEROSPACE INDUSTRY AND ANOTHER WAR

In 1927, in an old building that once housed a fish cannery, a small aircraft company was working frantically to finish constructing a special airplane. Ryan Airlines, co-owned by aviation pioneers Claude Ryan and B. F. Mahoney, began regular flights between San Diego and Los Angeles in 1925 and had a sideline division for aircraft construction. What they were constructing then, a plane Ryan built in just 60 days, was the *Spirit of St. Louis.* Soon after, Charles Lindbergh made his historic flight from New York to Paris and planted the seeds for San Diego's budding aircraft industry.

From 1880 until 1912 a red-light district flourished in San Diego. It was called the "Stingaree," after the stingrays that are commonly found in local bays and on beaches.

Following closely behind Ryan and Mahoney was Maj. Reuben H. Fleet, who moved his Consolidated Aircraft Corporation from New York to San Diego. With mergers, his company eventually would become Convair and then General Dynamics, a giant in the U.S. defense industry and one of the largest employers in San Diego. Fred Rohr, a metalsmith who had worked on the *Spirit of St. Louis,* formed his own aircraft company, which is still located just south of the city limits in Chula Vista. Rohr Industries (now called the Aerostructures Group) also would become one of San Diego's largest employers and now has manufacturing and maintenance facilities around the country and the world.

World War II was rapidly approaching, and the aircraft industry thrived, fed by defense contracts. Already a dominant presence in San Diego, the military increased dramatically as war loomed on the horizon. The army set up two new camps, Camp Callan near La Jolla and Camp Elliott on Kearny Mesa. Not to be outdone, the navy purchased Camp Pendleton for a marine base. (San Diego's largest *rancho* in the days before U.S. annexation, Camp Pendleton is a 133,000-acre parcel stretching north from Oceanside all the way to the Orange County line. Today this is the only undeveloped coastal land between San Diego and Los Angeles.) The navy also installed its 11th Naval District headquarters here, as well as the Naval Training Center (now closed) and the Miramar Naval Air Station, the latter now also operated by the U.S. Marines.

Consolidated Aircraft fared well during the war. More than 2,000 PBY Catalinas, a twin-engine flying boat, were manufactured by Consolidated and used extensively by the American and British air forces. They proved their value time after time. A Royal Air Force Catalina tracked the *Bismarck* for nine days and nights until the British sank the German sub. A U.S. Navy Catalina spotted a Japanese submarine lurking at the entrance to Pearl Harbor.

At the war's end, many active-duty military personnel stationed in town decided to stay. The population boomed to more than 330,000, and San Diego enjoyed a postwar prosperity throughout the 1950s.

A NEW DIRECTION

Peacetime had its price, and those who paid were in the aircraft and aerospace business. The industry suffered a severe decline that threatened the economy of the entire city. Economic experts around the country were predicting that San Diego was about to bust once again. But seasoned locals scoffed. They knew the history of their town, and that history was a long tale of booming and busting. This time they realized that the key to prosperity lay in looking in a different direction.

Dr. Jonas Salk, developer of the polio vaccine that bears his name, opened the Salk Institute for Biological Studies in 1963. Located in scenic La Jolla, it has become a world-renowned research facility specializing in molecular and cellular biology and neuroscience. Around the same time, the University of California, San Diego opened its 1,000-acre campus, also in La Jolla. The origins of the university lie with the Scripps Institution of Oceanography, which had long been a member of the University of California's statewide system. Saturated with scientists, the institution needed larger facilities not only to enhance its own capabilities but also to attract the best research scientists in the world.

The military was firmly in place, even in peacetime, and tourists kept coming in greater numbers every year. Real estate values were ebbing and flowing just as they always had. And now with the establishment of a world-class research facility and a science- and engineering-based university, the groundwork was firmly in place for San Diego's new course. It was almost as if the city could anticipate the explosion of high-tech and biotech that was about to rise to the top of the world's research and manufacturing industries. When that explosion came, San Diego was ready.

The California Room at the San Diego Central Library, 820 E Street, (619) 236-5834, has a comprehensive collection of excellent books on both San Diego and California. The California Historical Society (619-232-6203, www.sandiegohistory.org), begun by George W. Marston in 1928, has museums at Presidio Park, Balboa Park, and several other San Diego venues.

HIGH-TECH, BIOTECH, AND BRAIN POWER

The 1980s and 1990s saw an influx of high-tech and biotech companies that was beyond the wildest dreams of industry pioneers. Pharmaceutical companies, biotech researchers, and electronics and telecommunications companies made up the bulk of the newcomers, and this sector is still thriving despite the demise of the "dot.coms" and the bear market in general.

San Diego is prospering as we continue into the new millennium. Manufacturing is our number one industry, followed by defense and tourism. Surprisingly, agriculture is San Diego's next most important industry. Avocados, nursery plants, and flowers are the leaders in this field. Acres of strawberries, lettuce, and tomatoes are a familiar sight in the northern reaches of the county, though agricultural lands are shrinking as the population expands.

The icing on the cake of San Diego's prosperity is its growing enclave of higher learning. Known by locals as the "alphabet soup," UCSD (University of California, San Diego), SDSU (San Diego State University), USD (University of San Diego), and CSUSM (California State University, San Marcos) head the list of prestigious institutes. Also respected is Point Loma Nazarene University, a liberal arts college situated on the bluffs of Sunset Cliffs, overlooking the ocean. Added to this collection of four-year universities is an impressive array of community colleges. The result is a stunning production of brain power. (See our Higher Education chapter for more details.)

Many graduates stay in San Diego once they finish school. The biotech and computer software companies attract bright young minds as well. So it's no surprise that San Diego has one of the higher ciphers in the country for percentage of adults with higher learning. About 33 percent have earned a college degree, and more than half of those have a master's or Ph.D. We're proud of our brainiacs. They are a generation of movers and shakers who are well prepared to lead us in the 21st century.

Two Academy Award-winning actors were born in La Jolla: Gregory Peck and Cliff Robertson. Peck graduated from San Diego High School, Robertson from La Jolla High.

THE FLAVOR OF SAN DIEGO

The image many Easterners have of San Diego is blond surfer boys and even blonder girls in bikinis languishing under palm trees on the beach. Granted, most inhabitants take advantage of the beach as often as they can, but they do have jobs.

San Diego is a city that constantly contradicts its small-town image. It was host to the 1996 Republican Convention and also to a presidential debate that same year. Three Super Bowls have been contested here, the last in 2003, when watching our archrivals, the Oakland Raiders, get trounced almost made up for the Chargers' dismal year. San Diego is home to a first-rate opera company, dozens of theaters, and even more superb art galleries.

The city has a large and diverse ethnic population that is well reflected in its neighborhoods. Cultural events and festivals regularly celebrate the heritage of a multitude of ethnic groups. Its proximity to the Mexican border has naturally resulted in a well-established and growing Hispanic community. Of course, the city was Mexican before it was American, and Hispanic traditions and culture can be seen in buildings public and private, place names, and cultural events.

Although San Diego prides itself on being a modern, cosmopolitan city (seventh largest in the country), it still clings tenaciously to its roots. Its Spanish and Mexican heritage runs deep. The pace is a little slower than in most big cities, and San Diegans are more often identified as laid-back than hard-driven. Most believe they have found the best of all worlds. The industries of the future are already here. Educational opportunities abound. And then there's the weather.

Cabrillo could see it. So could Vizcaíno, de Portolá, and Father Serra. Alonzo Horton and John Spreckels figured it out, too. Paradise lies here sandwiched between the mountains and the ocean in a place called San Diego.

HOTELS AND MOTELS

It didn't take San Diego's founding fathers too long to figure out that their city by the bay had the potential to become an irresistible destination for visitors. Along with the first buildings in downtown San Diego—the general stores, saloons, and rooming houses—came places for guests to hang their hats. As increasing numbers of tourists targeted San Diego for their vacations, hotels began to spring up around the beaches and downtown.

Today there are hundreds of places from which to choose. If your idea of a room is only a place to hang your clothes and grab a few hours sleep, you'll find it here. But if you plan to spend a lot of time in your room or enjoy the touches of luxury that only top hotels can offer, you'll find that, too. You need only decide what best fits your style and budget.

Even though San Diego is a year-round destination, it does have a high season during the summer months. Summer is when you're least likely to find your first choice in accommodations unless you plan ahead. The good news is that there are so many hotels and motels spread throughout the county that you can almost always find an available room, even on short notice. Even during Super Bowl week in 2003, when hotels were sold out a year in advance, rooms were available here and there. If you're the spontaneous type who likes to pack a bag on Friday night and see what you can find once you arrive, chances are a nice room will be waiting for you somewhere in the county.

Your choice of accommodation depends on your plans. If you're visiting friends or relatives, it makes sense to book a room close to their neighborhood. If hiking and nature walks are high on your itinerary, you might look at facilities in the East County or North County Inland to be near the foothills and local mountains. If sun and sand are your first priority, you would naturally want to investigate beach-side hotels and motels.

If you plan to do it all—sightseeing, shopping, dining, the beach, and nightlife—you can stay just about anywhere in the county, although it's best to stay close to freeway entrances for easy driving. If you're without a car, though, we recommend that you check out some of the more centrally located facilities in downtown San Diego, Mission Bay or Mission Valley, and Carlsbad so you can take advantage of the bus system, the Coaster, and the San Diego Trolley for transportation.

Downtown has become an ever more popular destination for leisure travelers as well as conventioneers. Several hotels have opened around the baseball park and the convention center, and older hotels throughout downtown have been renovated. Many business hotels have special weekend packages for leisure travelers and families, with considerable discounts in room rates.

Whatever your idea of the perfect holiday may be, this chapter includes a good cross-section of available accommodations. Each facility is described to give you an idea of what makes it unique and desirable. We also list special amenities such as workout rooms or business centers. If the hotel has a great restaurant, we mention it.

Hotels and motels frequently change management companies and affiliations. Don't be surprised if you call one of our listings and the facility has a different name. If this happens, be sure to ask if the accommodation has undergone any significant changes. Remember, too, that the quality of chain hotels can vary from city to city. What might be an outstanding hotel in your city might be a little less desirable someplace else. Read our descriptions carefully, and we promise to steer you in the right direction. We've focused on the one-of-a-kind hotels that Insiders recommend to their friends and listed only exceptional chain hotels.

We've divided this chapter into our usual regional designations: Central San Diego, North County Coastal, North County Inland, East County, and South Bay. For your convenience, San Diego has been further divided into the areas most visitors target in their search for a hotel or motel. Bed-and-breakfast inns and vacation rentals are covered in separate chapters; campgrounds and RV parks are noted in our Recreation chapter.

PRICE CODE

San Diego's room rates are very high, especially during holidays. Prices are based on one night's stay for two people during summer months. Keep in mind that room rates can be somewhat lower during the rest of the year. San Diego's 10.5 percent hotel tax is not included in these rates.

$	**Less than $100**
$$	**$101 to $175**
$$$	**$176 to $250**
$$$$	**More than $251**

RESERVATIONS

It's always a good idea to make your reservations as far in advance as possible, especially if you have your heart set on a specific facility or part of the county. If you're planning a beach vacation and decide to take your chances when you get here, you might find yourself spending much of your time commuting to the beach from a hotel in an outlying area. Beach accommodations typically fill up far in advance of summer months.

When you make your reservation, most facilities require a major credit card to hold your reservation. Should you decide to cancel, policies vary so be sure to inquire when you make the reservation. Most require a specified lead time for cancellation to avoid a charge to your credit card. Unless we designate otherwise, all listings accept major credit cards.

Be sure to ask about check-in and checkout times, too. Most check-in times are around 3:00 P.M., and checkout is usually around noon. If those times don't fit with your schedule, ask about early check-in or late checkout. Many facilities are happy to accommodate your plans for no extra charge or offer to store your luggage, but some will charge extra fees if you're too early or hang around too long after checkout time.

Also keep in mind that most of the hotels and motels we list here offer smoking and nonsmoking rooms. If this is important to you, be sure to specify your preference when making your reservation. If you can't bear the thought of leaving your pet at home while you're vacationing, you may be in luck. Many hotels and motels welcome pets, though some request a cleaning deposit. We've noted any restrictions or special policies. In accordance with federal law, all hotels have accommodations for the disabled. Just be sure to specify your needs to the reservations clerk.

CENTRAL SAN DIEGO

Beaches and Mission Bay

Best Western Blue Sea Lodge **$$$-$$$$**
707 Pacific Beach Drive, Pacific Beach
(858) 488-4700, (800) 258-3732
www.bestwestern-bluesea.com

At the Blue Sea Lodge you can choose from 128 luxury oceanfront rooms or standard rooms with private balconies or patios. Some rooms feature sunken tubs and skylights. Start your morning with coffee on the patio by the oceanfront pool and hot tub, which has direct access to the beach. Then spend the rest of the day sightseeing, swimming, or strolling along the beach boardwalk.

No restaurants are on-site, but dozens are within 4 or 5 blocks. If eating in is more your style, ask about suites with kitchens. A few are available.

Catamaran Resort Hotel $$$$
3999 Mission Boulevard, Pacific Beach
(858) 488-1081, (800) 422-8386
www.catamaranresort.com

Long a fixture in the beach area, the Catamaran has 315 rooms with unparalleled access to both the beach and the bay. All rooms and suites are decorated in muted greens and pinks. Most rooms have a refrigerator, and all have a balcony or lanai.

The Catamaran has a water sports center on the bay, a spa, and a fitness center. The authentic stern-wheeler *Bahia Belle* cruises Mission Bay nightly from the Catamaran, offering cocktails and dancing. The Atoll Restaurant serves breakfast, lunch, and dinner daily, including an award-winning Sunday brunch.

Crystal Pier Hotel & Cottages $$$$
4500 Ocean Boulevard, Pacific Beach
(858) 483-6983, (800) 748-5894
www.crystalpier.com

These Cape Cod-style cottages on the Crystal Pier in Pacific Beach may be the most romantic lodgings in the county. The surf swirls around the pilings under the pier, lulling you to sleep in a comfy double bed or on the futon couch in the living room. The cottages have full kitchens and one or two bedrooms. They also have private decks right over the water. There are only 26 units, and they book up months in advance. There's a two-night minimum stay in winter, three nights in summer. Insiders consider them one of the best hometown escapes imaginable.

The Dana on Mission Bay $$-$$$
1710 West Mission Bay Drive, Mission Bay
(619) 222-6440, (800) 445-3339
www.thedana.net

Once a pleasant, modest family hotel, the Dana is now a full-scale resort with 270 rooms and suites, a conference center, marina and boat launch, fitness center, two pools, and a bayside wedding site. Sleek teak and mahogany furnishings, granite countertops, and plantation shutters give rooms a modern, airy feel; some have balconies overlooking the bay.

Free shuttles to the airport, SeaWorld, and Mission Beach are a major plus, and you can spot the summer nightly SeaWorld fireworks from the property. Facilities include a water sports center, a private marina, and bicycle rentals (biking is the perfect way to tour Mission Bay). The casual Blue Pearl restaurant serves breakfast, lunch, and dinner and offers children's menus.

Hilton San Diego Resort $$$-$$$$
1775 East Mission Bay Drive, Mission Bay
(619) 276-4010, (800) 445-8667
www.hilton.com

The Hilton San Diego is an oasis of palm trees and sand with a mirage-come-true in the form of beautiful Mission Bay right alongside the hotel. The Mediterranean-style resort has 357 rooms. Standard guest rooms have courtyard and garden views; suites have expansive bay views.

Activities galore await you at the Hilton. Take a walk down to the bay, which is just steps away, or play tennis on the lighted courts. Maybe you'd like to swim in the hotel's huge pool or hot tub—both have a bay view. The excellent activity center has bikes, catamarans, and other water toys for rent. Bayside Terrace Grill, which serves all meals, has outdoor seating.

Hostelling International Point Loma $
3790 Udall Street, Point Loma
(619) 223-4778
www.sandiegohostels.org

Located on the public bus line to Ocean Beach, this neighborhood hostel has 58 dorm beds available at $17 to $19 per night and five private rooms with shared bed at $42 to $48 per night. Laundry, Internet, and kitchen facilities are available, as is free parking. The Point Loma library is just down the street, and there's a grocery store and Laundromat across the street.

The immediate neighborhood is mostly residential, but the beach is a 10-minute bus ride away. Reservations are advised.

Inn at Sunset Cliffs **$$-$$$**
1370 Sunset Cliffs Boulevard, Ocean Beach
(619) 222-7901, (866) 786-2543
www.innatsunsetcliffs.com

If you love the sound of crashing waves, you'll be thrilled with this refurbished small hotel in Ocean Beach. A few suites sit right beside the ocean; even those farthest from the water are close enough for guests to smell the salty sea. All rooms have coffeemakers, microwaves, mini-refrigerators, and high-speed Internet access; some suites have one or two bedrooms and full kitchens.

The heated pool is a plus (it gets chilly by the ocean). Nearby beaches are favored by surfers and experienced swimmers. Ocean Beach's main beaches and pier are about a 10-minute walk away. There's no restaurant, but small markets and take-out delis are located within a couple of blocks, and Ocean Beach has a wide range of restaurants.

Paradise Point Resort & Spa **$$$$**
1404 West Vacation Road, Mission Bay
(858) 274-4630, (800) 344-2626
www.paradisepoint.com

For the best combination of luxury and a beach vacation, Paradise Point Resort is a great choice. The 462 single-level bungalow rooms have a variety of layouts, and all have patios and a spectacular garden, lagoon, or bay view. Studio and one-bedroom suites are also available.

The resort is perfect for quiet strolls, where you'll find surprises at every turn: lagoons with water lilies, fountains, waterfalls, bridges, and botanical treasures. For more active pursuits, try one of five pools or swim and sunbathe on the mile of sandy beach surrounding the resort. Tennis, sailing, volleyball, and bicycling are available, and an 18-hole putting course will help you refine your stroke. Paradise Point also has a fully equipped fitness center and Spa Terre, which incorporates an Indonesian style of relaxation treatments along with sports massage and other traditional treatments. Be sure to stop in at the Barefoot Bar, a legendary hangout for locals. Also on the premises is the excellent Baleen Restaurant & Bar, serving breakfast, lunch, and dinner with an emphasis on fresh seafood.

Tower 23 **$$$**
723 Felspar Street, Pacific Beach
(858) 270-2323, (866) TOWER23
www.t23hotel.com

Named for a lifeguard tower on Pacific Beach, Tower 23 is the hippest hotel on any San Diego beach. Splurge on a Sanctuary Suite with whirlpool tub and rain shower or go for the Surf Pad with the spot-on view of the boardwalk and beach. A Zen theme prevails from the cushy Serenity beds to the glass walls and water features that seem to change with the sun's light. Flat-screen LCD TVs and X-Box entertainment centers are available in all 44 rooms, and the whole building has wireless Internet access. The in-house JRDN (Jordan) restaurant throbs with youthful exuberance on weekend nights, as tanned hipsters dine on sushi and seafood. Noise can be a problem, but it's great fun to slip into a surf-sun-and-fun attitude and slip off to sleep to the sound of crashing waves long after the partiers have gone home.

Coronado

Best Western Suites Coronado **$$**
275 Orange Avenue, Coronado
(619) 437-1666, (800) 780-7234
www.bestwestern.com

One of the best values in Coronado, the Best Western's 63 rooms and suites offer comfort and convenience to all of Coronado's attractions. The Old Ferry Landing, with its shops and restaurants, is a 10-minute walk away, and the downtown village of Coronado is about 6 blocks in the other direction.

CLOSE-UP

Hotel del Coronado

Rarely does a mere hotel achieve legendary status, but the Hotel del Coronado has accomplished just that. Built in 1888 in the early stages of the development of the seaside village of Coronado, The Del has maintained a tradition of lavish service in a fairy-tale setting surrounded by mystery and wonder. The grounds sprawl across 26 acres of lush beachfront property, and the hotel itself is an architectural marvel. Some say it is as elaborate and frilly as a wedding cake. Locals have long claimed that Frank L. Baum, who wrote *The Wizard of Oz,* based his design of Emerald City on the hotel's turreted architecture. Actually, the book was written before Baum ever visited Coronado, but he completed other Oz books at the hotel and in a small cottage on the island. His child was even born at the hotel, and Baum is credited with designing the elaborate crown chandeliers that once hung in the hotel's ballroom, aptly called the Crown Room. Everywhere you turn is a nook, a cranny, a gazebo, or an alcove that makes you feel you're uncovering a secret that no one has ever found before.

Two Midwestern builders dreamed up The Del. Back in the 1880s, before Coronado was developed, Elisha Babcock and H. L. Story could see promise in the barren landscape. They spared no money or effort, importing lumber and laborers from San Francisco to help construct their vision. A mahogany bar was built in Philadelphia and delivered fully assembled to Coronado by ship, traveling all the way around South America. Babcock and Story spent a cool $1 million to realize their dream—$600,000 for construction and $400,000 for furnishings—an amount unheard of in those days.

The Del quickly became world famous, and even though it now is more than a century old, it has never sacrificed its old-world charm and elegance.

The hotel has attracted its share of legendary guests. Ten U.S. presidents have stayed at The Del, starting with Benjamin Harrison in 1891. Over the years William Taft, Franklin D. Roosevelt, Richard M. Nixon, Ronald Reagan, and Bill Clinton have all been guests.

But more than just politicians have added their luster to the hotel. Charles Lindbergh was honored at The Del after his historic 1927 flight across the Atlantic Ocean. And in 1920 England's Prince of Wales (who later became King Edward VIII) was an honored guest. It has long been rumored that the prince met Wallis Simpson at The Del; he later abdicated the throne to marry her. The story is a bit more complicated, and it's not known for sure that they actually met at the hotel. But the romantic rumor lingers.

Hollywood was quick to discover The Del, too, and frequently used the hotel grounds and interior for filming movies. Most famous, of course, is the romantic

Hotel del Coronado is a legend in its own right. PHOTO: COURTESY OF MARIBETH MELLIN

comedy *Some Like It Hot,* filmed in 1958 and starring Marilyn Monroe, Jack Lemmon, and Tony Curtis. Naturally, in 1995, when the Marilyn Monroe postage stamp was released, the only logical place for the unveiling was The Del. More recently The Del served as the main stage for *The Stunt Man,* starring Peter O'Toole, and it has served as a backdrop for scenes in *Mr. Wrong,* with Ellen DeGeneres, and *My Blue Heaven,* with Steve Martin. There has never been a shortage of fine entertainers either. During the summers of 1949 and 1950, the flamboyant pianist Liberace entertained in the Circus Room.

For those who have an affinity for the supernatural, The Del does indeed have a resident ghost. Hotel management had long hoped that particular legend would die; it now encourages repetition of the story of Kate Morgan, who was shot on a stairway outside the hotel in 1892. It is said that Morgan's spirit haunts room 3312. Some have felt the presence of a ghost in the room Morgan's maid used as well. In fact, the 1972 television series *Ghost Story* was filmed at The Del. If you'd like to add a little adventure to your holiday, ask the receptionist for the haunted room when you make your reservation. Stories of ghost sightings are all just part of the allure.

Today the Hotel del Coronado is as modern as the discriminating traveler demands, but it has never lost its original design and beauty. Thanks to ongoing renovations, the hotel retains the polish of its youth. A recent five-year makeover totaled $55 million. All guest rooms, public spaces, and meeting rooms were refurbished, including the oceanfront ballroom. The beautifully landscaped Windsor Lawn was created to replace the unsightly tennis courts that long marred the view of the ocean from the rooms. A birdcage elevator in the lobby was restored and now has a uniformed operator on duty 24 hours a day. Babcock and Story are honored in a bar and lounge bearing their names. It's a great place for a sunset drink or bedtime brandy.

The Hotel del Coronado has been designated by Congress as a National Historic Landmark and is dedicated to protecting its architectural integrity. Locals insist that the hotel remain the same and strongly protest any significant changes. This is no small task for the owners, when you consider that every modern service and comfort must continually be provided for guests to keep coming back. Ongoing building projects include Beach Village, with 78 oceanview rooms and suites, some with multiple bedrooms, fireplaces, and private patios. The exclusive enclave will have its own pools and hot tubs, a separate front desk, and an on-site concierge. A new state-of-the-art spa and fitness center is slated to open in late 2006 beside the Windsor Lawn.

Over the years, even though ownership of The Del has changed hands several times, the owners have never missed a step. The hotel is as beautiful as it was the day it first opened to the public in 1888, and it will continue to be a source of great pride in San Diego for generations to come.

All the rooms and suites are decorated in a contemporary style, and some have a view of the quiet courtyard in the middle of the hotel. Government and military travelers especially appreciate the Best Western Coronado because it's close to North Island Naval Air Station. Also available for guests are on-site laundry facilities and a complimentary continental breakfast. The streetside balcony rooms are excellent viewing stations for Coronado's Fourth of July parade.

Crown City Inn **$$**
520 Orange Avenue, Coronado
(619) 435-6750, (800) 422-1173
www.crowncityinn.com

One of the nicest features of Coronado is that it's a small island, jam-packed with things to do. And the Crown City Inn is right in the middle of it all. Walk 5 blocks in one direction and you'll find beautiful beaches. Five long blocks in the other direction brings you to San Diego Bay and the Old Ferry Landing.

The inn itself has 35 rooms, including a few one-bedroom suites. If you're not in the mood for a day at the beach, relax by the pool in the courtyard, or catch up on your laundry at the on-site facilities. The inn's Cafe Bistro, open for breakfast, lunch, and dinner (closed Sunday), is known for its good French/American cuisine. You're welcome to bring the family pet for an additional $8.00 to $25.00 per night.

Hotel del Coronado **$$$$**
1500 Orange Avenue, Coronado
(619) 522-8000, (800) 468-3533
www.hoteldel.com

Don't let The Del's 674 rooms lead you to believe you'll get lost in a maze of structures and people. Despite its size, The Del has created a comfy, cozy, and luxurious atmosphere that will make you feel like its most treasured guest. All the rooms in the main building have been painstakingly restored and are one of a kind in their decor. Rooms in the Ocean Tower combine the grandeur of the past with the conveniences of the present and a sense of quiet privacy. No matter where you choose to stay, you'll be overwhelmed by the surrounding beauty of the Pacific Ocean and the beautifully landscaped grounds of the hotel.

Guests need not stray far from the hotel to enjoy all the elements of a true Southern California vacation. Within the hotel are two restaurants and two lounges, and many more are just a few blocks' stroll away. You can enjoy tennis on The Del's oceanside courts or golf at the nearby Coronado Golf Course. The Del has its own boathouse from which all sorts of water activities can be enjoyed: sailing, fishing, and whale watching, to name a few. Round out your day with a few laps in one of the heated pools or a sunset stroll on the gorgeous long beach. And, of course, the hotel has its own shopping arcade, which is sure to provide you with the perfect memento of your stay.

Look for the Close-up on the Hotel del Coronado in this chapter for the history of this fascinating landmark. Locals have traditionally chosen the hotel's Sunday brunch as the setting for their Mother's Day and Easter celebrations. Served in the grand Crown Room, the brunch is a busy, bustling affair yet still feels elegant and special. Make reservations far in advance. In 2006 the hotel replaced its venerable Prince of Wales restaurant with 1500 OCEAN, an intimate, elegant dining room serving Southern California cuisine. Sheerwater, the more casual restaurant, is open for all three meals, and Victorian High Tea is served on Sunday in the Palm Court overlooking the gardens.

Loews Coronado Bay Resort $$$$
4000 Coronado Bay Road, Coronado
(619) 424-4000, (800) 815-6397
www.loewshotels.com

If you're ready to splurge and indulge yourself in the ultimate luxury hotel, the Loews Coronado Bay Resort is the place for you. Located on a private peninsula just a few miles south of Coronado, the resort has 438 guest rooms and suites, all with spectacular views of San Diego Bay, Loews' private marina, or one of the sparkling pools. This is a true destination resort (see our entry in Spas and Resorts), so get ready to be pampered.

Everything you'd expect in a resort is here: a full-service spa and fitness center, three swimming pools, and three full-size tennis courts. In addition, Loews Coronado Bay Resort has a business center with everything you'd need to combine work with pleasure. Azzura Point, one of the resort's award-winning restaurants, offers exquisite classic California cuisine, an inviting atmosphere, and superb service (see our Restaurants chapter for all the details). In a more casual setting, guests can enjoy dockside dining at the Market Café for breakfast, lunch, and dinner. The Market Café's award-winning Sunday brunch is a seafood lover's delight, with gorgeous displays of crab legs, sushi, and marinated seafood salads, as well as carved meats, waffles, and all your brunch favorites. If you simply can't drag yourself away from the sunshine and swimming pool, La Cantina, the outdoor bar and grill, is the perfect solution. Guests can relax after a long day in the Cays Lounge, which offers evening entertainment, cocktails, and hors d'oeuvres alongside an intimate fireplace.

Downtown/Gaslamp Quarter

Courtyard Marriott San Diego Downtown $$$
530 Broadway, Downtown
(619) 446-3000, (800) 321-2211
www.marriott.com

The 1927 San Diego Trust and Savings Bank, once a cornerstone of downtown, was uninhabited for several years before Marriott stepped in to revive the ornate building. The hotel's lobby has the original painted ceilings and bank tellers' counters, and the vault is now a meeting room. The 245 rooms are suitably decorated with carpeting and drapes in rich reds and blues. A restaurant and bar take up much of the lobby space. There is no on-site parking, but valet parking is available for $24 per day.

Embassy Suites Hotel **$$$**
601 Pacific Highway, Downtown
(619) 239-2400, (800) 362-2779
www.embassysuites.com

Downtown's Embassy Suites is in an ideal location: slightly removed from the hustle and bustle of downtown, yet close enough to walk to many of its attractions and restaurants. On one side of the hotel, the view is of San Diego's sparkling harbor. The other side offers a view of the stately skyscrapers that populate the heart of downtown. Each of the 337 suites has a living area (complete with refrigerator, microwave, and wet bar) and a separate bedroom and bath. An indoor pool and whirlpool are perfect for unwinding after a long day of sightseeing. There's also a full fitness center.

Seaport Village, with its shops and restaurants, is only 1 block away from the hotel (see our Shopping and Attractions chapters for the lowdown on Seaport Village), and the convention center is a long 3 blocks away. Allow 10 minutes to reach the center for meetings. Plus, all the shopping, dining, and nightlife of downtown and the Gaslamp Quarter are within a short walking distance.

Children younger than age 18 stay for free with their parents.

Hilton San Diego
Gaslamp Quarter **$$$-$$$$**
401 K Street, Downtown
(619) 231-4040, (800) 445-8667
www.hilton.com

Located directly across Harbor Drive from the convention center and near a trolley stop, the Hilton is an urbane, chic hotel. Some of the 282 rooms and suites are designed to resemble artists' lofts, and all are decorated with original art. The terrace-level outdoor pool and sundeck overlook the convention center. The fitness center has all the latest equipment, and you can jog along Martin Luther King Promenade, a linear park that runs alongside the trolley tracks. Take a break from sightseeing to enjoy a bit of pampering at the Artesia Spa. The breakfast buffet at the hotel's New Leaf restaurant is one of the best you'll find in a hotel, and the outdoor terrace seating is tranquil (except when a trolley passes by).

Holiday Inn on the Bay **$$**
1355 North Harbor Drive, Downtown
(619) 232-3861, (800) 877-8920
www.sixcontinentshotels.com

The 600-room twin high-rise towers of the Holiday Inn lie at the foot of downtown on the embarcadero, close to everything there is to see and do. Rooms have a view of either San Diego Bay or the city lights and lots of special amenities including high-speed and wireless Internet access. The rooms are renovated frequently, but this is an older hotel with some noise problems.

Workouts are a breeze in the poolside exercise facility, and a waterfront jogging trail is right across the street. The Elephant & Castle is an English-style pub and restaurant that's open for breakfast, lunch, and dinner and comes equipped with pool tables and dartboards. You can dine in style at the nearby Ruth's Chris Steakhouse, or grab a sandwich at Hazlewood's Deli. All of downtown's attractions are a few blocks away, and harbor cruises, the Maritime Museum, the *Star of India,* and the San Diego-Coronado Ferry are right across the street from the hotel. You may bring your pet along, but you must pay a $100 deposit, $75 of which is refundable. Pets are not allowed in public areas.

Horton Grand Hotel **$$$**
311 Island Avenue, San Diego
(619) 544-1886, (800) 542-1886
www.hortongrand.com

In 1986 the Horton Grand was built, brick by brick, from two original Victorian hotels in San Diego's Gaslamp Quarter. Today you can enjoy the elegance of the early-20th-century era in this painstakingly re-

The Horton Grand Hotel is made up of two Victorian-era historic buildings. PHOTO: COURTESY OF HORTON GRAND HOTEL

created hotel. None of the 132 rooms are alike, but all are furnished with Victorian draped queen-size beds, antiques, and gas-burning fireplaces. Be sure to check out the fabulous 100-year-old oak staircase in the lobby bar, lovingly restored at a cost of $200,000.

The Ida Bailey Restaurant is located on the premises, serving breakfast, lunch, and dinner as well as a sumptuous Sunday brunch. High tea is served on Saturday from 2:30 until 5:00 P.M. for $19.95. Shopping, restaurants, and nightlife are all within 2 or 3 blocks.

Hostelling International-USA, San Diego **$**
521 Market Street, San Diego
(619) 525-1531, (800) 909-4776
www.sandiegohostels.org

Located in the Gaslamp Quarter, this hostel has an ideal location and both dorm and private rooms. Free breakfast is served in the dining area, and guests gather in the lounge to share budget-travel tips. Internet, laundry, and kitchen facilities are available, as are lockers. Reservations are strongly advised. Rates for dorm rooms are $19 to $26, for private rooms $47 to $62—a real bargain in downtown.

Hotel Solamar **$$$$**
435 Sixth Avenue at J Street, Downtown
(619) 531-8740, (877) 230-0300
www.hotelsolamar.com

As befits a hotel in the stylish Kimpton chain, the Solamar is a study in modernistic design. You can't help swiveling your head and looking around as you approach the front desk beside a lounge area called the living room. A fireplace glows beside cozy chairs where guests study maps and brochures or use the hotel's WiFi on their laptops. A Casablanca flair prevails in the lobby and around the rooftop pool and bar.

The 235 rooms have a whimsical flare, with polka-dot fabrics and overstuffed chairs. Large desktops with ergonomic chairs and a Yoga channel on the flat-screen TVs please stressed business travelers who enjoy after-work gatherings by the fire pit in JBar on the roof. Pets are welcome.

San Diego's skyline rises behind the pool at the Manchester Grand Hyatt. PHOTO: COURTESY OF MARIBETH MELLIN

J Street Inn **$**
222 J Street, San Diego
(619) 696-6922
www.thejstreetinn.com
This budget gem is located just a couple of blocks from the convention center and is a model for inexpensive accommodations for visitors and city dwellers alike. The 200 clean, bright units are available on a daily or weekly basis, though you must stay three weeks to get the special weekly rate. Underground parking is available for a fee, and there are plenty of restaurants in the neighborhood.

La Pensione Hotel **$**
600 West Date Street, San Diego
(619) 236-8000, (800) 232-4683
www.lapensionehotel.com
Located in the rapidly developing downtown area of San Diego known as Little Italy, this modern hotel is a real find for the bargain traveler. The hotel has 75 rooms, all with refrigerators, cable TV, and dataports. There are plenty of excellent Italian restaurants and pizzerias, nightclubs, and bars nearby. Construction is taking place throughout this neighborhood as condo and townhome complexes rise to provide more downtown housing; noise can be a problem. The hotel is right by the trolley line and public bus stops. Underground parking and laundry facilities are available.

Manchester Grand Hyatt San Diego **$$$$**
One Market Place, San Diego
(619) 232-1234, (800) 233-1234
www.manchestergrand.hyatt.com
With boasting rights as the largest and tallest hotel on the West Coast, the Hyatt towers over San Diego Bay near the convention center. Naturally the 1,625 guest rooms and large meeting rooms make the Hyatt a popular convention and meetings hotel; the 30,000-square-foot ballroom is said to be the largest in Southern California. A terrace-level pool deck separates the hotel's two towers and even has an outdoor fireplace by the hot tub for chilly evenings. Rooms are standard Hyatt style with a somewhat jarring decor mixing plaid and floral fabrics. Nearly all the rooms are non-

smoking; all have coffeemakers, irons and ironing boards, and hair dryers. The 62 wheelchair-accessible rooms have all the necessities, including roll-in showers, easy pool access, and TDD phones.

Restaurants and bars include Sally's Seafood on the Water, with floor-to-ceiling views of the bay; Lael's, serving a prime rib buffet on Thursday nights; and the Top of the Hyatt on the 40th floor, where sunset cocktails are popular with downtown workers. The hotel has a full spa and salon, a fitness center, four tennis courts, and two pools.

Omni San Diego **$$$-$$$$**
675 L Street at Sixth Avenue
(619) 231-6664, (888) 444-6664
www.omnihotels.com

Few hotels can claim direct access to a major baseball park. The Omni actually has a sky bridge from a second-story corridor lined with baseball memorabilia to Petco Park. Private condos fill the top floors of the hotel's glass tower; naturally, the Padres' top brass claims prime views of the ballpark. A few of the 511 guest rooms also overlook the ballpark and are booked months in advance of home games.

You needn't be a baseball fan to enjoy the hotel's comfortable and highly functional rooms. All details are user-friendly, and the large desk and office chair take some of the pain out of business travel. The large bathrooms have plenty of shelves for toiletries, and the Get Fit rooms come equipped with treadmills. Guests gather around the fireplace by the rooftop pool on chilly evenings.

W San Diego **$$$-$$$$**
421 B Street, San Diego
(619) 231-8220
www.starwoodhotels.com

The sleek W, where trendy young professionals meet in the lobby bar for after-work martinis started downtown's hip hotel trend. The heated sand-floored rooftop beach bar is beyond cool, as is Rice, the main restaurant, serving Latin-Asian fusion cuisine. But on to the rooms—this is a hotel, after all. The decor is stark yet soothing, with pillow-top mattresses, Aveda toiletries, CD and DVD players, and broadband high-speed Internet access. It pays to be trendy if you decide to stay here, just to make it past the evening cocktail crowd in the Living Room lounge. Still, the very presence of a W hotel in San Diego means the city has achieved the cutting-edge status of Los Angeles or Manhattan.

U.S. Grant Hotel **$$$$**
326 Broadway, San Diego
(619) 232-3121, (800) 237-5029
www.usgrant.net

The historic U..S Grant has been a San Diego landmark and gathering spot since 1910. Ulysses South Grant Jr. commissioned the Italian renaissance palace to honor his father, President Ulysses South Grant. The hotel was quite grand, with an indoor pool and 400 rooms. Several investors have taken charge of the grand hotel over the years, remodeling the space and adding rooms. The hotel has been closed for yet another renovation, this one totaling $52 million. Scheduled to reopen in late 2006, the new U.S. Grant will have 273 opulent guest rooms and 47 suites, a rooftop terrace, and a fitness center. The hotel is now a part of Starwood Hotels' worldwide Luxury Collection, on par with the Gritti Palace in Venice and the Phoenician in Scottsdale, Arizona. When the hotel reopens, San Diegans will be thrilled

i

San Diego native Doug Manchester's 1,625-room Manchester Grand Hyatt is the largest hotel in downtown and commands the most impressive views. The 750-room tower is only 66 feet wide, yet the guest rooms have 30-foot-wide views of the bay or city. Dubbed the "screwdriver," the hotel's two narrow towers appear to pierce the waterfront skyline by the San Diego Convention Center.

CLOSE-UP

Rooms by the Sea

San Diego is an obvious beach destination, yet few hotels actually sit by the sand. If you're determined to hear waves crashing and the surf swooshing as you sleep, make sure your room really is close to the sea. Don't fall for enticements that claim a hotel is "steps from the sand" and has "oceanview" rooms. It's amazing how many things can stand between the beach and your room with a view. For absolute proximity to the sea you can't beat the Crystal Pier Hotel & Cottages. Book a cottage on the pier and the waves will crash right beneath your bed. In Ocean Beach, the surf has carved deep ridges into the cliffs beneath the Sunset Cliffs Inn.

Depending on the season, waves slam onto or slither over the sand in front of the La Jolla Beach & Tennis Club, which sits on a private beach at La Jolla Shores. The adjacent Sea Lodge shares its beach with the public; kayakers, swimmers, anglers, and scuba divers all enter the water at the nearby boat ramp. In North County, the Oceanside Marina Suites faces the open ocean and the harbor from its perch on a private peninsula.

Several other hotels are close enough to the sand to live up to oceanview standards. The Hotel del Coronado poses above one of the most gorgeous beaches in the county. You'll have to wander through gardens and lawns to reach the sand, but you should be able to hear the ocean from an oceanview room. Tower 23 in Pacific Beach sits right on the boardwalk, so you can wander barefoot from your room to your beach towel.

You'll pay dearly to fulfill your dream if you want to sleep by the sea in summer. Demand is incredibly high even as room rates rise between Memorial Day and Labor Day. Take advantage of lower rates and more availability by traveling to the beach in September and October, often the sunniest months in San Diego.

to once again dine at the clublike Grant Grill and enjoy afternoon tea under the lobby chandeliers.

Westgate Hotel **$$$$**
1055 Second Avenue, San Diego
(619) 238-1818, (800) 221-3802
www.westgatehotel.com

Voted by readers of *Travel & Leisure* magazine as the best business hotel in San Diego, the Westgate is filled with priceless antiques. The decor is reminiscent of an elaborate and ornate anteroom found in the Palace of Versailles in Paris. Each of the 223 guest rooms is unique in its design and offers a variety of amenities, including two-line phones and dataports and European antiques. The Westgate is located in the heart of downtown, across from the Westfield Shoppingtown Horton Plaza shopping center and the historic Gaslamp Quarter. Lunch, dinner, and a lavish Sunday brunch are served beneath crystal chandeliers in the hotel's Fontainebleau Restaurant. The restaurant's Friday night gourmet Seafood Soiree is utter heaven for those who crave oysters, mussels, and lobster. For more lively entertainment, try the Plaza Bar. Afternoon tea is served in the elegant lobby while a harpist plays in the background.

La Jolla/Golden Triangle

Embassy Suites Hotel **$$$**
4550 La Jolla Village Drive, San Diego
(858) 453-0400, (800) 362-2779
www.embassysuites.com

Like its sister hotel in downtown San Diego, the Embassy Suites in the Golden Triangle offers 335 full suites consisting of living room, bedroom, and bath. This is a popular hotel among business travelers, but many visitors enjoy it as well because of its proximity to La Jolla and to Westfield Shoppingtown University Town Center (UTC), one of San Diego's nicest shopping malls. (Check our Shopping chapter for all the details on UTC.) The mall is within easy walking distance of the hotel and has an abundance of stores, restaurants, and a multiplex theater.

The Coast Cafe restaurant on the premises is open for breakfast, lunch, and dinner, and many top-notch restaurants are within a few blocks. Room rates include a full cooked-to-order breakfast. For visitors who plan to do a lot of sightseeing, this is a centrally located spot that's hard to beat. La Jolla is a 5-minute drive away, downtown San Diego is 15 minutes south, and North County Coastal's hot spots are 15 minutes north. Children younger than age 18 stay for free with their parents.

The Grande Colonial **$$$**
910 Prospect Street, La Jolla
(858) 964-5400, (800) 826-1278
www.thegrandecolonial.com

The perfect blend of European ambience and American hospitality is found at this classy hotel, a member of the Historic Hotels of America. Its 75 luxury rooms and suites have a French country decor with some antique furniture. Eight of the suites are in a vintage beach cottage set amid flower gardens behind the main building. Rooms at the back of the hotel on the top floors have great views of La Jolla Cove.

A pool is on the premises, and the hotel can recommend a nearby gym or spa. The superb Nine-Ten restaurant is onsite, serving breakfast, lunch, and dinner daily. The inn is virtually steps away from La Jolla's numerous fine restaurants, shops, and galleries, so be sure to go exploring. Smoking is not allowed in any of the rooms.

New rooms are under construction in an adjacent building.

Hotel Parisi **$$$$**
1111 Prospect Street, La Jolla
(858) 454-1511
www.hotelparisi.com

The Zen-like ambience of this ultrachic hotel has made it the darling of celebrities and locals enjoying a special night out. The 20 rooms (all nonsmoking) were designed along feng shui principles and have a beige, cream, and white sleek decor that feels comfortable and soothing. The rooms are located above Victoria's Secret and other shops. Those facing the street can be noisy. There's no restaurant, but nearly every type of food you crave is available within easy walking distance. There is nightly room service from 5:00 to 10:00 P.M. provided by the nearby Tapenade Provencal Restaurant.

Hyatt Regency La Jolla **$$$**
3777 La Jolla Village Drive, La Jolla
(858) 552-1234, (800) 233-1234
www.hyatt.com

Located in the heart of the Golden Triangle, the Hyatt Regency offers all the amenities travelers have come to expect from fine hotels. Eleven acres of lush gardens surround this 419-room hotel, and the architecture and decor reflect the

The Hard Rock Hotel San Diego is scheduled to open in spring 2007 and will surely be downtown's hottest hotel and nightlife venue for many months. The 12-story hotel is rising just a few blocks from the ultrahip Hotel Solamar and will up the stakes in the competition for chic clientele.

style of architect Michael Graves's version of an Italian palace. The hotel's Aventine Sporting Club is a 32,000-square-foot health spa that's sure to challenge even the most fitness oriented. And, of course, tennis and a swimming pool are part of the package, too.

The hotel is part of the Aventine complex, which includes the sporting club, an office tower, and a restaurant enclave with several trendy eateries. Westfield Shoppingtown University Towne Center (as detailed in our Shopping chapter) is 3 blocks away.

La Jolla Beach & Tennis Club $$$$
2000 Spindrift Drive, La Jolla
(858) 454-7126, (800) 624-2582
www.ljbtc.com

Smack on the sand at the south end of La Jolla Shores, the La Jolla Beach & Tennis Club sprawls across 14 acres of prime oceanfront real estate. F.W. Kellogg, who established the resort in 1927, knew a good thing when he saw it. The prosperous newspaper publisher wanted to build a yacht club at the edge of the burgeoning La Jolla community, but deep water and the Depression quashed those dreams. Instead, he established a beach club and framed the property with stately Washington palms.

Today there's a four-year wait for membership. Outsiders can experience the club only with a member or as a guest in one of the 90 hotel units. Many guests return annually with families and friends and claim the prime rooms a year in advance of their summer vacations. Snagging a summer reservation for a one- or two-bedroom suite with kitchenette and full-on ocean view is difficult for first timers, but not impossible. There are pockets of availability in summer, and demand decreases considerably between Labor Day and Memorial Day.

The club's 90 rooms and suites are functional and comfortable, designed for sandy feet and damp bodies. Twenty rooms underwent a complete makeover in 2006. Wireless and high-speed Internet connections are available on the property. Facilities include a nine-hole golf course, 12 tennis courts, and a playground.

The club's beach is private (California beaches are public only to the high-tide line). Brightly striped beach umbrellas and toy boxes with buckets and shovels are thoughtfully placed along the beachfront esplanade. Guests can order barbecues, fire pits, steaks, and even s'mores from the clever Beach Services menu. The aroma of wood fires fills the air on summer evenings. Guests wander barefoot between their rooms and the sand, mingling with the club members who delight in their private beach. A mood of laid-back camaraderie prevails.

The classy, superb Marine Room restaurant sits at the south end of the property (see our Restaurants chapter). All meals are also served in the club's gardenlike dining room and on the pool terrace. Lounge chairs come equipped with flags for ordering food and drink service on the sand.

La Jolla Beach Travelodge $$
6750 La Jolla Boulevard, La Jolla
(858) 454-0716, (800) 578-7878
www.travelodge.com

One of the best bargains in La Jolla, the Travelodge is located outside the village area but close to Windansea Beach, where you can watch surfing pros ride the waves. The 44 rooms have coffeemakers, irons and ironing boards, and hair dryers. The pool is heated, and there is a hot tub. This is a good choice for those who plan to spend more time out playing than using the hotel facilities.

La Valencia **$$$$**
1132 Prospect Street, La Jolla
(858) 454-0771, (800) 451-0772
www.lavalencia.com

A landmark in La Jolla, La Valencia is the essence of old-world elegance and luxury. Overlooking La Jolla Cove, its 117 guest rooms and suites are custom decorated with a European flavor, and rooms have either a garden or a sweeping ocean view. Fifteen luxurious villas have whirlpool tubs, king-size beds, and an abundance of marble and granite accents in the Mediterranean decor. A private butler tends to the villa guests, unpacking their luggage, stocking the wet bar, and collecting the appropriate CDs for the in-room player. It doesn't get much more luxurious than this.

Even though you're just a whisper away from the ocean, the hotel has a heated swimming pool, whirlpool hot tub, and a fitness room with a sauna and massage rooms.

The Mediterranean Room/Tropical Patio serves breakfast, lunch, and dinner daily. For a more intimate dining experience, try the Sky Room Restaurant on the tenth floor, overlooking the cove. Be sure to stop by the Whaling Bar & Grill for lunch, dinner, or cocktails; La Jolla's Old Guard families tend to think of it as their private club.

The Lodge at Torrey Pines **$$$$**
11480 North Torrey Pines Road, La Jolla
(858) 453-4420, (888) 826-0224
www.lodgetorreypines.com

A veritable museum devoted to California Craftsman architecture and furnishings, The Lodge has received every kudo imaginable since opening in spring 2002. Owner Bill Evans purchased an old hotel on the bluffs above the ocean, beside the Torrey Pines Golf Course, several years ago. His passion for the architectural style of the early 1900s led to this faithful reproduction, with post-and-beam construction, shingle and sandstone exteriors, natural rock walls, and hardwood floors. The lobby and 173 guest rooms have William Morris-style furnishings mixing leather and wood.

Though the design is historical, the services are state of the art, with high-speed Internet access in the rooms and deep soaking tubs and separate showers in the bathrooms. The restaurant A.R. Valentien is also an award winner for both its warm, inviting ambience and its generous portions of beef, venison, salmon, and other hearty fare. Staying here is like immersing yourself in the best California has to offer.

Sea Lodge **$$$-$$$$**
8110 Camino del Oro, La Jolla
(858) 459-8271, (800) 237-5211

Step onto the balcony of your room at the Sea Lodge and you can almost touch the waves. It has become one of California's favorite oceanfront retreats, with its 128 rooms set amid fountains, courtyards, fresh flowers, and ocean breezes. The rooms have a casual, comfortable feeling, so you needn't worry about your wet, sandy beach gear. The architecture is reminiscent of old Mexico, and Mexican antiques are everywhere you turn on the grounds of the hotel.

The Sea Lodge offers an array of amenities: fitness center, tennis, pool and spa, sauna, and volleyball on the beach. The oceanfront Shores restaurant offers breakfast, lunch, and dinner daily. The menu, designed by chef Bernard Guillas of the Marine Room, offers exceptional cuisine at affordable prices.

Mission Valley

Doubletree Hotel San Diego/ Mission Valley **$$**
7450 Hazard Center Drive, Central San Diego
(619) 297-5466, (800) 222-TREE
www.doubletree.com

Located in the heart of Mission Valley's shopping district, the Doubletree has the added bonus of being right across the street from a San Diego Trolley station,

Searching for reduced rates on the Internet can often produce favorable results. Be aware, however, that hotels treat clients who have booked their rooms through Internet hotel reservation centers differently than those booking through the hotel. General managers tell us that guests who book directly through the hotel or its 800 number are more likely to get what they request, including nonsmoking rooms, extra beds or cribs, views, and other amenities.

which will take visitors to all points of interest in San Diego. The hotel's 300 guest rooms and suites all have minibars and PC dataports for those who don't like to be disconnected.

Swim in the indoor or outdoor pools, or get a good workout in the fitness center. Casual all-day dining is available at the Fountain Cafe. Enjoy the freshly baked chocolate chip cookie that awaits you on arrival. Pets are allowed at no additional charge. There's also a Doubletree Club Hotel in Mission Valley at 1515 Hotel Circle South.

Handlery Hotel & Resort **$$**
950 Hotel Circle N., San Diego
(619) 298-4135, (800) 843-4343
www.handlery.com

Each of the 217 contemporary rooms at the Handlery provide spacious comfort with a calm beige and yellow decor. Guests enjoy a workout in the fitness center, followed by a swim in the large heated pool. Complementary shuttle service is available to many of San Diego's most popular attractions. Golfing enthusiasts may want to book a tee time at the nearby Riverwalk Golf Course. Westfield Shoppingtown Mission Valley and Fashion Valley shopping centers (check out our Shopping chapter for details) are nearby, as are movie theaters and tons of restaurants. Or if you prefer to stay close to home, dine at Postcards American Bistro, which serves breakfast, lunch, and dinner daily.

Marriott Mission Valley **$$**
8757 Rio San Diego Drive, San Diego
(619) 692-3800, (800) 842-5329
www.marriott.com

Mission Valley can't be beat for its easy access to all of San Diego's attractions, and the Marriott Mission Valley is well situated to take advantage of the best the city has to offer. The 17-story, 350-room hotel has a swimming pool, a health club with a whirlpool and sauna, and a business center. Two blocks away are the Rio Vista shopping area and Westfield Shoppingtown Mission Valley. Qualcomm Stadium is just minutes away by car or trolley. The Café del Sol serves breakfast, lunch, and dinner, or grab a bite at any of the nearby restaurants in the valley.

Mission Valley Resort **$$**
875 Hotel Circle S., San Diego
(619) 298-8282, (800) 362-7871
www.missionvalleyresort.com

This beautifully landscaped 20-acre retreat has an ideal location, casual elegance, generous amenities, and attentive service. The 202 rooms are family friendly, with lots of room to spread out and relax. Kids will be pleased by the swimming pool and in-room Nintendo, while adults will enjoy the cocktail lounge with pool tables, the whirlpool spa, and the 27,000-square-foot athletic and racquet club. Pay attention to the location of your room. The property is large and has two pool areas and several parking lots. Rooms at the very back are quietest, while those by the pools can be noisy.

A 24-hour restaurant is located onsite, and room service is available, too. For even more convenience, there's a liquor store and small market. The resort provides complimentary transportation to shopping, trolley stations, and Old Town.

Red Lion Hanalei Hotel $$
2270 Hotel Circle N., San Diego
(619) 297-1101, (800) 882-0858
www.hanaleihotel.com
Here's an Insiders' secret: The Hanalei Hotel is one of the best bargains in San Diego County. It's a full-service luxury hotel for a price that fits most budgets. Surrounded by Southern California's signature palm trees and tropical plants, the Hanalei feels like an exotic resort set amid freeways.

The hotel's 402 rooms and suites are fairly standard, and the swimming pool, whirlpool, and fitness center are there to please the most discriminating traveler. Islands Restaurant serves Pacific Rim cuisine for dinner, and the Peacock Cafe is open daily for breakfast, lunch, and dinner. A $50 deposit will secure accommodations for your small pet.

Town & Country Hotel $$-$$$
500 Hotel Circle N., San Diego
(619) 291-7131, (800) 772-7527
www.towncountry.com
Spread across 40 acres of landscaped grounds, the Town & Country is a San Diego landmark. Amid dozens of palm trees are two guest-room towers and a sprawl of ranch-style garden bungalows. All together, the Town & Country has 1,000 rooms. It also has an on-site convention center, which makes it a favorite place for small conventions and gatherings of all kinds.

Kick off your shoes and jump into one of four swimming pools, or choose from five restaurants, which offer everything from fine cuisine to casual fare. Other facilities include a spa and the adjacent Riverwalk Golf Course (see the Golf chapter).

Old Town

Best Western Hacienda Suites $$-$$$
4041 Harney Street, San Diego
(619) 298-4707, (800) 888-1991
www.bestwestern.com
Terraced on a hillside overlooking Old Town State Park is the all-suite Hacienda. Decorated with handcrafted Southwest-style furnishings, each of the 198 guest suites opens onto a courtyard or a balcony, inviting in those fresh Southern California breezes. Suites have either one or two queen-size beds and come equipped with microwave ovens and refrigerators. You can take an afternoon dip here in the pool or hot tub. The rooms are spead down the hillside, and you may have a long hike back up to the lobby. Ask for something on a high floor if you have mobility issues.

Holiday Inn Express $$
3900 Old Town Avenue, San Diego
(619) 299-7400, (800) 465-4329
www.ichotels.com
Located in the heart of historic Old Town, the Holiday Inn Express has 125 standard rooms and 6 suites in an older motel-like building. Each room comes complete with a microwave oven and refrigerator you can stock with goodies. The hotel provides complimentary continental breakfast.

When you're ready to unwind, there's a central courtyard with its pool, spa, and sundeck. After a day of sightseeing or basking in the sunshine, you can take a 5- or 10-minute stroll to more than 30 restaurants, which offer everything from casual Mexican fare to fine seafood or ethnic cuisine. There's a charge to park in the underground lot.

La Quinta Inn San Diego Old Town $$
2380 Moore Street, San Diego
(619) 291-9100, (866) 725-1661
www.lq.com
The price is right and the location ideal at the edge of the Interstate 5 freeway and Old Town. The rooms all feature a refrigerator and microwave and two queen-size or one king-size bed. The rooms are nicely decorated in a Southwest style. Another plus is the on-site guest laundry facility. The pool is heated (it does get cold here in winter). Guests can also enjoy a complimentary continental breakfast, and there are several restaurants nearby.

Point Loma/Harbor and Shelter Islands

Best Western Island Palms Hotel & Marina **$$**
2051 Shelter Island Drive, Shelter Island
(619) 222-0561, (877) 484-3275
www.bestwestern.com

A common sentiment among visitors is, why come to San Diego if you don't stay on the water? The Island Palms sits beside the blue waters of San Diego Bay and offers a resortlike atmosphere for guests who want to get away from it all and still be close to San Diego's attractions.

The 97-room hotel has a bayside swimming pool and spa (but no swimming in the boat-filled bay), and most rooms and suites have spectacular bay views. If you plan to settle in for a while, take advantage of the oversize suites with full kitchens. The hotel's waterfront restaurant is perfect for dining and unwinding with friends in the lounge. All rooms are designated nonsmoking.

Hilton San Diego Airport **$$$**
1960 Harbor Island Drive, Harbor Island
(619) 291-6700, (800) 445-8667
www.sandiegoairport.hilton.com

Located on Harbor Island (near the airport), the Hilton's 207 rooms overlook San Diego Bay and the lively marina. Most rooms have a view, either of the city or the bay, and all have balconies or patios.

The Sierra Pacific Restaurant is open for breakfast, lunch, and dinner.

Humphrey's Half Moon Inn **$$-$$$**
2303 Shelter Island Drive, Shelter Island
(619) 224-3411, (800) 542-7400
www.halfmooninn.com

A tropical paradise on the bay is the best way to describe the Half Moon Inn on San Diego's Shelter Island. Its 182 rooms and suites are nestled among lush gardens, palm trees, ponds, and waterfalls. Some are in need of remodeling. Ask to see a selection of rooms if you're unhappy with your first choice. Humphrey's Restaurant is on-site and in charge of room service. Guests who visit from June through October are in for a special treat. Humphrey's Concerts by the Bay series (see our Nightlife chapter) takes place right on the grounds of the hotel. Enjoy the evening breezes by the pool or from your balcony while you enjoy music from jazz and pop entertainers such as Kenny G, Ringo Starr, and more. Kids will enjoy the pool and the continuous Ping-Pong games.

Vagabond Inn Point Loma **$$**
1325 Scott Street, San Diego
(619) 224-3371, (800) 522-1555
www.vagabondinns.com

This is strictly a bare-bones accommodation, but for convenience to Point Loma's fishing docks, it's a gem. Directly across the street are deep-sea fishing boats waiting to take guests on half-day or daylong ocean fishing trips. And for those to whom fishing is secondary, shopping and many restaurants are within a few blocks.

The 40 guest rooms underwent gradual remodeling in 2006, and the motel is within a 10- or 15-minute drive to most of San Diego's attractions. Pets are welcome for an additional $10 per night.

NORTH COUNTY COASTAL

Best Western Encinitas Inn and Suites **$$**
85 Encinitas Boulevard, Encinitas
(760) 942-7455, (866) 362-4827
www.bwencinitas.com

Do you need sea breezes? How about great sunsets? How about highway convenience? Then this North County Coastal Best Western is the right choice. It has 94 rooms, some with kitchenettes. Of course, it has the prerequisite pool and lounging features and is especially popular with seminar groups and corporations that use the hotel for retreats and meetings. If you're traveling with your pet and want to stay here, there's a $50 nonrefundable charge.

Best Western Stratford Inn Del Mar $$
710 Camino del Mar, Del Mar
(858) 755-1501, (800) 446-7229
www.bestwestern.com

One of the best bargains in Del Mar, this hotel is within walking distance of village eateries, boutiques and bookstores, and nifty pubs where you can find some live music. There are 93 rooms, and for days when you'd rather not deal with beach sand, there are two pools. The hotel also has a French day spa offering massages, manicures, and other services.

If you're staying for a week, ask about discounts. The hotel has some rooms with kitchenettes, but these are reserved early during both the summer and winter seasons. Book ahead if you want a place to cook.

Carlsbad Inn Beach Resort $$$
3075 Carlsbad Boulevard, Carlsbad
(760) 434-7020, (800) 235-3939
www.carlsbadinn.com

This popular hotel is a block from the ocean and attracts families because of its casual atmosphere. While it's pricey, keep in mind that you're right across a small street from huge sandy beaches and within walking distance to the shops and restaurants in Carlsbad and about 5 blocks from the Coaster station. When you get here you do not need to move the car for the entire vacation. You'll find 62 rooms, some with adjoining rooms and some minisuites. Some rooms are in disrepair, and you may have to deal with noise from adjacent rooms.

There's all you'd expect here, from a pool to rooms with tiny kitchens. Alas, there's no room service, but there are cafes and restaurants by the dozen in downtown Carlsbad.

Del Mar Hilton $$
15575 Jimmy Durante Boulevard, Del Mar
(858) 792-5200, (800) 445-8667
www.hilton.com

Stay at this Hilton and you can walk to the Del Mar Fairgrounds, including the on- and off-site horse racetrack. If you hope to stay here during the racing or fair season, make plans well ahead. There are 245 rooms and suites. Some have separate bedrooms and whirlpool tubs. There's a spacious pool, and the Aponi Restaurant has a pleasant courtyard and serves breakfast, lunch, and dinner. The hotel is 100 percent nonsmoking.

Doubletree Hotel Del Mar $$-$$$
11915 El Camino Real, Del Mar
(858) 481-5900, (800) 222-8733
www.doubletree.com

Just east of the ocean communities of Solana Beach and Del Mar, the Doubletree Hotel Del Mar offers 220 luxuriously appointed rooms and 12 suites, all oversize and warmly decorated. Rooms come with everything from coffeemakers to two-line phones with modem hookups. Wheelchair-accessible and nonsmoking rooms are available.

Along with that fresh-baked chocolate chip cookie you'll receive at check-in, you'll be able to relax even if you're visiting on business. Breakfast, lunch, and dinner are served in the hotel's restaurant and on the patio. There is an exercise room and outdoor pool. Families love the children's activities and separate wading pool. Within minutes, guests can be splashing in the Pacific or swinging a golf club at one of the many courses in the area. The hotel is near the Del Mar Fairgrounds and racetrack, too. There is complimentary shuttle service within a 6-mile radius of the hotel.

Four Seasons Resort Aviara $$$$
7100 Four Seasons Point, Carlsbad
(760) 603-6800, (800) 819-5053
www.fourseasons.com/aviara

With 329 rooms, many oversize and all with wonderful views, this is a destination location for anyone who loves luxury. (See the Spas and Resorts chapter for more details.) The lavish facilities include a championship golf course, two pools (one for quiet relaxation and one for family play), Internet hookups at poolside cabanas, and a full spa. Dining

Sumptuous suites await guests at the La Costa Resort and Spa. PHOTO: COURTESY OF LA COSTA RESORT AND SPA

in the hotel's restaurants is a delight. The four-diamond gourmet restaurant Vivace serves Northern Italian dinners, while the more casual California Bistro is open for breakfast, lunch, and dinner (see our Restaurants chapter). Pets weighing less than 15 pounds are welcome.

Holiday Inn Carlsbad-by-the-Sea $$$
850 Palomar Airport Road, Carlsbad
(760) 438-7800, (800) 266-7880
www.carlsbadhi.com
Close to Carlsbad's many attractions, this comfortable hotel is an obvious choice for many travelers. You can't miss it: A 50-foot Dutch-style working windmill sits atop the buildings. There are 147 rooms, a swimming pool, fitness center, and on-site TGIFriday's restaurant. Guests rave about the size and quality of the rooms and the convenient location.

Directly across the street from the hotel is the not-to-be-missed Bellefleur (see Restaurants) and the quicker eateries in the Carlsbad Company Stores mall.

L'Auberge Resort and Spa $$$$
1540 Camino Del Mar, Del Mar
(858) 259-1515, (800) 245-9757
www.laubergedelmar.com
Many people think of L'Auberge as a spa (see Spas and Resorts) and they're right. It has wonderful possibilities for relaxation and rejuvenation, yet it's also a convenient and enjoyable hotel located in the seaside village of Del Mar. Be sure to read more about the lovely beaches in Del Mar in our Beaches and Water Sports chapter.

There are 128 deluxe rooms and elegant suites, two tennis courts, indoor and outdoor fitness areas, and a pool. J. Taylor's restaurant, with patio dining beside a waterfall and a blazing fireplace in the dining room, is a lovely spot for romantic escapes. The village's delightful restaurants, sidewalk cafes, boutiques, and bookstores are all within walking distance.

La Costa Resort and Spa $$$$
2100 Costa Del Mar Road, Carlsbad
(760) 438-9111, (800) 854-5000
www.lacosta.com

La Costa Resort and Spa has been known for quality and outstanding sports facilities since it opened in 1965. An ongoing multimillion-dollar renovation is bringing the rooms and facilities back up to par. The buildings and gardens are exquisite, with a Spanish hacienda design. Best of all, the resort claims 400 acres in the rolling hills of North County just a few minutes from the coast. It feels as though you've escaped to a countryside hideaway, yet the beach, Legoland, and other North County attractions are just a few minutes' drive away.

The 511 rooms and suites are decorated with gleaming wood furnishings and plush fabrics and have large bathrooms with plenty of polished marble. Four restaurants and cafes serve everything from spa cuisine to burgers by the pool. Diversions include a spectacular spa (see our Spas and Resorts chapter), an Athletic Club fitness center, two championship 18-hole golf courses, and a Racquet Club with 17 tennis courts. The on-site Chopra Center, founded by spiritual guru Dr. Deepak Chopra, offers a variety of mind and body healing opportunities and programs.

La Costa hosts several champion-level tennis and golf tournaments, and frequent guests include legendary golfers and tennis players. Children can enjoy Camp La Costa with year-round activities for children age 3 through 12. For parents who want to enjoy a romantic evening, the hotel has a Night Camp from 6:00 to 10:00 P.M. on Friday and Saturday.

Oceanside Marina Suites **$$**
2008 Harbor Drive N., Oceanside
(760) 722-1561, (800) 252-2033
www.omihotel.com

Small (only 64 rooms) and convenient to the marina, this is the hotel of choice for those who motor or sail in for a vacation. There are some rooms with tiny kitchens, many with wonderful views, and the hotel has a pool. If you're looking for a romantic getaway, ask about the rooms with fireplaces and balconies. The hotel sits at the end of a private peninsula in the harbor, about as close to the open ocean as you can be without getting wet.

Are you planning to work during your stay? Ask about computer hookups, dataports, large desks, modems, fax machines, and rooms with multiple telephone lines when making reservations.

There isn't a restaurant on-site, but dining is close by and guests are offered free continental breakfast. You can rent a sailboat or book a fishing trip just steps from your hotel. Rates for a standard room start at a very reasonable $135; one-bedroom suites start at $205. Reserve early.

Rancho Valencia Resort **$$$$**
5921 Valencia Circle, Rancho Santa Fe
(858) 756-1123, (800) 548-3664
www.ranchovalencia.com

About 30 minutes from downtown San Diego, Rancho Valencia is elegant and a top choice for spa and resort fans (see our Spas and Resorts chapter). The only Relais & Chateaux property in Southern California, Rancho Valencia has been ranked as a favorite North American resort of *Tennis, Wine Spectator, Andrew Harper's Hideaway Report,* and *Travel & Leisure.* The resort was also listed on *Condé Nast Traveler*'s 2006 Gold List.

You'll find upscale touches throughout the 49-unit resort. The centerpiece is the Hacienda, a restored adobe brick home that was built in the 1940s. There are three suites in the Hacienda, and the entire building is often booked by such power players as Michael Jordan and Bill Clinton.

Luxurious villas with whirlpool tubs inside and out and plasma-screen TVs are scattered around the lush grounds. Even the most modest suites have fireplaces and private gardens. There are several pools and hot tubs, spa services, and fine dining at the resort's signature restaurant. You may want to venture out onto one of the 18 tennis courts, since the resort was recently designated by *Tennis* magazine as one of the nation's top tennis resorts.

There are also great hiking and biking trails right outside the hotel's door. You may become addicted to the ambience of Rancho Valencia. It's that lovely.

San Diego Marriott Del Mar $$
11966 El Camino Real, Del Mar
(858) 523-1700, (800) 228-9290
www.marriott.com
As North County continues to grow, hotel chains are finding a lucrative market with both business and leisure travelers. This lavish Marriott is centrally located on the inland side of I-5 near the coast. The excellent Arterra Restaurant draws a local following with its American bistro cuisine and sushi bar. The 281 rooms fill 11 stories—go for the views at the top. Self-serve laundry facilities are a boon for traveling families; other amenities include a fitness center and outdoor pool. The hotel fills quickly during the horse-racing season, so book early.

NORTH COUNTY INLAND

Best Western Escondido $
1700 Seven Oaks Road, Escondido
(760) 740-1700, (800) 752-1710
www.bestwestern.com
With 100 rooms and a location that's near the highway and the heart of Escondido, this hotel works well for visitors with relatives living nearby. It's about 10 minutes to shopping at Westfield Shoppingtown (see Shopping), 15 minutes from championship golf courses (see Golf), and 20 minutes to the Wild Animal Park (see Attractions).

There isn't a restaurant on-site, but many Escondido restaurants are nearby, and continental breakfast is provided. Pets weighing less than 15 pounds are welcome for a fee.

Comfort Inn $
1290 West Valley Parkway, Escondido
(760) 489-1010, (800) 541-6012
www.comfortinn.com
Whether you're just passing through or stopping to sample some of North County Inland's fun attractions, the Comfort Inn is a budget-right choice. The 93-room facility has a pool and the amenities that you'd expect.

Doubletree Golf Resort $$
14455 Penasquitos Drive, San Diego
(858) 672-9100, (800) 222-8733
www.doubletree.com
Situated just off Interstate 15 in the Carmel Mountain area, about 23 miles north of downtown San Diego, this hotel/resort offers 174 rooms and 2 bi-level and 4 two-room parlor suites. The rooms are oversize and inviting.

If you need a quiet hideaway, you'll enjoy the hotel. On-site you'll find an 18-hole golf course (par 72), five lighted wind-sheltered tennis courts, a state-of-the-art 5,500-square-foot health and fitness center, and heated outdoor pools. There are also whirlpool spas, steam rooms, and therapeutic massage treatments.

Holiday Inn Express $-$$
1250 West Valley Parkway, Escondido
(760) 741-7117, (877) 717-5337
www.holidayinnexpress.com
The Holiday Inn Express has 84 rooms, many with minikitchens, and offers two-room suites to give that extra elbow room often necessary when traveling. Rooms include microwave ovens and refrigerators. Services include free continental breakfast, a fitness room, heated pool, and spa. Golf packages can be arranged. It's a good family hotel close to the Wild Animal Park.

Lake San Marcos Resort & Country Club $$
1025 La Bonita Drive, Lake San Marcos
(760) 744-0120, (800) 447-6556
www.lakesanmarcos.com
Situated on the shores of Lake San Marcos, this resort offers a variety of accommodation options, from standard rooms to spacious one- and two-room suites and cottages, some overlooking the lake. Room amenities include coffeemakers and hair dryers. The hotel is very popular with retirees and provides activities and social mixers. It's also a special wedding venue,

booked solid with wedding parties on spring weekends.

Guests here have access to the 18-hole championship Lake San Marcos Country Club, known for its 6,515-yard, par 71 course. Its third hole is rated one of the toughest in San Diego County. There's also a challenging executive course for those who are perfecting their game. The facility includes a fitness room, four tennis courts, two swimming pools, and rental paddle-boats. There are three restaurants at the resort, which is close to San Marcos's "restaurant row," where the dining possibilities range from seafood to Mexican favorites (see our Restaurants chapter).

Pala Casino Resort & Spa $$-$$$
1114 Highway 76, Pala
(760) 510-5100, (877) 946-7252
www.palacasino.com

With more than 2,000 slot and video machines, 85 gaming tables, and 8 restaurants, Pala is one of the largest casinos in the county. The 2,000-seat events center hosts performances by top-notch comedians and rock and jazz bands. Gamers and concertgoers need not worry about driving home. The resort has 507 luxurious guest rooms, an Olympic-size pool, and a full-scale spa and fitness center.

Pala Mesa Resort $-$$$
2001 Old Highway 395, Fallbrook
(760) 728-5881, (800) 722-4700
www.palamesa.com

About a 90-minute drive north of San Diego and just off I-15, you'll find one of the area's nicest resorts. Peaceful and serene, the resort has 133 rooms, all with nearly 500 square feet of space for lounging about on the cushy pillow-top mattress or on the private patio.

Bestowed with the coveted four-star rating by *Golf Digest*, the impeccable golf course is designed in a classic style that challenges players at every turn. There are also four lighted tennis courts, a workout room, dining at the hotel's restaurant, and relaxing at the lounge.

Many San Diego hotels have celebrity chefs running their restaurants. Deborah Schneider oversees the menu at JSix, Hotel Solamar's sleek street-level restaurant. Bernard Guillas is so popular you need advance reservations to sample his cuisine at the La Jolla Beach & Tennis Club's Marine. Other stellar hotel chefs include Jason Knibb at the Grand Colonial's Nine-Ten, Jeff Jackson at A.R. Valentien in the Lodge at Torrey Pines, and Gavin Kaysen at the Rancho Bernardo Inn.

Radisson Suite Hotel $-$$
11520 West Bernardo Court, Rancho Bernardo
(858) 451-6600, (800) 333-3333
www.radisson.com

With 180 suites offering beautiful amenities, this work and pleasure hotel is close to Rancho Bernardo's technology hub. Year after year the hotel receives the Radisson President's Award for quality. In addition to the complimentary full American buffet breakfast, there are complimentary evening cocktails at poolside in the cabana cafe.

For business travelers and for meetings, there's 800-number access, dataports, computer and printer options, and spacious work areas in each room. On the fun side, there's an exercise room, heated pool and spa, nearby golf, tennis, and walking and hiking trails.

The hotel is about 20 minutes from the Wild Animal Park and a half hour from the mountain hamlet of Julian.

Rancho Bernardo Inn $$$
17550 Bernardo Oaks Drive Rancho Bernardo
(858) 675-8500, (800) 770-7482
www.ranchobernardoinn.com

This historic hacienda surrounded by golf greens is a favorite weekend getaway for San Diegans. The restaurant, El Bizcocho, is one of the main draws (see our Restau-

Many San Diego hotels have strict no-smoking policies. Some don't allow smoking in any rooms, others only in a few. You may be asked to sign a waiver saying you will pay a substantial fee if you smoke in your room; ask about such policies. Some hotels have rooms with a balcony or patio where you can smoke.

rants chapter). Here's a hint—plan on staying over Sunday night so you can savor the fabulous Sunday brunch and then go back to your room for a rest. The 288 rooms have been remodeled with puffy beds and large work desks; extraordinary suites have fireplaces, whirlpool tubs, and terraces by the inn's 18-hole golf course. A fitness center and 12 tennis courts also provide places to work off the calories. The spa and peaceful swimming pool add to the sense of pampering.

Super 8 Motel **$**
528 West Washington Avenue, Escondido
(760) 747-3711, (800) 800-8000
www.super8.com
Whether you're on a travel budget or just like the convenience of Super 8 motels, this Escondido location is a good choice. The hotel is near the Wild Animal Park, close to the corporate centers of Rancho Bernardo, and blocks from the freeways. This Super 8 is a 75-room hotel that offers AAA and senior discounts. There's no restaurant on-site, but there is a complimentary continental breakfast and guest laundry facility. You'll find all your favorite fast-food restaurants within walking distance; more upscale dining is just minutes by car.

Welk Resort Center **$$$**
8860 Lawrence Welk Drive, Escondido
(760) 749-3000, (800) 932-9355
www.welkresort.com
Many people select this hotel for its two 18-hole golf courses. Companies and corporations use it for retreats and seminars, and families love it for the outdoor attractions, including the golf, swimming, and biking and walking trails.

Located in North County Inland, about 45 minutes from downtown San Diego off I-15 and 10 minutes from the city of Escondido, the resort is situated on 600 beautiful acres. There are 38 rooms and suites available as hotel rooms, many right on the greens, along with two-bedroom villas. There's a pool, spa, beauty facilities, and a workout room, too. All-inclusive packages are available, and many units are used for vacation ownership guests.

EAST COUNTY

Barona Valley Ranch Resort & Casino **$$**
1932 Wildcat Canyon Road, Lakeside
(619) 443-2300, (877) 287-2624
www.barona.com
San Diego's Native American casinos have become full-scale resorts. Barona, a major casino with 2,000 slot machines, now has a championship golf course and a ranch-style hotel with 397 rooms. The hotel's facade and lobby are far grander than the rooms—guests are supposed to be playing in the casino rather than lounging around watching TV. Facilities include a fitness center, business center, pool, and lakeside wedding chapel. The resort is popular with residents of central San Diego seeking a quick getaway.

Best Western Continental Inn **$**
650 North Mollison, El Cajon
(619) 442-0601, (800) 882-3781
www.bestwestern.com
This AAA two-diamond-rated hotel makes you feel comfortable. It's a good choice for families who want to stay near the San Diego freeway or who are coming to visit San Diego State University. Golfing buffs choose it since it's close to the East County and San Diego courses. Some

suites have hot tubs; some have kitchenettes. There is a honeymoon suite, and there are meeting rooms, too.

La Casa del Zorro Desert Resort $$$$
3845 Yaqui Pass Road, Borrego Springs
(760) 767-5323, (800) 824-1884
www.lacasadelzorro.com

This is one of the jewels of East County, the kind of place families return to annually for reunions and special celebrations. The hotel is about two hours from San Diego and features 77 units, including rooms, suites, and two- and three-bedroom casitas; most include fireplaces and individual patios. Some of the casitas have private swimming pools; some have baby grand pianos. Located in Anza-Borrego Desert State Park, the resort offers numerous outdoor possibilities, from hiking to sunbathing to tennis. Several pools are scattered about the 42-acre property; some are reserved for adults seeking quiet time. The restaurant is pricey, but the portions of beef, duck, venison, and salmon are large and well prepared. The dining room also has a wine room with tastings of local wine. The hotel is popular throughout the dry, warm winter months and especially in the spring when the desert bursts with flowers. If you're planning a March or April visit, make reservations ahead of time.

Motel 6 $
550 Montrose Court, El Cajon
(619) 588-6100, (800) 466-8356
7621 Alvarado Road, La Mesa
(619) 464-7151, (800) 466-8356

Like other Motel 6's throughout the country, the East County motels are clean and functional. Kids accompanying an adult stay free. There are various discounts available, including ones for AARP members.

If you're going to spend your time here visiting the local attractions or doing business, then it's tough to go wrong with the basics, and Motel 6 has them down pat. As with other Motel 6 hotels, your pet is welcome in these two facilities.

Palm Canyon Resort $
221 Palm Canyon Drive, Borrego Springs
(760) 767-5341, (800) 242-0044
www.pcresort.com

Spacious grounds with oodles of hiking, biking, walking, and sunset-watching possibilities, this is a perfect choice for a getaway. The hotel has 60 rooms; all have refrigerators and coffeemakers. The adjacent RV park has 132 spaces. Guests at both places have access to the fitness center, pool, and restaurant. The 14-acre complex is situated next to Anza-Borrego State Park, so if you're planning to come to the desert to see Mother Nature's spring flower show, make plans early. All hotels fill up quickly between November and May. Note that the restaurant is closed from June through September.

Pine Hills Lodge $-$$
2960 La Posada Way, Julian
(760) 765-1100
www.pinehillslodge.com

An intimate 16-room hotel that's rustic and attractive, the lodge also serves as Julian's social center, with holiday parties and a festive Sunday brunch. A stay here is popular with those who want to escape from hectic San Diego living and breathe in pine-filled mountain air. This hotel isn't for every traveler. If you need a TV in your room, find another place to stay, since the Pine Hills Lodge doesn't have them. Some cabins have fireplaces or wood-burning stoves. All are comfy, with down comforters on the beds and wood and wrought-iron furnishings that suit the location.

Travelodge El Cajon $
471 Magnolia, El Cajon
(619) 447-3999, (800) 578-7878
www.travelodge.com

This is a thrifty, popular choice of hotel for those who visit the East County. The hotel has 43 rooms, each with a fridge and microwave. There's a small pool and free cable and HBO in all rooms. Complimentary continental breakfast is included, and there's dining nearby.

SOUTH BAY

Holiday Inn Express **$**
4450 Main Street, Chula Vista
(619) 422-2600, (800) 628-2611

For freeway convenience, sparkling clean rooms, and proximity to South Bay's attractions, the Holiday Inn Express can't be beat. Furnished in Spanish-Southwestern style, the 118 spacious and beautiful rooms make you feel like you're in a bed-and-breakfast inn. A complimentary continental breakfast only reinforces that notion. The inn is located just west of Interstate 805.

Beaches are a 15-minute drive from the inn, but what might impress the kids even more is the fact that Knott's Soak City, with its wave pools and waterslides, is just a five-minute drive away. We describe it in detail in our Attractions chapter.

La Quinta Inn **$$**
150 Bonita Road, Chula Vista
(619) 691-1211, (800) 687-6667
www.lq.com

The La Quinta Inn in Chula Vista is an ideal choice for business travelers working with major companies that have Tijuana factories. You can choose from 143 rooms and suites with either a king-size bed or two double beds. The spacious rooms, furnished in contemporary style, offer comfort and proximity to all of South Bay's attractions.

When you pry open those sleepy eyes, La Quinta's First Light breakfast is ready for you in the lobby: cereals, fresh fruit, pastries, bagels, juice, and coffee. Or if a Grand Slam is more your style, take a short walk next door to Denny's. Then it's back to the inn for a dip in the refreshing pool. Small pets are welcome here.

Red Lion **$$**
801 National City Boulevard, National City
(619) 336-1100, (888) 478-7829

For the business traveler or visitors who simply like to spread out, the Red Lion is an exceptional bargain. It is located just east of I-5 near the border. Each of the hotel's 168 suites has either a city or a bay view. Modern and comfortable, all suites are equipped with computer modems, and all have Internet access.

Laundry facilities are available for guests, as is a complimentary continental breakfast and room service with reasonably priced meals. Red Lion's central location makes access to beaches and to Mexico just an easy drive. If your favorite family pet does not reach your knees, it's welcome here for a $35 fee.

BED-AND-BREAKFAST INNS

Bed-and-breakfast inns in the San Diego region have a flavor that's strictly Southern California. Each has an easygoing ambience that makes you long to check in and dread saying good-bye. These inns are special, warm, restful, and inviting. They've been chosen because we would enjoy revisiting them or would recommend them to our closest friends.

These are not the bare-bones accommodations found in some parts of Europe. You know the places: one bath down the hall, "take a number please," and a pint-size sleeping room where if you sneeze, your next-door neighbor might respond, "Bless you."

All of the rooms at the bed-and-breakfast inns described in this chapter have private baths unless otherwise noted. Most have enticing, easy-to-get-to locations, which also happen to be some of our favorites places in San Diego County.

For instance, the Britt Scripps Inn is elegant and luxurious, like a boutique hotel from the Victorian era. It's the perfect choice for a romantic getaway close to Balboa Park and excellent restaurants. The Pelican Cove Inn in North County Coastal is so close to the Pacific that you're surrounded with ocean breezes—just the right prescription for even the most ragged spirit. Everything you could want for a relaxing weekend is there, and all within walking distance.

As you look over our listings, keep in mind that it's wise to call and double-check rates and availability of rooms. All of the bed-and-breakfast inns encourage reservations. If you want to book for a holiday, say Christmas or Valentine's Day, we recommend you do so months ahead so you won't be disappointed. Unless otherwise noted, the inns we've included all accept MasterCard, Visa, or cash but do not accept indoor smoking or pets. Assume, too, that children are discouraged, unless we tell you otherwise.

Some of the bed-and-breakfast inns featured here serve a continental breakfast, with plump muffins and fresh juice along with coffees and teas. It's simple but enough. Others have a full European-style (sometimes called gourmet) breakfast. These are the breakfast feasts of which fantasies are made, that spoil you to the bone while you're enjoying every minute of munching. Some of the inns have in-room eating options, too—nice if you'd prefer to have a romantic breakfast on the balcony or in your room. Our entries will tell you what to expect.

In all of the bed-and-breakfast inns we've featured there is a comfortable sitting room, parlor, or library. You may find overstuffed chairs loaded with pillows, lots of reading material, perhaps a puzzle in progress or a stack of board games, maybe a player piano, a decanter of sherry and some crackers, and maybe—but not always—a television. (Some inns only have a television in the main part of the house, not in individual bedrooms; some don't have televisions at all.)

Even when the bed-and-breakfast inn's parlor is deliciously old-fashioned, it's not unusual to find the rooms decorated in anything from African safari themes to South Seas motifs. Most are furnished with antiques and fresh flowers, lovely furnishings, and plump comforters. The morning paper will probably be placed by your door as might a rose or decanter of coffee. Some of the inns have lovingly placed extras in each of the rooms, such as bowls of local fruit or plates of home-made cookies to nourish your inner child.

If you haven't tried a bed-and-breakfast inn and need a few days off or want to stay somewhere unique when you're visiting San Diego, these entries will help you design the perfect getaway.

PRICE CODE

Our prices indicate a one-night double occupancy at high-season rates. Most inns have at least one ultrafancy room that garners a steep rate because of its views of the ocean or amenities such as a fireplace or whirlpool tub.

$	**Less than $95**
$$	**$95 to $135**
$$$	**$136 to $175**
$$$$	**$176 to $225**
$$$$$	**More than $225**

SAN DIEGO COUNTY

Balboa Park Inn **$$-$$$**
3402 Park Boulevard, Hillcrest
(619) 298-0823, (800) 938-8181
www.balboaparkinn.com

Does Paris in the '30s appeal to you? What does The Jungle Nook conjure in your imagination? These are the names of just two of the Balboa Park Inn's 26 uniquely decorated luxury rooms in a complex of four Spanish-colonial buildings. Paris in the '30s has a romantic wood-burning fireplace and a dreamy canopy bed. The Jungle Nook has hand-painted floor-to-ceiling murals in a jungle motif, a separate kitchen, and a private door to the sun terrace. The Beach House is wheelchair accessible.

Nestled in a quiet residential neighborhood on the north edge of Balboa Park, the inn is a short walk to the San Diego Zoo, museums, shops, restaurants, and the Old Globe Theatre. And it's just a few minutes' drive from downtown and the Gaslamp Quarter. Fruit and pastries are standard breakfast fare served either in your room or suite, on the sun terrace, or in the peaceful courtyard.

This is one of the rare bed-and-breakfast inns that welcomes children. In fact, kids younger than age 11 stay free when sharing accommodations with their parents. Cancellations must be made seven days in advance of your scheduled stay.

The Bed & Breakfast Inn at La Jolla **$$-$$$$**
7753 Draper Avenue, La Jolla
(858) 456-2066, (800) 582-2466
www.innlajolla.com

Here is a rare opportunity to stay in an architectural gem that is also a registered San Diego Historical Site. Designed by noted architect Irving Gill, the house was built in 1913 and is one of Gill's finest examples of Cubist-style architecture. The lush, original gardens were planned by renowned horticulturist Kate Sessions, who was also responsible for planting many of the gardens in Balboa Park.

Get ready to be pampered. Fireplaces and ocean views are available in many of the nine guest rooms in the main house and six in the annex. Fresh fruit, flowers, a glass of sherry, and a terry robe await you upon check-in, and wine and cheese are served as an aperitif every evening. A gourmet breakfast is yours to enjoy in the dining room, on the patio or sundeck, or in your room.

Each room is decorated differently, from the nautically themed Pacific View Room to the Oriental-style Windansea Room, with its rattan furniture. If a splurge is in order, try the Irving Gill Penthouse, a spacious suite at the tip of the house with an incomparable view of the Pacific Ocean. Smoking is not allowed, and pets are prohibited. None of the rooms are wheelchair accessible.

Britt Scripps Inn **$$-$$$**
406 Maple Street, Hillcrest
(619) 230-1991, (888) 881-1991
www.brittscripps.com

Just a few blocks from Balboa Park, this turn-of-the-20th-century mansion has recently been restored to its original Victorian luster. Follow the commanding, curving oak staircase to the second-story bedrooms, each decorated in bold combinations of period color such as mauve, cranberry, dill, and taupe. Beds with 1,000-thread-count sheets, downy duvets, and multiple pillows are simultaneously romantic and sleep inducing. At the foot of the staircase—and the original stained-glass window decorated with birds, butterflies, and other natural elements—are a baby grand piano and a parlor where evening hors d'oeuvres and wine are served. Breakfast is made to order each morning in the adjoining dining room, or you can eat outside on the wraparound porch. The converted carriage house at the back of the property is the most private of the nine guest rooms.

Elsbree House **$$-$$$**
5054 Narragansett Avenue, Ocean Beach
(619) 226-4133, (800) 607-4133
www.bbinob.com

If you're craving a vacation at the beach but still want the homey atmosphere of a bed-and-breakfast inn, Elsbree House is the solution. This Cape Cod house is just 500 feet from the Ocean Beach (OB) Pier and public beach and only 2 blocks from the OB business district, with its restaurants and antiques shops.

Innkeepers Katie and Phil Elsbree have created a modern escape to paradise. The six rooms are decorated in country English style. Each has a private entrance and a balcony or patio all to itself, where you can relax with a book or write your own great American novel. In the morning enjoy a self-serve continental breakfast of homemade bread and muffins, granola, cereal, fruit, and yogurt in the dining room. At sunset stroll along Sunset Cliffs for a panoramic view of the Pacific Ocean.

The Elsbrees also rent out a three-bedroom condo right by the beach. It can be separated into smaller units. The condo has a full kitchen, big porch, and washer and dryer. Children are welcome, but not pets. Smoking is not allowed, and none of the rooms are wheelchair accessible.

Heritage Park Bed & Breakfast Inn **$$-$$$$**
2470 Heritage Park Row, Old Town
(619) 299-6832, (800) 995-2470
www.heritageparkinn.com

This magnificent 1889 Queen Anne mansion has 12 antiques-filled guest rooms and suites featuring feather beds, claw-foot tubs, whirlpools, and robes so fluffy, you'll hate to take them off.

Heritage Park is the centerpiece of a collection of Victorian mansions located on a hill above historic Old Town, one of San Diego's favorite visitors' destinations. Peace and quiet are the norm, yet the bustle of shops, restaurants, and the theater are just steps away. It's a great place for a family vacation because of its proximity to Old Town, and children are welcome here, but leave the pets at home. Since 1992 owners Nancy and Charles Helsper have delighted their guests with a full candlelight breakfast, as well as afternoon tea on the veranda. Should you opt for an evening in, classic films are shown nightly in the sitting room.

The Drawing Room, a professionally designed and decorated room, is a romantic fantasy come true, complete with soft colors, lighting, and fabrics and a whirlpool for two. It's so romantic, it practically whispers in your ear. Some rooms are wheelchair accessible.

Keating House **$$-$$$**
2331 Second Avenue, Bankers Hill
(619) 239-8585, (800) 995-8644
www.keatinghouse.com

Immerse yourself in 19th-century Victorian luxury. Keating House, a beautifully restored 1888 home (and a San Diego Historical Site), sits proudly in a residential neighborhood full of elegant homes. The splendor of the Victorian era is re-created in each of the nine rooms. Because of its faithful restoration, the inn does not have any wheelchair-accessible rooms.

A full gourmet breakfast is served every morning in the dining room, and a cozy parlor offers the perfect setting for conversation or the opportunity to curl up in front

Some bed-and-breakfast inns have a resident dog or cat. If you're allergic to animals or prefer to stay in an animal-free environment, ask about pets when making reservations.

of the fireplace with a favorite book. Lush tropical grounds surround the house, and several seating areas in the garden and on the front porch allow visitors to drink in the sweet aroma of roses and jasmine and the vibrant colors of bougainvillea, orchids, and jacaranda. Smoking is allowed in the gardens, but not in the house. Close to downtown, Hillcrest, and Balboa Park, Keating House is ideally located for the visitor seeking quiet rejuvenation combined with lots of activities. Children are welcome as long as they are well behaved. This is not the place for energetic toddlers, but teens might enjoy the feeling of home.

Scripps Inn **$$$-$$$$$**
555 Coast Boulevard South, La Jolla
(858) 454-3391
www.scrippsinn.com

Right across the street from Ellen Browning Scripps Park in La Jolla, the Scripps Inn has been transformed from a run-down motel into a delightful bed-and-breakfast. The 14 rooms and suites have a clean white and beige decor that perfectly suits the location. A few suites have fireplaces, and the fabulous Vista Ocean Suite has a spot-on view of the sea. Guests begin the day with coffee and pastries from a nearby French cafe and can easily walk to La Jolla's many excellent shops, galleries, and restaurants. Reserve extra early here, as many guests return annually.

NORTH COUNTY COASTAL

The Cardiff-by-the-Sea Lodge **$$$-$$$$$**
142 Chesterfield Avenue, Cardiff
(760) 944-6474
www.cardifflodge.com

Overlooking the Pacific in the beach town of Cardiff, this sparkling clean and luxurious inn offers lush gardens and an open-pit fire ring that is high on the rooftop. Imagine roasting marshmallows as you watch the sun shimmering in the west. These attributes are tough to top.

Owned by Jeannette and James Statser, longtime Insiders themselves, the inn's interior is graced with original art and handcrafted touches. The Southwest Room, for instance, looks like it's straight out of New Mexico with hues of tan, pale pink, and the palest of blues. The crowning glory is the Sweetheart Room, and it's Jim's favorite, too. Here you'll find hearts everywhere, from the ceiling to the heart-shaped tub for two. Breakfast is simple and good and all homemade—Jim's the chef—with muffins, fruit, coffees, and teas.

All rooms are equipped with queen-size beds, custom furnishings, oversize baths, and showers. There are 16 rooms and a roof garden that's popular for weddings and receptions. Rates here go up during holiday weekends, and you can also expect to pay more for luxury suites or a spectacular view.

Pelican Cove Bed and Breakfast Inn **$$-$$$$**
320 Walnut Avenue, Carlsbad
(760) 434-5995, (888) 735-2683
www.pelican-cove.com

Only 200 yards from the Pacific, the inn is strolling distance from the antiques shops and fine eateries in the village area of Carlsbad. (If you love to antiques shop, be sure to read our Shopping chapter for tips on things to do in Carlsbad.) What makes this inn special is the soft luxury and romance of the rooms and the TLC poured on by all the staff members.

There are only 10 nonsmoking rooms in this small inn, but each one comes with a fireplace, television, and European (make that fat and fluffy) bedding that surrounds you like a huge hug. Some rooms have spa tubs, and some are wheelchair accessible. The Balboa, with twin beds, is done in rose florals. The Del Mar, an Insiders' favorite, is done in tones of white with floral accents; staying in this room feels rather like walking in the foam from ocean waves. Unlike some other bed-and-breakfast inns, Pelican Cove isn't a frou-frou antiques-strewn establishment. The decor is inviting and uncluttered, and children feel as comfortable as grown-ups.

The grounds are studded with flower gardens and trees. There's a sunporch and garden for lounging. The innkeepers make beach chairs, towels, and picnic baskets available for those who can break away from the inn for a day on the beach. Be aware that rooms cost more over holiday weekends, so be sure to ask when you call for reservations.

NORTH COUNTY INLAND

Fallbrook Country Inn $$-$$$
1425 South Mission Road, Fallbrook
(760) 728-1114
www.pinnaclehotelsusa.com

Popular as a getaway, the Fallbrook Country Inn specializes in wedding accommodations. In addition to the graciously appointed bridal suite, the inn offers 28 country-style rooms for family and friends. The garden, a riot of cascading annuals, makes a perfect setting for the ceremony.

All rooms have king- or queen-size beds, cable and color television, spacious baths, and patios. Some of the rooms have kitchenettes, and one is designated for smoking. Children are welcome, but pets are not.

You can spend your days lounging poolside, visiting the antiques stores that are aplenty in Fallbrook, or checking out the art galleries and handcrafted jewelry stores that dot the main street.

EAST COUNTY

Butterfield Bed & Breakfast $$-$$$
2284 Sunset Drive, Julian
(760) 765-2179, (800) 379-4262
www.butterfieldbandb.com

Beneath majestic pine and oak trees on a serene hillside that's just footsteps from the historic town of Julian is the comfortable, inviting Butterfield Bed & Breakfast.

Breakfast is a grand affair, with country gourmet served in the Garden Gazebo in the summer and by the crackling hearth when winter sets in. The Back Porch Pantry is stocked with fruit, coffee, cider, microwave popcorn, and afternoon sweets.

There are five rooms at the inn. All have televisions, and three have fireplaces. The Rosebud Cottage is decorated in country decor with a potbelly stove, sitting area, and knotty pine ceilings and is a world away from reality. Smoking is not permitted, and none of the rooms have wheelchair access. Children are welcome; pets are not.

Orchard Hill Country Inn $$$$$
2502 Washington Street, Julian
(760) 765-1700, (800) 716-7242
www.orchardhill.com

Far more than a B&B, Orchard Inn has 22 rooms with deluxe amenities, including a split of wine, Belgian chocolates, and fragrant toiletries. Some rooms have whirlpool tubs, others have fireplaces, and all have TVs and VCRs (there's a tape library in the main lodge). The rooms have been featured in many decorating magazines; some have wheelchair access. The sophisticated restaurant serves breakfast and afternoon hors d'oeuvres daily and fantastic dinners on some night of the week. Ask in advance if dinner will be served; it's $35 to $43 per person.

Victoria Rock Bed and Breakfast Inn $$
2952 Victoria Drive, Alpine
(619) 659-5967
www.victoria-rock-bb.com

Julian, snuggled in the mountains above San Diego, has more than 20 bed-and-breakfast inns and has a Bed and Breakfast Guild. To get up-to-the-minute information about rates and availability, call the guild at (760) 765-1555; www.julianbnbguild.com.

This bed-and-breakfast inn is small (just four rooms), and Insiders believe that's what makes it inviting—along with the fact that it's in the mountains and off the beaten path. The Victoria Rock Bed and Breakfast Inn, owned by Darrel and Helga Daliber, is not to be missed if you love staying in intimate inns sans children and pets.

The rooms are lovely, bright, and fresh. One Insider says his favorite has to be the South Seas room with a strong nautical theme. The room has a full bath as well as an Enchanted Grotto Shower. That's Victoria Rock talk for an 8-foot waterfall/shower.

Another Insider says her favorite place to stay at this inn is the Antique room. It features an oversize four-poster bed, delightful Victorian furnishings, and an early-20th-century ambience.

Breakfast is hearty and scrumptious. On the day one Insider stayed at the inn, breakfast was the specialty of the house, Southwest-style eggs Benedict. "This recipe was once a secret, but that's not so now since so many guests have asked for my recipe," says Darrel. Smart guests book well ahead for holidays and longer-than-weekend stays.

SPAS AND RESORTS

Spas, fitness centers, and alternative therapies have been part of the San Diego scene for decades. The Golden Door, still one of the finest spas in the country, has been attracting celebrities since the 1960s, as has La Costa and other lavish destination spas in the county. Today most San Diego hotels offer some sort of massage and spa treatments, and many have low-calorie selections on their menus. The full-scale resorts, however, take pampering and wellness to a whole different level. If you're on vacation with your family and want some me-time for self-improvement, these resorts are the perfect solution. They'll keep the kids busy with special activities, distract spouses with golf and tennis, and make it possible for spa lovers to truly enjoy their experiences. Couples on romantic getaways get special treatment with spa rooms designed for two, allowing partners to be pampered together.

In this chapter we've only included those spas and resorts that have special health, beauty, recreation, or relaxation programs and whose main thrust is to nurture the mind and body. These are not places to leave your belongings while you go out sightseeing; they're destinations in themselves—places where time slows, relaxation begins, tensions melt, and you leave your worries behind.

And they are the cream of the crop. These are the places we'd like to revisit or would suggest to a best friend. In fact, San Diego has some of the most prestigious spas and resorts in the world. If you're looking to relax, rethink fitness goals, revitalize your spirit, or play some sports, read on. The spas and resorts in this chapter will give you plenty of opportunities.

The first thing you may notice is that they're all different. Some, like the Golden Door, cater to women (although they do have a few weeks a year when men are invited). Others have incomparable spa and beauty facilities, but do not offer separate healthful or calorie-conscious meals. Some of the spas and resorts included in this chapter have day-spa packages where you can have all the fitness classes and pampering you want and then go back home or to your hotel at day's end.

We've tried to give you an idea about current prices for accommodations and treatments. Some spas charge by the week and do not allow guests to stay for just a few nights. Spas within hotels typically have a separate menu of services and rates that's not affected by the room rate—though spa packages may be available. If you plan to spend a lot of time at a hotel spa, check out the full-day programs that include several treatments and perhaps a spa lunch. Some of the resorts in this chapter are also included in the Hotels and Motels chapter—we've given you more information on their spa and health services here. For even more detailed information, you may want to call the spas to get their brochures and to be put on their mailing lists for upcoming spa-related events. (You might even receive a discount coupon that could make your spa visit even more delicious.)

Be aware that sometimes spas offer two-for-one specials and group discounts (in case everyone in your office or investment club wants to come, too). A few of the spas have seasonal packages, and there are discounts available. However, here in San Diego it's resort time 365 days a year, so don't expect to save a lot by visiting in an off-season.

Cal-a-Vie
2249 Somerset Road, Vista
(760) 945-2055, (866) 772-4283
www.cal-a-vie.com

Cal-a-Vie, nestled away in North County Inland, is a refuge from the stresses and strains of modern living. With only 24 guests and a staff that outnumbers their clients, the privacy and pampering are

Many of the spas in this chapter are open to nonguests, though some may do so only on weekdays. Locals splurge on "mental-health days" by taking some time off from work and checking into a spa from 9 to 5. There's nothing like a bit of pampering to put stress into perspective.

beyond compare. The low-calorie cuisine is an adaptation of classical gourmet foods, minus the fats. The emphasis is on flavor and the exquisite art of presentation.

The fitness course, tailored for each guest, is invigorating. You'll find classes from aerobics and body shaping to pool activities and stretching. There's a long morning and afternoon hike within the 200-acre landscaped compound. Even the most indulgent guests feel spoiled by soothing European therapies such as massage, body scrubbing, and aromatherapy. A favorite is the seaweed wrap, said to promote detoxification and replenish nutrients in the skin.

The main objective of Cal-a-Vie is to re-educate guests about the fundamentals of a healthier lifestyle. Evening lectures cover topics such as fitness, nutrition, safe and sane weight loss, and stress management. There's also a class on cooking low-fat, highly delicious food.

The Bath House at Cal-a-Vie features a hot-stone massage room, aromatherapy room, outdoor tented massage room, and a lounge with a vaulted wood-beam ceiling illuminated by a skylight, beneath which guests can rest on luxurious daybeds and sofas. The Bath House's hand-hewn plaster walls are painted in cool blue and aqua colors and are dimly lit by 18th- and 19th-century gilded lanterns and chandeliers imported from France and Italy, while its pale stone Turkish floors lead guests to the Jacuzzi area.

Cal-a-Vie offers packages for three, four, and seven nights, including spa cuisine meals, fitness classes, spa treatments—even workout clothes. Theme weeks, including one on women's wellness and another on high-intensity fitness, are interspersed with regular spa weeks—make sure you choose a week that suits your expectations.

Women-only and coed sessions are available, and there's complimentary transportation from Lindbergh Field. The spa also offers package plans. The European Plan includes meals, accommodations, all therapeutic treatments, and fitness classes for about $6,595 a week. The California Plan includes meals, accommodations, all fitness classes, and six body treatments for about $6,095.

Four Seasons Resort Aviara
7100 Four Seasons Point, Carlsbad
(760) 603-6800, (800) 332-3442
www.fourseasons.com/aviara

About 40 minutes north of downtown San Diego, just off Interstate 5 at the Poinsettia Lane exit, that spa and resort feeling hits. You feel it the minute you pull into the winding drive and make it up the incline to the white Spanish colonial–style building atop the hill. If you love Four Seasons quality, you'll be gaga over this gem.

The resort features 329 generously sized guest rooms and suites. Each upper-story room opens onto a private balcony; ground-level rooms have private landscaped terraces. All feature the famous Four Seasons beds, the best in the universe as far as we're concerned.

The grounds are lush, and the adjacent golf course, designed by Arnold Palmer, has been featured in several golf magazines. (See our Golf chapter for the scoop on this aspect of Aviara.) There is a rose garden where plenty of couples have said "I do."

The spa and fitness center are open to outside guests Monday through Thursday and hotel guests only the rest of the week. It's worth checking in for the night to luxuriate in the pampering, however. The serene solarium's fireplace is so inviting, you'll be tempted to nap in a comfy cashmere chair after your massage. Tea, water, and bowls of fruit are set about the entryway and locker rooms, which have saunas and steam baths. The 20 treatment rooms and sublime couple's suite with whirlpool tub and Vichy shower are all designed for ultimate comfort. Try the clary sage body gommage (50 minutes cost $120) for a gentle loofa experience, followed by the avocado body wrap that costs $150 for 50 minutes.

The hair salon is operated by the internationally known stylist Jose Eber. If you'd like to have Mr. Eber coif your hair, make plans ahead of time as he visits the salon only sporadically. The fitness center is beyond high-tech: Tiny televisions are attached to the treadmills and cardio machines so you won't lose track of CNN while you're racking up the miles. When fitness and pampering are complete, you can take a dip in one of the resort's two pools, have a healthful and beautiful lunch poolside or in one of the private cabanas (or hook up your laptop to the Internet by the pool), then lounge away the afternoon in the library.

This really is a family place, too, with a special Kids for All Seasons program offered during weekends, summer months, traditional school breaks, and holidays. There are supervised outdoor activities, including nature hikes and games set around an authentic outdoor tepee, and indoor play in a playroom that features a LEGO station and big-screen TV. Kids for All Seasons is complimentary for children ages 4 to 12; guests pay for the lunches. Children younger than age 4 must be accompanied by a parent; the concierge can also arrange babysitting. Staff members are CPR certified.

Golden Door
777 Deer Springs Road, San Marcos
(760) 744-5777, (800) 424-0777
www.goldendoor.com

Town & Country magazine pretty well sums up this spa: "The Golden Door is everything everyone has always said it is—and much, much more."

The Golden Door has been rated as America's number one spa by numerous spa guides and travel books. If you need some extra TLC and can afford the exclusive pampering, then pick up the phone and reserve your spot now at about $7,500 a week.

Packing for a stay at the Golden Door is simple because the spa provides everything. It suggests you bring personal basics (like toothbrush, aerobic and hiking shoes, swimsuit, and undergarments); the rest will be waiting for you.

Nestled in 350 acres, including orchards and gardens, the Golden Door provides plenty of room for hiking and other outdoor activities. The formal landscaping here was designed by the famed Takendo Arii. Among the resort's features are three guest lounges, a dining room, indoor and outdoor exercise studios, the Dragon Tree Gym, swimming pools, tennis courts, and plenty of graduated walking trails. Activities are geared to individual guests' requests according to their level of fitness, which is evaluated along with their range of motion, as staff create one-on-one fitness plans. There's also a customized take-home training program.

The Beauty Court is where you'll find steam rooms, saunas, showers, Swiss hoses, a fan-shape therapy pool, and sequestered rooms for body scrubs and lulling herbal wraps. There are fitness classes, too, taught by well-qualified instructors. These are small classes (only 39 guests attend the spa each week, and staff outnumber guests four to one), so everyone receives plenty of attention. The clientele include movers and shakers from around the planet and those you see on the big and little screen. In other words, the Golden Door is an exclusive hangout.

For most of the year, this is a women-only spa, though there are coed and men's weeks. There are also weeks for parents and young adults, who are charged half the parent's rate. The menu is gourmet and healthful, providing innovative cuisine that's low in sugar, sodium, and cholesterol yet rich in fiber and good taste. Evening programs might range from cooking demonstrations to lectures.

L'Auberge Resort and Spa
1540 Camino Del Mar, Del Mar
(858) 259-1515, (800) 245-9757
www.laubergedelmar.com

CLOSE-UP

Afternoon Tea (and More) at Aviara

Have you dreamed of quietly elegant afternoons sipping tea and sampling delicate morsels that taste even better than they look?

If the grandeur of afternoon tea is your idea of good living, then the Four Seasons Resort Aviara should be included on your dance card, whether you're a registered guest or a visitor. While you might find afternoon tea provided at some tea shop in San Diego, Aviara does it with Four Seasons style. We're talking top drawer.

At Aviara tea comes with a plethora of finger sandwiches, Sultana scones with rose petal jelly (that's to die for), lemon curd and Devonshire cream, delicate pastries, and petit fours. As for the tea, there are plenty of choices, including herbal and fruit infusions and the standards such as Darjeeling, English breakfast, black currant, and Zen.

While you're waiting in the lounge of the Carlsbad resort, allow your mind to contemplate the origins of teatime, an addictive custom. The first afternoon tea was ordered by Anna, seventh Duchess of Bedford, in 1840. Apparently Anna was tired (or grew hungry) during the long, dull space between meals. One afternoon about four, during her weary, low-energy time, she regally asked something like, "Bring me some tea, bread, butter, and cakes." This refreshing, light meal lifted Anna's spirits and blood-sugar level. Her idea spread like honey on a hot scone. Friends, family, royals, and commoners decided it was the "in" thing, and the practice became as English as Buckingham Palace. In 1865 the Aerated Bread Company opened London's first tea shop for the public.

Just a note for trivia lovers: Afternoon tea is a grand affair with delicate cakes and sandwiches. High tea is the American equivalent to supper, a sturdier meal, and may have been most popular originally with those who lived in the north of England.

Now to return to Carlsbad and the Four Seasons Resort Aviara. Afternoon tea is served Wednesday through Sunday in the hotel's Lobby Lounge, from 2:30 until 4:00 P.M., and it is deliciously accompanied by a harpist who sets the mood. You can lean back in one of the richly decorated sofas or overstuffed chairs, admire the tables decorated in

Located in the heart of Del Mar, one of Southern California's most picturesque coastal villages, this boutique resort offers 128 luxury guest rooms and suites. Rooms are well appointed and inviting; some have fireplaces. Prices range from $250 to $950 for the rooms.

As a guest, you may use the Sports Pavilion, featuring the latest in exercise and fitness equipment. You can have a fitness instructor develop and supervise a personal workout plan—or just have the teacher accompany you on a sunrise or sunset walk along the sand or a vigorous trail hike in Torrey Pines State Park. The resort has two tennis courts with a pro

Whether you're lingering next to the fountain or lying by the pool, the Four Seasons Resort Aviara is a treat for the senses. Days can be as busy or idle as you like. There's golf, tennis, nature trails, hiking possibilities, beauty and pampering treatments, a well-stocked fitness center, and private cabanas. Everything you need or want is minutes away from your room.
PHOTO: COURTESY OF FOUR SEASONS RESORT AVIARA

crisp linens, and breathe in the scent of fresh rose petals sprinkled around the tables. The view is the focal point, with floor-to-ceiling windows that frame views of the Pacific and the resort's luxurious Palm Courtyard.

Afternoon tea is $20.00; with the addition of a glass of sparkling wine, port, or sherry, the cost is $27.50. Insiders recommend making reservations for afternoon tea, especially during the holidays. The number is (760) 603-3773.

available for lessons, and there's golf nearby. Afterwards you can choose from a tantalizing menu of massages, skin and body treatments, and hair, nail, and facial treatments. The green tea and water lily wrap moisturizes tired skin, and the caviar facial and pearl facial sure smell and feel better than Botox. The spa is open to the public and has half-day packages starting at $150. Overnight spa packages start at $440.

La Costa Resort and Spa
Costa Del Mar Road, Carlsbad
(760) 438-9111, (800) 854-5000
www.lacosta.com

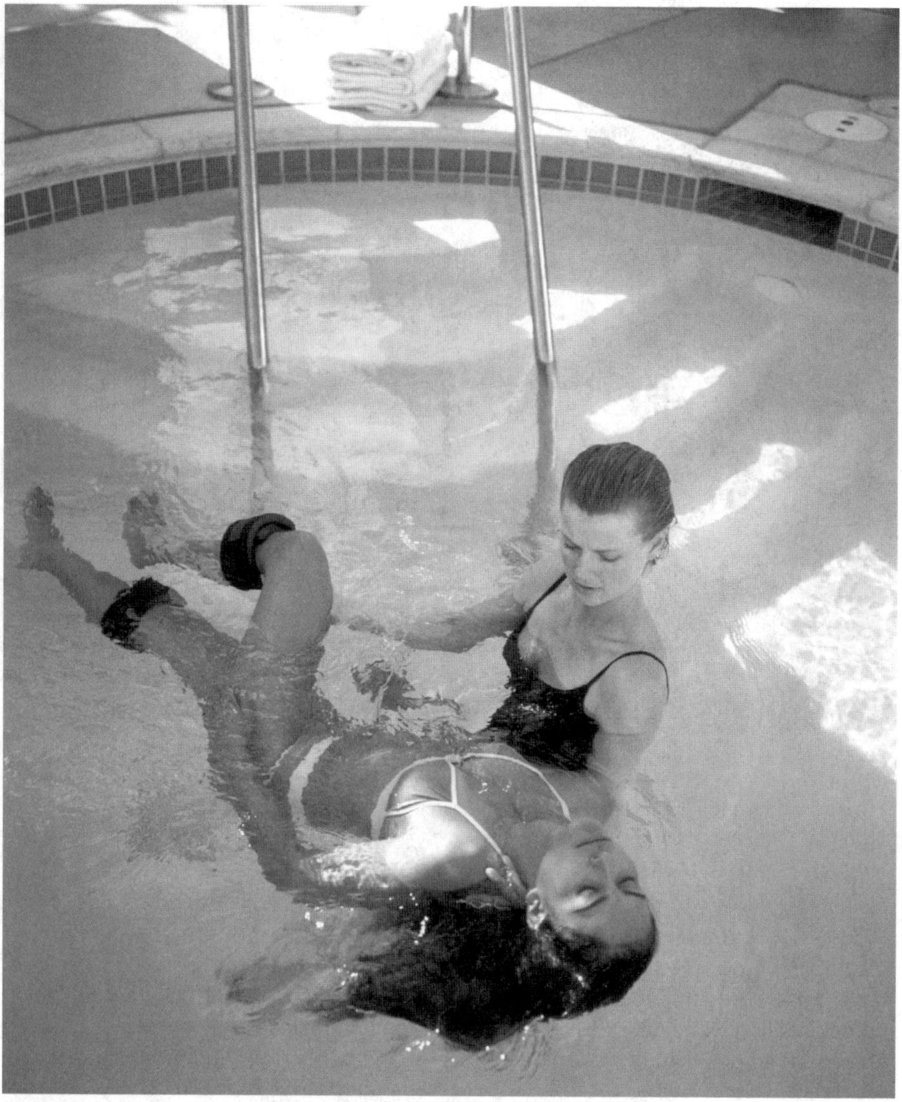

A therapist guides a guest through a soothing Watsu Massage in the Loews Coronado's spa pool. PHOTO: COURTESY OF LOEWS CORONADO BAY RESORT AND SPA

Thirty miles north of San Diego, minutes from I–5, is the 450-acre luxury resort of La Costa. Along with the two 18-hole championship golf courses, a 17-court racquet club, the award-winning restaurants and lounges, you have the spa.

The La Costa Spa was designed with feng shui features in a Spanish colonial–style complex with an outdoor courtyard and private VIP suites. The spa experience begins with a whirlpool bath, followed by a muscle-soothing session under the Roman waterfall. Clients relax in the cedar sauna, lounging pool, and spa courtyard between treatments. Half-day sessions are designed with tranquility, inspiration, and anti-aging elements and cost between $260 and $460. Several packages are designed for couples, who have use of a private suite with a fireplace, minibar, outdoor terrace with private pool, and a TV and Internet access for information junkies. Individual treatments are pricey—a 30-minute mineral bath costs $90, and an 80-minute Thai massage costs $215.

One of the major health-oriented aspects of La Costa is the Chopra Center, founded by physicians and authors Deepak Chopra and David Simon. The center's treatments are based on Ayurveda principles, a healing system from India that uses oils, herbs, and aromas to help detoxify and heal the body. On the beauty side, the Yamaguchi salon offers a variety of facials, manicures, pedicures, and other treatments.

Loews Coronado Bay Resort
4000 Coronado Bay Road, Coronado
(619) 424-4000, (800) 815-6397
www.loewshotels.com

Located just 20 minutes south of downtown San Diego, Loews Coronado Bay Resort has an exclusive location on a private peninsula in San Diego Bay. All rooms include custom furnishings, a fully stocked minibar, and a king-size bathroom with an oversize tub. The bay-side villas are in a class of their own, with private decks and bedrooms separated from elegant parlors. Splurge on one of these villas, and you'll feel like you've been transported to an exotic island.

Be sure to take the resort's herb-garden tour; it's free and the beds of flowers and pungent herbs are sure to please and impress you. Free "Dive-in Movies" are shown on a large screen poolside in summer months and on holidays. Guests also have access to bikes and in-line skates; sail-, motor-, and paddleboats; golf; wave runners; and tennis.

A 10,000-square-foot spa and fitness center offers all the latest pampering treatments. The design takes advantage of San Diego's perfect weather and affords guests a soothing Zen-like retreat. Fourteen indoor and outdoor treatment

If you're staying at a spa to achieve higher nutritional goals, ask about healthy gourmet food choices. Sometimes it's easier to stay at a spa that only serves low-calorie foods than one where you eat all meals in the main dining room.

rooms, including a couple's suite, are perfectly designed for a variety of massage, facial, and body services. A state-of-the-art fitness center features steam, sauna, and a luxurious relaxation lounge. An enclosed pool is used for water massage called Watsu. Do you want to charter a yacht? Just talk to the concierge. Want a romantic evening? Book a sunset gondola ride around the Coronado Cays, one of the island's most exclusive communities. The Commodore Kids Club has a supervised program providing entertainment for children age 3 to 12. Activities include arts and crafts, Ping-Pong, board games, and movies. As an extra service to you and your children, the management will gladly "kidproof" your room to help keep yours safe and happy during your visit.

The accommodations range from $265 for a standard bay-view room to $1,500 for the presidential and hospitality suites.

Rancho La Puerta
Tecate, Baja California, Mexico
(760) 744-4222, (800) 443-7565
www.rancholapuerta.com

Nestled in 3,000 acres of scenic countryside, just 3 miles south of the border, Rancho La Puerta is in a world of its own. Just 160 guests a week visit this valley where hiking trails cross the habitats of the spa's eco-sanctuary.

Unlike some other health and beauty spas, Rancho La Puerta is coed. Yet from its beginning more than 60 years ago, it was recognized that men and women require distinct fitness regimens, therapy, and workouts, so there are separate exercise centers and beauty treatment facilities. Be sure to sample the Kneipp herbal

Book an exfoliation treatment early on during your stay to prepare your skin for tanning. Also add moisturizing treatments frequently, since San Diego's air tends to be dry. Some local spas offer spray tans that last a few days, giving you that summer glow without sun exposure. If you happen to get sunburned, indulge in a cooling aloe vera wrap.

wrap (it will relax even the most Type A overachiever). The Ranch, as Insiders call it, provides multiple facilities for saunas, steams, nude sunbathing, whirlpool, and hot tubs. It also boasts one of the highest ratios of staff per guests of any spa.

The feeling throughout the Ranch is one of relaxation and comfort. There are more than 60 fitness classes and conditioning programs. There's plenty of pampering. And if you needed any more reasons to consider the Ranch, think about this: Rancho La Puerta is the birthplace of spa cuisine, with most of the fresh produce served here coming straight from the Ranch's organic gardens. It's honest food, offered at the peak of flavor. Everything is first-rate and appealing.

Accommodations at the Ranch consist of individual Spanish colonial-inspired cottages, most with private patios and fireplaces. The secure grounds are landscaped with lovely gardens. The facility includes six lighted tennis courts, six aerobics gyms, a weight-training gym with advanced equipment, three pools, five whirl-jet therapy pools, and three saunas and steam rooms. Specialty weeks focus on yoga, swimming, Pilates, and dance.

The question about drinking water was on the mind of one Insider during a visit to the Ranch. The tap water is filtered and fine for drinking. Bottled mineral water is always available, too.

The second question most people ask is: How do I get there? If you're coming in from San Diego's Lindbergh Field, a regularly scheduled spa bus can take you to the Ranch. Locals can also use the spa bus from the airport. Guests are asked to arrive on Saturday for the seven-day program; the Ranch is about an hour's drive from the airport. During the drive, chipper staff members offer mineral water, snacks, and information on what to expect and what one can expect to accomplish.

Spa packages are for seven days; prices range from $2,725 to $3,955 and are all-inclusive except for Mexican tax and modest charges for special treatments. Ask about special discounted packages, such as the Summer Savings program, with prices ranging from $1,970 to $3,090.

Rancho Valencia Resort
5921 Valencia Circle, Rancho Santa Fe
(858) 756-1123, (800) 548-3664
www.ranchovalencia.com

About 30 minutes and seemingly 3 million light years away from the city of San Diego, Rancho Valencia is elegant and secluded. Located in the North County Coastal area, it is a neighbor to the elite Rancho Santa Fe community. The resort's Hacienda, a restored adobe brick home built in the 1940s, has hosted countless notables such as Bill Blass, Merv Griffin, Kelsey Grammer, and Ted Danson. Guests choose from the 49 luxurious suites and villas spread around the lush grounds; returnees usually have their favorite rooms. The two-night package ranges from $1,525 to $1,825 per couple.

The Spa at Rancho Valencia, which opened in the summer of 2006, is a blissful spot with 10 treatments rooms, a steamy rain room with Vichy shower for wet treatments, and a Watsu pool for one of the most awesome mind and body treatments you'll ever experience. Hour-long massages start at $115; the 90-minute signature massage costs $175. Scents of the surrounding countryside are used in almond and orange oils and essences. Day spa packages start at $295.

VACATION RENTALS

We're about to let you in on the secret to becoming a real San Diegan, if only temporarily. Whether your stay in San Diego is short, long, or indefinite, one of the best ways to enjoy the true San Diego experience is by living it in a vacation rental. Within minutes of unpacking your bags, you'll find yourself doing the same things the natives do. The only difference is, you don't have to go to work.

Vacation rentals are plentiful and offer a cost-effective way to spend some time in San Diego, especially if you're bringing the whole family along. From a quaint 1940s cottage to a modern, fully appointed condominium to a grandiose house in La Jolla, if you can imagine it, you'll find it.

The vast majority of vacation rentals hug the beach, mainly because that's where most people gravitate. Picture waking up to the sound of the ocean waves gently breaking on the shore and having that first cup of coffee on a deck or patio just steps away from the sand. Or perhaps you're more inclined to be inland a few miles, in the wooded enclave of Rancho Santa Fe, or on the fairway of a world-class golf course.

From Oceanside in North County Coastal to Imperial Beach in the South Bay, rentals are available with an array of amenities and price ranges. The primary appeal to staying in a fully furnished house, condo, or cottage, aside from the lower cost, is that you can fend for yourself, and not rely on hotels and restaurants for your needs. It's a much more casual existence. Plus, many people love being absorbed by the local culture, mingling with neighborhood residents, browsing nearby shops, even making the obligatory trip to the local Laundromat.

So pack your bags lightly (remember, we're very informal here), bring along your sunscreen, and become a bona fide San Diegan. Imagine lazy days on the beach, a glass of champagne while watching the sunset, a leisurely dinner, and an evening stroll along the water. Then you'll understand why so many people have discovered that a vacation rental is the ideal way to go.

RENTAL AGENTS AND INDEPENDENT OWNERS

Even though most vacation rentals are independently owned, the majority are managed by property management companies. Although you can find beautiful properties that are rented directly by their owners, unless you have a reliable word-of-mouth referral or good photos that show the interior and exterior, we strongly recommend that you use an established agency. Properties managed by rental agents are uniformly well maintained, the renting agents are completely familiar with the units they are renting, and you will have few surprises. Agents will be more likely to have brochures, too, so you can get an idea of what you're renting ahead of time.

One of the benefits of vacation rentals in San Diego is that many of the properties are occupied by their owners at least part of the year. As a result, most are beautifully upgraded and maintained.

Some vacation rental companies advertise their properties only on the Internet, but the ads come complete with pictures and detailed descriptions of the house or condo. This is especially true for rentals in the inland and southern regions of San Diego. A browse around the Internet might be time well spent, particularly if you're looking for something other than beach property. Just search on "San Diego Vacation Rentals," and you'll be overwhelmed by the number and variety of rentals.

SHORT-TERM AND LONG-TERM STAYS

Although shorter stays are usually available during the winter season, most rentals require a minimum of a one-week stay during the summer. Some of the higher-end properties in La Jolla and Rancho Santa Fe, for example, might require a one-month commitment during the tourist season. Long-term stays, usually considered to be for the whole summer, are also an option. If you plan to stay longer than that, you may as well rent privately if for no other reason than to avoid local hotel taxes, which must be collected on vacation rentals.

Noise can be a considerable deterrent to renting a vacation home by the beach. It's particularly invasive around the Mission Beach boardwalk and the main sections of Ocean Beach and Pacific Beach. You may be happier a few blocks away from the sand or in the quieter residential areas of Mission Bay.

RATES AND RESERVATIONS

Not surprisingly, rates fluctuate greatly between the summer and winter seasons. The summer season generally runs from June through September; winter is considered to be October through May. Summertime rates are higher than winter rates, ranging from $600 per week to $3,500, while some winter rates drop by about $300 to $500 per week. So if you'd like to join the ranks of "snowbirds" who flee the harsh winters of the Midwest and the East for a respite in temperate San Diego, you'll probably find some good values.

Keep in mind, too, that quoted rates do not include the required 10.5 percent hotel tax. You will also be required to pay an advance reservation fee and security deposit. Most properties require a 30-day or 60-day cancellation notice to refund the full amount of your deposit. Some will withhold a portion of your reservation fee regardless of how early you cancel.

We highly recommend that you make your reservations well in advance of your visit. Some properties are booked for the summer by January, so the earlier you can make plans, the better.

KIDS AND PETS

Nearly all rentals welcome children. In fact, most encourage Mom and Dad to bring the kids. San Diego has much to offer the whole family. Most rentals have a limit on how many people can occupy a property, but they are designed to accommodate as many as possible. Property managers are happy to work with you to make sure your entire group is comfortably accommodated.

For the most part, pets are not allowed. If you're set on bringing Fluffy or Fido along, you might have more luck renting from individual homeowners, most of whom list their properties in the classifieds section of the *San Diego Union-Tribune* or on the Internet. If you play detective and search thoroughly enough, you should be able to find a place willing to host your four-legged family member.

PARKING

If there were a way to sugarcoat this issue, we would. But the truth is, parking at the beach is always a challenge. If you're driving into town and considering a beach rental, a garage or reserved parking space may be one of the amenities you'll wish to place near the top of your list. Even if you're lucky enough to find an overnight parking place on the street, should you decide to go for a drive the next morning, by 10:00 A.M. you will not find another place to park when you return. You'll be forced to park in a lot miles away and shuttle back and forth.

Just in case you're tempted to squeeze your car into a likely spot in one of the alleys, be forewarned. If one of your wheels even kisses the red line that screams "no parking," your car will be towed. And parking enforcement is a constant, vigilant presence at the beaches during the summer months. You'll have to pay not only the towing charges but also a painful parking fine. The good news is that even though parking is difficult at best, the payoff is worth it. Most people take it in stride and simply plan ahead. You might end up having to hike a little, but you should always be able to find something.

RENTAL AGENCIES

Beachfront San Diego Rentals
4603 Mission Boulevard, Pacific Beach
(858) 483-6116, (800) 248-5262
www.beachfrontsandiego.com

This company handles condo rentals at Capri by the Sea, an upscale beachfront property in Pacific Beach. There are several different-sized units with separate bedrooms and kitchens. The location is ideal, right on a slight cliff over the ocean between Pacific Beach and La Jolla. The company also handles homes and condos in other beach areas. Some have nightly as well as weekly rentals.

ERA Coastal Properties
731 South Highway 101, Suite 1P, Solana Beach
(858) 793-3600, (800) 636-7368
www.sandiegovacationhomes.com

ERA specializes in vacation condos and houses from La Jolla north to Oceanside and occasionally offers a property in Rancho Santa Fe or a condo in the Four Seasons Resort Aviara. Included in their territory are Del Mar, Solana Beach, La Costa, and Carlsbad, areas that are highly sought after for their proximity to the Del Mar Racetrack and North County Coastal golf courses. Most of the properties are high end, but all are exquisitely maintained and appointed to provide a memorable San Diego experience.

Consider exchanging a stay in your home for one in San Diego. Home exchanges have become a popular means of vacationing without spending a fortune. One of the most established companies is HomeExchange.com, which has listings of available homes throughout the world. Contact them at (310) 798-3864, (800) 877-8723; www.HomeExchange.com.

Pace Realty
5693 La Jolla Boulevard, La Jolla
(858) 454-1123

If you're looking for the ultimate luxury vacation, Pace offers magnificent individual homes for rent in La Jolla, the tony beachfront village that has some of the country's most valuable real estate. You're not likely to find any bargains here, but if you're willing to part with upward of $10,000, you'll get a month in a La Jolla house that is the stuff of which dreams are made.

Penny Property Management
4444 Mission Boulevard, San Diego
(858) 272-3900, (800) 748-6704
www.missionbeach.com

Since 1965 Penny Property Management has been helping vacationers find the perfect beach rental. Specializing in Mission and Pacific Beaches, Penny also has

Rental rates go down when the winter season officially begins at the end of September. However, San Diego has some of its nicest weather in October, when blue skies and warm temperatures are the norm. Book your vacation during October, and you'll have your pick of the best properties for the lowest prices.

You may be able to rent a condo overlooking La Jolla Cove. PHOTO: COURTESY OF MARIBETH MELLIN

rentals in downtown, Ocean Beach, and La Jolla. All of Penny's booking agents are familiar with each property they rent and can help you find exactly what's right for you, from a no-frills unit to a luxury penthouse in the sky.

San Diego Vacation Cottages
2422 San Diego Avenue, San Diego
(619) 291-9091, (888) 271-5496
www.sandiegovacationapts.com

Even though June signals the beginning of the summer season, it often is a gray, overcast month. The marine layer that locals wryly refer to as "June Gloom" settles in along the coast, and often the sun makes only an occasional appearance during the entire month. Keep this in mind if you're planning a beach vacation.

This company handles classic beach cottages in Ocean Beach, a casual community with less traffic and congestion than other areas. The cottages are within walking distance of the beach and are available by the night, week, or month. The company also books charming cottages in Old Town.

San Diego Vacation Rentals
3701 Ocean Front Walk, San Diego
(619) 296-1000, (800) 222-8281
www.sdvr.com

Like its cohorts, San Diego Vacation Rentals specializes in beach rentals, focusing on Mission Beach, Ocean Beach, and La Jolla. Whether you're looking for a large luxury house located right on the beach or bay-front sand, or a secluded cottage tucked away on one of Mission Beach's courts, San Diego Vacation Rentals can help you find a dreamy vacation home.

RESTAURANTS

The most delicious dilemma facing San Diegans most days isn't where to play, it's what to eat. In San Diego County you're facing nearly 3,000 restaurant choices, from drive-through taco stands to elegant gourmet dining rooms. In this chapter we've given you an overview of your dining options throughout San Diego County.

Certain areas are culinary hotbeds where you'll find a dozen or more intriguing restaurants sitting nearly door-to-door for several blocks. La Jolla has long been the Insiders' destination for culinary curiosities and excellence. But downtown's Gaslamp Quarter has overtaken all competition. More than 30 restaurants within a 16-block radius offer everything from Irish corned beef and cabbage to paella Valenciana. This long-neglected historic district has become nightlife central for Insiders, who simply spend the night in a Gaslamp hotel rather than driving home a tad inebriated late at night.

San Diego's finest hotels are home to excellent restaurants that are so popular, maitre d's have trouble juggling reservations for hotel guests and locals. Be sure to make reservations in advance at any upscale restaurant recommended in this chapter. Most are extremely popular.

Since San Diego abuts the U.S.–Mexico border, Mexican food is a regional specialty. Local grocery stores sell far more salsa than catsup, and jalapeño chilies, guacamole, and corn chips are among our basic food groups. For the most part, the best Mexican food is found in tiny hole-in-the-wall neighborhood hangouts. If you walk past one that's crowded, you can be sure they serve great tacos, enchiladas, burritos, and huevos rancheros. Some more upscale restaurants are now serving good regional cuisine from throughout Mexico, and a few places specialize in serving premium brands of tequila. Be sure to sample a few fish tacos, a local specialty.

As always, remember that San Diego is a casual place. Very few restaurants have any kind of a dress code. The key phrase seems to be "casually elegant." However, a few of the top-notch (meaning expensive) restaurants do insist that men wear jackets and that both men and women refrain from wearing shorts or jeans. If such a requirement exists, we'll be sure to mention it. It's not a bad idea to call ahead if you have any doubt, though.

Most restaurants accept reservations, except for the ultracasual places, and we recommend that you make them, especially on weekends. Most also accept all major credit cards; the exceptions are noted. The exceptions are usually small fast-food places that just aren't equipped for credit cards but are certainly worth experiencing. If a restaurant is especially family friendly, we've mentioned it, but you're likely to see children dining right along with Mom and Dad just about everywhere.

California has tough smoking laws. Smoking is prohibited in all restaurants and bars, unless you're seated in an outdoor patio or terrace. Even then, your fellow diners may object if you light up.

As usual, we've divided the chapter by geographic region, with one slight deviation. Restaurants in the city of San Diego have been further broken down into groupings by neighborhoods for your convenience. Each restaurant has also been identified by its cuisine.

So go exploring and try something new. We know you'll be pleased by what you'll find.

PRICE CODE

Our price code includes the average price of entrees for two people, excluding cocktails, tax, and tip.

$	**Less than $20**
$$	**$21 to $35**
$$$	**$36 to $45**
$$$$	**$46 and higher**

CENTRAL SAN DIEGO

Coronado

Azzura Point **$$$$**
Loews Coronado Bay Resort
Californian
4000 Coronado Bay Road, Coronado
(619) 424-4477

The decor is sophisticated and exotic, with Venetian-style chandeliers and hand-painted suede and silk drapes. The menu is a study in exquisite delicacies. The service is attentive but not fawning or overly friendly. These are just three of the reasons why Azzura Point is consistently named one of San Diego's top restaurants.

Chef de cuisine Martin T. Batis mixes Alaskan king salmon with Peruvian potato hash, muscovy duck breast with fava beans, grilled tenderloin of beef with caramelized onions, Roquefort tart, and morel mushrooms. You get the idea. His cooking is innovative and highly alluring. Your first time around, you might want to try the Chef's Tasting Menu to get an overview. Then you'll be able to order your favorite entrees with confidence. There's also a vegetarian Herb Garden Menu (drawing from the hotel's fragrant garden). The bittersweet chocolate hazelnut cake with caramel ice cream, chocolate lace, and coffee sauce is enough to make you want to spend the night at the Loews Coronado Bay Resort so you can go back for more.

If you want just a sampling of the chef's magic, the adjacent Azzura Point Lounge serves tapas-style hors d'oeuvres. The sommelier has managed to narrow his wine list to just 275 selections; fortunately, he's there to help guide you to the right choice. Dinner is served nightly except Monday.

Chez Loma **$$$**
French/Continental
1132 Loma Avenue, Coronado
(619) 435-0661
www.chezloma.com

The finely restored house Chez Loma calls home is a Coronado historical monument, and its award-winning cuisine has received nationwide distinction. The restaurant is broken up into several intimate dining areas that almost make you think you're dining at home—if you have a resident chef who can prepare updated French and continental classics.

Menus change with the seasons, but some standouts are the horseradish-encrusted Atlantic salmon with smoked tomato vinaigrette. Duck, lamb, seafood, and pasta dishes are also treated to the chef's special touch. A carefully selected wine list complements the menu, and the bar offers premium selections. The early dining special is a great deal. Chez Loma serves dinner nightly. Locals stop by for a glass of wine and an appetizer or coffee and dessert in the enclosed patio and don't bother dressing up. But you'll want to look a little spiffy if you dine inside.

Rhinoceros Cafe **$-$$**
American
1166 Orange Avenue, Coronado
(619) 435-2121
www.rhinocafe.com

American bistro-style cooking is featured here in this cozy cafe. Choose from steaks, poultry, fresh fish, and shellfish dishes as well as a selection of delicious pasta entrees. Light eaters lean toward the pasta dishes or the herb-sauced poached salmon. A good selection of beer and wine is offered.

The atmosphere is casual, and all menu items are available for takeout. Lunch and dinner are served daily.

Coronado's Orange Avenue is lined with sidewalk cafes. PHOTO: COURTESY OF MARIBETH MELLIN

Downtown/Gaslamp Quarter

Athens Market **$$**
Greek
109 West F Street, San Diego
(619) 234-1955
www.athensmarkettaverna.com

Located in the historic and beautifully restored Federal Building, the Athens Market is a haven for the relaxed dining crowd. Proprietor Mary Pappas offers a comprehensive Greek menu with large portions and high quality. All the traditional favorites are covered, including moussaka and spanakopita, but if you like lamb, don't miss the roasted lamb served here. It's especially nice.

Pappas has a longtime following of legal and financial leaders, along with regular folks who've come to feel like family. There's a full bar that keeps things lively. Dinner is served Monday through Saturday, and the restaurant is open for lunch Monday through Friday.

Bella Luna **$$$**
Italian
748 Fifth Avenue, San Diego
(619) 239-3222

For a long while, you couldn't throw a cannoli without hitting an Italian restaurant in the Gaslamp Quarter. Many have come and gone, but the ones that remain are those that have got it right from the beginning. Bella Luna continues to offer the excellent regional food of Capri in its small but chic establishment. The name translates to "Beautiful Moon," and moon-themed artwork covers the walls.

The menu is light and imaginative, including lots of fresh seafood and pasta, as well as a tasty breaded veal chop covered with a blend of arugula and fresh tomato. Daily risotto dishes are Insiders' favorites, but if it's available, try the shrimp salad or the tender crepe stuffed with salmon. One specialty always available is the grilled half chicken. Lunch and dinner are served daily.

The Cohn group has four restaurants in downtown and nearly a dozen around town, including The Prado in Balboa Park. All have excellent chefs and intriguing menus. Check their Web site at www.cohnrestaurants.com for special offers and information on wine dinners and featured chefs.

Bertrand at Mr. A's **$$$$**
French Mediterranean
2550 Fifth Avenue, San Diego
(619) 239-1377
www.bertrandatmisteras.com

Take the elevator to the top floor and settle in at a linen-topped table and watch the planes fly over downtown, as San Diegans have done for years at Mr. A's. Many were sad when this venerable institution closed in the late 1990s and delighted when it reopened in 2000. Chef de cuisine Stéphane Voitzwinkler presides over this casually elegant restaurant overlooking the city's skyline. Start your feast with traditional lobster bisque or Maine lobster and mushrooms in filo dough with cognac lobster sauce, then move on to braised sweetbreads or a classic New York steak. Open for lunch Monday through Friday, dinner nightly.

Blue Point Coastal Cuisine **$$$**
Seafood
565 Fifth Avenue, San Diego
(619) 233-6623
www.cohnrestaurants.com

You'll feel like you're walking into a San Francisco supper club when you enter Blue Point. With its large wooden booths and dining tables off to one side and a massive bar dominating the other, the mood is elegant and upbeat. In fact, you'll probably be inspired to order one of the dozens of specialty martinis to complement appetizers, which can be ordered at the bar.

Our favorite entree is the Hawaiian ahi, served with wild mushrooms and ginger butter. But you can't go wrong with any of the seafood items here, like crab cakes or catfish, all of which are served with lots of organic vegetables. Dinner is served nightly.

Cafe 222 **$**
American
222 Island Avenue, San Diego
(619) 236-9902
www.cafe222.com

Downtown loft dwellers and hip travelers congregate in this wacky cafe for pumpkin waffles, homemade granola, and veggie omelettes at breakfast and grilled meat loaf sandwiches for lunch. Regulars tend to linger at the sidewalk tables or inside under the chandeliers made of spoons (you gotta see it to believe it). The food is great, the clientele fascinating, and, if you want to be left alone, there's a huge stack of magazines for your perusal. Owner Terryl Gavre is usually there chatting with friends while overseeing the grill. Dogs are welcome "with well-behaved owners." It's open daily for breakfast and lunch from 7:00 A.M. to 1:45 P.M.

Croce's **$$-$$$**
International
802 Fifth Avenue, San Diego
(619) 233-4355
www.croces.com

Croce's nearly defies description, as it is much more than a restaurant. It's actually two restaurants, a jazz club, and a sidewalk dining spot. They all flow into one another with an electric mix of great food, divine music, and fun-loving folks. For dining, Croce's is truly an experience; to find out more about it as an entertainment spot, check our Nightlife chapter. Owner Ingrid Croce, widow of legendary singer Jim Croce, opened the first arm of her restaurant when the Gaslamp Quarter was in the early stages of its revitalization. Over the years the restaurant has spread out into adjacent buildings.

Ingrid Croce and chef de cuisine James Clark keep diners coming back by changing the menu. There's always a chicken dish or two. Try the one with forest mushroom risotto if it's available, or go for the Contemporary meat loaf with creamy mashed potatoes. Croce's is open for breakfast, lunch, dinner, and late-night dining daily.

Dobson's **$$$**
Californian
956 Broadway Circle, San Diego
(619) 231-6771
www.dobsonsrestaurant.com
For power lunches and after-theater dinners, Dobson's is a great choice. Downtown bigwigs know they'll be treated courteously whether they dine in the saloon-style bar downstairs or the upstairs loft dining room. The hands-down Insiders' favorite menu item is the signature mussel bisque with a puff-pastry crust.

You'll also find lots of seafood specialties on the seasonal menu, as well as meats and poultry that mingle Italian tradition with modern California style. Many go to Dobson's just to hang out at the bar, which is next to a huge front window, affording a view of the constant parade of downtown movers and shakers. Dobson's is open for lunch Monday through Friday and for dinner Monday through Saturday.

The Field **$**
Irish
544 Fifth Avenue, San Diego
(619) 232-9840
www.thefield.com
The food at this eatery/pub is down-home Irish, corned beef and cabbage being the main menu item. Thick slabs of corned beef are accompanied by tender sautéed cabbage. We know that boiled potatoes don't sound too sexy, but give them a try. Combined with the other flavors on your plate, they're a winner.

The interior of the restaurant is furnished with tables, farm tools, and equipment all imported, piece by piece, from Ireland. If you have even a smidgen of Irish in you (as we all do on St. Patrick's Day), you'll feel right at home here. The menu also includes fish and chips and some outstanding breakfast selections. Lunch and dinner are served daily.

Ingrid Croce, the ever-inventive owner of Croce's restaurant in downtown, has published* The San Diego Restaurant Cookbook, *which is filled with more than 260 recipes from Insiders' favorite restaurants. The book is available at Croce's and other restaurants and through the Web site www.sandiegorestaurantcookbook.com.

Las Cuatro Milpas **$**
Mexican
1857 Logan Avenue, San Diego
(619) 234-4460
A Barrio Logan mainstay since 1933, Las Cuatro Milpas is a storefront eatery offering authentic Mexican specialties, including chorizo, a spicy Mexican sausage, with beans. The dangerously fiery salsa concocted on the premises is a mandatory addition to every dish, and the warm tortillas are unlike anything you'll ever find in a supermarket. Over the years the restaurant has expanded its seating into adjacent buildings, which provide plenty of room for family-style eating. But don't be surprised if you find yourself dining on savory pork or chicken tacos in your car or while perched on the curb, because lines often snake out the door and down the street during lunch time.

The specialty of the week is served on Saturday only, when Las Cuatro Milpas opens at 6:00 A.M. to dish up steaming bowls of *menudo,* a legendary hangover cure. The restaurant is open for breakfast and lunch every day except Sunday. Takeout is available as well as bulk purchases of most menu items. Be sure to bring cash; no credit cards are accepted.

Red Pearl Kitchen **$$**
Asian
440 J Street, San Diego
(619) 231-1100
www.redpearlkitchen.com
All senses are stimulated by the innovative, creative menu and exciting decor at

Watch for restaurant specials and coupons in Thursday's* San Diego Union-Tribune. *Oftentimes you'll find two-for-one or early-bird specials that can save you a bunch.

this 2006 downtown newcomer. It's nearly impossible to narrow your dinner choices to a sensible selection. That's why the restaurant serves family style and staffers encourage diners to share everything. For our first Red Pearl dinner we started with flash-roasted endamame (an unbeatable munchie) while perusing the menu. Then we were able to settle on spicy tuna tartare on tempura eggplant for starters, followed by wok-fired Kobe beef with red papaya. All around us diners raved about their curries and pad thai. Despite our tightening waistbands we shared banana cake drizzled with caramel and a trio of tropical sorbets—the kiwi sorbet was a standout. Next time we'll bring our beaus and dine in the private niche glowing red in the light from a circular lantern, or book the chef's table in the kitchen. Dinner and late-night dining are available nightly.

Sevilla **$$**
Spanish
555 Fourth Avenue, San Diego
(619) 233-5979
www.cafesevilla.com
The only way to truly appreciate Sevilla is to go at least twice, because the first time you visit, it's almost mandatory to have the paella Valenciana. This traditional Spanish dish is loaded with clams, mussels, calamari, shrimp, chorizo, and roasted chicken, all cooked in an aromatic saffron rice. There's even a vegetarian version. When you return, you can enjoy one of the other fine entrees, such as New York steak with Riojo sauce or roasted chicken in garlic sauce.

Should you wish to sit at the bar and make a meal of tapas, which are Spanish appetizers, try a sampling of croquettes of shrimp, mushrooms sautéed in a garlic wine sauce, or fried calamari. If you'd really like to make a night of it, make reservations for the flamenco or tango dinner shows. See our Nightlife chapter for more happenings at Sevilla. Dinner is served nightly.

Sushi Deli 2 **$**
Japanese
135 Broadway, Central San Diego
(619) 233-3072
The plentiful portions and low prices have made Sushi Deli 2 thrive over the decades, despite downtown's ever-changing dining scene. The original Sushi Deli at Eighth Avenue and Broadway has closed, but Sushi Deli 2 remains a downtown favorite. As the name suggests, you'll want to head here for everything from California rolls to raw tuna (sashimi) with plenty of hot wasabi. Most customers know exactly what they want since they've eaten here so often, but first-timers need a few minutes to study the extensive menu. The combo platters with a couple of entrees, rice, and salad are a great deal—go for the vegetable tempura or teriyaki beef. It's open Monday through Saturday for lunch and dinner. Telephone take-out orders are not accepted at lunchtime, which tends to be busy.

Hillcrest/Uptown

Cafe on Park **$**
American
3831 Park Boulevard, San Diego
(619) 293-7275
An American-style bistro, this small and cozy eatery offers hearty breakfasts and lunches daily. Even during the week the cafe is busy from the moment it opens until closing. Breakfast seems to be the standout of the day. You can choose from all the standards—eggs, pancakes, cereals—but they're all prepared with a twist. Eggs are

called "scrambles" and are combined with a variety of ingredients, including peppers, onions, chilies, beef, and more. The lines for weekend breakfasts are long, giving diners time to work up their appetites.

Most diners are regulars, and most have their favorite dishes, except for one Insider who says his favorite menu item is whatever's in front of him at the time. Imaginative sandwiches, salads, and pasta items distinguish the lunch menu.

Chilango's Mexico City Grill $$-$$$
Mexican
142 University Avenue, San Diego
(619) 294-8646
www.chilangosgrill.com

Mexican restaurants are never in short supply around town, but few of them feature regional cuisine like Chilango's. It has dishes such as shrimp with vanilla and mango sauce; chicken with nopales (cactus); and pescado veracruzano, fish topped with tomatoes, onions, and chilies.

Chilango's started as a simple takeout with a few tables, but has expanded to a full-scale restaurant with tablecloths and everything. The prices have risen, naturally, but the excellent cooking is worth every peso. Try to get a sidewalk table for a view of the Hillcrest street scene. The restaurant is open for lunch Monday through Saturday and for dinner nightly.

Karen Krasne's
Extraordinary Desserts $
Desserts
2929 Fifth Avenue, San Diego
(619) 294-7001

1430 Union Street, San Diego
(619) 294-7001
www.extraordinarydesserts.com

Who hasn't fantasized about skipping dinner and going straight to dessert? This is the place to indulge the fantasy. Owner Karen Krasne, whose sweet creations have been featured in *Bon Appetit,* has carved a niche for those who want to throw caution to the wind and relax with a dessert that's as beautiful as it is tasty. Picture a tender, flaky napoleon filled with whipped cream and fresh berries, dusted with powdered sugar, and topped with edible flowers.

Or if chocolate is your only idea of dessert, you'll have plenty of choices. Dense chocolate tortes, huge brownies and cookies, and luscious chocolate cakes are yours for the choosing. Tart and sweet lemon tortes awaken the sense buds, and several kinds of buttery shortbread rekindle memories of Grandma's kitchen. Extraordinary Desserts also serves a large selection of coffees and teas, the ideal accompaniment to your sweet delicacy. The Fifth Avenue cafe is open to satisfy your sweet tooth from morning to late night daily.

Krasne's second dining venture at the downtown side of Little Italy is an exciting, urbane bistro/bakery. Locals linger over cheese plates, bruschettas, breads and dips, and other small dishes or just dive right into the ultimate brownie, made with Vahlrona chocolate and roasted almonds. The front shelves are filled with treasures that caught Krasne's eye during her travels. The selection of teapots, cups, spices, and candles (all for sale) is nearly as stunning as the glass display cases filled with tortes and treats topped with fresh flowers.

Kemo Sabe $$$
Southwestern/Asian
3958 Fifth Avenue, San Diego
(619) 220-6802
www.cohnrestaurants.com

As pleasing to the eye as it is to the taste buds, Kemo Sabe grabs your attention as soon as you walk through the door with its unusual collection of sculpture and other art pieces. Even the entrees are works of art—you'll hear lots of oohs and aahs as dishes are placed before diners. And what dishes they are. The perennial favorite is Skirts on Fire, a skirt steak grilled and seasoned with spices that will ignite your senses (and your mouth—but pleasantly).

For appetizers, try the mixed satay, skewers of grilled chicken, shrimp, and steak seasoned with Thai spices and served with a peanut dipping sauce. To complement your dinner, Kemo Sabe's bartender has created a large selection of custom martinis. This Insiders' favorite is the Blue Glacier, a concoction of Bombay Sapphire gin, Skyy vodka, and blue curaçao, with an orange twist. It goes down quite nicely. Dinner is served nightly.

Saffron Noodles and Saté/
Saffron Thai Chicken **$**
Thai
3737 India Street, San Diego
(619) 574-7737
www.sumeiyu.com

These side-by-side eateries have the same ownership and serve Thai favorites for takeout or to eat in. Owner Su-Mei Yu has published a cookbook with her most popular recipes, including mouthwatering chicken saté served with jasmine rice, cucumber salad, and peanut dipping sauce. There's also a large selection of noodle dishes served in traditional Thai style, flavorful and spicy. Next door at Saffron Thai Chicken, tender Thai-style roasted chicken is served with your choice of five sauces and a terrific Vietnamese coleslaw topped with chopped peanuts. There's no seating on this side, but all menu items can be ordered from either restaurant if you're eating in.

Saffron was listed in *USA Today* as one of the 10 best places in the country for takeout. Insiders have discovered the place, and it's not uncommon for lines to be a bit long. But it's worth the wait for these savory Thai delicacies. Saffron serves lunch and dinner daily.

La Jolla/Beaches

Brockton Villa **$**
Continental
1235 Coast Boulevard, La Jolla
(858) 454-7393
www.brocktonvilla.com

Although the food is equally good at lunch and dinner, breakfast is what draws the big crowds to this quaint, century-old beach cottage overlooking La Jolla Cove and the Pacific Ocean. Wander in around breakfast time, put your name on the list, then help yourself to a cup of coffee and a newspaper and lounge around the deck with the rest of the crowd waiting to be seated.

Once you're seated either inside or on the outside terrace, choose from some amazing breakfast dishes like steamers, Greek-style eggs scrambled with feta cheese, or banana pancakes dotted with big banana chunks. Orange French toast is a keeper, too. The lunch menu features shrimp and chicken salads, and at dinner don't miss the California seafood stew. Breakfast and lunch are served daily, and breakfast lasts until 3:00 P.M. on weekends; dinner is served Tuesday through Sunday.

George's Cafe & Ocean Terrace **$$-$$$**
Contemporary Californian
1250 Prospect Street, La Jolla
(858) 454-4244
www.georgesatthecove.com

This is alfresco dining at its best, on a rooftop terrace with an unimpeded view of La Jolla Cove. The California cuisine is also memorable. Lots of pastas are offered, like the fettucine with rock shrimp in garlic Parmesan sauce. Seafood offerings include a pan-seared king salmon that's served with couscous. Or try the deep-fried prawns accompanied by sweet potato cakes.

The lunchtime menu has great sandwiches and salads, but the star is the quesadilla with spicy-hot Jamaican chicken. The Ocean Terrace is open daily for lunch and dinner. The cafe sits atop George's at the Cove restaurant, one of the finest dining establishments in La Jolla. Have a special romantic dinner here if you care to splurge. The cuisine is always exciting, and wall mirrors amplify the view of the sea so no one misses out on spectacular sunsets.

Marine Room **$$$$**
Global
2000 Spindrift Drive, La Jolla
(858) 459-7222
www.ljbtc.com

This treasured restaurant on the sand manages to be both venerable and exciting. It has withstood the test of time and has been reinvented a number of times over the years to appeal to new generations of diners. In addition to fine adventuresome cuisine, the restaurant is noted for its ocean view. And it's not an ordinary ocean view—it's right on the water. During storms waves often crash against the triple-thick glass windows facing the ocean, putting on a show of Mother Nature's ferocity.

But back to the food. Chef Bernard Guillas keeps the menu interesting with his flavor combinations and exotic ingredients. No many menus around have barramundi, a delicious Australian fish, or gooseberry-glazed venison. The chef likes to play with the menu, but his loyal fans won't let him do away with the goat cheese brûlée. The spinach-wrapped Pacific oysters are also on the must-have list. You might want to spend a Sunday morning lingering over brunch. It doesn't matter if the day is sunny or gray, the view will always take your breath away. Lunch is served Tuesday through Saturday; dinner is served nightly. Sunday brunch is served from 11:00 A.M. to 1:30 P.M.

Saska's **$$**
American
3768 Mission Boulevard, San Diego
(858) 488-7311

Let's say you've pushed the day into nighttime, it's midnight, and you haven't eaten yet. Where do you go to get dinner other than a Grand Slam at Denny's? Since the mid-1950s Saska's has been the solution for late-night diners looking for a steak, a lobster tail, or even a good plate of pasta. Saska's stays open until 2:00 A.M., adding first-rate breakfast items to the menu at 11:00 P.M.

Even if you tend to dine at more conventional hours, it's worth a trip to Mission Beach to experience this legendary restaurant. The food is consistently good, especially the teriyaki steak and chicken, and there's usually a member of the Saska family behind the bar or roaming about to make you feel at home. Saska's serves lunch and dinner daily and brunch on Saturday and Sunday.

Shades **$$**
American
5083 Santa Monica Avenue, Ocean Beach
(619) 222-0501

The view of the Ocean Beach Pier from this restaurant's huge windows is enough of a reason to dine here. But the food is even better than the scenery. Huge bowls of homemade granola with fresh fruit, portobello mushroom omelettes, and chocolate chip pancakes are just some of the reasons to come by for breakfast. Piles of crisp fish and chips and the Ensalada OB, with chicken breast and Mexican cotija cheese, are top lunch choices, and the lobster and shrimp tortellini is a must-try at dinner. Open daily for breakfast, lunch, and dinner.

Thee Bungalow **$$-$$$**
Continental
4996 West Point Loma Boulevard
San Diego
(619) 224-2884
www.theebungalow.com

Make a point of visiting this longtime resident of Ocean Beach. Now owned by the Cohn Restaurant Group, this neighborhood favorite has been around for more than 30 years. One dish that is almost always available here is the roast duck, and for good reason. It's superb, as are the fresh fish dishes, innovative soups, and veal creations. Locals say the cassoulet makes you feel like you're sitting in the French countryside, and the wine list is extensive.

You can dine in the dining room, formal in construction but relaxed in mood, or on the outdoor patio. Watch for value-priced midweek and early-bird dinners. Thee Bungalow is always trying something different and fun. Dinner is served nightly.

Mission Valley/Inland

Adams Avenue Grill $$
Global
2201 Adams Avenue, San Diego
(619) 298-8440

Whatever your favorite meal is, you're likely to find it on the menu here. Everything from Thai to Italian to American to Southwest is represented. The mystery is how they all come out so well. The angel-hair pasta with roma tomatoes, garlic, basil, and balsamic vinegar is finished with a splash of burgundy that gives this traditional dish a nice twist. Equally pleasing is the Thai salad, a mixture of snow peas, Napa cabbage, and mixed greens tossed with roasted peanuts and a spicy peanut dressing.

Although offered as an appetizer, the Southwest black bean soup served with shrimp and a jalapeño quesadilla makes a full lunch. Desserts include a chocoholic's delight, a molten lava cake with a warm chocolate ganache center. Plan on a trip to the gym if you finish the whole thing. Lunch and dinner are served daily.

Kensington Grill $$
New American
4055 Adams Avenue, San Diego
(619) 281-4014

The owners bill their restaurant as "New American cuisine," and while we might be hard-pressed to define it, we don't care. Whatever it is, it's great. This is a neighborhood restaurant with a large and lively bar on one side (the music can be annoyingly loud) and a smallish dining room on the other. A few tables line the sidewalk for outdoor dining.

We strongly suggest you start your meal with a delectable mango and Brie quesadilla. It sounds unusual, but it's sinfully good. Then move on to such dishes as pan-seared sea bass and meat loaf. You can even get a burger here if you're searching for comfort food. Dinner is served nightly.

Several San Diego restaurants are pet friendly and have water bowls outside the front door for thirsty animals. For a list of restaurants and hotels that welcome pets, check out www.dogfriendly.com.

Prego $$
Italian
1370 Frazee Road, San Diego
(619) 294-4700

As you approach Prego through the sunlit courtyard, you'll get the feeling that you're walking into a large Italian villa. Once inside, the sights and sounds of regional Italian cuisine being prepared in the open kitchen will get your mouth watering. Begin with the fresh garlic-rosemary bread baked in Prego's wood-fired oven, then graze through such tasty antipasti as the grilled radicchio, endive, eggplant, and portobello mushrooms accompanied by prosciutto-wrapped goat cheese.

Chicken, seafood, pork chops, and steak all get the Prego treatment, and be sure to ask about the risotto of the day, a creamy arborio rice dish that changes according to the chef's whim. Lunch is served Monday through Friday, and dinner is served nightly.

Seau's: The Restaurant $$
Californian
1640 Camino del Rio North, San Diego
(619) 291-7328
www.seau.com

San Diego's own Junior Seau, one-time star defensive back for the San Diego Chargers, opened this restaurant to immediate acclaim. Junior's aim was to have an all-out sports bar that was all things to all people. He's darn well done it, too. Food is not secondary here. It ranges from pizzas, salads, sushi, and pastas to sandwiches and grilled fresh fish. And most menu items are quite good, especially the Greek salad, a toss of greens, feta cheese, Greek olives, and tomatoes dressed with a tangy herb vinaigrette.

Of course, baseball, basketball, football, and every other sport on earth is continuously broadcast from TVs placed everywhere. There's a full bar and lounge. Located in Mission Valley Center, Seau's is open for lunch and dinner daily.

Trophy's Sports Grill **$**
Californian
7510 Hazard Center Drive, San Diego
(619) 296-9600

4282 Esplanade Court, La Jolla
(858) 450-1400

5500 Grossmont Center Drive, La Mesa
(619) 698-2900

570 K Street, San Diego
(619) 237-9700
We can't mention one sports bar/restaurant without giving equal space to the other standout in town. Trophy's predates Seau's, and it has held its own against the young upstart by sticking to its tried-and-true formula. The range of menu items is predictable—pizzas, pastas, burgers, and sandwiches—but you'll find some unusual variations here that are quite good, like the pizza with artichoke hearts and bacon.

Trophy's is a kid-friendly place, providing a place mat and crayons at each table setting. This tends to bring out the kid in most adults, too. Wide-screen TVs are in the bar, and smaller ones are sprinkled throughout the rest of the restaurant. The newest Trophy's is located practically next door to Petco Park downtown. You couldn't get a better location for a postgame celebration. Trophy's is open for lunch and dinner daily, and for Sunday brunch during football season.

Old Town/Point Loma

El Agave **$$-$$$**
Nouveau Mexican
2304 San Diego Avenue, San Diego
(619) 220-0692
www.elagave.com
Sipping tequila is an art form here. Once you make your choice from more than 200 varieties, it's served in a miniature carafe and is accompanied by a small glass of sangrita, a cool mixture of tomato juice and lime intended to cool the fire of the tequila.

Moving on to the menu produces even nicer surprises. This is food with a Mexican influence, but there are none of the combo plates with rice and beans typically found in Mexican restaurants. A good way to try a variety of appetizers is to order the sampler, which includes tiny quesadillas, tacos, and tamales, all with unusual but delicious regional Mexican fillings. The watercress salad is also a star. Peppery watercress is quickly wilted in bacon drippings and served with warm tortillas in which to wrap it. Entrees include a variety of seafood dishes and chicken with several variations of mole sauces. If you've never tasted mole, we strongly recommend it. It is a complex sauce that combines dozens of flavors and ranges from mild to fiery. Lunch and dinner are served daily.

Old Town Mexican Cafe **$$**
Mexican
2489 San Diego Avenue, San Diego
(619) 297-4330
www.oldtownmexcafe.com
No trip to San Diego is complete without stopping for lunch or dinner at "Old Town Mex," as Insiders call it. You'll be hard-pressed to tell the locals from the tourists here, because everyone is too intent on the lively conversation and the steaming plates of Mexican food. There's usually a wait, so a good place to hang out (if the bar is full) is on the front sidewalk, where you can watch fresh tortillas being made by hand.

You'll find the usual combination plates of enchiladas, tacos, and burritos, but the dish that keeps everyone coming back is the carnitas. You'll understand why when a plate of roasted, shredded, and seasoned pork is placed before you with its accompanying hot tortillas, avocado, onions, tomatoes, and cilantro. Warm chips and salsa are served with every meal. Breakfast, lunch, and dinner are served daily.

Pizza Nova **$$**
Californian
5120 North Harbor Drive, San Diego
(619) 226-0268

3955 Fifth Avenue, San Diego
(619) 296-6682

945 Lomas Santa Fe, Solana Beach
(858) 259-0666
www.pizzanova.net

When the first Pizza Nova opened on the harbor in Point Loma, it didn't take Insiders long to figure out that it served a multitude of purposes. It's a great restaurant for casual dining, for dates, for the whole family, for a quick bite, or for a leisurely meal. Other locations began opening around town, and they all have become fixtures in their respective neighborhoods.

Pizzas are innovative, like the ever-popular Thai chicken—ginger-marinated chicken breast, green onions, bean sprouts, carrot slivers, cilantro, and roasted peanuts. The chopped salad almost overflows with generous chunks of salami, fontina cheese, turkey breast, and tomatoes. And the sinfully good fettuccine with prawns and prosciutto in a garlic cream sauce spiced with crushed red peppers and topped with Parmesan has been a menu mainstay for years.

Pizza Nova is open for lunch and dinner daily. All menu items are available for takeout, and delivery is available. Look for discount coupons in the newspapers.

Point Loma Seafoods **$**
Seafood
2805 Emerson Street, San Diego
(619) 223-1109

Enter Point Loma Seafoods, make your way to the counter, and prepare to be dazzled by the display of fresh seafood for sale by the pound. Then remind yourself that the same seafood you see before you is the main ingredient in wonderful sandwiches, salads, soups, and platters of fried fish served with coleslaw and french fries. Sushi and ceviche appetizers fly out the door every day, as do the shrimp and crab Louie cocktails.

Favorite sandwiches are the imaginative crab cake sandwich and the squid sandwich on sourdough bread. Several outdoor tables are situated harborside, but they become extremely crowded around lunchtime. So if you have a picnic in mind, this is a great place to stop. Don't miss the large selection of smoked fish. Combine it with some fresh sourdough bread, and you'll have a tasty snack. Lunch and dinner are available daily, but closing hours are early—around 6:30 P.M.

NORTH COUNTY COASTAL

Al's Cafe **$**
American
795 Carlsbad Village Drive, Carlsbad
(760) 729-5448

Here's an old-fashioned downtown cafe where you can enjoy breakfast and lunch inside or beneath an umbrella at one of the tables set out on a quiet side street. There are specials served every day. The all-you-can-eat fish and chips (for about $6.00) is a bargain. It's in the heart of downtown Carlsbad.

Angelo's Burgers **$**
American
621 North Coast Highway, Oceanside
(760) 757-5161

1050 South Coast Highway, Oceanside
(760) 757-4064

2035 South Coast Highway, Oceanside
(760) 967-9911

608 First Street, Encinitas
(760) 943-9115

Angelo's has been a favorite beach restaurant hangout for Insiders since the mid-1970s and continues to serve up great big burgers and mountains of fries for about $5.00. The quality and price are hard to beat. This is a no-frills burger joint (that starts the day with large breakfast burritos and other morning specials). You order at the counter and spread your food on plastic tables. You can dine inside or outside.

The gyros sandwiches are excellent and under $3.00. Hungry for a giant hot pastrami sandwich? Angelo's is your place. Try the homemade onion rings and zucchini strips, deep-fried but cooked in cholesterol-free corn oil. Sure, you can't eat this way all the time, but, hey, once in a while is fun, and doubly so if you're on vacation, it's the middle of the week, or you need good fast food. All locations are open daily for breakfast, lunch, and dinner.

Bellefleur Winery & Restaurant $-$$$
Californian/Mediterranean
5610 Paseo Del Norte, Carlsbad
(760) 603-1919

This restaurant is a find, and it's convenient, too, right off Interstate 5 and Palomar Airport Road in Carlsbad. Service is fabulous. Lunch prices are reasonable, but bring your credit card for dinner if you plan to include an appetizer, drinks, dessert, and a cordial or sherry to end your experience.

Refuel after shopping at the Carlsbad Company Stores outlets (the restaurant is in the same center) with a barbecued prime rib sandwich with seasoned fries or a Spanish chicken salad with black beans. The wine is excellent and priced reasonably for a glass of the Bellefleur Winery brands (which we highly recommend). Bellefleur Winery is located in Fallbrook and has won numerous awards and recognition. This restaurant is open daily for lunch and dinner.

Bully's $$
American
1404 Camino Del Mar, Del Mar
(858) 755-1660

Do you love wine but hate to pay inflated wine list prices? Most restaurants will allow you to bring your own bottle of wine for a corkage fee. Call ahead for details.

Want a place you can count on every time for good food? Bully's is your answer. This steak house has been a tradition in San Diego County since the early 1970s and deserves many repeat visits. They have great steaks, fresh seafood, ribs, succulent chicken, and plump sandwiches (the burger is immense). But it's the prime rib that draws the repeat crowds. You could order the petite cut, but then you wouldn't have any left over for your essential doggy bag. If you must stick with a salad, go for the classic Caesar salads, either plain or loaded with shrimp or chicken.

Bully's is popular in the summer months, but you can sit outdoors or in the pub and sip and wait. It's open for breakfast, lunch, and dinner daily. There are two other branches, at 5755 La Jolla Boulevard, La Jolla, (858) 459-2768, and at 2401 Camino del Rio South, Mission Valley, (619) 291-2665.

California Bistro $$$-$$$$
Four Seasons Resort Aviara
Californian
7100 Four Seasons Point, Carlsbad
(760) 603-6800, (800) 332-3442

You might not expect a hotel's casual restaurant to be one of the top dining spots in the area, but the California Bistro consistently draws diners from throughout the county. It's actually difficult to get reservations for the Friday-night seafood buffet, an extravaganza featuring everything from sushi to lobster with drawn butter. The $39 tab doesn't discourage seafood lovers. Reserve your table early in the week. The Friday-night Surf & Turf dinner with a gourmet salad bar and special menu is another big hit.

The regular menu has its highlights as well. Breakfast might start with smoked salmon Benedict, or you could go lighter with rosy papaya and a huge muffin. We highly recommend the honey sunflower toast and the sticky pecan rolls.

If you're visiting the California Bistro for lunch, you cannot go wrong with the Bistro chopped salad, Pacific swordfish salad, or the wok-fried sweet and spicy prawns with fragrant rice and charred fruit salad. The dinner menu always includes a traditional home-cooked meal like Mom's Meatloaf, served with green beans, buttermilk-mashed potatoes with gravy, and button mushrooms.

The restaurant's menu is marked with choices that are lower in calories, cholesterol, sodium, and fat, so if you're visiting and enjoying the spa program, you can eat healthy foods. The California Bistro is open daily for breakfast, lunch, and dinner.

Chin's Szechwan Restaurant **$$**
Szechwan
2959 Madison Avenue, Carlsbad
(760) 434-7117

1506 Encinitas Boulevard, Encinitas
(760) 753-3903

4140 Oceanside Boulevard, Oceanside
(760) 631-4808

While Chin's has a lot of locations, it's a San Diego exclusive and some of the best Szechwan we've had.

The decor is what you'd expect from nearly any Chinese restaurant, but the food is better. Vegetable dishes are hot, crispy, and good. Chin's has the prerequisite family-style dinners and early-bird specials, too. Service is excellent. It's open daily for lunch and dinner. You can get takeout if you're headed to the beach or an outdoor concert. There are 10 Chin's locations in North and East County.

Fidel's **$**
Mexican
3003 Carlsbad Boulevard, Carlsbad
(760) 729-0903

607 Valley Avenue, Solana Beach
(858) 755-5292

If you've ever fantasized about perfect Mexican food—hot, fresh, and abundant—Fidel's is your ticket to taste-bud heaven. The restaurants have been in business since the 1940s, and both locations are popular. On a Saturday or Sunday, especially during the summer, you probably will wish that they took reservations; they don't, so have a seltzer or glass of wine on the patio and be patient. You'll be rewarded.

Here's a tip: Come before the dinner crowd. As a matter of fact, come for happy hour (4:00 to 6:30 P.M.), when the drinks are more reasonable and the appetizers plentiful. Lunch prices are affordable and in the $5.00 to $8.00 range; dinner is a bit more pricey but still easy on the wallet. Ask for the salsa fresca with any meal. It's an explosive combo of onion, chili, cilantro, and tomato and made on the spot just to thrill your taste buds.

Try the tender, piquant carne asada or the Tostada Suprema, which is a massive plate of shredded chicken (or beef) loaded down with guacamole, olives, tomatoes, beans, and lettuce. Both locations are open for lunch and dinner and have happy hour and early-bird specials.

Fish House Vera Cruz **$$**
Seafood
417 Carlsbad Village Drive, Carlsbad
(760) 434-6777

Just 3 blocks from the beach and 3 blocks south of the Coaster station, Fish House Vera Cruz is one of the best seafood restaurants in the county. Fish is grilled to perfection over mesquite wood and is always succulent and fresh. They have a standard menu and catch-of-the-day choices, too. If you're from out of the area, the thought of eating grilled shark might be a bit much. Get over it if you want some really great fish and a great price, because shark is a mainstay on San Diego menus. The Sopa de Pescado (a spicy soup loaded with bite-size pieces of delicate fish, tomatoes, carrots, and potatoes) is served with lemon and is so luscious that the kitchen sometimes runs out.

If you're determined to eat here, come at an off time, such as midafternoon or just before the lunchtime crowd to avoid a long wait. They don't accept reservations. Unfortunately this "find" isn't much of a secret to Insiders. Like its "sister" at 1020 San Marcos Boulevard, San Marcos, (760) 744-8000, the restaurant is open daily for lunch and dinner.

If you find that evening is approaching and you don't have a dinner reservation, go early. Most restaurants start serving as early as 5:00 P.M., but the dinner crowd doesn't start arriving until about 7:00 P.M. Chances are you'll be able to get a table.

Greek Corner Cafe **$$**
Greek
1854 Marron Road, Carlsbad
(760) 434-5557
If you love Greek food, you'll be happy here. The meals, such as the gyros plate for two, are bargains; most are priced in the $10 to $19 range. They have low-fat and vegetarian dishes, too. You can dine inside or on the patio. You can't rush this experience because you'll want to savor every bite. It is open for lunch and dinner.

Jake's Del Mar **$$-$$$**
Seafood
1660 Coast Boulevard, Del Mar
(858) 755-2002
Here's a classic waterfront restaurant and a sure thing if you're hungry for seafood and atmosphere. The location, right on the ocean, is impossible to beat, and it outshines the food. Take a hint, and call for a reservation or be disappointed with a long wait. It's a good party place and draws in a fun-loving Friday-night crowd. After you've partied, stay for the Asian seafood cocktail followed by the tortilla-crusted halibut with avocado-mango salsa. Open for lunch and dinner daily and on Sunday for brunch.

Karl Strauss Brewery & Grill **$$**
American
5801 Armada Drive, Carlsbad
(760) 431-BREW
Hearty portions of meat loaf, pizzas, turkey burgers, and beer-battered fish and chips all go well with this local microbrewery's beers. The staff and customers are a friendly bunch, and the place has a homey feel that makes you want to settle in for hours. There are also Karl Strauss restaurants in downtown San Diego and La Jolla. Open daily for breakfast, lunch, and dinner.

Meritage Restaurant & Bar **$$$$**
Modern American
897 South Coast Highway 101, Suite F-104, Encinitas
(760) 634-3350
www.meritage1.com
The shining new star in North County in 2003, this classy but unpretentious cafe is in the Lumberyard center. Owners Susan and Dan Sbicca have been players in the North County dining scene for more than a decade, and their Encinitas offering has an exciting menu and enthusiastic clientele. Starters include crunchy panko-cornmeal-crusted calamari and Maryland blue crabfritters, with servings large enough to combine with a salad or soup for a satisfying meal. The marinated flatiron steak with scalloped truffle cheese potatoes is sure to satisfy the largest appetites, though you'll want to save room for the chocolate bread pudding. Almost all bottles on the excellent wine list are 50 percent off on Monday and Wednesday nights; Tuesday there's no corkage fee if you care to bring your own bottle. Open daily for lunch and dinner.

Mille Fleurs Restaurant **$$$$**
French
6009 Paseo Delicias, Rancho Santa Fe
(858) 756-3085
www.millefleurs.com
Here's the benchmark for all French restaurants in the county and a venerable leader in the romance category. Mille Fleurs, in the upscale area of Rancho

CLOSE-UP

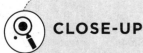

Sunday Brunch in San Diego

San Diego is a big brunch town, and chances are good that your favorite restaurant will have its own version of the weekend ritual. Most include complimentary champagne, and the serving style leans heavily toward buffet, although some restaurants have a special brunch menu.

The following list will give you an idea of where some of the best brunches in town are, but don't hesitate to do some exploring. Our price code is the same one we've used throughout this chapter and indicates the cost of brunch for two, excluding cocktails (although some brunches include complimentary champagne), tax, and tip. Most brunches start at 9:00 or 10:00 A.M. and wrap up by 2:00 or 3:00 P.M.

$$$ Bali Hai
2230 Shelter Island Drive
San Diego, (619) 222-1182

$$$ Bob's by the Bay
570 Marina Parkway, Chula Vista
(619) 476-0400

$$$ Catamaran Resort Hotel
3999 Mission Boulevard
San Diego, (858) 539-8635

$$$$ El Bizcocho
17550 Bernardo Oaks Drive
Rancho Bernardo, (858) 675-8500

$$$$ Four Seasons Resort Aviara
7100 Four Seasons Point
Carlsbad, (760) 603-6800

$$$$ Hotel del Coronado
1500 Orange Avenue, Coronado
(619) 435-6611

$$$ Humphrey's
2241 Shelter Island Drive
San Diego, (619) 224-3577

$$$$ Loews Coronado Bay
4000 Coronado Bay Road
Coronado, (619) 424-4000

$$ Marie Callender's
Rancho Santa Fe Road at Encinitas Boulevard, Encinitas, (760) 632-0204

$$$ 94th Aero Squadron
8885 Balboa Avenue, Kearny Mesa
(858) 560-6771

$$$ Quails Inn
1035 La Bonita, San Marcos
(760) 744-2445

$$$$ Rancho Bernardo Inn
17550 Bernardo Drive, San Diego
(858) 675-8550

$$$ Reuben's
880 East Harbor Island Drive
San Diego, (619) 291-5030

$$ Tomatoes
4346 Bonita Road, Bonita
(619) 479-8494

$$$ Westgate Hotel
1055 Second Avenue, San Diego
(619) 557-3622

Santa Fe, attracts national attention and constantly wins culinary awards. *Food and Wine* magazine has named it one of the top 25 restaurants in the country, and the James Beard House has named chef Martin Woesle one of the great regional chefs. Owner Bertrand Hug created this cozy cottage restaurant in 1984 and has made it one of the finest French restaurants in the country. Notables, celebrities, and the wealthy gather here when they want superb service and great food. In fact, your chances of spotting visiting celebrities are excellent here. People become hooked on Mille Fleurs and often try to think up special occasions so they can come here to celebrate.

The cuisine is fine dining at its best. The menu changes daily, as Woesle collects his ingredients from gourmet produce farms and other top-notch purveyors. Chances are you'll find sweetbreads, duck liver, partridge, and other treats you don't normally see on San Diego menus. The extraordinary wine list (with prices to match) makes connoisseurs swoon. Open for lunch Monday through Friday and dinner nightly. Be sure to dress up for the experience. If you come by on a Thursday, Friday, or Saturday night, you can join the patrons singing show tunes at the piano bar.

Pizza Port **$$**
Pizza
571 Carlsbad Village Drive, Carlsbad
(760) 720-7007

135 North Highway 101, Solana Beach
(858) 481-7332

Here's where you'll find praiseworthy pizza that's a cut above the most chi-chi pizzas you've had. Better yet, they brew on-site and provide just the right microbrewed beer to go with your choice. You can even have your pizza with a whole-grain beer crust.

Decor is of the wooden picnic-table variety with big-screen televisions flashing sports, and the music is sometimes loud and the conversation even louder.

Pizza specials and microbrew choices vary, and sometimes they sponsor beer-tasting contests in which the public can participate. The Pizza Port pizzerias are open daily for lunch and dinner.

Prontos' Gourmet Market **$**
Italian
2812 Roosevelt Street, Carlsbad
(760) 434-2644

Here's an eating jewel that's tucked away in the heart of the village of Carlsbad. Once you stop here, you may not want to tell any friends for fear it will become crowded.

Sandwiches are stuffed with meats and vegetables, prices are easy on the wallet, and everything is fresh and tasty. You get choices of breads and side dishes with each sandwich, and there are salads, too. Most folks take out and get back to work, but there's a shady patio where you can dine outdoors.

Prontos' is open 9:00 A.M. to 6:00 P.M. Monday through Friday. Stop and pick up a prepared meal, like the lasagna, or a sandwich for supper on the way home from work.

St. Germain's Cafe **$**
European Sidewalk Cafe
1010 South Coast Highway 101, Encinitas
(760) 753-5411

It's impossible to pinpoint a "type" for this quaint cafe set in Encinitas; locals just go there because the food is always wonderful. Here eggs Benedict are served all day long. You can also get eggs Acapulco (topped with zesty Spanish sauce) and a dozen other breakfast varieties. All food is served with fresh fruit or their yummy cafe potatoes. Belgian waffles, sandwiches, and soups are always good choices, too, and the juice bar serves up healthy thirst quenchers. Open for breakfast and lunch each day.

That Pizza Place **$**
Pizza and more
2622 El Camino Real, Carlsbad
(760) 434-3171

> *Many restaurants can package full meals for take-out service. Call ahead and pick up your order on the way to the beach or an outdoor concert.*

1810 Oceanside Boulevard, Oceanside
(760) 757-6212
That Pizza Place restaurants are neighborhood pizza eateries (that serve salads and subs, too) and have live entertainment on some evenings. They've been in North County Coastal since 1979 and are proud of the local connection. The places are the gathering holes for community sports teams; as you might expect, the atmosphere is supercasual, and no one will notice if your baseball shirt has grass stains on it or your soccer uniform is caked with mud.

The house special pizza is pepperoni, ham, salami, mushrooms, olives, bell peppers, and sausage—you have to ask for anchovies. It's always served up hot and fresh. We think the best things to eat at That Pizza Place are the Roll'N The Dough sandwiches. They're like a pizza burrito. You can dine in (with picnic-table elegance) or take it out. The restaurants are open for lunch and dinner daily.

Trattoria Positano **$$-$$$**
Italian
2171 San Elijo Avenue, Cardiff
(760) 632-0111
Welcoming and relaxing is the atmosphere of this cafe just a few blocks from the ocean in Cardiff. You'll find seafood, a slew of pasta choices, and vegetarian specialties, too. The decor is California/Italian, crisp and clean with great service. Lunch Monday through Saturday; dinner is served daily.

Vivace **$$$**
Northern Italian
Four Seasons Resort Aviara
7100 Four Seasons Point, Carlsbad
(760) 603-6800, (800) 332-3442
The decor of this popular restaurant is so inviting (some tables have fat easy chairs and sofas rather than straight-backed, restaurant-style chairs), you might try to stay forever. When the food arrives you'll be dazzled. It's one of those eating experiences where you can linger over your food, loving the antipasto and appetizers, adoring the soups, diving into the main courses, and cherishing every bite of the dessert. Ask for a table overlooking the balcony, the lagoon, and the Pacific beyond.

If you're a seafood lover, try the grilled swordfish with roasted fennel or the lobster risotto. It's impossible to go wrong with the lamb osso bucco or veal tenderloin. If you have room, try the Warm Bitter Sweet Chocolate Melt over cranberry ice cream. Vivace is open daily for dinner only.

NORTH COUNTY INLAND

Asia-Vous **$$$**
French-Asian Fusion
417 West Grand Avenue, Escondido
(760) 747-5000
www.asiavousrestaurant.com
Chef Riko Bartolome's creations bring diners from all over the county to his latest establishment in Escondido. His eclectic menu might feature crisp pork confit, veal sweetbreads with pineapple, pistachio-crusted duck breast, sea urchin risotto—you get the idea. Bartolome isn't afraid to seek out unusual ingredients and combine them with flair. The dining room glows with a soft purple hue; fabrics and seating arrangements are designed so diners feel pampered and comfortable. Asia-Vous is perfect for dinner before a performance at the nearby Center for Performing Arts. Lunch is served Tuesday through Friday and dinner Tuesday through Saturday.

Chieu-Anh **$$**
Vietnamese
16769 Bernardo Center Drive
Rancho Bernardo
(858) 485-1231

Chieu-Anh has to be included in a culinary tour of North County Inland because the foods are fresh and combinations unique even for this cuisine. It's tucked into a shopping mall, and you might walk past without hardly giving it a second thought, except for the fragrances emanating from the eatery. We love the specialty of feather-light Vietnamese crepe filled with grilled chicken and shrimp. There's a tangy and sour soup with tamarind flavor that's excellent, and the shrimp on sugarcane is a smoky, savory delight. The restaurant is open Tuesday through Friday for lunch and Tuesday through Sunday for dinner.

El Bizcocho **$$$$**
French
17550 Bernardo Oaks Drive
Rancho Bernardo
(858) 675-8500

If you're ready to propose to your darling or celebrate a momentous occasion, book a window-side table at the county's most elegant restaurant, which overlooks the golf course at the Rancho Bernardo Inn. Consistently rated among the top five restaurants in San Diego, El Bizcocho is overseen by chef Gavin Kaysen. The young, enthusiastic chef has been wowing insiders since he arrived in 2004. Locals swoon over his Hudson Valley foie gras with hazelnut crust and braised Kobe beef short ribs. The liqueur cart's selection of rare ports may well be worth more than some diners' cars. El Biz serves dinner nightly and a fabulous Sunday brunch. Reservations are essential.

Lake Wohlford Cafe **$**
American
25484 Lake Wohlford Road, Escondido
(760) 749-2755

You could call the decor at the Lake Wohlford Cafe "funky" and not be too far from the mark. The cafe is casual and makes you feel like it's okay to have fun. The cat fish dinner is a hit with anglers who've missed the bite on the lake.

Burgers and fries and lots of American food are on the menu. It's open Friday through Sunday.

La Paloma Restaurante **$$**
Mexican
116 Escondido Avenue, Vista
(760) 758-7140

Located outside of the usual restaurant area, La Paloma serves up fresh, savory, and spicy favorites. Although it's a struggle to name the best choices, we love the shrimp and lobster meat fajitas and the camarones con pollo cilantro (tender shrimp and sliced chicken breast sautéed in sauce and spices and topped with cheese, avocado, and cilantro).

All meals are served with rice, beans, and tortillas. You can be cautious with tacos and tostadas and burritos or reckless with bistec vaquero, a large steak charbroiled and topped with mushrooms, garlic, and onions. La Paloma is open daily for lunch and dinner, and you can dine indoors or on the patio.

Vincent's Sirinos Restaurant **$$$**
French/Continental
113 West Grand Avenue, Escondido
(760) 745-3835

Reservations are essential for dinner at this cozy dining room overseen by chef Vincent Grumel. The dining room is unassuming—some say uninspired—but any thoughts that this might be a dull place will end in a flash when you breathe in the fragrances coming from the kitchen, and ultimately onto your plate.

Grumel's specialty is duck, and diners rave about his Confit de Canard Grumel. Beef lovers can't miss with the filet mignon with Stilton cheese and a merlot sauce, and the ravioli stuffed with veal is superb. If you're not into meat, try the pastry Florentine, an overstuffed turnover bursting with spinach, Stilton cheese, and veggies. The eggplant ravioli is also a good option. Open for lunch Tuesday through Friday and dinner Tuesday through Sunday.

EAST COUNTY

The Barbeque Pit $
American
2388 Fletcher Parkway, El Cajon
(619) 462-5434

Since 1947 the Barbeque Pit has been serving up tender, succulent choices of carved-to-order beef, ham, and rib dinners that bring customers back again and again. Try the chicken, or if you're a hot-sausage fan, you can't go wrong with their spicy choice.

On Friday the specialty is shredded pork, not just on a sandwich, but piled high on a toasted bun. Side dishes include macaroni and potato salads, coleslaw, and french fries. The Barbeque Pit has good grub, the decor is without pretension, and it is open for lunch and dinner.

Dudley's Bakery and Cafe $
American
30218 Highway 78, Santa Ysabel
(760) 765-0488, (800) 225-3348
www.dudleysbakery.com

To visitors, Santa Ysabel might seem to be smack dab out in nowhere. Yet Insiders drive from all over Southern California for a loaf of Dudley's bread—raisin nut is a favorite. The small snack shop at the bakery serves hot dogs and cold drinks, but it's the bread that keeps folks stopping by on their way to Julian. Open Wednesday through Sunday from 8:00 A.M. to 5:00 P.M.

D.Z. Akin's $$
Delicatessen
6930 Alvarado Road, San Diego
(619) 265-0218
www.dzakinsdeli.com

East Coast transplants bemoan the lack of good Jewish delis in San Diego County. You're hard-pressed to find a good whitefish platter or chicken-in-the-pot with matzoh balls. That's why Insiders from throughout the county drive east on Interstate 8, past San Diego State, to this deli in a small strip mall. Divine rye bread is piled high with pastrami, tongue, liverwurst, brisket—nearly anything your taste buds desire. Try the scrambled eggs with lox and onions for breakfast and the tri-salad platter with chopped liver at lunch. You probably won't be able to pass by the bakery counter without buying rugalach, strudel, and eclairs to take home. It's open daily for breakfast, lunch, and dinner. The parking lot is usually packed. Have someone jump out and put your name on the waiting list while the driver waits for sated diners to waddle back to their cars.

Julian Grille $
American
2224 Main Street, Julian
(760) 765-0173

Go for the pie—apple pie, that is, and the pie that put Julian on the map. And be sure to save room after the large servings of American-style choices served at the Grille. This is where the Julian Insiders and visitors eat, and during Apple Days and when the art and photo shows are held, it can be busy. Service is good at the Grille, and the food worth the wait.

The Julian Grille is a nice tradition for every trip to the mountain community. It's open for lunch and dinner Tuesday through Sunday.

La Mesa Ocean Grill $$
Seafood
5465 Lake Murray Boulevard, La Mesa
(619) 463-1548

Here's the place if you've been craving lobster in a big way. They're big, sweet, and straight from New England. The whole Maine lobster (served seasonally) includes deviled clam, clam fritters, corn on the cob, red potatoes, and corn bread. The Big Kahuna Fried Fishermen's Plate will stuff you with Arctic cod, shrimp, scallops, calamari, crab cake, deviled clam, clam fritters, french fries, coleslaw, and corn bread. You may just want to order one dinner and split it between two. If you're not fond of fish, try the chicken scaloppini. Ask about the daily specials. La Mesa Ocean Grill, a find in East County, is open daily for lunch and dinner.

Mario's de La Mesa $
Mexican
8425 La Mesa Boulevard, La Mesa
(619) 461-9390

"This is down-home cooking," say some Insiders after sampling the food at this lesser-known, but wonderful nonetheless, Mexican restaurant. The food arrives in generous helpings, the menu is extensive, and the service is better than home. You can be sure to get smiles with every order here. There's a Don Gallo sauce that is a creamy covering for some of the seafood dishes. It's innovative and downright tasty, too. There's a "build your own" taco bar and all the standards you've come to expect from Mexican restaurants. It's open daily for breakfast, lunch, and dinner. On Sunday it opens for brunch and then heads straight to dinner.

Pinnacle Peak Steak House $$
American
7927 Mission Gorge Road, Santee
(619) 448-8882

Let's say you're in East County, maybe visiting Summers Past Farms or the casinos (see our Shopping and Attractions chapters). It hits you. You're hungry for a steak, and not just any steak will do. You want a cowboy-size portion with beans and bread and barbecue sauce that's rich and red. The answer to your need to feed is the Pinnacle Peak, a cowboy eatery where the staff, if necessary, will forcibly take your tie and suit jacket. All the beef (and chicken) choices are grilled to perfection over an open mesquite fire. Once you see the size of the steaks and burgers, you'll agree that they don't mess around with huge appetites.

The restaurant is a fun experience, a great place for families, and a favorite among residents from all over the county. Pinnacle Peak is open for dinner every day.

Romano's Dodge House $$
Italian/American
2718 B Street, Julian
(760) 765-1003

This restaurant is just a block off Main Street in a historic house in downtown Julian. The cuisine suits appetites stimulated by the mountain air. Try the pork loin in cinnamon, garlic, and whisky sauce or the spicy apple-cider sausage. Ask about the daily specials, and check out the pizza variations. Credit cards are not accepted here, but it is open for lunch and dinner Wednesday through Monday.

Viejas Casino & Turf Club $-$$
Buffet and Food Court
5000 Willows Road, Alpine
(619) 445-5400

For everything you can expect at this ultra-popular casino, be sure to read our entries in the Nightlife and Attractions chapters. You can also expect casual dining and fine dining, in very easygoing surroundings. Check out the Harvest Buffet (a smaller version of those seen in Las Vegas or Atlantic City). There's also the China Camp for Asian foods, the dignified Grove Steakhouse, and other 24-hour restaurants to make your gaming experience complete. Restaurants are open daily for breakfast, lunch, and dinner.

Village Garden Restaurant & Bakery $
American
8384 La Mesa Boulevard, La Mesa
(619) 462-9100

Home-style cooking with flair is what you'll find at the Village Garden Restaurant & Bakery. Go hungry—this is down-home, stick-to-your-ribs cooking. Consider the Yankee eggs, served with pot roast at breakfast, or the half-pound bruschetta burger with cheese, garlic, and olive oil. Have a hankering for chicken and dumplings? How about all-you-can-eat fish and chips (served Fridays). The mesquite grill on the terrace is fired up on Thursday and Friday nights in the summer, when diners clamor for the tender baby back ribs. You can dine inside or on the patio. The eatery is open for breakfast and lunch Monday through Wednesday, and Thursday through Sunday it's open for breakfast, lunch, and dinner.

SOUTH BAY

Anthony's Fish Grotto **$-$$**
Seafood
215 Bay Boulevard, Chula Vista
(619) 425-4200

1360 North Harbor Drive, San Diego
(619) 232-5103

9530 Murray Drive, La Mesa
(619) 463-0368
www.gofishanthonys.com

San Diego's Ghio family has established a long tradition of good, reasonably priced seafood at their grotto restaurants. When you enter the grottos, you'll feel you've been transported to an underwater cave, complete with sea animals, coral, and shells. The exception to this decor is the Harbor Drive restaurant, which is open to the bay to take advantage of the view.

Seafood salads are the gems of the lunchtime menu, especially the seafood combo—chunks of lobster, shrimp, crab, and avocado served over fresh greens and topped with Anthony's signature dressing. For more hearty appetites, choose from a variety of fish from both the lunch and dinner menus, including sole, sea bass, halibut, and swordfish that are grilled, sautéed, or broiled according to your desire. Anthony's is open for lunch Monday through Saturday and for dinner nightly.

Bob's by the Bay **$$**
American
570 Marina Parkway, Chula Vista
(619) 476-0400

Bob's is one of the most popular restaurants in the South Bay, and for good reason. The food is consistently well prepared, and the menu features perennial favorites. The grilled shrimp, two skewers of shrimp seasoned with citrus and butter, then grilled, is paired with fresh seasonal vegetables and basmati rice—just right for a dinner that's filling but on the light side. Grilled chicken Alfredo is another crowd-pleaser—marinated, boneless chicken grilled and served over fettuccine with a basil and Parmesan cream sauce.

This is a busy hangout for the after-work crowd, too, and a good place to meet friends for a drink before dinner. Bob's is located close to the water in the Chula Vista Marina and is open for lunch and dinner daily.

i ***Although it's been a few years since San Diego rationed water (because of the severe drought conditions), you may still have to order water with your meals.***

The Bonita Store **$$**
Mexican
4014 Bonita Road, Bonita
(619) 479-3537

If you're searching for a restaurant with strong influences of Baja California and Mexico in the South Bay, look no further than The Bonita Store (also known as Rockin' Baja Lobster). All the standard Mexican fare is served here, such as combination plates and a la carte tacos, burritos, and enchiladas, but the real treat is the bucket of Baja-style lobster for two.

The bucket includes slipper lobster tails, shrimp, grilled chicken, and carne asada, plus Caesar salad, rice, beans, and tortillas. The atmosphere is partylike and casual. Everyone has fun at The Bonita Store. It's open for lunch and dinner daily.

The Butcher Shop **$$**
American
556 Broadway, Chula Vista
(619) 420-9440
5255 Kearny Villa Road, San Diego
(858) 565-2272

As its name implies, The Butcher Shop specializes in beef: prime rib, top sirloin, and just about any other cut that strikes your fancy. Picture a darkened dining room with paneled walls and red fabric booths, a holdover from the days of three-martini lunches in a smoke-filled room.

The restaurant also caters to lighter eaters by offering chicken and fish dishes, but then spoils all your good intentions by serving them with irresistible, giant twice-baked potatoes and piping hot garlic bread. Dinner is served nightly, and lunch is served Monday through Saturday. On Sundays The Butcher Shop opens in the early afternoon for a late lunch or early dinner.

D'lish **$-$$**
Pizzas, pastas, and salads
386 East H Street, Suite 211, Chula Vista
(619) 585-1371
2260 Otay Lakes Road, Chula Vista
(619) 216-3900
5252 Balboa Avenue, San Diego
(858) 277-9977

Whether takeout is on the agenda or you're dining in, D'lish serves up gourmet salads, pizzas, and pastas with a different but delicious twist. The Caesar salad, for example, is made with roasted red peppers and kalamata olives, a tasty combination of flavors. Another menu favorite is the chicken sun-dried calzone, made with chicken, sun-dried tomatoes, marinara sauce, and sour cream. Or try the shrimp-scallop angel-hair pasta served with red onions, bell peppers, and zucchini.

The atmosphere is casual, with both table and booth seating. A fire pit keeps diners toasty warm on chilly winter nights. The menu may vary slightly at the different locations, and everything on the menu is available for takeout. Lunch and dinner are served daily.

Edelweiss **$$**
German
230 Third Avenue, Chula Vista
(619) 426-5172

If you're a schnitzel fan, Edelweiss is just what the doctor ordered. Try Wiener schnitzel, Jager schnitzel, or Holstein schnitzel. Or if you prefer to jump off the schnitzel bandwagon, sample one of the other authentic German entrees, like sauerbraten or hunter stew. Traditional treats such as potato pancakes and cabbage rolls are quite good, too. Open for dinner Tuesday through Sunday.

NIGHTLIFE

After a hard day playing outdoors, who wants to have more fun? Most of us in San Diego. While the city isn't known for the kind of trendy, chic, and wild nightlife you might find in Los Angeles or Manhattan, San Diego's after-hours persona is alive and well.

Here you can choose from a smorgasbord of nighttime pleasures. In this chapter we'll give you the rundown on clubs, bars, brewpubs, and independent coffeehouses. We didn't list Starbucks or other chains; just follow your nose to find them.

If there's a cover charge or a specific dress code for a nightspot, we've added that information, but keep in mind that things change. And don't be shocked if you're carded. Club owners and barkeeps have the right to ask anyone for ID at any time. Even if you're in the over-30 crowd, you'll need to carry identification. There's nothing more maddening than being turned away from a happening club, crow's-feet or gray hair notwithstanding.

Remember that in California there's no smoking in public establishments, and that includes bars, lounges, and restaurants. To cater to their smoking customers, quite a few bars have installed outdoor patios or rooftop lounges. Casinos and entertainment venues on Indian reservations, of course, are exempt. Most respect both smokers and nonsmokers, but call ahead if your preference is for an absolutely smoke-free zone or if you want to puff away with reckless abandon.

While there's plenty to do outside the Central San Diego area, the Gaslamp Quarter, in downtown San Diego, is definitely one of the hottest places to party. Relative to the old (in both senses of the word) venue in Hollywood, the House of Blues serves up food, firewater, and 'nothin' but the blues'—oh, and funk, jam, rock, and alternative tunes, too.

When we formulated our list, made phone calls, and took field trips (it was a tough job, but someone had to do it), one thing was clear: Clubs, pubs, coffeehouses, and other entertainment venues change. One spot might be hot with rock music and a month later spin house music or mashups. The next time you visit you might find a jazz band, a poetry reading, or a passel of square dancers. So though we've tried to make our listings as current and accurate as possible, it's best to call ahead and inquire about the types of music or entertainment you'll find.

With all these caveats out of the way, it's time to introduce you to San Diego's abundant hot spots. Enjoy!

NIGHTCLUBS AND CONCERT VENUES

Central San Diego

Gaslamp Quarter
Fourth to Sixth Avenues
between L Street and Broadway

There are too many Gaslamp Quarter nightspots to name them all, although we've reviewed some of our favorites (and our kids' favorites) below. **Confidential** (901 Fourth Avenue; 619-696-8888) offers excellent dining along with DJ-spun hip-hop and a "loft" for observing the youngish crowd below, tinted blue, purple, and red by the neon lights. Nearby **belo** (E Street between Fourth and Fifth Avenues; 619-231-9200) is a similarly hip new restaurant-nightclub. Serving American-fusion cuisine, it's located in the underground locale formerly called E Street Alley. For a more casual evening, head to the third-floor loft of **Dussini** (275 Fifth Avenue; 619-233-4323), which has billiards tables and a large flat-screen TV tuned to sports. A novelty is the bar, with a frozen

San Diego's most happening district, the Gaslamp Quarter, has more than 100 clubs, bars, and restaurants. PHOTO: COURTESY OF BRETT SHOAF

strip along the edge to keep your drink cold: The specialty is the rum-and-mint, Cuba-inspired mojito. **Stingaree** (454 Sixth Avenue; 619-544-9500) is named for the red-light district in Old San Diego. Very upscale, it's presided over by go-go dancers and a dance floor on the first of its three floors; on the smokers' rooftop bar is a crystal fire pit and a city view. **Dizzy's** (344 Seventh Avenue; 858-270-7467) is all about the jazz, not the scene, and since alcohol isn't served, all ages are welcome. These are just a few of the Gaslamp Quarter's 35 clubs. Some others are reviewed in these pages; as for the rest, well, we recommed that you wander the district's streets, and you'll discover many more on your own.

The Bitter End
770 Fifth Avenue, San Diego
(619) 338-9300
www.thebitterend.com

This classy joint at the corner of Fifth and F Streets is habituated by denizens of the Gaslamp Quarter. In the upstairs lounge there's a rather extensive dress code, including no baseball caps, tank tops, or sandals, and on Friday and Saturday, no printed T-shirts, tennis shoes, or hiking boots. Upstairs in the VIP room, stake out a coveted plush chair or sofa in front of one of two marble fireplaces; floors are hardwood and the ambience is comfortable yet elegant. On the ground floor the long wooden bar gleams, and the room is usually packed. For dancing, head to the

Looking for clubs, performances, and other fun stuff? Check the "Night and Day" section in the* San Diego Union-Tribune *or pick up a copy of the* San Diego Reader, *the weekly tabloid of film, music, theater, and cool stuff that's available free of charge at bookstores, libraries, and music outlets. The in-tune* City Beat *is available both online and at newsstands.

back of the bar and the Gaslamp Underground, where groups from the '70s, '80s, and today perform weekends and some weekday nights. After 8:00 P.M. on Friday and Saturday, when the line of hopefuls stretches around the corner, there's a cover charge of around $10.

Blind Melons
710 Garnet Avenue, Pacific Beach
(858) 483-7844
www.blindmelonspb.com
This is not a place to dress up. Throw on a pair of jeans and come listen to or dance to the tunes of nationally known blues, jazz, rock, and hip-hop artists. The cover charge varies according to the fame of the band, but it ranges from around $3.00 to $12.00. Monday is open-mic night; sign up in the morning or in the bar after 8:00 P.M. This is the epitome of a beach bar, so expect the crowd to have a free-and-easy attitude. Although music is the main attraction, there are pool tables and some patrons are always glued to a sporting event on one of several TVs.

'Canes Bar and Grill
3105 Ocean Front Walk, San Diego
(858) 488-1780
www.canesbarandgrill.com
This is a lively spot located in Belmont Park in Mission Beach. On a normal night the crowd is usually made up of 20-somethings, but special concerts will draw a mixed-age group. Some concerts are open to revelers as young as age 16. In addition to concerts, 'Canes has music festivals, local bands, and lots of special activities. The rooftop deck overlooking the ocean offers a nice respite from the activity below. Admission varies according to the event; usually it's between $6.00 and $12.00.

The Casbah
2501 Kettner Boulevard, San Diego
(619) 232-4355
www.casbahmusic.com
Open daily from 8:30 P.M. to the standard 2:00 A.M. closing, the Casbah is one of San Diego's cutting-edge clubs, offering happening young local and nationally known bands. It's a super bargain, as the cover usually ranges from $8.00 to $14.00 for the likes of Party of One, The Rugburns, Ben Harper, The Breeders, and Royal Crown Revue. The club has a smokers' patio and game room with a few pool tables and video games.

The Comedy Store
916 Pearl Street, La Jolla
(858) 454-9176
www.thecomedystore.com
What started in Los Angeles has made its way south to La Jolla. First-rate comedians entertain, and sometimes a big name will roll in. If you're an aspiring comic yourself, consider coming for the free "potluck Sunday," when you can try your act on a captive audience—at least for five minutes. Open Wednesday through Sunday, there's a two-drink minimum nightly and a $5.00 cover charge most nights ($20.00 to $25.00 on Friday and Saturday). Must be age 21 or older to enter.

Crudo
1953 India Street, Little India
(619) 398-2974
The gentrification of San Diego's Little Italy produced a vacuum where nightlife was supposed to be. So Michael Viscuso (of belo and On Broadway fame) created this intimate, Asian-themed sushi restaurant and nightclub for DJ-spun hip-hop and '80s vinyl fans. Drinks go for about $7.00 and up; cover charge is $10.00 to $20.00, although if you dine in the adjacent sushi restaurant, you can continue to the club for free.

Croce's Restaurant & Jazz Bar
802 Fifth Avenue, San Diego
(619) 233-4355
www.croces.com
Croce's has become an institution in San Diego for its fine dining and outstanding entertainment. Owned by Ingrid Croce, widow of singer Jim Croce, the bar features international jazz talents and an occasional appearance by A. J. Croce, son

of the legendary crooner. The bar showcases rhythm and blues nightly. The cover charge is $5.00 during the week, and $10.00 on Friday and Saturday. (There's no cover when you dine in the restaurant.) If there's a special event, the cover might be slightly higher.

Dick's Last Resort
345 Fourth Avenue, San Diego
(619) 231-9100
www.dickslastresort.com
Granted, this is a chain outfit with a reputation for being slightly uncouth. But take it from us, there's some great music going on here. Talented local bands play every night, and folks of all ages dance, have a beer, throw wadded up napkins at each other by way of introduction, and just generally let their hair down. Give it a try; you'll find all types of music, from rock or pop to R&B, every night except Monday. There's no cover charge.

Elario's Bistro & Sky Lounge
7955 La Jolla Shores Drive, La Jolla
(858) 551-3620
Located on the 11th floor of the La Jolla Inn, Elario's picture window frames the La Jolla coast. Featuring mainly local talent, the jazz here is on the light side, as is the food in the adjoining bistro. Within the lounge, order bar food and drinks. Musicians play on Wednesday and Thursday from 6:00 to 10:00 P.M., Friday and Saturday from 7:00 P.M. to 1:00 A.M., and Sunday from 6:00 to 8:00 P.M. No cover.

4th & B
345 B Street, San Diego
(619) 231-4343
www.4thandb.com
No wonder we're not sure in which category to put it: 4th & B bills itself as San Diego's "multipurpose, multicultural entertainment and special events venue." A wide variety of shows are held here, from the yearly Brazilian Carnival celebration to sit-down concerts featuring well-known rock or blues artists to stand-up Latino comedy. This indoor concert venue has really made its mark on San Diego's music scene. Hot bands as well as legends from the past appear regularly at 4th & B, including Mobb Deep, James Brown, and Alejandra Guzman. Tickets are available at the box office from 10:00 A.M. to 5:00 P.M. or by calling Ticketmaster at (619) 220-8497. You must be age 21 or older to get in.

House of Blues
1055 Fifth Avenue, San Diego
(619) 299-2583
www.hob.com
The warehouse-like main space serves drinks and sports a DJ, all without much charm. The back room is a concert venue where known jazzmen and purveyors of other types of tunes perform, but mostly its standing room only despite ticket prices of $20 to $40; there's a small balcony where for a surcharge you might get a coveted seat. Don't bring a camera or you'll have to check it at the ticket booth. The best thing about House of Blues is their Sunday gospel brunch. Say halleluiah!

Humphrey's
2241 Shelter Island Drive, San Diego
(619) 224-3577 (lounge and indoor stage)
(619) 523-1010 (concert info line)
www.humphreysconcerts.com
Humphrey's is a comfortable, if not terribly exciting, bar and restaurant and the place to hear live jazz Sunday evenings throughout the year. More exciting is Humphrey's unique summer concert series. The outdoor amphitheater has a tradition of hosting top-name performers such as Taj Majal, Joan Osborne, and Ringo Starr. If you have access to a kayak, Zodiac, dinghy, or small boat, you can cruise around the point and tie up to the concert site and listen to the music from the water, something that amuses some performers and annoys others. Patrons who prefer a less bootleg approach can purchase tickets through Ticketmaster, (619) 220-8497, or Humphrey's box office, (619) 523-1010. Food, beverages, and cocktails are all sold on-site; dinner show

packages are a bit pricey and must be reserved in advance.

In Cahoots
5373 Mission Center Road, San Diego
(619) 291-1184
www.incahoots.com
Polish up those boots and get ready for some line dancing and two-stepping. Dancing to DJ-spun country music is what's happening here, and this is a great place for singles of all ages to meet and mix in a friendly atmosphere.

Drink prices are inexpensive, but the main draw is the dancing. The cover charge ranges from $5.00 to $6.00, but there are free dance lessons on Tuesday through Saturday evenings before things really crank up. Learn a little bit of everything, everything from two-step to swing to "cowboy cha-cha."

On Broadway
615 Broadway, San Diego
(619) 231-0011
Opened in 2001, this large, super-sophisticated nightspot caters to the rich and the famous—or at least the well-heeled. VIPS should call (619) 565-0834 to reserve their own table for two or more. Choose the music and ambience that suits you, from DJ-spun house/techno or hip-hop to live salsa or jazz, and pay a table charge and/or bottle charge of several hundred dollars, and you'll be ensconced in one of many private or semiprivate rooms. Lesser folk can grace the 25,000-square-foot nightclub if they have the cash for expensive drinks and the patience to wait in the line that stretches down the block. In addition to a restaurant serving Euro-Asian cuisine, there's a dance club (open Friday and Saturday). Call (619) 565-0834 for reservations if you're willing to pay a hefty surcharge to avoid waiting in line. The building was originally built by mogul John D. Spreckels as the Walker Scott Bank Building, and the vault has been transformed into a billiards room.

Onyx/Thin
852 Fifth Avenue, San Diego
(619) 235-6699
Refined and often full of glamorous-looking 20-somethings, the intimate Onyx/Thin is a basement-level venue. The decoration of this retro-style piano lounge is classy, the mood is upbeat, and the lighting both red and subdued. Martinis are the specialty of the house, and there's a dress code: no athletic shoes or sandals, no jeans. It's closed Sunday and Monday, but otherwise open nightly until 2:00 A.M. In the back room a DJ spins records on Wednesday and Thursday, and there's live jazz at least once or twice a week. You'll pay $10 on Friday and $15 on Saturday, but there's no cover midweek.

Patrick's II
428 F Street, San Diego
(619) 233-3077
www.patricksii.com
When you've got a hankerin' for the blues, look no further than Patrick's II. A mainstay in the Gaslamp Quarter for years (long before this area was even called the Gaslamp Quarter, or was even halfway chic), this small club is usually packed with people of all ages soaking up the blues and soppin' up the brews. Quarters are close, but the crowd is friendly and the music can't be beat. During the week there's no cover charge; on Friday and Saturday it's $3.00; $5.00 after 9:00 P.M.

Sevilla
555 Fourth Avenue, San Diego
(619) 233-5979
Nibble on Spanish tapas or enjoy a full meal at this trendy restaurant/club in the Gaslamp Quarter. In the downstairs nightclub are dinner shows with a set menu for $40 midweek to $48 on weekends per person. It's tango on Friday night; on Saturday customers are served Spanish paella as the main course as they watch a flamenco dance show. In the club there's dancing every night of the week: Monday

to Latin hip-hop; Tuesday through Thursday to tropical tunes (with dance lessons for the uninitiated). On Friday Sevilla hosts a Latin-Euro Dance Club. During the week the cover charge is $5.00 to $10.00; on Friday and Saturday it's $10.00 and $15.00 respectively. Like most places in the Gaslamp, the age of the crowd varies.

Winston's Beach Club
1921 Bacon Street, San Diego
(619) 222-6822
www.blindmelonspb.com
This beach-casual club in Ocean Beach features standout bands ranging—or should we say *raging*—from reggae and ska to alternative, blues, funk, soul, and acid jazz. The crowd is mixed; you'll see all ages here, depending on what type of music is playing. The cover charge ranges from $5.00 to $15.00, based on the band and the night of the week. There's other stuff, too: Open-mic comedy for local talent, space for area artists to show (and sell) their art, and karoake are examples of nonmusical offerings with no cover charge.

North County Coastal

Belly Up Tavern
143 South Cedros Avenue, Solana Beach
(858) 481-8140
A classic in the county, the Belly Up Tavern has been bringing top performers and newcomer groups to the music scene since the '70s. Ticket prices vary, ranging from $3.00 to about $38.00. The name and assets (but not the building) were recently sold; some much-needed improvements have included a redesign with a new bar, a VIP section, some reserved seating, and an improved menu at the adjacent Wild Note Café.

Cafe Calypso
576 North Highway 101, Encinitis
(760) 632-8252
www.hwy101blues.com
North County Insiders swear this is the only gig in town—beyond the Belly Up, of course, which is the granddaddy of North County Coastal entertainment. In addition to great food (primarily seafood and Pacific Rim cuisine, with plenty of vegetarian options), this laid-back little cafe gets drop-ins from musicians who have fled the major music scene in addition to gigs with local celebs such as Candy Kane and Sue Palmer. It's got a nightly lineup of live music that ranges from blues to rock to island groove and zesty salsa.

North County Inland

The Boulevard
925 West San Marcos Boulevard, San Marcos
(760) 510-0004
www.theblvd.com
Talk about your all-purpose venue: This "music hall and sports grill" morphs into something different each day of the week. Sunday it's an all-ages reggae club with a $5.00 cover; on Wednesday it's country; Saturday reinvent the '80s, and so on. College kids take over on Thursday (no cover with college ID before 11:00 P.M.), but most any night the venue is dominated by the under-30 crowd. The Back Bar, with no cover and a less frenetic atmosphere, invites a more laid-back crowd seven days a week.

Club Tropics
740 Nordahl Road, San Marcos
(760) 737-9402
A hip club with a moderate cover charge, Club Tropics attracts a college-aged crowd and working folks, too. You'll be bombarded with music from the '70s, '80s, and '90s, from hip-hop to reggae all the way to old school and Latin tunes, and you can dance on multilevel dance floors or belly up to one of five bars. Doors open Wednesday through Sunday at 8:30 P.M.

Restaurant Row
1000 block of West San Marcos Boulevard, San Marcos
The dozen or so restaurants of San Marcos' eating/drinking scene double as the primary source of the city's evening entertainment. While some of the places are primarily restaurants, Zip and Zack's (1020 West San Marcos Boulevard; 760-591-9393) offers karoake, a sports bar, and dancing. Some of the others in Restaurant Row offer live or canned music as well. The San Marcos Brewery is described in our "Brewpubs" section.

East County

Dirk's Niteclub
7662 Broadway Street, Lemon Grove
(619) 469-6344
Dirk's fun party atmosphere is a big draw for the 35-to-50 age group—you know the people, the ones who remember Buffalo Springfield, Fleetwood Mac, and Sting. And college students who like this vintage music come here, too. Dirk's is popular, and the best part is that the classic rock is live on the weekends. Wednesday is karaoke night. Call to find out about upcoming special events such as the 1950s theme parties. Although the venue is super plain, everyone in the East County, from city mayors to college students, gives this club a thumbs-up. There's never a cover charge to get you in the door.

"Car nights" or "cruising nights" are lots of fun for families. Muscle cars, hot rods, vintage cars, and Harley Davidsons cruise the main streets of Escondido, El Cajon, La Mesa, and Chula Vista on summer nights, when the streets are blocked off for this purpose. See the Attractions chapter for details.

Sycuan Casino
5469 Dehesa Road, El Cajon
(619) 445-6002
www.sycuan.com
The Sycuan Casino, in East County's El Cajon, has live entertainment, usually classic rock, R&B, or smooth jazz. Summer hours are Tuesday through Sunday with fewer shows during the winter months. Name-brand entertainment such as The Doobie Brothers and Roy Clark perform in its Showcase Theater. Tickets run $15 to $50. Call or check the Internet calendar for upcoming performances.

Viejas Casino
5005 Willows Road, Alpine
(619) 445-5400, (800) 847-6537
www.viejas.com
As this ultrapopular Viejas Indian casino says, "We've got more fun," and when you go for entertainment, you won't be disappointed. Shows vary from season to season, but the club often offers blues bands on Friday after 8:00 P.M. and Big Band music for early evening dancing on Sunday. Neither show has a cover charge or a drink minimum, and the Dream-Catcher Showroom is renowned for its excellent acoustics. Of the three major East County Indian casinos, this is the only one that sells alcohol. The summer concert series, with names like Bill Cosby, B.B. King, and Jackson Browne, is held on the grass at the outlet center across the street.

South Bay

Coors Amphitheater
2050 Entertainment Circle, Chula Vista
(619) 671-3500
www.hob.com
This amphitheater adds a much-needed performance venue to the South Bay and to San Diego County. The outdoor theater seats 20,000 (nearly 10,000 reserved seats and 10,000 on the grass). You can

bring a blanket but no lawn chairs; food and drink cannot be brought but are sold on the premises. Tailgating is permitted in the parking lot before the show. Popular entertainers are booked at this modern venue; recent shows featured Korn, Maná, the Dave Matthews Band, Santana, and Pennywise. Tickets can be purchased at the box office the day of the event only or through Ticketmaster, (619) 220-8497.

Over the Border
3008 Main Street, Chula Vista
(619) 427-5889
www.overtheborder.com
Spanish rock, Mexican ska, funk, R&B, and soul . . . you'll find this and more, enjoyed by a mostly young, well-dressed Latino crowd (call for the dress code), Thursday through Saturday from 8:00 P.M. until 2:00 A.M. In addition to the house band, Liquido, you can see bigger name bands like Los Enanitos Verdes (Little Green Men), the popular Argentine rock band. Cover charge is usually $5.00 before 10:00 P.M., $10.00 after that.

BARS AND BREWPUBS

Central San Diego

Bar Dynamite
1808 West Washington Street, Mission Hills
(619) 295-8743
Hip-hop, reggae, Brazilian, house, and even the occasional disco tune are spun by DJs six nights a week. Young sophisticates are drawn to this comfy neighborhood bar weekend nights by its great sound system and refreshingly different tunes.

Coronado Brewing Co.
170 Orange Avenue, Coronado
(619) 437-4452
www.coronadobrewingcompany.com
Right in the heart of scenic Coronado is this lively brewpub, which has nearly a dozen varieties of beer on tap. You can lift

While Tijuana has a reputation as a party place for drunken U.S. sailors and exuberant teens, there's plenty of nightlife for the relatively sober crowd as well. See our South of the Border chapter for some of TJ's tried-and-true nightspots.

a pint and have a bite to eat for lunch or dinner. The menu includes casual fare: hamburgers, salads, wood-fired pizzas, and pasta. Two outdoor patios, one with a fireplace, are popular spots and often crowded, especially during happy hour.

Karl Strauss Brewery & Grill
1044 Wall Street, La Jolla
(858) 551-2739

1157 Columbia Street, downtown San Diego
(619) 234-2739

9675 Scranton Road, Sorrento Valley
(858) 587-2739

5801 Armada Drive, Carlsbad
(760) 431-2739
One of the first brewpubs to open in San Diego, Karl Strauss has maintained its quality and reputation through the years. From its first location in downtown San Diego, it now has four locations in the county and makes more than two dozen beers, including lagers, bitters, ales, and stouts.

Kensington Club
4079 Adams Avenue, San Diego
(619) 284-2848
This neighborhood bar has gained some panache, having been discovered by young, hip types fond of alternative music. (Still, it opens at 10:00 in the morning, so how classy can it be?) Live entertainment is now featured on Friday and Saturday, and the format varies. Weekdays DJs play an eclectic range of tunes from standards to hip-hop. The cover charge varies from nothing to $10.

The Lamplighter
817 West Washington Street, Mission Hills
(619) 298-3624
There's a pool table, a full bar, and a neighborhood crowd that couldn't be friendlier at the Lamplighter. Bartenders are exuberant in their attention to customers; some are a show in themselves. But if you want to put on your own show, some of the area's best karaoke starts at 9:00 P.M. nightly except Monday. The bar opens at 6:00 A.M.

McP's Irish Pub and Grill
1107 Orange Avenue, Coronado
(619) 435-5280
www.mcpspub.com
There's never a cover charge at McP's, and you get a lot for the price of a beer and a burger here. Bands play blues, rock, or "easy listening" seven days a week, although there's not a set schedule; Irish music is arranged for special days such as Saint Pat's. This is a favorite hangout of Coronado locals and visitors alike.

The Pennant
2893 Mission Boulevard, Mission Beach
(858) 488-1671
www.thepennantbar.com
Far from fancy, the Pennant is a quintessential Mission Beach bar that has been around forever. Patrons shoot the breeze, watch a game on TV, and generally just hang out in T-shirts and flip-flops. The upstairs deck is a godsend on warm summer evenings; smokers enjoy it year-round. The crowd is mixed, from college students to grizzled beach rats to tourists, so everyone fits right in.

Red Fox Room
2223 El Cajon Boulevard, San Diego
(619) 297-1313
There was a time when the Red Fox Room was one of the most elegant lounges in town. Its grandeur may have faded a bit, but its popularity has continued over the years. Today it's a piano bar where you can sing along while cozied up with your sweetie in its hallmark red vinyl booths. And be assured that your cocktail will be served full strength and with panache. The crowd is a great mix of ages and levels of eccentricity.

San Diego Brewing Co.
10450 Friars Road, San Diego
(619) 284-2739
If you're serious about beer drinking—and sports—this is the place to go. Fifty brews on tap will keep you sampling indefinitely. Talk with the knowledgeable staff about the different varieties, and be sure to try one new to you. Pace yourself with an extraordinary burger or bowl of chili, then sit back and enjoy the sporting events that are broadcast on 2 big-screen and 12 regular TVs.

Top of the Hyatt Lounge
Hyatt Regency, 1 Market Place, San Diego
(619) 232-1234
The Top of the Hyatt Lounge, on the 40th floor of its namesake hotel, is the best place in San Diego to have a cocktail with a view of the harbor on one side and a lit-up city skyline on the other. The interior of the bar is dimly lit so as not to distract from the glorious sights outside, and a recent renovation has produced more of the coveted seats with a view. It's comfortable, romantic, and breathtaking.

Trophy's Sports Grill
7510 Hazard Center Drive, San Diego
(619) 296-9600

4282 Esplanade Court, La Jolla
(858) 450-1400

5500 Grossmont Center Drive, La Mesa
(619) 698-2900
This homegrown sports bar/restaurant, filled with collections of sports memorabilia, has flourished in all three of its locations. The restaurant itself is good: Eats are cheap and quality is high. You can usually see at least one of the TVs from anywhere in the restaurant. The bar has big-screen TVs along with normal-size ones, and if there's a game in progress anywhere in the country, it's likely to be on. This is a fun place for families and singles.

The Waterfront
2044 Kettner Boulevard, Little Italy
(619) 232-9656
www.waterfrontbarandgrill.com

Once the domain of cannery workers and commercial fishermen, this bar has had a loyal clientele for longer than most of its barkeeps can recall. Along with many of the older properties in Little Italy, the narrow bar has been spruced up, but it's still a congenial, homespun, fun, and casual hangout. It's open for beer and breakfast from 6:00 A.M. There's live music in a variety of formats after 9:00 P.M. Thursday through Saturday and never a cover charge.

Whaling Bar
La Valencia Hotel
1132 Prospect Street, La Jolla
(858) 454-0771

Once an elite hangout for Hollywood types in town for the thoroughbred races at Del Mar, today the Whaling Bar has matured into an elegant gathering place for La Jolla locals and visitors. Entertainment is a piano bar, which naturally encourages the singer in us all to join in, and most folks do. A mammoth renovation in the late 20th century restored the bar while retaining its old-world style. If you want an ocean view, however, you'll have to go to the hotel's waterfront terrace upstairs.

North County Coastal

Coyote Bar & Grill
300 Carlsbad Village Drive, Carlsbad
(760) 729-4695

The age and musical tastes of Coyote's clientele change frequently. What seems to be constant, however, is the number of people spilling out the door, off the patio, and into the parking lot. When the weather is fine—and that's more often than not—young and middle-aged professionals can be found on the patio, some sipping one of the bar's hundred-odd brands of tequila. The popular hangout has loud music, lots of laughter, and live entertainment Wednesday through Sunday from 6:00 to 10:30 P.M. after which a DJ spins his (or her) magic. On weekdays partake of happy hour appetizers from 3:00 to 6:00 P.M. Tuesday is currently karoake night.

At the Indian gaming casinos you'll discover dancing and live music, but you may not be able to find a beer. Of the three major East County casinos, only Viejas serves alcohol. North County Inland's two biggies, Harrah's Rincon and Pala Casino, have both entertainment and alcohol.

Pizza Port
135 North Highway 101, Solana Beach
(858) 481-7332
571 Carlsbad Village Drive, Carlsbad
(760) 720-7007
www.pizzaport.com

Yes, you'll get pizza, but you'll also get some great microbrewed beers with it. The music makes this place feel like party time, even though it's not live and the loud and bustling place has a distinctly family-friendly feel. The microbrew choices vary, and the pub also has a large selection of imported beers if you prefer something continental with that garlic and feta pizza. Call for upcoming events such as the microbrew brewing contests, Real Ale Fest, and the Belgian Beer Party.

North County Inland

San Marcos Brewery & Grill
1080 West San Marcos Boulevard, San Marcos
(760) 471-0050

The number of microbrews on tap changes daily, and some Insiders say when the honey-wheat ale is available, get a pitcher because one glass won't be enough. The food is okay, the service is quick and friendly, but Insiders come for the brew.

This microbrewery—which is part of Old California Restaurant Row—draws the afterwork crowd, students from nearby Cal State San Marcos and Palomar College, and families, too.

South Bay

Edelweiss
230 Third Avenue, Chula Vista
(619) 426-5172
Come on, admit it. You like accordion music! But how often do you have the opportunity to hear it played seriously and at its best? Here's your chance. Get into the spirit at Edelweiss, formerly the House of Munich, which offers up Austrian food and ambience and—Friday through Sunday between about 6:00 and 9:00 P.M.—the accordion music of Gordon Kohl. It's a different experience and one well worth trying.

The Galley at the Marina
550 Marina Parkway, Chula Vista
(619) 422-5714
You'll find lots of South Bay locals as well as seafaring types bellied up to the wood and nautical-theme bar overlooking the marina. It's a comfortable place to hang out either at the dark bar or a comfortable booth, or outside in the sunshine at one of the white plastic patio tables overlooking the marina. You can order food from the restaurant, or just nurse a beer or well drink. Shows vary by season, but there's almost always some sort of low-key entertainment—from "interactive" comedy to acoustic guitar—on the weekends.

> ***While Starbucks and the chain coffee shops charge for Wi-Fi connect, some of the smaller venues and even neighborhood bars throughout the county offer it for free. These include, among others, The Aero Club (3365 India Street, Little Italy) and the nearby Gelato Vero (India Street at Washington Street) and Krakatoa (1128 25th Street, Golden Hill). Also included are Lestat's, E Street Cafe, and Couleur Cafe, which are included in this chapter.***

COFFEEHOUSES

Central San Diego

Lestat's Coffeehouse
3343 Adams Avenue, Normal Heights
(619) 282-0437
www.lestats.com
Nightly entertainment is featured here: ska, jazz, acoustic, folk, and even some music from the Middle Ages every once in a while. Monday is open-mike night for aspiring performers looking for an audience. Wednesday is currently comedy night. The clientele is largely but not exclusively gay at this 24-hour coffeehouse. The Wi-Fi connection is free.

The Living Room
5900 El Cajon Boulevard, San Diego
(619) 286-8434

1010 Prospect Street, La Jolla
(858) 459-1187

1018 Rosecrans Street, Point Loma
(619) 222-6852

2541 San Diego Avenue, San Diego
(619) 325-4445

1417 University Avenue, Hillcrest
(619) 295-7911
www.livingroomusa.com
Although we don't normally recommend chains, each of these coffeehouses is earthy, individual, and truly special. The name says it all. When you walk into The Living Room, you'll feel like you're in your own home. Relax on a comfortable sofa or sit at the polished bar or small tables, perfect for a tête-à-tête or a few hours of reading or journal writing. Choose from an outstanding selection of coffees and sin-

fully delicious desserts, from truffles and tortes to shortcakes and scones. There's some light bistro fare as well.

Twiggs Green Room
4590 Park Boulevard, University Heights
(619) 296-0616
www.twiggs.org
Something is going on at Twiggs nearly every evening. Most performances are acoustic/folk music, but occasionally a jazz or pop artist or a poet will make an appearance. This is a spacious coffeehouse with lots of room to spread out and get comfortable. Order a sandwich, homemade baked goods, or a wide variety of coffees or teas.

North County Coastal

E Street Cafe
130 West E Street, Encinitis
(760) 230-2038
Enjoy eclectic furnishing—you can lounge on the couch or at the dining-room table, to study—and free Wi-Fi at this comfortable coffeehouse near Highway 101. Sit at one of the few outside tables or under the lazily rotating ceiling fans inside. There's non-invasive live music most weekend nights; in addition to the usual surfeit of coffee drinks, bistro sandwiches, pastries, and desserts are served.

La Costa Coffee Roasting
6965 El Camino Real, Carlsbad
(760) 438-8160
This is a family-style hangout where people come to mingle, have coffee, and check their e-mail via free wireless connection after taking in a movie at the multiplex theater or visiting the branch of the Carlsbad City library right in the same shopping center. There's live entertainment—perhaps jazz or a guitarist, cellist, or bluegrass banjo player—on Friday and Saturday evenings starting at 7:00 P.M. If you're looking for a coffee-related gift to take back home, there are walls of designer, silly, and fun coffee mugs.

The Pannikin
2670 Via de la Valle, Del Mar
(858) 481-8007
510 North Highway 101, Encinitis
(760) 436-5824
Next door to the Book Works in Flower Hill Plaza, the Del Mar Pannikin is bright, playful, and cheery without being fussy. Choose from a wide variety of aromatic coffees and teas, along with desserts and gelato. There's a good variety of coffee-related accoutrements and kitchen paraphernalia for sale as well, some of which make great gifts. They usually have low-key live music Friday evenings beginning at around 8:00 P.M. The Encinitis venue, located in the old Santa Fe Railway Station, is full of charm and shares the space with the Off-Track Gallery, where local artists show their stuff.

North County Inland

Old California Coffee House
1080 San Marcos Boulevard
(760) 744-2112
www.oldcalcoffee.com
Most of the furniture looks like something from grandma's house: There are chintz-covered armchairs and pillow-strewn banquettes as well as a few tables where you can set up a laptop and work. There's free Wi-Fi indoors or out, and in addition to wraps, salads, and other light fare, an assortment of juices and smoothies. Live music sometimes materializes on the weekends.

Outdoor concerts are held in the summer at Quail Botanical Gardens (230 Quail Gardens Drive, Encinitas, 760-436-3036, ext. 206). This is an early night out on four weekends in July and August: Dinner begins at 5:00 and the concert at 6:00 P.M. Prices are $22 and include a light dinner.

East County

Coffee Merchant
5500 Grossmont Center Drive, La Mesa
(619) 460-7393
Whether you want one of many types of tea, espresso, decaf, or the real thing, this is a great little coffeehouse for grabbing a quick cup or hanging out with friends (or a good book). There's a complete espresso and dessert bar and live music every Friday evening, played by a jazz group, perhaps, or a guitarist singing Latino melodies.

Held each September, the San Diego Street Scene (www.street-scene.com) is the second-largest music and food festival in the United States. For three days local and regional talent perform, beginning in the early afternoon, while big-name bands top off the evening. Multiple stages are set up at the festival's new location: the parking lot of Qualcomm Stadium.

Chicano Perk
616 National City Boulevard, National City
(619) 474-7375

129 25th Street, San Diego
(619) 702-5414
www.chicanoperk.com
Welcome to the best of all worlds: good coffee (organic, fair-trade beans, no less), excellent digs, and on the weekends—live music. Spread out on the couch and tune in to *rock en espanol* (rock sung in Spanish) as well as Latin R&B or hip-hop. Sets usually start at 7:00 P.M. on Friday, 8:00 P.M. on Saturday, and around 5:00 on Sunday, when more mellow jazz is often on the menu. The newer National City location serves food too; both offer poetry readings and display art of local painters, all colored by the Hispanic traditions of these South Bay neighborhoods. The owners call themselves "Chicanos con conciencia": Chicanos with a conscience.

SHOPPING

If shopping is your hobby, passion, indulgence, or sport of choice, San Diego will satisfy you. The area's malls, shops, stores, and districts are seemingly endless and eclectic. We think San Diego has some of the most diverse shopping on the planet. The choices might even be a bit overwhelming. So in this chapter we've included need-to-know shopping information and then presented the best in shopping experiences. As shoppers at heart, we've put a lot of enthusiasm behind the lists we give you in this chapter. The places we've included are the ones we tell our friends not to miss.

Like the malls. Some, like the Fashion Valley Mall in Mission Valley, could easily become an addiction. Like the shopping districts—including Adams Avenue, with its blend of coffee pubs, new and used bookstores, and antiques emporiums. You'll find information on the Carlsbad Company Stores, too, where you can find specialty stores from Donna Karan to Ralph Lauren—not to mention Starbucks and Garden State Bagels. The shopping centers are often a blend of specialty stores like these, national chains such as Sears, and discount stores like Marshalls Department Store. That information is here, too.

We've included our favorite stores specializing in resale and consignment clothing, and then added swap meets and a few flea markets. Half the fun of shopping in these specialty places is that you never quite know what you'll find, and if you'll need it, until you see it.

We've also given you a taste of booksellers and antiques stores in the area. Our list is far from a telephone-book tabulation, though. Use it as a basic introduction only. If you're really hooked on antiquing, we recommend that you visit some of the stores and get a newsletter (we'll tell you about that, too), which should lead you to even more stores to try. And while you're off on your hunt, you might want to scan the listings for other possibilities. If you've traveled the hour and a half to East County's Julian Shopping District, for example, you may find some surprises to take home along with your antiques. This quaint mountain town is heaped with little shops that sell country collectibles and crafts—not to mention fudge, ice cream, apple pie, and apple cider.

After organizing all our favorite stores into tidy categories, we discovered something was lacking, so we created a new section. It's called "Unique and Intriguing." Here you will find stores that may tickle your fancy with unusual or hard-to-find offerings, like those little cookies you nibbled in Vienna, the right color chaps for your western-wear outfit, or perhaps a fragrant bouquet of dried herbs.

Within each shopping category you'll find the usual regional divisions. For ideas about places to play and relax in the areas of the county where you plan to shop, you might want to peruse those regions in our chapters on parks, recreation, attractions, nightlife, or restaurants. In fact, your companion or significant other might just insist on it!

MALLS

Central San Diego

Clairemont Town Square Shopping Center
4821 Clairemont Drive, San Diego
(858) 272-0992
www.clairemonttownsquare.com

Clairemont Town Square is anchored by Burlington Coat Factory, Circuit City, and Michael's, a giant arts and crafts store. Several fast-food places are sprinkled throughout the mall, and the Outback Steakhouse is nearby for a sit-down meal and a chance to rest your feet. Also located in the center is the Pacific Theatres Town Square, with 14 screens and stadium-style seating.

Horton Plaza is whimsical, but full of practical stores. PHOTO: COURTESY OF JOHN BAHU

Fashion Valley
7007 Friars Road, San Diego
(619) 688-9113
www.shopfashionvalleymall.com

This is San Diego's largest shopping mall, and it underwent a $120 million expansion and renovation at the end of the 20th century. The big department stores are Neiman Marcus, Nordstrom, Macy's, Saks Fifth Avenue, and JCPenney. And just about every other specialty store you can think of is there, too. Fashion Valley has more than 200 of them, including Tiffany & Co., Talbots, Gap, Banana Republic, Crate & Barrel, See's Candies, and many more. Restoration Hardware is one of our favorites. It's a hardware store that's enticing to both men and women for its one-of-a-kind reproduction treasures.

More than a dozen restaurants, bistros and eateries offer everything from a leisurely meal with wine and cocktails to a quick snack while on the run to the next store. The kiosks located throughout the mall offer unique gifts and mementos. If a movie is on your agenda, you can't go wrong with the AMC Theater in the mall. Eighteen screens and stadium-style seating provide the ultimate movie-going experience.

i ***Both the Mission Valley and Fashion Valley malls are right on the San Diego Trolley's Blue Line. Make a day of it, and use the trolley to travel between the two.***

Westfield Shoppingtown Horton Plaza
324 Horton Plaza, San Diego
(619) 239-8180
www.westfield.com/hortonplaza

Known for its highly acclaimed architecture and eye-catching color scheme, Horton Plaza is home to more than 180 shops. Nordstrom, Macy's, and Mervyn's are here, as are bebe, FAO Schwarz, 9 West, The Discovery Channel Store, Victoria's Secret, Ann Taylor, and Abercrombie & Fitch.

Some of our favorite restaurants are inside the mall, too, such as the Panda Inn for great Chinese food. The international food court can't be beat for a great variety of quick and tasty treats. For entertainment, check out the 14-screen theater or take in a play at the Lyceum Theatre, located on street level, one level below the mall's ground floor.

Westfield Shoppingtown Mission Valley
1640 Camino del Rio N., San Diego
(619) 296-6375
www.westfield.com/missionvalley

Just a hop, skip, and a jump away from Fashion Valley is Mission Valley. This is a mall that was in decline until it reinvented itself with the addition of a 20-screen AMC Theater and a bunch of new stores. It now is one of the most popular malls in the county, especially among teenagers. Besides Macy's Home & Furniture, Target, and Marshall's, there are more than 100 specialty shops and restaurants.

Nordstrom Rack, Loehmann's, and Bed, Bath & Beyond draw adults; teens like to shop at Express, Lerner New York, Old Navy, and Charlotte Russe and can be found in Starworks Arena, an interactive entertainment center that features virtual reality games and simulations. Ruby's Diner, O'Nami Japanese Restaurant, and Seau's: The Restaurant (check out the latter in our Restaurants chapter) are the main dining spots in the mall, but don't miss the food court, which has everything from soft pretzels to fish tacos.

Westfield Shoppingtown University Towne Center
4545 La Jolla Village Drive, San Diego
(858) 546-8858, (858) 453-2930
www.westfield.com/utc
With its grass and fountains, UTC has a parklike setting that encourages shoppers to slow down and linger. You'll find more than 180 stores, too, including Macy's and Sears and specialty stores like Sephora, bebe, Crate & Barrel, charles david, and Ann Taylor.

For dining, choose from Chinese, Japanese, Indian, Mediterranean, Mexican, or California bistro cuisine offered by full-service restaurants. Or sample the variety of treats available in the huge open-air food pavilion. A remodeled ice rink (see our Recreation chapter) guarantees to entertain both kids and adults.

North County Coastal

Del Mar Plaza
1555 Camino del Mar, Del Mar
(858) 792-1555
www.delmarplaza.com
On the corner of Camino del Mar and 15th Street, the many shops of petite, three-story Del Mar Plaza open onto a courtyard. Both Chicos and Tosca offer unique women's fashions, Banana Republic brings it down a notch, and Saddlebags has lots of accessories. Jewelry stores range from Just Pretend, selling costume baubles, to Logham, with high-end pieces. Find healthy foods and natural beauty-care products at the Harvest Ranch Market. In the evening you can dine or just stop for a drink at one of several comfortable but elegant restaurants: Epazote, Pacifica del Mar, or Il Fornaio. Outside the latter, the Enoteca del Fornaio wine bar faces west and gets a million-dollar view of the sun setting over the Pacific. Dress warmly and, wineglass in hand, watch the sun set over the ocean from a cushy lounge chair or cafe table.

The third-floor patio of Del Mar Plaza is actually open to the public, so there's nothing to stop you from bringing your own picnic basket, settling on the comfortable chaise lounges there, and watching the sunset. You needn't buy a thing.

The Forum
El Camino Real at Leucadia Boulevard
This is a large, one-story mall with designer duds and accessories. Non-shoppers can enjoy the pretty outdoor spaces with greenery and fountains, while shopoholics dive into Victoria Secret, Anthropology, Ann Taylor Loft (discounted Ann Taylor clothes and accessories), and Borders Bookstore, which has a wonderful selection of books, movie titles in DVD, and music CDs. There are also independent boutiques like Sur Le Table, where you can take cooking classes or spend from a dollar on a funnel to a lot more on the latest designer cookware.

Westfield Shoppingtown Plaza Camino Real
2525 El Camino Real, Carlsbad
(760) 729-7927
www.westfield.com
Plaza Camino Real is an enclosed regional mall that boasts more than 140 specialty stores, including those where you'll find

upscale women's clothing, shoes, toys, and kitchen gadgets. The anchor stores are Sears, JCPenney, and Macy's.

There are Walden Books and Boot World as well as more than 21 eateries where you can select everything from pizza to pretzels and a few Mrs. Fields cookies to ward off the shopping hungries. There are places to sit and people watch, clothing stores, and accessory boutiques.

North County Inland

Westfield Shoppingtown North County
272 East Via Rancho Parkway, Escondido
(760) 489-2332
North County Inland's largest enclosed mall is anchored by Nordstrom, Macy's, Sears, and JCPenney. You'll find 200 specialty shops, including Godiva chocolates, Crabtree & Evelyn, Mrs. Fields cookies, Lane Bryant, and O'Nami Japanese restaurant as well as a food court with everything from pizza to Indian food. Throughout the mall there are plenty of places to sit and people watch—a favorite pastime for those who come along with a true shopper. Parking on weekends can be tricky, but there always seems to be enough.

East County

Grossmont Center
5500 Grossmont Center Drive, La Mesa
(619) 465-2900
www.grossmontcenter.com
The Grossmont Center has attracted shoppers from East County and the mountain communities since it was founded in 1965; it's one of the few in the county not in the Westfield chain. Currently there are more than 100 stores. Anchor stores include Macy's and Target. You'll find specialty stores that are unique, including a half-dozen jewelry stores and Shavers and Small Appliances, as well as Barnes & Noble and a Cost Plus World Market.

Westfield Shoppingtown Parkway Plaza
415 Parkway Plaza (at Johnson), El Cajon
(619) 579-9932
www.westfield.com/parkway
This sprawling mall is anchored by Sears, JCPenney, and Mervyn's and has hundreds of specialty stores. Young girls love Afterthoughts, Claire's, Rave Girl, and Anchor Blue; for the grown-ups there's Victoria's Secret and Frederick's of Hollywood as well as the usual array of music, electronics, clothing, and specialty shops. The food court has fast food from different countries, and there's a Rubio's Fish Taco and a Jasmine Chinese Bistro here also. The multiplex theater is a good place to chill after a hard day of shopping.

South Bay

Chula Vista Center
555 Broadway, Chula Vista
(619) 427-6700
Located right in the heart of Chula Vista, this mall is home to Macy's, Mervyn's, Sears, and JCPenney as anchors. There are more than 100 specialty stores, including Express, Victoria's Secret, Hot Topic, and Casual Corner.

An Ultrastar 10 Theater is in the mall, and so are lots of fast-food places where you can grab a snack.

Westfield Shoppingtown Plaza Bonita
3030 Plaza Bonita Road, National City
(619) 267-2850
www.westfield.com/plazabonita
South Bay's only enclosed, climate-controlled shopping center, Plaza Bonita is anchored by JCPenney and Mervyn's. More than 150 specialty shops like Anchor Blue and Foot Locker will keep you shopping for hours. When you need a break, stop in at Applebee's, Outback Steakhouse, or one of the many restaurants in the food court.

DISCOUNT AND OUTLET SHOPPING

Central San Diego

Burlington Coat Factory
3962 Clairemont Mesa Boulevard
San Diego
(858) 272-1893
www.burlingtoncoatfactory.com

Located in the Clairemont Town Square Shopping Center, you'll find much more than just coats (although there's no shortage of those).

Burlington is one of the largest off-price clothing store in the country, offering fashions for the whole family. Most styles are in season, but in some cases sizes and selection are limited. Additionally, Burlington has shoes, accessories, linens, and baby furniture.

DSW
836 Camino del Rio N., Mission Valley Mall South, San Diego
(619) 296-4079

Think beautiful. Think bargains. Think twice before you come in with a few hundred dollars in your purse or checkbook; even the most frugal shopper usually leaves with no fewer than four boxes of fabulous shoes, many designer labels and all at wonderful discounts. There is a small section of men's shoes, but mainly it's aisle after aisle of women's footwear: sneakers, platforms, slingbacks, pumps, mules—you name it. The super-discount section is along the back wall; otherwise, it's a serve-yourself warehouse-style store with wide aisles. Socks, stockings, purses, and a few other accessories round out the inventory.

La Jolla Village Square
8657 Villa La Jolla Drive, La Jolla
(858) 455-7550

This almost qualifies as a mall, but it's really a discount shopping center, and a pretty spiffy one at that. It's a popular shopping destination because of its Starbucks, offbeat fast-food eateries, and 12-screen theater. Mixed in with the leisurely crowd, however, are the power shoppers looking for bargains at Marshalls, Cost Plus, Linens 'n Things, Famous Footwear, Ross Stores, and Crown Books Superstore.

Shop at Trader Joe's for international wines and delicacies.

Loehmann's
1640 Camino del Rio N., San Diego
(619) 296-7776

San Diego's version of this national discount store is located in the east wing of Mission Valley Center (see our entry under Malls). Famous for its discount women's designer clothes, it's also a great place to find bargains on sportswear, shoes, and lingerie. Loehmann's has a good children's department, too, and a menswear section. Don't forget to check out the back room, where top-of-the-line designer formal wear and more casual duds can be had for deep discounts. Wear your best underwear—fitting rooms are communal.

Nordstrom Rack
1640 Camino del Rio N., San Diego
(619) 296-0143

This is where a lot of the beautiful but pricey clothes from Nordstrom end up. You can get great deals on ladies', men's, and children's clothing as well as shoes, accessories, lingerie, and some home decor items. Don't expect the level of service you'd find at Nordstrom's regular department stores, but the volume is usually overwhelming and the values make it a worthwhile visit. The Rack is located in the east wing of Mission Valley Shopping Center.

Shoe Pavilion
4240 Kearny Mesa Road, San Diego
(858) 492-9833
3337 Rosecrans Street, San Diego
(619) 222-6787
www.shoepavilion.com

In these (and other locations; there are too many to list) warehouse-style stores you'll find quality brand-name men's and women's shoes for about half the retail price.

The shoes are displayed on counters with boxes piled up underneath, and it's strictly self-serve. Many shoes are constructed of man-made materials. Friendly salespeople are always glad to answer questions or help you find something special.

Westfield Shoppingtown Mission Valley Center West
1640 Camino del Rio N., San Diego
(619) 296-6375

Mission Valley Center's little sister, located just to the west of the main shopping center, has DSW (see listing above), Old Navy, and Marshalls, three discount giants. You'll also find a Borders Books & Music and Just for Feet athletic shoes. When you're ready to hit the links, stop in at Golfsmith for all your golfing equipment and supplies. A giant Gateway computer store should fulfill all your techno-wishes, while a Gordon-Biersch brewpub provides a place to wet your whistle (the food's not bad, either) after shopping.

North County Coastal

Carlsbad Company Stores
5620 Paseo del Norte, Carlsbad
(760) 804-9000

Carlsbad Company Stores is a potpourri of some 80 discount outlets, from Ralph Lauren, Jones of New York, and Donna Karan to Rockport, Tommy Hilfiger, Gap, and Hush Puppies. North County shoppers who love those exceptional brand names love coming here.

All in all, you can choose from 85 fine stores selling clothing, shoes, outerwear, accessories, and jewelry as well as luggage and baby accessories.

Should you start fading while you're picking the perfect little black dress or searching out some supercool sneaks, you'll find chain coffee cafes like Starbucks, an Asian fast-food restaurant, Ruby's old-fashioned malt shop with enormous burgers, and a real California smoothie (juice) bar. Or if you'd like to pop outside, you can find fine dining without even moving your car. Just a short block north is Bellefleur (see our Restaurants chapter), which features fresh and flavorful California-style cuisine and excellent local wines.

On weekends the stores are busy, and during the holidays the Christmas decorations are magnificent. There's lots of parking, and the mall is wheelchair accessible.

Marshalls Department Store
685 San Rodolfo Drive, Solana Beach
(858) 755-0791

While there are other Marshalls stores in San Diego, many Insiders consider this North County Coastal store to be the best. We're talking primo prices and larger selections, from shorts and T-shirts to business suits.

This store is bigger than the others, for one thing. It stocks higher quality merchandise at the excellent discount prices one expects from Marshalls. Close by are other specialty stores that move in and out of the strip mall. Currently you'll find an accessories shop, a lingerie store, an office supply store, and a bagel and coffee cafe.

North County Inland

UFO-Upholstery Fabric Outlet
1120 North Melrose Drive, Vista
(760) 941-2345
www.ufofabrics.com

No, you will not find E.T. at this store, but rather great bargains from the Upholstery Fabric Outlet. If you're in the market for fabric or for the accessories it takes to re-cover or design anything, this is the store. At UFO you'll be tempted by first-class merchandise. Although the sales happen rarely, the clearance table may hold a few finds.

East County

GTM Discount General Store
8967 Carlton Hills Boulevard, Santee
(619) 449-4953

7663 Broadway Avenue, Lemon Grove
(619) 460-2990
This is a discounter with a true no-frills ambience. These stores specialize in merchandise that's discounted because it's slightly damaged (for example, a somewhat crushed and taped-up box) or because the original store isn't carrying the item anymore. The products come from suppliers such as Costco and 130 other vendors. We've found bargains on everything from beauty aids and stretch pants to pet food and whole-bean coffee. Plan on a stop at GTM if you love a deal that feels like a real bargain, especially on items you use every day.

Viejas Outlet Center
5005 Willows Road, Alpine
(619) 659-2070
www.shopviejas.com
Landscaped with massive rocks and rushing water features among bronze statues and structures made to resemble those of a Native American village, this outlet center has a unique look that makes shopping a relaxing affair. There are nearly 60 retail store outlets, including Gap, Big Dog Sportswear, Liz Claiborne, Jones of New York, Eddie Bauer, and Perry Ellis. Shop for gifts and accessories, jewelry, and books, or pop into one of eight footwear outlets. In the evenings around 9:00 P.M. (earlier in winter months) there often is some form of free musical or laser-light entertainment. Those needing a break from the slot machine and bingo at the Viejas Casino across the road can sit down to pizza, ice cream, sushi, fast food, or tacos at Rubio's Baja Grill. This is also the home of San Diego's East County Visitors Bureau office, (619) 445-0180 or (800) 463-0668.

South Bay

Shoe Pavilion
304 East H Street, Chula Vista
(619) 691-0640
Like its sister stores in Central San Diego and North County Coastal, Shoe Pavilion offers no-frills shopping but excellent quality, selection, and price in brand-name and designer shoes for men and women. Don't miss the clearance racks, where prices are often as much as 75 percent below retail.

UFO-Upholstery Fabric Outlet
1919 Hoover Avenue, National City
(619) 477-9341
Even if you have no plans to reupholster any of your furniture, a visit to UFO will change that kind of thinking in a hurry. What seems to be miles and miles of racks of fabric will inspire your creative spirit, and you're sure to find something you can't live without or the perfect fabric to re-cover Aunt Matilda's antique chaise. UFO, along with its sister store in North County Inland, is an Insiders' secret not to be missed. It's closed on Sunday.

SHOPPING DISTRICTS

Central San Diego

Adams Avenue Business District
Between 30th and 40th Streets, Normal Heights
Informally known as San Diego's Antique Row, this stretch of Adams Avenue is filled with antiques stores, art galleries, used-book shops, collectibles, and home furnishings. This is a browser's paradise. It's a bit of a hike up and down the 10-block area; take a break at one of the pubs, coffeehouses, or restaurants that are mixed in with the stores. Rosie O'Grady's pub is a longtime fixture at 3402 Adams Avenue.

Most San Diego stores open at 10:00 A.M. and close anywhere between 6:00 and 9:00 P.M. On Saturday and Sunday evenings they may close earlier or later, depending on clientele, merchandise, and locations such as Pacific Beach or the Gaslamp Quarter.

Bazaar del Mundo
4133 Taylor Street, Old Town
(619) 296-3161

The popular and profitable concession started by Diane Powers was moved to its new location after losing its 20-plus-year concession at Old Town State Historic Park to the New York-based company Delaware North in 2004.

The colorful clothing, home accessories, and handicrafts shops are complemented by a book shop specializing in Latin American themes and by Guadalajara restaurant-bar.

Ferry Landing Marketplace
1201 First Street, Coronado

Not really a mall, not really a neighborhood shopping district, the Ferry Landing Marketplace is nevertheless a fun-filled shopping area. This is the perfect spot for souvenir shopping at places like Captain Coronado's Trading Company or the Coronado Ferry Company. Shop for fine art, collectibles, gourmet gifts, and T-shirts, or have an espresso drink or deli sandwich to eat there or take on a picnic.

You can also dine in style at Peohe's Restaurant overlooking San Diego Bay and the city skyline.

Gaslamp Quarter
Fourth to Sixth Avenues, between Broadway and L Street, San Diego
(619) 233-5227
www.gaslamp.org

Interspersed among the nightclubs and restaurants in the Gaslamp are about 90 unique shops, ranging from the well-known home-furnishings store Z Gallerie at 611 Fifth Avenue to the Gaslamp Books, Prints & Wyatt Earp Museum at 413 Market Street. Part of the appeal of shopping in the Gaslamp is that many of the stores are open late: until 9:00 P.M. on weekdays and 11:00 P.M. on weekends. So after dinner in one of the more than 100 restaurants, grills, or brewpubs in the Quarter, you can browse leisurely through the shops.

You'll find vintage clothing stores and boutiques that specialize in offbeat fashions. For collectors, there are a smattering of art galleries and rare print stores. And if you're having trouble deciding what to buy, you might consult the Gaslamp Psychic at 507 Fifth Avenue.

Hillcrest
Fifth Avenue, between Robinson and Washington Streets, and University Avenue, between Fourth Avenue and Park Boulevard

A funky and cool collection of shops and eateries lines Fifth Avenue in Hillcrest. You'll find vintage clothing in several shops, including Wear It Again Sam at 3832 Fifth Avenue, a San Diego icon for at least a generation. Although timeless bookshops such as the Blue Door have fallen prey to the megabookstore trend, Bountiful Books at 3834 Fifth Avenue manages to hang on, to the delight of book lovers who love to wander the neighborhood.

Also in this neighborhood, University Avenue between Fourth and Park has tons of resale clothing and furniture boutiques and trendy home-furnishing stores tucked among the timeless bars and liquor stores and a few prosperous minimalls. In the Uptown District, apartments and grocery stores mingle in smart 21st-century fashion with good restaurants and specialty shops.

La Jolla
Prospect Street and Girard Avenue

La Jolla is famous for its upscale shopping district, and it's hard to argue that there's a better location. Sunshine, the ocean, and streets teeming with happy shoppers combine to make this an out-of-the-ordinary shopping excursion. Here you'll find trendy boutiques and designer clothing stores, art galleries, and just enough offbeat stores, bars, and restaurants to keep things interesting.

One of our favorites is, believe it or not, family-run Ace Hardware, where you'll find lots more than screws and mousetraps. You'll find lots of eateries along both Prospect Street and Girard Avenue, including San Diego's Hard Rock Cafe at 909 Girard, plenty of casual bistros, and lots of full-service restaurants.

Ocean Beach
Newport Avenue, between Sunset Cliffs Boulevard and the beach

Downtown OB is overflowing with antiques stores, along with a sprinkling of interesting art galleries, card and gift shops, jewelry stores, and bikini and surf shops (you are at the beach, after all). Often on summer weekends there's a festival or fair happening, complete with craft booths for even more shopping.

Plaza del Pasado
Juan and Calhoun Streets,
Old Town State Historic Park
(619) 297-3100
www.plazadelpasado.com

Despite the rage that many San Diegans felt when Bazaar del Mundo lost its lease here in the historic state park, time heals (most) all wounds and Plaza del Pasado fills many of the same functions, albeit in a less colorful, more historically accurate way. The shops, restaurants, and even benches and trash cans are period-specific to 1821 to 1872. The shops and outdoor areas are anchored by period-authentic eateries as The Jolly Boy Restaurant & Saloon, The Cosmopolitan, and Casa de Reyes, each specializing in seafood and/or Mexican food.

Seaport Village
849 West Harbor Drive at
Kettner Boulevard
(next to the Hyatt Regency San Diego)
(619) 235-6133
www.seaportvillage.com

We included Seaport Village in our Attractions chapter simply because there's so much to do here. But we just had to

Downtown La Jolla is known for its upscale shopping district. PHOTO: COURTESY OF BRETT SHOAF

include the 14-acre waterfront zone in Shopping, too, because some of San Diego's most interesting stores are here.

Where else can you find a store like the Captain's Cove, which specializes in nautical treasures? You'll also find shops selling candles, kites, hammocks, and everything you need to perform magic tricks. There's an Upstart Crow bookseller where you can get a great cup of coffee or a pound of beans as well as magazines or books. More than 50 unique stores make up Seaport Village, and for the dedicated shopper, it's a place not to be missed.

North County Coastal

Cedros Avenue Shopping and Design Centers
Cedros Avenue, Solana Beach

Here you'll find wonderful shops from Adventure 16 (the outdoor gear and camping specialty store) at 143 South

CLOSE-UP

Fresh and Fabulous Farmers' Markets

Picture succulent produce, aromatic herbs, and field-fresh flowers. Now put that vision smack-dab in the center of a convenient neighborhood street or parking lot, and you'll get a vision of what our farmers' markets have to offer.

At all the places mentioned, you'll find fresh-picked vegetables and fruits, many cut for sampling. Flowers like the exotic protea compete with multihued sunflowers and perky Gerber daisies. Each stall holds something different: herbs or organic eggs, pies, and breads. Some of the markets listed have specialties, too, like tamales, wraps, or roasted-on-the-spot peanuts. As you visit them, you'll find that each has a flavor all its own. It's a good idea to cruise the entire market before buying and to bring plenty of single dollar bills to make purchasing quick and easy. Most of the outdoor farmers' markets are open for about three or four hours. Winter rainstorms do tend to discourage customers, but it usually takes a good soaking before the vendors pack up and leave.

Remember that the produce found at the farmers' markets is seasonal, which is part of its old-fashioned, noncommercial appeal. If you're looking for vine-ripened strawberries in December, you'll certainly be out of luck. Check that same market around June, though, and you'll be impressed by the selection.

We've listed the markets by days of the week rather than regions. So if your dinner party is on Thursday and you really need field-perfect squash, mouthwatering melons, and magnificent mushrooms, just find a market that's open that morning, and you'll know which direction to head. For more info, visit www.sdfarmbureau.org. On that Web site there are phone numbers where you can double-check the markets' locations and hours.

SUNDAY: La Jolla, Girard Avenue at Genter Street (La Jolla Elementary School), 9:00 A.M. to 2:00 P.M.; **Solana Beach,** 410 to 444 South Cedros Avenue at Rosa Street, 2:00 to 5:00 P.M.; **Hillcrest,** at the

Cedros Avenue to a host of high-end and lower-scale antiques stores. Be sure to stop at Cedros Gardens, 330 South Cedros Avenue, a wonderful, quaint garden store where the plants are as unique as the gifts and garden art that surround them. In the same district you'll find cafes and pubs, including Belly Up (which is mentioned in the Nightlife chapter).

There are more than 50 store owners who support one another in the shopping and design center for the North County Coastal area. Parking is mostly on the street, but there are lots places on side streets. FYI: The district stretches about 3 blocks south from the Coaster/Amtrak train stop in Solana Beach. Check the Coaster schedule to make sure you can get to and from the district at convenient times.

DMV parking lot, 3960 Normal Street, 9:00 A.M. to 1:00 P.M.; **Encinitis/Leucadia,** Paul Ecke Elementary School, Union and Vine Streets, 10:00 A.M. to 2:00 P.M.

TUESDAY: Coronado, at the Old Ferry Landing, corner of First Street and B Avenue, 2:30 to 6:00 P.M.; **Escondido,** Grand Avenue and Broadway, 4:00 to 7:00 P.M.; **UCSD,** Price Center at Library Walk and Lyman Lane, 10:00 A.M. to 2:00 P.M., September through June only.

WEDNESDAY: Ocean Beach, Newport Avenue between Ebers and Bacon Streets, 4:00 to 8:00 P.M. (7:00 P.M. in winter); **Carlsbad,** Roosevelt Street between Grand Avenue and Carlsbad Village Drive, 2:00 to 5:00 P.M.

THURSDAY: Oceanside, Coast Highway and Pier View Way, 9:00 A.M. to 12:30 P.M.; **Chula Vista,** Third Avenue at Center Street, 3:00 to 6:00 P.M.; (7:00 P.M. in winter); **Downtown San Diego, Horton Square,** 225 Broadway, 11:00 A.M. to 3:00 P.M. (March through mid-October).

FRIDAY: Chula Vista, 1360 Eastlake Parkway, 3:00 to 7:00 P.M.; **La Mesa Village,** Allison Street east of Spring Street, 3:00 to 6:00 P.M.; **Pacific Beach,** Cass Street at Chalcedony, 3:00 to 6:00 P.M. (7:00 P.M. in summer); **Rancho Bernardo,** Bernardo Winery, 13330 Paseo del Verano Norte, 9:00 A.M. to noon.

SATURDAY: Carlsbad, Roosevelt Street between Grand Avenue and Carlsbad Village Drive, 9:00 A.M. to 1:00 P.M.; **Clairemont,** Lindbergh Schweitzer Elementary School, Balboa Avenue and Hathaway Street, 3:00 to 6:30 P.M.; **Del Mar,** City Hall parking lot, Camino Del Mar between 10th and 11th Streets, 1:00 to 4:00 P.M.; **Point Loma,** High Tech High School, Womble and Truxtun Roads, 9:00 A.M. to 1:00 P.M.; **Scripps Ranch,** Ellen Browning Scripps Elementary School, 10380 Spring Canyon Road, 9:00 A.M. to 1:00 P.M. **Poway,** in Old Poway Park, Midland Road and Temple Street, 8:00 A.M. to noon; **Pacific Beach,** at Promenade Mall, Mission Boulevard between Reed Avenue and Pacific Beach Drive, 8:00 A.M. to noon; **Vista,** Eucalyptus and Escondido Avenues (City Hall parking lot), 8:00 to 11:00 A.M.

State Street Stores
Between Oak Street and Beech Street on both sides of State Street, Carlsbad
If you're looking for an antique or an addition to your baseball-card collection, are just nuts about rare books, or need a good cup of coffee, you'll find it all in this shopping area. Within the 4-block-plus shopping district, you'll be treated to about 40 antiques stores, boutiques, and small shops.

Be sure to browse through DeWitts Antiques and Collectibles for jewelry and glassware (there are more than 50 dealers combined in this store at 2946 State Street, and there's a licensed appraiser on-site). Don't miss Vinge Antiques, 3087 State Street, where you'll find rugs, books, and paintings along with the usual antique fare.

Mixed among the shops and cafes are boutiques like Kobos, at the corner of

Carlsbad Village Drive and State Street (2998 State Street). This shop features trendy and sensible beach clothes and California-casual sportswear. If you're headed up to North County from downtown San Diego, check the Coaster train schedule to make your trek more enjoyable. The station is right in the middle of this shopping district.

North County Inland

Carmel Mountain Plaza
San Diego
11602-11744 Carmel Mountain Road
(858) 350-2600

Carmel Mountain Plaza is a nice little neighborhood shopping mall with a 12-plex Pacific Theatres for movies, Cold Stone Creamery for cold, sugary treats, a major bookseller for reading material, and anchors such as Mervyn's, Target, and Marshalls. Additionally, there are some 50 or more boutiques and retail stores. For fans of good fast food there's an In 'N Out Burger joint.

East County

Julian Main Street Shopping District
Julian

Julian's antiques stores are mostly located around Main Street in the downtown area, which is about 5 easy blocks long. That said, if you don't look out the car windows while driving into town, you'll miss other stores along California Highway 78 as it winds up to this mountain village.

When you get to town, stop at the Julian Town Hall (on Main and Washington Streets) and pick up an antiques newsletter giving brief descriptions of shops and any specialties. You can also ask about the best places for the famous Julian apple pie and cider, but you may just have to do the sampling yourself. (The truth is, all the pies and cider we've tasted—and we've tried to be fair—are luscious. Be sure to buy enough to take back with you.)

About 3 miles *before* (west) of Julian, a string of small shops line Highway 78 at its juncture with Wynola Road, in Wynola. In a series of brightly painted, mainly historic buildings are a ranch market, a bookstore, an Orfila vintner, and a pizza restaurant. A group of antiques sellers share a rejuvenated packing shed at 4326 Highway 78, (760) 765-4758.

La Mesa Shopping District
La Mesa Boulevard at Spring Street

Sometime in the 1980s store owners along La Mesa Boulevard looked around and decided it was time to spiff things up. And so they did. This shopping district now includes coffee pubs, tidy cafes, inviting boutiques, and antiques shops—nearly 20 at last count—all within the downtown area of La Mesa.

South Bay

Chula Vista
Third Avenue, between E and G Streets
Chula Vista

Once a declining business district, Third Avenue has been revitalized and is now the hub of downtown shopping in Chula Vista. Restaurants, an old-fashioned movie theater, a performing arts theater, and, most important, lots of shops now line the busy street. As you amble up and down the pedestrian-friendly street, you'll find card shops, antiques stores, a specialty food market, and a few boutiques, too.

RESALE AND CONSIGNMENT

Central San Diego

Consignment Classics
1895 Hancock Street, San Diego
(619) 491-0700

Formerly called Terri's Consign & Design,

this shop offers new and slightly used name-brand furniture and accessories on consignment. Lots of new merchandise arrives each week, so it's a good idea to stop by whenever you're in the neighborhood. The owners are always happy to talk shop and help customers create an eclectic or traditional look for their home or office. They accept consignments from individuals in addition to purchasing from manufacturers.

Dress to Impress
4242 Camino del Rio N., San Diego
(619) 528-9797
If you're looking for a special dress to wear for a formal occasion, Dress to Impress may be your answer. You'll find a large selection of women's wear in all sizes: long gowns, cocktail dresses, and formals as well as slacks, jackets, blazers, and shoes. Better-quality sportswear, dresses, and suits are also available. Clothing for consignment is seen daily by appointment only.

Encore of La Jolla
7655 Girard Avenue, La Jolla
(858) 454-7540
www.encorelajolla.com
Occupying what was once an upscale department store, Encore specializes in women's high-end resale designer clothing. All the big labels for men and women are here. You might not find the bargain-basement prices that you would at other resale and consignment shops, but the selection and quality are fabulous.

Wear It Again Sam
3823 Fifth Avenue, San Diego
(619) 299-0185
This store is worth a visit just to see the latest finds. Specializing in vintage clothing from the 1900s through the 1960s, there's always something unusual to be found. Quality men's and women's clothing, shoes, and accessories that you haven't seen in years are sure to capture your imagination.

North County Coastal

Always Fabulous
1217 Camino del Mar, Del Mar
(858) 481-8866
From jewelry, hats, belts, sunglasses, and purses to clothing and shoes, you can select top-of-the-line styles (yes, that have been placed here on consignment) for a fraction of the original cost. As with all resale and consignment shops, the merchandise changes often. Are you after something special or a period piece of clothing? See if a staff member might give you a call when items like you're looking for come in.

Carolyn's Affordable Elegance
1310 Camino del Mar
(858) 793-9829
What can we say, except that among many worthwhile resale boutiques in North County, Carolyn's remains a top contender. Many barely worn designer rags are dropped off by ladies from Rancho Santa Fe and Del Mar who wouldn't dream of wearing the same outfit twice, and the best thing is, prices are extremely reasonable.

Double-Take
731 South Highway 101, Solana Beach
(858) 794-5451

2931 Roosevelt Street, Carlsbad
(760) 434-0101

509 South Highway 101, Encinitis
(760) 479-2501
This is a great place for accessories and that perfect bit of rhinestone jewelry. The store features designer brand-name clothing from Liz Claiborne to Vera Wang, worn once by those who can afford to then clothe the less fortunate among us.

Farmers' markets are fun outings for the whole family. If you discover an unusual fruit or vegetable, just ask the vendor for cooking or eating recommendations.

Two Sisters Consignment Home Furnishing
616 Stevens Avenue, Solana Beach
(858) 755-4558
If you love to browse through medium- to high-end modern furnishings as well as antiques, this store is a find. Most of the pieces are well within a family's budget.

There's a large supply of home furnishing in nearly perfect condition, and the best part is that consignments arrive daily. (While you're in the neighborhood, check out the Cedros Avenue Shopping and Design Center.) It's closed Sunday.

North County Inland

Deborah's
1624 East Valley Parkway, Escondido
(760) 743-8980
This is a huge, one-stop resale store for items for the entire family. In business since 1974, Deborah's has jewelry, shoes, clothing, accessories, furniture, household items, and gift items. The store sells only items in very good and nearly perfect condition and has a large supply of department-store brands.

East County

Conceptions
10438 Mission Gorge Road, Santee
(619) 596-2229
Conceptions offers resale accessories and clothing for babies and children and maternity clothes for mothers to be. They purchase gently used clothing, furniture, toys, strollers, and other baby accessories.

Don't forget to check out the bookstores at San Diego's local universities. Not only do they carry a good selection of books, they also have clothing and other items with the school's name and logo.

South Bay

Disabled American Veterans Thrift Store
881 Broadway, Chula Vista
(619) 420-1371
If you're a dedicated bargain-hunter, get ready to dive into the largest of the Disabled Vets' stores. You may have to plow through a lot of stuff before you come upon what you're seeking, but that's half the fun. And there's a ton of quality mixed in with the stuff that might be best classified as "junque." Clothing for the whole family, accessories, and home furnishings are just some of the treasures you'll find. Be sure to check out the collection of silk ties. It's a great way to add to your collection for a fraction of the retail price. Closed Sunday.

BOOKSTORES

Central San Diego

B. Dalton Bookseller
Horton Plaza, 407 Horton Plaza
San Diego
(619) 615-5373
B Dalton has been around a long time. Even though it doesn't compete with the superstores in terms of volume of titles, it's a consistently good bookstore with up-to-date stock and friendly salespeople. Inside the entertaining Horton Plaza Mall, it's easy to stop in while you're shopping for other things, too.

Barnes & Noble
7610 Hazard Center Drive, San Diego
(619) 220-0175
www.bn.com
With more than 150,000 titles, Barnes & Noble is one of the giants in town. The Hazard Center location is roomy and spread out, and there's a coffeehouse next door where you can spend a few quiet moments with your new book. Part of the special appeal of Barnes & Noble is the huge children's department.

Bay Books & Cafe
1029 Orange Avenue, Coronado
(619) 435-0070
Coronado's Bay Books has national and international newspapers and magazines to go along with its extensive collection of new books. Best sellers, fiction, mysteries, travel guides, children's books, cookbooks, and gardening books highlight the collection. You'll have plenty of opportunity to peruse your selection in the reading room or at the espresso bar.

Bookstar
3150 Rosecrans Place, San Diego
(619) 225-0465

8650 Genesee Avenue, San Diego
(858) 457-7561
Owned by mammoth Barnes & Noble, Bookstar is a smaller version of the giant superstores. Don't think for a moment you won't find a huge selection of titles; these stores are just a little smaller and have a cozier atmosphere. The Rosecrans store, for example, is in the old Loma Theater and still sports the bright blue neon marquee outside. As you move through the store toward where the screen used to be, the floor gently slopes, just the way it did when theater seats occupied the floor instead of bookshelves. Many patrons whisk their purchases next door to the Pannikin coffeehouse and restaurant and begin reading in seats rescued from the adjacent movie house when it was gutted to make Bookstar.

The sales staff at Bookstar is great for helping you locate a title in their computerized inventory. And if what you want isn't in stock, they'll be happy to order it for you.

Borders Books, Music & Cafe
1072 Camino del Rio N., San Diego
(619) 295-2201
www.borders.com
This mammoth 25,000-square-foot bookstore is located in the Mission Valley Center West shopping mall, and like its counterparts (see the Web site for more county locations), it is a combination bookstore, music store, and cafe.

In addition to carrying more than 200,000 book titles, DVDs, and videos, the store features the Borders' Cafe Espresso, where customers are encouraged to sip a cup of coffee while they read their latest purchase.

Something special always seems to be going on at Borders, whether it's a book signing, a live music performance (usually on Friday), or a children's event. The comfortable interior induces shoppers to hang around and enjoy all the activity.

Controversial Bookstore
3021 University Avenue, San Diego
(619) 296-1560
www.controversialbookstore.com
Since 1964 this bookstore has been selling just about everything except mainstream books. Spirituality, religion, metaphysics, and wellness are among the popular subjects here. Also offered are new age music and videos, crystals, jewelry, tarot cards, and other gifts.

Family Christian Store
3231 Sports Arena Boulevard, San Diego
(619) 224-2863
Serving the Christian community, this store has a wide selection of religious books, CDs, tapes, and gift items. It's also a treasure trove of church and Sunday school supplies. If there's something you need that is not in stock, the staff is great for handling quick mail orders.

Gaslamp Books, Prints, & Wyatt Earp Museum
413 Market Street, San Diego
(619) 237-1492
For that one-of-a-kind find, this is the place. Although the shop is diminutive, it has an interesting selection of old magazines, prints, and books. Complimenting all the reading material is a nice collection of antiques. And don't miss the Wyatt Earp Museum on the premises. It's a little-known tidbit of history that Wyatt Earp

Many specialty stores also sell books. If you're looking for a book on climbing opportunities, a sporting goods specialty store such as Adventure 16 or REI might have a better selection than a bookstore.

was a saloon owner in the early days of San Diego. Closed Sunday.

Upstart Crow Bookstore & Coffee House
Seaport Village, 835 West Harbor Drive
San Diego
(619) 232-4855
www.upstartcrowtrading.com

Long before coffeehouses became popular, and eons before anyone thought to combine a coffeehouse with a bookstore, Upstart Crow was doing it, and doing it well. Located right in the middle of sometimes chaotic Seaport Village, it's an oasis of calm. You can enjoy a steaming cup of coffee or tea while you're surrounded by stacks and stacks of books, all begging for a reader. Although small, the store has a good cross-section of titles, plenty to keep you occupied. Open 9:00 A.M. to 9:00 P.M.; until 10:00 P.M. during the summer.

Wahrenbrock's Book House
726 Broadway, San Diego
(619) 232-0132

No one knows exactly how many books are in Wahrenbrock's—not even the owners. But look around and you'll surely guess that there must be at least a million. Most of the books are used, but Wahrenbrock's does have some new ones scattered about its three floors. Loosely organized by subject matter, the books offer a browser's paradise. And if you're looking for something specific, ask a pleasant, helpful staff member. Even with all those titles and no real system to catalogue them, the staff usually knows exactly what they have and where it can be found. If you have a rare book, this is a great place to get an appraisal. Closed Sunday.

Warwick's
7812 Girard Avenue, La Jolla
(858) 454-0347
www.warwicks.com

If a celebrity author comes to San Diego for a book signing, Warwick's is where he or she will likely end up; Senator Hillary Clinton has been one of the most popular speakers to date. Other well-known personalities who have recently appeared are Maya Angelou, Anne Rice, Suze Orman, and senators Barbara Boxer and John McCain. Large for an independent, Warwick's carries 40,000 titles along with books on cassette, large-print books, maps, and globes. One half of the store is dedicated to gifts and stationery, so chances are you'll find a nice, albeit pricey, memento in addition to a new book. The store carries some of the children's books once stocked at the venerable White Rabbit, now closed.

North County Coastal

Barnes & Noble
2615 Vista Way, Oceanside
(760) 529-0106

12835 El Camino Real, Del Mar
(858) 481-4038
www.bn.com

The Barnes & Noble chain is justly proud of its commitment to customer service. If you need a book, they'll help you find it, and if it's not in the store, they'll special-order it for you. Since the stores are open 9:00 A.M. to 11:00 P.M. daily, they're convenient to visit, too. Both have large children's departments and sometimes have story times or special kids' events. In these locations there are more than 150,000 titles close to your book-loving fingertips.

Book Works
2670 Via de la Valle, Del Mar
(858) 755-3735
www.book-works.com

Book Works has been helping book lovers

satisfy their reading needs since the late 1970s. Located at the Flower Hill Promenade, it offers new and best-selling books, as well as some used ones. The shop hosts several author discussions and book signings a month. It also offers magazines (both foreign and domestic), unusual cards and stationery, English garden statuary, and wonderful vintage decorative accessories.

You can also get a cup of coffee or tea next door at an Insiders' cafe paradise, the Pannikin Cafe.

Paperback Book Exchange
578 Carlsbad Village Drive, Carlsbad
(760) 729-4100
If you love to read and are looking for bargains, you must stop in at the Paperback Book Exchange, which has been doing business in Carlsbad for 20 years. This store is just ½ block east of the antiques, cafe, and coffeehouse shopping district of downtown Carlsbad and about 2 blocks south of the Coaster station.

Most of the books have been pre-read (i.e., they're used), and the prices are right. If you're hooked on an author of paperback fiction, call the store to see which titles are in stock, since inventory turns over quickly. They specialize in no particular genre, purveying everything from science fiction and horror to contemporary fiction, historical romance, westerns, and war. Closed Sunday.

Sacred Pathway
282 North El Camino Real, Encinitas
(760) 436-7740
www.sacredpathway.com
Here you'll find candles, oils, and jewelry along with a fine collection of books on topics ranging from traditional metaphysics to spirituality.

If you simply must know your future or have questions about a specific forecasting technique, you're in luck: There are daily psychic readings (tarot, palm reading, or astrology; it's best to call ahead for an appointment) and monthly psychic fairs that host guest metaphysical experts. If you're looking for a spiritual piece of artwork (including ones in glass, wood, or pottery), you'll especially enjoy the gallery.

Soulscape
765 South Coast Highway, #106, Encinitas
(760) 753-2345
In the Lumberyard Mall, Soulscape is a metaphysical and spiritual bookstore with tomes on well-known topics like astrology as well as lesser-known ones like Celtic crop circles and sacred altars. There are some books for children, too. It also has a wonderful selection of cards and gifts, including music, jewelry, incense, crystals, and spiritual art.

North County Inland

Barnes & Noble
810 West Valley Parkway, Escondido
(760) 480-2760

11744 Carmel Mountain Road, Rancho Bernardo
(858) 674-1055
www.bn.com
Part of the fine chain of bookstores found throughout the country, these stores, with their atmosphere of calm, are especially inviting on a hectic weekend. While some bookstores have noisy, boisterous events, here you'll find people who've come to quietly browse, and the staff is happy to have them.

In no time at all, shoppers can be directed to a special book or have it special-ordered. As at other Barnes & Nobles, there's a sizeable selection of children's books and a place for kids and parents to sit and preview them.

Borders Books, Music & Cafe
11160 Rancho Carmel Drive, San Diego
(858) 618-1814
www.borders.com
While the address says the store is offi-

cially in San Diego, it's really in the Carmel Mountain region. The store is immense, as you'd expect a Borders to be. It's a busy place with lots going on. If you're the type who loves a cozy, peaceful (read that quiet) bookstore, you won't find your bibliophile heaven here. It can get noisy, busy, and crowded on weekends. The children's area is in the back of the store; this is where the many story times are held and where parents can sit and read to their little ones. Pick up a newsletter of current events, including poetry readings and author book signings.

There's a cafe on-site for a cup of tea or coffee and a sweet treat, and no one looks twice if you take the snack to a comfortable reading area.

Waldenbooks
200 East Via Rancho Parkway, Escondido
(760) 746-4859
Located at the North County Faire Shopping Mall, this Waldenbooks is especially inviting when you've been on a shopping spree. There's a calm atmosphere in the store, and the staff is very willing to allow you to browse. They'll special-order books, too, if they don't have them in their large stock.

Ask about book clubs and upcoming events, including signings by local and national authors.

East County

Barnes & Noble
5500 Grossmont Center Drive, La Mesa
Grossmont Center
(619) 667-2870

Santee Trolley Square, Santee
9938 Mission Gorge Road
(619) 562-1755
www.bn.com
Like others in the chain, these have a real commitment to customer service.

All Barnes & Noble stores are open seven days a week and have large children's departments. If you need help finding one of the more than 150,000 titles in stock, the staff will be glad to assist. Pick up a newsletter to find out about their children's story hour and author book signings. They have special book clubs for seniors and contemporary fiction. It's open Sunday until 10:00 P.M.; other days until 11:00 P.M.

Romance World
854 Jackman Street, El Cajon
(619) 588-5494
www.romanceworldbooks.com
If you adore romantic fiction, head to Romance World for oodles of books from authors ranging from Debbie Macomber to Barbara Cartland. Even if you have to make the drive from another part of the county, if you love this genre, you have to visit this store. Here you'll find romance books from the top to the bottom of the shelves. You might get to see one of your favorite authors, too, as the store occasionally attracts big-name romance authors for signings. Call for an events schedule or to find out what's going on in the store. The staff will special-order hard-to-find books.

Yellow Book Road
7200 Parkway Drive, La Mesa
(619) 463-4900
This children's and teachers' bookstore attracts people from throughout the county because of its wonderful books and good selection of resource materials for teachers. If the staff doesn't stock what you're looking for, they will get it. There's a newsletter and calendar of events, and they draw in famous children's authors for signings.

South Bay

B. Dalton Bookseller
Plaza Bonita Shopping Center
3030 Plaza Bonita Road, National City
(619) 267-1294
For the largest selection of titles, this is South Bay's best bet. You're likely to find

exactly what you're looking for in this pleasant, well-organized store. Like all B Daltons, this store is open daily and has friendly and helpful salespeople.

Family Christian Store
639 Broadway, Chula Vista
(619) 425-4223
Like the other stores in this chain, Family Christian Store serves the Christian community with a wide selection of religious gifts as well as books, CDs, and tapes—some in Spanish. Although they don't carry them in stock, Sunday school supplies can be special-ordered.

Gracie's Book Nook
1722 Sweetwater Road, National City
(619) 474-4464
For the best in bedtime reading material, Gracie's is the place. The "gently read" selection of titles includes mystery, romance, general fiction, true crime, and science fiction. It's always a pleasure to search the shelves for the latest gem to hit Gracie's, and you can't beat the prices. If you're like most Insider bibliophiles, you know what a treat it is to find a great used bookstore, and Gracie's is tops in South Bay in the Sweetwater Crossing Shopping Center.

ANTIQUES

Central San Diego

Adams Avenue Antique Row
Adams Avenue, between Texas Street and 40th Street, San Diego
www.adamsaveonline.com
You could make a day of browsing through the nearly two dozen antiques shops that stretch along Adams Avenue. Stop in at Zac's Attic at 2922 Adams Avenue if you're looking for the perfect piece to complete a room. The Kensington Antique Parlour at 2938 Adams Avenue is overflowing with a variety of antiques, including toys, jewelry, porcelain, art, and furniture as well as historical items and textiles.

Insiders love to do their holiday shopping at the juried Harvest Festival. During the three-day event at the Del Mar Fairgrounds, hundreds of vendors sell handmade items—everything from furniture to fine art. The entrance price is steep ($8.00 for adults), but die-hard shoppers make a day of it, and local shops offer coupons. For information call (415) 447-3205 or visit www.harvestfestival.com.

D.D. Allen Antiques
7728 Fay Avenue, La Jolla
(858) 454-8708, (877) DDALLEN
www.ddallen.com
Shopping in La Jolla always results in something special, and nowhere is that more true than at D.D. Allen Antiques. You'll marvel at the antique linens and quilts or the baskets and beadwork. If figurines are on your list, D.D. Allen has tons of them, along with antique furniture, oil paintings, silver, bronze, crystal, and glass.

House of Heirlooms
801 University Avenue, San Diego
(619) 298-0502
This upscale shop is an Insiders' favorite for its comprehensive selection of quality antiques. Among the treasures you'll find here are English furniture from the '30s and '40s, silver, china tea sets, cut glass, brass, and oodles of decorative accessories.

Ocean Beach Antique Mall
4926 Newport Avenue, San Diego
(619) 223-6170
Dozens of antiques stores line Newport Avenue, some in malls or centers, some standing alone. This one has a dood selection of antiques and collectibles, or cruise up and down the street to check out the competition.

North County Coastal

Antique Warehouse
212 South Cedros Avenue, Solana Beach
(858) 755-5156

Under one warehouse roof (15,000 square feet and perfect when you want to shop for antiques and it's wintry outdoors), this mall has more than 100 shops, and new merchandise arrives daily. If you're on a Cedros Avenue antiques hunt, this is a good starting point for your journey.

There's great variety here: shops that specialize in bottles, brass, Depression glass, vintage clothing, western gear, and pewter. There's always coffee and refreshments for the weary shopper. Parking and all shops are on ground level. Ask at the front desk to be steered toward specific genres or periods. They are closed on Tuesday.

Estate Sale Warehouse
1719 South Coast Highway, Oceanside
(760) 433-6549

This store is more on the collectible end of antiques than others, but if you're looking for good-quality used furniture—perhaps doing a room in '60s retro—then head to Oceanside. You'll find unusual period pieces and truly great prices. Like the name says, these are estate sale pieces—and they move in and out fast.

McNally Company Antiques
6033 Paseo Delicias, Rancho Santa Fe
(858) 756-1922
www.mcnallycompanyantiques.com

McNally's is the place if you're looking for 18th- and 19th-century furnishings or just love to browse through classic furniture. Here you'll find estate pieces, objets d'art, and investment collectibles. They also carry quality items in silver. The store isn't open on Sunday or Monday; other days of the week the hours are 10-ish to 5-ish. Really, that's what the sign on the door says.

Vinge Antiques
3087 State Street, Carlsbad
(760) 729-7081

Discover their china (lovely teapots were everywhere during our last visit), Depression glass, and glassware that some of us used in the '60s and '70s (which is selling for collectible prices now), along with paintings, too.

North County Inland

Antique Village
983 Grand Avenue, San Marcos
(760) 744-8718
www.antiquevillageinc.com

Antique Village has more than 65 stores, and that makes for excellent shopping. You'll find everything from unique collectible garden accessories to glassware collectibles here. And if you love oak and vintage furniture, there's sure to be a piece to tempt you.

This store has one of the largest selections of antiques in North County Inland. If you're looking for something distinctive and adore the country look, head in this direction.

Hidden Valley Antique Emporium
333 East Grand Avenue, Escondido
(760) 737-0333
www.hiddenvalleyantiques.com

Imagine more than 10,000 square feet of antiques shopping. It's here at Hidden Valley Antique Emporium. Currently there are more than 60 shops under one roof, and they have layaway. They're open until 5:00 P.M. on Sunday; other days the hours are from 10:00 A.M. until 5:30 P.M. Parking can be found along nearby side streets.

South Bay

Gibson & Gibson Antique Lighting
180 Mace Street #C9, Chula Vista
(619) 422-2447
www.gibsonandgibsonantiquelighting.com

Antique lighting is the specialty at Gibson & Gibson in Chula Vista, both originals and reproductions. Does your home need an antique lamp to set off your favorite room?

This is the place to find it. The store has two warehouses full of fixtures and lamps, and upon learning of your decorating desires, will show you pieces from its vast collections. It's essential to call first to make sure an employee is on-site when you want to visit.

While on vacation in San Diego or just spending the day in galleries and boutiques, consider buying fine art or unique crafts to stockpile as gifts. You'll not only avoid the less-than-festive shopping hysteria around major holidays, you'll support local artisans as well.

SWAP MEETS AND FLEA MARKETS

Central San Diego

Kobey's Swap Meet
3500 Sports Arena Boulevard, San Diego (at the Sports Arena)
(619) 226-0650
www.kobeyswap.com
Opened in 1980, Kobey's has become San Diego's largest open-air swap meet. Both new and used merchandise as well as many a hidden treasure can be found at Kobey's, and you don't need a fortune to come home with lots of goodies. Clothing, jewelry, collectibles, electronics, fresh flowers, baked goods, and produce are just some of the items to be found. Hot dogs, hot pretzels, and other survival-genre food and beverages are available on the premises. The swap meet is open Friday through Sunday from 7:00 A.M. until 3:00 P.M. Admission is 50 cents on Friday; $1.00 on Saturday and Sunday. Children younger than 12 are admitted free.

North County Coastal

Oceanside Drive-In Swap Meet
3480 West Mission Avenue, Oceanside
(760) 757-5286
The swap meet is held 7:00 A.M. to 3:00 P.M. each Saturday and Sunday and on holiday Mondays at this Oceanside location. Treasures to trash are found here.

There's new and used merchandise, and bargaining is encouraged by many of the regular vendors. This swap meet is said to be one of the biggest in Southern California. Most Insiders agree that it's definitely one of the largest in North County. Admission is 75 cents on Saturday and $1.50 on Sunday.

Seaside Bazaar
1 block south of Encinitas Boulevard on South Coast Highway 101, Encinitas
(760) 753-1611
Every weekend for the last 25 years, vendors and shoppers have been coming to this import craft bazaar to sell, buy, and marvel at the merchandise: books, jewelry, and clothing imports from around the world as well as crafts, antiques, collectibles, flowers, plants, and home-decorating items. *Sunset* magazine once called it one of the "secret finds along the coast." A secret no more, this North County Coastal sale still offers opportunities to find a bargain, if not an outright prize. It's open weekends 10:00 A.M. to 4:00 P.M. year-round. There is no admission fee.

North County Inland

Escondido Drive-In Swap Meet
600 West Washington Street, Escondido
(760) 745-3100
The swap meet is held year-round, Wednesday and Thursday 7:00 A.M. to 3:00 P.M.; Friday 3:00 to 9:30 P.M.; Saturday and Sunday 7:00 A.M. to 4:00 P.M. There are food booths, a farmers' market, and lots of treasures in new and used merchandise. Admission ranges from $1.00 to $1.50; it's free on Thursday.

If you enjoy browsing, the Cedros Shopping District supplies great galleries along with antiques stores. It's about 3 blocks from the Coaster commuter train stop in Solana Beach.

East County

Spring Valley Swap Meet
6377 Quarry Road, Spring Valley
(619) 463-1194

If beauty is in the eye of the beholder, then you may find some beautiful items for sale at this East County swap meet. When you go you can never predict what will be there. And isn't that half the fun?

Generally speaking, there's new and used merchandise, antiques, collectibles, farmers' market produce, foods, and stuff that you probably just have to take home. The admission is 50 cents for adults, and the vendors are open from 7:00 A.M. to 3:00 P.M. on Saturday and Sunday throughout the year.

South Bay

National City Swap Meet
3201 D Avenue, National City
(at the Harbor Drive-in Theater)
(619) 477-2203

Every Saturday and Sunday 50 cents will get you into this swap meet that's primarily of the garage-sale variety. Household items and collectibles are abundant, but you will find some new items, too. Show up early; things usually start rolling by about 7:00 A.M. It ends around 4:00 P.M. Half a dozen snack bars and food vendors are scattered throughout the swap meet. Be sure to wear a hat and bring your sunscreen.

UNIQUE AND INTRIGUING

Central San Diego

Ace Hardware
1007 University Avenue, Hillcrest
(619) 291-5988

7756 Girard Avenue, La Jolla
(858) 454-6101

Looking for some nuts and bolts? You'll find them here, along with thousands of things you'd never expect to see in a hardware store. Time after time we hear locals say they stopped into the Hillcrest or La Jolla Ace Hardware and had a hard time leaving. There's just so much to look at. Along with traditional hardware items, check out the plants, gift items, antique hardware pieces, and all those other little things you never thought you needed until you saw them here.

Adelaide's
7766 Girard Avenue, La Jolla
(858) 454-0146
www.adelaidesflowers.com

This world-class florist sells live plants (they have lovely orchids), pretty vases, scented candles, and clever things for the garden. But it's their floral arrangements that will make you swoon. As you near the storefront, the aroma of Julian lilac or other seasonal plants will stop you in your tracks, as will the dazzling displays of flowers not found elsewhere—like peonies, tulips, and lilies of the valley. Their arrangements are top-notch as well.

The Black
5017 Newport Avenue, San Diego
(619) 222-5498

Back in the '60s and early '70s, this was the best-known "head shop" in town. Today it's fun, if only for the sake of nostalgia, to take a trip back through time as you enter The Black, which still sells beads, bongs, incense, psychedelic art, and candles, along with calendars, beachwear, and cigars, pipes, and pipe tobacco. The adjacent Black Bead sells everything you might need in small baubles and beads.

IKEA
2149 Fenton Parkway, San Diego
(619) 563-4532
www.ikea.com

It's not unique, because there are IKEA stores around the world. But this massive, endless, and inexpensive store certainly qualifies as intriguing. About 0.5 mile west of Qualcomm Stadium, this superstore has a huge inventory of everything needed for the home. Styles vary, but most of the furniture—from bedroom to kitchen and beyond—is based on Swedish modern. You'll find Persian rugs, modern and wacky lamps, lots of kitchen accoutrements, beds, and office furniture as well as essentials such as wastebaskets and cutting boards. In fact, there's so much here that you'll eventually give up and run screaming to the small cafeteria, which serves hot food as well as coffee, tea, sodas, and soft drinks. Merchandise found in the second-floor showroom can be picked up in the warehouse below; in other departments you just pop the item into your cart.

Museum Shops of Balboa Park
Balboa Park, San Diego

Every single museum in Balboa Park has a gift shop offering distinctive gifts from around the world. You could plan an entire day around nothing but shopping in Balboa Park, especially if you're looking for something a little different.

Books, textiles, jewelry, and ceramics are available at the Mingei International Museum. At the Museum of Photographic Arts you'll find photo kits, cards, posters, and frames. Or how about some sports-related gift items from the San Diego Hall of Champions? See our chapter on Balboa Park for a complete listing of museums and their locations.

My Own Space
7840 Girard Avenue, La Jolla
(858) 459-0099
www.mosmyownspace.com

Upscale and modern bedding, lighting, and home accessories can be found within My Own Space's online catalog, but they are best appreciated in the La Jolla store, where you can run your fingers through the expensive wool rugs that look like they're made of rose petals, and other innovative products. Even the designer cat and dog food bowls are fun, and expensive.

99 Ranch Market
7330 Clairemont Mesa Boulevard
San Diego
(858) 565-7799
www.99ranch.com

Have you ever wandered into those mysterious, small Asian markets that are stuffed with unusual food items you've never seen before? Imagine that small market expanded to supermarket size, and you'll have an idea of what 99 Ranch is like. It's huge—make no mistake—and if you're seeking an obscure Asian food or ingredient, you'll find it here. Don't miss the fresh fish display, and there are mounds of vegetables, both exotic and pedestrian, to complete your Asian feast. In the front of the store are stalls selling exotic drinks, frozen things, and hot food. Definitely worth a try!

Walter Andersen's Nursery
3642 Enterprise Street, San Diego
(619) 224-8271

When you step into Walter Andersen's, you'll find the usual assortment of trees, shrubs, bedding plants, bulbs, and garden tools—in spades. But what makes this nursery a treasure—and one of the most expensive in town—is the staff. If you need advice,

---

i

In the San Marcos Shopping District, furniture is the name of the game. The stretch along 2 miles of Los Vallecitos Boulevard, in the heart of San Marcos, sells everything from bedding to bar stools at excellent prices. After a day of shopping, head over to restaurant row, on San Marcos Boulevard.

Here in San Diego, shopping attire is California casual. Sneakers or sandals, shorts, and a shirt are suitable for malls and stores. In the shops in La Jolla, Del Mar, and Rancho Santa Fe, you may feel more comfortable with a slightly upscale version of this very same dress code.

an opinion, or just some conversation about what's growing in your garden, the certified nursery professionals are only too happy to oblige. You'll learn more here in an hour than you would in a month of horticultural study. In other words, these folks know their stuff, and they're glad to share it. Just in case you're looking for something exotic, Walter Andersen's has that, too, along with many native plants and trees.

The White House Black Market
7927 Girard Avenue, La Jolla
(858) 459-2565

1555 Camino del Mar, Del Mar Plaza
(858) 794-0355

1911 Calle Barcelona, The Forum, Carlsbad
(760) 942-7846
Here's an interesting twist—women's clothing and accessories all in shades of white and black. Just walking through this classy store makes you feel like you're shopping for the perfect outfit for an afternoon sipping Bellini cocktails on a terrace overlooking Italy's Lake Como. From casual to dressy, the prices are affordable, and the clothes are adorable. The White House has a store in the Del Mar Plaza shopping center, too.

Whole Foods
711 University Avenue, San Diego
(619) 294-2800

8825 Villa La Jolla Drive, La Jolla
(858) 642-6700
www.wholefoodsmarket.com
Farmers' markets are ideal for picking up organic produce and other goodies, but they're usually open only one day a week. Whole Foods, with a similar selection of freshly picked strawberries and whole-grain breads, is open every day. You won't find a larger array of organically grown produce, whole grains, fresh fish, poultry and meats, and herbs and vitamins. The Hillcrest neighborhood store has Jamba Juice, with smoothies and fresh-squeezed everything, while the La Jolla location features healthful meals or coffee and dessert at Mrs. Gooch's Cafe.

North County Coastal

Anderson's La Costa Nursery
400 La Costa Avenue, Encinitas
(760) 753-3153
www.andersonslacostanursery.com
Possibly the best nursery and garden specialty store ever conceived, Anderson's La Costa Nursery is far from a secret, though their "secret garden" is not to be missed. This is the place to wander and dream of what your garden can be and then to select perfect plants (that will thrive after they're home).

In addition to plants, trees, and specialty items (such as bromeliads and proteas and huge potted palms), you'll find an enticing collection of wind chimes, bird feeders, statuary, and garden art. The herbs and perennials are worth the drive from all points in the county, and in the winter months you can get David Austin and Old English roses here that are hard to find at other nurseries. Call ahead if you're searching for something special; their knowledgeable staff can answer your plant-care questions.

Carlsbad Danish Bakery
2805 Roosevelt Street, Carlsbad
(760) 729-6186
If you're visiting the antiques shopping district in Carlsbad, you may want to take a short walk (1 block east and 1 block north) to Roosevelt Street, where you'll find this hidden secret of sweet temptation. The Carlsbad Danish Bakery can

offer you a perfect muffin or sweet treat (try the oatmeal cookies and the bran muffins—they're to die for) and a hot cup of coffee or tea. Take home a loaf of their multigrain bread, too.

Their wedding and special-occasion cakes are known as the best throughout North County Coastal. They are beautiful and taste even better.

This is a popular Insiders' hangout—often packed—so you may have the chance to browse through the offerings before it's your turn at the counter. You can eat here, too, inside or in the fresh air; try coffee and cake at an umbrella-covered table. The bakery choices run out after about 3:00 P.M. and the bakers don't make the same treats every day, so it's best to come early. The bakery is closed on Sunday.

Mary's Tack & Feed
3675 Via De La Valle, Del Mar
(858) 755-2015
This is a horse lover's and pet lover's shopping heaven and the best place along the coast if you need a bale of hay or a new set of spurs. Frequented by the upscale residents of Rancho Santa Fe and Fairbanks Ranch, the store is a fun browse, and the staff is friendly and knowledgeable on pet-oriented topics.

Weidners' Gardens
695 Normandy Road, Encinitas
(760) 436-2194
Every day except Tuesday, the gardens are open from 9:30 A.M. to 5:00 P.M. for retail sales. This family-owned nursery was formerly called Begonia Gardens, but Mary Weidner changed the name because many thought that was the only flower for sale. In fact, you'll find perfect tuberous begonias of all varieties, from tiny hanging plants to monster-size specimens, but you'll also find fuscias, impatiens, and other flowers. The nursery sells many new introductions—plants that the public hasn't seen before—and specializes in hanging baskets. At Christmastime there's a fine collection of superfresh poinsettias.

North County Inland

Orchid Source
2426 Cherimoya Drive, Vista
(760) 727-2611, (888) 727-2760
www.orchidsource.com
If you're hooked on orchids, you'll have to include this place on any plant-seeking expedition. Here you'll find cymbidiums, oncidiums, phalaenopsis, cattleyas, and dendrobiums by the score. All plants are of premium quality, and the helpful staff will tell you what each one requires to keep it happy. They'll also give you plenty of instruction on how to get started in the exotic world of orchids.

East County

Branding Iron
629 Main Street, Ramona
(760) 789-5050
An old-fashioned Western apparel and tack store, the Branding Iron has everything from silver bits and spurs to horse blankets and felt cowboy hats. You'll also be tempted with jeans, Western clothing, boots, moccasins, and Western collectibles; and if you happen to need some hay or oats for Trigger, you're in the right place, too. This is a real Western-wear store, and shopping is just part of the experience as you tour the aisles.

Dudley's Bakery
30218 Highway 78, Santa Ysabel
(760) 765-0488, (800) 225-3348
www.dudleysbakery.com
This bakery is a treasure, and while visitors might see it as being smack-dab out in nowhere, they have to admit it's busy. In fact, people drive from all over Southern California for a loaf of Dudley's bread. And if you're going to Julian, it's an absolute "must stop." (But remember—it's closed both Monday and Tuesday.)

The bread is so good, you'll want to take some home, but which loaf? There are 17 different types to tempt you, including loaves of bright orange cheddar cheese bread and enormous, 1.5-pound rounds of date-nut, sheepherder, or jalapeño bread. Dudley's also has a cafe, which is especially busy during holidays and on weekends. But that's okay. While you wait you can snack on the bread you've bought.

Summers Past Farms
15602 Old Highway 80, Flinn Springs
(619) 390-1523
www.summerspastfarms.com
A friendly place where cats tend to wind about your ankles, this nursery attracts gardeners, plant lovers, and those looking for a special gift with an herbal or natural theme. Visit the herbal soap shop and factory, children's garden, vegetable garden, cutting garden, and fragrance garden. The store also holds craft demos and classes. If you're hooked on crafts like wreaths and soap-making, call the shop or visit the Web site to see what's planned during your visit.

We recently attended a free seminar on how to grow, enjoy, cook with, and soothe the body with lavender. The shop and gardens are closed on Monday and Tuesday.

South Bay

General Bead
317 National City Boulevard, National City
(619) 336-0100
www.genbead.com
Whether you're looking for a few beads to decorate your favorite jacket or you need hundreds of beads for that special craft project, you won't be disappointed at General Bead. Choose from among 18,000 items spread out across 3,000 square feet. Beads of all sizes, shapes, and colors will dazzle you and inspire your creative nature. It's closed Monday.

My Bridal Gown
281 Third Avenue, Chula Vista
(619) 407-4075
You'll be overwhelmed by the more than 1,000 designer bridal gowns that this store stocks. Expert bridal consultants will help you select the perfect gown in sizes 4 to 40 for a storybook wedding. If there's something special you have in mind, My Bridal Gown can order direct from the manufacturer at a substantial savings. Your attendants will be delighted by the large selection of bridesmaids' dresses and accessories.

National City Mile of Cars
National City Boulevard, between 24th and 30th Streets, National City
If you're in the market for a new car but are undecided about exactly what you want, drive to National City, park, and start walking. Car dealers line National City Boulevard. Every make and model you could possibly think of is here, so you can test-drive all your favorites without having to visit dealers all over town.

ATTRACTIONS

Besides the glorious climate, why do so many people visit and settle in San Diego? Attractions. We have them by the boatload, and they're as varied as the county itself.

Sure, we have the places to go and the things to see that you've read about in glossy publications and books. We're justly proud of the famous San Diego Zoo and its "sister," the Wild Animal Park, a 2,300-acre park that's home to 3,000 critters great and small. We love to talk about the history of Old Town, the family of creatures at SeaWorld, and the San Diego Hall of Champions, with its collection featuring numerous sports and a mountain of memorabilia. These are great, but there's more.

For instance, take the Surf Museum in Oceanside, where you can learn the history of surfing (it began in 1907), or downtown's floating museum aboard the aircraft carrier *Midway*. Want to visit some lovely gardens? You can't beat the tranquil beauty and luscious variety of plants at Quail Botanical Gardens.

Now blend this cauldron of interesting places with the excitement of casinos, high-energy fun at water parks, and the thrill of roller-coastering at Belmont Park in Mission Beach. Include the things you'll learn at the Stephen Birch Aquarium and the Chula Vista Nature Center, and you've taken just a sip of the attractions that are all within an hour's drive of downtown San Diego.

In this hefty chapter we've included our favorite attractions, including the quirky ones, the notable ones, and the ones we always share when friends come to town. Prices and hours are as current as we can make them. You may want to call ahead, however, in case these have recently changed.

As you browse through this chapter, keep in mind that these activities and not-to-be-missed places may also be described in other chapters. For instance, there is so much to see and do at Balboa Park that you'll find an entire chapter devoted to this jewel of San Diego. Other entries may reappear in Kidstuff or Parks or Nightlife. So to get the most of our chunk of paradise, you'll want to refer to the index to get all the details on your favorites. Like most of our other chapters, this one is organized by geographic region and then by alphabetical listings within each region.

So grab your camera, pack a lunch or some snacks for the road, and let's hit it. There's plenty to do in San Diego and just so many hours in a day.

CENTRAL SAN DIEGO

Balboa Park
1549 El Prado, San Diego
(619) 239-0512

Balboa Park is truly the heart of San Diego, both geographically and culturally. You could spend a whole day in the park and barely scratch the surface of all there is to do. Rather than try to cram Balboa Park into a few short paragraphs, we've devoted an entire chapter to an in-depth description of all it has to offer. But just to give you a taste of what you'll find, we'll start with, of course, the world-famous San Diego Zoo. That's a day's expedition all by itself. Another day could easily be spent going through its museums—the Aerospace Museum, the Natural History Museum, the Museum of Photography, and the Model Railroad Museum, just to name a few. The miniature railroad and the historic merry-go-round are favorites with the kids, and both adults and youngsters flock to the Ruben H. Fleet Space Theater and Science Center for IMAX films and hands-on exhibits. If you plan to spend the day at Balboa Park, turn to its chapter and we'll give you the whole low-down, including some tips on scheduling your time. You'll find even more informa-

Decommissioned in 1981, the Point Loma lighthouse is still a major and beautiful San Diego icon. PHOTO: COURTESY OF CHARLIE MANZ

tion about entertainment in the park in The Arts chapter.

Belmont Amusement Park
3146 Mission Boulevard, San Diego
(858) 488-0668
www.giantdipper.com

Home of the Giant Dipper, one of two remaining antique wooden roller coasters in California, Belmont Park is a small amusement park featuring rides, restaurants, and attractions for the whole family. In the tradition of Coney Island in New York, Belmont Park sits alongside the beach, and the ocean view from the top of the Giant Dipper is spectacular, though the roller coaster itself is quite tame by today's standards.

Besides the roller coaster, you can enjoy an arcade, the Bumper Cars, an endless wave machine, the Vertical Plunge (a three-story drop), the Liberty Carousel, the Sea Serpent ride, a Crazy Submarine, and Baja Buggies. If those seem too much for the young ones, they may enjoy Pirates Cove, a play facility with more than 7,000 square feet of tunnels, slides, and a ball pool. Adults and kids will enjoy the arcade game center and CyberStation, which has a collection of the latest electronic games.

One of the park's oldest and best-loved attractions is the indoor Plunge, a nice alternative to the salty ocean. Built in 1925, it's Southern California's largest indoor swimming pool. When you get hungry, stop at the food court, which has numerous fast-food establishments, or enjoy one of the oceanfront restaurants within the park.

Admission to the park is free; rides and attractions are priced separately, or you can buy a wristband for unlimited riding. For good, old-fashioned family fun, try combining a day at the beach with a visit to Belmont Park.

Boomer's
6999 Clairemont Mesa Boulevard
San Diego
(858) 560-4211
www.boomersparks.com

Like its sister venue in El Cajon, this Boomer's has enough going on to entertain and occupy kids (and Mom and Dad, too) for a full day or evening. In addition to the attractions offered by the other centers—miniature golf courses, batting cages, bumper boats, go-karts, and huge arcades—this one also has a laser-runner venue and a Country Fair Fun Zone with amusement park rides for smaller children.

Summer hours correspond to traditional summer vacation months and school holidays. The park is open daily at 10:00 A.M. and closes at 11:00 P.M. Sunday through Thursday, midnight on Friday and Saturday. Winter hours are reduced, so be sure to call before you go. The various attractions are priced separately, or you can purchase an all-day wristband: $21 for bigger kids, $16 for smaller fry. Every Tuesday and Thursday, play unlimited video games for $10.

Cabrillo National Monument
1800 Cabrillo Memorial Drive, San Diego
(619) 557-5450
www.nps.gov/cabr

High above San Diego Harbor, at the tip of the Point Loma peninsula, is the Cabrillo National Monument. The monument commemorates the 1542 landing of Juan Rodríguez Cabrillo in what is now San Diego and acknowledges that he was the first European to set foot on the West Coast. After stopping at the visitor center, which has information about the park, exhibits, and films, make a beeline to the Old Point Loma Lighthouse for a trip back in time. Your tour of the lighthouse, built in 1854, will remind you of the days of sailing ships and oil lamps. Back when it was a working lighthouse, its light could be seen 39 miles out to sea.

Once you've taken in the panoramic views of the harbor from the lighthouse, stroll along the 2-mile bayside trail that descends 300 feet through the cliffs and is surrounded by native sage scrub, prickly pear cactus, and yucca. It passes remnants of the defense system used to protect the harbor during both world wars. Finally, take a short drive down to the tide pools and check out the shore crabs, bat stars, dead man's fingers, sea hares, and many other fascinating sea creatures there.

Since fall 2003 the tide pools have been included in the paid part of the park—no more freebies! Keep in mind that the rocks around the tide pools are slippery, and the barnacles can be sharp. Wear sturdy, nonslip shoes. And remember, federal law prohibits collecting marine animals, shells, or rocks.

The park is open daily from 9:00 A.M. to 5:15 P.M. (6:15 P.M. in summer). Admission is $5.00 per vehicle and $3.00 per bicyclist, jogger, walker, or city bus passenger.

Buy a one-, two-, three-, five-, or seven-day Go San Diego Card ($49 to $159 for adults, $39 to $109 for kids) for big savings on multiple San Diego attractions and even tours to L.A., Temecula wine country, and Tijuana. Major parks that honor the pass are LEGOLAND and the San Diego Zoo, but there are dozens of other attractions, bay and walking tours, and other forms of entertainment, making this a great deal for visitors on the go, or even Insiders who want to get out and enjoy their county. A number of good restaurants and shops offer discounts, usually 10 to 20 percent, to cardholders. You can buy it locally at The International Visitor's Information Center, 1040 ⅓ West Broadway at Harbor Drive, (619) 236-1212, at other San Diego locations, or on the Internet at www.gosandiego.com, where you also can see a complete list of participating attractions.

Dave & Buster's
2931 Camino del Rio N., San Diego
(619) 280-7115
www.daveandbusters.com

In 1985 the Cabrillo National Monument was the most-visited national monument in the United States, attracting 1,720,000 visitors. The next year it lost its number one status to the Statue of Liberty, but it's still one of the most visited monuments in the country.

Spotting a gray whale requires patience and luck, but an ideal place to try is the observation deck at the Cabrillo National Monument. High-powered viewers may help you spot one or more of the leviathans on their annual winter migration to Mexican waters.

Designed with adults in mind, this interactive video-game facility has a bar, restaurant, and billiards room. The Mission Valley venue (open Sunday through Wednesday 11:30 A.M. to midnight, Thursday until 1:00 A.M., and Friday and Saturday until 2:00 A.M.) boasts more than 200 games, and it's easy to drop a wad of cash in a big hurry.

Gaslamp Quarter
Between Fourth and Sixth Avenues below Broadway, San Diego
(619) 233-5227
www.gaslampquarter.org

No matter what you're seeking—dining, entertainment, history, or shopping—you'll find it in the Gaslamp Quarter. Covering an area of more than 16 blocks, the Quarter was named for the gas lamps that lit the evening sky in the late 19th century.

By day, stroll through the district and go back in time to the days when lawman Wyatt Earp operated three gambling houses and the area was a thriving red-light district. Drink in the beautifully restored Victorian houses, including the William Heath Davis House, the Gaslamp's oldest surviving structure. Browse among more than 65 retail stores, including antiques shops, art galleries, boutiques, and specialty shops.

By night, join the crowds who fill the streets as the gas lamps begin to glow.

A fun way to get around the Gaslamp Quarter is by pedicab. There's no set fee: The strong-legged guys and gals will pedal you around for your (generous) tip.

Head to an Irish pub for a lively happy hour or enjoy fine dining at one of more than 100 restaurants serving a variety of cuisines: Italian, French, Spanish, Greek, Asian, and even Californian. After dinner, have a cup of coffee or tea at one of the many coffeehouses that dot the area.

Then the fun begins. Choose from Dixieland jazz, hip-hop, country, or Spanish flamenco in the clubs and cabarets that have made the Gaslamp one of Southern California's finest entertainment centers. If you're looking for nightlife in San Diego, you won't be disappointed by the Gaslamp Quarter.

Old Town State Historic Park
San Diego Avenue at Twiggs Street
San Diego
(619) 220-5422
www.oldtownsandiego.org

No visit to San Diego is complete without time spent where California began. Even Insiders frequently feel the need to rediscover their roots in historic Old Town, where there's often a fiesta in progress. After Mexico's independence from Spain, the first adobe houses were constructed in the fledgling settlement in the 1820s and 1830s. Father Junipero Serra established his first mission in 1769, with the adjacent presidio (fort) for protection, on a hill overlooking the site.

The 6-block park includes a main plaza, where Kit Carson was among those who raised the first American flag in 1846. Surrounding the plaza are historic buildings, including a dentist's office and blacksmith's shop, the Mason Street School (San Diego's first schoolhouse, still in use), and La Casa de Bandini, now housing a popular restaurant. Two of San Diego's other original adobe structures, La Casa de Estudillo and La Casa de Machado y Stewart, have been restored and are open to the public.

On the streets leading to the plaza are surprises galore: the haunted Whaley House, a professional theater, artisans, galleries, and shops with old-fashioned wares. On the south end of Heritage Park, near the Old Town theater, is a cluster of gift

The USS Midway *takes up residency as a major San Diego museum.* PHOTO: COURTESY OF JOANNE DIBONA

shops and restaurants where you'll often find entertainment as well. When the aroma emanating from a dozen fine restaurants proves irresistible, give in to temptation. Most serve Mexican cuisine, and strolling mariachi bands only add to the flavor.

Free historic walking tours are offered daily at 11:00 A.M. and 2:00 P.M., and Saturday again at 4:00 P.M. The schedule may be reduced in winter months, so call ahead. The Visitor's Information Center is at 4002 Wallace Street, just across from the western edge of Old Town Plaza. If you prefer a self-guided walking tour, pick up a booklet for $2.00 at the visitor center.

While you're out walking, be sure to tour Heritage Park Village, a collection of restored Victorian homes that were moved to their current site at the edge of Old Town in the early '70s.

Finally, if you're searching for the perfect gift to take home, head for Plaza del Pasado. Many San Diegans were distraught when this shopping concession replaced the original and highly colorful Bazaar del Mundo with this plainer if more historically accurate enclave of shops. (Entreprenuer Dianne Powers has moved Bazaar del Mundo a few blocks away to 4133 Taylor Street, near Juan Street.) But it sells much the same lineup of dolls, toys, colorful home accessories, and souvenirs. Plan to spend the better part of the day in Old Town to fully enjoy the food, fun, and history of old San Diego. The park is open every day except Thanksgiving and Christmas, from 9:00 A.M. to 5:00 P.M. There is no admission fee.

San Diego Aircraft Carrier Museum
910 North Harbor Drive, San Diego
(619) 544-9188
www.midway.org

Visit the USS *Midway,* retired in 1992 after nearly 50 years of service, for an unusual experience. The gray behemoth is more than 1,000 feet long and 250 feet wide. At full capacity it had a crew of 4,500 and a monthly payroll of $1.2 million. Check out

On Harney Street in the center of Old Town, you can buy blown glass, ceramics, paintings and more locally produced art at the artisan's market each Saturday between 9:00 A.M. and 4:00 P.M.

the claustrophobic sleeping quarters, the galley where 13,000 meals a day were prepared, and the 4-acre flight deck. There are dozens of aircraft on exhibit; more are added to the collection as they are restored by enthusiastic volunteers at North Island Naval Air Station in Coronado. The museum is open daily 10:00 A.M. to 5:00 P.M., with last admission at 4:00 P.M. Tickets cost $15.00 for adults, $8.00 for kids age 6 through 17. Children age 5 and younger and active-duty military pay nothing.

San Diego de Alcalá Mission
10818 San Diego Mission Road
San Diego
(619) 281-8449 (gift shop),
(619) 283-7319 (parish office)
www.missionsandiego.com

In 1769, when Father Junipero Serra established the first of 21 missions at what is now Presidio Park, it must have seemed an idyllic spot overlooking the valley and the sea. In just a few years, however, the need for a better water supply and the lack of local Indians to convert prompted the move to the present location in Mission Valley, where today it is a favorite visitor attraction as well as an active parish church.

Completely restored in 1931, the mission is truly San Diego's most famous historical landmark. The on-site museum displays artifacts unearthed during archaeological digs over the years. It also gives visitors a detailed history of Father Serra's work as well as a chronicle of the early days of San Diego. The serene gardens surrounding the property are a favorite spot for relaxation and contemplation, as is the beautiful chapel. The mission is open daily from 9:00 A.M. to 4:45 P.M. Admission is $2.00 for adults and $1.00 for seniors, students, and children younger than age 12. Cassette players are provided for self-guided tours at no additional cost. Mass is held several times a day, including a Spanish Mass at the larger St. Francis church just behind the original church; call or see the Web site for times.

San Diego Maritime Museum
1492 North Harbor Drive, San Diego
(619) 234-9153
www.sdmaritime.com

Immerse yourself in San Diego's exciting maritime history by touring a collection of historic ships docked along the picturesque embarcadero. The 1863 *Star of India* is the oldest actively sailed square-rigged ship in the world. Aboard the ship you can learn about its colorful history of collisions, mutiny, dismasting, and entrapments. The 1898 ferryboat *Berkeley,* which steamed around San Francisco Bay in its glory days, has exhibits as well as a research library, model shop, and gift shop; it can also be rented as a party venue. During its time, the *Berkeley* was used to evacuate survivors of the 1906 earthquake and ensuing fires. The recently restored *Pilot* hosts school kids on educational trips around the bay, as does the 145-foot sailing vessel *California,* the "official tall ship of the state." Last but not least is the 1904 *Medea,* one of three surviving great steam yachts. It saw service in both world wars, under three navies and six national flags.

The floating maritime museum exhibits the history of each boat, demonstrations of nautical skills, maritime art, and interactive activities for children. Hours are 9:00 A.M. to 8:00 P.M. daily every day of the year. Admission is $12.00 for adults and $8.00 for children age 6 to 17. Children younger than age 6 are admitted free.

SeaWorld
500 SeaWorld Drive, 1 mile west of Interstate 5 San Diego
(619) 226-3901, (800) 257-4268
www.seaworld.com

Although some folks find the sight of marine mammals leaping and cavorting on command distasteful, SeaWorld does play a part in marine conservation, and when possible rehabilitates injured or sick whales or other fauna and returns them to the wild. However, their main business is entertainment, and there are lots of impressive attractions and exhibits to thrill both children and adults in the 190-acre park.

At the Wild Arctic attraction you can journey to the frozen North on a simulated 400-mph jet helicopter expedition. When you land you'll find yourself eye-to-eye with polar bears, beluga whales, walruses, and harbor seals. Or visit the Manatee Rescue attraction, Forbidden Reef (featuring bat rays and moray eels), or the shark and penguin encounters. How about a trip to Rocky Point Preserve, home to bottlenose dolphins and California sea otters? And don't forget the favorite thrill of all: seeing Shamu, the Killer Whale, perform. The sea lion and bird shows are also impressive and a big hit with kids and adults.

SeaWorld features a half-dozen excellent shows and more than 20 exhibits for the whole family. The most recently added attractions are Pets Rule, in which shelter-adopted animals perform zany antics; Fools With Tools, marine mammals with their own home-improvement show; and the 4-D movie *R. L. Stein's Haunted Lighthouse*.

Park hours vary; it opens at 9:00 or 10:00 A.M. and closes anywhere between 6:00 and 11:00 P.M. Call ahead for the current schedule. Admission, which includes almost all shows and attractions, is $53 for adults and $43 for children age 3 to 9. Children age 2 and younger are admitted free. Ticket packages and annual passes are also available. Parking is $7.00.

Seaport Village
849 West Harbor Drive, San Diego
(619) 235-4014
www.spvillage.com

Nestled at the foot of San Diego's skyline along the embarcadero, Seaport Village is a compact if somewhat cutesy spot for dining, shopping, entertainment, and strolling. Four restaurants provide views of San Diego Bay as well as eclectic and continental cuisine, seafood and steaks. Or if you're in the mood for something a little more casual, sample an international treat at one of eight eateries situated throughout the village—everything from deli sandwiches or Greek food to an authentic Italian cappuccino.

If shopping is the order of the day, you'll find handcrafted gifts, original art, souvenirs, toys, and fashions are among the unique items awaiting your scrutiny. The kids are sure to head for the restored 1890s Looff carousel, and they will delight at the ongoing parade of mimes, clowns, and street performers. Then stroll along the boardwalk for an up-close view of the embarcadero, or hop aboard a horse-drawn carriage for a romantic and scenic tour of the area.

Shops are open daily from 10:00 A.M. to 9:00 P.M.

Stephen Birch Aquarium-Museum
2300 Expedition Way, La Jolla
(858) 534-3474
www.aquarium.ucsd.edu

Have you ever been eye to eye with a fish bigger than you? Here's your chance to get up close and personal with more than 3,000 native fish from the cold waters of the Pacific Northwest to the balmy seas of Mexico and the South Pacific. The largest oceanographic museum in the country, the Stephen Birch Aquarium-Museum gets you as close to ocean life as possible without getting wet. The aquarium-museum is part of the world-renowned Scripps Institution of Oceanography and is dedicated to educating the public about marine science.

Kids especially enjoy the re-created tide pool on a plaza overlooking the coastline and the interactive oceanographic museum with its hands-on exhibits of seawater recycling, global warming, and earthquakes. Also part of the aquarium-museum is a specialty bookshop featuring a wide selection of educational gifts, books, and souvenirs. Hours are 9:00 A.M. to 5:00 P.M. daily, except New Year's Day, Thanksgiving Day, and Christmas Day, when the museum is closed. Admission for adults is $11.00, seniors age 60 and older $9.00, students (with ID) $8.00, kids age 3 to 17 $7.50, and children younger than age 3 are admitted for free.

The Flower Fields in Carlsbad draw BIG crowds, including organized groups, tour buses filled with visitors, and lots of people from Southern California. To avoid the crushing traffic, visit before noon on a weekday during the blooming season, usually from March to Mother's Day.

Whale Watching
H&M Landing
2803 Emerson Street, San Diego
(619) 222-1144
www.hmlanding.com

Hornblower Cruises & Events
1066 North Harbor Drive, San Diego
(619) 686-8700, (888) HORNBLOWER
www.sandiegowhalewatching.com

Islandia Sportfishing
1551 West Mission Bay Drive, San Diego
(619) 222-1164

San Diego Harbor Excursion
1050 North Harbor Drive, San Diego
(619) 234-4111
www.sandiegoharborexcursion.com

Seaforth Sportfishing
1717 Quivira Road, San Diego
(619) 224-3383
www.seaforthlanding.com

Every year visitors and locals have the opportunity to experience the excitement of seeing one of the largest creatures on earth, the California gray whale. Between mid-December and March an estimated 25,000 of these magnificent creatures pass San Diego as they leave their feeding grounds in the Bering Sea for their calving grounds in the lagoons of Baja California, 5,000 miles to the south. Theirs is one of the longest migration of any mammal on earth.

Most whale-watching cruises are two to three hours long and have comfortable indoor and outdoor seating. Commentary by experienced captains and naturalists accompany each tour. Food and beverages are available on most tours, but amenities and prices vary from company to company; call for information and reservations.

NORTH COUNTY COASTAL

California Surf Museum
223 North Coast Highway, Oceanside
(760) 721-6876
www.surfmuseum.org

"Don't wait for the tide to come in, come over to the California Surf Museum" is the slogan of this slightly offbeat and wonderfully fun museum. Located at the top of the Oceanside pier, this attraction is a must for surfers and surfer wannabes, too. The goal of the museum is to preserve the surf lore and legends of California and the Pacific Rim. There's a gift shop with surf stuff you just might have to buy.

You'll find colorful displays and photos that chronicle surf history, and learn trivia—did you know surfing began in 1907? The featured surfing legend changes every six months. Through photos, clothing, and memorabilia, you'll find out about surfers, surfing records, and possibly more than you thought possible about surfboards. For instance, you'll see redwood and mahogany "planks" from the '30s, hollow wood boards, and boards constructed from balsa, foam, and fiberglass.

The museum is open daily 10:00 A.M. to 4:00 P.M.; closed major holidays. Admission is free; donations are appreciated.

Carlsbad Flower Fields
Palomar Airport Road and
Paseo Del Norte, Carlsbad
(760) 431-0352

Though more commercial and crowded than it once was, this annual event is greatly anticipated by many San Diegans. The six- to eight-week flower show between March and early May is breathtaking. You'll see acres of ranunculas in brilliant whites, yellows, oranges, pinks, and reds. There are also rows of mixed colors.

Plan to stay at least an hour. You can pick up makings for a picnic from the coffee cart and on-site catering service. Adult admission is $8.00; children age 3 to 10 pay $5.00; seniors pay $7.00. Purchase bouquets, tubers, and flower-field boutique items at the gift shop on the grounds.

Heritage Park Village and Museum
220 Peyri Road, Oceanside
(760) 439-0995

This attraction, adjacent to the San Luis Rey Mission, celebrates the beginning of the city of Oceanside, one of the oldest incorporated cities in San Diego County. Walking down the main thoroughfare of Heritage Park Village is like walking down Main Street in the old American West. Kids especially enjoy it. A small-fry Insider recently said, "It's just like a movie set."

You'll stroll by the first general store, a blacksmith shop, a small museum, and livery stable. Along the way you'll pass by Oceanside's original city jail, Libby School (the first public school), and the newspaper office. And you'll also see Mrs. Nellie Johansen's house, built in 1886 and complete with living-room furnishings and kitchen appliances from the era. Guided tours are available by arrangement, and the entire area can be reserved for special events, including weddings. The grounds are open 9:00 A.M. to 4:00 P.M.; the buildings are open for visitation Sundays only, from 1:00 to 4:00 P.M. Call for special tour information. Admission to the park is free.

LEGOLAND California
One LEGOLAND Drive, Carlsbad
(760) 918-5346
www.legoland.ca.com

Home of the educational amusement park devoted to those ever-popular LEGO bricks, this is a not-to-miss experience for kids and parents. Here you won't find that thrill-a-minute excitement of Magic Mountain and Disneyland; the excitement here is a different kind and every bit as good.

Open since March of 1999, the park is about 40 minutes north of San Diego in Carlsbad, on a 128-acre hill overlooking the ocean. (Take the Cannon Road exit off Interstate 5.)

LEGOLAND is a mix of education, adventure, and fun designed for kids to age 12, but it is most appreciated by those age 4 to 8. It took more than 30 million LEGO blocks to build the models and displays here; 20 million alone were used in Miniland. Be sure to kneel down and get close to them—many displays have "hidden" design elements that will make you and your kids laugh out loud.

LEGOLAND has six theme areas, each leading easily into the next. Village Green includes an opportunity to drive your own Jeep on an African safari; you'll see life-size LEGO giraffes, zebras, lions, and other wildlife. A boat ride takes you through storybook adventures. In Fun Town kids drive real electric cars and earn their official LEGOLAND driver's license at the Driving School. There are also kid-size LEGO helicopters (yes, kids pilot them) and Skipper School where you can captain real boats.

At The Ridge you can enjoy the Sky Cycle, where you pull yourself up to the top of a tower for an overhead view of the park, and then free-fall down to the ground. (No, there are no jerky, scary crashes; they're all controlled, easy landings.) At Castle Hill there's a fun Dragon roller coaster, a royal joust, and a chance for kids to enjoy a treasure hunt before moving over to the Hideaway to climb balance beams, walls, and curvy slides. In Imagination Zone families are invited to play with LEGO toys. Little ones can start with the larger-sized DUPLO blocks. Older kids can test out LEGO's latest innovations in this area. This is where they can build and program cutting-edge computerized LEGO blocks into robots. The last area (and the favorite of these Insiders) is Miniland, where you'll see reproductions of American landmarks. You can get up close by walking around Miniland or by taking the Coast Cruise grand tour.

There are more than 25 specialty shops and carts and open-air restaurants where you can get everything from a quick snack or salad to a sit-down dinner of ribs and chicken. The park prides itself on fresh, wholesome foods that will enhance the experience.

The park is open daily in July and August, and closed Tuesday and Wednesday during the rest of the year. Adult admission is $53, $43 for children age 3 to 12 and seniors 60 and older. Parking is

CLOSE-UP

Transportational Tours

Contactours
1726 Wilson Avenue, San Diego
(619) 477-8687, (800) 235-5393
www.contactours.com
This charter service and tour operator has buses for 47 to 58 passengers. Visitors can hop aboard daily sightseeing tours to major San Diego attractions or to Tijuana or do both, with a quick harbor excursion, on the Grand Tour. The four-hour city tour costs $29 per adult. Kids are $15 each, but two children may attend free with two paying adults.

Corporate Helicopters of San Diego
3753 John J. Montgomery Drive
San Diego
(858) 505-5650, (800) 345-6737
www.corporatehelicopters.com
For a thrilling bird's-eye view of San Diego, take the tour that adventurous souls swear by: a sky tour over the best of San Diego. Soar past the San Diego skyline in a quiet, jet-powered helicopter. See Old Town, the zoo, Petco Park, and the Coronado Bridge as you fly across San Diego Bay. View the beauty of Sunset Cliffs, Mission Bay, and La Jolla. Soon you're safely back on the ground with a never-to-be-forgotten memory. The 30-minute San Diego tour is $150 per person. Other tours are available, too, including a Temecula winery tour that lasts three and a half hours (flight time is one and a half hours) and costs $1,125 for a maximum of four passengers. Custom aerial adventures can be arranged.

Harbor Tours
Hornblower Cruises & Events
1066 North Harbor Drive, San Diego
(800) 467-6256
www.hornblower.com

San Diego Harbor Excursion
1050 North Harbor Drive, San Diego
(619) 234-4111, (888) 442-7873
See San Diego the way Cabrillo first viewed it—from the water. Both Hornblower Cruises and San Diego Harbor Excursion offer one- and two-hour narrated tours of San Diego's diverse natural harbor. Among the sights you may see are the U.S. Navy fleet, the *Star of India* sailing ship, the Cabrillo National

$8.00 for cars. If you plan to visit the park and want to stay close by, we recommend you make hotel reservations in advance. And take our advice: Wear comfortable shoes, use sunscreen, and bring a hat.

For more details, be sure to read about LEGOLAND in our Kidstuff chapter.

Misión San Luis Rey de Francia
4050 Mission Avenue at Rancho del Oro Drive, Oceanside
(760) 757-3651
www.sanluisrey.org
Of the 21 California missions, this is probably the least known and one of the prettiest. It was founded in 1798 as the

Monument, the San Diego-Coronado Bay Bridge, and the historic Hotel del Coronado. Enjoy the sights and the sea air from pleasant sundecks or comfortable inside seating. Snacks and beverages are available onboard.

Prices for the one-hour tour are about $17.00 for adults, and $8.50 for children age 4 to 12. Two-hour tour prices are $22.00 for adults, and $11.00 for children age 4 to 12. Three-hour dinner cruises are available too, if you'd like to take in the nighttime skyline; cost is $58.00 to $61.00 per person (Hornblower raises the price by $5.00 on Saturday). Both companies offer champagne brunch. Even on warm days, the air can get chilly on the water, so it's a good idea to bring along a light jacket or sweater, even in summer.

Old Town Trolley Tours
San Diego Avenue at Twiggs Street
San Diego
(619) 298-8687
www.oldtowntrolley.com

Hop aboard an open-air trolley on wheels and take a leisurely approach to sightseeing. Start your two-hour narrated tour at any of the trolley's stops, including Old Town State Park (the main location, with free parking), the Gaslamp Quarter, Seaport Village, Horton Plaza, Coronado Island, the San Diego Zoo, the embarcadero, or Balboa Park. You can stay on and take a standard two-hour tour, or use the trolley as a means of transportation, getting off at any of the stops to shop, sightsee, or dine. The latter is an excellent, economical way to see the city's highlights, which is why a two-day pass also should be considered. When you're ready, climb back aboard the next trolley and resume your tour, which is narrated with anecdotes, ghost stories, and historical facts. Call Old Town Trolley Tours for a complete list of their stops, or check to see if your hotel has a map. Hours are 9:00 A.M. to 5:00 P.M. (to 4:00 P.M. in the winter). Tour prices are $30 for people age 13 and older and $15 for children age 4 to 12.

SEAL: Sea and Land Adventure
SEAL booth at Seaport Village, San Diego
(619) 298-8687

Old Town Trolley Tours began operating this "amphibious adventure" in August 2001. Passengers board a 40-foot Hydra Terra truck for a land-and-water tour beginning at Seaport Village cruising on San Diego Bay via Shelter Island. Narration emphasizes the ecological and maritime aspects of San Diego's history, past and present. Tours last approximately 90 minutes and cost $30 for adults and $15 for children age 4 to 12. Kids younger than age 4 are free. You must call in the morning after 8:30 to see when the day's tours are departing.

18th in the string of missions that dot the state.

Strolling through the grounds, church, garden, and museum, you'll be treated to early artwork, historical artifacts, and Native American historical displays. Be sure to visit California's first pepper tree and the *lavanderia,* or laundry area, used by the mission Indians and settlers. It's across the road from the main site. You can also visit the mission cemetery, which dates from 1798 and is still being used by members of all faiths.

Admission to the museum is $5.00 for adults, $3.00 for students and children; families pay a maximum of $20.00. Hours

February is Museum Month in San Diego. Free Culture Cards available at San Diego County Robinsons-May stores entitle the bearer and up to three others to half-price admission to county historic sites and museums. Among those participating are Birch Aquarium, the Children's Museum, Quail Botanical Gardens, and many Balboa Park museums.

are 10:00 A.M. to 4:00 P.M. daily. The gift shop/bookstore is worth a visit. Worship services are held at the old mission Saturday at 5:30 P.M. (7:00 P.M. in Spanish) and in the newer parish chapel Sunday at 8:00 and 10:00 A.M. and 5:00 P.M. (noon in Spanish).

One Wednesday a month, join the friars for dinner and an inspirational talk. There are also weekend retreats specifically for married couples, seniors, families, and women as well as those for individuals.

Oceanside Harbor
Harbor Drive, Oceanside

This is the quintessential California pleasure harbor. Here you'll see beautiful boats, restaurants dotting the waterfront, and sailors, strollers, in-line skaters, and artists all capturing their own vision of fun.

The harbor is used by more than 900 pleasure crafts and sportfishing boats. Unlike other ports, the boats are visible from the two-lane road that hugs the harbor. You'll find fine restaurants to simple fish-and-chips hangouts and shops that sell everything from shell wind chimes to upscale clothing.

Insiders visit the harbor for a leisurely walk and to admire the sunset. Families and working folks picnic on the grass and share lunch with the ever-present, ever-hungry flock of seagulls.

You'd be amazed how many San Diego venues are available for rent. Quail Gardens, Bates Nut Farm, and most of the museums at Balboa Park can be booked for weddings, bar mitzvahs, silver wedding anniversaries, and kids' birthday parties.

Oceanside Museum of Art
704 Pier View Way, Oceanside
(760) 721-2787
www.oma-online.org

This museum features changing exhibits of a wide variety of genres, from art glass to traditional sculpture, photography, or paintings. Topics range from San Diego subject matter to national or universal themes. Special features of the museum are art openings, discussions of art with the artist, and a host of art classes. Museum hours are Tuesday through Saturday 10:00 A.M. to 4:00 P.M. and Sunday 1:00 A.M. to 4:00 P.M. Admission is $5.00, members get in for free.

Oceanside Pier
West end of Mission Avenue, Oceanside

The pier is a popular fishing, meeting, and whale-watching spot for Insiders and visitors alike. At its current length of 1,942 feet, it is one of the longest wooden recreation piers on the West Coast.

A license is required to fish from the beach; no license is required to fish from the pier, where there's a bait shop. If you don't catch any, you might stop at Ruby's, a '50s-style restaurant that's drawing interest from around the county. This outing is easy on the wallet, as there's no admission fee.

Quail Botanical Gardens
230 Quail Gardens Drive, Encinitas
(760) 436-3036
www.qbgardens.com

In the midst of developments, Quail Botanical Gardens is a favorite retreat for nature lovers. Ask five people about their favorite parts of the garden, and you'll receive five different answers. There's a tropical area, desert display, and a cool bamboo forest with specimens from around the world. You'll see cork oak, the bird garden that attracts birds and butterflies, and a large display of local plants used by Native Americans for food and medicine among other wonderful living exhibits.

There are guided tours Saturday at 10:00 A.M.; group tours are available for a small fee. Self-guided tours are available with the user-friendly brochures found at the trailhead. Changing activities for children and parents introduce the young ones to plants, bugs, and, hopefully, a love of gardens and gardening. There's also a bookstore/gift shop and a small attached nursery, which sells plant starters. Plant sales scheduled throughout the year are a hit in the community. Recently, Quail Gardens has become a popular place for garden weddings, so your visit might just include a bit of romance.

The gardens are open daily from 9:00 A.M. to 5:00 P.M., except Thanksgiving, Christmas, and New Year's Day; the shop is open from 10:00 A.M. to 4:00 P.M. Adult admission is $8.00; seniors pay $5.00; children age 3 to 12 pay $3.00. It's free to all the first Tuesday of each month.

NORTH COUNTY INLAND

Antique Gas and Steam Engine Museum
2040 North Santa Fe Avenue, Vista
(760) 941-1791, (800) 587-2286
www.agsem.com

Located about an hour's drive from downtown San Diego, this museum is devoted to early engines and early-20th-century farm equipment. If you want to see what early farm life was like, this is the place. Located on more than 40 acres, most in cultivation, the museum collects and displays working historical gas-, steam-, and horse-powered equipment. Period displays include a blacksmith shop, gristmill, country kitchen and parlor, steam-operated sawmill, and small gas-powered train.

Fairs are held the third and fourth weekends of June and October, with demonstrations of how the engines and apparatuses on-site actually work. During these events visitors of all ages can enjoy food, crafts, and music.

The museum is open 10:00 A.M. until 4:00 P.M. daily. Admission is $3.00 for adults, $2.00 for children.

At local attractions food can be pricey and not always the most nourishing. Consider packing a picnic or stopping at one of the less expensive restaurants listed in the Restaurants chapter.

Bates Nut Farm
15954 Woods Valley Road
Valley Center
(760) 749-3333
www.batesnutfarm.biz

At Bates Nut Farm you'll find nuts. That's a given, but you'll also find an eight-acre park and farm zoo and special events.

Insiders enjoy the shaded park for family picnics—especially popular for Mother's Day and the Fourth of July. Kids of all ages adore the pumpkin patch, but it can become terribly crowded on the weekends preceding Halloween, when there are live bands and craft shows. Later in the year Bates is the place for Christmas-oriented crafts.

The grounds also include a nostalgic country gourmet food store and the Farmer's Daughter gift shop. Cultural events and arts and crafts fairs are held throughout the year. Admission is free.

Cruisin' Night
Grand Avenue between Center City Parkway and the Grand/Valley Parkway Split, Escondido

Every year between April or May and September, the city of Escondido shuts down Grand Avenue in the early evening for the weekly Friday-night cruise. Like its counterparts in El Cajon and La Mesa, Escondido becomes a meeting place for car enthusiasts from throughout the county, and even beyond. They converge on Broadway and contiguous streets to show off their muscle cars, hot rods, and even their Harleys and to check out what the "competition" is driving. The restaurants do a brisk business, the weekly farmers' market provides artisan bread and organic produce, and there's always at least one local band playing. It's a great way for locals and visitors to cruise and enjoy Escondido's quaint older section of town.

Escondido Historical Society's Heritage Walk and Grape Day Park
321 North Broadway, Escondido
(760) 743-8207
www.escondidohistory.org

Besides nature, you can enjoy a bit of history in this downtown park, which is lovely, shady, and the home of some of Escondido's historic buildings. On a typical Sunday you'll find lots of Insider families here.

The Escondido Historical Society maintains the buildings, which you can visit. So come see the city's first library, a barn with a windmill, a Victorian house, the 1888 Santa Fe Railroad depot, a railroad car, and the model train. You can also visit a working blacksmith shop.

There is no entry fee although a $3.00 donation is suggested, and buildings are open Thursday through Saturday from 1:00 to 4:00 P.M.

Harrah's Rincon Casino & Resort
777 Harrah's Rincon Way, Valley Center
(760) 751-3100, (800) 427-7247
www.harrahs.com

One of San Diego County's newest Las Vegas-style casinos, this one in the far north of North County Inland offers banquet facilities, six restaurants, a coffee bar, two lounges (one with live music), and a 200-room resort hotel with a pool and gym. In the 24-hour gaming rooms, you'll find the usual suspects: 8 poker rooms, 50 gaming tables, and 1,600 one-armed bandits. Alcohol is served in the restaurants, bars, and gaming rooms.

Palomar Observatory
Highway of Stars (off California Highway 76) to County Road S6
Palomar Mountain
(760) 742-2119
www.palomarsummit.com

When you wish upon a star and desire to learn more about the heavens above, you might want to visit this observatory owned and operated by the California Institute of Technology. It's a working observatory, so there's no peering through the huge 200-inch Hale telescope or taking a nighttime star tour. What you do get is a self-guided tour, an educational video, and a visit to the gallery dome to see the telescope.

The facility is open daily (except Christmas Eve and Christmas) from 9:00 A.M. until 4:00 P.M. The gift shop, jammed with star- and galaxy-related stuff, is open weekends only, with extended summer hours. There are hiking trails, and here on the top of the mountain, there are great views in all directions. Bring a picnic lunch to eat at Silver Crest picnic area, just outside the park boundaries, or you can pick up a snack at the Palomar Mountain General Store or get takeout (or eat in) at the vegetarian Mother's Kitchen (760-742-4233; www.motherskitchenpalomar.com).

San Diego Wild Animal Park
15500 San Pasqual Valley Road Escondido
(760) 747-8702
www.wildanimalpark.com

With more than 2,100 acres, this may be the largest, most authentic animal park outside of Africa and worthy of more than 1 or 10 visits. It's a favorite hangout of Insiders, who buy a yearly zoological society pass and spend many days visiting the animals, the lovely gardens, and the shows.

Included in the entrance fee is a 50-minute monorail ride through the "field exhibits": hundreds of acres of open land simulating the habitats of Africa and Asia. It's fabulous to see herds of giraffes, zebra, antelope, and buffalo as they roam free among other species. This is a great way to start the day. Be sure to bring a sweater or jacket if you're visiting in the early morning or in winter; it's usually cool and breezy on the monorail. It's worth every goose bump, though, for the photo and viewing opportunities.

The park is noted for its educational programs, African village, and the higher-than-average birth rate for captive endangered species. By reservation, tour the park's animal hospital, take a VIP or photo safari, or participate in seasonal events (like the summer sleepovers) that will make your visit super special. Bird, elephant, and other shows take place throughout the day.

Set in the dry hills of Escondido, the expansive park has dozens of wonderful exhibits. Feed brightly colored lorikeets, scout for acrobatic gibbons in the trees, or watch a family of lowland gorillas groom each other. Head down the 2-mile Kilimanjaro Walk to see plants and animals native to that area and get your exercise, too. No matter what parts of the park you visit, there's lots of walking involved, so wear comfortable shoes.

Winter hours are 9:00 A.M. to 5:00 P.M. (last entrance at 4:00 P.M.); summer hours are extended until 9:00 P.M. (last entrance at 8:00 P.M.). Admission for people age 12 years and older is $28.50 (seniors get a 10 percent discount); those age 3 to 11 pay $17.50; children age 2 and younger get in free. Parking is $8.00. Ask about the combination ticket for the Wild Animal Park and the Zoo or a three-for-one pass that includes SeaWorld, too. Call ahead to inquire about group or theme tours or to reserve the Hunte Nairobi Pavilion for a corporate or private event.

The Wave Waterpark
101 Wave Drive, Vista
(760) 940-9283

It's a strange feeling to put on a swimsuit or grab your beach towel for a day in the waves and then head away from the ocean, but Insiders do it all the time. The Wave Waterpark is a dynamite place to cool down on any San Diego day from May through September.

If you're planning a visit to the tide pools, check the tide tables before you go. Low tide is the optimum time for an up-close look at the vast array of marine creatures.

This $3.8 million state-of-the-art aquatic park is municipally operated and geared to families. Its attractions include the Flow Rider, four waterslides, a Crazy River, a competition pool, and a children's water playground. Admission for those taller than 42 inches is $14.00; it's $10.50 for seniors and kids under 42 inches tall. Children younger than age 2 are welcome at no charge. The park is open daily from 10:30 A.M. to 5:30 P.M. June through the end of August. Throughout the year it's available for kids' parties and swimming lessons; in summer there are weeklong day camps for kids age 7 to 15.

EAST COUNTY

Back to the 50s Car Show
La Mesa Boulevard, from Date Street to Grant Street, La Mesa

Those in East County know that a visit to the Car Show means a good time will be had by all. Every Thursday June through August from 5:00 to 8:00 P.M. you'll be treated to live music performances and DJs spinning CDs; food vendors; and most important, hot rods, muscle cars, and buffed-out motorcycles.

Barona Casino
1932 Wildcat Canyon Road, Lakeside
(619) 443-2300, (888) 722-7662
www.barona.com

Grown-up fun is the bill of fare at this Barona Indian gambling center. You can try your luck at more than 2,000 Las Vegas-style slots and 70 gaming tables as well as satellite wagering and high-stakes bingo. Dining options include gameside service within the casino, a Las

Vegas-style buffet and food court, and fancier restaurants. Barona Casino is alcohol-free, air-conditioned, and open 24 hours a day. A multimillion-dollar expansion project, Barona Valley Ranch, includes a new 400-room hotel, spa, 18-hole golf championship course, parking structure, and events room.

Boomer's El Cajon
1155 Graves Avenue, El Cajon
(619) 593-1155
www.boomersparks.com

Boomer's is an East County institution for kids, teens, and tweens. Hit the batting cages, play a round of miniature golf, or enter the cacophonous video arcade. Climb aboard bumper boats to get wet or the go-karts to get dusty. There's a party room and, of course, a junk food eatery.

Heritage of the Americas Museum
12110 Cuyamaca College Drive W., El Cajon
(619) 670-5194
www.cuyamaca.net/museum

Set on the campus of Cuyamaca College, this museum attracts some folks who just come for the view. It's located atop a hill that overlooks the entire El Cajon valley area, and that's quite a sight on a perfect San Diego day.

The museum is known for its cultural and educational displays, which reflect the natural and human history of the Americas. Don't expect the Smithsonian, but rather a carefully selected collection of minerals and meteorites, fossils, seashells, tribal tools, effigies, baskets, jewelry, and indigenous artifacts. There's a small art gallery, too. The museum is open Tuesday through Friday from 10:00 A.M. until 4:00 P.M., Saturday from noon to 4:00 P.M. Admission is $3.00 for adults; kids younger than age 17 (with an adult) are admitted free.

Although the "big three" in Indian gaming are the Sycuan, Viejas, and Barona casinos, smaller reservations also have casinos. These include Pala Casino (760-742-2268) in Pala and the Golden Acorn Casino (619-938-6000) in Campo. Each offers slots, games, and dining facilities, and new casinos are in the planning stages.

Sycuan Resort and Casino
5459 Sycuan Road, El Cajon
(619) 445-6002, (800) 272-4646
www.sycuan.com

The Sycuan Resort and Casino, in East County's El Cajon, isn't just another place for adult fun: There's also a golf course and golf school, a resort hotel with nearly a dozen lighted tennis courts, and the Showcase Theater for evening entertainment. You'll also find satellite wagering and a 24-hour card room but no cocktails; this is an alcohol-free casino complex. No alcohol is served in the restaurants either, which include an all-you-can-eat buffet, a sit-down restaurant, and a 24-hour cafe and deli. High-stakes bingo is the biggest draw, right along with the buffet and the restaurants. Call for a schedule of live entertainment. You must be age 21 to gamble in California, even on Indian reservations.

Viejas Casino & Turf Club
5000 Willows Road, Alpine
(619) 445-5400, (800) 847-6537
www.viejas.com

As this ultrapopular casino says, "We've got more fun." They really work at the fun portion, too, and include high-stakes poker, video tournaments, satellite wagering, and Indian blackjack; there's a nonsmoking area. Like other area casinos, it's open 24/7. *San Diego Union-Tribune* restaurant critic Leslie James raved about Viejas's Grove Steakhouse but was unimpressed by the ho-hum Harvest Buffet. Food and drinks are served throughout the gaming rooms.

Across the street, an outlet center offers shops selling housewares, apparel, gifts, and shoes as well as restaurants such as Subway and Rubio's Baja Grill.

SOUTH BAY

ARCO U.S. Olympic Training Center
2800 Olympic Parkway, Chula Vista
(619) 656-1500, (619) 482-6215
www.cvonline.biz/olympic_training_center.html

One of only four official Olympic Training Centers in the country, the ARCO Center is where Olympic hopefuls train for international competition. Unlike its sister facilities in Lake Placid and Colorado Springs, the ARCO Center is the only year-round warm-weather venue for track and field, kayaking, field hockey, cycling, soccer, archery, tennis, softball, and rowing.

Officials at the Training Center like to say that visitors get the "red, white, and blue carpet treatment" when they come for a tour. From the Olympic Path, guests can view the entire 150-acre campus, including the athletes' dormitories, training fields, and tracks. The Chula Vista site has the largest permanent archery range in North America, four soccer fields, an all-weather hockey field, a 15,000-square-foot boathouse, and four tennis courts. In addition to those stellar facilities, the center provides a 400-meter track, six acres for field events, and a cycling course.

Free guided tours are offered at 1:30 P.M. Tuesday through Saturday; more often during the summer. Or take a self-guided tour any day between 10:00 A.M. and 5:00 P.M. Be sure to stop in the Spirit Store (closed Monday), where you'll find a wide variety of Olympic merchandise and memorabilia. Although tours are free, donations are accepted to further the Olympic dream for the Training Center's athletes.

Chula Vista Nature Center
1000 Gunpowder Point Drive, Chula Vista
(619) 409-5900
www.chulavistanaturecenter.org

Did you know that burrowing owls imitate the sound of a rattlesnake to fool potential predators? Hear it for yourself at the Chula Vista Nature Center. Located in the Sweetwater Marsh National Wildlife Refuge, it's one of the few remaining habitats of its kind on the Pacific coast. A haven for more than 215 species of birds, some endangered, the Nature Center's observation tower provides the perfect venue for watching the birds go about their daily routine.

---

i

Visit the Downtown Information Center (closed Sunday; 619-235-2222) for maps, literature, and videos. It's located at the NBC Building, 225 Broadway Circle at Second Avenue. The first and third Saturdays of the month, take advantage of free, hour-long, narrated bus tours at 10:00 A.M. and noon.

In addition to birds, a variety of seemingly fierce creatures native to San Diego Bay can be found—and petted. Don't miss the $1 million, 4,000-gallon tank with above- and underwater viewing stations and interactive displays. Bat rays and leopard sharks are among the intimidating but harmless water babies awaiting the attention of the curious.

If a bird, bug, and nature walk appeals to you, check with the Nature Center for its schedule. Many such tours and walks are provided to the public.

Hours are 10:00 A.M. to 5:00 P.M. Tuesday through Sunday; it's closed on major holidays. Admission is $4.00 for adults, $2.00 for seniors age 55 and older, and $1.00 for juniors age 6 to 11. Children younger than age 6 are admitted for free.

To reach the Nature Center from I-5, take the E Street exit in Chula Vista, and go west to the parking lot.

Free shuttles from the parking lot (near the Baysite/E Street trolley stop) to the facility run about every 20 minutes.

Knott's Soak City USA
2052 Otay Valley Road, Chula Vista
(619) 661-7373
www.soakcityusa.com

Despite San Diego's often-stellar winter weather, Soak City is open daily only in summer, when Insiders can enjoy the park's 17 waterslides, four-story interactive family play structure, and other attractions more appropriate for toddlers. There are fast-food stands and picnic areas, several shops, changing rooms, and pay lockers.

The park is open weekends from 10:00 A.M. to 6:00 P.M. between April and Memorial Day and from Labor Day to the end of September. Between those two holidays it's open daily from 10:00 A.M. to 7:00 P.M. It's closed from the end of September until April. Adults pay $27.00 ($22.00 for SoCal residents); kids age 3 to 11 pay $15.00. Summer season passes cost $75.00 for adults and $45.00 for children. Parking is $7.00.

KIDSTUFF

It's not hard to find things for kids to do in San Diego. Most of what makes San Diego special—the zoo, SeaWorld, Wild Animal Park, the beaches—appeals to kids just as much as it does to adults. Even though kids can have as much fun doing all the things that grown-ups enjoy, there are times when they need something a little different, something that's designed just for them. And that's what we'll help you discover in this chapter.

We've found the special little treats just for kids and given you the lowdown on them all. For kids that like to touch without being chastised, visit the Children's Museum, where they can get their hands on interactive displays.

Or maybe the kids would enjoy seeing a performance by the San Diego Junior Theatre. Lots of one-time events are staged especially for kids, too, and though we can't predict what's coming, we'll tell you where to find Easter and Halloween festivities and science programs. Some bookstores have story times; we've clued you in on the ongoing ones. Libraries are a good place to check out, too. Most have reading programs for kids ranging in age from toddlers to teens.

A great resource for kidstuff is in the "Calendar" section of the *San Diego Reader,* a weekly tabloid that comes out on Thursday and can be picked up at bookstores, libraries, convenience stores, and hundreds of other locations throughout the county. The "Night & Day" section of the Thursday *San Diego Union-Tribune* will give you ideas as well.

Here you'll find listings for places geared especially for children, like LEGOLAND and the Children's Museum. Also check out the Parks, Balboa Park, Beaches and Water Sports, Attractions, and Recreation chapters for other things that appeal to kids as well as their unpaid chauffeurs.

If an adult's presence is required at a children's event or attraction, we've made note of it. If your child needs to bring along anything extra, we've tried to mention that, too. Keep in mind, though, that it's always a good idea to phone ahead and get all the particulars.

CENTRAL SAN DIEGO

Boomer's
6999 Clairemont Mesa Boulevard
San Diego
(858) 560-4211

We covered the Boomer's located throughout the county in our Attractions chapter. But they're worthy of a mention here, too, simply because kids go wild over the variety of activities they can dive into, such as batting cages, miniature golf, arcade games, go-karts, and amusement park rides.

"Summer" hours apply to traditional summer vacation and school holidays, when the park is open. Boomers opens at 10:00 A.M. on weekends and 11:00 A.M. on weekdays; call for closing hours, as they change by season. Winter hours are reduced, so be sure to call before you go. The various attractions are priced separately, but all-day passes cost $21 for bigger kids, $16 for smaller fry. Kids younger than age 5 are free with a paying adult. Every

Many libraries throughout the county offer story time for children, as do major bookstores such as Barnes & Noble (7610 Hazard Center Drive, San Diego, 619-220-0175, www.bn.com) and B Dalton Booksellers (Bookstar, 3150 Rosecrans Place, San Diego, 619-225-0465). Call your local library or the above booksellers to find out about story time near your neighborhood.

To find out about county picnic grounds and playgrounds or special events like Easter egg hunts or Halloween activities, contact Parks and Recreation at (619) 685-1350 or (619) 235-1100.

Tuesday and Thursday they can play unlimited video games for $10.

Camp SeaWorld
500 SeaWorld Drive, San Diego
(619) 226-3834, (800) 237-4268
www.swbg-adventurecamps.com

For preschoolers through high school seniors, SeaWorld has some of the coolest camp programs around. It's an adventure filled with animals, games, crafts, and learning. Camps for preschoolers are designed for children ages 3 and 4 (with parent involvement), and the level of activities and learning experiences accelerate for older kids.

Half-day camps run during the morning hours, and there's an extended camp that lets kids stay in the park to enjoy an afternoon of games, shows, and animal attractions. Extended camp ends at 5:00 P.M.

Prices run about $88 for a three-day morning program for preschoolers through grade-3 kids and $185 for a five-day-long, half-day program for older children.

Another event popular with kids is the overnight adventure. Parents or grandparents can come with the kids; schoolchildren from grade 2 to 8th grade arrive in the late afternoon and have a pizza party, games, and crafts designed to teach them about marine life. They then sleep in their sleeping bags next to the penguin, manatee, or shark enclosures. In the morning they get a light breakfast, a T-shirt, and a tour of the park before it opens to the public, with the option of spending the rest of the day in the park. The cost is $135 per person. Private reservations are also accepted.

High-brow high school students can share their poetry non-competitively with others the first and third Monday of the month at the San Dieguito Boys & Girls Club (3800 Mykonos Lane, Del Mar, 858-720-2180). A competition for best poetry is held the last Thursday of the month.

During spring break and summer, kids in grades 4 through 12 can attend a six-night ocean adventure camp. For $950, youngsters get meals, lodgings, transportation, equipment rentals, and a T-shirt as they learn kayaking, boogie boarding, and other water sports. Children divide their time between San Diego's beaches and bays and SeaWorld itself.

Children's Pool
Coast Boulevard, south of Jenner Street
La Jolla

City engineers gave Mother Nature a helping hand when they built a seawall to partially enclose a natural inlet. The result is Children's Pool, which would more appropriately now be called the sea lions' pool. Up to 200 of these marine mammals take up residence each winter on the sand and rocks, giving kids a close-up look at these amazing sea creatures. Humans, however, are now banned from the water due to contamination from sea lion waste. And although most kids would change places with the pinnipeds any day, they still get a kick out of watching the social creatures dive from the rocks and roll around in the sand. Nearby beaches like La Jolla Shores are great for kids.

Chuck E Cheese's
550 Grossmont Center Drive, La Mesa
(619) 698-4351

3146 Sports Arena Boulevard, San Diego
(619) 523-4385
www.chuckecheese.com

Put on your best game face, Mom and Dad, and prepare for an assault on the senses. Kids absolutely love Chuck E Cheese's for its noise, shows, constant activity, games, rides, prizes, and pizza. The motto is "It's a magical place where a kid can be a kid."

Shamu and company make a splash at SeaWorld. PHOTO: COURTESY OF SEAWORLD

Although it may be a bit much for adults looking for a peaceful meal, the smiles on the kids' faces makes it all worthwhile. Large groups are welcome (call in advance), and birthday parties and other gatherings can be arranged ahead of time. Admission is free, and the restaurant is open for lunch and dinner every day but Monday.

J.W. Tumbles
3125 Rosecrans Street, Suite B, Point Loma
(619) 224-5437

An activity center and gym strictly for kids age 4 months through 8 years old, J.W. Tumbles offers kid-style fitness and exercise programs and classes. The staff here can also help you create great birthday parties.

La Jolla YMCA Day Camps
8355 Cliffridge Avenue, La Jolla
(858) 453-3483
http://lajolla.ymca.org

La Jolla's YMCA has traditional and special-interest day camps that run for one week during the summer. An intense, five-hours-per-day program at the Mission Bay Aquatics Center teaches kayaking, wakeboarding, and waterskiing. Professionals from the Fern Street Circus teach clowning and trapeze, among other valuable circus skills. Dozens of other camps are available, too, including cooking, mountaineering, science, surf, drama, skateboarding, ice-skating, and art. There's something for any kid between ages 3 and 17. Prices vary, beginning at $150 and running to several hundred dollars

Kids and parents share quality time at fabulous outtings offered through the San Diego Museum of Natural History. Learn to kayak, join a mock dinosaur dig, or travel south of the border. Call the museum at (619) 232-3821, ext. 8, for the current schedule and information.

In early spring issues of San Diego Parent *and* San Diego Family Magazine, *you'll find listings of summer activities and camps for kids. If your offspring have their hearts set on a special camp, make reservations early.*

for the one-week session. YMCA members get a discount.

Marie Hitchcock Puppet Theater
2130 Pan American Road W.
Balboa Park, San Diego
(619) 685-5990
www.balboaparkpuppets.com

Named for San Diego's original Puppet Lady, who charmed local kids for decades with her amusing puppet acts, the Marie Hitchcock Puppet Theater offers year-round performances at the theater, with marionettes, shadow puppets, and hand-puppets. Occasionally the troupe will stage a ventriloquist act, too. The theater also hosts traveling shows that produce a variety of events.

It's a small theater—only 230 seats—so it's a good idea to get there a little early. No refreshments are sold during performances, and food isn't allowed in the theater. Shows usually run about 30 to 45 minutes. Tickets are available at the theater on the day of the performance; no advance reservations are required. Show times are 10:00 and 11:30 A.M. Wednesday through Friday; 11:00 A.M., 1:00 P.M., and 2:30 P.M. on Saturday and Sunday, with additional performances in the summer. Admission for adults is $5.00; children age 3 to 17 are charged $3.00. Children age 2 and younger are admitted free.

Another great resource for all sorts of summer programs is www.summer-daycamps.com, where you can search by topic or by area code for a camp teaching anything from digital media and robotics to math or horsemanship.

Mission Valley YMCA
5505 Friars Road, San Diego
(619) 298-3576
www.ymca.org

The Mission Valley Y has summer camps for kids of all ages. They can make a music video, play laser tag or card games, or learn hip-hop, painting, kiteboarding, karate, or wakeboarding. Sports camps focus on learning techniques and strategies needed to excel at baseball, basketball, gymnastics, skating, and other types of athletics. Winter day camp is available to kids age 3 to 15 and offers field trips, arts and crafts, and age-appropriate games and sports. Cost ranges from around $100 to several hundred dollars.

San Diego Junior Theatre
Casa del Prado Theatre
1650 El Prado, Balboa Park, San Diego
(619) 239-1311 (information)
(619) 239-8355 (box office)
www.juniortheatre.com

Since 1948 the San Diego Junior Theatre has provided kids age 4 to 18 with classes in acting, voice, dance, and other specialties like intro to improv, dialects, and stage makeup. One- or two-week classes, held at Balboa Park, the Chula Vista campus (corner of Davidson and Third Streets), and La Jolla campus (7877 Herschel Avenue) are offered during spring break and the summer, and once-a-week sessions of 10 weeks are available during the rest of the year.

Students age 8 or older who have taken or are currently enrolled in Junior Theatre classes are eligible to audition or be part of the stage crew for the year's dozen or so productions, which are as varied as *Holes* and Shakespeare's *Twelfth Night*.

Even if the kids aren't interested in classes, the productions themselves are always crowd-pleasers, enjoyed by children and adults alike. Ticket prices are $5.00 and $10.00 for seniors and for children younger than age 14 and $10.00 or $15.00 for adults. Class prices vary depending on the type of class and the age of the child, but the usual fee is between $85 and $125.

San Diego Zoo and Wild Animal Park Adventures and Programs
Balboa Park and Escondido
(619) 234-3153
www.wildanimalpark.com

The San Diego Zoo and Wild Animal Park host great educational programs and adventures for children year-round. During the summer (late June through early September) don't miss Nighttime Zoo, when the facilities stay open late for performances and shows. Night is when the animals are most active, as many choose to snooze during the afternoon's heat. Kids age 4 to 6 enjoy Kids' Night Out, for 90 minutes of animal-related activities and encounters. Five-day summer camp for kids in grades K through 7 involve children with animals and teach cooking and other fun skills.

Summer Sports Camps
University of San Diego
5998 Alcalá Park, San Diego
(619) 260-2999, (800) 991-1873, ext. 2

The University of San Diego Sports Camp program is dedicated to providing a unique athletic experience tailored to the individual needs of each child. The emphasis is on personalized instruction and increased performance. Sessions of three days to two weeks in day or resident programs are offered to children ages 8 to 17. Camps hone skills in baseball, basketball, softball, swimming, soccer, volleyball, tennis, or water polo. Overnighters stay in dormitories on the beautiful USD campus. Costs range from about $295 to $350 for day camp to $495 to $575 for overnight per week.

All-Sports Camp combines team sports and activities such as Frisbee, golf, street hockey, and archery as well as recreational games. Half-day clinics cost $120 a week; full-day costs $200.

Some of San Diego's less affluent neighborhoods offer children a safe and supportive environment at the Boys & Girls Club (619-298-3520, 760-746-3315; www.bgcsd.com). Kids can get help with homework as well as practice sports or learn arts and crafts, swimming, and other activities. Some sites offer summer camp or day care.

NORTH COUNTY COASTAL

Cole Library
1250 Carlsbad Village Drive, Carlsbad
(760) 434-2870

Kids are king at the Cole Library. Along with a huge collection of books, videos, and tapes, there are reading programs and story hours for toddlers and preschoolers. After-school activities, from magic workshops to cultural activities, are free and fun. There are lots of arts and crafts programs designed to please even the most particular child.

The library sponsors teen book clubs and the incredibly popular (for more than 30 years!) summer reading program for all ages. Do like the Insiders: Park off Elmwood Street, just east of the library, in the unpaved parking lot. Stop in for a program and newsletter that details the free activities.

Chuck E Cheese's
2481 Vista Way, Oceanside
(760) 439-1444
www.chuckecheese.com

If you and the kids need a shot of intense family fun, steer the car to Chuck E

At the Zoo and the Wild Animal Park, you can rent lockers. The lockers are wonderful for a picnic lunch, film, and the extra items families need. You can also rent strollers and wheelchairs.

LEGOLAND is coastal North County's top attraction for kids. PHOTO: COURTESY OF BRETT SHOAF

Cheese's. It's a restaurant like no other because here kids really are encouraged to be kids. You'll get pizza and salad and then the family can wrap it up with plenty of activity and excitement.

No one has to be quiet or use proper manners here—the noise and enthusiasm level is always on full blast. Call ahead if you're bringing a big group or planning an event.

Joe and Mary Mottino YMCA
1965 Peacock Boulevard, Oceanside
(760) 758-0808
www.mottino.ymca.org
This newish facility has lots to offer, and it serves residents of Vista and Fallbrook as well as Oceanside. The Pee Wee sports program trains tykes as young as age 3, as do the Pee Wee soccer and T-ball clubs. Before- and after-school care frees working parents from worry, and, speaking of no worries, there's free on-site child care while parents work out. In addition to dance, yoga, and sports for children, this Y offers traditional summer day camps where your little Insiders can learn basic carpentry or hone cheerleading, dance, archery, or even survival skills.

J.W. Tumbles
292-A North El Camino Real, Encinitas
(760) 942-7411
www.jwtumbles.com
This location offers the same programs as the other locations (see Point Loma entry under Central San Diego).

At this location, however, every other Friday from 5:30 to 9:30 P.M. is Kids Night Out. Parents can drop off children ages 3 through 9 for supervised activities (from coloring to games) and fun theme parties. The food that's available runs along the pizza and soda line. The cost is $30 per child for the four hours, $35 for nonmembers. This activity is popular with both kids and parents, so reservations are recommended.

LEGOLAND California
One LEGOLAND Drive, Carlsbad
(760) 918-5346
www.legolandca.com
Devoted to those ever-popular LEGO

bricks, this theme park is most appropriate for smaller children. Wholesome fun for kids and their parents, it has no scary breath-snatching rides and nothing that will make even the youngest have bad dreams.

It took more than 30 million LEGO blocks to build the models and displays here; 20 million alone were used in Miniland, the heart and soul of this 128-acre theme park, which is divided into six theme areas. Village Green includes an opportunity to drive your own Jeep on an African safari; you'll see life-size LEGO giraffes, zebras, lions, and other wildlife. A boat ride takes you through storybook adventures. In Fun Town, kids drive real electric cars and earn their official LEGOLAND driver's license at the Driving School. There are also kid-piloted LEGO helicopters as well as Skipper School boats. Waterworks offers kids a place to play with water and is best on a hot summer day. There's also DUPLO for younger guests, a puppet theater, a magic theater, and a snack shop.

You can then move on to the Ridge, LEGO maze, and Sky Cycle, where you cycle your way around in a zany people-powered car. The way it's planned, this self-propelled ride will take you up Kid Power Tower. At the top—guess what?—you can experience the exhilarating "free-fall" to the bottom. This is all very safe and won't scare even the youngest child.

There's more child-oriented pleasure in Castle Hill (for medieval scenes and encounters), the popular Imagination Zone, and the sports center, where the kids can play basketball, soccer, and other games. New starting in the summer of 2006 is Pirate Shores, with four water-based attractions designed to get kids happily wet.

Several of the park's restaurants actually serve fresh, healthy foods. Open daily in July and August, LEGOLAND is closed Tuesday and Wednesday the rest of the year. Adult admission is $53, $43 for children age 3 to 12 and seniors. Parking is $8.00.

Best photo ops for the park? From the Garden Restaurant near Castle Hill, on the promenade heading into the Imagination Zone, and anywhere in Miniland.

After conducting an international poll, the monthly trade magazine* Amusement Today *rated LEGOLAND California "the best of the best" of children's parks, giving it the Golden Ticket Award in 2005 for the second straight year.

Magdalena Ecke YMCA
200 Saxony Road, Encinitas
(760) 942-9622
http://ecke.ymca.org

The Y has been an important source of kidstuff throughout the county for years. Its varied programs are well supervised, age-specific, and lots of fun. Choose to have the kids experience horseback riding, surfing, skating, crafts, gymnastics, or a dozen other fun camps, workshops, and ongoing classes. There's a very popular skateboard park and a brand-new aquatic center with retractable roof. There are also classes and sporting teams for parents and teens as well as family campouts. Call or check the Internet for prices, locations, and a current schedule; Y members receive a discount on events and trips.

San Diego County Fair, aka the Del Mar Fair
Del Mar Fairgrounds
2260 Jimmy Durante Boulevard
Del Mar
(858) 755-1161
www.sdfair.com

We mention this huge county fair in the Annual Events chapter; you can read the details there. Some of the kids' favorite attractions, in addition to the food and the midway rides, are the collection contests,

San Diego Kids (www.sdkids.com) has an extensive listing of activities to do with children. Their calendar is kept up to date, and there are tons of links to others Web pages.

Take the kids to Blue Sky Ecological Reserve (see the Parks chapter for full details) around Halloween, when docents dressed as animals lead walks. Other children's activities are sometimes offered throughout the year, and khaki-clad docents lead guided walks most weekends.

the animals, the horse shows, and the special events like sheep shearing and herding demonstrations. Pick up a free listing of events for the day just past the fairground entrance.

During the three-week event, Tuesday is kids' day; they get in free. Otherwise, kids ages 6 through 12 pay $6.00; there's no charge for kids age 5 and younger. On Thursday seniors pay the usual price, but events and musical groups are geared to their tastes. General admission is $11.00, but pre-fair tickets and family passes are available. Find out where you can get these by calling the hotline at (858) 793-5555 (or 858-755-1161 to talk to a real person); also ask about the free shuttles available from various locations.

Silver Bay Kennel Club Dog Show
Del Mar Fairgrounds
2260 Jimmy Durante Boulevard, Del Mar
(858) 792-4252

Grown-ups (along with dog breeders and handlers) go to the show to see the competition. Kids love it to see how working dogs work, the pampered pooches compete, and the demonstrations. All animal-loving kids and future vets will talk about this premier dog event for years. Kids can get up-close to elite canines (with permission from the handlers) before and after competition times.

There is no admission fee for this event that happens each February. If your kids love dogs, keep a watch at pet-food centers and in the newspaper for other dog shows around the county. Show dates change each year, so watch the paper or call the fairground's info line.

Be sure to check out our Annual Events chapter for more information about this and other free, kid-oriented things to do.

NORTH COUNTY INLAND

Bates Nut Farm
15954 Woods Valley Road, Valley Center
(760) 749-3333
www.batesnutfarm.biz

At Bates Nut Farm kids can be kids as they discover and touch farm animals. There are wonderful places to let the smaller set run as you put out a picnic lunch. In the fall plan a trip here to pick a pumpkin. Bates fields will be blanketed with bright orange, plump pumpkins. You might want to bring along a wagon as you go out to find your own. Don't forget your camera; the snapshots are sure to make the aunts, uncles, and grandparents smile.

At Christmastime you can select the perfect tree at Bates Nut Farm, and while you're there, you might want to take a horse-drawn hayride, too. For many families, that's become a holiday tradition.

Mom and Dad will enjoy the craft shows that are scheduled during the fall and December holidays. Parents will also like the gourmet foods found at the Bates general; after all this fun you'll need some healthy snacks.

See Attractions for a full idea of what's in store for kids and grown-ups at Bates Nut Farm.

Chuck E Cheese's
624 West Mission Avenue, Escondido
(760) 741-5505
www.chuckecheese.com

If as a parent or chaperone you can handle loud music, yelling kids, and costumed creatures cavorting on stage, there's fun aplenty at this kids-oriented restaurant. This restaurant is probably the one most requested by the 7-and-younger set, and plenty of teens go there, too. If you and the kids need a shot of intense fun, steer the car to Chuck E Cheese's.

J.W. Tumbles
11501 Rancho Bernardo Road, Suite 150, Rancho Bernardo
(858) 673-4700

1605 South Melrose Drive, Vista
(760) 734-4400
These locations offer basically the same programs as the other locations; see the Point Loma entry under "Central San Diego." The Vista gym offers open gym for kids of all ages Monday through Thursday around noon, and it employs an occupational therapist for kids with special needs.

Roar and Snore Sleepovers
San Diego Wild Animal Park, 15500 San Pasqual Valley Road, Escondido
(619) 718-3000
www.wildanimalpark.com
This fabulous experience has evolved over the years, and there are now two separate camping nights for children and their parents: for kids age 4 and older and kids age 8 and older. Both start with orientation and then dinner; younger kids do a walk and scavenger hunt and have a campfire with stories about animals and African culture and singing before bed. Older kids get to take a longer nighttime hike where they get to see (but mainly listen to) the animals as they feed, play, and generally go about their nocturnal activities before hitting the hay near the African section of the park. In the morning there's breakfast and a ride through the park on the railway for both groups. The cost of the camping experience is $129 to $199 per adult and $109 to $129 per child (it's more for snazzier tents with cedar flooring and electrical outlets). Additionally, one must pay the usual Wild Animal Park entrance fee, which allows campers the option of staying two full days in the park, or the day of the campout or the day after.

The camp happens on Friday, Saturday, and some Sunday evenings May through October. Call for reservations and a recommended equipment list. See our Attractions and Balboa Park chapters for more details on the Wild Animal Park.

i

A terrific family outing is a sail aboard the historic* Californian*—a replica of a schooner built in 1847 and California's official Tall Ship. The San Diego Maritime Museum offers three-hour sails, weekend jaunts to Catalina Island, and at least one longer trip up the coast each summer. Maritime-themed movies are screened aboard the* Star of India *on summer weekend nights.

The Wave Waterpark
161 Recreation Drive, Vista
(760) 940-9283
This is a wet and wild adventure for kids and parents. Be sure to read all about it in the Attractions chapter, then come sample the fun at this $3.8 million, state-of-the-art, municipally operated family aquatic park. It's open from May through September. If you're interested in swimming lessons for the kids, it's wise to reserve a space ahead of time.

The attractions include the Flow Rider, four waterslides, a Crazy River, a competition pool, and a children's water playground. Admission for those taller than 42 inches is $14.00; it's $10.50 for seniors and kids under 42 inches tall. There's no charge for kids age 2 and younger. During the summer (June through the end of August) it's open daily from 10:30 A.M. to 5:30 P.M.

YMCA
1050 North Broadway, Escondido
(760) 745-7490
http://palomar.ymca.org
You can depend on the Y for quality year-round fun. There are summer day camps, overnight campouts, crafts, and classes in CPR and first aid. The Escondito Y has after-school programs and an indoor sports arena. Open to community members, its incredible teen center has 3 pool tables, a recording studio, giant-screen TV, and 13 computers. Members have free access to the adjacent Stensrud Youth

and Hockey Center. Call for a current schedule of activities.

EAST COUNTY

Boomer's El Cajon
1155 Graves Avenue, El Cajon
(619) 593-1155
www.boomersparks.com
In our Attractions chapter you'll find all the details about this great activity center. Here you'll find old- and new-fashioned fun: miniature golf courses, batting cages, and bumper boats, as well as go-karts, an arcade with the latest video games, the Kids Country Fair, and a 32-foot rock-climbing wall.

Chuck E Cheese's
5500 Grossmont Center Drive, La Mesa
(619) 698-4351
www.chuckecheese.com
Okay, so it's loud inside. Okay, kids run around a lot. And that's more than okay if you and the kids need to laugh, get wild, and have some fun. This La Mesa restaurant is a carbon copy of others—same pizza, soda, and video and arcade games. This is a popular place for pint-size sports teams. If you're new in the community, it's a great place to meet other families.

Cuyamaca Rancho State Park
California Highway 79 between Highway 78 and Interstate 8
(760) 765-0755
www.cuyamaca.statepark.org
If you're a camping family and love to explore, this state park should be on your must-do list. (Parts were destroyed by the Cedar Fire of 2003, but this ecosystem has a dramatic ability to regenerate.) You and the kids will be treated to wilderness areas, a museum with Native American artifacts, and more than 100 miles of walking and equestrian trails. Some of the trails are easy walks, perfect for smaller children; others are more challenging.

The wilderness area covers more than 25,000 acres in East County, including heavenly wildflower meadows (usually blooming in April or May), Green Valley Falls, and the fenced ruins of a gold mine, the Stonewall mine. There are two developed campgrounds with group campsites and cabins. You'll want to look at the Parks chapter for a full overview of this natural adventureland and of other parks throughout the county that have special kids programs. Most programs are seasonal and change themes often.

East County Family YMCA
8881 Dallas Street, La Mesa
(619) 464-1323

8669 Magnolia Avenue, Santee
(619) 449-9622
The Y is more than just a great place to work out—it's a kidstuff favorite with important learning programs, child-care resources, summer classes, and camps that are run on age-specific levels. Two facilities offer a great range of services. At the main facility on Dallas Street, there are four lighted tennis courts, a short running path, a skate park, playground, well-equipped, air-conditioned gym with many fitness classes, and a heated outdoor lap pool. The Cameron Family YMCA, at Town Center Community Park in Santee, has a large gym with an excellent gymnastics training program and dance studio as well as an aquatic center. Y members receive a discount on camps and programs.

J.W. Tumbles
2522 Jamacha Road, El Cajon
(619) 670-6212
See the write-up under Point Loma, Central San Diego. This location offers the same activities for kids up to 9 years old.

Mother Goose Parade
West Main and Chambers Streets, El Cajon
(619) 444-8712
www.mothergooseparade.com
The parade is held the Sunday before Thanksgiving and really gets the family in the mood for holiday fun. The parade begins at noon on West Main and Chambers Streets and continues east on Main to Second Street then north on Second to Madison. This is an old-fashioned children's affair with lots of local turnout. You'll see floats, clowns, bands, equestrians, civic leaders, and representatives of charitable organizations. There's no admission fee. Bring your own lunch or buy food from vendors, then try some of the peanuts or candy for sale.

SOUTH BAY

Border View YMCA
3085 Beyer Boulevard, Suite A-103
San Diego
(619) 428-1168
http://borderview.ymca.org
Like most YMCAs, Border View offers a safe and nurturing environment for kids. As well as sports and after-school care, this Y offers mentoring and tae kwon do. Subsidized programs make prices here economical. During the summer sign the kids up for one (or all) of the 12 weeklong day camp sessions. Designed for children ages 5 to 12, they offer arts and crafts, sports, swimming, and field trips to attractions around the county that have maximum "kid appeal." One-week sessions cost just $85 for members, $115 for nonmembers.

Chuck E Cheese's
1143 Highland Avenue, National City
(619) 474-6667
www.chuckecheese.com
This is a carbon copy of the other Chuck E Cheese's kids' restaurants in the county. You'll notice that they've popped up in every one of our regions, and for good reason: Kids absolutely love them. For more information, see our entry under Central San Diego.

A perfect vacation spot for kids is San Elijo State Beach (800-444-7275; www.cal-parks.ca.gov) in Cardiff. There are tent and RV sites. Nearby is Glen Park, with basketball courts and picnic tables, as well as the Cardiff Library, Seaside Market (with a great deli), Starbucks, and Yogis Bar and Grill. Area restaurants have ocean views.

Fun-4-All
950 Industrial Boulevard, Chula Vista
(619) 427-1840, (619) 427-1473
www.fun-4-all.net
Fun-4-All is open Monday through Thursday from 10:00 A.M. to 10:00 P.M., Friday 10:00 A.M. to midnight, Saturday 9:00 A.M. to midnight, and Sunday 9:00 A.M. to 10:00 P.M. Miniature golf is $6.00 for adults and $4.75 for children younger than age 12.

J.W. Tumbles
734 Otay Lakes Road, Chula Vista
(619) 397-0029
This location offers the same programs as the other locations; see the Point Loma entry under "Central San Diego."

Knott's Soak City USA
2052 Otay Valley Road, Chula Vista
(619) 661-7373
www.soakcityusa.com
Something about water parks is irresistible to kids, so when you toss out the idea of a day at Knott's Soak City, the suggestion is sure to be met with cheers and shouts of approval. Even if adults don't like to admit it, they get a kick out of water parks, too. It must be that combination of warm sunshine, cool water, and knowing your kids are having an excellent time.

You'll find body slides, tube slides, a giant wave pool, a four-story interactive family play structure, and a scaled-down structure for younger children.

There are picnic areas and junk-food stands as well as changing rooms and pay lockers. From Memorial Day to Labor Day, it's open daily from 10:00 A.M. to 7:00 P.M. It's closed from the end of September until April. Otherwise it's weekends only from 10:00 A.M. to 6:00 P.M. Adults pay $27 (SoCal residents pay $22); kids age 3 to 11 pay $15. Summer season passes cost $75 for adults and $45 for children. Parking is $7.00.

BALBOA PARK

San Diego is famous for its natural attributes—the sparkling beaches, the curving harbor, the imposing ocean bluffs, the blooming desert. It's also noted for its man-made landmarks, such as the Hotel del Coronado, the San Diego-Coronado Bay Bridge, and SeaWorld. But the best combination of San Diego's natural and man-made attributes is on display at Balboa Park.

Most San Diegans believe that Balboa Park was born during the Panama-California Exposition, held in 1915 and 1916 to celebrate the opening of the Panama Canal. But the seeds of the park were planted—literally—in 1892. Kate Sessions, a noted horticulturist, leased 30 acres of Balboa Park from the city to use as a nursery. In exchange, she agreed to plant 100 trees a year in the park for the next 10 years. Today the park is landscaped with some 15,000 trees of more than 350 different species, with vast displays of exotic and drought-resistant plants and trees.

The man-made attributes of the park came later. San Diego's leaders hired some of the finest local and national architects to construct the buildings for the Panama-California Exposition. A cantilevered bridge was constructed over a deep canyon as the entryway to the exposition, leading to the Spanish colonial-style California Building. The building's 200-foot-high California Tower, topped with yellow and blue tiles, has become one of San Diego's most endearing landmarks.

Some buildings were restored for the California Pacific International Exposition in 1935 and 1936, and others were added to the park. This often rushed and confused approach resulted in a melange of styles, from Beaux Arts to Baroque to Spanish Renaissance. Somehow, the combo worked. These historic buildings make Balboa Park an architectural museum of sorts. Many have been lovingly reconstructed and renovated to house some of the city's finest museums.

At the conclusion of the first exposition, Dr. Harry Wegeforth, a local physician, gathered together a few animals left from various exhibits to start a small zoo. His prescient act led to the formation of the San Diego Zoological Society and the world-famous San Diego Zoo. From those beginnings grew Balboa Park as we know it today, the jewel in the crown of San Diego's attractions.

The park is not something you can absorb in a day. Like a rich dessert, it's better savored at a leisurely pace. The zoo alone can take up the better part of a day. You need another day to see and appreciate the rest of the park. As you read this chapter, you will undoubtedly choose the sights that match your interests. But we recommend that you try not to stick too closely to a strict agenda. It's inevitable that you'll get distracted by something. That's half the fun.

In this chapter we'll describe the zoo, museums, gardens, and other attractions so you can get an overview and see what appeals to you. The park is spread across 1,200 acres, and even though that sounds enormous, most everything is within walking distance—the zoo excepted—of any place you park. (Parking in all lots, by the way, is free.) Should you get tired of walking, just hop on the free Balboa Park Tram that runs continuously from 8:30 A.M. to 6:00 P.M. (later in summer) daily. Tram stops are located throughout the park; the starting point is the parking lot of Inspiration Point, at Park Boulevard and President's Way.

i

Be one of 6 million people this year to visit Balboa Park, the largest urban cultural park in the nation, with 15 major museums.

If you think you'll miss out on shopping while you're discovering Balboa Park, guess again. Every museum has an expansive gift shop stocked with items related to the museum as well as gifts with general appeal. Also, the Reuben H. Fleet, Natural History, Hall of Champions Sports Museum, and Japanese Friendship Garden have cafes.

Loads of places to picnic are scattered throughout the park, and it's a great way to take a midday break from all the activity. One prime spot is the grassy area surrounding the Moreton Bay fig tree, which was planted in 1915. Located behind the Natural History Museum, this magnificent tree has been a San Diego icon for generations. Lawns surrounding the lily pond and the botanical garden are other prime locations for picnicking or just relaxing. If lunching alfresco isn't your style, there's no lack of spots that provide food and beverage, from hot dog stands to The Prado, a "Latin-Italian fusion" restaurant.

The park is loaded with museums and several noteworthy theaters. These are covered in greater detail in The Arts chapter. We'll include some references to attractions with particular appeal to kids, which are also included in our Kidstuff chapter. Specific festivals and events are listed in the Annual Events chapter.

Balboa Park is located in the heart of the city, just north of downtown San Diego. It's accessible by Metropolitan Transit bus or by car via Interstate 5, off California Highway 163. Once you're there, a good place to start is the visitor center, located in the House of Hospitality building at 1549 El Prado, (619) 239-0512. Friendly receptionists can answer questions, give you maps, and sell you a Passport to Balboa Park: a good deal if you plan to visit several attractions—or more. The park is open daily 9:30 A.M. to 4:30 P.M. The park's very comprehensive, up-to-date Web site is www.balboapark.org.

Signage pointing the way to just about everything is excellent in the park, but it's a good idea to carry a map showing locations of the various plazas and buildings. Most hotels have Balboa Park maps, and they are also available at the visitor center. So carve out a day or two from your schedule, gather up the family, and don't forget your *Insiders' Guide*. Art, science, culture, history, animals, bugs, and botany all await.

During the summer from mid-June to end of August is Twilight in the Park. Tuesday through Thursday evenings at 6:15 there are free musical programs from Barbershop Quartets to flamenco performances at the Spreckels outdoor auditorium.

Alcazar Garden/Palm Canyon
Located adjacent to the House of Charm

Though much smaller, the park's Alcazar Garden is patterned after those of Alcazar Castle in Seville, Spain, with ornate fountains and colorful Moorish tiles. It's a beautifully symmetrical garden, with individual areas bordered by boxwood hedges and planted with more than 7,000 annual flowers for year-round drama.

Just across the road and behind Alcazar Garden is Palm Canyon, a tropical oasis of more than two acres graced by 450 palm trees representing 70 species. Most prominent in the canyon are Mexican fan palms planted in the early 20th century.

Both Alcazar Garden and Palm Canyon are open daily, and there is no admission fee.

Botanical Building and Lily Pond
North side of El Prado, between Timken Art Museum and Casa del Prado

Walking down El Prado, the main pedestrian mall in the park, you can't miss the reflecting lily pond, where creamy white lilies and lotus flowers float. It's hard to imagine that the pond was used as a therapy pool during World War II for injured sailors sent over from nearby Balboa Naval Hospital.

Less striking from the outside, but glorious on the inside, is the Botanical Building that sits behind the pond. At 250 feet long by 75 feet wide and 60 feet tall, it was the largest wood lath structure in the world when it was built in 1915. Inside you'll find more than 2,100 specimens of tropical plants and trees, including many types of orchid. The Botanical Building underwent extensive renovation in 2001 and 2002. Workers replaced more than 70,000 linear feet of redwood lath to restore the building's grandeur.

The Botanical Building is open daily, except Thursday and on city holidays, from 10:00 A.M. to 4:00 P.M. Admission is free.

Carousel and Miniature Railroad
Park Boulevard and Zoo Place, behind the Spanish Village Art Center

Built in 1910 and imported from New York, the "merry-go-round" has been a park fixture since 1922. Its menagerie of animals were hand-carved by European craftsmen. It's one of the few remaining carousels in the world where you can still go for the brass ring and win a free ride.

From mid-June through Labor Day the carousel operates from 11:00 A.M. to 6:00 P.M. every day. The rest of the year it opens on Saturday, Sunday, holidays, and during school vacations from 11:00 A.M. to 5:30 P.M. Tickets are $1.75; children younger than a year old ride free. Adults should accompany smaller children.

Next door to the carousel is the miniature railroad. The ⅕-scale locomotive takes a three-minute, 0.5-mile ride around four acres of Balboa Park. It's a replica of the General Motors F3 diesel, which pulls the Santa Fe's Super Chief. Adding to the atmosphere is the conductor in a railroad cap and overalls who not only shouts "All aboard!" but also serves as engineer for every ride.

The miniature railroad runs on Saturday, Sunday, and school holidays from 11:00 A.M. to 4:30 P.M. (mid-June through Labor Day until 6:00 P.M.). Admission for "children 1 to 99" is $1.75; children younger than a year old ride for free. Kids younger than age 5 must ride with an adult.

Almost all of the museums here are closed on major holidays: Thanksgiving, Christmas, and New Years Day; some close on Easter, but that changes year to year. Only the zoo and the Reuben H. Fleet Space Center are open those days. Most of the museums also have salons or gardens for private events, fund-raisers, wedding receptions, or birthday parties.

Centro Cultural de la Raza
2125 Park Boulevard
(619) 235–6135
www.centroraza.com

Located just south of the Pepper Grove picnic area, the Centro Cultural de la Raza is an internationally recognized art space that hosts exhibitions and performances showcasing Latino, Chicano, and Native American culture. Stroll around the perimeter of the circular building, and you'll see that the exterior is one long mural depicting themes from Maya, Native American, and Chicano cultures. The Ballet Folklorico Aztlan usually offers a dance performance on the second Sunday of the month while artisans sell their wares on the third Sunday at the Centro Mercado.

For more information about the Cen-

If you plan to spend more than a day or two discovering Balboa Park, you may want to purchase a "Passport to Balboa Park." The $30 passport is valid for a week and allows entrance to 13 attractions (an $85 value). Passports can be purchased at the visitor center in the House of Hospitality building, (619) 231–1640, or at any participating museum.

Insiders who work near the park love to lunch at the informal Waters' Cafe@SDMA, which overlooks the Sculpture Garden. The push-cart-style cafe serves yummy soups, sandwiches, salads, and desserts. It's open Tuesday through Sunday from 11:00 A.M. to 4:00 P.M.

tro's exhibits, community outreach programs, and performances, see The Arts chapter. The Centro is open Tuesday through Sunday, noon to 4:00 P.M. Admission is free.

House of Pacific Relations, International Cottages
Pan American Road W.
(619) 234-0739
www.sdhpr.org

Founded in 1935, the House of Pacific Relations is an organization dedicated to fostering cooperation and understanding among its international groups. More than 30 countries are represented in the organization, and most of them have their own cottages in Balboa Park. The cottages are furnished and staffed by members of the respective groups and present exhibits that showcase their history, culture, and traditions.

Cottages are open on Sunday from noon to 4:00 P.M. at which time group members, dressed in traditional costumes, welcome visitors and answer questions. Adjacent to the International Cottages is the Hall of Nations, which also has international exhibits. Groups that do not have cottages rotate their exhibits in the Hall of Nations.

On Sunday from March through October, special Lawn Programs are held on the outdoor stage in the cottage area at 2:00 P.M. Admission is free to all House of Pacific Relations events (except films); donations are gratefully accepted.

Inez Grant Parker Memorial Rose Garden/ Desert Garden
Located across Park Boulevard, opposite the Natural History Museum

Stopping to smell the roses has never been sweeter. This stunning, award-winning garden shows off more than 2,400 rose bushes in 178 varieties. Peak bloom time is during April and May, but some of the roses bloom clear through December. If you're in the mood for romance, the Rose Garden is the most popular wedding spot in Balboa Park.

With the heady fragrance of roses still lingering, walk a few yards north and visit the two-and-a-half-acre Desert Garden. Kate Sessions, the horticulturist who was largely responsible for turning Balboa Park into a botanical wonder, was fascinated by drought-resistant plants. The Desert Garden displays many of the specimens Sessions introduced to the park, as well as succulents and other drought-resistant varieties from around the world.

The Rose Garden and the Desert Garden are open daily, and admission is free.

Japanese Friendship Garden
Located between the House of Hospitality and the Spreckels Organ Pavilion
(619) 232-2721
www.niwa.org

Peaceful and serene describe the atmosphere within the two-acre Japanese Friendship Garden. Funded by a grant from the San Diego Art and Culture Commission, the garden was built as a tribute to San Diego's sister city of Yokohama. Enjoy sushi, noodles, salads, and snacks in the tea garden from 10:00 A.M. to 4:30 P.M.

Exhibits within the garden include a meditation garden, a koi pond, and a sweet-scented wisteria arbor. Weekend classes such as sushi making and calligraphy are offered. The Friendship Garden is open Tuesday through Sunday from 10:00 A.M. to 4:00 P.M. (daily till 5:00 P.M. in summer). Admission is $3.00 for adults, $2.50 for seniors age 65 and older, and $2.00 for disabled persons, military, students, and children ages 7 to 17. Children age 6 and younger are admitted free. The garden is open free of charge on the third Tuesday of every month.

Marie Hitchcock Puppet Theatre
Pan American Plaza
(619) 685-5990
www.balboaparkpuppets.com
Named for San Diego's original "puppet lady," the Marie Hitchcock Puppet Theatre has been charming local kids since the 1940s with marionettes, shadow puppets, hand puppets, and ventriloquists.

Show times are 10:00 A.M. and 11:30 A.M. Wednesday through Friday; 11:00 A.M., 1:00 P.M., and 2:30 P.M. Saturday and Sunday, with additional performances in the summer months. Admission for adults is $5.00, children age 3 to 17 $3.00. Admission is free for children age 2 and younger.

Mingei International Museum
1439 El Prado, Balboa Park
(619) 239-0003
www.mingei.org
Many cultures are adopting the word "mingei" to mean "art of the people." The mission of the San Diego Mingei International Museum is to further understanding of art of all cultures of the world. The goal is to open a window to a broad view of the creative potential of all people.

The Mingei Museum displays arts and crafts of unsurpassed beauty. Frequently changing and touring exhibitions present essential art forms, such as ceramics, textiles, baskets, pottery, toys, furniture, and other objects of daily use. Also in the collection are hundreds of pieces of pre-Columbian artifacts from North and South America. Numerous videos are available for viewing.

The museum is open Tuesday through Sunday from 10:00 A.M. to 4:00 P.M. Admission is $6.00 for adults and $3.00 for students and children ages 6 to 17. Admission is free for children younger than age 6. Admission is free for everyone on the third Tuesday of each month.

Model Railroad Museum
1649 El Prado, Casa de Balboa
Lower Level
(619) 696-0199
www.sdmodelrailroadm.com
Check out the largest operating model-railroad exhibit in America. More than 24,000 square feet of model train exhibits await your delighted observation. It's a toss-up which attraction kids love more: the train exhibits or the interactive Toy Train Gallery, where they (and you, too) can play engineer.

Along with the impressive scale and model trains is an in-depth exhibit that details the colorful history of railroads in the American Southwest.

The museum is open Tuesday through Friday 11:00 A.M. to 4:00 P.M., Saturday and Sunday 11:00 A.M. to 5:00 P.M. Admission is $5.00 for adults, $4.00 for seniors, $3.00 for students, and $2.50 for military. Children younger than age 15 are admitted free when accompanied by an adult. The first Tuesday of the month is free admission day for the Model Railroad Museum.

Museum of Photographic Arts (MOPA)
1649 El Prado, Casa de Balboa
(619) 238-7559
www.mopa.org
If you're like many Insiders, your photo treasures are limited to snapshots of family, friends, and favorite vacations. But we all appreciate those who have the talent to create spellbinding works of art with the camera. Some of the best are on display at the Museum of Photographic Arts, one of the country's finest.

Changing exhibits display critically acclaimed historical and contemporary works by some of the world's most celebrated photographers. In addition to its exhibits, the museum offers lectures and workshops. If you'd like more insight into exhibits, docents are on hand between 10:00 A.M. and 4:00 P.M. When the museum was completely remodeled in 2000, a new 238-seat theater was added; art films in a variety of formats are screened here Thursday evenings and for special screenings. General admission price is $10.

The museum is open daily from 10:00 A.M. to 5:00 P.M., Thursday until 9:00 P.M. Admission is $6.00 for adults and $4.00

For a look at an arts and crafts-style home turned museum, visit Marston House (3525 Seventh Avenue, 619-298-3142). Designed by local architects Irving Gill and William Hebbard, it is filled with original furnishings. Located at the northwest corner of the park, it's open Friday through Sunday 10:00 A.M. to 4:00 P.M. for a nominal fee.

for students, seniors, and military; children younger than age 12 are admitted free when accompanied by an adult. Admission is free to all on the second Tuesday of every month.

Museum of San Diego History
1649 El Prado, Casa de Balboa
Upper Level
(619) 232-6203
www.sandiegohistory.org

San Diego's history is rich with tales of townspeople determined to turn a town into a city. Despite numerous obstacles and bumps in the road, our founders persevered. This museum traces the city's development from 1850 to the present with permanent and changing displays of historical photos, costumes, and artifacts.

The museum is operated by the San Diego Historical Society, which also makes its research archives available to the public. History buffs spend hours in the archives, poring over photos and documents from the early days of San Diego. Research archives are open Thursday through Saturday from 11:00 A.M. to 4:00 P.M., and the fee for using the archives is $5.00; $2.00 for juniors age 6 to 17. The museum is open daily from 10:00 A.M. to 5:00 P.M. Admission is $5.00 for adults; $4.00 for seniors, students, and military; and $2.00 for children ages 6 to 17. Children younger than age 6 are admitted free. Admission is free to all on the second Tuesday of each month.

Ranger tours are scheduled for 1:00 P.M. on Tuesday and Sunday, giving insight into the park's "botanical, architectural, and historical treasures." Meet in front of the visitor center.

The Old Globe Theatres
Located behind the San Diego Museum of Man
(619) 234-5623
www.theoldglobe.org

Since 1935 the Old Globe Theatre has been presenting Shakespearean classics as well as contemporary plays and musicals. The Old Globe and its sister theaters in the Old Globe complex, the Cassius Carter Centre Stage and the outdoor Lowell Davies Festival Theatre, are nestled in a grassy enclave behind the San Diego Museum of Man. Visitors love strolling around the grounds and touring the Old Globe, which is a replica of the original Old Globe Theatre in London.

For more information about the Old Globe and its Tony Award-winning productions, please see the entry in The Arts chapter.

Pepper Grove

Pepper Grove is the perfect spot for a picnic. Lots of shady trees and wide, grassy areas give you the choice of eating in the shade at a picnic table or spreading out on the grass to bask in the sunshine.

Located behind the Reuben H. Fleet Space Theater (to the south of the theater), Pepper Grove is a great place for kids to burn off excess energy. It has three separate play areas with swings, climbing equipment, and interactive structures. A parking lot is conveniently located right next to the area.

Reuben H. Fleet Space Theater and Science Center
Plaza de Balboa
(619) 238-1233
www.rhfleet.org

If you've never experienced an IMAX film, you're in for a treat. The space theater surrounds viewers with images projected onto a giant domed screen; more than 150 state-of-the-art speakers are guaranteed to rock your world. Here you can see IMAX films such as *Everest,* the story of the tallest Himalayan peak and one of the world's greatest climbing adventures.

The Exhibit Galleries in the Science Center contain more than 100 hands-on displays. Put your hands on the Lightning Globe and become a link in an electrical circuit. Find out how your heart works, or test your reaction time and coordination skills. All exhibits are science-related and highly entertaining for both kids and adults.

The Theater and Science Center are open from 9:30 A.M. to 5:00 P.M. daily (until 8:00 P.M. in summer). Show times vary, but there usually is a show every hour. Ticket prices for IMAX shows (which includes entrance to the Exhibit Galleries) are $11.75 for ages 13 and older, $9.75 for seniors age 65 and older, and $8.75 for children ages 3 to 12. Admission to the Science Center Exhibit Galleries only is $6.75 for ages 13 and older and $5.50 for children ages 3 to 12. Children younger than age 3 are admitted free. Everyone is admitted free to the Science Center on the first Tuesday of each month.

San Diego Aerospace Museum
2001 Pan American Plaza
(619) 234-8291
www.aerospacemuseum.org

Have you ever wondered what it was like when the Wright Brothers made the first powered flight? You can relive that thrilling day in history at the San Diego Aerospace Museum, along with other landmark events and innovations in the history of aerospace. See the SPAD, the Nieuport 28, and the Albatros (the latter two, reproductions) from World War I and the Spitfire, Zero, and Hellcat from World War II, along with a working replica of the *Spirit of St. Louis,* built right here in San Diego.

The Aerospace Museum's collection has aviation memorabilia and more than 60 foreign and domestic aircraft, including present-day spacecraft. The Hall of Fame honors aviation legends. For an additional fee, jump into the Motion Simulator to experience life on an international space station or landing on an aircraft carrier. Film collections are available to educators free of charge.

Plan a child's birthday party at the San Diego Aerospace Museum. Bring 29 of your best buddies (15 kids, 15 adults total) for rides, crafts projects, a guided tour, and a goodie basket. Including admission, the cost is $300.

The museum is open daily from 10:00 A.M. to 4:30 P.M. (5:30 P.M. in summer). Admission is $9.00 for adults, $7.00 for seniors age 65 and older, $4.00 for children ages 6 to 17, and free for children younger than age 6. Active-duty military members are admitted free, too, and admission is free for everyone on the fourth Tuesday of the month.

San Diego Automotive Museum
2080 Pan American Plaza
(619) 231-2886
www.sdautomuseum.org

The automobile holds such fascination for Americans that it has become integrated into our culture, our lifestyle, and our technological advances. Along with automotive memorabilia, the San Diego Automotive Museum exhibits exotic road cars, the historic Model-A, gas-guzzling muscle cars, tiny economy cars such as the Nash Metropolitan, luxurious Rolls Royces, and actor Russell Crowe's Harley-Davidson. The research library, which is open to the public, contains rare publications, photos, and vintage films, and the museum offers a wide variety of lectures and workshops.

Museum hours are 10:00 A.M. to 5:00 P.M. daily. Admission is $7.00 for adults, $6.00 for active-duty military and seniors, $3.00 for children ages 6 to 15, and free for children younger than age 6. Admission is free on the fourth Tuesday of each month.

The San Diego Zoo provides special exhibits for guests with disabilities as well as appropriate parking, restrooms, telephones, and access to shows and exhibits. Special ASL "signed" bus tours are available, too. Call the zoo's info line at (619) 232-1515, ext. 4318, to arrange for an interpreter.

San Diego Hall of Champions Sports Museum
2131 Pan American Plaza
(619) 234-2544
www.sdhoc.com

Uniforms, trophies, photographs, and other memorabilia from San Diego's sports stars adorn the walls of the Hall of Champions museum. The jerseys of baseball legend Ted Williams are here: the ones he wore when he belted his first homers for the Padres' Pacific Coast League team, and ones he donned in his more famous days with the Boston Red Sox. Find information about your favorite amateur and professional sports (including surfing and skateboarding) at interactive exhibits. Local talents from Over-the-Line (see our Spectator Sports chapter for the lowdown on this homegrown sport), golf, the Holiday Bowl, swimming, and horse racing are all honored, too.

The Hall of Champions is open daily from 10:00 A.M. to 4:30 P.M. Admission is $6.00 for adults, $3.00 for children ages 7 to 17, and free for kids 6 and younger. Free for everyone the fourth Tuesday of the month.

San Diego Museum of Art
1450 El Prado
(619) 232-7931
www.sdmart.org

The San Diego Museum of Art has something for everyone: an Asian collection of paintings and sculptures, Spanish and Dutch old masters, American art, and numerous other collections. Besides these permanent holdings, the museum holds year-round special exhibits, too, such as the Jewels of the Romanov, devotional art from the Kathmandu Valley, Fabergé eggs, and a special collection of Monet's works. We describe the museum in detail in The Arts chapter.

Hours are 10:00 A.M. to 6:00 P.M. Tuesday through Sunday, until 9:00 P.M. on Thursday. General admission prices are $10.00 for adults; $8.00 for military and seniors age 65 and older and young adults ages 18 to 24, $4.00 for children ages 6 to 17; and free for children age 5 and younger. Admission is free on the third Tuesday of every month. There is an additional cost for some shows.

San Diego Museum of Man
1350 El Prado (under the California Tower)
(619) 239-2001
www.museumofman.org

San Diego's fine anthropological museum is filled with treasures of the ages. In 1915 the Smithsonian Institution gathered a collection of artifacts and physical remains that were displayed at the Panama-California Exposition. After the exposition the collection became the Museum of Man, and today it holds more than 70,000 items, each one a symbol of cultures from ancient times to the present.

Replicas of spectacular Maya stelae—stone pillars covered with symbols of Maya gods and historical events—stand at the museum's entrance. The artifacts of San Diego's indigenous Kumeyaay peoples are displayed in a permanent exhibit, as are others from indigenous groups from throughout the Southwest. Ancient hunting spears, ceramic vessels, and delicately woven textiles are just a few of the objects on display. Kids can dress up as pharaohs and their subjects at the interactive Children's Discovery Center's Discover Egypt exhibit.

The Museum of Man is open daily from 10:00 A.M. to 4:30 P.M. Admission is $6.00 for adults, $5.00 for seniors, $3.00 for children ages 6 to 17, and free for kids age 5 and younger. Everyone gets in for free on the third Tuesday of every month.

San Diego Natural History Museum
Plaza de Balboa
(619) 232-3821
www.sdnhm.org

Since 2001, when its new glass-fronted wing opened, the Natural History Museum has been transformed into an exciting and dynamic institution with cutting-edge exhibits and programs. The museum was one of the backers of *Ocean Oasis*, an extraordinary film on Baja California and the Sea of Cortez. The film is now one of two films shown on a giant screen within the museum several times daily and is just one of many new exhibits in the 21st-century research and educational institution.

The museum was conceived in 1874, when a group of amateur naturalists formed the San Diego Society of Natural History. The Balboa Park museum opened in 1933 with exhibits on paleontology, ecology, and mineralogy.

In 1991 the museum took on a new approach to education with a commitment to a strong focus on the binational region of San Diego and Baja California, Mexico. A Biodiversity Research Center of the Californias was established; the first exhibit featured fossils and live snakes and lizards collected in the region. In the Fossil Mysteries exhibit, which debuted in July 2006, interactive displays and satellite images complement dioramas, murals, fossils, and more in the 9,700-square-foot gallery. A 2,600-foot rooftop deck accommodates private meetings and parties.

Hours at the Natural History Museum are 10:00 A.M. to 5:00 P.M. daily. Admission is $9.00 for adults; $6.00 for college students, seniors, and military; and $5.00 for children ages 3 to 17. Children younger than age 3 are admitted free. The museum is open free of charge on the first Tuesday of every month.

San Diego Zoo
2920 Zoo Drive
(619) 231-1515
www.sandiegozoo.org

The world-famous San Diego Zoo was founded in 1916, at the close of the Panama-California Exposition, by an enterprising local physician, Dr. Harry Wegeforth. He gathered a collection of about 50 animals, some of which had been used during the exposition and some that were part of various local menageries. Today the zoo contains more than 4,000 rare and endangered animals from 800 different species.

The Great Panda exhibit is a must-see at the San Diego Zoo. PHOTO: COURTESY OF THE SAN DIEGO ZOO

More than just a place where animals hang out, the zoo has long been dedicated to animal research with the goal of preserving endangered species. And you won't find any tigers or polar bears sitting listless and bored in cages. Enclosures and open spaces have been created to replicate the animals' natural habitats. Visit Tiger River, Sun Bear Forest, Gorilla

CLOSE-UP

Offshoot Tours

Explore the exotic horticulture, the architectural beauty, and the historical wonders of Balboa Park by taking one of several free tours. Meet in front of the visitor center, 1549 El Prado, at the House of Hospitality at 10:00 A.M. on Saturday, except those falling within the holiday break from Thanksgiving through mid-January. No reservations are necessary, but tours are canceled if it's raining or the group is fewer than four people. All walking tours are easy paced and last about one hour. Tours are year-round except the period between Thanksgiving and mid-January. For more information, call the visitor center at (619) 239-0512.

History Walk—First Saturday
This tour blends a little bit of everything: history, architecture, and horticultural delights. You'll meander up and down the 2-block El Prado area while your tour guide describes the history and architecture of the various buildings. You'll also get background information on some of the many botanical specimens for which the park is noted.

Palm Walk—Second Saturday
Delve into the world of palm trees. Learn about their structure, growth, and landscape value as your guided tour takes you into Palm Canyon, where a huge collection of palm specimens awaits your inspection.

Tree Walk—Third Saturday
Famed horticulturist Kate Sessions made sure Balboa Park had a vast array of exotic trees. Your guide will introduce you to many of these rare beauties. You'll see some in the Botanical Building and many others that have been planted over the years, all within a few blocks walk.

Desert Walk—Fourth Saturday
Kate Sessions was also devoted to cultivating drought-resistant plants. See the wide variety of American, African, and Baja Californian desert plants as you tour the Desert Garden across from the San Diego Natural History Museum.

Tour del Dia—Fifth Saturday
Explore the Palisades area, where the California Pacific International Exposition was held in 1935 and 1936, and learn about its historical and horticultural roots. Like the other tours, this is a short walk that's equivalent to a few blocks.

Tropics, Hippo Beach, and Polar Bear Plunge, and you'll see what we mean. Indonesian orangutans and siamangs cavort amid tropical vegetation in the newest attractions, Absolutely Apes and Monkey Trails and Forest Tails.

The Children's Zoo is most interesting to kids age 5 and younger. Giant tortoises, goats, and other gentle critters roam freely, giving kids the opportunity for some hands-on interaction. Several animal shows are staged throughout the day in the main zoo, showcasing predators and prey from around the world.

Another must-see is the Giant Panda exhibit. Born in 1991, Bai Yun is the mother of Hua Mei, born in 1999 and the first giant panda born at the San Diego Zoo; she has now gone to live in China. But don't despair, you can see her equally adorable siblings Mei Sheng, born in the summer of 2003, and Su Lin (whose name means "A Little Bit of Something Very Cute"), born in 1995. Gao Gao, father to both cubs, was born in the wild.

When you get hungry, choose from a wide range of snacks and all-American favorites at stands throughout the zoo. Or dine in style at one of several full-service restaurants, including the Albert's Treehouse Cafe and the Flamingo Cafe. Picnic areas are also located in convenient spots around the zoo, and you're welcome to bring your own lunch. Lockers are available if you're not in the mood to tote your gear till lunchtime.

The zoo is open every day of the year from 9:00 A.M. until 5:00 P.M. (last entrance 4:00 P.M.), with extended hours during the summer, until 10:00 P.M. Admission includes the Children's Zoo and all the animal shows. Prices are $22.00 for ages 12 and older, $14.50 for children ages 3 to 11, and free for children age 2 and younger. Deluxe Admission includes a bus tour and Skyfari aerial tram ride and is priced at $32.00 for adults and $19.75 for children ages 3 to 11.

Spanish Village Art Center
1770 Village Place
(619) 233-9050
www.spanishvillageart.com

Constructed in 1935 for the California Pacific International Exposition, the charming collection of buildings was meant to depict a picturesque village in Spain. At the conclusion of the exposition, a group of dedicated artists established the village as an arts center. Its only departure from that designation was during World War II, when the U.S. Navy used the village for temporary barracks. Today the center offers the creations of more than 50 artists, many of whom use the buildings as both studios and galleries.

To see the zoo's giant pandas in live streaming video, click on "plants and animals" and then "videos and live cams" at www.sandiegozoo.org/zoo/. If the pandas aren't playing, try the polar bear, ape, or elephant cam.

Thirty-five individual studios house artists working in a variety of media: oil, watercolor, ceramics, sculpture, jewelry, wood carving, glass, photography, and enamel. You can shop or just browse among the one-of-a-kind items every day except New Year's Day, Thanksgiving, and Christmas from 10:00 A.M. to 4:30 P.M. Admission is free.

Spreckels Organ Pavilion
Pan American Road E.
(619) 702-8138

John D. Spreckels, one of San Diego's most enterprising entreprenuers, presented the city with a gift on New Year's Eve in 1914, just before the beginning of the Panama-California Exposition: a beautiful pipe organ and a grand pavilion to house it. The organ has been in almost continuous use since that time. It contains 4,530 pipes ranging in size from more than 32 feet tall to about the size of your little finger.

Year-round organ concerts are presented to the public on Sunday afternoons from 2:00 to 3:00 P.M. Special summer performances are held on Monday nights from mid-June through August at 7:30 P.M. Even if there's no concert scheduled for the day you're in the park,

In addition to the Offshoot Tours, one-hour walking tours emphasizing history, architecture, and plants are led by park rangers on Tuesday and Sunday at 1:00 P.M.

check out the pavilion and its stunning architecture; it's located at the south end of Plaza de Panama. Admission to all concerts is free.

Timken Museum of Art
1500 El Prado
(619) 239-5548
www.timkenmuseum.org

The Timken Museum of Art is devoted to the preservation of European and American paintings from the early Renaissance through the 19th century. Among its exhibits not to be missed is a collection of beautiful Russian icons.

Like Balboa Park's other art museums, we cover the Timken in greater detail in The Arts chapter. Insiders refer to it as San Diego's "jewel box for the arts."

Hours are 10:00 A.M. to 4:30 P.M. Tuesday through Saturday and 1:30 to 4:30 P.M. Sunday. Closed in September. Admission is free.

Zoro Gardens
Between the Reuben H. Fleet Space Theater and the Casa de Balboa

Zoro Gardens was a favorite attraction during the California Pacific Exposition of 1935–1936. Why? Because the gardens were the site of a nudist colony. The chief of police, however, insisted that the women wear brassieres and G-strings and that the men wear loincloths during daylight hours when visitors were likely to wander in.

Today there are no nudists, but the sunken gardens are an inviting and usually cool spot for a break during your exploration of the park. Myriad plants to attract and feed both butterfly larvae (milkweed, sunflower, passion vine, and California lilac) and adults (lantana, butterfly bush, verbena, and pincushion flower) have been planted. The winding paths travel far back into the canyons. There is no admission charge.

ANNUAL EVENTS

San Diego County's many cities, towns, and neighborhoods have good cause for celebration. There are so many activities taking place each week that it's hard to choose whether to participate in a marathon, build a sand castle, or shop for handicrafts at a street fair.

Our goal with the list is to bring San Diego's special fun to you. We've included plenty of free events and festivals from the Mother Goose Parade to the Rancho Santa Fe Rummage Sale (the primo sale of the year) to the Mainly Mozart Festival. We've also tried to blend the expected events with the unusual, notable, and eccentric ones, such as the Over-the-Line Tournament and the Pegleg Smith Liars Contest. If there's an adult-only aspect, we've included that; where it's family fun, we've stressed that, too.

Typically the outdoor events include food booths. If not, there's always a market or restaurant nearby. We've listed the current fee or cost, if it's known. We also let you know when the event is free.

Remember when looking at the calendar of events that we've organized this chapter by months rather than region. Keep in mind that you'll want to call to double-check locations and times or to verify prices. Some phones are handled by volunteers. Try to call during normal work hours.

Many communities have mini-events and cultural activities that are big news for neighborhoods but are too small to be listed here. If you've just moved into the San Diego area and wonder what's happening, ask a neighbor or call the city's parks and recreation office. Events, athletic tournaments, community picnics, and concerts are also often listed on bulletin boards in libraries and neighborhood shops.

We've tried to make it easy for you to use this list by ordering events chronologically. If an event happens in the beginning of any month, you'll find it among the first listings; if it's at the end of the month, you'll find it listed last.

JANUARY

Penguin Day Ski Fest
De Anza Cove at Information Center
Mission Bay
(858) 270-0840

During this ski fest, you won't see any of the penguins from SeaWorld; however, you will see brave (read that daring) water-skiers race around Mission Bay (no wet suits allowed) and lots of people swimming and skiing in chilly ocean water. It's kind of crazy to be going in the water in winter, but that's where the fun comes in. The ski fest is from 9:00 A.M. to 1:00 P.M. on New Year's Day. Call for details if you want to enter (watching is free). There is always a party afterwards, where you'll find food booths and places to picnic.

Carlsbad Marathon
Plaza Camino Real shopping center, 2500 El Camino Real, Carlsbad
(858) 792-2900
www.sdmarathon.com

This 26.2-mile marathon draws runners, walkers, and watchers from around the country. Last year the number of participants exceeded 10,000. This is a three-day weekend event with Friday activities

If you're looking for events at the Del Mar Fairgrounds (and something is always happening there), call (858) 755-1161 to reach the box office. Call (858) 793-5555 for a 24-hour event hotline or visit www.sdfair.com for information on monthly events and upcoming concerts.

featuring a golf tournament and Saturday activities including a Keebler Kids Marathon and a health expo, food, vendors, and activities. The actual marathon is on Sunday and begins in Carlsbad near Plaza Camino Real shopping center. Call for entrance fees, which vary; Saturday activities and watching the marathon are free.

Local Authors Exhibit
San Diego City Public Library
820 E Street, San Diego
(619) 236-5800
This is an important event for Insiders and visitors who are interested in local authors. There are some best-selling writers among our literary crowd. The month-long exhibit and author readings highlight the best the county has to offer. Call for library hours, information on readings, and, if you're a writer, information on submitting your work. Admission to the readings is free.

Martin Luther King Jr. Day Parade
County Administration Building to Seaport Village
885 Harbor Drive, San Diego
(619) 264-0542
School marching bands and homemade floats parade from the County Administration Building south along Harbor Drive to Seaport Village to honor Dr. Martin Luther King Jr. around his birthday. The festivities continue with an award ceremony and a festival with exhibits, dance demonstrations, and food vendors.

Robert Burns Supper
Town & Country Hotel
500 Hotel Circle N., San Diego
(619) 234-3525
www.oblaw.com
The Robert Burns Club of San Diego holds this annual event in honor of Scotland's national bard. The traditional banquet includes haggis; the entertainment includes pipe bands and Scottish dancing. Tickets are $45.

Whale Watch Weekend
Cabrillo National Monument
1800 Cabrillo Memorial Drive, San Diego
(619) 557-5450
The monument atop Point Loma is one of the best places to spot California gray whales spouting and breaching in the ocean. The park celebrates the whales' arrival with special exhibits, films, and lectures. The park is open every day from 9:00 A.M. to 5:15 P.M. Admission is $5.00 per vehicle and $3.00 per bicyclist, jogger, walker, or city bus passenger. The pass allows entrance for seven days.

Rose Pruning Demonstration
The Inez Grant Parker Memorial Rose Garden/Desert Garden, across Park Avenue from the Natural History Museum, Balboa Park, San Diego
(619) 235-0004
www.sdrosesociety.org
Sponsored by the San Diego Rose Society, this demonstration at Balboa Park's rose garden will teach you the how-tos and what-fors of growing gorgeous blooms. The event is held from 9:00 A.M. to noon. Rose Society members and volunteers trim, clip, and coddle the more than 1,300 bushes found in the park's knockout rose garden. Volunteers are encouraged to participate in the fun. Held sometime in January, depending on the weather, the event is free. Or you can participate in the luncheon, daylong demonstration, and a question-and-answer session with rose experts for around $20.

International Teddy Bear, Doll, and Toy Festival
Scottish Rite Temple
1895 Camino Del Rio S., San Diego
(815) 464-3470
You'll find everything imaginable at this weekend festival for professional collectors and those who appreciate the world populated by teddy bears, dolls, and toys. More than 200 vendors display their wares at this semi-annual event. Admission is $6.00.

Buick Invitational of California
Torrey Pines Municipal Golf Course
11480 North Torrey Pines Road, San Diego
(619) 281-4653, (800) 888-BUICK
www.buickinvitational.com
San Diego's Torrey Pines Municipal Golf Course shines during this all-star golf competition. The best of the best play at this PGA event, which attracts more than 100,000 spectators. The tournament has been especially exciting since 2002, when the course was remodeled with new challenges for the golfers. Ticket prices are $22 on weekdays and $28 on weekends. Call to verify ticket prices and availability, and plan to walk a ways from the parking locations. For more information about this event, check out the entries in our Spectator Sports and Golf chapters.

FEBRUARY

Anza-Borrego Desert Wildflowers Season
Anza-Borrego Desert State Park
Borrego Springs
(760) 767-4684 (recorded wildflower message)
www.parks.ca.gov
When spring comes to the desert, the colorful flowers can be a wonderful contrast to the otherwise stark environment. It's a short blooming season and worth the drive. If you haven't visited Anza-Borrego "for the flowers," you must do so at least once. Pack your camera, sunscreen, and sense of wonder. Flowers do not bloom on a strict schedule, so should rains come early, the blooms will, too. And not all species of desert plants bloom simultaneously. A call to the park's visitor center can give you the status of the blooms. There are plenty of roadside opportunities for viewing the flowers, but if you love nature and flowers, you'll want to visit the information center at the park. There's a $6.00 fee to enter the park beyond the visitor center and various charges for camping. See our Parks chapter if you're a hiker or camper and want more information about outdoor opportunities at the park.

Many Insiders attend a concert at Humphrey's by the Bay (2241 Shelter Island Drive, Shelter Island, 619-523-1010, www.humphreysconcerts.com). The May through October season caters to baby boomers with such acts as Joan Baez, the Indigo Girls, and George Carlin. Sit in the metal folding chairs at the outdoor venue or act like naughty Insiders and float your (small) boat around Shelter Island Point to listen for free.

San Dieguito Half Marathon
Lomas Santa Fe and Highland Drive, San Dieguito County Park, Rancho Santa Fe
(619) 298-7400
www.kathyloperevents.com
This race is half the size of the Carlsbad Marathon and more doable for less determined runners. The race begins at 8:00 A.M. and goes through the San Dieguito County Park and surrounding community. There are hills, so it can be a challenge. If you're not up to 12 miles, how about the 5K run/walk? Call for entrance fees. Spectators can cheer for free.

International Dance Festival
Balboa Park Club Building
Balboa Park, San Diego
(619) 286-0355
The fair is free; however, you'll want to bring some money since the ethnic clothes and pottery, especially the coffee mugs, are treats for any shopper. And there's plenty of food—from traditional American to exotic ethnic fare. The weekend event features more than 1,700 folk dances from all over the world. Some groups invite festivalgoers to join in the dancing.

Jamboree by the Sea
Del Mar Fairgrounds
2260 Jimmy Durante Boulevard, Del Mar
(858) 486-1691
There's so much fun to squeeze in that this event lasts for three days; it's held the first full three-day weekend in February.

You'll marvel at the skill, the precision, and the energy of the dancers. Come and watch them square, clog, and round dance—it might encourage you to join the fun. This is an enjoyable family event, and there's no charge for visitors.

Chinese New Year Faire
Third Avenue and J Street, San Diego
(619) 234-4447, (619) 234-7844
www.sandiegochinese.com

Go for the festival and stay for the fun with this celebration that presents the many cultures of China. There are traditional dancers, martial-arts demonstrations by pros and students, cultural information, craft booths, and food. The tea sets are especially worth a second look. The event is held for two days and is sponsored by the San Diego Chinese Center. Remember that Chinese New Year doesn't always happen in February. Free admission.

Cupid's Carnival
Spreckels Park
Seventh and C Streets, Coronado
(619) 522-7342

If it's romance you're looking for, head elsewhere. This is a high-intensity, giggling children's carnival that never goes out of style. It's Valentine fun for the family in this kidstuff event held annually in Coronado. There's a kissing booth, play area, games of chance (for a quarter a try), and an ice-cream sundae making event. The carnival is free.

Mardi Gras in the Gaslamp
Gaslamp Quarter, San Diego
(619) 233-5227
www.gaslampquarter.org

The Gaslamp Quarter hosts this parade and festival, which features music, food, and entertainment that makes you feel like you're in a small-scale New Orleans. The festival is held from late afternoon until midnight. The boisterous, sexy, and colorful parade, which starts at Fifth Avenue and K Street, begins around 8:00 P.M. Tickets are $20, and you must be 21 years or older. Call for details on the music and food venues.

Silver Bay Kennel Club Dog Show
Del Mar Fairgrounds
2260 Jimmy Durante Boulevard, Del Mar
(858) 793-5555

This is a premier dog event that usually takes place the last weekend in February, although you'll want to call to confirm the dates. The Silver Bay show attracts more than 2,200 canine contenders and a hundred breeds vying for Best in Show (that's what the top dog is called). Judging begins about 8:30 A.M. on Saturday and continues through Sunday as dogs in various categories compete for titles and trophies. At any given time there may be as many as 20 different competitions going on in the three huge indoor facilities. If you're a dog lover, this is the place to find everything you need for your pooch, from doggie hats to the latest in dog foods and canine treats. Be sure to catch the herding demos and dog obedience competitions; that's where training shines. The show is a family affair, and admission is free.

Vietnamese Tet Festival
Qualcomm Stadium
9449 Friars Road, San Diego
(800) 359-2002
www.sdtet.com

This festival will delight you with children's ethnic-costume contests, savory and satisfying foods, and dancing. Organizers gave it a big boost in 2006, moving the event to Qualcomm Stadium and adding a Miss Vietamese Pageant, a fashion show, free head shots, rides, and other activities to draw a younger and not exclusively Vietnamese audience. There are traditional games, martial-arts demos, crafts, and folk music. It's a multiday festival that involves the city's substantial Vietnamese community. Most Vietnamese-owned businesses are closed during Tet. Admission is $4.00 per day; call the number above for dates.

MARCH

Marine Gear Swap Meet
The Marina at Chula Vista
550 Marina Parkway, Chula Vista
(619) 691-1860

Calling the oars and craft crowd: This is the boat and water-sport-related swap meet of which dreams are made. What can you expect? A humongous parking lot heaped with good, used items. Here you'll find generators, compasses, scuba stuff, captain's hats, and other items a boater can't live without. There are plenty of interesting objects for boating-gear collectors, too. It's billed as a great day for the seafarer. There are shows in June and October as well, but this is the biggest. Admission is free, but if you have stuff to sell, you'll need to call for pricing to rent a space.

Spring Harvest Gift and Food Festival
Del Mar Fairgrounds,
2260 Jimmy Durante Boulevard, Del Mar
(858) 793-5555

This springtime festival presenting the arts and crafts of area artisans now offers the wares of gourmet food vendors whose pastas and pestos are packaged for sale. In addition to the artists' booths, enjoy music, jugglers, and other entertainers. Tickets ($7.00 for adults and $4.00 for kids) permit entry for all three days of the event; discount coupons are available at area stores such as Albertsons, Longs Drugs, and Mervyns.

Ocean Beach Kite Festival
4726 Santa Monica Avenue, San Diego
(619) 531-1527

This is a build-it-yourself festival filled with the magic known as kites. There are prizes, a parade, food booths, demonstrations, and, of course, the kite-flying competition, held on the nearby beach. Come fly your own; walk it along in the parade. Or just come for the sight of them: triple-deckers, Japanese kites, fish-shaped kites, and all manner of imaginative homemade flyers. This is great family fun, and it's free for everyone.

Saint Patrick's Day Parade
Sixth Avenue, San Diego
(858) 268-9111
www.stpatsparade.org

If you've seen *Riverdance* and loved the high-stepping Celtic dancers, you'll have a treat here watching experts and novices kick up their heels. The parade also features marching bands (including ones carrying bagpipes).

After the event there's an Irish festival. It's held in Balboa Park, and you needn't be Irish to have a great time. There's plenty of food and that traditional St. Pat's Day brew. Try one of the Irish varieties. Or if you're a hearty soul, you can sip a beer that's been "greened" just for the special day. There are drinks for the kids, too. This is fun for the whole family. The parade and festival are free; food prices vary.

Fred Hall's Fishing, Boat and RV Show
Del Mar Fairgrounds
2260 Jimmy Durante Boulevard, Del Mar
(805) 389-3339
www.fredhall.com

Fishing addicts swarm to this well-known show, where they get to test out the latest gear, shop for bargains on fishing line and lures, and brag about their catches. Many a boat lover finds his or her dream boat here. Although owners are known to say a boat is merely a hole to pour money into, they can't resist the new models. If you're a landlubber, you'll want to climb into a few souped-up recreational vehicles to fuel your fantasies.

America's Schooner Cup Charity Regatta
Harbor Island and Shelter Island
San Diego Bay
(619) 223-3138

The largest schooner race on the West Coast and the largest charity regatta in America is a must for anyone who loves the spray of the sea. The race, held near the end of the month, raises funds for the Navy/Marine Corps Relief Society (providing help for military personnel and military dependents in time of personal need).

Sponsored by the Kona Kai International Yacht Club, the course begins on Harbor Island and follows a course in San Diego Bay. Watching the event is free. Claim a spot on the grass along the bay-facing shores of Shelter and Harbor Islands. Call for information if you want to participate in the event.

San Diego Crew Classic
Crown Point Shores
Mission Bay, San Diego
(858) 488-0700
www.crewclassic.org

This championship has been attracting rowing teams from the United States, Canada, and Europe since 1973. Crowds line the shores along Mission Bay often gathered under flags representing the universities or organizations in the competition. It's a great way to spend the day outdoors listening to bands, checking out picnic layouts, and cheering on your team. Admission is $7.00 for anyone older than 12 years of age ($10.00 for both days). There is a $10.00 fee for preferred parking—go early, since the lots fill quickly.

APRIL

MS Walk
Various locations in San Diego
(800) 344-4867
www.mswalk.com

The walks are held in various locations in San Diego, and proceeds go to the Multiple Sclerosis Society. They're a great family activity for a worthy cause. Last year's participants included babies in strollers, folks in wheelchairs, and well-mannered family dogs (with leash, collars, and poop bags mandatory). The 5K gives you a chance to meet people, do some good, and even get a T-shirt—provided your collected pledges total at least $95. There are other gifts each year for those who raise even more money. If you're new in town and want to get involved, the society is always looking for volunteers. Call the MS Society or see their Web site for locations, pledge levels, dates, times, and sponsorship information.

Flower Fields of Carlsbad
Palomar Airport Road and Interstate 5, Carlsbad
(760) 431-0352
www.theflowerfields.com

Insiders say that this event is not to be missed, and with a six-week time slot (Mother Nature's in charge of the actual dates), you should be able to admire the awesome flower fields. The ranunculus, in shades too startling to describe, is the star in this explosion of colors. Months before the blooming season, growers stagger their plantings so that the flowering cycle stretches for a six- to eight-week period. And those flowers cover 50 acres. You can catch a glimpse of the fields driving north on I-5 or by visiting the Carlsbad Company Stores (see our Shopping chapter). But we recommend, no, urge you to stop and pay the entrance fee ($7.00) to walk the fields. Camera buffs will want to pack extra film, and gardeners will want to visit the garden store for bulbs and bouquets. Picking flowers is strictly prohibited, as these are commercial fields.

Easter Egg Hunts
Coronado (619) 522-7342
Encinitas (760) 633-2740
Escondido (760) 839-4382 ($2.00 fee)
Poway (858) 679-4366
Santee (619) 596-3141

The hunts are scheduled in many communities throughout the county. There may be games and hat-making contests, too. They are usually open and free for all egg and candy hunters younger than age 10. Check with your local parks and recreation departments for details, dates, and times.

Gaslamp Quarter Easter Bonnet Parade
Fifth Avenue and L Street
Gaslamp Quarter, San Diego
(619) 239-4287
www.gaslamp.org

Come and stroll the Gaslamp in your Easter bonnet for this annual event held the Saturday before Easter. There are hat-making activities for children and adults at 11:00 A.M. The parade starts after the hats are made and runs from Fifth Avenue and L Street along Fifth to the Horton Grand Hotel. There's an Easter egg hunt and treats for children. The cost is $12.00 for adults and $6.00 for children, and the proceeds go to a worthy cause.

The Lavender Fields
12460 Keys Creek Road, Valley Center
(888) 407-1489
www.thelavenderfields.com

Less touristy than the Carlsbad Flower Fields, these sweet-smelling, organically nurtured nine acres of fields are open to the public April through July. Products can be purchased, and on Fathers' Day, dads can purchase and plant a tiny lavender bush in the Peace Garden to symbolically encourage world peace.

Pegleg Smith Liars Contest
Anza-Borrego Desert State Park
Borrego Springs
(760) 767-5555

Like telling tall tales? Enjoy twisting the truth just a bit? You'll be delighted with the elaborate lies contestants create for this annual contest. Participants must make up a tale about lost gold, the desert, and colorful characters and spin it for the rapt audience. The free event takes place in the evening.

Adams Avenue Roots and Folk Festival
Adams Avenue at 35th Street, San Diego
(619) 282-7329

Folk, jazz, and blues musicians perform on a half dozen outdoor stages during this venerable weekend event. The Adams Avenue neighborhood is known for its ethnic diversity, cluster of antiques shops and bookstores, and colorful, funky attitude. The festival is family oriented, with plenty of games and activities for kids. Admission is free.

Coronado Flower Show Weekend
Spreckels Park, Coronado
(619) 435-3849
www.coronadoflowershow.com

The residents of this genteel community take great pride in their gardens and even have a competition for the best front-yard gardens every spring. The flower show is a must for gardeners; it's said to be the largest such show on the West Coast with a different theme each year and prizes for roses, orchids, community and home gardens, floral arrangements, and more. The weekend-long event includes a spring gala and plant sale.

Take time to walk the side streets around the park to check out the amazing front-yard gardens. Pick up a list of award-winning homes at the flower show. You'll be amazed at the towering hollyhocks and delphiniums, candy-colored tulips and poppies, and ingenious floral displays.

ArtWalk
Kettner Boulevard and India Street
San Diego
(619) 615-1090
www.artwalkinfo.com

This two-day art fest has become San Diego's premier arts event, with seminars and new events added yearly, it seems. It takes place in Little Italy near downtown and includes visual and performance art displays at galleries, studios, and other venues along the boulevard. Hundreds of artists participate in the event, which began in 1984. Kids are encouraged to join in art workshops and music performances, and food stands add to the festivities. Admission is free.

Avocado Festival
Main Street, Fallbrook
(760) 728-5845
www.fallbrookca.org/avofest.htm

Do you make a guacamole that has friends begging for the recipe? Would you like to taste avocado ice cream? Have you ever wondered if your child could be the next Little Miss or Mr. Avocado? Then don't miss this family-oriented outdoor

Flower shows are held monthly at Balboa Park's Casa del Prado. Call (619) 239-0512 for information; there is no admission fee. One favorite show is the spectacular Mother's Day event featuring epiphyllums. (What's an epiphyllum? Look it up—it's worth knowing about.)

street fair in downtown Fallbrook, which features recipe contests, booths selling arts and crafts, live music, and lots of food—everything from ribs and potato salad (with chunks of avocado in it, of course) to burgers smothered in avocado and, yes, even avocado ice cream. Of course, there's plenty of guacamole, too.

At various venues connected by free shuttles, the fair includes an organic farmers' market, art show, and antique aircraft display. And, lest we forget, "sports" such as pit spitting, avocado pit races, and the ever-popular avocado bowling competitions (all in good fun).

The event is usually held on a Sunday in mid-April, but call for dates. With no admission, it's high time you attended this event.

Rose Society Annual Show
Qualcomm Statium
9449 Friars Road, San Diego
(619) 448-0321
www.ars.org

Does a Double Delight or Queen Elizabeth rose that's blooming in your garden have what it takes to be Queen of the Day? Call for entry info, times, and rules. Spectators can watch as roses are judged by category, form, and even fragrance. Vendors sell rose plants of all types and related stuff. Parking is abundant and free. Admission is $4.00 for adults, free for children younger than age 17.

Lakeside Rodeo
California Highway 67 N.
and Mapleview Lakeside
(619) 561-4331
www.lakesiderodeo.com

Whoa baby, this much-anticipated event is locally known as the granddaddy of Western fun. Visit it and you'll know why. The three-day celebration includes performances by nationally known and up-and-coming country music groups and by school bands. There's a parade, crafts, clothes, and food. According to those who live in boots and cowboy hats, this is the main country-western event in Southern California. General admission to the Friday-night festivities is $7.00. General admission for Saturday and Sunday is $10.00; reserved seating is $15.00; kids age 12 and younger are $5.00.

MAY

***Union-Tribune* Run/Walk for Literacy**
Balboa Park and Downtown
(858) 792-2900

With proceeds going to the San Diego Council on Literacy, this is a win/win/win proposition. The main race is a scenic run from Balboa Park, down Highway 163, down Broadway, and through the Gaslamp Quarter to end at G and Union Streets. The kids participate in a "Magic Mile" on the west side of Balboa Park and get a book as well as a commemorate T-shirt. Participants are encouraged to collect pledges to support San Diego's literacy campaign. After the races there's a party with food and music.

Rancho Santa Fe Garden Club
Rummage Sale
Avenida de Acacias, Rancho Santa Fe
(858) 756-1554
www.rsfgardenclub.org

Sponsored by the Rancho Santa Fe Garden Club, this isn't your average rummage sale. Of course, you'd expect more from one of the county's premier communities. If you're a true bargain hunter, you'll be in buyer's heaven. The two-day sale begins at 8:00 A.M. and continues throughout the day. Proceeds are earmarked for charities and scholarships.

Carlsbad Spring Faire
Grand and State Streets, Carlsbad
(760) 945-3288
This event is billed as the biggest and best arts and crafts fair in Southern California. The fair satisfies your expectations with T-shirts, collectibles, antiques, books, tools, and gourmet foods. Then it takes you a step further with its size. If you miss it, don't despair—there's another faire in November. The entire village area of Carlsbad is closed to traffic and crowds mingle through the displays. There is no admission fee. Parking can be tricky, so be prepared to walk several blocks. Better yet, take advantage of free shuttles from the Plaza Camino Real shopping center and the Poinsettia Coaster station.

Cinco de Mayo
Various locations throughout the county, including:
Christmas Circle, Borrego Springs
(800) 559-5524

Chula Vista, Third Avenue from E to G Streets
(619) 422-1982

Gaslamp Quarter, Fifth Avenue, Downtown
(619) 233-5008

Old Town State Historical Park, San Diego
(619) 296-3236
Cinco de Mayo is a Mexican national holiday commemorating the battle in which Mexican troops defeated the invading French military in 1862. Though it isn't Mexico's most significant holiday, it is celebrated with great fanfare throughout San Diego. Most celebrations occur during the weekend closest to May 5. Look for folk dancing by kids and adults, Mexican foods, and activities for the whole family. Some festivals feature arts and crafts. Old Town's includes folkloric ballet performances and mariachi bands. Many restaurants and nightspots also feature Cinco de Mayo celebrations offering plenty of margaritas and cervezas. The scene can be rowdy, so be forewarned.

Portuguese Festa
2818 Avenida de Portugal, San Diego
(619) 223-5880
www.upses.com
The reds and greens of the flag, the huge scarlet swirling skirts of the traditional dancers, and the chords of the fado (a traditional Portuguese song) are what will stick in your memory. That and the aroma and taste of the foods you can try here. You might want to start with caldo verde (a green cabbage and spicy sausage soup) then move on to a hearty fish stew; be sure to save room for rice pudding with port, *doces de ovos* (egg sweets), or *cauacos* (a hard, sweet biscuit). One of San Diego's longest-running ethnic events (since 1910), it offers a parade, crowning of the Festa Queen and King, dancing, music, and Portuguese foods that tempt any appetite. The festa is held in Point Loma, home to many families of Portuguese descent. Admission is free. The event is usually held in May or June; call for the exact date.

JUNE

Surfing Contests
Various locations, San Diego beaches
www.sandog.com
Surfing contests take place all along the county's beaches throughout the year, hitting their peak from June through September. Most surf shops list upcoming events, or you can check out the comprehensive Web site above, which contains information on upcoming events and results of past contests. Watching most events is free, though some are staged as fund-raisers for environmental and health causes, and donations may be solicited.

Indian Fair
San Diego Museum of Man, Balboa Park, San Diego
(619) 239-2001
Representatives from Native American groups throughout the country assemble

Since the success of the 2005 Street Scene at Qualcomm Stadium, many festivals and fairs are being held there, such at the Vietnamese Tet Festival (which corresponds to Chinese New Year Festivities) and San Diego's Annual Rose Show. Unless organizers choose to charge for parking, it is free and super abundant here, solving the parking woes in San Diego's business districts and residential neighborhoods.

at the Museum of Man annually—since 1915. The fair includes dances, arts and crafts displays (bring your wallet), and ethnic food vendors. The museum has a large collection of American Indian artifacts; combine a visit to the museum with the fair at no additional charge. It's free to kids age 17 and younger, $5.00 otherwise.

A Taste of Gaslamp
Gaslamp Quarter restaurants, Downtown
(619) 233-5227
www.gaslamp.org

Downtown's historic district is packed with excellent restaurants. In fact, it may be the most diverse dining district in San Diego. Many of the finest restaurants participate in this annual event, where adventurous diners pay $25 (or $40 for both days) to sample the specialties of up to 20 fine chefs per day.

Greek Festival
3655 Park Boulevard, San Diego
(619) 297-4165

Are you hungry for gyros and moussaka? Are you amazed by the skill and precision of traditional Greek dancers? This annual event, sponsored by and held at Spyridon Greek Orthodox Church, gives you plenty to celebrate even if you can't claim Greek heritage. Be sure to check out the Greek imports and crafts. There's a small entrance fee for adults. Children younger than age 12 get in free.

San Diego County Fair
Del Mar Fairgrounds
2200 Jimmy Durante Boulevard, Del Mar
(858) 755-1161
(858) 793-5555 (24-hour event hotline)
www.sdfair.com

This may be the biggest county fair you've ever attended, but don't let the scope and size put you off—there's old-fashioned fun to be had. The three-week event draws top country and rock 'n' roll musical performers, but hometown talent is also a big draw. There are baking contests, hobby displays (you've got to see the lint collection!), woodworking prizes, weirdest vegetable competitions, kids' events, and even wine and microbeer competitions.

What are the most popular events with the crowds? With the age-10-and-younger set it's the midway rides and the animal displays (4H is active in San Diego). Teens enjoy the vendors, the carnival games, and competitive events sponsored by schools and clubs. The age-20-and-older group appreciates all of the above along with the displays, landscape exhibits, flower shows (be sure to see the roses), and food. The cinnamon buns are huge (and scrumptious), and the roasted corn on the cob is a bit of heaven. Food is pricey; some folks pack a lunch or eat before they go and then buy treats. Free shuttles are available from various locations in the county, which helps decrease the frustration that comes from waiting in lengthy traffic jams. General admission is $11.00, the price for seniors and kids ages 6 through 12 is $6.00. Kids get in free on Tuesday.

Watch the newspaper for a schedule of concerts and events. Also, some of the local grocery stores offer discount tickets that can be purchased before you go. This will save you money and time, since you'll avoid standing in line to buy tickets at the fair.

Mainly Mozart Festival
Various locations in San Diego and Mexico
(619) 239-0100
www.mainlymozart.org

You've just gotta love Wolfgang or forget going to this outstanding series of chamber music and piano concerts. The musical performances are sublime, to say the least, and are held in various locations throughout San Diego and Baja California, Mexico. Ticket prices vary, so call for dates and availability as the festival books up fast. (To read more about Mainly Mozart, see The Arts chapter.)

Pala Mission Fiesta
Pala Mission Road, U.S. Highway 76, Pala
(760) 742-3317
Help celebrate our Native American heritage with this little-known, movable feast of Corpus Christi. The fiesta is held on the grounds of Mission San Antonio de Pala, and it includes dancing, food (a pit barbecue and Indian fry bread are not to be missed), and wonderful music. The fiesta is an outstanding, wholesome experience, especially for the fourth grader in the family who studies California's rich heritage.

JULY

Fourth of July Fireworks and Parades
Various locations, including:
Coronado Beach, Coronado
(619) 522-7320

Marina View Park, Chula Vista
(619) 585-5682

Oceanside
(760) 754-4512

Ocean Beach, San Diego
(619) 224-4906
Several communities hold Fourth of July celebrations featuring everything from parades to street fairs to surfing contests to fireworks displays. Naturally, each town claims to have the best festivities, but we think Coronado takes the prize. The parade (which starts at 10:00 A.M.) is followed by U.S. Navy air and sea demonstrations (the parachuting is awesome), a concert in Spreckels Park, and fireworks over Glorietta Bay.

What's the Fourth without fireworks? Insiders think those at the Oceanside Pier in Oceanside, Ocean Beach, and Ferry Landing Marketplace in Coronado are the best in the West.

Check with your local parks and recreation department for what is happening on our nation's birthday. The newspapers and TV news programs also list the times and places of major fireworks displays.

Del Mar Thoroughbred Horse Racing
Del Mar Fairgrounds
2260 Jimmy Durante Boulevard, Del Mar
(858) 755-1141, (858) 793-5533
www.dmtc.com
The mid-July through mid-September horse-racing season is anticipated by locals and visitors alike. The races bring the country's most illustrious horses and jockeys to San Diego. The venue is billed as the place where the "turf meets the surf." From the grandstand you'll know why: The Pacific is the track's neighbor. Bing Crosby, W. C. Fields, Don Ameche, and other Hollywood stars flocked to the racetrack in the 1940s. Jimmy Durante became such a regular visitor, the turf course was named in his honor.

Today you'll see the elite movers and shakers of San Diego—if you happen to get a seat in the members-only Turf Club. There's on-track wagering, with bets starting at $2.00. The events start at 2:00 P.M., and the track is closed on Tuesday. General admission varies depending on spe-

Heading to the Del Mar Fairgrounds for the county fair? Traffic jams can be unpleasant, but there are alternatives. You can take the Coaster or one of the free shuttles. Watch the schedules, which can be found in the local newspapers. Some days kids and seniors need not pay admission fees.

CLOSE-UP

San Diego's Favorite Fruit

Did you know that San Diegans eat more avocados than any other regional group in the United States? If you love the shiny, sometimes bumpy, green and glorious avocado, you know why. They're good in and on about everything that Insiders serve.

Avocados are native to Mexico. Hernán Cortez, the Spanish explorer and adventurer, discovered them in Mexico in 1519. Montezuma II, the Aztec emperor, treated the avocado like a treasure, and according to legend, it was offered as a gift to the Spanish conquerors. Much later in 1848, a year before gold was found at Sutter's Mill, Henry Dalton planted avocado trees in Southern California. In 1911 Carl Schmidt traveled to Mexico and brought back new avocado varieties.

Schmidt, like others who first began farming the avocado, had some setbacks. His first grove was hit hard by the frost of 1913, and only one variety survived. Schmidt called it the Fuerte, the Spanish word for strong. About the same time Rudolph Haas discovered and named after himself a truly tasty avocado. Today the Haas is our most popular variety, followed by Fuerte, the Zutano, Bacon, Pinkerton, and Reed.

The Haas has a thick, pebbly skin that turns purplish-black when ripe. You'll find this one in the store nearly year-round. The smoother varieties, such as the Fuerte, do not change color when ripe. All are ripe when they yield to gentle pressure.

Avocados are persnickety and need some pretty fine conditions to produce. Luckily, in San Diego we have what it takes. Here avocados prefer living near the coastal strip (not more than 50 miles from the ocean) that stretches from San Luis Obispo to the Mexican border.

This decadent-seeming fruit is wonderfully healthy: It has no cholesterol; is low in sodium and saturated fat and is loaded with fiber and nutrients, such as vitamins B6, C, and E and potassium. (It's the cheese, sour cream, and other ingredients that many add to the fruit that make avocados dangerous for dieters.)

Okay, you're convinced—now you agree with Montezuma and most San Diegans. Avocados are worth their weight in gold and are far more attainable. But what do you do with avocados so hard you could break a window with them? It's simple. To ripen the fruit, place it in a fruit bowl at room temperature for a week. Or place the fruit in a paper bag with an apple to speed the process. Either way, check the ripening process every day or two.

After it's ripe, you can sprinkle with lemon juice to avoid browning and refrigerate it in an airtight container for two to three days. Or better yet, just eat the whole thing, and enjoy!

cial events, promotions, and coupons, but standard stretch run (no seat) is $6.00. Check the newspaper for special deals. Concerts are held on the infield after the races on Friday nights. See our Spectator Sports chapter for more information on the races.

Over-the-Line World Championships
Fiesta Island, Mission Bay, San Diego
(619) 688-0817
www.ombac.org

The big networks wanted to put this annual event on television so that all of America could watch the fun. The hitch? The competitors would have to clean up one of their traditions: X-rated team names. "No way," said the Old Mission Beach Athletic Club, which sponsors the beach softball fest. Therefore, the adult-oriented event can only be seen in person. But you'll hear a lot about it at local nightspots, on the radio, and in the press. Admission is free. To read more about the Over-the-Line competition, see the entry in our Spectator Sports chapter.

U.S. Open Sand Castle Competition
Imperial Beach Pier
Imperial Beach
(619) 424-6663
www.usopensandcastle.com

This competition makes any sand architect marvel. The three-day event begins Friday night with the annual Sandcastle Ball at 8:00 P.M. Saturday's events include a parade, family-oriented entertainment, food booths, crafts, rides, and fireworks. Sunday is the day for serious professional and amateur competition; pre-entry for the competition is required. Prize money is awarded for the sand structures, with $5,000 going to the best in the professional competition. About 300,000 visit the free spectator event, so parking is at a premium. With fireworks beginning at dusk on Saturday, it's a wonderful weekend at the beach that will truly spark your imagination.

Lesbian and Gay Celebration
University Avenue between Normal Street and Sixth Avenue, Hillcrest
San Diego
(619) 297-7683
www.sdpride.org

San Diego's large gay, lesbian, bisexual, and transgender community comes out en masse for this celebration of diversity. Events include a Friday rally and an elaborate parade complete with bands, floats, and outrageous costumes. The parade moves down Sixth Avenue to Marston Point in Balboa Park at Sixth Avenue and Ivy Lane, where revelers enjoy live bands, great party food from various stands, and a general sense of happy camaraderie. The weekend festival is a two-day affair, with tickets costing $12 per day or $20 for a two-day pass. It's generally held the last weekend of July.

Obon Summer Festival
Vista Buddhist Temple
150 Cedar Road, Vista
(760) 941-8800

This classical Japanese festival features the dances (odori) and displays of taiko (the incredible Japanese drums) along with ethnic foods and crafts. The festival is usually held between the end of July and the middle of August and begins about noon on Saturday and Sunday and continues to 8:00 P.M. The admission to this perfect outing is free.

Acura Tennis Classic
La Costa Resort and Spa, Costa del Mar Road and El Camino Real, Carlsbad
(760) 438-5683, (760) 438-9220
www.acuraclassic.org

San Diego's premier women's professional tennis event comes to North County at the La Costa Resort and Spa. Past lineups have included superstars Venus Williams, Martina Hingis, Martina Navratilova, and Steffi Graff. The nine-day event draws in excess of 70,000 spectators, including celebrities, movie stars, and notable Insiders. Tickets range from approximately $16 to $35 for individual days, with packages going for between $70 and $625. There is a charge for parking. See our Spectator Sports chapter for more information on this event.

AUGUST

World Body Surfing Championships
Oceanside Pier and Beach, Oceanside
(760) 802-7452
www.worldbodysurfing.com
Tried riding waves only to end up eating sand? Watch the experts use their fins to chase the wave's crest and ride atop the foam to shore. Approximately 200 amateurs compete in heats divided by age and gender. Each bodysurfer has 15 minutes to catch as many waves as possible, with the judges scoring on the best four waves. The contest begins at 6:00 A.M. with the finals beginning at noon, and runs to about 6:00 P.M. Admission is free.

Annual Julian Weed Show and Art Mart
Julian Town Hall, Main Street, Julian
(760) 765-1857
A weed is a weed is a weed when it's in your garden, but in this show a weed might be a work of art. Come see how the pesky plants can be arranged to delight the senses. Yes, arranged as one would a bouquet. The two-week event, held from 10:00 A.M. to 5:00 P.M. daily, includes a show of San Diego artists, so in addition to admiring weeds, you can also feast your eyes on paintings, sculpture, ceramics, weaving, and photography. Admission is free.

Midnight Madness Spring Bicycle Ride
County Administration Building
1600 Pacific Highway, Downtown
(619) 645-8068, (877) 224-4229
Don a whacky costume (pajamas are a popular theme) and hop on your bike for this 20-mile midnight ride through downtown San Diego—surely one of the strangest bike rides you'll ever enjoy. Before the ride there's a two-hour party and costume-perfecting event. The cost to participate is $25 if you apply beforehand, $30 if you just show up. Proceeds fund various local youth programs and scholarships. This crazy bike tour usually takes place in mid-August.

SEPTEMBER

Festival Del Mar
Del Mar Racetrack
2260 Jimmy Durante Boulevard, Del Mar
(858) 755-4844
www.festivaldelmar.com
This two-day weekend food and music event began in 2005, and it was so successful we feel sure it will continue for years to come. Held on the grassy infield of the Del Mar Racetrack, the event showcases a range of musical styles—from blues and gospel to funk, jazz, reggae, and the music of talented songsmiths Jason Mraz and Macy Gray—on four stages.

Julian Fall Apple Harvest
Throughout Julian
(760) 765-1857
www.julianca.com
San Diegans are accustomed to appreciating the small signs of seasonal changes. The best place to feel like you're in the crisp fall air is in the mountain town of Julian, where apples grow in abundance. The festival includes pie-baking contests, concerts, crafts fairs, and other events scheduled on weekends throughout September. Just driving through the mountains is a joy. Take along your hiking boots and hit the trails outside town to see trees with gold and red leaves.

Street Scene
Qualcomm Stadium
9229 Friars Road
(619) 557-8490, (888) 487-4347
www.street-scene.com
In 2005 San Diego's biggest musical party moved from its usual location in the Gaslamp Quarter to the parking lot of

Qualcomm Stadium. While the new venue didn't have the same cache, it is massively big (2.5 million square feet), is more centrally located, and offers excellent parking. And the trolley stops there, encouraging many concertgoers to use public transportation. The area covered by beer gardens alone at the 2005 event was bigger than the entire venue the previous year, which was held in the parking lot of Petco Stadium near the Gaslamp Quarter. All three days are now open to under 21s, and there were rides and other attractions for kids as well as a warren of food stalls.

Bigger also was the lineup, with no fewer than 15 bands per night, including the White Stripes, Snoop Dogg, and Social Distortion. Another change was a shift in music toward younger tastes with mainly punk rock and hip-hop music; stages for electronica and World Music may be included in the 2006 event. According to *San Diego Union-Tribune* music critic George Varga, festival founder Ron Hagey plans to make future Street Scenes more "intimate and interactive," adding more performance to the mix as well, with a drag queen extravaganza and Bindlestiff Family Cirkus freak show. Tickets cost $45 per day, $85 for a three-day pass.

Grape Day Festival and Parade
Grape Day Park, Grand Avenue, Escondido
(760) 743-8207

Come celebrate the annual Grape Day Festival and Parade with fun for the whole family, especially since this event is free. Celebrated on the first (sometimes second) Saturday in September, it goes from 9:00 A.M. to 5:00 P.M. There's a tour of the historical sites at the park, creative cooking (with grapes, of course), and performances by local bluegrass and country groups. One year we tapped our toes to the Texas Toothpicks and then sat in awe at the Ballet Folklorico de Cristo Rey dance group. You'll find mountains of food choices, free grapes, and plenty of kid and adult entertainment.

See the Kidstuff chapter for information about Roar and Snore Sleepovers: overnighting on the African savannah (of the Wild Animal Park). It's an excellent activity for parents and their kids. For grown-up fun without the munchkins, there are adults-only weekends at the park as well.

Día de la Independencia
Old Town State Historical Park
Old Town, San Diego
(619) 296-3161

Old Town celebrates Mexican Independence Day on or around September 16. (Mexican Independence Day actually begins at 11:00 P.M. on September 15 and continues throughout the next day.) You'll be treated to lots of music, dancers performing traditional steps, and even a salsa-tasting contest. The mariachi bands are incredible. Some cities and neighborhoods in the South Bay also celebrate this festival; check with your local parks and recreation department. There is no admission charge.

Rosarito-Ensenada 50-Mile Fun Bicycle Ride
Call for official starting location
(858) 483-8777
www.rosaritoensenada.com

The annual Baja cycling event attracts more than 10,000 riders of all skill and age levels. From Rosarito Beach the route runs south along the two-lane free (libre) road to Ensenada, where there's a nightlong fiesta. Though most of the ride is easy, there are some steep hills and nasty curves to overcome, and competition can be fierce. An earlier start time for better riders separates them from the hoi polloi. Entry is $40; the T-shirt is an extra $15.

All during the month of October, kids age 11 and younger can visit the San Diego zoo for free. On Zoo Founders Day, celebrated on the first Monday of October, everyone is admitted free.

OCTOBER

Marine Corps Air Station Miramar Air Show
Miramar Marine Base, San Diego
(858) 577-1000
www.miramarairshow.com

This is a three-day military and civilian air show and aviation expo that excites the entire family. Parking and admission are free. There are displays and performances that will snatch away your breath, including flights by the Blue Angels. There's a twilight show on Saturday. Special seating in the grandstand and box-seat area can be reserved for a fee by calling (619) 220-8497.

Oktoberfests
Various locations

Come celebrate fall with German-related festivals in many of San Diego's communities. Some have an entrance fee, but at others it's the food that carries a price tag. Insiders say the best Oktoberfest is in La Mesa, held the first full weekend in October in the downtown village area on La Mesa Boulevard, Allison Avenue, and Palm Avenue. There are 400 booths selling food and craft items, as well as the ever-popular beer garden and, of course, brass bands and polka dancing. For more information, call the chamber of commerce at (619) 440-6161.

Fans of off-road racing should look for the indie film **Chasing the Horizon,** *which debuted at the Newport Film Festival in 2006. Flying Canters Brothers Productions documents the story of three unlikely teammates in their attempt to win the Tecate Score Baja 1000 race.*

Halloween Festivals and Haunted Houses
Various locations throughout San Diego County, including:
Monster Bash, Gaslamp Quarter, San Diego
(619) 233-5008
www.gaslamp.org

The Scream Zone, Del Mar Fairgrounds
Del Mar
(858) 792-4252
www.thescreamzone.com

Almost every community in San Diego celebrates Halloween with fun houses, haunted houses, and activities such as pumpkin-carving contests and pin-the-tail-on-the-pumpkin games. Most of the activities are free. Adults (must be 21 years of age) like the Gaslamp Quarter's Monster Bash on Fifth Avenue between J and K Streets. Tickets are $15 in advance, $20 at the door. There are two costume contests (with the top winner nabbing a $2,000 prize), gourmet food booths, live entertainment, and plenty of partying in the clubs and restaurants in the Quarter. Kids love the fairgrounds' Scream Zone, which is open on weekends throughout the month as well as the 10 days before Halloween. The 25-room haunted house is filled with serious frights. Tickets are $13 to $25. Call your local parks and recreation department for what's happening in your neighborhood.

NOVEMBER

Tecate Score Baja 1000
Ensenada, Baja California
(818) 225-8402
www.score-international.com

This is an annual off-road race for cars, trucks, and motorcycles, and it is much anticipated in the dirt-racing community. The treacherous race covers some of the roughest terrain on the Baja California Peninsula. If you've ever driven in the area

December Nights offers the best of the holiday season. PHOTO: COURTESY OF BRETT SHOAF

or flown over it, you know it's desolate. There's a substantial entry fee for racing folks; viewing is free. The race starts early in the morning in Ensenada and attracts thousands. At the end in the city of La Paz, there's a fiesta and rowdy party that some parents might consider to be R-rated.

Mother Goose Parade
West Main and Chambers Streets, El Cajon
(619) 444-8712
www.mothergooseparade.com
Attracting nearly a half million spectators, the parade is usually held the Sunday before Thanksgiving. It begins at noon on West Main and Chambers Streets and continues east on Main to Second Street then north on Second to Madison. This is an old-fashioned children's affair with lots of local turnout. You'll see floats, clowns, bands, equestrians, civic leaders, and charitable organizations represented. There's no admission fee, so bring your lawn chairs or blankets for sidewalk sitting and some cash for the food, peanuts, toys, banners, and candy.

DECEMBER

Annual Festival of Lights
Various locations throughout San Diego
Cities and communities throughout the county create imaginative electrical displays to the delight of neighbors and those who drive around to see them. Fireside Drive in Oceanside (off Mission Avenue) puts on a prodigious display, as do numerous other San Diego county neighborhoods. For an official exhibition, bring the family to the drive-through display, with 350 installations, at the Del Mar Fairgrounds Festival of Lights (858-755-1161; www.holidayoflights.com). The cost is $12 per vehicle (up to five people; $17 for six or more people).

Balboa Park December Nights
(619) 239-0512, (619) 235-1100
www.balboapark.org
Balboa Park twinkles, glistens, and shines during the holidays. This weekend-long celebration, usually held at the beginning of the month, includes carolers, a candlelight procession, ethnic food and crafts stands, and general holiday merriment. Admission to the museums is free after 5:00 P.M. Stock up on goodies at the museums' shops.

Old Town Holiday in the Park and Candlelight Tours
Old Town State Historical Park, San Diego
(619) 220-5423

Walk through the historic districts of San Diego, view the holiday period decorations, and listen to stories about the early days of Old Town. The Las Posadas reenactment of Mary and Joseph's search for shelter is held midmonth. There's entertainment, caroling, and refreshments. Old Town's shop owners decorate their stores, and most are open late during the tours.

Boat Parades of Lights
Various harbors

The parades feature boats of all shapes and sizes decorated for the holiday season. To get the best view of the Mission Bay Christmas Boat Parade, Insiders suggest watching it from Crown Point. For Oceanside's boat parade, anywhere in the harbor is perfect. For San Diego Bay's, the best views are at Seaport Village and Harbor Island. If you want to enter your boat, call or contact the local parks and recreation office or chamber of commerce. Remember to wear a warm jacket. It can be breezy and cold on December evenings. Most parades start about 7:00 P.M.; watching is free but traffic can be gnarly. Take public transportation or carpool when feasible.

Holiday Parades and Celebrations
Various locations

Chula Vista's annual Starlight Yule Parade begins at 5:30 P.M. downtown at Third Avenue and includes floats and marching bands. There is also a crafts fair and tree-lighting ceremony. Ocean Beach has a parade and tree festival, too. The parade there goes down Newport Avenue and includes every children's organization in the community. At the end of Ocean Beach's parade, there is a holiday festival and community tree lighting. All are free events. For more information, contact the cities' chambers of commerce or parks and recreation offices.

San Diego International Auto Show
San Diego Convention Center
111 West Harbor Drive, San Diego
(800) 345-1487
www.sdautoshow.com

More than 32 domestic and foreign manufacturers roll out their newest and fastest and sleekest vehicles for this popular show. You'll see auto design exhibits, cars of the future and past, and exotic street machines. Admission is $10.00 for those age 13 and older; children ages 7 through 12 and younger enter for $5.00. There are discounts for seniors and the military. Sunday is Kid's Day, with special activities. Check newspapers, car dealers, chain supermarkets, and local restaurants for discount coupons for adult admission to this event.

Pacific Life Holiday Bowl
Qualcomm Stadium
9449 Friars Road, San Diego
(619) 283-5808
www.holidaybowl.com

The Holiday Bowl, held in late December, features a football face-off between nationally ranked teams from the Big 12 and either the WAC or the Pac 10. Begun in 1978, the Holiday Bowl has earned a reputation for close games. This is a popular event in San Diego, so get your tickets early; they range in price from $44 to $50. (Read more about the Holiday Bowl in our Spectator Sports chapter.)

First Night Escondido
Downtown Escondido near the California Center for the Arts, Escondido
(760) 420-9701
www.firstnightescondido.com

This is a G-rated New Year's Eve event, so you can celebrate with the family. It's a no-alcohol affair where you buy a button (that's your ticket) for $10—less if you buy it before the event, and kids age 6 and younger get in free. There's something for everyone, from fireworks to mimes and performances by steel bands and mariachi bands and acrobats. There's lots of food, too—everything from pizza and hot dogs to foot-long sandwiches, ribs, and chicken. Insiders always save room for the strawberry cheesecake and gourmet coffee. Each year events expand and vary; for 2006, a dramatically lit hot-air-balloon display and short-film festival provided drama and variety. First Night begins at 6:00 P.M. and goes until the midnight fireworks. Proceeds support the arts community. There's also a First Night San Diego celebration at Embarcadero Marina Park. Call your local parks and recreation department for other First Nights in the area.

THE ARTS

It's a long-standing myth that San Diego is bereft of culture. Take it from us—that may have been true 25 years ago, but it simply isn't the case any longer and hasn't been for some time. Once an idea is established, however, it's hard to convince folks otherwise. So we'll just let San Diego's fine arts establishments and performers speak for themselves. You'll soon see that no matter what region of the county you're visiting, you'll find an abundance of galleries, museums, classical music performances, theaters, and much more.

In North County Inland, Escondido, for example, has its own California Center for the Arts. And small but distinguished theaters are found throughout the county. Within the city of San Diego is everything you could possibly look for in the arts.

During its season the San Diego Opera features such internationally renowned singers as Ewá Podleś and Cecilia Bartoli. The Old Globe Theatre in Balboa Park, modeled after the original in London, not only continues with its cornerstone of Shakespearean plays, but has also presented everything from Molière to Mamet, from *Electra* to *Damn Yankees.* The La Jolla Playhouse has established itself by premiering several plays that have gone on to Broadway.

Around the county are hundreds of art galleries where you can find paintings, prints, and sculptures by emerging as well as established artists. In the East County are galleries featuring Western art from the likes Olaf Wieghorst and Remington; in La Jolla and North County you'll find African, Aboriginal, Scandinavian, Indian, Chinese, and Egyptian art—just about any type that piques your interest.

Traveling troupes have discovered that San Diego audiences enthusiastically embrace touring performances such as Broadway revues, ballet, and dance shows like *Riverdance* and *Stomp.*

The film scene has started to emerge in San Diego, too, and several film festivals make this their home. San Diegans have long enjoyed the Latino and Jewish Film Festivals; in 1998 the San Diego International Film Festival was added to the mix. All draw filmmakers from all over the world, giving locals the chance to learn more about the history of filmmaking and to see some off-the-beaten-path movies.

San Diego has also begun to attract a growing enclave of writers. Victor Villaseñor, author of the best-selling *Rain of Gold,* is a native of North County Coastal near Oceanside. Joseph Waumbaugh, author of *The Onion Field* and numerous other best-selling novels, has adopted San Diego as his hometown, and scores of lesser-known but highly successful writers pen their works from somewhere around the county.

You can see that San Diego indeed is no slouch when it comes to the fine arts. With unlimited time and an unlimited budget, you could be out every evening attending a play, a concert, a musical, or an art film. So when someone bemoans San Diego's lack of cultural accoutrements, you can just smile knowingly and head to the opera while the uninformed spend another night in front of the tube.

In this chapter we'll give you a comprehensive description of all San Diego has to offer in the way of arts. We'll tell you where the best clusters of galleries are, where the best art-film houses are, and how to get discount tickets. Like everywhere else in San Diego, dress tends to be on the casual side, even for nighttime performances of the symphony and the opera (opening night excepted!). Although only the most daring wear jeans to these events, tuxedos and full-length evening gowns are nearly as uncommon, and most patrons of the arts choose comfortable and casual yet elegant clothing.

For current listings of performances, festivals, and special gallery shows, check the "Night and Day" section of the *San Diego Union-Tribune*, their online version at SignonSanDiego.com, or the "Calendar" section of the free *San Diego Reader*, which can be picked up in convenience stores, libraries, and bookstores all over the county. Both newspapers come out on Thursday.

For half-price, day-of-performance tickets to local shows, check out the Times Arts Tix Booth on the southwest corner of Horton Plaza, half a block from the Lyceum Theater. Or call (619) 497-5000 for a list of each day's half-price shows.

CLASSICAL MUSIC

Central San Diego

La Jolla Music Society
(858) 459-3728
www.ljcms.org
All year long the La Jolla Music Society presents classical music ensembles featuring national and international musicians. Different series now stretch throughout most of the year, including the Revelle Chamber Music and Piano Series, which presents such notables as violinist Hilary Hahn and the Beaux Arts Trio in the Museum of Contemporary Art's Sherwood Auditorium. The Celebrity Series, staged at downtown San Diego's Civic Theater, brings together the world's most distinguished musicians and orchestras. Since 2004, there's jazz as well. In August the 19-day Summerfest, also held at the Sherwood Auditorium, dazzles music lovers with a series of daily concerts, workshops, and exhibitions.

Mainly Mozart Festival
(619) 239-0100
www.mainlymozart.org
The title of this festival spells it out: It's mainly a series of performances of the works of Mozart, but it also includes his 18th-century contemporaries, Baroque composers of the late 17th century, and the romantic masters of the early 19th century. Since 1988 the festival has successfully bridged the gap between the winter concert season of San Diego's primary performing arts groups and the major summer events. Many of North America's finest musicians are showcased every June in the All-Star Orchestra, led by artistic director and conductor David Atherton. Performances are held throughout the county and across the border in Tijuana.

The festival has expanded in recent years to include special events year-round, such as the Spotlight Series held January through April. For the most current performance schedule and to order tickets, call the number listed above. Ticket prices range from $20 for a single concert to package deals.

San Diego Chamber Orchestra (SDCO)
(858) 350-0290
www.sdco.org
More than 20 years after its inception, the San Diego Chamber Orchestra is still in the black, with twice its original budget and twice the number of annual performances. The new artistic director and conductor Jung-Ho Pak has served as guest conductor in the past. Very interested in reaching out to young people, he has produced nontraditional programs aimed at San Diego youth as well as the African-American, Asian, and Latino communities. Subscription concerts are most often held at St. Joseph's Cathedral, downtown San Diego; La Jolla's Sherwood Auditorium; and Fairbanks Ranch Country Club in Rancho Santa Fe. The 2006–2007 season includes the music of Hayden, Beethoven, and Mozart, among others. The SDCO, which has made seven recordings, collaborates at times with the San Diego Master Chorale and San Diego Children's Choir. General admission tickets generally run from $20 for students

The San Diego Opera has two free opportunities for opera fans. Backstage tours are conducted for the general public before Tuesday evening performances and Sunday matinees; reservations are required. Impromptu lunchtime concerts are sometimes held at the San Diego Concourse (A and C Streets, First and Third Avenues) opening night. Call (619) 232-7636 for further information.

to $40 for the general public, although some performances cost more.

San Diego Civic Youth Orchestra
(858) 484-9635
www.sandiegocyo.org
Gifted young musicians make up the San Diego Civic Youth Orchestra, a group dedicated to studying and performing the world's great orchestral works. Each year the organization embarks on a tour to perform around the world. Here at home, they delight and entertain audiences with the Tchaikovsky's *Nutcracker Suite,* Beethoven's *Symphony No. 5,* and John Williams's *Star Wars.*

Performances are held in various venues throughout the county, including the California Center for the Arts, Copley Symphony Hall, and Spreckels Theater.

The season runs year-round. Call for the current schedule.

San Diego Master Chorale
(858) 581-2203
www.sdmasterchorale.org
Originally founded as the choral element of the San Diego Symphony in 1962, the Master Chorale split off into an independent organization in 1979, producing its own concert season and joining other organizations for collaborative efforts. Frequently the chorale will join the San Diego Opera and the San Diego Symphony for special performances.

The 100-member group performs all around San Diego County in a variety of settings, from churches to outdoor stages. The repertoire includes a broad scope of music from master choral works to modern songs and show tunes.

San Diego Opera
1200 Third Avenue, Suite 1824, San Diego
(619) 232-7636 (administration),
(619) 533-7000 (tickets)
www.sdopera.com
There's little middle ground with opera: You either love it or hate it. But if you happen to be on the fence, we strongly suggest you take in a performance of the San Diego Opera; we suspect it'll make a convert of you. Since its 1965 debut, the San Diego Opera has matured into a major community asset for San Diego. With general director Ian Campbell at the helm since 1983, the character of the opera has evolved beautifully. Fiscally conservative and artistically daring, Campbell has led the opera to a point where its financial status is sound and its performances are a combination of the classics and the contemporary.

Campbell promises at least one contemporary opera each season, such as Mozart's *The Magic Flute,* André Previn's *A Streetcar Named Desire,* and Catán's *Rappaccini's Daughter,* the first Mexican opera ever to be performed in San Diego. Balancing out the new and unusual are the standard opera warhorses like Puccini's *Madama Butterfly* and Verdi's *Aida.*

Five or six operas are performed during the season, which runs from January through May. The opera performs in the Civic Theatre at Third Avenue and B Street in downtown San Diego. Information about subscriptions and tickets to individual performances are available by calling (619) 533-7000 or by stopping by the Civic Theatre box office. Ticket prices for individual operas range from $27 to $182.

San Diego Symphony
Copley Symphony Hall, 750 B Street
San Diego
(619) 235-0804
www.sandiegosymphony.com

Inaugurated in the early 1900s, the San Diego Symphony's financial woes were abruptly abolished in January 2002 when Qualcomm CEO Irwin Jacobs and his wife, Joan, announced a $120 million endowment, the most significant individual donation ever awarded a symphony orchestra. Half of the money benefits the symphony now, with the second installment to be endowed upon the philanthropists' deaths.

Under the leadership of Jahja Ling, appointed music director in 2004, the symphony produces several subscription concert series during its primary season from October through May, with performers such as Burt Bacharach, Dave Brubeck, Mark O'Connor, and Yo-Yo Ma. Formats range from the traditional pieces of the Masterworks Series to family-oriented concerts around the holidays and the Light Bulb Series, in which more unusual multimedia pieces are performed. Concerts are also presented at the California Center for the Arts in Escondido.

The Summer Pops are always an Insiders' favorite, featuring such productions as *Beatlemania,* Doc Severinsen's *Latin Show,* Roberta Flack in concert, and *Broadway, Just Off Broadway.* The Pops' venue is downtown's Navy Pier, at Harbor Drive off Eighth Avenue. Ticket prices for the above events range from $15 for gallery seating to $67 for a champagne table, and tickets can be purchased through Ticketmaster at (619) 220-8497 or at the Symphony Hall box office, (619) 235-0804.

San Diego Youth Symphony
Casa del Prado
1650 El Prado, Balboa Park, San Diego
(619) 233-3232
www.sdys.org

Founded in 1945, the San Diego Youth Symphony provides talented young musicians with the experience and discipline necessary for performing at a professional level. Musicians are between the ages of 14 and 25, and the 350 or so members come from all over San Diego County and Baja California.

A wonderful venue for concerts and other performances is the grounds of the historic San Luis Rey Mission. Receptions are sometimes held before or after a performance. See our Attractions chapter for more information on the mission, and call (780) 757-3651 for a schedule of performances.

The Youth Symphony performs in various locations around San Diego, sometimes breaking the ensemble into just strings or just winds. Occasionally the group will join with the San Diego Master Chorale for a special concert. Whatever is on the agenda, these talented youngsters are always a pleasure to hear.

Starlight Theatre
2125 Park Boulevard, San Diego
(619) 544-7827
www.starlighttheatre.org

This organization has been delighting its patrons for decades with such easy-to-digest performances as *Hello Dolly, Camelot,* and *Seven Brides for Seven Brothers.* All shows are held in the Starlight Bowl Amphitheater in Balboa Park, where you'll see lots of families picnicking on the grassy areas in the park before the show. It's traditionally a summer season, running between June and mid-September.

Once the performance begins, be prepared for one of the quirks peculiar to Starlight Bowl. It's right under the flight path to San Diego International Airport, so every time a plane comes over, performers will freeze the action until the plane has passed and the actors can be heard once again. This may happen 30 to 40 times during the performance, and kids especially get a kick out of watching for incoming planes and guessing when the action will freeze.

General admission ticket prices range from $10 to $75 and can be ordered by calling (619) 544-7827. Bring a sweater or jacket and a cushion or a blanket to sit on—the hard seats may become uncomfortable. Box dinners can be ordered ahead for a pre-performance picnic on the grounds. (For kids there's a $5.00 PB&J with fruit salad; adults choose from a classier selection of entrees.)

DANCE

Central San Diego

City Ballet School & Company
941 Garnet Avenue, San Diego
(858) 272-8663
www.cityballet.org

San Diego's City Ballet is a nonprofit corporation that has been producing high-quality ballet performances and outreach presentations since 1993. Each August the company offers free performances in the Organ Pavilion in Balboa Park, and, of course, the traditional *Nutcracker* is a must-see at Christmastime. City Ballet tends to stay with familiar ballets such as Shakespeare's *A Midsummer Night's Dream,* though it's beginning to add more contemporary programs in its November-through-May season. The venues vary as do ticket prices, but most tickets are in the $25 to $40 range, with some discounts for seniors and students.

City Ballet also has a strong educational program that provides training for professional and pre-professional dancers. Its Discover a Dancer program provides free ballet training and performances for disadvantaged children in San Diego.

Malashock Dance & Co.
3103 Falcon Street, Suite J, San Diego
(619) 260-1622
www.malashockdance.org

This small company of dancers is led by its founder, John Malashock, a former principal dancer with Twyla Tharp in New York. The company maintains rehearsal and teaching studios in Balboa Park. Its mission is to advance the art and experience of modern dance through creative self-expression.

Malashock has an active year-round schedule, performing all over San Diego County, including fall performances at Balboa Park's Old Globe Theatre. Workshops are held each summer. Call the number above for a current schedule of performances and for ticket information.

FILM FESTIVALS

Central San Diego

San Diego International Film Festival
Festival offices and are located at
7974 Mission Bonita Drive, San Diego
(619) 582-2368
www.sdff.org

This festival gives movie lovers a chance to see noncommercial live-action and animated features and shorts in many genres, from comedies and kids' movies to documentaries and dramas. Many are foreign films that have not been optioned by U.S. distributors, so they are otherwise unavailable to San Diego audiences. Format is varied, too: projected are DVDs and videos as well as films, further broadening the moviegoer's options. Reorganized in 2004, the festival now offers up parties and VIP functions at some of the hippest clubs in its new Gaslamp Quarter venue. Get a VIP pass for all of the events, plus gifts ($250 in advance) or a $99 pass for some of the events; both passes include film admission, but popcorn is extra. Individual tickets go on sale as available for $10 a pop.

San Diego Jewish Film Festival
(858) 457-3030
www.sdiff.org

More than 40 films from nearly a dozen countries—including features, short subjects, and documentaries—are shown in this February festival. Documentaries, shorts, and feature films examine such weighty topics as genocide, racism, and anti-Semitism; some, however, use satire or comedy as a vehicle to discuss the human condition. Along with the films there are panels, forums, and guest speakers. Films are screened at theaters in La Jolla, Poway, and central San Diego. Ticket prices range from about $6.00 to $12.00 for the general public.

San Diego Latino Film Festival
Madstone Theaters Hazard Center 7
7510 Hazard Center Drive, San Diego
(619) 230-1938
www.sdlatinofilm.com
This event is presented annually in March by the Media Arts Center of San Diego (www.mediaartscenter.org). Latino filmmakers, writers, and actors are showcased in a series of short and feature-length films. The goal of the festival is to make the masses aware of talented Latinos who are making commercially successful films. Special guests have included noted filmmakers such as Moctezuma Esparza and actors Edward James Olmos and Joe Mantegna. Tickets for each screening are $8.50. Festival passes for all screenings can be purchased for $175 and include such perks as inaugural parties, VIP seating, a free event T-shirt, and no waiting in line. Packages can be purchased online or by phone; individual tickets can be purchased at the theater box office the day of the screening. The Media Arts Center promotes Latino culture in other ways throughout the year, offering monthly films in Spanish from around the world, as well as other events.

Spike & Mike's Sick and Twisted Festival of Animation
Museum of Contemporary Art
700 Prospect Street, La Jolla
(858) 454-0267, (858) 459-8707
www.spikeandmike.com
Spike & Mike's "classic" animation of years gone by has been replaced by the irreverent but not degenerate program of today. Some of the short films have foul language, and others may have some sexual (but not X-rated) content; for example, the theme of *Stick Girl* is a safe-sex message. The films are therefore not appropriate for children. Screenings are held Friday and Saturday evenings from the end of September through the end of October. Tickets cost $9.00 per program.

GALLERIES

Central San Diego

Chuck Jones Studio Gallery
2501 San Diego Avenue, San Diego
(619) 294-9880
www.chuckjones.com
Animation is the cornerstone of this gallery, which features original work by such legendary artists as Chuck Jones, animator of Warner Brothers characters Bugs Bunny and Daffy Duck, as well as the art of Dr. Seuss and Walt Disney. Fine art by internationally acclaimed photographers and artists such as Phil Borges and Sid Avery is generally also displayed. The gallery is open Sunday through Thursday from 10:00 A.M. to 7:00 P.M., Friday and Saturday 10:00 A.M. to 8:00 P.M.

Cosmopolitan Fine Arts
7932 Girard Avenue, La Jolla
(858) 456-9506
www.cosmopolitanart.com
La Jolla boasts many fine galleries, and Cosmopolitan is an Insiders' favorite. The gallery represents well more than a hundred artists. This vintage gallery offers mainly plein air and figurative treatment of still lifes and cheerful scenery, mainly by American and European artists. Hours are from 10:00 A.M. until 6:00 P.M. seven days a week.

The grand reopening of the historic Balboa Theatre, which opened to vaudeville acts in the 1920s, is slated for 2007. The theater, whose elaborately decorated interior blends classic Mediterranean and the Spanish revival style of most Balboa Park structures, has excellent acoustics and is well-suited to nonamplified performances.

A great introduction to the San Diego art scene is the yearly Open Studios Tour, held each September. Self-guided tours allow lookie-loos and prospective buyers access to the studios of more than 50 artists. Call the convention and visitor's bureau at (619) 232-3101 for details.

Expressions of Mexico
1122 Cesar E. Chavez Parkway, Logan Heights
(619) 232-1699
www.expressionsofmexico.com

A couple of blocks from the Chicano Park murals under the Coronado Bridge, this gallery represents Mexican, Latino, and Chicano artists whose themes represent those cultures. Artists range from newbies to more recognized and experienced artists creating crafts, folk arts, and representative and abstract paintings and sculptures. Open Wedneday through Saturday noon to 6:00 P.M.

Michael J. Wolf Fine Arts
363 Fifth Avenue, Suite 102, San Diego
(619) 702-5388
www.mjwfinearts.com

It's essential to stop in at this wonderful small gallery when visiting the Gaslamp Quarter. Among their most endearing and enduring artists is Josue Castro, whose paintings and sculptures are imbued with the luminous colors of his native Mexico. Although his imagery is contemporary, the artist gets inspiration from cultures such as the Zapotecs of Oaxaca, whose society was cutting edge in sixth-century Mesoamerica. Alexander Sheversky's photo-realism acrylics are nothing less than amazing. The gallery is closed Sunday and Monday.

Morrison Hotel
1230 Prospect Street, La Jolla
(858) 551-0835

Like its sister gallery in New York City, this one has photos of rock and roll stars, but these are shots you don't see elsewhere, and so intriguing they'll make you consider changing your home's interior design. Mick Jagger, Janis Joplin, and Davie Bowie share several salons with more current icons. If nothing else, it's an excellent foray into rock history.

Scott White Contemporary Art
2400 Kettner Boulevard, Loft 238
San Diego
(619) 501-5689
www.scottwhiteart.com

This upscale gallery offers contemporary painting, sculpture, and photography by such internationally recognized artists as William Glen Crooks, and Carol Hepper. There are fascinating modern wood or steel sculptures as well as paintings. Hours are from 9:00 A.M. to 5:00 P.M. Tuesday through Friday, Saturday 11:00 A.M. to 5:00 P.M.

San Diego Art Institute
1439 El Prado (House of Charm)
Balboa Park, San Diego
(619) 236-0011
www.sandiego-art.org

See the Museums section for more information.

Spanish Village Art Center
1770 Village Place, Balboa Park, San Diego
(619) 233-9050
www.spanishvillageart.com

Spanish Village is a unique, concentrated collection of studio/galleries that display the work of local artists. Many of the artists are on-site, creating their work as you watch. You'll find artwork in a variety of media, including oil, watercolor, ceramics, sculpture, jewelry, wood carving, glass, photography, and enamel. There's no admission to Spanish Village, and it's open every day from 11:00 A.M. to 4:00 P.M.

Stephen Clayton Galleries
1201 First Street, Suite 111, Coronado
(619) 435-6474
www.stephenclaytongalleries.com

Lithographs by contemporary artists such as Michael Parks and MacKenzie Thorpe are the specialties at this gallery. You'll find both lithographs and original art by Hessam and lithos and serigraphs by the late Ted Geisel, children's author Dr. Seuss. In addition to lithographs, you'll find a nice selection of modern sculpture. Hours are Sunday through Thursday 10:00 A.M. to 7:00 P.M., Friday and Saturday 10:00 A.M. to 9:00 P.M.

Wentworth Gallery
1025 Prospect Street, Suite 110, La Jolla
(858) 551-7071
www.wentworthgallery.com
As much an Internet gallery as a physical one, the La Jolla venue is nonetheless worthy of a visit. Pictures range from the romantic, feminine portraits by Lefing to the sculptures and bas relief by Schluss. The gallery strives to keep on-hand the astonishing work of Charles Fazzino, glittering 3-D serigraphs cut into zillions of pieces and reassembled with scenes including the Coronado Bridge and other San Diego County icons.

North County Coastal

101 Artists' Colony
90 North Coast Highway, Encinitis
(760) 632-9072
www.101acevents.com
This nonprofit's mission is both to bring art to the public and provide a forum for fine artists and art-related works and events. Frequent receptions usher in shows by the colony's numerous artists; both the gift shop and gallery are open daily except Monday. There's poetry, drumming, and music several times a week. Some events are free, others are a nominal charge. Visit the Web site for a list of upcoming events.

Cedros Design District Galleries
Cedros Avenue south of the Coaster station at Highway 101, Solana Beach
(858) 755-0444
www.cedrosdesigndistrict.net
Sprinkled within the 3 blocks of garden and interior accessories shops that make up this North County shopping enclave are numerous art galleries, including the Ordover Gallery, Susan Street Fine Art Gallery, Devine Gallery, and others whose wares include photography, sculpture, and classical and modern-style paintings. The Hands on Cedros gallery specializes in functional, useable art. Most are closed on Monday. On the third Thursday of the month, these art galleries, along with some of the other shops on the avenue, stay open until about 8:30 P.M. and offer live music, wine, and hors d'ouevres.

Looking for the perfect gift to take back home to family or coworkers? The galleries often have less-expensive collectibles and cards worth framing as well as pieces of art.

Enchanted Gallery
2690 Via De La Valle, #230, Del Mar
(858) 792-6704
This truly is an enchanted gallery featuring the fine art of jewelry designers and acclaimed artists. You'll be treated to extraordinary blown glass, sculptures, and paintings. In addition, the store offers mineral and crystal specimens for sale. In the Flower Hill Mall, the gallery is open Monday through Saturday 10:00 A.M. to 6:00 P.M. and Sunday noon to 5:00 P.M.

North County Inland

Escondido Municipal Gallery
142 West Grand Avenue, Escondido
(760) 480-4101
The shows at this intimate gallery change focus often, so it's worth stopping in to browse when you're in the neighborhood. At a recent exhibit there was an all-media exhibition of two- and three-dimensional art by local artists. More than 60 local artists form this partnership that showcases sculpture, prints, paintings, and mixed-media pieces. The gallery is open

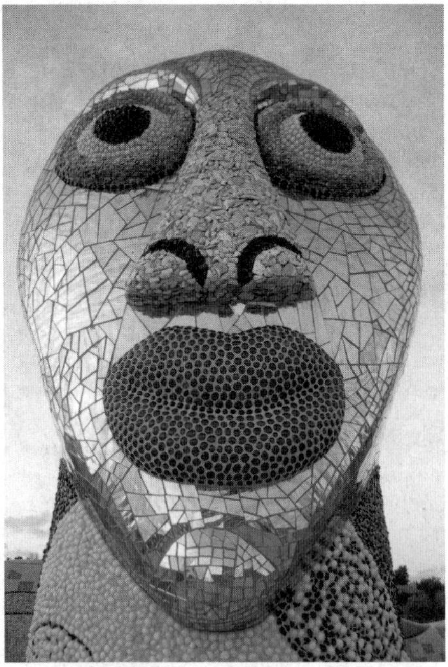

Queen Califa's Magic Circle sculpture garden in Escondido's Kit Carson Park is a wonder to behold. PHOTO: COURTESY OF CHRIS ARENDS

Tuesday through Saturday 11:00 A.M. to 4:00 P.M.

Poway Center for the Performing Arts
15498 Espola Road, Poway
(858) 748-0505
www.powayarts.org
The gallery at the Poway Center exhibits the work of new and established artists. A recent exhibit included the inaugural show of the North County Printmakers of San Diego. The gallery is open Monday through Friday 9:00 A.M. to 4:00 P.M. and Saturday 11:00 A.M. to 3:00 P.M.

At the foot of the San Diego-Coronado Bay Bridge, at the intersection of National Avenue and Crosby Street on the San Diego side, is Chicano Park. Within the park Chicano artists have painted the abutments of the bridge with murals representing their history and social concerns. The result is an internationally acclaimed public art project.

East County

Art World-Western Heritage Gallery
1266 Broadway Street, El Cajon
(619) 440-1041, (800) 269-8081
www.4westernart.com
According to Insiders who love Western or wildlife art, this is the primary gallery in Southern California. Many people travel from Los Angeles to visit it. More than 50 artists are represented here, including Bev Doolittle, G. Harvey, Mark Martensen, Frank McCarthy, and many more. The store also carries numbered fine-art prints and limited editions. The gallery is open Tuesday through Friday 10:00 A.M. until 6:00 P.M., Saturday 10:00 A.M. until 4:00 P.M.

El Cajon Art Association
1246 East Main Street, Suite 113, El Cajon
(619) 588-8875
www.eastcountyartassociation.com
More than 200 East County artists belong to and show at this cooperative art gallery. Although the media are nearly always two-dimensional, there's a wide range of styles and themes to be found in the 11 exhibits shown each year. The gallery usually has three juried shows per year and offers life drawing and watercolor classes. It's open Wednesday through Saturday 11:00 A.M. to 4:00 P.M.

MUSEUMS

For a more comprehensive list of museums, see the Balboa Park chapter.

Central San Diego

Mingei International Museum
1439 El Prado, Balboa Park, San Diego
(619) 239-0003
www.mingei.org

The word "mingei" is used transculturally for "art of the people." Thus, traditional and contemporary folk art, crafts, and design representing the many cultures of the world are the focus at the Mingei Museum. You'll see exhibits such as *Dolls—Mirrors of Humanity,* which showcases more than 200 objects, including an 18th-century dollhouse and a parade of dolls in vehicles of all kinds. All permanent and changing exhibits portray the essential arts that are satisfying to the human soul.

The museum is open Tuesday through Sunday from 10:00 A.M. to 4:00 P.M. Admission is $6.00 for adults and $3.00 for students and children ages 6 to 17. Admission is free for children younger than age 6.

Museum of Contemporary Art
700 Prospect Street, La Jolla
(858) 454-3541
1001 Kettner Boulevard, San Diego
(619) 234-1001
www.mcasd.org

Both locations of this museum have a long-established reputation for thought-provoking exhibitions as well as highly regarded permanent collections; both can truly be labeled "cutting edge." For those who want to understand contemporary art, docent tours are free. At the La Jolla MCA, the Edwards Sculpture Garden and surrounding area have been improved with pieces from the collection that have been awaiting exhibition space, including works by Niki de Saint Phalle, Judith Shea, and Roman de Salvo. Temporary sculptures and installations can be found there as well.

Lectures and commentaries are frequently scheduled, too. Both locations are closed Wednesdays. The downtown museum is free and open year-round Thursday through Tuesday 11:00 A.M. to 5:00 P.M. The La Jolla museum is open Friday through Tuesday 11:00 A.M. to 5:00 P.M., Thursday 11:00 A.M. to 7:00 P.M. During the summer it's open weekdays (except Wednesday) until 8:00 P.M. Admission there costs $6.00, $2.00 for children. Both locations have worthwhile gift and book shops and offer many lectures, films, and community events.

Art museums in Balboa Park offer free admission one day every month. The Museum of Photographic Arts offers free entry on the second Tuesday. Visits to the San Diego Museum of Art and Mingei International Folk Art Museum are free on the third Tuesday. Admission is always free at the Timken Museum of Art.

Museum of Photographic Arts (MOPA)
1649 El Prado, Balboa Park, San Diego
(619) 238-7559
www.mopa.org

Photography is one of the more intriguing art forms, and the Museum of Photographic Arts consistently displays stunning examples of the work of some of the finest international photographers. In addition to its permanent collection, changing exhibitions highlight the museum's dedication to displaying outstanding photography. MoPA puts on approximately six shows a year.

After a one-year expansion and remodel, the museum reopened in March 2000. Renovations include additional gallery space, a print-viewing room and 25,000-volume library, and the 238-seat Joan & Irwin Jacobs Theater, where art films are screened regularly. The museum is open Monday through Sunday 10:00 A.M. to 5:00 P.M., Thursday until 9:00 P.M.

Each spring the San Diego Museum of Art presents Art Alive, a fabulous show in which artists and gardeners interpret paintings and sculpture form the museum's collection using flowers, ferns, moss, and anything green or growing.

One of many sculptures by iconoclastic artist Niki de St. Phalle, Queen Califa's Magic Circle, in Escondido, has both detractors and admirers. The former say it's incongruous with the muted, scrubby landscape of Kit Carson Park. Check it out at 3315 Bear Valley Parkway and decide for yourself.

Admission is $6.00 for adults and $4.00 for seniors, students, and military. Children younger than age 12 are admitted free when accompanied by an adult. General admission for films, generally shown Thursday evenings, is $10.00. Double-check current show times.

San Diego Art Institute (SDAI)
1439 El Prado (House of Charm)
Balboa Park, San Diego
(619) 236-0011
www.sandiego-art.org

The mission of the SDAI is to stimulate the public's appreciation of media of all types created by San Diego's diverse artists. Shows in the 10,000-square-foot gallery in the heart of Balboa Park are juried by art experts, yet quality is sometimes mediocre. Held every four to six weeks, each solo exhibit features multiple works by a featured SDAI member. The art of local schoolchildren is regularly shown, and the Institute has various kid-oriented programs. Life drawing, computer animation, and multimedia classes are available for adults. Gallery entrance is $3.00 for adults; $2.00 for senior, military, and students; kids age 12 and younger get in free.

San Diego's newest museum is the Aircraft Carrier Museum. The retired carrier **Midway** *will be docked at the North Embarcadero, showcasing planes and helicopters from its service years (1945–1992) on deck and other exhibits below.*

San Diego Museum of Art
1450 El Prado, Balboa Park, San Diego
(619) 232-7931
www.sdmart.org

This venerable museum has a respectable permanent collection consisting of Italian Renaissance, Spanish old masters, American art, 19th-century European paintings, and 20th-century paintings and sculptures. There's also a gallery dedicated to California art and salons dedicated to Asian antiquities.

It's the traveling exhibitions that draw the big crowds, though, and recent years have seen the Jewels of the Romanov visit the museum, as well as a huge collection of Fabergé eggs. Less stirring was a 2003 exhibit of bronze Degas ballerinas, built in wax by the artist as studio studies and presumably never intended to be either cast or viewed by the public.

Hours are 10:00 A.M. to 6:00 P.M. Tuesday through Sunday and Thursday 10:00 A.M. to 9:00 P.M. Admission prices are $10.00 for adults; $8.00 for seniors, young adults ages 18 to 24, and military; and $4.00 for children ages 6 to 17. Children age 5 and younger are admitted free.

Timken Museum of Art
1500 El Prado, Balboa Park, San Diego
(619) 239-5548
www.timkenmuseum.org

Known locally as San Diego's "jewel box for the arts," the Timken Museum is devoted to its select collection of European and American masterworks, which includes a small sampling of beautiful Russian icons. The Putnam Collection spans five centuries of art, from the early Renaissance through the 19th century. You'll see the works of artists such as Veronese, Bruegel, Cézanne, Clouet, Rembrandt, and Reubens.

American artists are well represented, too, including Bierstadt, Copley, Heade, and others. This is an outstanding small museum that's known nationwide for its critically acclaimed, tasteful, and well-lit setting for viewing its collection. Because its small but important collection includes pieces prized by other museums, the Timken has ample bargaining power and can put together one or two focus shows every year, with pieces from other collections catalogued by a guest curator. The hours are 10:00 A.M. to 4:30 P.M. Tuesday through Saturday, 1:30 to 4:30 P.M. Sunday. Admission is free; closed the month of September.

North County Coastal

Oceanside Museum of Art
704 Pier View Way, Oceanside
(760) 721-2787
www.oma-online.org
Located in the historic Gill Building, which was the Oceanside city hall in the 1920s, the museum features local and international art. Its rotating exhibits include traditional paintings in watercolor and oil as well as glass, weaving, pottery, sculpture, and even furniture. The museum is open Tuesday through Saturday 10:00 A.M. to 4:00 P.M., Sunday 1:00 to 4:00 P.M. Admission is $5.00.

North County Inland

The Visual Arts at the California Center for the Arts
340 North Escondido Boulevard Escondido
(760) 839-4120, (800) 988-4253
www.artcenter.org
An always changing group of exhibits are on display here. Recently there was an exhibition of 20th-century still-life paintings from the Phillips Collection with works by Pablo Picasso, Georges Braque, Stuart Davis, and Georgia O'Keeffe.

With your ticket to a performance at the center, you can visit the museum and sculpture court for free. Otherwise, ticket prices are $5.00 for adults and $3.00 for children age 12 and older and students with identification. It's open Tuesday through Saturday 10:00 A.M. to 4:00 P.M. and Sunday noon to 4:00 P.M. It's free the first Wednesday of every month.

Mingei International Museum
155 West Grand Avenue, Escondido
(760) 735-3355
www.mingei.org
A new North County satellite on Grand Avenue in Escondido, just down the street from the California Center for the Arts, opened in December 2003. The new facility has a multimedia education center as well as a 5,000-square-foot exhibition gallery for displaying some of the museum's 12,000-piece collection. Hours are Tuesday through Saturday 1:00 to 4:00 p.m. Admission is $6.00 for adults and $3.00 for students and children ages 6 to 17.

PERFORMANCE VENUES

Art Film Houses

CENTRAL SAN DIEGO

Hillcrest Cinemas
3965 Fifth Avenue, San Diego
(619) 819-0236
www.landmarktheatres.com
This five-theater complex tucked away in the Village Hillcrest Shopping Center shows first-run foreign films and independent American films. The theaters are on the small side, lending a cozy atmosphere to the experience, but the amenities are modern and first-rate.

Ken Cinema
4061 Adams Avenue, San Diego
(619) 819-0236
Old-style theaters are rapidly falling by the wayside since the tidal wave of multiplex cinemas began taking their place. The Ken remains, however, and manages to hang on and to draw crowds to its retrospectives and bodacious films not shown elsewhere. For instance, the theater has shown a retrospective of Kurosawa films, a series of Humphrey Bogart thrillers, Monty Python collections, and all the *Godfather* movies. During "Sing-a-Long Sound of Music," theatergoers were encouraged to join in singing with Maria

the governess and the Family von Trapp. There's always something interesting or provocative showing, though the venue itself is worn.

NORTH COUNTY COASTAL

La Paloma
471 South Coast Highway 101, Encinitas
(760) 436-7469
www.lapalomatheatre.com
Inaugurated in 1928 as a silent-movie house with a wonderful organ, La Paloma is now the place for watching art films and viewing wild, weird, or funny classics. Don't expect highbrow stuff at this beach-town film house; most of the films are on the contemporary side of classic. For instance, if you must see the 1960s surf classic *Endless Summer* on the big screen once again, La Paloma is the place. La Paloma also hosts various community events and programs.

Cultural Centers

CENTRAL SAN DIEGO

Centro Cultural de la Raza
2004 Park Boulevard, Balboa Park
San Diego
(619) 235-6135
www.centroraza.com
Murals that cover the exterior walls of this institute of Mexican, Chicano, and indigenous arts and culture depict the historical and mythological roots and traditions of these cultures. Both traditional and experimental forms of visual and performing arts are presented in the classroom/workshop space, including film screenings, literary presentations, and numerous workshops such as African drumming, video production, and salsa dancing. Recent years have seen an increase in theatrical music and dance performances as well as art exhibits. Admission is free, but donations are gratefully accepted.

San Diego Concourse Convention and Performing Arts Center
1100 Third Avenue, San Diego
(619) 570-1100
This is a grand title for what actually is pretty much restricted to the Civic Theatre. Although the Concourse gets heavy use by conventions and trade shows, the performing arts are intelligently confined to the theater, which has the acoustics and the ambience the Concourse does not. From January through May the Civic Theatre is the exclusive home to the San Diego Opera. But once the opera season is over, watch out! Everything from *Beauty and the Beast* to *The Full Monty* and *Jesus Christ Superstar* has made an appearance at this gracious and graceful theater. If there's a popular Broadway production to be seen, chances are good that it will show up at the Civic Theatre.

As the holidays approach, you can take it to the bank that a traveling performance of *The Nutcracker* will turn up, and this is where you'll find the rare ballet that comes to town. The theater holds just fewer than 3,000 people, but the seats in the upper regions virtually demand binoculars. So if you have your heart set on seeing a special concert or show, get your tickets early. Tickets can be purchased at the box office at the Concourse or by calling Ticketmaster at (619) 220-8497.

Simon Edison Centre for the Performing Arts
Old Globe Theatre, Cassius Carter Centre Stage, Lowell Davies Festival Theatre located behind the Museum of Man in Balboa Park
(619) 239-2255, (619) 234-5623
www.oldglobe.org
Beautifully situated in Balboa Park, this complex consists of three theaters, including the Tony Award-winning Old Globe Theatre. The other two are the 225-seat Cassius Carter Centre Stage, which is a theater-in-the-round, and the 615-seat Lowell Davies Festival Theatre,

an outdoor venue used between July and October.

The three theaters stage performances ranging from the traditional Shakespearean classics to world premieres such as *Getting and Spending* and *Paramour*. Christmastime always brings something to please the young ones, like *How the Grinch Stole Christmas*. Ticket prices range from $25 to $50 and can be purchased at the box office or by calling (619) 239-2255.

NORTH COUNTY COASTAL

Oceanside Museum of Art
704 Pier View Way, Oceanside
(760) 721-2787
www.oma-online.org

Located in the old Oceanside city hall, the museum sponsors musical performances, including chamber music concerts, in addition to garden parties, an annual Mardi Gras brunch, and other activities. Admission prices vary. Performances are usually held in the afternoon. The museum itself is open from 10:00 A.M. to 4:00 P.M. Tuesday through Saturday, 1:00 to 4:00 P.M. Sunday.

NORTH COUNTY INLAND

California Center for the Arts
340 North Escondido Boulevard
Escondido
(760) 839-4100, (800) 988-4253
www.artcenter.org

Will it be Bill Maher, Itzhak Perlman, the Los Angeles Guitar Quartet, or Mancini at the Movies? Handel's *Messiah* or *Forbidden Hollywood?* The performances at the California Center for the Arts run the gamut from classic and serene to madly modern. The world-class arts center is located on a 12-acre campus and includes fine educational programs. Designed by the late renowned architect Charles Moore, it includes a 1,538-seat concert hall, a 408-seat theater, and a full-service conference center. In December 2001 philanthropist Edna Sahm pledged $663,000 dollars to the center, bringing its total endowment to nearly $1 million.

The theater brings troupes from around the globe to the inland community and brings Insiders and visitors from nearby counties to enjoy the varied programs. There are musical theater and Broadway shows, classical productions, dance, and music from around the world, holiday programs, jazz and Big Band shows, and family theater. Prices vary from about $10 to $60. Call or check the Web site for current programs.

Poway Center for the Performing Arts
15498 Espola Road, Poway
(858) 748-0505
www.powayarts.org

This cultural center provides live stage and musical performances for Insiders and visitors. Programs are varied and include plays you can attend with children, chamber music, Broadway-style reviews, and even performances by the San Diego Opera and the New Shanghai Circus, with its dramatic and elegant acrobats. This center seats 800 people, but it's a popular venue, so be sure to make reservations early. Call for a schedule of upcoming events. Ticket prices depend on the performance and seating location.

Theaters

CENTRAL SAN DIEGO

Horton Grand Theatre
444 Fourth Avenue, San Diego
(619) 232-9608

Located in the heart of the Gaslamp Quarter, this small theater continuously presents crowd-pleasing plays that more often than not are held over. A case in point is *Triple Espresso: A Highly Caffeinated Comedy,* which was brought back by popular demand and has been running, although not consecutively, since 1998. It's a fairly small theater but is comfortable

CLOSE-UP

La Jolla Playhouse

This is a story of three Hollywood actors who were at the peak of fame and fortune in their film careers but still longed for the purity of the stage. Gregory Peck, Dorothy McGuire, and Mel Ferrer had dreams of opening a playhouse to bring live theater to California, where it was sadly lacking, and much to the good fortune of San Diego, they chose La Jolla.

Peck had grown up in San Diego and attended local schools, so it was only natural that he would return to his roots. With the financial support of David Selznick and a solid core of local theater lovers, the La Jolla Playhouse opened its first season in 1947 in the auditorium of La Jolla High School. The first production starred Dame May Whitty in *Night Must Fall,* a play in which she had been triumphant in both London and Hollywood. It was a great success and quelled all doubts about the threesome's venture. The future of the La Jolla Playhouse looked bright.

Peck himself performed in three plays at the La Jolla Playhouse during the next few years. Ferrer acted in three as well and McGuire in six, among them Tennessee Williams's *Summer and Smoke* and Oscar Wilde's *The Importance of Being Earnest.* In 1997 a new production of that same play opened the 50th anniversary season of the La Jolla Playhouse, and Peck and Ferrer were in the audience.

The early days of the playhouse were filled with remarkable performances by notable actors including Jennifer Jones, Groucho Marx, Charlton Heston, and David Niven. La Jolla quickly became a playground for the stars, and after each opening night the three founders could be found carousing with the likes of Desi Arnaz and Lucille Ball in the Whaling Bar at the La Valencia Hotel.

The playhouse occupied La Jolla High School's auditorium for 18 seasons. Production ceased after the 1964 season for a number of reasons, the biggest being economic. It would take 19 years before the Playhouse presented another play; however, the dream of a La Jolla Playhouse never died. As early as 1954 local supporters were raising funds for the construction of a new theater, but that feat wasn't accomplished until 1982, when construction was completed on the current La Jolla Playhouse. Supporters were able to enlist the aid of UCSD's Dr. Roger Revelle, and as a result, the new Playhouse found a home in the Mandell Weiss Theatre on the campus of the university, where it remains today.

Under artistic director Des McAnuff, the La Jolla Playhouse reopened in 1983 with Peter Sellars's production of *The Visions of Simone Machard,* which was later distinguished by the *Village Voice* as one of the 10 best regional theater productions of the 1980s. But it was the 1984 production of *Big River* that started the real buzz about the playhouse. With its score by Roger Miller, *Big River* went on to Broadway and won seven Tony awards.

This was just the beginning of a tradition of Broadway-bound productions making their debut at San Diego's homegrown theater. *A Walk in the Woods* followed a few years later and quickly made its way to Broadway. So did Frank Galati's adaptation of *The Grapes of Wrath.*

But the real test of McAnuff's genius came in 1993, when playgoers gathered on a summer evening in July, anxiously awaiting the debut of The Who's groundbreaking rock opera *Tommy*. It was wildly successful among both the traditional playgoers and rock fans. Naturally it went on to Broadway, and the next year *Tommy* won five Tonys, including one for McAnuff. But those weren't the only Tonys San Diego felt pride in that year. During the same award ceremony, the playhouse received the Tony given annually to an outstanding regional theater.

That same year McAnuff stepped aside and passed the torch to Michael Greif, whose 1997 production of *Rent* garnered a Tony nomination for Best Director. After less than a half-decade of experimenting with theater in other venues, McAnuff returned to the playhouse, much to the delight of longtime fans.

But it's more than just a charismatic and innovative director that endears the playhouse its patrons. Education and outreach programs help inspire future actors, directors, and even playgoers. In spring and summer kids and teens study acting, movement, improv, and stage combat with professional actors. Internships are offered each year in disciplines from costume development and wardrobe to electrical technician and production. The POP Tour brings theater to schools and libraries in communities where many people may have not experienced, or regularly experienced, live theater.

The 45,000-square-foot Joan and Irwin Jacobs Center, made possible by a key grant by its namesakes, houses additional theater space, learning centers, public spaces, and a restaurant/cabaret. It opened in late 2004.

It has been 60 years since three actors with a germ of an idea started the La Jolla Playhouse. And each year San Diegans take more and more pride in the quality of productions at the Playhouse. The combination of classics, popular musicals and plays, and groundbreaking productions has put the little theater on the national theatrical map.

and elegant. The theater is within a few blocks of all the Gaslamp's restaurants and clubs, so a performance can easily be combined with dinner and after-theater entertainment.

La Jolla Playhouse
La Jolla Village Drive at
Torrey Pines Road, La Jolla
(858) 550-1010
www.lajollaplayhouse.com

This distinguished theater, founded by actors Gregory Peck, Dorothy McGuire, and Mel Ferrer, is constantly on the cutting edge of world-premiere plays and musicals that have a habit of finding their way to Broadway. Several Tony Award–winning plays have debuted here, including Roger Miller's *Big River* and The Who's rock opera *Tommy.* Classics are never ignored at the La Jolla Playhouse, however, and recent seasons have included such venerable plays as the Pulitzer Prize–winning *Our Town* and Michael Ondaatje's *The Collected Works of Billy the Kid.* For detailed history of the La Jolla Playhouse, be sure to read the Close-up in this chapter.

Lamb's Players Theatre
1142 Orange Avenue, Coronado
(619) 437-0600
www.lambsplayers.org

The history of the Lamb's Players Theatre is one of extremes. It started out in a Quonset hut in the East County and now occupies a historic theater in Coronado. Along the way it has grown into San Diego's third-largest theater organization, behind the Old Globe Theatre and the La Jolla Playhouse. Its resident acting company stages performances year-round, including plays like *A Man For All Seasons, The Survivor,* and *Godspell.*

Mystery Cafe
505 Kalmia Street, San Diego
(619) 544-1600
www.mysterycafe.net

Serious patrons of the arts might sniff at the idea of dinner theater, but sometimes ya just gotta do it. And the Mystery Cafe at the Imperial House Restaurant is one of the best. Audience participation is not only encouraged, it's expected, and plenty of laughs are guaranteed.

The long-running *Murder at the Café Noir* entertained guests with its hilarious blend of mystery and red herrings; another performance, *The Catskills Conspiracy,* is billed as "*Dirty Dancing* meets *Dragnet.*" Along with the performance, a four-course meal is served. Tickets usually go for $55 to $60.

San Diego Repertory Theatre
79 Horton Plaza, San Diego
(619) 231-3586 (box office),
(619) 544-1000
www.sandiegorep.com

Two subterranean theaters house the San Diego Repertory Theatre, the 550-seat Lyceum Stage, and the 270-seat Lyceum Space. The season runs from autumn through spring, and the performances are eclectic: musicals, dramas, and comedies. Many are fairly well-known, and Shakespeare makes at least one appearance each year, though often with modern staging. The Rep stages a two-week run of *A Christmas Carol* every December, presenting a different version each year. Community-based events include February's Kuumba festival, showcasing local African-American performers, and in May/June, the Lipinsky Family San Diego Jewish Arts Festival, with concerts and plays by international Jewish artists.

Sushi Performance Gallery
964 Fifth Street, San Diego
(619) 235-8466
www.sushiart.org

Since 1980 Sushi has gained national acclaim as an adventurous alternative performance-art theater. Whoopi Goldberg got her start here, and feminist performance artists Karen Finley and Holly Hughes have appeared, too. Performances are held at various venues, more often than not intimate locales. Ticket prices are modest; dress is always casual. Sushi's performances require an open mind; most are edgy and thought provoking. The annual fund-raiser, The Red Ball, is one of the company's most popular events.

Theatre in Old Town
4040 Twiggs Street, San Diego
(619) 688-2494
www.theatreinoldtown.com
An indoor, amphitheater-style house, the Theatre in Old Town presents familiar, favorite plays and often musicals. Shaped like a huge barn, the venue is actually intimate, with just 250 seats wrapping around the thrust stage, ensuring easy viewing for all. Whether it's *Forever Plaid, Beehive,* or another show, this theater is worth a visit. The atmosphere is relaxed and casual, and all of Old Town is right outside the door.

NORTH COUNTY COASTAL

North Coast Repertory Theatre
987D Lomas Santa Fe Drive, Solana Beach
(858) 481-1055
www.northcoastrep.org
You might see a drama, comedy noir, or, as often is the case, classics like *Auntie Mame, Fiddler on the Roof,* and *Our Town* in this intimate 194-seat theater. The theater is elegant and comfortable, and you can come as casually dressed or as gussied-up as you choose. Thursday through Saturday performances start at 8:00 P.M. On weekends there are matinees; Wednesday and Sunday performances are at 7:00 P.M. Call or check the Web site to see about "off-night" performances, which include comedy and musical shows.

NORTH COUNTY INLAND

Avo Playhouse
303 East Vista Way, Vista
(760) 726-1340, ext. 1523 (information)
(760) 724-2110 (for tickets)
www.moonlightstage.com
Owned by the city of Vista, this 382-seat neighborhood playhouse was elegantly restored in 1948 in art nouveau style. The proscenium stage has a modified thrust, which allows actors to get closer to their audience. During the winter season, November through March, a small handful of productions are staged here. It's also an important North County venue for youth and community productions.

Join a free self-guided romp through downtown Escondido's art district the second Saturday of each month. Many of the more than 20 participating galleries schedule openings at that time, so expect lots to offer wine, hors d'oeuvres, and sometimes live music. In the morning an artist usually speaks on an art-related topic at the Escondido Municipal Gallery. Call (760) 480-4101 or check www.escondidoarts.org for more info.

Moonlight Amphitheater
1200 Vale Terrace Drive, Vista
(760) 724-2110
www.moonlightstage.com
An outdoor theater in North County Inland, each summer the Moonlight hosts five plays: musicals, comedies, and dramas that you can watch under the stars. The theater has recently produced *Seussical the Musical, The Sound of Music,* and *Singin' in the Rain.* There is some seating, but if you plan to sit on the grass, bring low lawn chairs only or blankets and pillows. Lots of Insiders bring picnic suppers or, if they're coming from work, fast food.

Patio Playhouse Community Theater
201 East Grand Avenue, Escondido
(760) 746-6669
www.patioplayhouse.com
The Playhouse is a not-for-profit, volunteer organization presenting a range of live performances in comedy, drama, mystery, and musicals. There are seven or eight different shows presented each year, including youth theater shows. For the kids in the family there are plays such as *Puss & Boots* and for adults such entertainment as Jay Mower's *The Diary of Anne Frank.*

Call or check the Web site for a schedule of events and ticket prices.

Welk Resort Center
8860 Lawrence Welk Drive, Escondido
(760) 749-3448, (888) 802-7469

In our Hotels and Motels chapter we covered the things you can do at the Welk Resort Center, but there's a whole lot more than spa-ing and golfing here. The Welk Resort's production team offers such classic shows as *Showboat, Carousel, Guys and Dolls,* and *Singin' in the Rain.* Each week there are about five matinees and three evening performances, and both are available with the lunch or dinner buffet or for the performance only. Prices range from $37 to $58 including the buffet.

EAST COUNTY

Christian Community Theater
1545 Pioneer Way, El Cajon
(619) 588-0206, (800) 696-1929
www.cctcyt.org

The theater presents productions that the entire family will enjoy, and often there are children's classics on the live theater "menu." The Christmas programs at the El Cajon Performing Arts Center are especially popular, and many Insiders make attending them a family tradition. Eight different productions are staged each year. The company's emphasis, however, is on education for young people—their values and goals as well as their acting skills.

East County Performing Arts Center
210 East Main Street, El Cajon
(619) 440-2277
www.ecpaclive.com

Built in the 1970s by the city of El Cajon and the Grossmont-Cuyamaca Community College District, the 1,142-seat theater is back in the black after being acquired by the Arts Center Foundation in 1997. Since then the concert and performance venue has been revamped, with a new state-of-the-art sound system, stage curtain and carpeting, and heating and air-conditioning systems. Recent programs have included Natalie Cole, Patti Austin, Crystal Gayle, and the San Diego Symphony Orchestra. The season runs mid-September through May. Seats in all price sections are wheelchair accessible.

SOUTH BAY

Onstage Playhouse
Park Village Theatre, 291 Third Avenue
Chula Vista
(619) 422-7787
www.onstageplayhouse.org

If you like to get up close to the stage and see every little thing that's going on, try one of Onstage Productions' fine plays: the season is July to June. The theater is intimate—only 60 seats—and sitting so close to the stage, you could almost believe you're part of the play. The quality of the plays is excellent. Recent productions include *Steel Magnolias* and *Prelude to a Kiss.* Call or check the Web site for the current schedule and ticket reservations.

PARKS

In this chapter you'll find parks where you can have lunch, fly kites, take a walk, discover a nature center, or have a wonderful family outing. As in other chapters of the book, we've divided the material into regions and then listed those entries alphabetically. Of course our list isn't exhaustive; we've tried to list the brightest stars in a galaxy of possibilities. If you want to visit a beach park, check out the sites listed in our Beaches and Water Sports chapter.

Although we mention some wilderness areas in this chapter, see our Recreation chapter if you want to know about other ones and the serious hiking, biking, climbing, and other rugged activities that happen in them. Further camping possibilities are listed there, too.

Besides the smaller parks listed here, where people can jog after work or picnic at lunchtime, we've included some national forests and large regional parks and preserves, and we've sometimes narrowed in on certain areas within them. Cleveland National Forest, for instance, takes up a major section of the East County and offers some superb places to picnic, camp, walk, and hang out. Since Cleveland National Forest is huge, we haven't just said, "Head east, friends." Instead we've done some of the scouting for you and selected parks within the area that are special, such as Palomar Mountain State Park and Cuyamaca Rancho State Park.

But large or small, all the parks here offer outdoor fun for adults and are just right for families, too. See the Kidstuff chapter for suggestions on where to let the rug rats run free.

Whether you're hiking alone or with another person, it's wise not to roam into unfamiliar and isolated areas after dark. Pets, on 8-foot leashes and with a responsible owner, are normally welcome in county parks, but not in all city parks. They must be attended at all times, and it might be smart to call to find out if Fido is welcome.

We've included special information to make your park visits more enjoyable. For example, at Blue Sky Ecological Reserve you might see vultures and foxes, but you won't find drinking fountains. You'll need to bring your own water. At Laguna Mountain Recreation Area, you can reserve a place for some thrilling nightlife—if you're into stargazing. Star parties are held during the summer months. When there are specific hours of operation or if the park has unusual restrictions, we've noted that.

Laws against picking wildflowers, removing plants, and tampering with archaeological artifacts or the animal and natural features in state, county, and city parks are enforced.

Some parks let you reserve picnic areas for parties and reunions. For some camping areas, the reserved list is long. It's always sound advice (in our popular county) to make park reservations well in advance of the date you plan to visit. See the sidebar in this chapter for phone numbers of major camping locations and the individual parks for more details.

Wait no more. Pack a lunch; grab a hat. Now let's head out and explore San Diego's parks.

Love the outdoors? Want to make new friends? The County of San Diego Department of Parks and Recreation is eager for reliable volunteers to run programs and become docents. Call (858) 694-3049 for more information.

CENTRAL SAN DIEGO

Kate O. Sessions Memorial Park
5115 Soledad Road and Loring Street in Pacific Beach, San Diego
(858) 581-9927

Named for famed horticulturist Kate Sessions, this 79-acre park is a tranquil spot overlooking Mission Bay. During summer months it's an ideal location for picnicking, especially for those who want to avoid the traffic and congestion of the beach areas but still want to take advantage of those ocean breezes (which, by the way, make this a favorite spot for kite flying).

For those who crave a hike, a 2-mile trail, lined with coastal sage scrub and other native plants and trees, winds its way through the park and up and down a canyon. If you prefer something less challenging, there's also a paved walking path—perfect for working off that big picnic lunch. This is a well-equipped park with plenty of picnic tables, barbecues, playgrounds for the kids, and restrooms.

Marian Bear Memorial Park
Accessible from either Regents Road or Genesee Avenue, south off California Highway 52, San Diego
(858) 581-9952, (858) 581-9961
www.sannet.gov/park-and-recreation/parks/marbear2.shtml

One of the nicest things about San Diego is that it has maintained so much open space within its urban areas. Marian Bear Park is a 466-acre expanse of woodland and trails that runs the length of San Clemente Canyon. You'll feel like you've left the city far behind as you make your way through the dense live oak trees, sycamores, willows, and tons of native grasses and shrubs.

Hikers will enjoy the 7 miles of trails, and mountain bikers are welcome to use the park's maintenance roads. You'll often see mountain bikers practicing their moves here. This is a peaceful spot for a picnic, and there are lots of picnic tables to accommodate you.

Naturalists and knowledgeable volunteers from the Canyoneers Club of the San Diego Natural History Museum lead hikes most weekends to a variety of environments throughout the county. Walks, which generally last from two to six hours, are free. See www.sdnhm.org/canyoneers or call (619) 255-0203 for information or to request a schedule.

Miramar Reservoir
10710 Scripps Lake Drive, off Scripps Ranch Boulevard, San Diego
(619) 668-2050, (619) 465-3474 (for recorded information)
www.sannet.gov/water/recreation/miramar.shtml

Do you like to just get out and walk? So do many Insiders, and Lake Miramar is one of the most popular places for walkers, joggers, and skaters. Circling the lake entirely is no longer permitted, but the 4-mile paved path that ends at the reservoir is perfect for a workout, whether you're strolling, running, or on wheels. The lake is a good spot for fishing, too, and you're likely to reel in rainbow trout, largemouth bass, sunfish, and channel catfish.

Plenty of picnic areas are available, as are concession stands and restrooms. The lake closes for 30 to 60 days each fall, generally in October and November.

Mission Bay Park
2125 Park Boulevard, San Diego
(619) 235-1169

As this is technically classified an aquatic park, we'll cover Mission Bay Park more thoroughly in our Beaches and Water Sports chapter. But we also mention it here because it offers more than just water sports.

What was once a stretch of mud and marshlands began its transformation into Mission Bay Park in 1960. At 4,235 acres, it's the largest facility of its kind in the world created by dredging, filling, and landscaping. The park and picnic areas are used for volleyball, softball, kite flying, and horseshoes. The 27 miles of bayfront and 17 miles of oceanfront beaches are probably the county's most popular place for bicycling, skating, jogging, or just strolling along and people watching.

Facilities are extensive and varied—boat rentals, docks and launches, beaches, picnic tables, fire rings, restrooms, and playgrounds for the kids all make the park perfect for whatever recreation you have in mind. Even if you plan no more than a snooze on the grass while listening to the seagulls and the water lapping on the shore, you can't go wrong with Mission Bay Park.

Mission Trails Regional Park
1 Father Junipero Serra Trail, San Diego
(619) 668-3281
www.mtrp.org

Imagine this: 5,820 acres of open space with nearly 40 miles of hiking and biking trails—right in the middle of San Diego. Add to it the highest point within the city of San Diego, Cowles Mountain (read about what a great hike this is in our Recreation chapter), and stone outcroppings for rock climbers. Mission Trails Regional Park even has its own lake—Lake Murray—and it's open year-round for fishing on Wednesdays and weekends.

The impressive Visitor and Interpretive Center provides videos and interactive exhibits that describe the geology, history, plants, and animals in the park. Interpretive walks, stargazing, wildlife tracking, and many other activities are held at the center. The best spot for picnicking is around the Old Mission Dam. The paved trail around the lake is ideal for jogging and walking. Campsites at Kumeyaay Lake (there are 46) have no water or electricity, but the campground itself has restrooms with running water and solar showers; it's open Friday through Monday. 2 Father Junipero Serra Trail, off Mission Gorge Road (619-668-2748). Reservations can be made via the Web site.

Many of the California state parks now offer Wi-Fi Internet access.

Presidio Park
Taylor Street and Presidio Drive
San Diego
(619) 297-3258

This is the site of Father Junipero Serra's first mission and adjoining presidio, or fort, in California. The mission was moved to a new location a few years after it was built, but the museum, built in 1929, is in mission style and contains an abbreviated visual history lesson of the beginnings of San Diego. Open 10:00 A.M. to 4:30 P.M., cost is $5.00 for adults and $2.00 for kids ages 6 through 17. If you're just looking for recreation and a picnic, surrounding the presidio is a tree-filled park with sloping grassy hills—directly above Old Town and within a few miles of the sea. Plenty of picnic areas are available, and a pitch-and-putt golf course is within the park for those looking to work on their short game. A rec center (619-692-4918) offers indoor basketball and an outdoor softball field.

Tecolote Canyon Natural Park
Tecolote Road, off Interstate 5, San Diego
(858) 581-9952, (858) 581-9961
www.sannet.gov/park-and-recreation/parks

For the explorer, this is one of the best parks in town to while away the hours, absorbing the quietness and observing native plant and animal life. Hiking trails meander back and forth across Tecolote Creek in this 970-acre park, and you'll wander through wooded glades of willows, live oaks, and sycamores.

Tecolote has a nature center open Monday through Friday 9:00 A.M. to 4:00 P.M. and Saturday 9:00 A.M. to 2:00 P.M. featuring exhibits on canyon ecology, natural history, and Native Americans. The nature center also offers lectures and

Phone Numbers for Major Camping Locations

San Diego County Parks:
(858) 563-3600 information;
(877) 565-3600 for reservations;
www.sdparks.org

California State Parks:
(619) 688-3260 information;
(800) 444-7275 for reservations;
www.parks.ca.gov

National Park Service:
(619) 557-5450 information; (800) 365-2267 for reservations; www.nps.gov

USDA Forest Service:
(858) 673-6180 Cleveland National Park; (877) 444-6777 National Forest Recreation Reservations; www.fs.fed.us

guided walks through the park. Birders meet at 9:00 A.M. at the interpretive center the fourth Sunday of the month for guided walks. Sturdy shoes or hiking boots are recommended.

NORTH COUNTY COASTAL

Guajome County Park
3000 Guajome Lakes Road, Oceanside
(858) 565-3600, (877) 565-3600 (toll-free in San Diego County for reservations)

To find this 557-acre park, exit Interstate 5 on Mission Avenue in Oceanside and drive about 7 miles east. Nature trails ramble for miles through the lush riparian wilderness here. There are equestrian trails, too. The marsh area is popular with serious bird-watchers, and the lakeshore is a well-liked fishing spot. You'll find camping available in 35 RV sites (with showers for campers). There are plenty of picnic and barbecue areas along with a play area and convenient restrooms. Near the parking lot is an information kiosk that has brochures about the area. Nature walks and docent-led tours of the historic adobe home on-site are held most weekends; call for dates and times.

San Elijo Lagoon Ecological Reserve
2710 Manchester Avenue, Encinitas
(760) 436-3944
www.sanelijo.org

There are nearly 300 different species of birds that can be seen at this North County Coastal reserve. One Insider spotted egrets, blue herons, coots, and an array of ducks. This is one of the county's best-preserved wetlands. The 900-acre reserve has more than 5 miles of walking trails that wind through chaparral and marshes. Depending on the season, you'll see ferns and wildflowers.

Docent-led nature walks are held every second Saturday of the month at no cost. The walks begin at 9:00 A.M. Call for starting points and routes.

Torrey Pines State Reserve
North Torrey Pines Road, 1 mile south of Carmel Valley Road, San Diego
(858) 755-2063
www.torreypine.org

This is the sanctuary for the Torrey pine, the rarest pine in the United States. On the 2,000-acre reserve you could count more than 4,000 of these once-endangered trees, but it's more fun to visit the indigenous plant garden surrounding the interpretive center and wildlife museum. In the spring and early summer, you'll find native wildflowers mixed among the sage and chaparral-loving plants. Nature walks are held on weekends and holidays at 10:00 A.M. and 2:00 P.M.

The reserve is open daily from 8:00 A.M. to sunset. Dogs are not allowed, and picnicking is prohibited except on the beach.

NORTH COUNTY INLAND

Blue Sky Ecological Reserve
Espola Road, 0.5 mile north of Lake Poway Road, Poway
(858) 668-4781

A wonderful addition to the "outback" parks in the county, Blue Sky Ecological Reserve has 700 acres of wilderness. There's a mixture of chaparral, riparian woodland, and coastal sage scrub that gives off a wonderful aroma when warmed by the San Diego sun. The area is home to coyotes, deer, foxes, and snakes of many varieties. For the bird-watcher, of special note might be gnatcatchers, California quail, and hawks.

Drinking water isn't available at the park, which is open during daytime hours. Horses are allowed, but bikes are not. Near the parking lot is an information kiosk with a display of native plants and animals. Guided nature walks are offered on weekends at 9:00 A.M. Wildlife talks around the campfire are presented April through September on the fourth Saturday of the month. Call for information and reservations.

Lake Hodges
20102 Lake Drive off Via Rancho Parkway Escondido
(619) 668-2050, (619) 465-3474 (recorded information)
www.sannet.gov/water/recreation

The shoreline park on Lake Hodges is a popular place for walking, horseback riding, bike riding, and picnicking. Surround trails pass through open grassland to marshlands and stands of stately oaks, although the park has a decidedly urban feel. This is a wonderful place to see birds and other wildlife. Fish from shore, from float tubes, or from private or rental boats for largemouth bass, crappie, and catfish. Swimming isn't allowed in the lake.

When hiking in the mountains and deserts, stick to the trails and watch where you sit. While rattlesnakes are not aggressive creatures, they will strike when threatened or surprised.

The lake and adjoining parking lot are open February or March through October on Wednesday, Saturday, and Sunday from sunrise to sunset. Otherwise, park near trailheads and access the lake trails on foot.

Lake Poway Recreation Area
14644 Lake Poway Road off Espola Road, Poway
(858) 679-4343 (reservations), (858) 486-1234 (general information)

Lake Poway is a 35-acre recreational area that's popular in this youthful community. There is a 60-acre reservoir for boating and fishing, and it's stocked with trout in the fall and winter and catfish in the summer. Paddleboats, rowboats, and motorboats are available for rental Wednesday through Sunday year-round (no private boats are allowed). There are two playgrounds for the younger set, as well as two sand volleyball courts and horseshoe pits. There are picnic areas, a nature trail, and a concession stand that's open year-round.

Los Peñasquitos Canyon Preserve
Black Mountain Road, west from Interstate 15
Rancho Penasquitos
(858) 565-3600
www.sannet.gov/park-and-recreation/parks

The reserve is about 3,300 acres, and you'll find woodlands, scrub oak, and chaparral in these coastal canyons. There are walking trails, but bikes are allowed

Frequent visitors to California's state parks can purchase an annual day-use pass. Good for most state parks, beaches, recreation areas, and reserves, the $125 pass lasts a year from date of purchase and can be transferred from one vehicle to another. For more information see www.parks.ca.gov or call (619) 688-3260.

only on the service roads. Depending on the season, some of the trails may be closed; the preserve is open from dawn to sunset daily.

Within the park are remnants of San Diego County's first Mexican rancho. The adobe structures, built between 1825 and 1862, can be toured Saturdays at 11:00 A.M. and Sundays at 1:00 P.M. They are located at the end of Canyonside Park Driveway, off Black Mountain Road. Call (858) 484-7504 for more information.

Palomar Mountain State Park
19552 State Park Road, Palomar Mountain
(760) 742-3462, (800) 444-7275 (camping reservations)
www.palomar.statepark.org

As you reach the fork in County Road S7, one way leads to Palomar Mountain State Park and the other takes you to the national forest and the observatory. The sign is clear, but the choice may be hard. This picnic, walking, and camping area is popular year-round but nicest in spring and fall. In winter the snow brings San Diegans in droves. Be sure to bring chains during the winter if you head toward Palomar Mountain for some fun in the snow. You may not be allowed to drive up to the top without them. Elevation at the park ranges from 4,000 to 5,500 feet.

At the park you'll find some rambling walking trails. The Doane Valley Nature Trail is an easy 3 miles; most of it is on flat ground. The hike to the observatory, according to the self-guided trail markers, is about 4 miles with some climbing; kids older than age 10 will probably love the challenge. Request a trail brochure from the ranger station staff as you drive into the park.

For those who love to picnic, you'll find eating areas and camping spots with barbecues. Many Insiders picnic on Thanksgiving and Christmas, and the outings have become family traditions. There are also 31 developed campsites. Speaking of picnics and camping, become "bee wary." The bees and yellow jackets (a hungry, hazardous wasp) can be a serious fun-deterrent during the late summer and fall, when they swarm around campgrounds and picnic areas. Leashed dogs are allowed at the campsite but not on the trails.

The observatory and visitor center, at the end of County Road S6, are open from 9:00 A.M. to 4:00 P.M. daily throughout the year. The park is open from dawn to dusk. There's a small gift shop that's open daily and an adjacent bakery and vegetarian restaurant.

San Pasqual Battlefield State Historic Park and Museum
15808 San Pasqual Valley Road
Escondido
(760) 737-2201
www.parks.ca.gov

Just about a half mile from the San Diego Wild Animal Park and a million miles away in focus is the San Pasqual Battlefield. It's a historic park honoring those who participated in the 1846 San Pasqual Battle, called the bloodiest battle of the Mexican-American War. There's a visitor center, a hiking trail, and the requisite stone marker that describes the historical significance of the area. At the center you'll find an exhibit and videos. Visit between 10:00 A.M. and 4:00 P.M. the first Sunday of the month from October through June for Living History Day reenactments, or in December each year for a reenactment of the battle itself.

The center is open weekends only, 10:00 A.M. until 5:00 P.M. Admission is free. There are picnic tables and volunteers on staff to answer questions.

EAST COUNTY

Anza-Borrego Desert State Park
Borrego Springs
(760) 767-5311,
(760) 767-4205 (visitor center),
(800) 445-7275 (camping reservations)
www.anzaborrego.statepark.org

There are more than 600,000 acres of desert within this state park for camping, picnicking, walking, biking, and hiking. Here you'll see plants from the silver cholla and jumping cholla (a prickly cactus that will earn your respect if you mess with it) to the century plant (a type of agave) and indigo bush (with its cobalt blue flowers). There's wildlife, too, from big jackrabbits to bigger coyotes—and four species of rattlesnakes.

Though some see the desert as a dry, barren wasteland, others love it for its vast open spaces, starry skies, and strange plants. See our Attractions chapter for details about the wildflowers that bloom here in late winter or early spring and turn the desert into a breathtaking burst of exotica.

At the park you'll find 110 miles of trails (remember to take water—carry some with you and leave more in your car). Borrego Palm Canyon has 117 developed campsites for tents and RVs, 5 group sites, and a hiking trail that leads to an oasis of palms and shaded pools that's always unexpected, even if you've hiked the park 20 times. Tamarisk Grove has 25 developed campsites. Call the park and ask to have the latest newsletter sent, or scout out books on the park at bookstores and libraries.

If you're adventurous, there are primitive campsites here and there throughout the park that are given out on a first-come, first-served basis; backcountry camping is allowed; no fee or permit required. Remember, you'll need to pack in your water and pack out the trash. The equestrian camp has 10 sites and a corral. The visitor center, located 1 mile west of Borrego Springs on West Palm Canyon Drive, is a great place to begin your visit. Watch a slide show, visit the labeled cactus and succulent garden, and get a map of the park. It's open from 9:00 A.M. to 5:00 P.M. October through May; weekends and holidays June through September. There's a $6.00 day-use fee to park at the two main campgrounds; otherwise, access to the enormous wilderness park is free.

Cuyamaca Rancho State Park
California Highway 79 between Highway 78 and Interstate 8, eastern San Diego County
(760) 765-0755, (800) 444-7275 (camping reservations)
www.cuyamaca.us,
www.cuyamaca.statepark.org

This is a state park that's worth visiting again and again, whether you come for a short walk or plan to disappear for a while in the wilderness. Equestrians, mountain bikers, and hikers share more than 100 miles of paved and unpaved road. The wilderness area covers 25,000 acres in East County, including heavenly wildflower meadows, Green Valley Falls, and the ruins of a gold mine, the Stonewall. There are two developed campgrounds with 166 units, group campsites, and cabins. Equestrian campsites accommodate both groups and families.

Lake Cuyamaca is popular for fishing, boating, and bird-watching. Playing on the shore is allowed, but swimming isn't. Motorboats and rowboats are rented throughout the year. During the summer canoes and paddleboats are available.

---

i

Mountain lions (aka cougars) are found in some San Diego wilderness areas. There you should avoid hiking alone, especially at dawn and dusk, when the big cats tend to hunt. If you see a cougar stalking you: MAKE EYE CONTACT; act large and menacing, raising your arms and yelling; pick up small children but avoid crouching; don't let the lion get behind you.

Santee Lakes Regional Park has a playground for physically challenged kids, and on Lake #4, the pier is designed for handicapped anglers.

Call (760) 765-0515 for rental information. The park has a museum, too, displaying Native American artifacts; it's open weekdays 8:30 A.M. to 4:30 P.M., weekends 10:00 A.M. to 4:00 P.M., with extended hours in summer. The lake is open daily 6:00 A.M. to sunset.

Laguna Mountain Recreation Area
County Route S-1, 6 miles northeast of Pine Valley
(619) 445-6235 (information)
(619) 473-8547 (visitor center)
(877) 444-6777 (camping reservations)
www.lmva.org, www.sandiegoriver.org

Located within Cleveland National Park, you'll find 8,600 acres of recreation area with more than 35 miles of trails. Included is part of the Pacific Crest Trail, where every turn presents Kodak opportunities. You can ride horses or mountain bikes or hike through most of the park, which is regenerating after the 2003 Cedar fire.

The visitor center has information on safety, hiking, and campfire programs, along with the summertime stargazing parties. The center is open Friday 1:00 to 5:00 P.M., Saturday 9:00 A.M. to 5:00 P.M., and Sunday 9:00 A.M. to 3:00 P.M. (weekends only in winter). There are several hundred developed campsites, some open year-round, others only during the summer months.

Birders should fly to San Elijo Lagoon, a shallow-water estuary with more than 5 miles of hiking trails and 295 species of birds, including 65 nesting species. For information, visit the Web site www.sanelijo.org or call (760) 634-3026 or (760) 436-3944.

Lake Morena County Park
2550 Lake Morena Drive, off California Highway 94, or Buckman Springs Road off Interstate 8, near Campo
(858) 565-3600

Part of Cleveland National Forest, which stretches through San Diego County and into Orange County, Lake Morena is a lakefront park that covers about 3,250 acres. The terrain is rocky foothills with scrub oak and chaparral. Here you'll find part of the Pacific Crest Trail that excites hikers of skill. You'll also find easy walking trails for young kids.

If you're into camping, this is a choice park. There are 86 developed campsites, 58 with RV hookups, and 2 campsites for disabled campers. There are also scores of picnic areas. Due to low water levels, the primitive campsites at the northern end of the park are closed indefinitely.

If you're into fishing, call the "fish report hotline" at (619) 478-5473 for the latest report. Fishing is popular here, and bass, bluegill, catfish, crappie, and stocked trout crowd the lake—at least that's what we've heard from those who love the sport. There's a boat launch and motor- and rowboats are available for rent. The park is open daily from just before sunrise to just after sunset.

Santee Lakes Regional Park
9040 Carlton Oaks Drive, Santee
(619) 596-3141
www.santeelakes.com

Popular Santee Lakes Regional Park offers a profusion of picnicking, jogging, lounging, boating, and fishing opportunities around a chain of seven lakes. The backdrop of this urban campground and lake is dry hills; there's definitely not a "forest" feel to it. There's a developed campground with 300 sites with RV hookups, a general store, a swimming pool, and a rec center along with a laundry room. To add to the fun, there are horseshoe pits, volleyball courts, and a large playground. Tent campers may use the RV sites but pay full hookup price. Campers have access to the pool and other facilities. Dogs are not permitted in the day-use area.

SOUTH BAY

Sweetwater Regional Park
3218 Summit Meadow Road, off San Miguel Road, Bonita
(858) 694-3049
www.co.san-diego.ca.us/parks

If your idea of the perfect day at the park includes hiking or horseback riding, Sweetwater may be the place for you. Its 580 acres of open space and trails include more than 36 miles of hiking and equestrian trails that run along the Sweetwater River and the southern shore of the Sweetwater Reservoir. A 4-mile paved bicycle and equestrian trail runs from the western end of the park to San Diego Bay.

Sixty developed campsites are in the park (see our Recreation chapter for more camping information), and picnic sites are available. Sweetwater is a wilderness park that is dedicated to preserving the area's riparian habitat and grasslands.

Tijuana River National Estuary Research Reserve
301 Caspian Way, Imperial Beach
(619) 575-3613

A bird-watcher's delight, this 2,500-acre salt marsh reserve boasts more than 370 species of birds, including a dozen endangered species. The landscape of buckwheat and lemonadeberry bushes is generally unremarkable, but the 3.5-mile South McCoy hike skirts marshy wetlands with many birds and ends at the beach. There's a visitor center that has exhibits on local ecology and the species of birds you're likely to see. The center offers easy, one-hour guided nature walks at 3:00 P.M. on Sunday. Junior ranger programs (kids ages 7 through 12) reflecting various nature-related themes happen Thursday afternoons.

Winter is the best time to see migratory waterfowl; in springtime acres and acres of chaparral-covered hillsides are blanketed with colorful wildflowers, putting on a display that only Mother Nature could create. The visitor center is open daily.

The Coast to Crest Trail is an ongoing project to link the coast and interior with hiking trails through both public and private land, following the San Dieguito River to its source around Volcan Mountain. There are currently trails around Del Mar, Lake Hodges, Ramona and Volcan Mountain. See the Web site www.sdrp.org/trails.htm for details.

RECREATION

San Diego is famous for its abundance of recreational activities, both indoor and outdoor. The perception that locals and visitors spend much of their time in pursuit of recreation is no myth. From bicycling to bowling to hang gliding to in-line skating, the opportunities are almost endless. So numerous, in fact, that we've devoted entire chapters to water sports and golf. In this chapter we'll cover everything else and give you enough information to get you started on your favorite sport.

We'll tell you where to find the county's best hiking and walking trails. If being airborne appeals to you, we'll direct you to places where you can hook up with a hot-air balloon or a hang glider. And we promise to keep earthbound enthusiasts busy but safely anchored.

Part of the appeal of San Diego is that you can combine relaxation with fresh air, exercise, and a ton of fun. We encourage you to try something new while you're in town. Rent a pair of in-line skates and glide around Mission Beach. Or join an impromptu game of volleyball at the beach or in one of the county's many parks.

A couple of good sources for organized (and usually free) hikes, walks, bicycle tours, and many other activities are Thursday's "Night and Day" section of the *San Diego Union-Tribune* and the *San Diego Reader*. The *Reader* also comes out on Thursday and is distributed free at record stores, bookstores, grocery stores, and many other businesses throughout the county. They both have comprehensive listings of things to do around town. Whatever you decide to do, keep in mind that San Diego's balmy climate can be deceiving. Don't forget your sunscreen, even when the temperature is mild, and a sweatshirt or windbreaker in case the day turns brisk.

BALLOONING/BIPLANES

Ever since the movie *Around the World in 80 Days* focused attention on ballooning as a mode of transportation, the fascination for those brightly colored, soaring globes has held steady. If you'd like to quietly glide through the sky above San Diego, several balloon companies are eager to make your dream come true.

Balloon or Biplane Adventures by California Dreamin'
(800) 373-3359
www.californiadreamin.com

Soar high above the earth on a first-light ride over the wine country in Temecula or a sunset ride over Del Mar. Riders receive a photo and certificate at the conclusion of the ride. The sunrise ride is $128 per person ($148 on weekends; kids rate is $118 any day) and includes a continental breakfast and champagne mimosa; the sunset ride ($168 per person Monday through Friday, $188 per person Saturday and Sunday) includes champagne. Considering the morning flight is longer (45 to 75 minutes as opposed to 40 to 60 minutes for the afternoon journey), includes breakfast, and costs less, it seems the better deal. Or take one of several different backcountry biplane adventures (25 to 55 minutes; $248 to $448 for two).

Skysurfer Balloon Co.
2658 Del Mar Heights Road, Suite 198, Del Mar
(858) 481-6800, (800) 660-6809
www.sandiegohotairballoons.com

Soar above the Temecula Valley on an early-morning balloon flight, juice or mimosa in hand, or watch the sun set over the ocean above Del Mar to the taste of champagne on an hour-long flight with San Diego's original balloon operator, flying since 1979. Rates for the approximately one-hour flights are $150 for Temecula and $165 ($175 on weekends) for Del Mar. Kids older than age 6 welcome; they pay the same price. Start to finish the tours take three to three-and-a-half hours.

BICYCLING/MOUNTAIN BIKING

Whatever your pleasure—gentle, flat surfaces or more challenging hills and terrain—you'll find it somewhere around town. Designated bike paths are clearly marked on many San Diego streets, and great off-road trails are located throughout the county. One of the best street rides is along the coast, from Mission Beach north to La Jolla. It hugs the shoreline for most of the way, but when it does veer inland for a block or two, you'll be treated to a peek at some magnificent homes. For mountain bikers, the Iron Mountain Trail in East County is a moderately difficult favorite. Trailheads are located on California Highway 67 at Poway Road and CA 67 at Ellie Lane.

Distance riders recommend a trip around San Diego Bay, continuing on to Imperial Beach and up The Strand in Coronado, returning downtown on the ferry. Other popular longish rides include Alpine to Pine Valley, in the East County, and in the South Bay, Chula Vista to Tecate and back. Beginning cyclists and those interested in a more leisurely outing like the paved pathway between College Avenue and the Oceanside Harbor.

Bicycles can be rented at several locations; we've listed a few below. Rental rates vary, but you usually can rent a cruiser for $6.00 or $7.00 per hour. Rent cruisers, hybrids, or mountain bikes for a half-day, day, or 24-hour period; prices range from $20 to $45. Most bike shops provide maps that highlight street bike paths and off-road trails all over the county, or you can pick up a map at the Caltrans office at 2829 Juan Street, San Diego, (619) 688-6699. Remember, bicycle helmets are recommended for all and required by law for children younger than age 18.

B&L Bike and Sports
211 North Highway 101, Solana Beach
(858) 481-4148
www.blbikes.com

B&L specializes in road bikes, triathalon bikes, cruisers, mountain bikes, and hybrids (a cross between a road bike and a mountain bike). Rentals are available by the hour, day, or week.

Bike Tour San Diego
509 Fifth Avenue, San Diego
(619) 238-2444

This shop specializes in hybrid and mountain bikes. Also available for rent are mountain bikes with front suspension or with dual suspension. Free pickup and delivery are offered, and all bike rentals come with roadside assistance, locks, helmets, repair kits, and maps.

Bikes and Beyond
1201 First Street, Coronado
(619) 435-7180

Beach cruisers and mountain bikes can be rented by the hour, half-day, or full day. The shop is located in the Ferry Landing Marketplace. A wide variety of cycles is available for adults and kids; price includes helmet and lock.

Cheap Rentals
3689 Mission Boulevard, Mission Beach
(858) 488-9070, (800) 941-7761
www.cheap-rentals.com

Wow! Their rates are cheap. And there's a wonderful variety of equipment for use on the boardwalk, the bay, or the beach a block away. In addition to beach cruiser bikes, the baby joggers, in-line skates, and skateboards go for $5.00 an hour or

---

For a comprehensive list of biking clubs, routes, and events throughout the county, as well as links to other biking sites, check out www.efgh.com/bike.

Lots of San Diego organizations offer sports camps for children, including the YMCA, the University of San Diego, San Diego City College, and The Lawrence Family Jewish Community Center, which is open to people of all faiths.

$17.00 for 24 hours. They also rent beach chairs and umbrellas for $5.00 a day. Or pay $20.00 for a day of fun: you get a bike, snorkel gear, and map leading you to La Jolla Cove for a day of snorkeling. Or pay $35.00 for the whole weekend.

Hike Bike Kayak San Diego
2246 Avenida de la Playa, La Jolla
(858) 551-9510, (866) 425-2925
www.hikebikekayak.com
Several inexpensive tours per day will help put you in touch with your inner athlete. Tours are geared to folks of different ages and abilities: from the family-oriented Mission Bay ride (for kids as young as age 2!, $35 per person) to coast rides for children age 8 and older (with their parents, $30) to longer mountain bike treks ($75, ages 10 and older). Check their Web site for adventures that, as the business name implies, combine biking with other adventure activities.

Bicycle Clubs

For organized cycling adventures, we suggest you contact one of the following clubs:

North County Cycle Club (NCCC)
P.O. Box 127, San Marcos, CA 92069
www.northcountycycleclub.com
Three groups make up the membership of NCCC: The Cruisers, who are laid-back and like to enjoy the scenery while they ride; The Roadies, who are fast, intermediate to advanced riders who like to pick up the pace a little; and The Spokey Dokes, who are the mountain bikers of the group. All three groups schedule regular rides.

San Diego Bicycle Club
P.O. Box 80562, San Diego, CA 92138
(858) 495-2454
www.sdbc.org
This is the oldest bicycle club in San Diego and has members of all ages. Its focus is on racing, and members are trained by experienced cyclists who have both racing and coaching backgrounds. The club organizes several races throughout the year.

San Diego Bicycle Touring Society
P.O. Box 1941, Chula Vista, CA 91912
(619) 426-8192
www.bicyclingsandiego.com
Geared mostly for the bicyclist who likes distance, this club offers some challenging rides. Members schedule weekly Tuesday evening and weekend rides that take place in locations all over the county.

BILLIARDS

The game of billiards has been enjoying a resurgence in recent years, a fact borne out by the increasing number of billiards parlors in San Diego.

The Hungry Stick
4664 Clairemont Mesa Boulevard, Clairemont Mesa
(858) 272-1412
Watch big-screen TV, eat great food, and play pool with some of the best in San Diego. You can play all day (until 6:00 P.M.) for $5.00 a table; after that it's $7.00 an hour.

Joltin' Joes
717 North Escondido Boulevard
Escondido
(760) 743-7665
With a full sports bar, grill, and 22 pool tables, you can't go wrong here. Rates for two people range from $6.00 per hour for daytime hours during the week to $10.00 per hour for weekend nights.

Pacific Q Billiards Club
1454 Encinitas Boulevard, Encinitas
(760) 943-9929
www.pacificqbillards.com
Play pool on one of eight gorgeous tables for $5.00 to $7.00 per player per hour, with a table maximum making it more economical for four players. Domino's Pizza delivers from next door, and the bar itself serves basic pub grub: chicken wings, fries, burgers, and so on. It's an all-ages billiards room despite the fact that more than 30 brands of beer are served.

Society Billiard Cafe
1051 Garnet Avenue, San Diego
(858) 272-7665
In addition to 15 regulation pool tables, Society Billiard Cafe has a bar that serves cocktails, beer, and wine from around the world. Pizza, salads, and sandwiches can be enjoyed at the on-site restaurant, which also has patio dining. Rates range from $6.00 per table per hour midday during the week to $12.00 per table per hour on weekend nights. Or take advantage of the special: $10 per person for unlimited pool until 7:00 P.M., including food.

BOWLING

One sport that never goes out of style is bowling. San Diego has several bowling alleys where you can enjoy a leisurely game or two, or if league play is more to your taste, all alleys provide that, too. Prices vary depending on the facility, day of the week, and the time of day. You can bowl a lane for just over $2.00 during bargain hours or as much as $8.00 per person per hour. Most facilities have discounts for seniors and kids, and some offer special events with music, disc jockeys, and laser lights on weekends.

AMF Eagle Bowl
945 West San Marcos Boulevard
San Marcos
(760) 744-7000
Forty lanes with automatic scoring make AMF Eagle Bowl a modern, up-to-date facility. If you're looking for something a little different, try Extreme Bowling on Friday and Saturday nights (9:00 and 8:00 P.M., respectively; $5.00 per person). Classic rock 'n' roll plays, the house lights go off, and the black lights go on while pins and balls go all glowy and weird. You'll find a snack bar, lounge, and pro shop on the premises.

Brunswick Premier Lanes
845 Lazo Court, Chula Vista
(619) 421-4801
Brunswick Premier has 48 lanes, a pro shop, a cocktail lounge, a snack bar, and a Pizza Hut Express. This is a busy facility, so reservations are highly recommended (weekdays only; on weekends it's first come, first served). There are competitive and "just-for-fun" leagues as well as leagues for kids and seniors. Weekend price is $4.70 per person per game, or take advantage of multiple midweek specials, like on Tuesday and Thursday shoes, soda, and game for $1.50 an hour.

Kearny Mesa Bowl
7585 Clairemont Mesa Boulevard, San Diego
(858) 279-1501
www.kearnymesabowl.com
Forty lanes provide ample opportunity for bowling on even the most crowded days. Pay $14 to $18 per hour or take advantage of many midweek specials. Bowl to loud rock music on Thursday afternoon or Friday or Saturday nights until 1:00 A.M., when there's also karaoke in the bar.

Mira Mesa Lanes
8210 Mira Mesa Boulevard, San Diego
(858) 578-0500
Mira Mesa Lanes is a typical modern bowling alley with a color-coded, automatic scoring system. On the premises is everything you'll need to make your bowling day a complete experience: a sports bar,

snack bar, well-stocked pro shop, and video arcade. On Fun Fridays and Saturdays ($16 per person) from 10:00 P.M. to 1:00 A.M., a DJ spins records and colored lights create a disco effect.

Parkway Bowl
1280 Fletcher Parkway, El Cajon
(619) 448-4111
www.parkwaybowl.com
Parkway Bowl has long been a family entertainment center in East County. Its 68 lanes are equipped with bumpers just for kids—which means no gutter balls. All lanes have automatic scoring, and the facility has a pro shop, bar, Mexican restaurant, and pizzeria, as well as laser tag and 17 pool tables. Prices here are reasonable, and the lanes stay open on Friday and Saturday until 3:00 A.M. Monday through Friday from 8:30 A.M. to 5:00 P.M., adults pay just $2.25 per person.

CAMPING

Is your idea of camping truly roughing it with just a tent and a few essentials? Or do you prefer a more upscale form of camping, say, in an RV or a park that has all the luxuries of home? Whatever your heart's desire, San Diego has the perfect campsite for you.

We have listed private and government campgrounds pertaining to the county or within state parks and national forests, all with as many or as few amenities as necessary to satisfy the adventurer in you. Here we give you a sampling of some of the area's best and most popular campgrounds. You may want to check some of the camping sites described in our Parks chapter, too. But if you want an in-depth listing of the dozens of sites throughout the county, contact the county's parks and recreation department at (858) 694-3049, www.sdcounty.ca.gov/parks/ or the state's parks and recreation department at (800) 444-7275, www.reserveamerica.com. Or look for camping guides and books at your local library or bookstore, especially those listed as Insiders' Tips on these pages. Most but not all campgrounds accept advance reservations and dogs. Rates change frequently, so be sure to check for current prices.

Agua Caliente County Park
39555 County Route S2
(877) 565-3600, (858) 565-3600
Two naturally fed mineral pools are the main attractions here. One is a large outdoor pool kept at its natural 96 degrees; the other is indoors, heated, and boasts Jacuzzi jets. The 140 campsites accommodate tents or RVs with full or partial hookups. In addition to miles of hiking trails, there are a children's play area, horseshoe pits, and shuffleboard courts to amuse kids and adults. Campsites rent for $14 to $18 per night, and reservations can be made 12 weeks in advance. Closed between Memorial Day and Labor Day. Dogs are not allowed.

Campland on the Bay
2211 Pacific Beach Drive, San Diego
(858) 581-4200, (800) 422-9386
www.campland.com
Every campsite at Campland comes with a beach, a bay, and a rollicking good time. Right on the shores of Mission Bay, this private urban campground has nearly 600 spaces; almost all have fire rings. Tent sites offer water, cable TV, and electricity (summer rates $56 midweek, $84 on weekends); 420 RV sites have full hookups (pay according to location and day of the week: $61 to $259). "Winter" rates are considerably lower, and then you can also rent by the week or month. Campers can enjoy a wide range of equipment and activities, including two Jacuzzis and heated pools, showers, picnic tables, a large playground, a recreation room, and a marina with boat launch and tons of water activities; bikes, pedal boats, kayaks, and catamarans can also be rented. A full-time rec director organizes Ping-Pong tournaments, bingo, line-dancing lessons, etc. Primitive sites ($39 to $44) are open

only when the rest of the camp is full. At the other end of the spectrum is the Supersite ($200 to $375), a private site overlooking the bay with a Jacuzzi, washer and dryer, telephone, landscaping and lawn furniture, gas grill, and cable TV. Reservations are accepted up to two years in advance.

Laguna Campground (Cleveland National Forest)
3 miles northwest of Mount Laguna, off County Road S1
(619) 445-6235 (information)
(877) 444-6777 (reservations)
www.reserveUSA.com

Camping in the Laguna Mountains is back-to-nature with just the basics, but a more beautiful and peaceful spot would be hard to find. The federally owned Laguna Campground has 101 tent and RV sites. There are no hookups, but there's a sanitary dump station about 4 miles away at Buckman Springs. You will find running water, flush toilets, barbecues, showers, fire rings, and picnic tables, as well as access to the Laguna Rim and a portion of the 2,627-mile Pacific Crest Trail, which stretches between the borders of Canada and Mexico. Rates are $15 per night. Some sites are open year-round.

From North County, take California Highway 78 east through Ramona toward Julian; turn right (east) at a stop sign after 4 blocks and turn right on to California Highway 79; follow to the junction with S1 (Sunrise Highway); turn left. It's about 5 miles to the campground. Heading east on Interstate 8, take the Sunrise Highway (S1) exit; the entrance is about 3 miles north of the Laguna store and post office.

South Carlsbad State Beach
5 miles south of Carlsbad, via County Road S21
(760) 438-3143 (information)
(800) 444-7275 (reservations)
www.reserveamerica.com

This is a rare campground set on the bluffs above the beach at Carlsbad and perfect for those who wish to combine camping

Based in Idyllwild in the San Jacinto Mountains northeast of San Diego, Wilderness Outings offers monthly climbing clinics in San Diego's Mission Trails Regional Park and more advanced lessons in Joshua Tree National Park, one of the country's premier climbing spots. Contact them at (877) 494-5368 or see the Web site www.wildernessoutings.com.

with water sports. Surfing, fishing, or simply swimming are all right at your feet here. The site includes a coin-op laundry, a convenience store, showers, restrooms, fire rings, and picnic tables. The campground has 220 tent or RV sites (no hookups), all $31 per night. Ten sites are wheelchair accessible. Reservations can be made up to seven months in advance.

Sweetwater Regional Park
3218 Summit Meadow Road, Bonita
(858) 565-3600, (877) 563-3600

Sixty campsites accommodate tents, RVs, campers, and horse trailers. Several sites have horse corrals, and all have water and electricity. Horse trails galore are the main attraction here. Other amenities include restrooms, showers, barbecues, picnic tables, and a large group area.

As with all county parks, reservations are accepted up to 12 weeks in advance. Rates are $16.00; for horses, add $2.00 to the fee. To get to the campground, take Bonita Road east until it becomes San Miguel Road, and turn left onto Summit Meadow Road.

CLIMBING

Indoors or outdoors, rock climbing is quickly becoming the sport of choice for many locals and visitors alike. Indoor facilities are available for climbing, lessons, and equipment purchase or rental. For outdoor climbing, we highly recommend you take advantage of an organized climb, especially if you're a newcomer to the

If you plan to test your skills at one of San Diego's indoor climbing facilities, morning hours are the least crowded time. By early afternoon there may be more climbers around you than you want to contend with.

sport or unfamiliar with the area. Outdoor climbing areas are abundant throughout San Diego County, but you can't go wrong with the recommendations and guidance of professionals.

Solid Rock
2074 Hancock Street, San Diego
(619) 299-1124

13026 Stowe Drive, Poway
(858) 748-9011

992 Rancheros Road, San Marcos
(760) 480-1429
www.solidrockgym.com
This indoor climbing facility has three San Diego locations, all offering 30-foot, seamless, textured climbing walls and a multitude of apparatuses for practicing techniques such as bouldering, top-roping, and lead climbing. Day passes can be purchased for $12 Monday through Friday, $15 on weekends. Children age 16 and younger pay $13. Private and group lessons are available but are not required of inexperienced climbers.

Vertical Hold Climbing Center
9580 Distribution Avenue, San Diego
(858) 586-7572
www.verticalhold.com
This center has an indoor 17,000-square-foot climbing wall with hundreds of routes for beginners to advanced climbers. Beginning climbers are required to take instruction. A $38 private beginner's lesson includes equipment and a day-climbing pass. Day passes are $14.00, half-day passes cost $12.00, and lunchtime passes go for $8.00. Die-hard indoor climbers can get a monthly or annual pass.

Thinking of trying hang gliding? Wind conditions at Torrey Pines are consistently the best from February through April, even though you'll be able to fly whenever a good wind comes up. Insiders swear that when accidents do occur, it's among hot-dogging experts, not the more cautious novice flyers.

HANG GLIDING

Hang gliding, or paragliding as it is frequently called, is as close as you can get to flying without actually having wings. For the thrill of a lifetime, soar above the beautiful Torrey Pines coastline and enjoy unparalleled stillness and serenity while navigating either a hang glider or paraglider. All fliers must have an advanced license to soar on their own, but you can experience the thrill right away by taking a tandem flight with a licensed pilot.

Torrey Pines Gliderport
(Air California Adventures)
2800 Torrey Pines Scenic Drive, La Jolla
(858) 452-9858
www.flytorrey.com
Located at the historic landmark Torrey Pines Gliderport, Air California Adventures offers training courses ranging from beginner to advanced. The three-to five-day beginner course ($895) teaches the basic skills necessary to fly under direct instructor supervision. To achieve the next level, where solo flights are permitted, you'll need an instruction packet costing $1,625. For a one-time thrill, try a tandem flight. No instruction is necessary—you glide with an experienced pilot. The cost is $175 for a 20- to 30-minute flight.

HIKING

We proudly declare that there is no better place in the world than San Diego for hiking over a variety of terrain, from mountain to desert to coastal trails. While we may be overstating the case just slightly, if you're a dedicated hiker, you will not be disappointed here. If you'd like to meet new friends and prefer to hike with a group, check Thursday's *San Diego Union-Tribune*. It usually has a list of organized hikes from which you can choose.

If you prefer selecting your own location, we'll highlight a few of the best hikes here. For comprehensive maps and lists of hiking trails, check with any sporting goods store or bookstore. Be sure to pack lots of water and sunscreen, and if you're planning to make a day of it, include a picnic lunch and some basic first-aid supplies. San Diego does have its share of dangerous critters, too, so be alert for rattlesnakes (even on the coast) and on some of the more remote inland trails, mountain lions.

Cuyamaca Rancho State Park
10 miles northeast of Alpine
(760) 765-0755
www.cuyamaca.statepark.org
www.cuyamaca.us

If diversity in hiking is what you're after, this park is the ticket, with more than 100 miles of hiking trails: along streambeds and through pine-oak forests, meadows, and sagebrush. The park is bisected by CA 79, and a variety of signed trails depart from parking lots along the road. One of the most rewarding, moderate hikes is a portion of the East Side Trail. Some climbs await you, but the reward is an unequaled scenic vista. This trail is not marked well in some places, so we advise you to get a map from the ranger station before you set out. The trail length is 4.7 miles, and it should take you about two hours. As always, be sure to take more water than you think you'll need. To get to the trailhead, take I-8 east to CA 79, turn left (north), and drive about 4 miles to a large parking lot on the right.

Los Peñasquitos Canyon Preserve
10 miles north of downtown San Diego
(858) 538-8066

Hike through oak trees and lush meadows on this 6.5-mile trail before descending to the canyon floor, where you'll be surrounded by giant boulders. During winter and spring a stream forms small waterfalls between the boulders, making this a perfect spot for a picnic. You'll hike up a canyon for a while before returning to the grove of oaks and the main trail back to the parking lot. The hike takes about two and a half hours. To get to the trailhead, take Interstate 15 north to Mira Mesa Boulevard. Turn left (west) and travel 0.5 mile to Black Mountain Road. Turn right and drive to the parking lot, which is 1 mile ahead on the left.

Mission Trails Regional Park
1 Father Junipero Serra Trail, San Diego
(619) 668-3275, (619) 668-3281
www.mtrp.org

Mission Trails contains almost 6,000 acres of hiking, mountain biking, and equestrian trails that meander through mountains, valleys, and lakes. Guided hikes depart from the Visitors/Interpretive Center on Wednesday, Saturday, and Sunday, usually at 9:30 A.M., and from the park's only campground on the second and fourth Saturdays of the month at 8:30 A.M. One of the best hikes in the park is to the top of Cowles Mountain. At 1,591 feet, it's the highest point in the city of San Diego. There are three different routes to the top. The trailhead and parking lot for the most popular and crowded route is found at Golfcrest and Navajoa Roads. More scenic is the trail departing from Barker Way at Navajoa Road.

San Elijo Lagoon Ecological Preserve
Encinitas and Solana Beach
(760) 436-3944
www.sanelijo.org

This is a wonderful place to combine a

Are you an amateur photographer? Capture some of San Diego's most beautiful images at Mission Trails Regional Park. The dramatic stone outcroppings are captivating subjects for shutterbugs.

Three gems of information on some of the best hiking trails in San Diego County are Sean O'Brien's **12 Short Hikes: Coastal Areas; 12 Short Hikes: Mountain Areas;** *and* **Best Easy Day Hikes: San Diego.** *All are available at most local bookstores.*

lovely estuary hike or jog with fantastic birding. To see most of the preserve, choose the Rios Trail. To get to the trailhead, exit Interstate 5 on Loma Santa Fe Drive and go west. Turn right on Rios; at the end of the street is the trailhead. The trail leads through many of the 900-acre preserve's distinct habitats, including mixed chaparral, coastal sage and riparian habitats, and salt- and freshwater marshes. The path ducks under I-5 from its staging area near the sea, where this watershed is fed by Escondido and Orilla Creeks.

HORSEBACK RIDING

Grab your cowboy hat, pull on those boots, and climb on a horse for a different view of San Diego. Whether you prefer riding on the beach or in the wilderness, both are available for short rides of one hour or longer rides up to a full day.

Happy Trails
12115 Black Mountain Road, San Diego
(858) 271-8777
www.happytrails-usa.com
This company has been around a long time and hopes to open a branch in the mountains of East County. Currently they offer rides into the Los Peñasquitos Canyon Preserve, following part of the original stagecoach trail that connected Julian to Old Town. Guided rides are offered seven days a week; cost is $45 for one hour, $60 for one and a half hours, $75 for two hours.

How about ice-skating at the beach? Coronado's storybook Hotel Del Coronado creates a skating rink overlooking the beach each year around Christmas.

ICE-SKATING

Hard to imagine ice-skating in San Diego? Believe it or not, it not only exists, it thrives. Several local skating rinks have public hours for amateur skaters to test their skills gliding across the ice. Remember, even in summertime it can get chilly inside the rinks, so dress appropriately.

Ice Town
4545 La Jolla Village Drive, San Diego
(858) 452-9110
www.icetown.com
Located in the University Towne Center mall, Ice Town offers public ice-skating seven days a week. If you need lessons, teachers are on hand to help get you upright and moving forward. The rink is available for private parties, too, in case you're looking for someplace unique for your next gathering. Because the rink is located in the UTC shopping mall (see our Shopping chapter), there's the added benefit of a food court surrounding the rink, and parents can shop while kids skate. Rates are $12 ($10.00 if you have your own skates). There are youth and adult hockey leagues and hockey lessons for future Wayne Gretskys. Public hours vary from day to day, so be sure to call ahead.

Iceoplex
555 North Tulip Street, Escondido
(760) 489-5550
www.iceoplex.com
This modern facility in North County Inland has public skating, as well as individual and group lessons for ice hockey, adult and youth hockey leagues for men and women, camps, and hockey clinics. Join a pickup hockey game most days of the week, or form your own team. Figure-skating and hockey lessons are available. Private activities that can be scheduled include broomball (easygoing

Julian in winter. San Diego County is home to beaches, deserts, and snow-covered mountains. PHOTO: COURTESY OF JULIAN CHAMBER OF COMMERCE

"hockey" where kids in tennis shoes hit a soft ball) and "snow days," where kids play on the ice and in piles of snow and later warm up with cocoa and cookies. There's a pro shop and a pizza parlor on-site, as well as a lap pool, gym, steam room, and sauna. Kids pay $9.00 with skate rental and $6.50 without; adult admission is $10.00 including skates, $8.00 without. There are morning and afternoon sessions on weekdays, afternoon sessions only on weekends.

San Diego Ice Arena
11048 Ice Skate Place, San Diego
(858) 530-1825
www.sdice.com

This rink offers public skating every day (except when rented for parties) and most evenings. Hours change from day to day, so call ahead for current times. A complete sport shop is on the premises, and both individual and group lessons in figure skating and hockey are offered. Skating rates are $7.00 per person; skate rental is $3.00. Group activities range from Christian Music Night to swing parties to activities for local schoolchildren and Girl and Boy Scouts. This is the best spot in the county to learn to play hockey.

LASER TAG

Advanced technology has created new and innovative ways to play, and nowhere is that more true than in a laser-tag venue. Laser tag is an interactive adventure that combines computer technology with action-oriented team play. Players don a special pack and take a laser-pulse phaser into intricately designed play areas where they score points for their team by "tagging" opposing team members.

CLOSE-UP

Carlsbad Marathon

Imagine this: It's a perfect early morning winter's day in San Diego. That means the sun is out and it's in the high 40s or low 50s, but sure to jump 20 degrees by lunch. The scene could be tranquil; however, with more than 10,000 people warming up, stretching, and psyching up to compete in this event, all is far from serene.

The annual Carlsbad Marathon is the second-oldest marathon on the West Coast. Begun in the late '50s by the San Diego Track Club, it was originally run from Oceanside to Mission Bay. It moved to North County in December of 1990.

Change is constant in San Diego and usually brings improvements. This new race was no exception. When the current organizing company, In Motion, Inc., was hired to orchestrate the event, it moved the race to North County in 1990, which increased its national exposure and changed the race into more than a recreational activity. It's a community event now.

The company also coordinates a fitness-training program for those interested in running but who might not be in shape. The 25-week regimen is designed to help everyone, regardless of age or fitness level, to participate in the race—and have some fun, too.

Even if you don't run, there are still exciting things to do at the free three-day All About Fitness Expo, which is held in conjunction with the race. Thousands come to see the latest in exercise equipment, sample healthy snacks, and meet some minor local celebrities, from the mayor to the winners of previous years' races.

The featured event is the marathon (26.2 miles), where runners run north along San Diego's coastline. Lynn Flanagan, founder of In Motion, explains: "The marathon and half marathon are run on a gently rolling out-and-back course along the ocean. All marathon events are run on a closed course.

The half marathon is recognized as one of the fastest races of that distance in the United States, and organizers say that it draws the very best field of American runners competing for the $1,000 purse.

The marathon is held in the middle of January. If you'd like details for the next run, contact In Motion at (858) 792-2900 or (888) 792-2900, or visit www.sdmarathon.com.

All ages are welcome, but players should be at least 7 years old to get maximum enjoyment from the game.

Laser Storm
9365 Mission Gorge Road, Santee
(619) 562-3791
Players receive a brief introduction to the game, put on lightweight vests and headsets, then enter a futuristic arena with phasers in hand. The object here is to seek, find, and deactivate opposing team members and their base station. The arena is full of barriers, strobe lights, police beacons, sentries, roboscanners, and many more obstacles to add to the fun and the challenge. Games last for 10 minutes, and the cost is $4.00 per person for the first game and $3.00 for subsequent games.

Laser Storm is generally open Friday 6:30 to 11:00 P.M., Saturday and Sunday 1:30 to 4:00 P.M., and Saturday 6:30 to 9:00 P.M. Groups of eight or more can reserve the facility at other times.

Ultrazone
3146 Sports Arena Boulevard, Suite 21
San Diego
(619) 221-0100
www.playultrazone.com
Laser tag at Ultrazone starts in the Briefing Room, where players get their "assignments." Once inside the 4,000-square-foot arena, players are confronted with a fog-filled environment full of mazes and all sorts of other challenges.

The game typically lasts for about 15 minutes, and the cost is $7.00 per game. The facility can be rented 24/7 for private parties.

PAINTBALL

Here's a treat for those looking for something a little different. Paintball has taken firm root as a game filled with fun, thrills, and strategy. Players seek out opponents with the intent of eliminating them with a brightly colored blob of paint. Come alone, bring a friend, or organize a group, and get ready for a unique experience.

***The bible of the San Diego outdoor enthusiast is Jerry Schad's* Afoot & Afield in San Diego County. *Providing incisive information about nearly every inch of the county, Schad describes trail length/difficulty, terrain, and suitability for kids, dogs, mountain bikers, etc. Further insight can be found in the outdoorsman's weekly column in the* San Diego Reader.**

Camp Pendleton Paintball Park
Camp Pendleton, Oceanside
(800) 899-9957
www.cppaintball.com
Paintball competition consists of two teams playing the classic "capture the flag" game in an outdoor park. The staff is always on hand to assist you with equipment needs, explanation of the rules, and general tips to enhance your paintball day. The Marine Corps base park is open to the public (bring proper identification) Saturday and Sunday from 9:00 A.M. to 4:30 P.M. or on weekdays for prearranged private parties only. Any age can play, but those younger than age 18 must have a signed parental consent form. Admission is $12; packages including equipment, 500 paintballs, and admission go for $44.

Mr. Paintball
25320 Lake Wohlford Road, Escondido
(760) 737-8870
www.mrpaintballusa.com
Owner Mr. Paintball (otherwise known as Stan Burgis) likens the sport to the cops-and-robbers games we played as kids. Mr. Paintball emphasizes safety while ensuring that participants have a good time. Folks can play either on outdoor fields or inside.

Play on weekends and most holidays from 8:00 A.M. to 4:00 P.M. Full-day admission, including a deli-sandwich lunch, is

$25 for those with their own equipment, or pay $45 to $65 for a package including equipment of varying sophistication.

RACQUETBALL

Although racquetball isn't the rage that it once was, there are still dedicated players who hit the courts with regularity. Some fitness centers and clubs have racquetball courts and will allow the public to play without purchasing a membership. But your best bet is to try one of the public courts listed below. They charge a per-person rate for one hour's play, but if the courts aren't busy, you can often keep playing at no additional charge.

American Athletic Club
2539 Hoover Avenue, National City
(619) 477-2123
Rates range from $7.00 to $8.00 per person depending on the time of day. The club has six courts and is open Monday through Friday 6:00 A.M. to 10:00 P.M., Saturday 7:00 A.M. to 6:00 P.M., and Sunday 9:00 A.M. to 2:00 P.M.

La Mesa Racquetball
4330 Palm Avenue, La Mesa
(619) 460-3500
www.lamesaracquetball.com
Racquetball can be played on nine courts here, 365 days a year. The courts are open Monday through Thursday 11:30 A.M. to 10:00 P.M., Friday 11:30 A.M. to 8:00 P.M., and weekends 7:00 A.M. to 2:00 P.M. You can also play Wallyball here: that's indoor volleyball that incorporates the walls for a whole new aspect to the game. Rates range from $8.00 to $10.00 per person.

Find more racquetball clubs at www.californiaraquetball.org or call (714) 966-9329. The Web site also has an online newsletter and excellent links where you can read about pro players and area tournaments or learn the rules of the game.

San Diego Workout
1010 South Santa Fe Avenue, Vista
(760) 724-6941
www.workout4life.net
Four racquetball courts are available for public play at this facility, and reservations are accepted up to a week in advance. Rates are $10 per person per hour for non-members. Hours are 5:00 A.M. to 10:00 P.M. Monday through Thursday, 5:00 A.M. to 9:00 P.M. Friday, 6:00 A.M. to 5:00 P.M. Saturday, and 7:00 A.M. to 5:00 P.M. Sunday. Their Del Mar club (Workout4Life, 2010 Jimmy Durante Boulevard, Del Mar, 858-481-6226) offers fitness classes for kids as well as kickboxing, yoga, Pilates, and more for adults. The Escondido branch (409 West Felicita Avenue, Escondido, 760-871-6600) offers the same classes for adults and babysitting for children.

SKATING/SKATEBOARDING

As in most cities, the popularity of skating and skateboarding seems to be in direct proportion to the intolerance for the sports. The city of Del Mar, for example, discourages skating and skateboarding wherever it can within the city limits. Both are also prohibited in Balboa Park, but for good reason. There's always such a large group of people milling about that combining wheels with slow-moving feet would be a recipe for disaster.

Never fear, however. We'll get you rolling safely and legally in some of the best spots in the county. Do it on your own, or join an organized skate to meet new friends and discover new skating places.

Coronado Skate Park
Tidelands Park, 2000 Mullinex Drive
Coronado
(619) 522-7342
Skaters pay a yearly fee of $10 (which includes first-session equipment rental

and entrance fee) to skate at this smooth park just across the bridge in Coronado. Summer hours are daily 10:00 A.M. to dusk; during the school year the outdoor park opens at 1:00 P.M. Year-round weekend hours are Saturday and Sunday 10:00 A.M. to dusk. Helmets, knee pads, and elbow pads are required and can be rented, as can skateboards. Wrist guards are recommended. Call ahead for session hours, as these change frequently. Cost is $5.00 per session.

Escondido Sports Center
3315 Bear Valley Parkway, Escondido
(760) 839-5425
www.escondido.org/sportscenter

The 22,000-square-foot park for board skaters has a good rep with out-of-towners as well as locals. As the park is open daily and lighted for nighttime use, you or your kids will have ample opportunity to check out the miniramp with bowl and spine and the smaller 3-foot ramp, a street course with rails, and other features. For in-line hockey, there are two arenas, and soccer facilities on-site as well. Cost is $4.00 on weekdays and $5.00 on weekends for those with a $19.00 yearly pass, $10.00 for others. It's best to check the Web site for the rather complicated daily sessions schedule.

Krause Family Skate Park
3401 Clairemont Boulevard, Clairemont
(619) 279-9254

One of San Diego's best parks, this 53,000-foot, wood-and-concrete skate giant has a vertical ramp like those used in the X-Games. The pool has depths of 4, 8, and 10 feet, and there's a street course and an area for little dawgs and novice skaters. Open weekdays 2:00 to 5:00 P.M., with two sessions (11:00 A.M. to 2:00 P.M. and 2:00 to 5:00 P.M.) on weekends. In the summer there's an additional session from 5:00 to 8:00 P.M. Members pay $22.00 per year and $4.00 per session; nonmembers pay $10.00 a session.

At Mission Bay Park, miles and miles of paved (and wide) walkways are shared equally by walkers, joggers, skateboarders, and skaters. Choose from the beach or bayfront boardwalk or the pathway that meanders from the beach all the way around the various bays and inlets that make up the park. There are no restrictions here, except for an 8-mph speed limit on the boardwalk.

Magdalena Ecke YMCA Skatepark
200 Saxony Road, Encinitas
(760) 942-9622, ext. 1603
www.ecke.ymca.org

This is probably San Diego's best skate park, with 37,000 square feet of fun. The outdoor park has a street course with a great variety of ledges, pipes, rails, and ramps of all sizes and shapes, as well as a combo bowl that really rocks. Since our idea of radical skating is gliding carefully around Mission Bay Park, we'll just tell you that this skate park is a favorite with veteran skaters and kids alike. Minimum age is 6; the little ones can begin to work on their "radical" at the tot lot. Summer hours are two sessions, Monday through Friday from 3:15 to 8:00 P.M.; on the weekends there are four sessions between the hours of 9:00 A.M. and 7:30 P.M. Cost is $4.00 for members ($6.00 on weekends) and $10.00 for nonmembers. Kids love the summer skate camp for in-line skaters and skateboarders ages 6 to 12. There's a dirt-bike park here as well as all the features of a well-equipped YMCA.

Robb Field Skate Park
2525 Bacon Street at West Point Loma Drive, San Diego
(619) 525-8486

Forty thousand square feet of outdoor skateboarding and in-line bliss can be purchased for $5.00 per day at the eastern end of Robb Field in Ocean Beach; yearly passes cost just $30.00. Kids younger

Studying martial arts helps develop not only the physical body but also confidence, peace of mind, strength, and flexibility. San Diego County has dozens of centers teaching everything from meditation and tai chi to jiujitso, karate, and judo. To help find the right sport and dojo *(training studio) for you, purchase* Black Belt *magazine (www.blackbeltmag.com) or visit www.usadojo.com.*

than age 18 need a permission form signed by a parent to use the facilities. Hours are Monday through Friday 10:00 A.M. to dusk, weekends 9:00 A.M. to dusk.

TENNIS

Looking for a game of tennis? You're in luck. Many hotels have their own courts, but if yours doesn't, you'll find quite a few public courts throughout the county. Here we list the most centrally located within our five regions.

Balboa Tennis Club
2221 Morley Field Drive, San Diego
(619) 295-9278
www.balboatennis.com
This tennis center at Morley Field (part of Balboa Park) has 25 courts (19 are lighted) and is open from 8:00 A.M. to 8:00 P.M. weekdays and from 8:00 A.M. to 6:00 P.M. on weekends. An all-day individual permit is $5.00. Courts are assigned on a first-come, first-served basis, except for members, who pay no court fees and can schedule their games ahead. The best time to get a court is between 11:00 A.M. and 5:00 P.M.

Coronado Tennis Association
1501 Glorietta Boulevard, Coronado
(619) 435-1616
Eight courts, three of them lighted, are available on a first-come, first-served basis. Play is free, and courts are open from dawn until dusk; the lighted courts until 10:00 P.M.

George E. Barnes Tennis Center
4490 West Pt. Loma Boulevard, San Diego
(619) 221-9000
www.tennissandiego.com
Twenty hard courts and four clay courts are available for public play daily. Adult walk-on prices are $5.00 for the day for hard courts and $7.50 for clay during the day (add $4.00 after dark for lighted courts). Courts are open Monday through Friday 8:00 A.M. to 9:00 P.M., Saturday and Sunday 8:00 A.M. to 7:30 P.M.

La Jolla Tennis Club
7632 Draper Avenue, La Jolla
(858) 454-4434
www.ljtc.org
The courts never close here, so if you can see, you can play. The lights, however, do go off at 9:00 P.M. No reservations are accepted for the nine courts; play is strictly on a first-come, first-served basis. Previously free, the facility now offers memberships: $85 a year permits unlimited daily access to the courts. Nonmembers pay $3.00 if accompanied by a member or $5.00 on their own. Two full-time pros give lessons and clinics for adults and juniors and organize round-robins and outings to the U.S. Open and other tournaments.

Lake Murray Tennis Club
7003 Murray Park Drive, San Diego
(619) 469-3232
www.lakemurraytennis.com
A fee of $5.00 allows singles an hour and doubles one and a half hours of play on any of 10 courts; members pay a $155 annual fee but play for free. Members can reserve four days in advance. Hours are 8:00 A.M. to 9:00 P.M. Monday through Thursday, 8:00 A.M. to 8:00 P.M. Friday, and 7:00 A.M. to 8:00 P.M. on weekends. There's an on-site pro shop, and the club sponsors round-robins, tournaments, and social events throughout the year.

Southwestern College Tennis Center
900 Otay Lakes Road, Chula Vista
(619) 421-6622

This is a small tennis center with 14 courts located on the campus of Southwestern College. Though courts are sometimes in use for classes or clinics, there's no charge for play. Check at the pro shop for current open-play hours. The courts are staffed by tennis pros, and group and private lessons are available for beginning, intermediate, and advanced players, be they juniors or adults. Clients as young as age 4 can begin honing their skills. Clinics, skill development sessions, and match play are available. Courts are open from 9:00 A.M. to 6:00 or 7:00 P.M., and play is on a first-come, first-served basis. Sundays excepted, make sure to purchase a $2.00 day-parking permit and park in the student lot to avoid a fine.

VOLLEYBALL

Volleyball in San Diego is a big deal, especially beach volleyball. Most games consist of groups of friends who set up a net and start playing when the mood strikes them. As popular as the game has always been in Southern California, it gained even more recognition since Misty May and Kerri Walsh kicked some seriously sandy butt at the 2004 Olympics in Athens, winning the gold.

The premier spot in San Diego for sand play is South Mission Beach—the epitome of a laid-back beach scene—about a mile south of Belmont Park, where there are 17 permanent sand courts. In Ocean Beach players bring their own nets to affix to permanent poles.

Several organizations sponsor tournaments and other events throughout the year: the California Beach Volleyball Association (800-350-2282, www.cbva.org) and West Coast Beach Volleyball (619-572-4316, www.wcbv.com).

One way to meet others who share an interest in the sport is to sign up for lessons.

Beach Volleyball Classes
(888) 742-4763
Instructor and certified personal trainer Rich Roe teaches V-ball classes during the summer months in Ocean Beach; you can register as early as April, which is a good idea as classes usually fill up. There are two nine-week sessions each summer, simultaneously, for beginners/intermediate and advanced players. The cost is $129 per person.

Beach volleyball is big in sunny San Diego County. PHOTO: COURTESY OF BRETT SHOAF

Starlings
(619) 742-9418
www.starlings.org/sandiego
The San Diego chapter of this national not-for-profit association offers kids and teens the opportunity to grow as people and as athletes as they learn skills and

Look for* Walking San Diego *by Lonnie Hewitt and Barbara Moore. If you're a dedicated walker, this is a great book that tells you where to go to get away from it all and what to do when you get there.

participate in tournaments and social events. There are more than a dozen clubs throughout the county from Ramona to National City.

WALKING/HIKING

Sometimes there's a fine line between walking and hiking, but for those who truly love to stroll around city streets or even take an easy nature walk, hundreds of spots exist for both.

The beauty of walking is that, other than a good pair of shoes, no special equipment is needed, no reservations are required, and you can do it just about anywhere. If you like to confine your walks to paved sidewalks, no prettier places can be found than the walkway around Mission Bay or the coastal streets and walkways in La Jolla. But any neighborhood in the county will provide the requisite fresh air and exercise.

Some prefer walking as a solitary pursuit; others like to walk with a friend or a group. If an organized walk sounds like it might be of interest to you, check out one of the many walking organizations listed below. You'll have your pick of organized nature walks, neighborhood walks, backcountry walks, or any other kind of walk you can possibly imagine. And you'll have the added pleasure of making new friends.

Gaslamp Quarter Walking Tours
410 Island Avenue, San Diego
(619) 233-4692
www.gaslampquarter.org
Combine exercise with a little bit of history as you take a two-hour guided walking tour through San Diego's historic Gaslamp Quarter. Prices are $10.00 for adults and $8.00 for seniors and students. Tours depart at 11:00 A.M. every Saturday. It's best to arrive a bit early to pay your fee.

Sierra Club
3820 Ray Street, San Diego
(619) 299-1744
The Sierra Club offers a number of hikes in different locations throughout the county. Call for a free copy of the *Hi Sierran* newsletter, which lists a variety of walks and hikes for singles, dog owners, and others, or look under "Walking" or "Hiking" in the "Night and Day" section of the *San Diego Union-Tribune* (Thursday edition) or the weekly *San Diego Reader.*

Walkabout International
4639 30th Street, Suite C, San Diego
(619) 231-7463
www.walkabout-int.org
Walks are scheduled almost every day of the year by this well-known group. Walks are organized by pace: Walk with those who like to amble or those practically run. Many outings end with socializing over coffee or a meal. Call for the current schedule of events.

BEACHES AND WATER SPORTS

What's the first thing everyone, including locals, thinks of when they think San Diego? Beaches, of course. Long stretches of tan sand, sparkling blue ocean, sunny days basking in the warm California sunshine with your toes buried in the sand—all these images float through the minds of those hankering for sun and surf. Guess what? It's no myth. Those magical beaches do exist. Even better, there's never a fee to use any of San Diego's beaches, just an occasional parking charge.

For those of you who want to interact with the blue Pacific but prefer a little more activity than just dreaming away the day with maybe a splash in the water to break things up, we also have a whole bunch of water sports you can enjoy. We'll show you where to rent Jet Skis, surfboards, scuba equipment, and more. If fishing is what sends you to nirvana, we'll point you to the best piers and sportfishing expeditions. We'll give you the scoop on licensing requirements and where to get your equipment. We'll even tell you what fish you can expect to reel in.

Picture yourself sailing across the smooth waters of Mission Bay in a kayak or a sailboat. You can even rent powerboats and take the whole family water-skiing. Or try something new and rent a sailboard. With just a short lesson, you can be sailing across the water with nothing but a sail and a surfboard to move you along. And don't think you need to bring a lot of stuff with you. Virtually everything you need, from basic equipment like a boat to wet suits and life jackets, is either easily rented or comes as part of a package.

Now we have a few words of caution for you. The Pacific Ocean can be deceptive. It looks calm and beautiful, but it can pack a wallop. Even the most serene lake or swimming pool has its dangers, so we urge you to bring your common sense along and take the advice of a couple of longtime beach rats: If you plan to go in the water, know how to swim. If you're not a swimmer, don't you dare go in the pool or ocean past your ankles. Rip currents in the ocean are hard to spot and can get ahold of you before you know what's happened. A rip current is sort of like a narrow but very powerful river that's heading back out to sea. They tend to form in the deepest points along the ocean floor, pulling everything with them as they flow seaward. Even the strongest swimmers have a healthy respect for rip currents.

If you're in a boat, always wear a life jacket and make sure all children wear them, too. Should a mishap occur, you won't have time to put one on, so you're well advised to just keep it on at all times.

If you heed some simple guidelines about rip currents and other potential dangers, though, you should have no problem. First and foremost, whether you're swimming in the ocean or a pool, be sure it's protected by a lifeguard, and pay attention to all warning signs, especially those regarding rip currents. Lifeguards can spot them and will post red flags where they have formed. That's a clear signal to avoid swimming in that area. Should you get caught in a rip, swim parallel to the shore in either direction until the pull of the current subsides. Then you can swim in to shore.

Lifeguards advise you to swim in the ocean with fins. They use them; you should, too. Also, never swim when you've been drinking. Alcohol impairs your judgment and your physical capabilities. Avoid using things like Boogie Boards or rafts as

San Onofre State Beach is bordered by both a nuclear power plant and the Camp Pendleton Marine Corps Reserve, which help create a 20-mile-long greenbelt between San Diego and Orange Counties.

swimming aids if you're a weak swimmer. You shouldn't venture any farther with a raft than your swimming ability would normally take you. Finally, if you get into trouble, simply wave your arms. Lifeguards recognize this as a distress signal, whether you're in the water or on the shore. You'll get immediate attention. We've indicated which beaches are staffed by lifeguards. Their schedules change with the seasons, however, so check to see if the lifeguard towers are manned before entering the water. Don't go in the water alone if there's no lifeguard around.

In addition to heeding safety tips, you'll need to follow the few rules and regulations that exist to make going to the beach a pleasure for everyone. The permissibility of alcoholic beverages varies from beach to beach. Some don't permit alcohol at all, but most will allow it between certain hours. Signs are posted at all beaches advising you of current regulations. Bottles are never permitted on beaches, so bring your beverages in cans or in plastic. Fires can be built in provided fire rings only, and many beaches have them. Never bury coals in the sand—they don't go out for hours, and some unsuspecting beachcomber may stumble upon them and end up with a bad burn.

You might expect that San Diego overflows with marinas since we spend so much time in and on the water. Although there are quite a few, they're mostly private. You can rent a temporary slip at a hotel marina if you're a guest, but arrangements should always be made in advance. Vacant slips are hard to find, so we don't advise that you sail into town and expect to find a marina to accommodate you.

Now that we've given you the heads-up on how to stay out of trouble, let us urge you to throw caution to the wind and explore all the possibilities that coastal life has to offer. And remember, you don't have to have any special knowledge or skill to take advantage of most water sports. Experienced captains are always on hand to pilot a boat for you, or to take you on a tandem Windsurfer, or teach you to water-ski. But if that sounds like just too much activity, then do as we do. Grab a beach towel, some no-brainer summer reading, lots of sunscreen, and hit the sand. You'll feel remarkably mellow at the end of the day.

We've listed the beaches in geographical order, from north to south, and have tried to point out the characteristics and quirks that distinguish each. We've included a few that don't have lifeguard service or facilities such as restrooms, but do have something special that tends to attract locals. Just be advised that these aren't places to take the kids. Water sports are listed by activity, with a description of the sport along with where to go to get the necessary equipment.

So put the sightseeing aside for a day and head to the water.

Most locals claim to have seen it, but only a lucky few really have. We're talking about the green flash, a brilliant green light that appears for a split second right at sunset. Watch for it in the western sky over the ocean at the precise moment the sun dips below the horizon.

BEACHES

San Onofre State Beach
Interstate 5 and Basilone Road
San Onofre

This is one of the most popular surfing beaches along the coastline in San Diego County. Surfers call it "Trestles," and it's known around the world for awesome surfing. Many people say it's the best surfing spot in the entire state.

Once you exit the freeway (at the Basilone Road exit), follow the blue signs for beach access and parking. There's a $5.00 entrance fee to park your car. The north end of the beach has a wide sandy shoreline that's good for walking, swimming, and sunset watching. The south end is more narrow and covered with large beach stones—here's where the surfers hang out. The beach is walkable for about 4 miles in either direction. The beach has lots of restrooms, cold showers, running water, some picnic tables, and fire rings. Shade is limited. There are public phones near all the restrooms. Lifeguards are on duty from Memorial Day through Labor Day. For lifeguard updates call (760) 725-7979. During the rest of the year, call 911 for emergencies.

Oceanside Beaches
Oceanside

Oceanside beaches all have wide sandy shores, which are great for lounging, picnicking, sunbathing, and, yes, even swimming. Families congregate at Oceanside Beach, also called The Strand. The surf is gentle close to shore, and youngsters can safely practice riding the waves on Boogie Boards. Restrooms, parks, and an excellent playground line the boardwalk edging the sand. Surfing is especially good between Tyson Street Park and the Oceanside Pier, just south of Mission Avenue.

Pacific Street runs all along the ocean from Oceanside Harbor to the Buena Vista Estuary. There is free and metered parking, with handicapped spaces provided. Parking is at a premium, however, so be prepared for a walk to the water during the summer months and especially on the Fourth of July when beaches are busy.

Buccaneer Beach, 1506 South Pacific Street, is popular with families because of its wide sandy shore. Various organizations bring summer day campers here for surfing lessons. The beach is patrolled 24 hours a day by police, and there are lifeguards at Buccaneer, too. The beach has picnic tables, barbecues, some shade, and a public telephone.

Just south of Buccaneer Beach is a popular surfing place with a width that varies with the seasons and the tides. Parking is scarce, and illegal parking will nearly guarantee you a ticket. There's no lifeguard on duty here.

Gated communities at the south end of Pacific Street have private security guards who may try to keep you off the property, but all beach below the high-tide line is public, so you can still walk through without fear of trespassing. Alcohol is not permitted on any Oceanside beaches.

Carlsbad Beaches
Carlsbad

The beaches begin south of Buena Vista Lagoon. Carlsbad City Beach, the first of the string we present here, has some sand at high tide; at low tide it's a wide and popular spot for surfers rather than walkers and swimmers. There are no facilities at the north end of this beach, which is open from 6:00 A.M. to 11:00 P.M. daily.

To access the beaches where there are facilities and lifeguards, you can walk the beach steps down from streets running straight to the sea. After Carlsbad Village Drive stops at the ocean, turn left to Ocean Street and then merge into Carlsbad Boulevard. Here you'll find street parking (although it's at a premium) and flights of stairs to reach the sand. Beach access signs, indicating how to get to the water, are everywhere. The Carlsbad beaches, by the way, are only about 3 blocks west of the Coaster station. So if you'd like to visit this community's water and sand and would rather not drive north, check the Coaster's schedule.

Whatever you decide, be sure you're wearing comfortable shoes, either to walk from the station or from that parking place wherever you may find it (at least most parking is free).

There are cold-water, open public showers at Christiansen Way and Tamarack Avenue and restrooms, telephones, and lifeguard stations all along the shore.

Be sure to use established trails and stairways to reach the beaches. Other entryways may seem obvious and easy, but they might be blocked by high tide when you try to leave.

You'll see fire rings along the beaches as well. Where Tamarack Avenue ends at the Pacific Ocean there is a public parking lot. You can't, however, expect to find a spot on beautiful sunny days.

Directly above the beach is the well-maintained Carlsbad Seawall, a 4-foot-high barrier between the cliffs and the sea. It was built to help maintain the integrity of the cliffs, since erosion and generations of ground squirrels, who also love beach life, have weakened the earth. You can stroll on the walk that follows the seawall.

Or, at street level, there's the popular beach-view sidewalk for strolling, skating, jogging, or briskly walking from Carlsbad Village Drive all the way to Cannon Drive—a good 5-mile trek. Lots of folks who work in Carlsbad take brown-bag lunches, or buy fast food, and eat at the tables along the beach. And lots of folks walk here in the evenings—including many with leashed canine companions. Dogs are allowed on some beachside walkways but not on the sand. At the street level there are picnic tables and benches, and there's some shade, too.

South Carlsbad State Beach
Poinsettia Drive and Carlsbad Boulevard
Carlsbad
To reach this state beach, exit Interstate 5 at Poinsettia and drive west. There are no day-use facilities here. It's a popular beach campground, and those who want to camp here make reservations months in advance. Even in winter it's nearly always full. From the campground, there are trails to the narrow pebbled beach. There are lifeguard towers. Surfing is best at the south end in an area locals call "Ponto." At the campground there are restrooms, tables, fire rings, shade, and a food store.

Beacon's Beach
Encinitas
Exit I-5 at Leucadia Boulevard and head west, then follow the BEACH ACCESS signs toward Diana Street. Beacon's Beach has a small parking lot that's open from 6:00 A.M. until 10:00 P.M. There is a public telephone and a steep path down to the beach. There are no lifeguards. This is a surfers' beach, and parking is often a problem since it's so limited. Insiders park legally where they can find a place and walk a number of blocks to the beach.

Moonlight State Beach
Encinitas
Exit I-5 at Encinitas Boulevard and drive west. There is parking on B Street and Third Street. This is one of the nicest beaches in North County: a place where kids can run and parents can play. There are restrooms, public phones, a snack bar, showers, fire rings, volleyball courts, and picnic tables. Moonlight State Beach is a popular swimming beach with lots of wide sandy areas that make walking fun. This beach is about a 5-block walk from the commuter train station.

Swami's
Encinitas
Just below Sea Cliff County Park, where First Street and Coast Highway 101 merge, is Swami's. There are restrooms, tables, barbecues, and public telephones at Sea Cliff park on the bluff, a romantic sunset-watching spot and an excellent place to whale watch during the winter months. To get to the surfing beach—no sand, just pebbles—there are stairs. Swami's is known worldwide as an excellent surfing beach and is best left to the pros. It's a dangerous place for casual swimmers or amateur surfers, since the seasoned surfers are more interested in riding their waves than looking out for swimmers.

San Elijo State Beach
Cardiff
Just south of Swami's is San Elijo State Beach. There's a campground here and

facilities from showers to snack foods; there's a $3.00 charge if you want to park in the campground. There is limited street parking along Highway 101. You'll find the stairs to the beach at the campground, too. It's another San Diego pebble beach, so you'll need to wear sneakers unless your feet are tough. San Elijo State Beach is locally known as "Cardiff Pipes." There are lifeguard stations.

Tide Beach
Solana Beach

You can reach this sandy beach by exiting I-5 at Lomas Santa Fe Drive. Drive west past First Street (which in places may be marked Highway 101) to Acacia Avenue. Turn right to Solana Vista Drive, and you'll see the sign for Tide Beach. Parking is limited. There is a lifeguard tower manned during the summer months and a wide shoreline that's good for walkers. The large reef just offshore is perfect for snorkelers (if the surf is calm). It's also a great spot to look for sea creatures in the tide pools when the tide is low.

Fletcher Cove
Solana Beach

Just south of Tide Beach, you'll notice this one has sand. Fletcher Cove, also locally known as Pillbox Beach, is popular with fitness walkers and families. There are restrooms, showers, telephones, and fire rings. Lifeguards are on duty between 8:00 A.M. and 8:00 P.M. in summer and 8:00 A.M. to 6:00 P.M. in winter.

North Beach
Del Mar

Dogs are permitted to run free on this Del Mar beach between September 15 and June 15. During the summer months Fido can accompany you, but only tethered to a leash. The beach is located north of 29th Street. Exit I-5 at Via de La Valle and turn right onto Highway 101. There's roadside parking; access is somewhat difficult since you'll be crossing dirt paths and must hike up and down some cliffs. Look for the BEACH ACCESS signs. North Beach is found between Via de La Valle and the San Dieguito River. The area is also called "Rivermouth."

Be forewarned that not all dog owners bring friendly, kid-loving pets to the beach. If you're planning a family outing, talk to the kids about dog safety before you hit the sand. Make sure your canine companion is current with all vaccinations, isn't aggressive, and doesn't infringe on others. Then you can hope that others do the same.

Thanks to rude smokers who use the beach as a big ashtray, some cities, including San Diego, have banned smoking on public beaches. Look for no-smoking signs. If you do smoke at the beach, please put your butts in a trash can.

Del Mar Beaches
Del Mar

The beaches in Del Mar are wide and are wonderful for family times, beach walking, and swimming. The Del Mar beaches are typical of postcard photos friends and family have sent you when they've visited San Diego. The central lifeguard tower is staffed between 9:00 A.M. and 8:00 P.M.; additional towers add staff as beach use demands. Rip currents are common in this area, so pay attention to warning signs. There are no fire rings or tables here, but portable barbecues are permitted. Parking is always at a premium.

Above Del Mar Beach is Seagrove Park, with a small playground, picnic tables, benches, grassy picnic areas, and places to spread a blanket, but no other facilities. This is a popular brown-bag lunchtime area for those who work in Del Mar. There's metered parking, and controls are enforced. Adjacent to Seagrove Park is the historic Powerhouse Community Center, which was a power plant in the early 1900s, a nightclub in the 1950s, and an experimental desalination plant.

Good news in Del Mar—there's disability access to the sand. There are two spe-

One of our favorite beach activities is absolutely free. It's called tidepooling, and it involves clambering about on wet rocks looking for sea creatures in pools of water left by the receding tide. You can find starfish, sea anemones, hermit crabs, and other critters in tide pools at Ocean Beach, Tourmaline, La Jolla Cove, Moonlight, and any beach with a rocky shoreline.

cial beaches where wheelchairs are kept at the main lifeguard station (lifeguards on duty year-round), and many beach entrances are wheelchair accessible.

Torrey Pines State Beach
Del Mar
Exit I-5 at Carmel Valley Road and turn left at Torrey Pines State Beach. There is some roadside parking, but you'll have to climb over some rocks to reach the sand. There is a parking lot with a $4.00 entry fee where you'll have access to restrooms and public telephones. There's beach access from the parking lot and no fee for visitors on foot.

Torrey Pines State Beach includes a 1,750-acre park with picnic tables, walking trails, sandy and pebbled beaches, and restrooms. Lifeguard towers are located on the main part of the beach but not in the area below steep cliffs. Picnics are permitted on the beach but not in the wildlife preserve area.

Unique along the coastline is the Torrey Pines State Beach underwater park. It is protected and maintained for marine research and enjoyment by scuba divers and snorkelers.

Black's Beach
Torrey Pines
Black's Beach is famous (or infamous) as San Diego County's nude beach. Actually, the nudity is not legal, but officials look the other way. The access to the nude area involves a climb down a steep path from the Torrey Pines Gliderport at 2800 Torrey Pines Scenic Drive. The path can be slippery and dangerous; lifeguards perform a few cliff rescues here each year. You can also reach the clothing-optional area by walking south along the sand from Torrey Pines State Beach. There are no facilities or lifeguards.

La Jolla Shores Beach
La Jolla
La Jolla Shores is a favorite hangout for teenagers and families. It's a wide sandy beach nearly a mile long, with a gently sloping ocean floor. Waves are usually fairly gentle—just the right size for those who want a taste of wave action without being bowled over every time a set rolls in. Separate water areas are reserved for swimming and surfing. restrooms and showers are located 100 yards north and south of the main lifeguard tower, which is staffed daily. Kellogg Park, a nice grassy area for those who don't like sand in their peanut butter and jelly, is located behind the tower. Just south of the tower at Avenida de la Playa is the only beachfront boat launch in San Diego.

To get to La Jolla Shores, take La Jolla Village Drive west from I-5 south or La Jolla Parkway from I-5 north. Follow the signs to Torrey Pines Road and head south. Turn right onto La Jolla Shores Boulevard and left onto Camino del Oro to the beach. A free parking lot runs the length of La Jolla Shores, but it fills up quickly during summer months. Then you're on your own. You can park on adjacent streets, but you will probably end up with a big hike ahead of you. It's a good idea to drop your companions and all your gear at the beach if the lot is full, then only one of you has to make the trek from car to beach. Alcohol is not allowed on this beach.

La Jolla Cove
La Jolla
To reach La Jolla Cove, follow the directions for La Jolla Shores but continue on Torrey Pines Road to Prospect Street. Turn right

and follow the road to Coast Boulevard. The cove is in the 1100 block. Swimming, snorkeling, and scuba diving are permitted at the cove; surfing is not allowed. It's a north-facing cove and has unusually coarse sand, but water visibility can be excellent, sometimes as much as 30 feet, which is why so many divers and snorkelers frequent the waters here. Grassy Ellen Browning Scripps Park is immediately adjacent to the cove and is a fine place for a picnic. Lifeguards are on duty year-round, and a public restroom with showers is located in Scripps Park. This is a great place to bring the family, especially the little ones who might be overwhelmed by big waves. Come early, though: Parking is limited to what's available on the street.

La Jolla Children's Pool
La Jolla
The beach at the Children's Pool has been taken over by harbor seals, who lounge on the rocks and sand and swim about in the calm waters. The seals give birth on the sand and raise their babies. Debates over whether humans or seals should lay claim to this extremely popular beach have raged for several years. For now the seals are winning, and volunteers patrol the beach and encourage humans to watch the seals from afar.

Marine Street Beach
La Jolla
This is a locals' hangout for those who like to toss Frisbees, sunbathe, and surf. From La Jolla Boulevard, the main street that runs north/south through La Jolla, turn west onto Marine Street and drive to the foot of the road. Parking is limited to what's available on adjacent streets. The drawback to Marine Street Beach is that there are no facilities and no lifeguard service. Perhaps it's the isolation that draws people here, but surfers know there's something else, too: a wicked shore break that challenges even the most experienced body surfers. If rough and tumble in the waves sounds like a day in heaven, this may well be the ideal spot for you. Otherwise, you might prefer to stick to one of the more conventional beaches.

Colorful fish, including the bright-orange garibaldi, are protected in the La Jolla Underwater Park and Ecological Preserve off La Jolla Shores and La Jolla Cove. The sea life is abundant, making this a great spot for snorkelers and divers.

Windansea Beach
La Jolla
Windansea is both a swimming and surfing beach distinguished by its sandstone rocks that take the place of sand. It offers a secluded and scenic atmosphere for sunbathing; swimming and surfing are a bit more of a challenge, and this is not a recommended place for diving. To reach Windansea, turn west off La Jolla Boulevard to Neptune Place, and park wherever you can find a spot on the street.

Like Marine Street Beach, Windansea has a shore break, a condition on steep beaches that produces hard-breaking surf right at the shoreline. Experienced swimmers and surfers know to take care while entering and exiting the water to avoid injury. Lifeguards are present only during the summer months.

Bird Rock
La Jolla
Take Bird Rock Avenue west off La Jolla Boulevard and drive to the end of the street to find this unusual beach. Bird Rock is not a beach for swimmers or sunbathers, but surfers, divers, and bird-watchers love it. Conditions for both surfing and diving are usually top-notch, but the big draw is the beach's namesake: Bird Rock. It's a huge boulder that sits right off the coast and plays host to scores of visiting seabirds. Bring your binoculars. No facilities or lifeguard staffing is available at Bird Rock. Parking is limited to what's available on the surrounding streets.

Dangerous sea critters aren't too much of a problem at San Diego's beaches. But watch out for the occasional floating jellyfish that can inflict a painful sting. Also, when you first enter the ocean, it's a good idea to shuffle your feet along the sandy floor to shoo away stingrays that lie in the sand.

Tourmaline Surfing Park
Pacific Beach

No swimming is allowed at this designated surfing park, but surfers flock to Tourmaline in droves. Turn west off La Jolla Boulevard onto Tourmaline Street and head for the large parking lot. Surfers love the year-round reef break, and there's enough room for novices to practice without being overrun by more seasoned surfers. There's a nice picnic area for those who'll be staying shoreside, and restrooms and showers are conveniently situated near the parking lot.

North Pacific Beach
San Diego

This mile-long beach stretches south from Tourmaline Surfing Park to Crystal Pier, which is located at the foot of Garnet Avenue, the main drag through Pacific Beach. To reach the beach, take the Grand Avenue/Garnet Avenue exit from I-5 and drive west to the beach. It's a beach that's protected by high cliffs, and it has separate areas for swimming and surfing. Lifeguards staff the beach year-round, but hours vary with the season. Scuba diving is not recommended here because of the heavy use by surfers and sailboarders. Restrooms and showers are located at the foot of Diamond Street and Law Street on the south end and at Tourmaline on the north end. You can park either in the Tourmaline lot or on nearby residential streets.

Overnight parking is prohibited at most beaches, and your car will be ticketed or towed away. Camping is allowed at a few state beaches, and reservations should be made many months in advance of your stay. For information on California state beaches, contact the state office at (916) 653-6995, (800) 777-0369, www.parks.ca.gov. To make reservations for camping, contact ReserveAmerica, (800) 444-7275, www.reserveamerica.com.

Pacific Beach/Mission Beach/
South Mission Beach
San Diego

A continuous 2 miles of sand bordered by a cement boardwalk stretches south from Crystal Pier, at the foot of Garnet Avenue, to the channel entrance to Mission Bay. It's the busiest and most popular beach in the county year-round. People watching is a preferred activity, and the boardwalk provides plenty of it. Joggers, walkers, in-line skaters, skateboarders, and bicyclists combine to form a never-ending parade of entertainment. The beach itself has separate water areas for swimming and surfing. Lifeguards staff the main lifeguard towers at the foot of Grand Avenue in Pacific Beach, West Mission Bay Drive in Mission Beach, and Avalon Court in South Mission Beach. During the summer months additional lifeguards staff seasonal towers that are sprinkled along the beach. Public restrooms and showers are located at all three beach areas.

Alcohol is permitted on the beach between noon and 8:00 P.M., but not on the boardwalk. There is much debate among local politicos and those who own homes near the beach about the wisdom of allowing alcohol here. Some feel it lends to the general rowdiness; others say it's their right to quaff a few cold ones while sunbathing on the sand. The issue has not been resolved. Be sure to read the signs posted along the beach, and don't carry alcohol in your cooler if it's not permitted—you can be ticketed. Scuba diving is not recommended here because the water is usually crowded with swimmers and surfers. To reach any of these beaches, walk along any of the streets west from Mission Boulevard, but don't bother trying to park there. You're best off heading for the lots along south Mission Boulevard, by Belmont Park.

Mission Bay Park Beaches
San Diego
More than 4,200 acres make up Mission Bay Park—half water and half land. The park has 27 miles of shoreline, 19 of which are sandy beaches. Both Interstates 8 and 5 border the park exits and signs are plentiful. You'll see just about everything here: powerboaters, sailboaters, rowers, waterskiers, picnickers, joggers, and even swimmers. The many coves and inlets provide scenic spots for a day at the beach, and the gentle bay is often preferred by families with small children. East Mission Bay Park's facilities include an information center, playgrounds, and plenty of space for picnics. Thrill seekers with Jet Skis and Wave Runners swarm to Fiesta Island (the only place dogs are allowed) and most of the eastern side of the park. Lifeguard staffing usually begins around springbreak time and continues through until summer. Restrooms and showers are liberally sprinkled throughout Mission Bay, and there are several large parking lots. Pay attention to water contamination signs.

Ocean Beach
San Diego
A wide sandy beach, O.B. is populated mostly by locals and visitors who are staying in the area. Drive west on I-8 until the freeway ends at Sunset Cliffs Boulevard. Follow Sunset Cliffs Boulevard to Newport Avenue. Turn right, and park in the large lot at the Ocean Beach Municipal Pier or in one of the auxiliary lots along Abbott Street. Surfing is especially popular just north of the pier, and there are separate water areas for swimming. The main lifeguard station is staffed year-round, and additional stations are set up during the summer.

Several beaches have a supply of large-wheel sand chairs for beach lovers with disabilities. They are available on a first-come, first-served basis at the main lifeguard towers at Imperial Beach, La Jolla Shores, Ocean Beach, South Mission Beach, Pacific Beach, Oceanside, and Torrey Pines State Beach.

At the north end of Ocean Beach, separated by a long rock jetty, is Dog Beach. Dog owners are allowed to let their pets run free on the beach. Their owners are a congenial group who strive to keep the beach clean. Keep in mind that even though disposal facilities are provided, some people do not pick up after their dogs. Dog Beach has become something of a local legend; the owners and their pets even march together in the Ocean Beach Christmas parade. If you're traveling with a dog, be sure to let it have its day at the beach here. Swimming here is not allowed.

Restrooms and showers are located at the foot of Santa Monica Boulevard and Brighton Avenue.

Sunset Cliffs Park
San Diego
Take I-8 west to Sunset Cliffs Boulevard and follow it until you see an impressive sight: crumbling cliffs with surf pounding at the base. This is one of the best spots in San Diego to watch a sunset; every local has a pile of Sunset Cliffs snapshots. A few pathways and staircases lead down to small beaches where experienced divers and surfers enter the sea. Novices are best off staying on top of the cliffs. The surf can

Pacific and Mission Beaches are packed with sun lovers on summer weekends, and parking is a nightmare. The police block entry to the beach areas except for local residents when parking lots are full. Arrive before 10:00 A.M. or go elsewhere.

Many of San Diego's beaches lose their sand during winter storms and become rocky and difficult to walk on. At some beaches, such as the popular Moonlight Beach in Encinitas, sand is trucked in every spring to replenish the beach. At others, such as Ocean Beach, the sand is piled into berms to prevent flooding during winter high tides, then smoothed out in spring.

be rough here, and swimmers can find it hard to get back to shore without crashing into rocks. Lifeguard rescues are common, and residents in the area are accustomed to hearing the blare of sirens as lifeguards and ambulances rush to the scene. It's important to note that the cliffs are soft and continuously eroding, so mind the warning signs and use only specified approaches to the beaches. A few parking lots are sprinkled along the cliffs; otherwise, street parking is usually easy to find. There are no lifeguards or other facilities.

Coronado City Beach
Coronado
Aside from being one of the prettiest beaches in San Diego, Coronado serves as a backdrop for the historic Hotel del Coronado. Marilyn Monroe frolicked on the sand during the filming of *Some Like It Hot,* and the beach often appears in promotional videos and advertisements. It's a great family beach with lots of room to spread out. Crowds are well-behaved, and the beach is always spotlessly clean. Fishing, swimming, and surfing are all given separate water areas, and nearby Sunset Park is a large grassy area for picnickers and Frisbee throwers. There is a wheelchair ramp leading down the sand almost to the waterline. Once you're on the island of Coronado, take Orange Avenue southwest to Isabella Avenue, which ends at Ocean Boulevard and the beach. Park wherever you can find a spot on residential streets. Plenty of lifeguards and restrooms are provided.

Silver Strand State Beach
Between Coronado and Imperial Beach
From Coronado, take California Highway 75 south to the signs that point the way to the beach. From Imperial Beach, take the Palm Avenue exit from I-5 and drive west until it veers north to Silver Strand Boulevard. The 2-mile-long beach has a wild, away-from-it-all feeling, despite the RV campsites lining the parking lot. Anglers wade into the surf as they cast their lines, hoping to reel in a few perch for dinner. In the spring, tiny grunions flop on the sand in the moonlight as they spawn. Also look for the tiny silver shells for which the beach was named. They cover the shoreline on the narrow spit of land between the ocean and San Diego Bay. There are facilities galore here: picnic areas, restrooms, lifeguard stations, and RV camping.

Imperial Beach
Imperial Beach is a vast sandy beach that's popular with swimmers, surfers, and Boogie-Boarders. It's also home to the annual sand-castle competition (see our Annual Events chapter for more details on this ultrafun event), which draws a ton of people every July. The Imperial Beach Pier, at the south end of the beach, is a favorite with folks who like to fish. Grassy picnic areas are available, as are restrooms and year-round lifeguard service. Drive west on Palm Avenue from I-5 until you reach the ocean. Parking is tight, as it is at most beaches, but you should be able to find something either in one of the lots or on nearby residential streets.

WATER SPORTS

Freshwater Fishing

Freshwater fishing is a popular hobby with lots of Insiders and visitors, and there are several lakes that have rental boats available. The popular fishing lakes are regularly stocked with rainbow trout, catfish, and other popular catches. All anglers older than age 16 must have a California state fishing license and a freshwater fishing permit.

At **Lake Miramar,** Scripps Lake Drive off Scripps Ranch Boulevard, Central San Diego (619-668-2050), you can fish for rainbow trout, bass, catfish, and channel catfish. The lake is closed for fishing during October and November.

Lake Murray at Mission Trails Regional Park, 1 Father Junipero Serra Trail, Central San Diego (619-668-3281), is open for fishing and boating Wednesday, Saturday, and Sunday. Shore fishing is allowed daily. It is closed during October and November, when it is stocked with trout.

Lake Poway Recreation Area, Lake Poway Road off Rancho Bernardo Road, Poway (858-679-5466), has a 60-acre reservoir for boating and fishing. Fishing hours vary with the season, but usually occur Wednesday through Sunday from sunrise to sunset. The lake is stocked with rainbow trout weekly from November through mid-May and with catfish in the summer months.

Lake Morena County Park, Lake Morena Road, off California Highway 94, or Buckman Springs Road, off I-8, near Campo (619-478-5473). Fishing is popular here, and bass, bluegill, catfish, crappie, and stocked trout crowd the lake. There's a rowboat launch, too.

Guajome County Park, Guajome Lakes Road, near Mission Avenue, Vista (760-724-4489), gives you the chance to fish and picnic or bird-watch all in the same developed park and wilderness area. The park is nearly 600 acres, with trails. The lake has shore fishing and is popular with kids from the area.

Lake Cuyamaca, California Highway 79 between California Highway 78 and I-8 in eastern San Diego County (877-581-9904) has year-round trout fishing, along with smallmouth bass, channel catfish, bluegill, and sturgeon. The 110-acre lake is an angler's delight, populated by fans of both fly fishing and boat fishing. Free fishing classes are offered every Saturday at 10:00 A.M.

Be sure to read our Parks chapter for information on all the lakes that have fishing, boating, and water-sporting possibilities. If you prefer to cast your line in the ocean, see this chapter's section on sportfishing.

Wherever you go, you are required to have a California state fishing license. A resident sportfishing license costs $34.90. A nonresident license costs $89.50. The license is good from January through December; it's not good for a year from the date you purchased it. You may also need special permits for catching certain fish. A two-day sportfishing license costs $16.80 and allows you to fish in fresh and salt water. For up-to-date information on licenses, call the California Department of Fish and Game at (619) 237-7311. Or log onto www.dfg.ca.gov. Most bait and tackle shops and sportfishing outfitters sell licenses. There is a $250 fine for fishing without a license. You may fish from piers without a license. If you are age 16 or younger, a license is not required.

Kayaking/Canoeing/ Wave Riding

One of the best ways to experience San Diego's waterways is in a kayak or canoe. Be sure to check posted signs before putting your vessel in the water; boating regulations vary. Boating is not allowed in certain wildlife preserve areas, including Buena Vista Lagoon and Batiquitos Lagoon in Carlsbad.

Aqua Adventures Kayak School
1548 Quivera Way, Central San Diego
(619) 523-9577, (800) 269-7792
www.aqua-adventures.com

This full-service center offers kayak rentals, sales, and tours. The fee for a full-day kayak rental is $50, and the shop has a frequent-renter program with reduced rates. Rentals include life jackets, and the shop has a selection of wet suits you can rent for an additional fee.

Kayakers find calm, clear water at Mission Bay. PHOTO: COURTESY OF BRETT SHOAF

You can also arrange for kayak instruction and take advantage of the ocean and river kayaking trips and tours, including trips to Baja.

California Water Sports
4215 Harrison Street, Carlsbad
(760) 434-3089
Located at Snug Harbor Marina in North County Coastal, this store provides everything you need for a water-sporting good time, including instruction on use and safety.

Many of San Diego's lakes are actually reservoirs for the city of San Diego's municipal water system and are run by the city's water department. For information on schedules and regulations, call (619) 668-2050 or check www.sandiego.gov/water. For lakes operated by the city of San Diego, call (619) 465-3474.

You can rent kayaks and canoes for $15 to $20 an hour. You can rent wave runners for $70 for a half hour or $125 for an hour, and the equipment can be shared with up to three people. When you rent motorized equipment, you'll also be shown a seven-minute safety and instructional video. They like having first-timers come to Snug Harbor Marina and make sure there are plenty of instructors on the beach for additional help. You can also take classes on these sports at the marina. Snug Harbor also has a pro shop, snack bar, and picnic tables.

Carlsbad Paddle Sports
2002 South Coast Highway, Oceanside
(760) 434-8686
This store is far more than a place to rent equipment. Kayakers think of it as their North County club, where knowledgeable staff members provide instruction, lead adventure trips, and know all the local paddling possibilities. If you need equipment, it's $80 for an eight-hour kayak rental.

The company offers all sorts of adventurous trips from Baja to Kauai. Closer to home, they teach newbies how to paddle into the ocean at the Oceanside Harbor and how to surf the waves in a sit-on-top kayak at Carlsbad State Beach. They'll also guide you to the best spots for kayak fishing and for spotting sea creatures.

Hike Bike Kayak San Diego
2246 Avenida de la Playa, La Jolla
(858) 551-9510, (866) 425-2925
www.hikebikekayak.com
Perfectly located at La Jolla Shores, this one-stop adventure shop offers imaginative kayaking tours that include a nighttime paddle in Mission Bay to watch the SeaWorld's fireworks and a Saturday-morning trip where paddlers bring their dogs along for the ride. Single kayaks rent for $28 an hour and $45 a day, and they'll deliver your kayak to your launching point.

REI (Recreational Equipment, Inc.)
5556 Copley Drive, San Diego
(858) 279-4400
www.rei.com
If you don't want to transport your kayak to San Diego or if you want to try the sport without buying one, REI is your ticket. It's $40 to $50 rent an ocean kayak for one day. Rates are higher for those who are not members of the REI association; membership costs $15. The store's savvy staff reminds you to reserve a kayak if you want it for a holiday weekend. The store also has a full line of outdoor accessories for sports from camping to biking and rents lots of other equipment.

Resort Watersports
Catamaran Hotel, 3999 Mission Boulevard
Pacific Beach
(858) 539-8696

Bahia Hotel, 998 West Mission Bay Drive
Mission Beach
(858) 539-7696
www.resortwatersport.com
For rentals of water-sporting equipment and lessons, Resort Watersports is a one-stop shopping and outfitting emporium. Single and double kayaks range from $17 to $20 for an hour's rental. There is a discount if you want to rent them for a day. The staff shows you how to use the equipment and then lets you get out on the bay or ocean. Call first to reserve equipment since this is a popular shop.

Windsport
844 West Mission Bay Drive, San Diego
(858) 488-4642, (888) 488-7656
www.windsport.net
This is a full-service kayaking and windsurfing shop where you can buy and rent kayaks and accessories. The price for a single sit-on kayak is $15 for an hour, $45 for four hours, and $75 for a full 24-hour day. You'll get some basic instructions from the craft-smart staff before they set you free to paddle the bay. If you'd like further instruction, a one-hour lesson is $40. You can combine learning and touring on their two-hour trips, led by an instructor, to Mission Bay, the La Jolla Sea Caves, and the open ocean.

Sailing and Powerboating

San Diego is a sailor's dream come true. You can sail on San Diego Bay, around Shelter and Harbor Islands, up and down the coastline and never lose sight of land. You can head for Catalina, the Channel Islands, or even Hawaii (as long as you know what you're doing).

You can also sail on some of our local lakes. Lake Hodges, at Lake Drive off Interstate 15 and Via Rancho Parkway, Escondido (760-735-8088), has a small boat launch and a boat-rental concessionaire. There's a shady picnic area, parking, and tiny grocery stores in the area should you forget to bring lunch. (See our Parks chapter for more places to boat and sail on our lakes.)

For an overview of San Diego's pools and aquatics programs, call the recorded information number at (619) 685-1322 or check out www.sandiego.gov/park-and-recreation/aquatics.

Many marinas have sailboats to rent, and depending on the size and length of time you'll be on it, they are priced accordingly. If you want to sail around San Diego Bay, you can get a 14-foot Capri for as little as $18 an hour. Visitors and locals rent the boats for a few hours to see the city from a different viewpoint and experience the joys of being on the water.

With the small two-person sailboats, you may be restricted to the bays and marinas and will be asked to show that you're competent with the boats before you leave the dock. There's usually a security deposit required when you rent a boat. For larger sailing craft, you may have to take a test cruise with an instructor (for a fee), and only then will you be able to set sail. Many of the sailboat rental companies have sailing clubs and lessons. Local parks and recreation offices in coastal communities like Oceanside will have sailing and other water-sport classes, too.

Harbor Sailboats
2040 Harbor Island Drive, San Diego
(619) 291-9568, (800) 854-6625
www.harborsailboats.com

You don't have to take lessons here to get into a sailboat. You will have to show you know what you're doing, though, when a staff member checks you out before untying the mooring ropes. Prices range from $70 to $100 for four hours on a 22-foot Capri to $730 for a full day aboard a 411 Beneteau. If you're headed to San Diego and have made up your mind to sail, just call and reserve a craft. Remember that over the holiday weeks and the summer months, boat availability may be limited. By renting boats here, you get yacht club discounts and instruction for all levels and can enjoy other club and cruising experiences. There's a pool, deli, and restaurant on-site at the Harbor Island Sailing Club.

San Diego's extensive sailing scene is covered in full on the Web site www.sandiegosailing.com. If you're thinking about sailing into San Diego, check out the section on local marinas.

Resort Watersports
Catamaran Hotel, 3999 Mission Boulevard
Pacific Beach
(858) 539-8696

Bahia Hotel, 998 West Mission Bay Drive
Mission Beach
(858) 539-7696
www.resortwatersport.com

As mentioned above, Resort Watersports is the place to rent everything from kayaks to wave runners. They also rent powerboats (a 16-foot powerboat will cost you $80 for an hour, $240 for four hours). They rent sailboats, too. The Capri sailboats, 14-, 18-, and 22-foot lengths, range from $25 to $40 for an hour, and there's a savings if you want to rent in four-hour periods. Call to reserve boats and for more information.

Scuba Diving

San Diego has some excellent locations for scuba diving, if you don't mind cold water and wet suits. In fact, some of the earliest divers perfected the sport in San Diego's waters. Divers from the Scripps Institute of Oceanography have photographed incredible underwater sights here, and there is a strong and enthusiastic scuba community. As is common everywhere, you must be a certified diver to get your tanks filled and to dive legally with local operators. If you're in town for a week or so, you can get certified in as little as four days and then be able to discover and explore the fascinating underwater world. However, even though the intrepid diver can find lots of interest in local waters, most novice scuba divers head elsewhere. The water here tends to be cold most of the year, and a consistent surge can keep things murky underwater. Sometimes visibility is limited to a foot or less.

Once you're a certified diver, the best spots for diving are the La Jolla Underwater Ecological Reserve and the kelp beds off Point Loma. You're likely to see California's state fish, the brilliantly colored orange garibaldi, as well as countless varieties of large fish. Keep in mind that if you're diving in any ecological reserve, you may not remove anything—even a shell. Look, but don't touch.

Boat diving is also popular here; you can choose from half- and full-day trips to the Coronado Islands in Mexico or trips around local waters. Safety is a big issue with scuba diving, so always remember what you've been taught: Dive with a buddy, and observe all the safety rules your instructor has pounded into your head.

The Diving Locker
6167 Balboa Avenue, San Diego
(858) 292-0547
www.divinglocker.com

Since 1958 the instructors at the Diving Locker have been teaching the skills of scuba to thousands of would-be divers. Lessons start at around $150 and include four pool sessions, four classroom sessions, and five ocean dives. Students are required to provide their own mask, snorkel, gloves, and booties. The Diving Locker also offers certified divers full equipment rentals for $38. The shop often offers reduced fees for classes, especially in the winter months.

Ocean Enterprises
7710 Balboa Avenue, San Diego
(858) 565-6054
www.oceanenterprises.com

This excellent dive shop offers all levels of PADI certification courses starting at about $150. They run several specials throughout the year at reduced rates. The shop is a diver's delight and displays all the latest gear in the brightest neon colors. They also offer rental gear, boat dives, and dive trips to prime spots around the world.

OE Express Dive & Kayak Center
2158 Avenida de la Playa, La Jolla
(858) 454-6195

617 Quivira Road, Suite B, Mission Bay
(619) 224-6195

1453 Rosecrans Street, Point Loma
(619) 758-9531

With outlets at San Diego's most popular diving, snorkeling, and kayaking spots, this company covers all the bases. Open-water PADI dive certification is available, and experienced divers can increase their skills with Master Scuba Diver and Scuba instructor classes. The shops also have kayak tours and rentals and rent snorkeling gear.

Snorkeling

If the time and expense involved in full scuba certification put you off, try snorkeling. With just a mask, snorkel, and fins, you can explore the underwater world for as long as you wish. There's much to be seen that's close to the surface and the shore of the beach, and equipment is easily rented or purchased. All sporting goods stores sell snorkeling equipment. If you're serious about the sport, it's nice to have your own mask that fits well. You can

It you decide to visit the beaches in Del Mar and Ocean Beach, where dogs are permitted, keep in mind that dogs are dogs. Some dogs are friendly, and some dogs are not. And there are irresponsible beachgoers who "forget" to clean up after Fido. You may have to watch where you step, sit down, or play in the sand. If you are not a dog lover, head to another of our area's fine beaches.

Dedicated anglers are hooked on finding out how many fish the charter boats catch each day. The following numbers have recorded information on the types and quantity of fish caught. It's best to call the numbers after 7:00 P.M. For recorded information call (619) 223-1626, (619) 224-2800, or (619) 224-6695.

even get a mask that matches your eyeglass prescription if need be.

The best place by far for snorkeling in the county is La Jolla Cove, where there are rarely any waves or strong currents. At most other beaches you'll need to check the waves before trying to breathe through a snorkel. There are good snorkeling spots at Tourmaline Beach, Sunset Cliffs, and Bird Rock.

O.E. Express
2158 Avenida de la Playa, La Jolla
(858) 454-6195
www.oeexpress.com

This is the closest place to La Jolla Cove where you can rent or purchase snorkeling equipment. Daily rental rates are $8.00 for a mask and snorkel and $8.00 for fins. O.E. Express also offers full scuba training and equipment and kayak rentals.

Play It Again Sports
1401 Garnet Avenue, San Diego
(858) 490-0222

9841 Mira Mesa Boulevard, San Diego
(858) 695-3030
www.playitagainsports.com

If you're in the market to purchase snorkeling equipment (or any sport equipment, for that matter), check out the selection in these showrooms. The stores carry both new and used equipment. You can find everything from a mask to a wet suit here, all at a big discount.

Sportfishing

Most sportfishing boats operate year-round in San Diego, regardless of the weather. The waters off San Diego are home to albacore, yellowfin, and bluefin tuna, marlin, shark, yellowtail, barracuda, bonito, calico bass, sand bass, halibut, and rock cod. There are specific seasons for the various types of fish. The best season is from May to October. If you have your heart set on catching a big tuna, ask if they're in the nearby waters before forking over the money for a trip. The sportfishing companies we've included offer half- or full-day excursions, along with overnight trips. Before deciding on an expedition, consider what's included in the price, such as gear and food. Other factors are important, too, like how the boats are equipped, the number of passengers they carry, the facilities on board, the size of the boats, and the experience of the crew. You must have a California fishing license even when going out with a charter boat. Most bait and tackle shops and sportfishing outfitters sell licenses. A two-day sportfishing license costs $16.80 and allows you to fish in fresh and salt water. There is a $250 fine for fishing without a license. See the Freshwater Fishing section for further information on fishing licenses.

Fisherman's Landing
2838 Garrison Street, Point Loma
(619) 221-8500
www.fishermanslanding.com

Charter boats are available with Fisherman's Landing for one-day, two-day, or long-range trips lasting several nights. The captains will head for whatever type of fish is in the waters and do their best to make sure even novices catch something. The cost of a one-day trip on a 65- to 95-foot boat, which leaves at night and returns the next evening, ranges from $110 to $200; gear rental is extra. Equipment is available for purchase.

H&M Sportfishing
2803 Emerson Street, Point Loma
(619) 222-1144
www.hmlanding.com
H&M offers half-day and longer trips. Their half-day trips stick close to shore and are a good option for those trying fishing for the first time. Tackle sales and equipment rental are available. Full-day trips depart at night and return the next night to provide optimum fishing time. Some boats have private staterooms; others have shared bunk rooms. Rates run between $75 and $125 for an overnight trip.

Point Loma Sportfishing
1403 Scott Street, Point Loma
(619) 233-1627
www.pointlomasportfishing.com
This outfit arranges fishing trips on several different charter boats. They offer short, inexpensive trips to long-range trips lasting 16 days or more. Half-day trips are great excursions for first-timers who aren't totally hooked on fishing yet. They cost only $37 and last about five hours. These trips are great family excursions. If you go in the winter months, you might even spot gray whales while you're fishing for everything from bass to tuna.

Seaforth Sportsfishing
1717 Quivira Road, Mission Bay
(619) 224-3383
www.seaforthlanding.com
Seaforth has half-day, full-day, and twilight trips and is conveniently located at Mission Bay Park. The company has tackle and bait for sale, and equipment can be rented. Specialty trips include shark and rock cod in season. For the partial-day trip, 6:30 A.M. until 4:00 P.M., the cost is $57 for adults and $47 for children age 15 and younger. For the one-and-a-half-day sportfishing trip, 10:00 P.M. until 6:00 P.M. the following day, the cost is $250 per person and includes sleeping accommodations.

Surfing

San Diego County has world-renowned surfing beaches, including Trestles, Windansea, and Swami's. These are the premier spots to ride big waves when the surf is high. If you're visiting and have to see the sport San Diego-style or are into the surfing scene, check out these beaches and the surfers by the pier at Ocean Beach or at Tourmaline Beach. See this chapter's Beaches section for information on these and other surfing spots. We also have some pretty cool surf shops. Following are a few favorites.

Emerald City Surf Shop
3126 Mission Boulevard, Suite G
San Diego
(858) 488-9224
1118 Orange Avenue, Coronado
(619) 435-6677
www.ecboardsource.com
Insiders swear that Emerald City Surf Shops have the best prices on brand-name surf gear, so some trek from outlying areas to come to the stores. Emerald City is also a store for buying wave boards and other surf and water-sport supplies.

Hansen's Surf & Ski
1105 South Coast Highway 101, Encinitas
(760) 753-6595
www.hansensurf.com
Hansen's is the place to go for all the fashion-conscious surf lines of clothing and

Check out the daily catch by visiting the Municipal Sportfishing Pier on Scott Street at the foot of Garrison Street in Point Loma. Multiday fishing boats bearing 200-pound tunas usually arrive around 9:00 A.M., while short-range boats return at midday and early evening.

Kids get expert instruction surfing with dad at Tourmaline Beach. PHOTO: COURTESY OF BRETT SHOAF

water-sport accessories. That said, many Insiders think of Hansen's as too touristy. They still come here, though, during sales and if they need something the other stores just don't have. The store carries body boards, water skis, wet suits, new and used surfboards, and in-line skates, too. The store is about 2 blocks north from Swami's (see our Beaches section in this chapter). If you want the surf report in Encinitas, you can call (760) 753-6221.

Longboard Grotto Surf Shop
978 North Coast Highway 101, Encinitas
(760) 634-5250
www.thelongboardgrotto.com
Want to browse and buy at a store that real surfers enjoy? Then Longboard Grotto is it. The store has been selling long boards and books, videos, and memorabilia on surfing and the sport since the 1980s.

Offshore Surf Shop
3179 Carlsbad Boulevard, Carlsbad
(760) 729-4934
www.offshoresurfshop.com
Offshore Surf Shop can outfit you in everything from a perfect-fit wet suit to reef sandals and shoes. Yes, they sell new and used surf boards and rent surf gear. If you're looking for something special, say an antique long board, put in your request here. The store has a full line of men's and women's beachwear, from shorts to logo T-shirts to bathing suits. They can also tell you about the surf along Carlsbad beaches.

South Coast Surf Shop
5023 Newport Avenue, San Diego
(619) 223-7017
www.southcoast.com
This is your place to find out about up-coming surfing contests and to buy surfing and water gear and other equipment. The store also has surf and sports clothing and sometimes has used equipment for sale.

Sun Diego Surf & Sport
Fashion Valley Mall, 7007 Friars Road
San Diego
(619) 299-3244

Westfield Shoppingtown North County, 272 East Via Rancho Parkway, Escondido
(760) 743-4133
www.sundiego.com

These surf shops in malls are a stretch for serious surfers. Many shun them as gauche, others as too commercial. But these same folks also admit that the stores have a place in the county. So if you find yourself far from the beach and at the mall and say you need some surf wax, a T-shirt, or want the latest copy of a surfing magazine, stop in. The stores have equipment that goes beyond surfing, including snowboarding and skateboarding merchandise. They have an extensive line of apparel for kids, men, and women, too.

Surf Ride Board Shop
1909 South Coast Highway, Oceanside
(760) 433-4020

If you're looking for surf gear, shoes, and accessories, Surf Ride always offers a big selection of top-quality merchandise, including designer labels.

Witt's Carlsbad Pipelines
2975 Carlsbad Boulevard, Carlsbad
(760) 729-4423

If you were to create a surf shop for a movie set or television show, you'd build it just like Witt's. It's a bit crowded, loaded with surf stuff, and all of the staff has that truly-San Diego surf look down pat, including the warm friendly smiles. If you're from a part of the country or world that doesn't have surf shops and you want to see the ultimate example, head to Witt's and take some snapshots of the store to show the folks back home.

Witt's is a welcoming, low-key place with a dedication to service. No surfing question is too basic. They want you to succeed at the sport, and while the more upscale stores might sell you unnecessary stuff, at Witt's you can depend on solid advice.

For information on surf contests, publications, and other surf news, check out www.sandog.com. The site includes profiles of San Diego's top surfers. Links to environmental organizations bring you up to speed on the many issues surrounding the cleanliness of San Diego's beaches and water.

Swimming

Swimming isn't limited to just beaches; you can get a pool fix at any number of public and municipal pools around the county. Or you might enjoy spending a day at one of the two water parks in the county, Knott's Soak City in Chula Vista or The Wave Waterpark in Vista (check our Attractions chapter for all the details). Many health and fitness clubs have pools that are open to the public for a small fee. And if you're staying at a hotel, you probably need venture no farther than a few steps outside your room.

Municipal pools offer swimming lessons for all ages, from toddlers up to adults, in groups or individually. Lessons start at around $28 per child for 10 group lessons and go up from there, depending on age and type of lesson. Recreational swimming hours vary from pool to pool, so be sure to call before you go. At San Diego pools admission is $5.00 for adults and $1.50 for children younger than age 16. Admission prices for pools in other cities around the county are indicated separately. The San Diego municipal pools listed here are the ones that are open year-round. For a complete listing of San Diego pools, call the Swim Hotline at (619) 685-1322.

The San Diego branch of the Surfrider Foundation monitors local ocean and beach conditions and holds a wide range of community events to help protect the coastal environment. For information check out www.surfridersd.org.

Water contamination is a serious problem at San Diego's beaches, unfortunately. Contamination is most common at Mission Bay, Ocean Beach, and Imperial Beach. Keep an eye out for signs warning swimmers to stay out of the water, and follow their advice. You may see some hard-core surfers ignoring the signs, but their bravado often results in ear infections and other illnesses.

SAN DIEGO MUNICIPAL POOLS

Allied Gardens
6707 Glenroy Street, San Diego
(619) 235-1143

Bud Kearns Memorial Municipal Pool
2229 Morley Field Drive, Balboa Park, San Diego
(619) 692-4920

Clairemont
3600 Clairemont Drive, San Diego
(858) 581-9923

Swanson
3585 Governor Drive, San Diego
(858) 552-1653

Tierrasanta
11238 Clairemont Mesa Boulevard, San Diego
(858) 636-4837

Vista Terrace
301 Athey Avenue, San Ysidro
(619) 424-0469

NORTH COUNTY COASTAL

Carlsbad Community Swim Complex
3401 Monroe Street, Carlsbad
(760) 434-2860
Designated hours for lap swimming and recreational swimming are offered here; call for the schedule, which tends to vary because of special events. Admission is $3.00 for adults who are Carlsbad residents, $4.00 for adult nonresidents, and $2.00 for children age 17 and younger.

NORTH COUNTY INLAND

Woodland Park Aquatic Complex
671 Woodland Parkway, San Marcos
(760) 744-9000
Operated by the city of San Marcos, this pool has a 50-foot waterslide as well as a water basketball hoop. Admission is $2.00. Call for public swimming hours. The pool is closed during the winter.

EAST COUNTY

Fletcher Hills Pool
2345 Center Place, El Cajon
(619) 441-1672
Public swimming hours are available every day but tend to vary and are scheduled around lessons. Admission is $2.00 for adults and $1.00 for children ages 3 to 17. Closed in winter.

SOUTH BAY

Parkway Pool
385 Park Way, Chula Vista
(619) 691-5088
You can get your laps in here or merely splash around if the spirit moves you. Admission is $3.00 for adults, $2.00 for seniors and children ages 6 to 17.

Waterskiing/Jet Skiing/Windsurfing

San Diego is a water-sport paradise. You can Jet Ski, water-ski, and windsurf in the ocean, the bays, or many of the local lakes. The cove on the south side of Fiesta Island in Mission Bay is designed for wave riders. Mission Bay is action-central for water-skiers, many of whom launch at Crown Point. Windsurfers head to Mission Bay's Sail Bay and the area by the Hilton Hotel and to the Silver Strand in Coronado. Lake Hodges, at Lake Drive off I-15 and Via Rancho Parkway, Escondido (760-735-8088), is one of the best places in the county for windsurfing and has a windsurf school and rental facility. Some other lakes may allow sailing but not Jet Skiing, so ask first. For information on rental equipment, see our listings under Kayaking/Canoeing/Wave Riding.

Seaforth Boat Rental
1641 Quivira Road, San Diego
(619) 223-1681
www.seaforthboatrental.com
A one-stop shop for watercraft rentals, Seaforth rents speedboats and waterskiing equipment, wave runners, and sailboats. The waterski package includes boat rental along with inner tubes, wakeboards, knee boards, or skis and runs just under $100 for a one-hour rental. Full-day and overnight rentals are also available.

GOLF

It's five-star golf," say avid players about the courses in San Diego. That's why golfers throughout the country drag along their clubs when they're headed to our fair city and why championship golf tournaments are held here. We're looking forward to hosting the prestigious U.S. Open at Torrey Pine Golf Course in 2008.

For duffers, there are plenty of courses where one can have fun, enjoy the sport, and keep some self-respect intact.

In this chapter we'll give you the goods on the good places to play. As you look over the listings, be aware that these aren't the only places in the county. The yellow pages of your phone book and Web sites such as www.sandiegogolfer.com, www.golfsocal.com, and www.golfsd.com will give you lots of info although they're not always up to date.

What you have here are the ones we like and recommend to friends and family. And we've included all the extraordinary ones, like Reidy Creek, the ultimate executive course located in Escondido. In each case we've tried to sketch out what makes them especially worthy of inclusion—what makes them winners.

If there's an extra cost for the cart or something special you need to know, like a dress code, we've added that. Most of the courses here have driving-ranges and putting greens. However, we haven't repeated those under the driving-range category. The driving range entries are strictly that, except for Surf & Turf in Del Mar, in North County Coastal, with its miniature golf area. Here you can play a really short game, and it's also fun for the kids.

Like restaurants and shopping districts, golf courses sometimes change with time. So it's smart to call to make sure you'll get what you expect and to verify the greens fees, too.

We've divided our chapter into public golf courses, executive courses, and driving ranges, with entries under each category following our usual geographic order. At all of the courses and ranges, you can rent clubs, and at most you have to look clean and casual. At the Four Seasons Resort Aviara, for instance, you'll want to spiff up a bit more, since this is an upscale course.

We've omitted those country club and resort courses where you need to be a member or guest to play. Keep in mind, however, that at courses connected to hotels, like Carlsbad's La Costa Resort and La Jolla's Lodge at Torrey Pines, you can get great golf-package deals.

If you're determined to golf when visiting San Diego, if you want to play at a popular time, or if you're traveling a distance, call ahead. Some courses, like Torrey Pines, which hosts the PGA tour, hold tournaments. We provide phone numbers so you can get the scoop and be sure you'll get a tee time.

GOLF COURSES

Central San Diego

Balboa Park Municipal Golf Course
2600 Golf Course Drive, San Diego
(619) 570-1234 (reservations)
(619) 239-1660 (pro shop)
Despite its 1999 renovation, the Balboa Park course isn't one of San Diego's finest. However, we include it here because of its primo location in the heart of San Diego and its status as one of the city's first courses—it was built in 1915. Greens fees for this municipal course are reasonable, too: $36 on weekdays and $41 on weekends. San Diegans pay a discounted fee if they carry a resident card, which can be purchased for $12 at the course. The city residents' greens fees are $23 during the week, $25 on weekends and holidays. Golf cart rental is $26. There are no restrictions on walking.

Coronado Municipal Golf Course
2000 Visalia Row, Coronado
(619) 435-3121, ext. 3 (reservations)
(619) 435-9485 (pro shop)
www.golfcoronado.com
This is one of the most underrated courses in the county, mainly because it can be tricky getting a tee time, so lots of golfers don't even try. Call two days in advance, beginning at 7:00 A.M., to reserve. A beautiful new clubhouse opened in 1997, and the 9th and 18th holes were rebuilt soon thereafter. But the course's greatest claim to fame is that on June 10, 1996, President Bill Clinton shot a 79 here, breaking 80 for the first time in his golfing career.

The par 72, 6,317-yard course is flat and open, and it stays in the shadow of the San Diego-Coronado Bay Bridge for most of the front nine. Still, you'll face two par 5s within the first four holes, so keep your driver polished. A couple of ponds guard the 8th and have been known to swallow many an errant ball. The approach to the 8th is long and requires accurate shooting to avoid the ponds. Fortunately, the back of the green slopes down to hold those shots from far back in the fairway.

Greens fees are $25 for everyone, every day. Cart rental is $14 per person. The twilight rate is $13, $23 with cart rental.

Mission Trails Golf Course
7380 Golfcrest Place, San Diego
(619) 460-5400
Nestled in a canyon at the foot of stately Cowles Mountain, Mission Trails is a par 71, 5,603-yard course that has lots of ups and downs in the fairly rugged terrain.

The signature hole is the 16th, the longest par 4 on the course. It's noted not so much for its difficulty—it's a not-too-daunting dogleg right—but for the beautiful view of Lake Murray as you approach the green. If you're walking, keep in mind that the climb to the 18th green is a steep one. Greens fees are $20 Monday through Friday and $35 on weekends. Cart rental is $15 per person. The course also has a grass-and-mat driving range and putting, chipping, and sand practice areas.

Try walking on at some of the more popular courses like Torrey Pines and Balboa. Singles and even twosomes can usually get a game with a minimum wait because of cancellations and no-shows.

Riverwalk Golf Club
1150 Fashion Valley Road, San Diego
(619) 296-4653
www.riverwalkgc.com
Reopened in the spring of 1998 in the heart of Mission Valley, this centrally located course was formerly the Starlight County Club course. Three nine-hole courses combine to produce the par 72, 6,156-yard Mission/Presidio Course, the par 72, 6,033-yard Mission/Friars Course, and the par 72, 6,277-yard Presidio/Friars Course. Presidio is longer and straighter than Mission and is favored by brute-force hitters. Mission has several doglegs and lots of water, so accurate golfers tend to fare well here. Friars has long, undulating fairways that tend to produce unexpected bounces. Thirteen of the 27 holes are protected by four lakes and the San Diego River. If you can distract yourself from your game for a few moments, you'll appreciate the beauty of the waterfalls, wildlife, and wetlands flora that are all over the course.

The second hole on Mission is a short par 4 with a dogleg left and a narrow landing area. It calls for precision shots. Slice it, and you're in the water. Hook it, and your ball will be bouncing among the cars driving by on Fashion Valley Road. Greens fees include a cart and are $95 Monday through Thursday and $105 Friday through Sunday. Residents get a $26 to $40 price break depending on the day of the week. You can walk, but the greens fee will be the same as with a cart. There's a two-sided, lighted driving range with practice greens adjacent to the course.

Held at Torrey Pines Golf Course, the Buick Invitational is a San Diego staple for golfing fans.
PHOTO: COURTESY OF JOEL ZWINK

Torrey Pines Golf Course
11480 North Torrey Pines Road, La Jolla
(619) 570-1234 (reservations)
(858) 452-3226 (pro shop),
(800) 985-4653
www.torreypinesgolfcourse.com

When the PGA makes its tour stop at Torrey Pines in January of each year for the Buick Invitational, millions of television viewers across the country are awed by the splendor of the course, with its emerald green fairways and stunning views of the towering cliffs and the ocean beyond. As a result, when visiting golfers find their way to San Diego, playing Torrey is a must. We won't lie to you—it's hard to get on, but not impossible. For those who manage to get a tee time, it's an experience of a lifetime.

Divided into two courses, the North and the South, it's a day of golf that can bring even seasoned golfers to their knees. Most prefer to play the tougher South Course, mainly because that's where the pros play the last two rounds of their tournament. This course was completely redone by Rees Jones in time for the 2002 Buick Invitational, to the tune of $3.3 million. According to Scott Simpson, a San Diegan who won the 1998 Buick Invitational on the course, "It's a much prettier course because of the holes they moved closer to the ocean, and it will definitely be tougher." Simpson also approved of the styling of the greens and bunkering, which have been vastly improved. The course was made longer, too, now 6,885 yards but still par 72.

Until the remodel, many golfers preferred the par 72, 6,326-yard North Course, with a tricky par 3 overlooking the ocean

i

JC Golf (www.jcgolf.com) offers membership and discounts at nine San Diego courses. Among the many member benefits are junior league for golfers age 12 and older, clinics, classes, tournaments, and a wide range of other activities.

as well as a view south to downtown La Jolla. Once you recover from the splendor of the view, the hole itself is waiting to humble you. The green slopes from back to front and is guarded by bunkers on both sides and in front. Shoot over the green and kiss your ball bye-bye. It'll be gone forever in a sharp, brush-covered dropoff.

Greens fees have gotten a bit complicated since renovation of the South Course. Weekday rates for those 18 holes are $115.00 for visitors, $85.00 for county residents, and $40.00 for city residents with a $12.00 photo ID card. (Add $20.00, $15.00, or $5.00, respectively, on the weekends.) North Course rates are $75.00 for visitors, $60.00 for county residents, and $29.00 for city residents. Visitors add $10.00 on weekends; city and county residents add $5.00. Cart fees are $32.00. Twilight rates are available after 2:00 P.M. The driving range and practice facilities are top-notch.

North County Coastal

Encinitas Ranch Golf Course
1275 Quail Gardens Drive, Encinitas
(760) 944-1936

Opened in 1998, this course features no fewer than 15 holes with views of the mighty Pacific. Proximity to the ocean keeps the temperatures moderate, and when the weather is clear, the views are astonishing, making this course one of the most enjoyable in the county.

Winding through the sloping hills and valleys of the quintessential beach community of Leucadia, the 5,820-yard course has fairly wide fairways and larger-than-average greens. Though water is a factor on only 3 holes, there are more than 50 sand traps, and afternoon winds can have a substantial effect on your score. The course is quite playable, however, if you don't allow the back tees to tempt you and keep the ball off the fairways' sloping sides.

Encinitas Ranch has a double-sided driving range, practice bunker, chipping area, putting green, and snack shop; lessons are available. Price depends on who you are and when you play. Midweek prices are $38.00 for Encinitis residents, $55.00 for Southern California residents, and $60.00 for the general public. Add $5.00 to $6.00 on Friday, $15.00 to $20.00 on weekends and holidays, and $12.00 per person per cart.

The Four Seasons Aviara Golf Club has one of the longest and toughest courses in the county.

Four Seasons Resort Aviara Golf Club
7447 Batiquitos Drive, Carlsbad
(760) 603-6900

Here's the only Arnold Palmer-designed course in San Diego County, and it's also considered one of the longest and toughest. Golfing Insiders say it's one of the best, too. Every hole has a panoramic view of the mountains, the lagoon, or the azure Pacific (or all three).

The course has been featured in *Golf Digest* and *Golf* magazines as one of the top courses in the United States. There are four sets of tees measuring 5,007 to 7,007 yards. This allows golfers of various abilities to enjoy the play. The course is open to all, but the driving range and practice facility is available for guests only. Greens fees range from $195 to $205 and include a cart. Walking is not allowed. For slightly more cost, you can reserve a tee time up to a month ahead.

The signature hole is the 18th, a par 4. When asked about the hole, Arnold Palmer said, "A picturesque finishing hole with a wide fairway." Then he added this Insider's tip: "Direct the tee shot towards the fairway bunkers away from the lake. The shot to the fairway is visually exciting, with the rock and waterscape highlighting the approach." For a complete look at all that happens at this resort, check out our Spas and Resorts and Restaurants chapters.

Remember this is a lavish resort. If you stroll into the pro shop in cutoffs and flip-flop sandals, you'll be reminded that upscale golf attire is required.

Call the resort for information on golf and spa package deals.

The Meadows Del Mar
5300 Meadows Street, Del Mar
(858) 792-6200
www.meadowsdelmar.com
Winding through the Carmel Valley mesa in a links-style format, The Meadows has spectacular natural formations and landscaping truly unique in Southern California. Just 3 miles from the sea, the course is subject to the cooling afternoon breezes that can affect play. Accuracy is important, as the deep rough can consume balls at an alarming rate. Fairways tend to be narrow and greens undulating; in other words, it's a wonderful course. Designer Tom Fazio's creation features remarkable flexibility: A variety of tee locations allow the length to be stretched from 4,974 to 7,054 yards, creating a course that will please any skill level.

Reserve a tee time up to 60 days in advance. The dress code requires a colored shirt with a collar; jeans are not allowed. Greens fees are $145 weekdays and $175 on weekends (including cart). There's a restaurant as well as a putting green and driving range.

North County Inland

Castle Creek Country Club
8797 Circle R Drive, Escondido
(760) 749-2422
www.castlecreekcc.com
If your idea of a good game of golf is to play on a course that has big trees, beautiful fairways, and flawless greens, then Castle Creek Country Club is your course. Castle Creek's golfers come here to play golf and have fun.

It's a par 72, 6,400-yard, 18-hole course, and the signature hole is number 14. To make this one, without losing balls or adding a lot to your score, you'll be expected to drive over a creek, hit to the right, and then make it over a small lake. Oh yes, don't forget that there's a huge oak tree guarding the hole.

Challenging and fun, Castle Creek's greens fees are $48 Monday through Thursday, $50 on Friday, and $64 on weekends ($31, $33, and $37 respectively after noon). Weekdays, seniors play for $35. Prices go down considerably after 11:00 A.M. and again after 2:00 P.M. You can reserve a tee time up to 10 days in advance of your game time. There's a chipping and putting green, pro shop, bar, and restaurant (closed Sunday and Monday for dinner).

Maderas Golf Club
17750 Old Coach Road, Poway
(858) 451-8100
www.maderasgolf.com
Snaking through the canyons, cliffs, forests, and creeks of a rural section of North County Inland, this Johnny Miller-designed course opened to rave reviews in 2000. It has since been awarded many accolades, including Zagat's "#1 Course in San Diego County" and "Best New Golf Club" by *Golf Digest* magazine.

Playing Maderas is like belonging to a private club for a day. From the grand entrance to the clubhouse's elegant bar and restaurant to the sweeping panoramic views of the finishing holes from the terrace, it truly is a testimony to opulent golf course design. Managed by Troon Golf, this welcome "newbie" offers players services and amenities unrivaled by its competitors.

Greens fees are $120 on weekdays, $150 on weekends (cart included for residents of San Diego and Riverside Counties; others pay $150 and $195, respectively). Visit the well-stocked pro shop, the restaurant, or bar. There's a driving range and a short-game facility.

Pala Mesa Resort
2001 Old Highway 395, Fallbrook
(760) 731-6803, (800) 722-4700
www.palamesa.com

Tucked away in Fallbrook, just off Interstate 15 in North County Inland, Pala Mesa is considered one of the best truly traditional courses in the county because of the stately trees, manicured greens, and extensive fairways. Lots of seniors and those with weekday flexibility come here Monday through Friday. Golf and overnight packages are available.

The course is lush and especially delicious, we think, in the fall when the trees hugging the fairways change colors. Pala Mesa has rolling fairways, edged with pines and sycamores, and a challenge at every turn. The mountain views are spectacular on the 6,502- to 6,131-yard course. It's a par 72 with a 131 slope.

The signature hole is the 11th because of the view. You get a 360-degree panorama portrait of the area. Don't be shy about admiring it. If you have room for a camera in your golf bag, it's worth taking one along to take this shot back home.

Prime-time greens fees (noon to 3:00 P.M.) are $74 Monday through Thursday, $79 Friday through Sunday. Reduced rates apply for morning, twilight, and supertwilight hours. A GPS-equipped golf cart is included in the price; the dress code (collared shirts, no denim) is enforced.

San Luis Rey Downs
31474 Golf Club Drive, Bonsall
(760) 758-9699, (800) 783-6967
www.slrd.com

This par 72 course measures 6,750 yards, and while the overall length isn't that long, it is formidable. For duffers, the better word might be difficult. It's not that the course isn't beautiful—it is. You see, there are large trees dotting the fairways and many other hazards. There are also wonderful ocean breezes...wonderful when your opponent is at the tee and you've already placed your ball on the green.

Monday through Thursday fees are $34; the shared cart (mandatory on holidays and weekends) is $10 for each player. Friday greens fees are $36; Saturday, Sunday, and holiday fees are $64, including the required cart. There's a pro shop where lessons are offered, as well as a driving range and putting greens.

The signature hole is the 15th. It's long and narrow and deceptive. Just when you think everything is perfect, a caboose gets in your way. Yes, a train caboose is on the golf course with a resort sign attached. With the wonderful breeze, your ball could be swept straight at that obstacle. Trust us on this one.

East County

Carlton Oaks Country Club
9200 Inwood Drive, Santee
(619) 448-4242
www.carltonoaksgolf.com

Carlton Oaks Country Club has a challenging 7,088-yard course designed by Pete Dye. This is the course where Curtis Strange hit a 1-iron to the 18th and made eagle to win the NCAA individual title and assure Wake Forest of the team title.

There are tinkling creeks, clusters of tall trees, and a strategically undulating peninsula fairway. Carlton Oaks greens fees Monday through Thursday are $55; Friday, $60; weekends and holidays, $80. Cart included. There are package deals that include lodging, breakfast, and dinner with prices that could entice you; call for information.

The signature hole here is the 12th, a par 3 that's partially surrounded by water. (Take extra balls if you play like we do!) Be aware that the driving range closes about four hours before sunset on Wednesday and opens only between 10:00 A.M. and noon on Thursday.

Sycuan Resort Golf Courses
3007 Dehesa Road, El Cajon
(619) 442-3425, (800) 457-5568
www.sycuanresort.com

Once family owned and operated, Singing Hills is now part of the Kumeyaay Indian tribe's Sycuan Resort and Casino. The course is spread over gently rounded fairways and hugged by rugged mountains.

There's a choice of three 18-hole courses, two 18-hole championship courses and an executive course, offering golfers of all abilities challenging and fun play.

You may have already seen Singing Hills on ESPN. It has been the site of numerous PGA, LPGA, and SCGA championships, in addition to hosting the School of Golf (for women, juniors, and seniors). The courses were designed by Ted Robinson.

Greens fees here are inexpensive: $16 weekdays, $22 weekends for the Pine Glen Course; $45 to $62 for Willow Glen or Oak Glen (weekdays and weekends, respectively). Carts are $12 per player. The course is busy on weekends, so call ahead to reserve a tee time.

This is a sunny course, so you may want to wear a hat and use sunscreen. East County can be warm in the summertime, so pack a bottle of water in your golf bag.

Steele Canyon Golf and Country Club
3199 Stonefield Drive, Jamul
(619) 441-6900
www.steelecanyon.com

The 27-hole championship course in this golf community was designed by Gary Player.

The Canyon Ranch Course requires strength; the signature 5th hole is elevated—and we're talking high up. On the meandering Ranch Course, it's the 3rd hole, called Parachute, that's the challenge—again, its the elevation. The Meadow Course highlights the dry, dramatic scenery of inland San Diego County. You might spy rabbits and lots of birds. For the Meadow Course, it's the 6th hole that most remember. Here you must hit the ball over a deep ravine to make it to the green. The Canyon Course is 3,206 yards, the Ranch Course is 3,205 yards, and the Meadow Course is 3,273 yards, with six different combinations of play for all types of players.

There's a practice facility, including a target-oriented driving range and two large putting greens. The fees for residents and nonresidents are $55 and $84, respectively, Monday through Thursday; $89 and $124 Friday through Sunday. There's no extra charge for carts. You can reserve starting times in advance, paying extra to reserve eight days ahead or more. The dress code prohibits jeans, cutoffs, short shorts, and collarless shirts. Clubs can be rented at the well-stocked pro shop.

South Bay

Bonita Golf Club
5540 Sweetwater Road, Bonita
(619) 267-1103
www.bonitagolfclub.com

Most of the fairways are lined with trees at this South Bay course, which is scenic if you hit straight, but trouble if you hook or slice. It's a fairly short par 71 course at 5,832 yards, so concentrate on accuracy rather than long drives. Watch out for water, too. The Sweetwater River meanders through six holes, and a large pond comes into play on another two. Bunkers are sparse, thankfully.

The signature 13th hole presents a couple of choices, both of them doubtful. It's a par 5 dogleg left that has both the river and a big pond to contend with. If your tee shot is too short, you just might have to lay up short of the river on your second shot. Conversely, if you blast your drive into the stratosphere, you're likely to plunk it into the pond.

Warm up on the driving range with both mat and grass tee stations, putting green, and chipping/sand practice area that are all set around a large clubhouse with a nice sports bar and restaurant. Greens fees are $26 on weekdays and $38 on weekends. Carts are an additional $13 per person. Twilight golf is $16 during the week and $24 on weekends.

Chula Vista Municipal Golf Course
4475 Bonita Road, Bonita
(619) 479-4141

Former PGA star Billy Casper helped design this municipal course in the early 1960s. It's short on trees and pretty flat, but don't let the lack of scenery fool you. It's a par 73 course that plays longer than its 6,186 yards. Only a few holes don't have water to bedevil you, and the last three holes on the back nine are straight into the wind, which is usually strong in the afternoon.

The par 4 6th is the toughest hole on the course. The wind comes in from the west and has a habit of knocking your drives down to a conveniently located bunker. Second shots demand a long iron or fairway wood to reach a skinny little green that has bunkers on both sides.

A nice grass-tee driving range is on the grounds, as is a putting green and chipping/sand practice area. Greens fees are $27.00 on weekdays and $34.00 on weekends. Carts are $13.00 per person extra. Twilight fees are $17.50 during the week and $33.50 on weekends. Chula Vista residents with an $8.00 annual ID card receive discounted greens fees.

Eastlake Country Club
2375 Clubhouse Drive, Chula Vista
(619) 482-5757
At first look, you might think the computer-equipped carts at Eastlake are little more than a gimmick. But once you get used to the information you can get at the push of a button, you may well be hooked. Screens on every cart provide exact distances to the pin, along with helpful hints about the idiosyncrasies of each hole. They can't help your swing, though, so that part is up to you.

The par 72, 5,726-yard course has fairways that are lined with nearly 2,000 young trees, 6 lakes, 3 waterfalls, and dozens of sand traps. Most holes have bunkers placed right about where your drive should land. Approaches are narrow but clear, with bunkers guarding either one side or the rear of the green. It's usually the par 3s that are the sticklers, and the 12th at Eastlake is one of them. A head wind can play havoc with your tee

Would you love to play golf in the border area of Mexico? Look over our South of the Border chapter for some suggestions on challenging courses.

shot, and water laps right at the putting surface. It's also protected by a couple of bunkers to the right and directly behind.

Greens fees are $59 Monday through Friday, $79 on weekends, and include the computerized cart. Twilight golf (after 2:00 P.M.) is $29 on weekdays and $39 on weekends. A luxurious three-building clubhouse complex offers all the after-golf amenities, and there's a grass driving range, two chipping/sand practice areas, and two putting greens.

EXECUTIVE AND 9-HOLE COURSES

Central San Diego

Balboa Park 9-Hole Course
2600 Golf Course Drive, San Diego
(619) 570-1234 (reservations)
(619) 239-1660 (pro shop)
If you're too short on time or talent to tackle the main course at Balboa, the 9-hole is more than adequate as a second choice. It underwent a renovation at the same time the main course did, and the effort actually improved a course that was already too much fun. It's a par 32, 2,175-yard course that has some of the same hazards as the big course—big trees and bunkers.

Most fairways are lined with trees, and errant shots can easily end up in the next fairway over on the several holes that are adjacent, going up and back. Players tend to be accepting of this, and it's probably one of the few places where you look ahead and behind before you hit the ball. This is a good course for walk-ons in the late afternoon. Greens fees are $21.00 every day; $9.00 with a $12.00 resident card.

The private course at La Costa Resort and Spa earned one of Links *magazine's 50 Best of Golf Awards for its dedication to the preservation of golf played with caddies.*

Mission Bay Golf Course
2702 North Mission Bay Drive, San Diego
(858) 581-7880
This is the only course in San Diego that has lights for nighttime play. It's a fun course with 18 holes that stretch into a par 58 of 2,719 yards. Each nine has seven par 3s and two par 4s. The best is saved for last, with the 18th being the longest hole on the course at 291 yards.

If you play at night, our best advice is to hit it straight. The lights—which go out at 10:00 P.M.—are bright, but should you wander too far from the fairway, you'll probably have some trouble finding your ball because the lights are aimed at the tee boxes and the greens. Greens fees are $19 on weekdays and $23 on weekends. Most everyone walks on this course, but pull and electric carts are available. You can also play nine holes for a discounted rate of $12 during the week and $14 on weekends. There's a snack bar, driving range, and putting green.

Tecolote Canyon Golf Course
2755 Snead Avenue, San Diego
(858) 279-1600
Designed by Robert Trent Jones Sr. and Sam Snead, this course is widely known as one of the toughest par 3s in California. You might not pull every club in your bag, but we guarantee you'll be challenged. The course is in a narrow canyon with swirling winds that make club selection a creative sport. Four par 4 holes range from 299 to 339 yards, and the total yardage is 3,161 on the par 58 course. Both greens and bunkers were improved in 2002.

The fun starts at the 1st hole, where you tee off from the top of a cliff to the green below. It's a feel-good hole that's easy and gives you false confidence for the rest. By the time you get to the killer 11th, you'll have figured out that this is no walk in the park. The 299-yard, par 4 11th begins at the farthest point of the course, and lots of trees and the edge of the canyon provide trouble on the right. Most lay up short of the creek that runs through the fairway, then play a 9-iron up to the green, which is guarded by a trap.

Greens fees during the week are $18; on weekends, $25. Shared carts cost another $24. There's a lighted driving range with half-grass and half-mat stations, a practice putting green, a small chipping area, and a snack bar.

North County Coastal

Emerald Isle Golf Course
660 South El Camino Real, Oceanside
(760) 721-4700
www.emeraldislegolf.net
Emerald Isle is billed as North County's "most challenging executive course," and it's the hills that get your attention if you're walking the course with its full 18 holes. Emerald Isle is a comfortable, unpretentious place to play and have family fun. If you've never been into mingling with the Rolex watch crowd or you're a beginner, Emerald Isle could become your favorite.

Prices are right here, just $17.00 on weekdays and $20.00 on weekends. Carts are $18.00 for two people weekdays; add $2.00 on weekends. There's a putting green, spacious driving range, and snack bar. Emerald Isle's staff offers instruction, whether you need a few tips or a series of lessons with the pro.

Rancho Carlsbad
5200 El Camino Real, Carlsbad
(760) 438-1772
www.ranchocarlsbad.com
This executive golf course, "Rancho" as it's

known by Insiders, is right off El Camino Real, near LEGOLAND California (see our Kidstuff chapter), the Carlsbad Flower Fields (see our Annual Events chapter), and shopping (see our Shopping chapter). It is an Insiders' favorite. Not that many people frequent it, so you'll rarely have to wait long, even if you don't call ahead to reserve a tee time.

While executive courses usually don't have signature holes, we like the 9th. There's a long narrow fairway, and the green is elevated. Should you hit the ball way out in the rough on this hole, remember you're playing in the backcountry and watch where you step. Snakes have been known to think that the brush adjacent to the 9th is their home.

There's a shady putting green and a driving range (buy your tokens for the ball machine at the pro shop). You can browse through the pro shop and visit the snack bar. You can eat on the patio. The entire package here is wrapped in mature trees, with plenty of shade even on warm days. If it's been raining or looks like a storm's on the way, call to make sure Rancho is open. On wet days management closes the course to avoid destroying the fairways. It's $14 during the week and $17 on weekends to play a round on the full 18-hole, par 56 course. After 3:00 P.M. it's $11 ($14 on weekends) to play as many holes as you want. This course is tucked out of traffic and it's quiet.

North County Inland

Oaks North Golf Course
12602 Oaks North Drive, Rancho Bernardo
(858) 487-3021
(888) 703-2537 (reservations)

This is it: our Insiders' favorite executive course. Actually there are three 9-hole courses that easily add up to a pleasurable day out.

Oaks North is stunning, with long and short fairways that make it fun for experienced golfers (you see lots of them) and duffers, too. There is a dress code here—you'll need to wear nice shorts or khakis and golf shirts (or shirts with collars). The prices range from about $30 weekdays to $34 on weekends. The twilight rate is a bargain as it starts at noon on weekdays, 1:00 P.M. on weekends. A cart will cost you $8.00 extra per person, and unless you always get a cart when you golf, forego it here. The walk is worth the price of admission.

Call ahead to reserve a tee time. There's a snack bar and shaded patio for lunch or an after-golf iced tea, soda, or beer.

Travel packagers such as San Diego Golf Vacations (www.sandiego-golf vacations.com; 888-292-4966) and Showtime Golf Vacations (www.show timegolfvacations.com, 866-661-2334; ext. 1) offer San Diego golf vacations that combine some of San Diego's best courses and a range of accommodations. Their informative Web sites give lots of course info and even the latest weather reports.

Reidy Creek Golf Course
2300 North Broadway, Escondido
(760) 740-2450
www.reidycreekgolf.com

Accuracy counts at this 2,602-yard course in a rural part of Escondido, where you'll see some great canyon views. It's a challenging course with quick, undulating greens and 54 sand traps; there are water hazards on one-third of the holes. The short 7th hole is guarded by a bunker on the right side, while the 8th, the longest of the front nine, is protected by the course's namesake creek. The signature 13th is fronted by a trenchlike bunker, making the approach difficult and club choice all-important. Ask at the pro shop about golf lessons and PGA clinics. There's a cafe and a large putting green where chipping is also allowed. Greens fees are $23 during

Twilight (and sometimes "supertwilight") golf is your best bet for getting in a round at your preferred course. And of course the rates are substantially cheaper.

the week and $28 on weekends (less for Escondido residents). After 2:00 P.M. in winter (3:00 P.M. in summer), supertwilight fees are $14 on weekdays and $16, cart included on weekends.

Welk Resort Center
8860 Lawrence Welk Drive, Escondido
(760) 749-3225 (pro shop),
(800) 932-9355
www.welksandiego.com

Hidden away in the foothills about an hour's drive from downtown San Diego, the courses here delight avid players and novices, too. Surprisingly, the cost of playing at the resort can be reasonable. At the Oaks Executive Course, the fees are $16.00 weekdays to walk and just $11.00 after 1:00 P.M. Weekends are only slightly more at $18.00 ($12.00 twilight). Carts cost $8.00 per person, although most people walk. The Fountains Course has a rather complicated pricing system, with rates sliding down as the day progresses. The cost is the same to walk or ride. Weekday rates range from $39 to supertwilight rates of $17 after 4:00 P.M.; on weekends it's $42 to $29.

Every hole is beautiful, and with the warm, sunny days of summer that last well into the evening, you might be wise to play late in the afternoon. Some of the fairways are steep, but they make for a good bit of exercise if you're walking the course.

The yardage, designed by David Rainville, is 1,837 at the Oaks and 4,002 at the Fountains. If you want a golf getaway, call about golf packages. Some include lodging at the resort (see our Hotels and Motels chapter) and unlimited golf with a cart to play either course.

South Bay

National City Golf Course
1439 Sweetwater Road, National City
(619) 474-1400

This is a quick-play par 34 nine, and many golfers play around twice, completing a full round in about four hours. It's a narrow canyon course that can be lots of fun for straight hitters. Those who lean left or right are in for some creative second shots. The fairways are narrow, especially on the only par 5, the 525-yard second. Water comes into play on three holes.

Greens fees are $10.00 for 9 holes, $17.00 for 18 on weekdays; weekend fees are $14.00 for 9; $22.00 for 18. Carts are $7.00 per person.

DRIVING RANGES

Central San Diego

Stadium Golf Center
2990 Murphy Canyon Road, San Diego
(858) 277-6667
www.stadiumgolfcenter.com

When this range first opened, passersby thought aliens had landed because the lights were so bright and visible from such a distance. What evoked images of E.T. in some is a benefit to those who use the range because you can see just where your shots land, even in the dead of night.

With 48 mat tees and 24 grass tees, there's rarely a problem finding an open tee here. The landing area is long and grassy and has seven target greens. One of the nicest features is the 10,000-square-foot bent-grass putting green that's available for play (along with the chipping and sand practice areas) for $4.00. Bucket prices range from $6.00 for 45 balls to $17.00 for 200 balls.

North County Coastal

Carlsbad Golf Center
2711 Haymar Drive, Carlsbad
(760) 720-4653
www.thecarlsbadgolfcenter.com

The Carlsbad Golf Center is tucked behind a hill and a strip shopping center right off California Highway 78. Exit at El Camino Real. You might not know it's there until you're past the exit. Call for directions if you don't have a good map because the location is extra nice; it's worth going out of your way to find this driving range.

The center is big, with 58 stations where you hit the ball off imitation grass. It's rarely crowded. There's a well-stocked pro shop and you can arrange for lessons here, too. The putting green now has real grass, and there's a practice sand bunker. Eight dollars will get you a big bucket of 100 balls. Get the tokens in the pro shop.

Olympic Resort Hotel & Spa
6111 El Camino Real, Carlsbad
(760) 438-8330, ext. 142

Here's a driving range for the serious golfer and anyone who wants a challenge. At Olympic Resort there are 48 deluxe stations. There's a practice bunker and four—count 'em—four putting greens. You can also arrange for PGA instructions and take advantage of video lessons on state-of-the-art equipment. Downside? The range is situated so that in the late afternoon or early evening (depending on the time of year), you're hitting straight into the sun. So for about an hour you'll need sunglasses, or simply schedule your practice session for another time. A large bucket (105 balls) costs $6.00, medium is $4.00, and small (25 balls) just $2.00.

Surf & Turf Driving Range
15555 Jimmy Durante Boulevard, Del Mar
(858) 481-0363

Surf & Turf is easy to get to. Just exit Interstate 5 at Via De La Valle in Del Mar and head toward the ocean. Make the first left turn onto Jimmy Durante Boulevard. You can't miss it. The range is across from the Del Mar Fairgrounds. The staff here offers individual and group lessons. The range is lighted and open daily from 8:00 A.M. until 9:00 P.M. Both grass and Astroturf mats are available.

Keep in mind that when the horses are running (during racing season) and during the Del Mar Fair (mid-June though early July) is being held, traffic can be unpleasant. If you're uncertain of what's happening at the fairgrounds or the track, call the driving range about traffic conditions before you set your sights on hitting golf balls here. If you want to play some strictly-for-laughs golf after hitting a bucket of balls ($6.00 to $11.00). Surf & Turf has a place to play miniature golf, too—30 holes for $5.00.

North County Inland

Thunderbird Driving Range & Training Center
26351 North Centre City Parkway Escondido
(760) 746-0245

Conveniently located right off I-15 (take the Deer Springs Road exit), the Thunderbird is popular. The downside is that the highway traffic can be noisy. There's a pro shop and snack bar. Cost is up to $10 for 105 balls. Private and group lessons are available.

South Bay

All Golf
540 Hollister Street, San Diego
(619) 424-3213

Located just off I-5 in the South Bay, the 48 hitting stations here are half grass and half mat. The landing area is grassy, and target flags and yardage markers are sprinkled throughout. A bonus is a nice chipping course with nine holes ranging from 30 to 70 yards. Buckets of balls are

Check out www.golfsd.com for course information, greens fees, and other useful information about San Diego County courses.

$5.00 and $7.00. The range is lighted and is open from 8:00 A.M. until 10:00 P.M. daily.

Bonita Golf Center
3631 Bonita Road, Bonita
(619) 426-2069
Rent a bucket of balls and swing away on this lighted range that has 30 grass tees and 18 mat stations. The first 175 yards of the range have small target areas that are marked by flags for those accuracy shots. If you just want to swing away and see how far you can drive, distance markers are placed beyond the target areas.

Next to the pro shop is a putting green and a large sand/chipping practice area. (Bring your own balls to use in this area.) If you bring your own balls, it's $4.50 per hour to use the practice facilities, but if you rent a bucket, it's free. Balls rent for $4.00 for a small bucket of 30, $6.00 for 60, and $7.00 for 100. Hours are 7:30 A.M. to 8:00 P.M. daily.

SPECTATOR SPORTS

San Diegans have a reputation for being fair-weather fans—literally and figuratively. Whether or not that reputation is deserved is up for debate, but the fact is that professional sports teams struggle at times to generate sustained interest among local fans—unless, of course, the team is in the hunt for a championship. If the Padres or the Chargers are having a dismal season, chances are that more than a few Insiders will look elsewhere for entertainment, mainly because there's so darn much to do here. Why waste an afternoon or evening watching the hometown boys turn in yet another lackluster performance when you could bask on the beach or sip champagne at an outdoor concert by the bay?

That said, don't think for a moment that San Diegans don't appreciate our sports teams. Scores of die-hard fans attend every home game (and many away games, too) simply out of sheer devotion and loyalty, regardless of the standings. And when the team is winning or an out-of-town superstar is making an appearance, tickets can be hard to come by.

In addition to the standards—football, baseball, golf, tennis, and auto racing—San Diegans are blessed with a couple of oddball (but highly entertaining) sports spectacles. Among them is Over-the-Line, a three-person-per-team softball game invented by some beach guys who believed that running the bases interfered too much with their beer drinking. From that philosophy was born a game celebrated every summer in a two-weekend tournament that draws players and spectators from all over the world. Somewhere along it's line has earned some actual credibility.

The X Games have been to San Diego twice, bringing along such extreme sports as sky surfing, bicycle stunt riding, and the downhill luge. Everyone hopes they'll be back for future meets. Another repeat performer is the Super Bowl. In 1998 both the event itself and its weeklong festivities were so successful that the NFL brought it back in 2003. San Diegans were thrilled to watch the total rout of their archrivals, the Oakland Raiders, by the Tampa Bay Buccaneers.

Although San Diego does not have an NBA basketball team, there is no lack of exciting sporting events to fill the gap. Thunderboats—high-speed racing boats—roar across Mission Bay in an annual competition, thrilling onlookers with their death-defying speeds. A short trip south of the border is all you need to see the ancient and historic sport of bullfighting. And the beautifully renovated Del Mar Thoroughbred Club plays host to the sport of kings every summer.

We'll fill you in on them all in this chapter. Some sports are annual events; some are held during a regular season. We'll give you dates, ticket prices, and venues—all you have to do is make up your mind what appeals to you most. You're likely to find a sporting event to watch on any day of the year. And if it's a nice day, which it usually is, ignore the lure of the beach. The sun will be out at the stadium, too, and we guarantee you'll have a great time.

Qualcomm Stadium
9449 Friars Road, San Diego
(619) 641-3131
www.ci.san-diego.ca.us/qualcomm

Home games for Chargers and San Diego State University Aztec football and the annual Holiday Bowl are all held at

---

For the latest parking info for football games, call the San Diego Chargers Parking Hotline at (619) 281-PARK.

Kids love the interactive games in the plaza concourse of Qualcomm Stadium. During baseball season they can try their luck at the batting contest or have the speed of their pitching gauged by radar.

Qualcomm Stadium. Located in Mission Valley, the stadium is just north of Interstate 8, between California Highway 163 and Interstate 15. The Chargers instituted new parking fees and regulations for the 2006 season, creating an uproar among die-hard fans. A new RV parking area was designated apart from general parking, forcing tailgaters to limit their activities. A reserved tailgating area was created with parking costing $75 per game for a car and $100 for an RV when reserved in advance. All RVs must park in a reserved space, which costs $150 on game day. Tailgate companion parking costs $20 per car with a limit of two cars. General parking also was raised to $20. Bus service to home games is provided from parking sites around the county; call (619) 685-4900 for route information. If you taxi your way in, rest assured that you'll find one waiting for you following the game in the stadium parking lot. One of the best ways to get to Qualcomm is by way of the San Diego Trolley. The trolley departs from locations all over town and takes you right to its station in the stadium parking lot, just a short walk from Gate J. The closest trolley stations with ample parking are Old Town and Hazard Center.

Bottles, cans, and liquid containers are not allowed inside the stadium. The exception is baby bottles and containers with formula. Food may be brought into the stadium, but since 9/11 coolers and large backpacks are prohibited, and bags and purses are subject to inspection at the gate. Smoking is not allowed in any of the seating areas or in the field-level concourse. Smoking is permitted in the plaza, loge, and view concourses.

Tailgating is a popular way to kick off a game. Gather your friends, some food and drink, and have an impromptu party in the parking lot. Just remember that tailgaters must confine themselves to their own parking space.

AUTO RACING

Barona Drag Strip
Wildcat Canyon Road, about 5 miles northeast of the Barona Casino
(619) 445-3559
www.baronadrags.com

The ⅛-mile strip is adjacent to the Barona Speedway, at the Barona Indian reservation. Located on an old sand drag pit, it now boasts some 250,000 square feet of asphalt and grandstands accommodating 4,000 spectators. There's parking for cars and RVs. On Saturday the strip hosts NHRA (National Hot Rod Association) meets, with competition among Open Comp classes, stock, gas, and imports.

BASEBALL

San Diego Padres
Petco Park, 100 Park Boulevard
San Diego
(619) 280-4636
www.padres.com

May 27, 1968, was an exciting day for baseball fans—San Diego was awarded a National League franchise, the San Diego Padres. Now in its fourth decade as a major-league team, the club has amassed some statistics that have little to do with hits and runs: The Padres have seen 4 owners and 15 managers over the years. And it was 1975, seven years after the team's inception, before the club climbed out of the cellar.

It took another eight years of fluctuating between fourth place and last before everything clicked. In one memorable season, in 1984, the Padres soared. Not only did they beat Atlanta to win their division, they came back from an early deficit in the National League Championship Series to snatch the pennant away from the Chicago Cubs. The beleaguered Padres were going to the World Series!

No matter that the Series proved to be anticlimactic—the Pads dropped four of five to the Detroit Tigers—they had made it to the big show. Never was a city more proud of its team. Winning seemed almost irrelevant. It's a good thing, too, because subsequent years brought more of what fans were used to. The team dropped to third place in their division the following year, then fourth, and then last, a position they seemed almost comfortable with.

Days of glory finally returned, though. In 1994 John Moores and Larry Lucchino bought the team, and a new and better era began. The quality of the team improved dramatically with the acquisition of players such as Ken Caminiti, Steve Finley, Wally Joyner, Greg Vaughn, and Kevin Brown, who joined longtime Padre Tony Gwynn. And by the end of 1998, the Padres had returned to the World Series, only to suffer an even more ignoble fate than before—being swept by the New York Yankees. After that season several of the hottest players moved or retired. So the Padres were once again rebuilding.

Perhaps San Diegans remain true to the Pads because the club is really involved in the community. Owners and players fund the Padres Scholars program, giving $5,000 scholarships to talented but financially challenged middle-school students. To date more than 250 students have received more than $1.4 million for college tuition. The Little Padres Parks program will build or refurbish 60 youth baseball fields across the region. And through the Cindy Matters Fund, the club has donated more than $1,050,000 to the UCSD and Children's Hospital Cancer Care Programs to honor the memory of a young Padres fan who lost her life to cancer.

The Padres' history includes such notable players as Randy Jones, Rollie Fingers, Gaylord Perry, Ozzie Smith, Steve Garvey, Gary Sheffield, and Fred McGriff.

Even though days are warm during the summer, nights can be chilly. If you go to a nighttime Padres baseball game, especially during the early summer months, be sure to bring a warm jacket or even a blanket.

More than a dozen Gold Glove Awards belong to Padres' players (five to Tony Gwynn alone), and the team boasts three Cy Young Awards for pitching. But history doesn't win today's pennants, and Tony Gwynn, whom local sports writer Nick Canepa calls "the greatest pure ball-striker of his generation," is history as well; he retired at the end of the 2001 season.

Despite its lackluster record, the team remained popular enough to convince fans (and voters) of the need for a new baseball-only ballpark right in the middle of downtown San Diego. A joint venture by the Padres and the city of San Diego, it opened in April 2004. (See the Close-up for details.) The stadium seems to have inspired the team. By mid-season 2006 the Pads had won seven of eight home games. Ticket prices range from $8.00 to $57.00 for individual games. Season tickets start at $810.00 for the full season. Tickets may be purchased at Gate F in the stadium. Call (619) 699-6100 for information on season ticket packages or (877) FRIAR-TIX for single-game tickets.

BULLFIGHTING

El Toreo de Tijuana
Boulevard Agua Caliente at Boulevard Cuauhtémoc, Tijuana
Plaza Monumental
Playas de Tijuana, Tijuana
(619) 232-5049

Dating from 2000 B.C., bullfighting is a combination of ritual and mortal combat, pitting man against beast in a graceful but deadly battle. El Toreo de Tijuana and Plaza Monumental, both less than 15 min-

CLOSE-UP

Petco Park: A Hit or an Error?

In 1998, 60 percent of San Diego voters approved a $225 million ballot measure as first money toward a new, baseball-only downtown ballpark. That's a slim majority for such a substantial project. Seventeen lawsuits and four years later, the stadium was nothing more than a large hole in the ground. The ballpark had become a bureaucratic boondoggle.

The Padres threatened to move elsewhere if the stadium wasn't built. And boosters stressed that the project would revitalize the dilapidated East Village, downtown's largest neighborhood, which borders the popular and vital Gaslamp District. The team prevailed in January 2002, and bond sales were allocated to finance the project. Five years after voters first approved the project, the San Diego Padres began their 2004 season at intimate, asymmetrical Petco Park.

Before the Padres' season opener on April 8, 2004, thousands of fans attended nearly a dozen San Diego State University Aztec baseball games at Petco Park. As head coach of the Aztecs, retired Padre all-star Tony Gwynn had the honor of playing the ballpark before his former teammates. The stadium's inauguration was auspicious: The Aztecs soundly defeated the University of Houston Cougars on the pristine natural-grass field.

More than 40,000 people filled the 42,000-seat venue on the Aztecs' opening night. This preseason run-through helped stadium coordinators work out the inevitable snafus regarding concession sales and pedestrian flow, and it also

utes south of the border, present some of the world's leading matadors.

Bullfights are generally held between May and September, but not every Sunday. Tickets are available in San Diego through Five Star Tours (Santa Fe Train Depot, 1050 Kettner Boulevard, 619-232-5049), which is by far the easiest way to arrange the excursion. Five Star adds a $5.00 service charge to the price of the ticket and also offers bus transportation, $17.00 ($9.00 one way) per person round-trip. Ticket prices vary based on the fame of the matador and other factors but generally cost $15.00 for general admission (nosebleed seats in the sun) to around $50.00 (plus $5.00 service charge if booked in San Diego) for reserved seats.

FOOTBALL

Pacific Life Holiday Bowl
Qualcomm Stadium, 9449 Friars Road
San Diego
(619) 283-5808
www.holidaybowl.com

Since 1978 the Holiday Bowl has featured a football face-off between nationally ranked teams from the Big 12 and either the WAC or the Pac 10. Since its inauguration, the majority of games have been won by a margin of one touchdown or tested the capability of the bright red trolley, which struggled to transport more than the expected 12,000 riders.

Trolley riders can park at Qualcomm Stadium—the Padres' former playing field—where there are 5,000 free parking spots unless the stadium is hosting a concert or other event. From the North County the train also connects to the trolley at the Santa Fe depot. Lucky downtown residents can walk, bike, or take a pedicab to the event.

Revitalization of the East Village is a cornerstone of the ballpark project. A mixed-use office, residential, and retail development, East Village Square has been designed to surround a 40,000-square-foot urban park. The low-rise Kimpton Hotel provides a link to the past with its brick façade, while the 32-story Omni, adjacent to the ballpark and accessible via a footbridge, is sleek and modern.

Downtown redevelopment aside, what excites baseball fans is the 16-acre, $458 million ballpark itself. All seats down the lines are angled toward home plate, and there are just six roomy seats per aisle. The seating bowl is "fractured" by first- and third-base towers housing among other things, nine clubs and restaurants. Park at the Park is a grassy, one-acre spot overlooking the stadium where folks can get a glimpse of the game, or on nongame days, picnic or attend community events.

The project was protracted and painful, but most San Diegans are excited about their downtown ballpark. Traffic flow and parking may be a concern, but who knows? Maybe this will finally get San Diegans out of their cars and onto public transportation. That alone would make the project worthwhile.

less, and most have been decided in the final two minutes. It's no wonder the Holiday Bowl has earned a reputation as America's most exciting bowl game.

The hometown San Diego State Aztecs made an appearance in the Holiday Bowl in 1986 and put on one of the best shows ever. The Aztecs held off the Iowa Hawkeyes until the final four seconds, when an Iowa field goal gave the team a one-point edge over the Aztecs and a final score of 39 to 38.

Holiday Bowl tickets are available in advance by calling the Bowl ticket office at (619) 285–5059. Ticket prices range from $48 to $60. The game is held in late December.

San Diego Chargers
Qualcomm Stadium, 9449 Friars Road
San Diego
(619) 280–2121, (877) 242–7437
www.chargers.com

The histories of the San Diego Chargers and the Padres have followed an eerily parallel course. Just as the Padres are not frequent contenders in the World Series, the Chargers have made it to the Super Bowl but one time, in 1995. And like both the Padres' World Series contests, the Chargers faced a powerhouse opponent in the Super Bowl—the San Francisco 49ers—and were soundly trounced.

The loss didn't totally squelch the enthusiasm of fans, though. Game day

Try one of Rubio's famous fish tacos while you're attending a game at Qualcomm Stadium. Available on the concourse of the Plaza, these delicacies originated just south of the border.

always finds a sea of blue-and-gold-clad aficionados who are ever loyal to their beloved "Bolts." (The Bolt refers to the streak of lightning on the Chargers' uniforms.) After two terrible seasons under head coach Mike Riley (with 11 straight losses in his second year of coaching, and 9 straight to end his third and final year), fans cheered on head coach Marty Schottenheimer when he brought the team to the AFC Championships in 2004.

Team members have shown a devotion to San Diego by diving headfirst into charitable ventures. Charger Champions scholarship funds, charity golf tournaments, and Junior Charger Girls are just a few of the ways in which players give back to the community. Earlier Chargers players such as Lance Alworth, Rolfe Benirschke, and Dan Fouts set the example, and today quarterback Doug Flutie has also established his own foundations in support of the San Diego community.

Whether the Chargers are having a winning season or not, you can always count on sellout crowds whenever their perennial nemesis, the Oakland Raiders, are in town. One step below the Raiders in terms of rivalry are the Denver Broncos. But whomever the team is playing, the excitement is unparalleled. The Chargers' commitment to San Diego became tenuous in 2006 when the city refused to build a new stadium to replace Qualcomm. With the city of San Diego in dire financial straits, a new football stadium fell to the bottom of the priorities list. In May 2006 the city agreed to allow the Chargers to look elsewhere in the county for a new stadium deal. The likely contenders include Chula Vista, Oceanside, and National City. The Chargers will be allowed to relocate after the 2008 season if the team makes the final payments for a 1997 expansion of Qualcomm Stadium.

Individual home-game tickets for the 2006 season are available at the Chargers' ticket office, Gate E at the stadium, or by calling Ticketmaster at (619) 220–8497. Prices range from $29 to $72. For information on season tickets, call (877) 242–7437. Season-ticket prices range from $240 to $650.

San Diego State University Aztecs
Qualcomm Stadium, 9449 Friars Road
San Diego
(619) 283–7378
www.goaztecs.com

Many Insiders, but especially SDSU alumni, are just as loyal to the Aztecs football team as they are to the Chargers. Home games commonly draw more than 40,000 fans to the Q (as Qualcomm Stadium is often called) to cheer on the team led by head coach Tom Craft. Prior to the opening of Qualcomm Stadium in 1967, San Diego State played its games in Aztec Bowl, located on campus, or in Balboa Stadium downtown. Neither facility was large enough to hold the masses clamoring for tickets, so the move to Qualcomm was a welcome one.

The Aztecs competed in the Western Athletic Conference until the end of the 1999 season against teams such as UNLV, BYU, Air Force, and Wyoming. After that the Aztecs split off with several other members of the WAC to form a new conference called the Mountain West Conference. Despite their less-than-illustrious performance in this conference, the NFL draft does keep an eye on SDSU.

Tickets to home games range in price from $10 to $32; there are discounts for military, seniors, youths, and students. Tickets are available at Gate G in the stadium or at the SDSU ticket office on campus.

Horses take off at the Del Mar Thoroughbred Club. PHOTO: COURTESY OF DEL MAR THOROUGHBRED CLUB

GOLF

Buick Invitational Golf Tournament
Torrey Pines Golf Course, 11480 North Torrey Pines Road, La Jolla
(858) 570-1234
www.buickinvitational.com

The annual PGA Tour men's tournament makes its way to Torrey Pines every January for a week of special events topped off with the four-day professional competition. Sponsored by the local Century Club, this is the only PGA Tour event held on a municipal course—and a more beautiful one would be hard to find. Beautifully manicured fairways and greens are located on the bluffs above La Jolla, and the views are spectacular. Crowd favorite Tiger Woods took his fourth Buick Invitational Championship in 2006.

Practice rounds are held Monday and Tuesday, a Pro-Am featuring local and national professionals is Wednesday, and the competition runs from Thursday through Sunday. For exact dates of the tournament and to order tickets, call the Century Club at (619) 281-4653, ext. 313, or order online.

HORSE RACING

Del Mar Thoroughbred Club
Del Mar Fairgrounds, 2260 Jimmy Durante Boulevard, Del Mar
(858) 793-5533, (858) 755-1141
www.delmarracing.com

At the races everyone has a unique wagering technique, including betting on the jockey's silks. To learn more sophisticated techniques, attend Del Mar's free handicapping seminars, weekends between 12:30 and 1:15 P.M. For more fun, don't miss "donut days," Saturday mornings in August. For two hours beginning at 8:00 A.M., you can grab a free OJ, donut, and coffee as you watch the thoroughbreds work out.

Driving on Interstate 5 around Del Mar can be downright impossible during horseracing season at the Del Mar track. You'll probably spend more time sitting still than moving. Try to stay off the freeway in midday when fans are rushing to the 2:00 P.M. post timer. Unless you're a horseracing fan, plan to explore Del Mar on Tuesday when the track is closed.

Bing Crosby and his Hollywood buddies envisioned a horse palace by the sea where they could play all day and party all night, and thus was born the Del Mar Thoroughbred Racing Club. Bing was there to greet the first fan through the gate on July 3, 1937, and even now, each racing day begins with a recording of Bing singing "Where the surf meets the turf in old Del Mar." The track is still a favorite of Hollywood celebs, as well as families, singles, and crusty-voiced race-bet veterans. The racing runs from mid-July through early September.

Some of racing's top California-bred horses have set records at Del Mar, including Bertrando and Best Pal. The track's most exciting day ever was in 1996, when the mighty Cigar attempted to break Citation's 16 consecutive wins record, only to be upset by an unheralded horse.

The racing season runs from mid-July to early September. Races are held daily except Tuesday. First post is at 2:00 P.M., except on some Fridays, when first post is at 4:00 P.M. Admission starts at $4.00 and varies with your choice of location, seating, and food service. Senior, military, and AAA discounts are available. You can also have a meal at restaurant tables, well placed in front of season boxes. Special events and jazz concerts (usually on Wednesday) take place at least once a week on the infield after the last race. Parking costs $6.00, $20.00 for valet parking.

HYDROPLANE AND POWERBOAT RACING

Thunderboats Unlimited
Mission Bay Park, San Diego
(619) 225-9160
www.thunderboats.net

Since 1964 Unlimited Hydroplanes and other classes of powerboat racing have been held on Mission Bay. The stars of the spectacle, three-ton monster Unlimited Hydroplanes, bring thrills and chills to spectators with their rooster-tail-spewing power. Also, you'll see Drag Boats, Formula Ones, Super Stocks, Unlimited Lights, and many more boats on the water. East Mission Bay's Bill Muncey Course is named for the sport's all-time greatest star, who was instrumental in bringing Unlimited Hydroplane racing to San Diego.

Nighttime fireworks, demonstrations by Navy SEAL teams, and performances by the Sea World Beach Band entertain spectators between and after races. Kids will love the in-line skating, skateboard demonstrations, and interactive games and rides.

Three racing venues are used during the September event: East Vacation Isle, Fiesta Island, and Crown Point Shores. Your ticket is good for all three locations, and shuttles run continuously between them. Tickets for a three-day pass are $50 in advance and $60 at the gate for adults, $20 for children ages 7 to 12, and free for children age 6 and younger. Single-day adult tickets start at $40. Preferred three-day parking is $40; single-day starts at $15 and varies with the day. Three-day general parking is $40. To order tickets, call (619) 225-9160 or check the Web site.

MOTOCROSS RACING

Carlsbad Raceway
6600 Palomar Airport Road, Carlsbad
(760) 727-1171, (760) 480-8369

This motocross track is home to a series of races for all classes: beginner, novice, intermediate, and expert. Races are scheduled at various times throughout the year, usually in a series of eight races spread over three or four months. Admission is $15. Gates generally open at 10:00 A.M., practice starts at 11:00 A.M. (8:00 A.M. on Sunday), and racing starts later in the day; times vary by event, so call ahead for information about upcoming races. A catering truck is located at the racetrack, or you can bring a lunch with you.

POLO

San Diego Polo Club
14555 El Camino Real, Rancho Santa Fe
(858) 481-9217
www.sandiegopolo.com

For pure primal excitement, nothing compares to the thrill of eight mounted riders thundering downfield in pursuit or defense of a goal. The object of polo is to move a ball through the goal in six periods of play called "chukkers." Each chukker is seven minutes long, and there are no time-outs except for injuries or penalties.

The San Diego Polo Club holds its matches on Sunday from June through September with a summer break in late July. The fall season in October sees play on Wednesday, Saturday, and Sunday. Admission is $5.00.

Pre-match festivities include picnics, tailgating, polo demonstrations, kids' activities, and complete food and beverage service. Spectators have one responsibility—during the intermission between the third and fourth chukkers, fans are asked to make their way to the field and stomp down the divots unearthed by the ponies. It's a great tradition and a chance to meet other polo aficionados, too.

SAND SOFTBALL

Over-the-Line World Championship Tournament
Fiesta Island, Mission Bay, San Diego
(619) 688-0817
www.ombac.org

The Old Mission Beach Athletic Club (OMBAC) consists of a group of friends who organized in 1954, mainly to sponsor beach volleyball. From the beginning OMBAC has been most famous for Over-the-Line, a novel takeoff on softball. Three players per team compete on a rectangular field with a triangle at its tip, pointing toward the batter. The spot where the base of the triangle abuts the rectangle is "the line." The object is for the batter to hit the ball over the line without being fielded by the opposite team. In keeping with OMBAC's philosophy of maximum pleasure with minimum effort, no base running is involved.

If you plan to attend OMBAC's Over-the-Line Tournament, remember the organizers' safety motto: No bowsers (dogs), bottles, or babies.

Now evolved into a major tournament, this annual ritual occurs every second and third weekend in July, and tens of thousands of fans flock to Fiesta Island to watch it. One of the signature characteristics of the tournament is the team names. Entrants are encouraged to be as creative as possible, and the result is a collection of names that are bawdy at best and downright crude at worst. This is not an ideal event for kids, but for people watching, lots of sunshine, and an interesting game, it can't be beat.

Hot dogs and soft drinks are sold at the tournament, but you're welcome to bring your own food and drink. Bottles are not permitted, though there's no ban on booze. The tournament runs from 7:30 A.M. to dusk, and admission is free. Parking on the island isn't permitted during the tournament, but you can catch one of the shuttles that run continuously between Fiesta Island and Mission Bay High School along East Mission Bay Drive or the South Mission Bay route that connects to Belmont Park. (Traffic getting to those spots can still be hairy, so take public transportation if you can.) Be sure to bring a beach chair or towel, a small cooler, a hat, and sunscreen.

TENNIS

Acura Tennis Classic
La Costa Resort and Spa, 2100 Costa Del Mar Road, Carlsbad
(760) 438-5683
www.acuraclassic.org

Every summer the women's professional tennis tour stops in La Costa, in San Diego's North County Coastal region. The tournament attracts top stars and the excitement is nonstop. Held on the grounds of the posh La Costa Resort and Spa, this is professional tennis at its best.

The end of July or the first week in August is the usual time for the tournament, but call the box office at (760) 438-5683 to get the exact dates. Tickets range in price from $20 for practice rounds to $40 for the finals. It's best to purchase your tickets as far in advance as possible, as they usually sell out early. Tickets are available at the box office at La Costa Resort or through Ticketmaster at (619) 220-8497.

COLLEGE AND HIGH SCHOOL SPORTS

San Diego State University's athletic teams are competitive. The school has baseball, basketball, football, golf, swimming, and tennis teams. As befits a sports-craxy town, students can also join water polo, volleyball, and crew teams.

Certain Aztec teams have a loyal local following, especially among the alumni who've never left town. Basketball, football, and baseball are especially popular. Tickets for these sports can be purchased at the Aztec box office at (619) 283-7378 or at goaztecs.cstv.com.

Insiders know that the University of San Diego's Toreros (www.usdtoreros.cstv.com) tend to shine in football, basketball, baseball, volleyball, and soccer. The Tritons of the University of California, San Diego, compete on a national level in a number of sports, and Point Loma Nazarene University has strong athletic teams, too.

Let's not forget our community colleges. Their intercollegiate sports can be every bit as competitive as their four-year counterparts. And for the ultimate sports experience, go to a high school game. With more than 70 county high schools, all of which have sports programs, you're sure to find a game of some kind on just about any day of the week. This is sports in its purest form, and the rivalries between teams are intense. Remember, these youngsters are the superstars of tomorrow. Join the parents, faculty, and boosters at any high school game.

DAY TRIPS

Why leave the San Diego area even for a day trip? That's a good question. We have nearly a never-ending supply of places to see and things to do right here in our amazing county. But folks here do like to visit the desert communities, Disneyland, San Juan Capistrano mission, and Temecula's wine country.

We selected the trips for this chapter using two simple principles: 1) they had to be ones we'd recommend to friends and family, and 2) they had to be doable in one day. Most are worth an overnight stay, if you have time.

We thought about including Los Angeles, but it's really far from doable. It takes a good three hours to drive there from downtown San Diego, and more frustrating hours trying to find your destination in gridlock traffic. That's not the way to spend an enjoyable day. If you want to see Los Angeles, drive up—you'll need a car once you get there since public transportation may not be an efficient way to get around. Spend a couple of nights in a hotel, see the sights, then drive back to San Diego. You'll be thrilled to get back to our comparatively clean air and relatively free-flowing traffic.

You can reach the desert communities of Palm Springs, Rancho Mirage, and Indio in about two hours, so it's possible to go there for the day. Traffic is normally light, compared to that of Orange County and Los Angeles. For fans of minimalism and subtlety, the desert scenery can be inspiring. And you'll be treated to the sight of snow-covered mountains in winter atop Mount San Jacinto and the electricity-generating windmill farm near the Palm Springs exit from Interstate 10. So get a map, gas up the car, and get ready to explore Southern California.

THE DESERTS

Whether you go for the hot display of spring flowers or the hotspots for shopping, eating, golfing, and celebrity-watching in Palm Springs, the desert communities are rewarding day trips. Many Insiders go to the desert cities when it's cool and damp along the coast. Some prefer to visit during the summer, when temperatures soar but there are great deals on tennis, golf, and dining packages.

Anza-Borrego Desert State Park
200 Palm Canyon Drive, Borrego Springs
(760) 767-5311 (the park)
(760) 767-4205 (recorded wildfire report)
www.parks.ca.gov

Every year about 600,000 visitors travel to the park to camp, enjoy desert hikes and walks, and see the spring flowers. (Please see our Annual Events and Parks chapters for more tips.) At the park's visitor center—the best place to start—you'll find information and brochures about the area. The center holds naturalist's talks, fossil programs, garden walks, nature hikes, campfire programs, and activities for "junior" rangers. The visitor center is open daily October through May, 9:00 A.M. to 5:00 P.M. During the hottest months (June through September) the center is

---

i

To check out the wild side of the desert, book a tour with Desert Adventures (760-324-JEEP, 888-440-JEEP, www.red-jeep.com). Bright red four-wheel-drive jeeps take visitors into the Santa Rosa Mountains and the high desert. The guides point out desert plants and creatures, teaching clients about the natural desert setting.

---

open weekends and holidays only. There's overnight camping and other options at the park, too.

The Desert Cities
Palm Springs Desert Resorts Convention and Visitors Authority
70-100 Highway 111, Rancho Mirage
(760) 770-9000, (800) 967-3767
www.palmspringsusa.com

Bureau of Tourism Palm Springs
2901 North Palm Canyon Drive, Palm Springs
(760) 778-8418, (800) 347-7746
www.palm-springs.org

A fashionable resort city, Palm Springs is known worldwide for its celebrity residents, perfect winter temperatures, and endless golf greens. Once considered the playground for the rich and famous, Palm Springs and the adjacent desert communities—including Palm Desert, La Quinta, and Rancho Mirage—have become family vacation destinations. Sure, there are still plenty of celebrities who live here full or part-time and plenty of celebrity sightings at golf tournaments and other events. Golf, tennis, and spa packages abound at the hotels and resorts, and during the winter "snowbirds" flock to the areas from colder climes.

From San Diego you reach the desert towns by traveling north on Interstate 15 to Interstate 215 and connecting with California Highway 60 or I-10. From there take California Highway 111 to Palm Springs. The trip from San Diego is about two and a half hours.

For shopping fun while you're in the area, don't miss a stop on I-10 about 17 miles west of Palm Springs at the **Cabazon Outlet Stores** (909-922-3000; www.cabazonoutlets.com). Here you'll find a rest stop (restrooms and food) blended with outlet shopping that Insiders say is the best in the area.

For special values on accommodations, attractions, and events in the desert communities, call year-round for a **Palm Springs Travel Planner** *brochure from the Palm Springs Visitor and Information Center at (800) 347-7746. There's also information for gay and lesbian travelers and people with mobility problems.*

For mildly adventurous types, photo buffs, and outdoor enthusiasts, the **Palm Springs Aerial Tramway** is a must-do when you're in the desert. Kids love it. Call for hours of operation as they change depending on the season, (760) 325-1391, (888) 515-TRAM, www.pstramway.com. To take the tram, exit I-10 at CA 111 and head toward Palm Springs. Exit again at Tramway Road and follow the signs. The entrance is about 4 miles up the road toward the mountain. Once the admission fee is paid (about $22 for those age 13 and older; about $15 for kids ages 3 to 12), you'll board the tram, which transports passengers 2.5 miles from Valley Station in Chino Canyon (at an altitude of 2,643 feet) to and from Mountain Station (at 8,516 feet) at the east edge of Long Valley. The trip in an enclosed hanging gondola isn't the proper jaunt for those who avoid heights or are uncomfortable in enclosed areas. If you love scenery from a bird's-eye view, this is a spectacular way to see the mountains and the entire Coachella Valley below. On any blistering summer's day, you can leave Palm Springs in 100-degree-plus weather and feel a chill on top of the mountain. At the summit you'll find a restaurant, cafeteria, observation area, picnic spots, museum, gift shop, and snack bar along with walking and hiking trails. Guided nature walks are free.

Once you're back down in the desert, you can take a celebrity-spotters bus tour (760-770-2700; www.celebrity-tours.com) with **Palm Springs Celebrity Tours.** The one-and-a-half to three-and-a-half hour tours start at $25 for adults and $12 for children. (You can call ahead for reservations, and they're recommended during the popular winter season and during the film festivals.)

Also down in the desert, you can shop along trendy **El Paseo,** with stores such as Escada beckoning you inside. Ice-cream parlors, classic coffee shops, and chic dining establishments will satisfy your appetite. Be sure to check out the **Palm Springs Art Museum** (101 Museum Drive, 760-325-7186), which has a gamut of fine art, concerts, and classes. The museum holds events from drama to dance in the Annenburg Theater. Call for dates and performance information; general admission is $12.50.

Golf is a major draw, with more than 100 courses in the greater Palm Springs area. Check out www.palmsprings.com/golf.html for a comprehensive listing of the most popular courses.

Just east of Palm Springs in Palm Desert is the **Living Desert Zoo and Gardens** (47-900 Portola Avenue, 760-346-5694, www.livingdesert.org). Here visitors can take a self-guided tour of the grounds and learn about the more than 400 animals representing 150 different species, such as coyotes, bighorn sheep, birds of prey, and cheetahs. Hours are seasonal, so call ahead. General admission from September 1 through June 15 is $12.00 for adults, and $7.50 for children ages 3 to 12. Summer rates are about 25 percent less expensive.

ORANGE COUNTY

In this section we're giving you a taste of what you'll find in Orange County. You may also contact the Anaheim/Orange County Convention and Visitor Bureau at (714) 765-8888, (888) 598-3200, www.anaheimoc.org.

Remember when driving in Orange County, it's well worth avoiding the freeways during peak commuter times and to find alternative routes if possible. Carry a map, should there be a snag in traffic. Listen to the radio channels that give traffic updates, too.

High school students fill Disneyland and California Adventure on graduation nights. Kids are bused to the park from all across Southern California for parties that last till dawn. It's a safe way to celebrate an important rite of passage, and even the coolest, most jaded teens enjoy the experience. Mother's Day is one of the least visited days at the park.

Disneyland and Disney's California Adventure
1313 South Harbor Boulevard, Anaheim
(714) 781-4565
disneyland.disney.go.com

Space Mountain, Frontierland, and Tomorrowland are just a sample of the fun that's in store at Disneyland. The theme park is as much Southern California as oranges, surfers, and blue-sky days. The park is about 90 miles north of San Diego, and there are signs to get you to Disneyland displayed on Interstate 5 at Katella Avenue in Anaheim.

Insiders and visitors from around the world make this wonderful family tradition part of their vacation plans. It's open every day, with more than 60 major attractions, 50 shops, and 30 restaurants, from sit-down places to snack-food walk-up counters.

The newest addition to the Disney Resort is California Adventure, a stone's throw from the original park. The park is divided into "lands": Golden State, A Bug's Land, Hollywood Pictures Backlot, Paradise Pier, and the Sunshine Plaza. Some of the more popular rides are Grizzly River Run (better experienced during the warm summer months since you will get quite wet on the final plunge) and Soarin' Over California, which uses state-of-the-art technology to combine suspended seats with a spectacular surround-style movie. Riders literally "soar" over California's picturesque sights.

On the major highways leading out of San Diego, there are checkpoints administered by the U.S. Border Patrol. Because the checks can slow traffic, especially if you're heading north into Orange County on I-5 during commuting hours, it pays to add an extra half-hour to any trip.

FASTPASS is an ingenious service allowing visitors to "save" their place in line for some of the more popular rides. With some minimal attention to scheduling, you can drastically reduce your time spent waiting in lines. The attractions that offer the FASTPASS service are listed on the map provided when you enter the park. You simply slide your admission ticket into a FASTPASS machine, and a paper will pop out with the time when you can come back and (usually) walk right on the ride. This service is available at both Disneyland and California Adventure.

Wedged between Disneyland and Disney's California Adventure is a shopping and entertainment complex called Downtown Disney. There is no charge to enter, and with ample parking, it's a good choice for grabbing a bite to eat and relaxing after a day at one of the parks. The AMC Theaters offer love-seat-style stadium seating and surround sound, while the ESPN Zone has two floors and 35,000 square feet of interactive entertainment, dining, and 175 TV monitors broadcasting different sporting events. Downtown Disney has more than a dozen eating establishments offering everything from Voodoo Shrimp (at the House of Blues) to pasta dishes at Catal Restaurant. If the kids are with you, be prepared to be dragged into the LEGO Imagination Center; they will surely want to check out the 23-foot giraffe built entirely of LEGOS, together with the hundreds of LEGO toys and products for sale.

Adult admission to Disneyland and Disney's California Adventure is $59 for each park; children age 3 to 9 pay $49 for each park; online and multiday, multipark packages are available. Park hours vary, so call ahead, but both are open daily, and hours are extended during the summer.

Mission San Juan Capistrano
26801 Ortega Highway, San Juan Capistrano
(949) 234-1300
www.missionsjc.com

Padre Junipero Serra founded this mission in 1776, and every year the swallows migrate to the grounds on or around Saint Joseph's Day, March 19. The swallows are not aware that humans try to clock their arrival and flock to see the birds coming back. Depending on weather conditions throughout the world, the birds may arrive early or late, but visitors come nonetheless.

Padre Serra's Chapel at the mission is the oldest building still in use in the state. For youngsters in the fourth grade who study California history, the trip to the mission is sometimes the most impressive field trip of the year.

On the 10-acre grounds you'll see the Serra Chapel, padres' quarters, the cemetery, and the Great Stone Church. There are often crafts demonstrations and various festivals.

The mission is within walking distance of the Amtrak train station depot in San Juan Capistrano, and many Insiders take the train and a picnic lunch for a day at the mission. If you're driving, exit I-5 at the California Highway 74 exit and drive west, following the signs to the mission. Admission is $6.00 for adults, $5.00 for seniors, and $4.00 for children ages 4 to 11. The mission is open daily from 8:30 A.M. to 5:00 P.M., except for Thanksgiving and Christmas (it closes at noon on Good Friday and Christmas Eve). Within a few blocks of the mission, there are boutiques, cafes, antiques shops, and bookstores.

Medieval Times
7662 Beach Boulevard, Buena Park
(714) 521-4740, (800) 899-6600
www.medievaltimes.com

About 90 miles north of San Diego is the popular Medieval Times. Step back in history to a place where knights, ladies-in-waiting, kings, and jesters exist as if they were really living in the castle showplace. A full-scale exciting show with jousting, falconry, and music accompanies dinner; the audience is encouraged to cheer and jeer as the knights battle. Admission is $48 for adults and $34 for children age 12 and younger and includes a four-course dinner, two-hour show, beverages, and tax.

Radisson Knott's Berry Farm and Knott's Soak City USA
8039 Beach Boulevard, Buena Park
(714) 220-5200
www.knotts.com

Knott's Berry Farm is a fun family theme park that celebrates California and the West. There are six areas: Ghost Town, Indian Trails, Wild Water Wilderness, Fiesta Village, The Boardwalk, and the world-famous Camp Snoopy (home of the Peanuts gang).

Within the park are 30 shops and restaurants. Here you can buy that fabulous Knott's boysenberry jam and lots of old-fashioned treats like salt water taffy, fudge, and peanut brittle. At the not-to-be-missed Mrs. Knott's Chicken Dinner Restaurant you can sample some of that famous delicious fried chicken. Park hours vary, so call or check the Web site before you go. To get to the park, which is about two hours from San Diego, drive north on I-5, then take California Highway 91 west to the Beach Boulevard exit, then head south. Unlimited-use tickets have been reduced: $40 for adults and just $15 for seniors age 60 and older and children ages 3 to 11. Southern California residents pay less for adult admission.

Next door to the amusement park is Knott's Soak City USA, a water-themed park sure to keep the tykes entertained all day. Open daily from late May or early June through Labor Day and weekends only during May and September, it has high-speed slides, inner-tube rides, and tube slides (probably best avoided by those claustrophobic sorts). There is also a large pool where "tidal waves" are generated every 15 minutes. The Sunset River gently floats folks of all ages down a leisurely ride on oversized inner tubes. Admission is $27 for adults and $15 for seniors and children ages 3 to 11.

TEMECULA

Temecula is a favorite day trip. Head north on I-15 past Escondido. You may want to stop along the way at one of the many farmers' stands filled to the brim with fresh vegetables and fruits and pick up plenty of healthy snacks for the day. You'll see these as you exit I-15 at California Highway 76, going either east or west. Just 6 miles farther along the interstate, you'll find the valley of Temecula in Riverside County.

Temecula and Rancho California are fast-growing, family communities. For the day-tripper, the area is a treasure trove of possibilities. Be sure to read this chapter's Close-up about the excellent skateboard park that's located in this sprawling community.

Hot-air balloons fill the sky over Temecula's vineyards. **A Grape Escape Balloon Adventure** (951-699-9987, 800-965-2122, www.agrapeescape.com) offers sunrise flights in hot-air balloons, usually followed by continental breakfast and a winery tour. Balloonists from throughout the Southwest gather every June for the annual **Temecula Valley Balloon & Wine Festival.** The festivities include wine tasting (for an additional charge), live musical entertainment, balloon rides ($150 per person; book in advance at 888-965-2122), balloon glows, a kids' fair, arts and crafts, a food court, and commercial exhibits. Friday nights 5:00 to 10:00 P.M., $15.00 for adults, children age 12 and younger free; Saturday 6:00 A.M. to 10:00 P.M., $22.00 for adults, $5.00 children age 7 to 12; Sunday 6:00 A.M. to 6:00 P.M., $15.00 for adults, $5.00 for children age 7 to 12. For more information, visit www.tvbwf.com.

CLOSE-UP

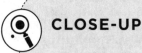

Good Golly Miss Molly—They're Grinding

And they're thrashing and getting some air. Yep, you guessed it. These folks are on skateboards and happily involved in a sport that's growing by the minute.

Once you tell your kids about this day trip to Temecula, just more than 80 miles from downtown San Diego, be prepared to be pestered until you actually make the trek north on I–15. It's worth the drive to see this model skateboard park and perhaps even try your own luck at the sport. You can rent safety equipment when you arrive, so the excuse, "Gee, honey, I don't have a helmet," won't cut it here.

Temecula's skateboard park is located at Rancho California Sports Park (42569 Margarita Road, 951-695-1409, www.ronaldreaganspsportspark.com) and shares space here with ball fields, places for in-line skating, and a roller-hockey rink. It's open to kids of all ages, seven days a week. Weekday hours are 4:00 to 9:30 P.M., Saturday hours are 10:00 A.M. to 9:30 P.M., and on Sunday it's open from 1:00 to 6:30 P.M. Hours are extended in summer and most school holidays.

The park features challenging areas for beginners and special times for anyone who has yet to learn to balance on a skateboard. Those who are really good at the sport will just have to try it to believe the air they get flying off a ramp.

There are bowls, lifts, and jumps to sample, in addition to a fun box and one area that looks like a pyramid with a flat top. A favorite is the Embarcadero steps, a series of cement stairs. Each obstacle holds a thrill for skaters who live and breathe the tricks and maneuvers that sometimes make a parent's heart stop.

Kevin Thatcher, skateboard guru and former editor for the skateboarding magazine *Thrasher,* was one of the park's designers. His patience paid off during the process, and he was impressed when he finally skated the park on its opening day—June 27, 1996. "It's bad, rad, gnarly, and groovy. . . . It should provide a lot of thrills, definitely. It's far and away better than any facility in America," he said modestly.

Why the excitement about an acre that's covered with cement shaped into hills and valleys and vaguely resembling a swimming pool that's been drained? That answer requires more questions, starting with: Is skateboarding illegal in your hometown and on your city's sidewalks? If you've said yes or have seen warning signs prohibiting skaters, you're not alone. But imagine for a minute outlawing baseball? Or soccer? Imagine telling fitness walkers to get off the hiking trails or face a fine?

In the spring of 1993, the city of Temecula heard pleas from skaters and skateboarders who wanted to practice their sport. While some store and business owners screamed that they wanted skating enthusiasts run out of Dodge, other citizens in this progressive area knew the truth: What skateboarders lacked was a safe, well-run venue. It took time and lots of planning, but public opinion and soil were turned. What emerged was the Ronald Reagan Sports Park (originally named the Rancho California Sports Park).

The park has been enormously successful, judging by the skate park's mountainous pile of waivers (each skater must sign one) and by the park's growing reputation. City officials from around the country have toured the facility. Herman D. Parker, deputy director of Temecula's Community Services Department, says, with a good measure of pride, that "there's even been interest in the park from planners in London, England."

Julie Pelletier, Temecula's recreation superintendent, points out one of the unique factors in the park's success: "Many cities have opened parks, but they are not manned. We have a staff of seven." Pelletier also mentions other reasons the skate park is so popular: "A lot of professional skaters live in Southern California." She adds that the park draws not only kids, but lots of adults, too. "It really caters to all ages," she says. Whatever explains it, the park has become a mecca for beginners and pro skaters alike.

And the rules don't drive them away either. Of course there are some—that's to be expected. You must sign a waiver form. Temecula residents with proof of residency must pay an annual $1.00 fee and a $2.00 entrance fee for each session. (A session lasts about two hours.) Nonresidents pay a $5.00 entrance fee. All skaters younger than age 18 must have a parent or guardian sign an information form or waiver to use the facility. Parents of skaters who live in Temecula must visit the park in person to fill out the form. Children younger than age 7 must be accompanied by an adult.

While spectators can't enter the park while skating is occurring, there are plenty of grassy areas. It's fun just to watch and marvel at the skill and balance of those who put on skates or ride skateboards. There's a snack bar outside of the rink, restrooms, an equipment rental service, a tot lot, and plenty of parking. On holiday weekends be prepared to wait for a turn. Only 35 skaters are allowed at a time.

No bicycles, food, or drink are allowed inside the skate park, and any skirmishes between skaters are dealt with promptly. But these disputes rarely happen. And broken bones? There have been a few, but the bad injuries are kept down since all patrons must wear appropriate safety gear (wrist guards, elbow pads, knee pads, and helmet) that is in good condition. Skateboards and skates must be in good condition, too.

The park fulfills the dreams of skaters of all ages. The roller-hockey rink accommodates state-of-the-art league play for more than 2,000 youths per year. That's quite an accomplishment, since only a short time ago these youngsters had nowhere to play but parking lots and public streets. Now rather than practice their sport on the blacktops of malls and public roads, the skaters can enjoy a safe, well-supervised, and challenging place to participate in their sport.

If you're interested in a fine meal or a perfect overnight retreat, check out the **Temecula Creek Inn** (44501 Rainbow Canyon Road, 951-694-1000, 877-517-1823, www.temeculacreekinn.com). The charming hotel set beside a dazzling green golf course has 130 guest rooms, including 10 suites, some with views of the course. The inn's Temet Grill is open daily for breakfast, lunch, and dinner. Dinner entrees include sautéed halibut with white wine sauce, and roasted vegetable ravioli with sautéed spinach, basil pesto, and shaved Parmesan cheese. There is a 27-hole golf course, a swimming pool, a hydro-spa and massages, and a fitness center. It's the perfect romantic getaway.

The **Antiques Shopping District** in Old Town Temecula along Front Street may be as close to heaven as any antiques hunter could imagine without going through the pearly gates—at least that's what some antiques lovers say. In a multiblock area, you'll find more than 40 antiques dealers in historic buildings flanked by wooden sidewalks and old-fashioned benches. The area also has family-style restaurants and specialty food spots.

If you're touring Temecula on a Saturday morning, be sure to linger at the **Farmer's Market** in Old Town Temecula. Along with fresh produce from nearby farms, vendors display gorgeous arrangements of fresh flowers and locally made arts and crafts.

TEMECULA WINE COUNTRY

Temecula Valley Winegrower's Association
(951) 699-6586, (800) 801-9463
www.temeculawines.org

This is Southern California's largest wine-producing area, and within the valley of Temecula you can visit more than 18 wineries, each offering samples of their wares.

According to the vintners, this is perfect wine country because of the combination of geography, microclimate, and well-drained soil. The 1,100-foot elevation and cool summer nights add to the grape-growing and wine-making magic.

The wineries range in size from one that produces about 1,000 cases a year to large-scale wineries with production exceeding 100,000 cases each year.

Avoid the worry of driving after sampling a few too many wines by hopping on the Grapeline Wine Country Shuttle, which runs on weekends. Call (951) 693-5755 or (888) 8-WINERY or check out www.gogrape.com for schedule and fares.

For more information on the area, contact the Temecula Valley Chamber of Commerce, (951) 676-5090, www.temecula.org.

The following are just a taste of the many fine wineries you'll discover in Temecula.

Baily Vineyard & Winery
33440 La Serena Way, Temecula
(951) 676-9463
www.bailywinery.com

This vineyard and winery produces award-winning wines available primarily at the tasting room. Open daily 11:00 A.M. to 5:00 P.M., there's a restaurant, picnic area, gift shop, and special events. Baily Vineyard & Winery is known for its Chardonnay, Muscot Canelli, and Riesling.

Hart Winery
41300 Avenida Biona, Temecula
(951) 676-6300

This winery specializes in handcrafted, barrel-aged red wines and dry, full-bodied white varieties. Tasting is available daily from 9:00 A.M. until 4:30 P.M. There's a cost of $2.00 per person, and it includes a winery logo glass you can take home. Hart Winery, according to in-the-know Insiders, does an excellent Fumé Blanc, and the Barbera and Merlot are outstanding.

Thornton Winery
32575 Rancho California Road, Temecula
(951) 699-0099
www.thorntonwine.com

Thornton's award-winning Methode Champenoise sparkling wine is Southern California's version of the more famous wine from France's Champagne region. Buy a few bottles for special occasions. The Café Champagne is open daily, serving Mediterranean-influenced cuisine in the courtyard. Jazz concerts are held here on summer evenings. Open daily 10:00 A.M. to 5:00 P.M. Winery tours are available on weekends only.

Van Roekel Vineyards & Winery
34567 Rancho California Road, Temecula
(951) 699-6961

This vineyard and winery has developed premium wines. Tasting is daily from 10:00 A.M. to 5:00 P.M. There's a picnic area and a shop that sells gourmet cheeses, deli items, and a wide selection of wine-related gifts. You'll want to taste and, of course, bring home Van Roekel's Chardonnay and award-winning Grenache.

SOUTH OF THE BORDER

¡Bienvenido a Mexico! Most visitors to San Diego (and most locals, too) sooner or later end up south of the border. Even though they are warned that Tijuana hardly represents the "real" Mexico, the idea of visiting a foreign culture proves a powerful lure. Added to that lure is the fact that the U.S.-Mexico border is only a 20-minute drive from downtown San Diego, which makes for an easy day trip or after-dark excursion. Many Insiders make regular forays to Tijuana for an evening on the town. Fine dining is abundant, and Tijuana has several nightclubs that are popular among revelers of all generations, but especially the young.

Beyond the border city of Tijuana lie the resort towns of Rosarito Beach and Ensenada. Either can be visited as a long day trip, or relax a little, visit both, and spend the weekend. With much smaller populations (Tijuana is Mexico's fourth-largest city) and decidedly less congestion and crime, Rosarito and Ensenada are worth the extra effort to get to. An isolated yet popular getaway for Hollywood stars during the '30s and '40s, Rosarito Beach has grown from a tiny enclave and suburb of Tijuana to a strip of restaurants, hotels, and shops fronted by a seemingly endless stretch of beach. A real city of some 370,000 people—dating from the Spanish colonial days—Ensenada itself is more attractive than Rosarito. Although bathing or surfing beaches there are found only north or south of town, several successful fishing fleets are based at the town's bustling port.

Between Tijuana and Ensenada are some favorite stops. One is Puerto Nuevo, once a collection of humble if compelling lobster shacks, which in recent years has evolved into a more formal enclave of restaurants and shops. If many of the spruced-up venues now accept credit cards, and a few savvy entrepeneurs have opened hotels in the vicinity, the menu hasn't changed at all: It still consists of boiled and broiled lobster, refried beans, rice, and baskets of hot tortillas. A few miles north of Puerto Nuevo is Foxploration (Free Road to Ensenada Km 32.8, Popotla, 011-52-661-614-9444, or toll-free from the United States 866-369-2252; www.foxploration.com). Emerging from the set of the major motion picture *Titanic,* filmed in 1997, the theme park has a film set, wardrobe room, and other areas that show how films get made. On-site are artifacts from *Pearl Harbor; Master and Commander: The Far Side of the World;* and *The Weight of Water,* also filmed here. There's also an outdoor stage, food court, and shopping arcade. Closed Mondays and Tuesdays. Admission is $12.00 for adults and $9.00 for children ages 3 to 11.

Golfers head for Bajamar, the posh resort overlooking the sea between Tijuana and Ensenada, or Real Del Mar, just a few miles south of the border. The golfing and facilities are good at both courses.

Tijuana is the city that draws the most visitors, though, and there's no shortage of attractions. Shopping, dining, and cultural performances and exhibits all await the intrepid explorer. We'll introduce you to the highlights in this chapter and give you lots of tips for planning your trip and finding things to do once you get there. Most places south of the border accept American dollars and major credit cards in addition to the Mexican peso. If credit cards are not accepted at an establishment, we've made a note of it.

GETTING THERE AND GETTING BACK

The border crossing at San Ysidro (at the southern end of Interstate 5) is open 24 hours; the Otay Mesa crossing at the eastern end of Interstate 905 is also open daily 24 hours. Travelers crossing the border into Mexico are usually waved through with few, if any, questions. When you return to the United States whether walking or driving, you must stop for inspection by U.S. Customs and Immigration officials. Usually you will be asked a few questions, like your place of birth, where you've traveled, and what you're bringing back with you, but occasionally drivers will be asked to stop for a secondary inspection. It's a fairly rare occurrence and only happens if customs inspectors suspect you might have exceeded your permissible duty-free articles or are attempting to smuggle contraband. Carry your driver's license, your passport (required if you are not a U.S. citizen and of U.S. citizens beginning in 2007), or certified copy of your birth certificate to pass through U.S. customs most efficiently.

Driving

If your idea of a trip into Mexico is a leisurely expedition, stopping here and there without a set agenda or time schedule, then you should drive. A word of caution, however. Driving in Tijuana is not for the weak of heart. Traffic is usually heavy, street signs and directions are often in short supply and are in Spanish, and the driving habits of exuberant locals may be disconcerting to first-time tourists. Tijuana is also chock-full of traffic circles. Getting stuck in one can be frustrating and disorienting. Just remember to bear right and follow the counterclockwise flow of traffic; if possible, it's best to keep moving. Also, watch for one-way street signs, which are numerous. If you're used to driving in large foreign cities such as Rome or Paris, Tijuana will be a piece of cake. If the prospect sounds a little intimidating, you might be better off taking taxis or signing on with a tour group.

If you drive south of Tijuana, you'll soon encounter a toll road. The fares total around $7.20 from Tijuana to Ensenada; you can pay in U.S. currency or Mexican pesos.

Should you decide to drive, take I-5 south to the San Ysidro border crossing. From Interstate 805, drive south to I-905, and go east to the Otay Mesa border crossing. The San Ysidro crossing is recommended for easiest access to downtown Tijuana; Otay Mesa is generally used for access to Tijuana's international airport. Once across the border and into the downtown Tijuana area, you'll find plenty of pay lots (recommended) and on-street parking. Most shopping centers offer free parking. You can also drive all the way to the border, park in one of several security-guarded lots, and walk across. The fee averages around $3.00 for half an hour, but tops out between $6.00 and $10.00 for 24 hours.

If you're driving a rental car, be sure to check with the rental agency to see if they allow their cars to be driven across the border. Of the larger rental agencies, Avis and Enterprise do allow travel into Mexico. But policies change, so be sure to check ahead of time.

INSURANCE

This is important. Be sure to purchase Mexican auto insurance before you cross the border. Mexican authorities recognize insurance policies issued only by companies licensed to transact insurance sales in Mexico. If you're involved in a traffic accident while in Mexico, a Mexican insurance policy will pave the road to resolution. The laws are different in Mexico, where you're presumed guilty until proven innocent. If it's determined that you are at fault and you don't have a Mexican policy, you will be expected to pay for the damages on

If you see a traffic sign that has a big E with a slash through it, that means "no parking."

the spot. If you can't, you'll be taken to jail. In any case, you might end up in jail while the whole thing is sorted out, even if you are not at fault. Having Mexican auto insurance will prevent this from happening. To purchase insurance (and to drive in Mexico) you'll need your valid driver's license and current vehicle registration.

Mexican insurance policies are available through the Auto Club of Southern California and from a number of companies that have set up shop near the border; their signs are clearly visible when you take the last U.S. exit off I-5. Several companies will sell you a daily or yearly policy by phone, including Sanborns (16264 East Whittier Boulevard, Whittier, CA 90603; 562-943-7174; www.sanborninsurance.com).

Alternative Transportation

Public transportation is a highly recommended method for a trip across the border. The San Diego Trolley Blue Line goes all the way to the San Ysidro border crossing, then you can walk across the border and catch a taxi for the short drive into town. Or you can join the crowd of people who enjoy walking into town, an easy stroll of less than a mile. A typical taxi fare from the border or for a drive within town runs about $5.00 to $7.00. You might be able to negotiate a lower fare, but be sure to establish what the fare will be before you take off.

Greyhound Bus Line (120 West Broadway, 619-239-6737, 800-231-2222) also has frequent service from downtown San Diego to its station in downtown Tijuana. Bus transportation to Tijuana airport or to attractions anywhere between Tijuana and Ensenada can be arranged through **Five Star Tours** (1050 Kettner Boulevard, San Diego; 619- 232-5040; www.efivestar-tours.com). From the last U.S. trolley stop or from the Border Station Parking & Visitor Information Center (next to San Diego Factory Outlet Center) at the last U.S. exit off I-5, big red **Mexicoach** buses charge $3.00 per person each way to deliver passengers to the other side of the border; $6.00 to Rosarito Beach (one-way). They run every 15 to 20 minutes daily between 8:00 A.M. and 9:00 P.M. To catch a ride back to the United States, go to the Terminal Turistico Tijuana, Avenida (Revolución 1025, between Sixth and Seventh Streets, (664) 685-1470.

One of the easiest ways to navigate Tijuana and regions beyond is by joining a tour group. You can sign up for half-day, full-day, or even overnight tours to Tijuana and beyond, and leave the worries of driving to the tour company. Here are three companies that offer south-of-the-border tour packages.

Baja California Tours
7734 Herschel Avenue, Suite O, La Jolla
(858) 454-7166, (800) 336-5454
www.bajaspecials.com
Excellent tours to Tijuana, Rosarito, and Ensenada are offered by this experienced company. Specialty tours—including visits to artists' studios, wineries, and lobster restaurants—are available, and the guides are bilingual and well informed. The day tours cost $31 for Tijuana, $40 for Rosarito, and $65 for Ensenada.

Five Star Tours
1050 Kettner Boulevard, San Diego
(619) 232-5051, (800) 553-8687
www.fivestartours.com
This San Diego-based tour company offers a variety of trips south of the border. On Sunday there's a seven-hour trip with sightseeing in Rosarito and Tijuana and a lobster lunch at Puerto Nuevo ($69; $35 for kids), just south of Rosarito. Or take a winery tour to the Guadalupe Val-

ley with lunch in Ensenada ($75), which departs San Diego on Saturday. They also offer singles' ($59) and other specialty tours.

San Diego Scenic Tours
2255 Garnet Avenue, Suite 3, San Diego
(858) 273-8687
www.sandiegoscenictours.com
Tour guides have been entertaining folks since 1993 with the history and culture of Tijuana. Once in T.J., you're on your own for shopping, taking in the sights along Avenida Revolución, the city's main shopping street, having lunch at one of many fine restaurants in the area, or simply sit, and enjoy mariachi music while sipping a frosty margarita. Food and drink are not included in the tour price. Both full- and half-day tours are available, with prices starting at $30 for adults and $15 for children ages 3 to 11.

More Travel Tips

Citizens of the United States and Canada do not need tourist cards if traveling within 100 miles of the U.S. border. However, if the length of your stay exceeds 72 hours or you plan to journey beyond Ensenada, a tourist card for each traveler is required. Tourist cards can be obtained in the United States from Mexican consulates or Mexican tourism offices, the Auto Club of Southern California, and most travel agents. Travelers must fill in the necessary information and have either a valid passport or a certified birth certificate. It's always a good idea to keep identification and proof of citizenship with you while traveling in Mexico (driver's license, military ID, passport, or birth certificate). Residents of countries other than the United States or Mexico must have passports to return to the United States.

English is spoken most everywhere in Tijuana, but knowing a few Spanish words can be helpful, especially *por favor* (please) and *gracias* (thank you). Don't be afraid to try a few words from your Spanish-English dictionary. You'll endear yourself to the locals. And remember that a smile is the universal language.

Most of the tourist-oriented shops, hotels, and restaurants accept U.S. dollars, Mexican pesos, and credit cards; some don't accept traveler's cheques. Returning U.S. citizens are allowed up to $400 worth of merchandise for personal use once in every 30-day period. You also are allowed one liter of alcoholic beverages and a carton of cigarettes. Keep in mind that most fruit and vegetables are not allowed to cross into the United States.

Now let's clear up some common misconceptions. Yes, Tijuana is a great place to buy fireworks. No, you may not bring them back into the United States. If you are caught, they will be confiscated, and you may be subject to a hefty fine. U.S. Customs also prohibits transporting guns, ammo, knives, and other weapons across the border.

You've probably also heard about the great deals you can get on prescription medications in Tijuana. You *must* have a valid prescription from a U.S. doctor to legally bring medications back across the border, although many people buy and bring back prescription medications without one.

Ready, Set, Go

Now that we've gotten all the caveats out of the way, get ready for a one-of-a-kind experience. Granted, Mexico is not for everyone. Close as it is to San Diego, it's a different country, with its own customs and laws and different food and language. But open-minded individuals will surely enjoy the experience and most likely return with a precious trinket, a great story, or some other interesting experience to share.

And don't forget to have a margarita for us. Lift your glass and say *"¡Salud!"* and *"¡Viva México!"*

ACCOMMODATIONS

Should you decide to stay for a spell, several nice hotels and resorts are available. Keep in mind that the amenities may not be what you're accustomed to back home, but in all the hotels we recommend, you should be quite comfortable.

PRICE CODE

The price code indicates the cost of accommodations for two for one night excluding tax. Prices are based on summer rates, which may be 15 to 25 percent lower during the winter at Rosarito and Ensenada's resort hotels. Geared to business travelers, Tijuana's rates do not typically drop during the winter.

$	**$50 to $100**
$$	**$101 to $150**
$$$	**$151 to $200**

Tijuana

Hotel Lucerna **$$-$$$**
10902 Paseo de los Héroes, Tijuana
(800) 582-3762
011-52 (664) 633-3900
www.lucerna.com
Authentic Mexican atmosphere combines with modern amenities to make the Hotel Lucerna an Insiders' choice. It has 168 rooms and 8 suites and features a sunken lobby, an open-air cafe, and a courtyard garden. The hotel's swimming pool is in the midst of the garden and is surrounded by palm trees. In addition to the cafe, there's a restaurant, a cocktail lounge, and a nightclub. Rooms have double, queen-, or king-size beds, cable television, and fully appointed baths. The more expensive rooms have a courtyard view. This hotel is geared toward businesspeople, and rates therefore are reduced on weekends.

The U.S. Consulate is located on Calle Tapachula 96 near the Agua Caliente Racetrack. The telephone number is 011-52 (664) 622-7400.

Rosarito

Las Rocas Hotel **$$**
Km 38.5, Old Ensenada Highway
(888) 527-7622, 011-52 (661) 614-9872
www.lasrocas.com
The best reason to visit this small resort south of Rosarito is the full-service spa. A variety of massages, facials, wraps, and other treatments is available. The pool area is fabulous as well. Many of the rooms have fireplaces and large living-room areas, though the furnishings are outdated and maintenance is not always up to U.S. standards. The basic, least expensive rooms are in the worst condition; suites are better. Especially enjoyable are the whirlpool baths in private rooms with wall-to-ceiling windows facing the sea. The restaurant serves adequate food, and the hotel is within easy driving distance of Rosarito, Puerto Nuevo, and Ensenada.

Rosarito Beach Hotel & Spa **$$-$$$**
Boulevard Benito Juárez 31, Rosarito
(800) 343-8582, 011-52 (661) 612-0144
www.rosaritobeachhotel.com
Made famous in the '20s and '30s by legions of Hollywood stars escaping the constraints of Prohibition, the resort has expanded and become more plebeian, but the lobby retains much of its original charm. Resting on its laurels, the staff can be perfunctory and downright curt, if not rude. Most of the 280 overpriced rooms and suites have been renovated over the years but still vary greatly in comfort and decor. Some are quite small; those facing the playground and pool are noisy. Rooms and two-bedroom suites are available in beachfront lowrises or in the tower. The upper floor ocean-view rooms are the most expensive.

The hotel sits on Rosarito's long,

coarse, creamy-sand beach; there are also two pools, one with a slide and shallow pool that caters to kids. Singles barhop among the three watering holes or relax in one of the three Jacuzzis. Play tennis or racquetball, billiards, or Ping-Pong. In a '30s mansion next door is the Casa de Playa Spa. It's a full-service European-style spa that offers massages, herbal wraps, saunas, and hot tubs. Chaberts, specializing in both steaks and French cuisine, is a dignified, stately restaurant where chandeliers, plush Middle Eastern carpets, massive oil paintings, and lovely table linens will make you want to don your finest apparel. Much more casual, and with good food, is the hotel's Acteza bar-restaurant. Room rates are less expensive on weekdays, and specials are often available.

Ensenada

Estero Beach Resort Hotel **$-$$**
On Highway 1, 6 miles south of Ensenada
011-52 (646) 176-6235, (646) 176-6230
www.hotelesterobeach.com

This is truly an Insiders' favorite. Tennis, horseback riding, and boating are just some of the activities to occupy your time while at Estero Beach. Located on a long estuary (for which it's named), the resort has a playground and large pool for the amusement of children and adults. A 15-minute drive from the shops and restaurants of Ensenada, this is a good bet for those who like enjoying the beach and hotel amenities.

The resort has a variety of cottages and suites, most with ocean view. The cottages with kitchenettes and patios are popular, as is the RV Park for big rigs and smaller campers. La Terraza restaurant serves pizza and sushi as well as the usual soups, salads, seafood, and steak.

Posada El Rey Sol **$-$$**
Avenida Blancarte 130, Ensenada
011-52 (646) 178-1601

Right in downtown Ensenada, El Rey Sol ("the Sun King") has comfortable if not flashy rooms with good beds, direct-dial phones, data ports, and hair dryers as well as other perks like inexpensive Internet access and free local phone calls. There's a spa and small exercise facility; the elegant French Restaurant of the same name, around the corner, is reviewed later in this chapter.

ATTRACTIONS

People often forget that Tijuana is a major city, and as such it has developed a number of worthy attractions over the years. When you've had your fill of shopping and dining, check out some of the attractions that are unique to Mexico or at least uncommon elsewhere.

El Toreo de Tijuana
Bulevar Agua Caliente at Bulevar Cuauhtémoc, Tijuana
Plaza Monumental
Playas de Tijuana, Tijuana
(619) 232-5049 (San Diego)
011-52 (664) 686-1510
www.toreodetijuana.com

If the ancient sport of bullfighting intrigues you, two bullrings in Tijuana present some of the world's top matadors. Dating from 2000 B.C., bullfighting is a combination of ritual and mortal combat, pitting man against beast in a deadly battle in which the humans enjoy better than 100 to 1 odds.

Bullfights are held between May and the end of September, but not every Sunday. Tickets are available in San Diego through Five Star Tours (Santa Fe Train Depot, 1050 Kettner Boulevard, 619-232-5049, www.fivestartours.com), which is by far the easiest way to arrange the excursion. Five Star adds a $5.00 service charge to the price of the ticket and also offers bus transportation to the event at $20.00 per person round-trip. Bullfight ticket prices vary based on the fame of matador and other factors, but generally cost from $12.00 for general admission (nosebleed seats in the sun) to around $50.00 (including the $5.00 service charge if booked in San Diego) for good reserved seats. Go earlier in the day for shopping or lunch; Five Star then provides transportation to the bullfight around 2:45 P.M. Box seats for up to four people are situated at ground level for up-close viewing of this deadly spectacle.

L.A. Cetto Winery
Cañón Johnson 2108 and Avenida Constitución
011-52 (664) 685-3031

An interesting outing just a short walk from downtown is a tour and tasting at the L.A. Cetto winery. Here you can sample (and purchase) sparkling and sweet wines, red and white, as well as brandy and tequila. The shop has accoutrements for the wine lover, including glasses with the winery's logo in gold. Individuals can tour without an appointment (though we suggest calling ahead); groups of 10 or more should call for an appointment. Tastings cost $2.00 for four samples, but you can taste more! Choose the vintages that most interest you, or let your guide introduce you to something new. Hours are Monday through Friday 10:00 A.M. to 5:30 P.M., Saturday 10:00 A.M. to 4:00 P.M.

Tijuana Cultural Center
Paseo de los Héroes and Avenida Independencia, Tijuana
011-52 (664) 687-9600
www.cecut.gob.mx/

For a little bit of Mexican history and culture, stop in at this modern complex. The museum (closed Monday, $2.00) features archaeological, historical, and craft displays, all labeled in English as well as Spanish. Other salons have changing exhibits, and an OMNIMAX theater (open daily, $4.50) has films in both Spanish and English. The 1,000-seat performing arts theater offers a variety of musical and dramatic performances.

Wax Museum
Calle 1 near Avenida Revolución, Tijuana
011-52 (664) 688-2478

Some travelers cannot visit a new city without seeking out the local wax museum, and the one in Tijuana is worth a look-see, if typically weird and even a bit scary for children. Mixed in with the standard representatives of Hollywood (Marilyn Monroe, Madonna) are figures from Mexican history such as Emiliano Zapata and Benito Juárez. International historical standouts are featured, too. You can get nose to nose with the likes of Mahatma Gandhi and Mikhail Gorbachev. Hours are from 10:00 A.M. to 6:00 P.M. daily. Admission is $1.60; free for children younger than age 6.

FISHING

In the border zone, Ensenada is the hot spot. At **Sergio's Sportfishing Center** (Sportfishing Pier, Boulevard Costero, 011-52-646-178-2185, http://sergios-sportfishing.com) you can sign up for a variety of fishing expeditions, including day trips and extended-trip charters. Prices begin at $55.

For longer trips, **Fisherman's Landing** (2838 Garrison Street, San Diego; 619-221-8500, www.fishermanslanding.com) offers everything from overnight party boats to the Coronado Islands ($110 for bait, bunk, and fishing permit) to 20-day-long trips to the Outer Banks. Longer trips are on vessels large enough to provide a good level of comfort for die-hard seekers of that trophy fish. The cost of such trips vary widely, beginning at $450 for a two-day adventure. Many varieties of fish inhabit the waters on both sides of the Baja peninsula; you're likely to hook tuna, halibut, sea bass, yellowtail, and mahimahi.

GOLF

Two full-scale golf resorts draw golfers from both sides of the border. Both have courses with unusual challenges, and both have fine hotels and restaurants.

Bajamar Ocean Front Golf Resort
Km-77.5, Ensenada Toll Road
(888) 311-6076, 011-52 (646) 155-0151
www.golfbajamar.com

Between Rosarito Beach and Ensenada is this Insider's favorite golf resort. It's about a 50-minute drive from the border, and golfers often stay for a day or two to take full advantage of the modified links-style courses. Three 9-hole courses combine to provide different challenges. The par 71 Lagos to Vista Course is 6,968 yards with a 74.9 rating and a 143 slope.

The rugged Baja California coastline provides an incomparable setting, and you'll undoubtedly see a few lizards sprinting through the fragrant desert sage. It's a tough course, and the brutal rough tends to swallow balls. Bring lots of them—one Insider lost 20 in one round. Hole number 11, a par 4, 500-yarder, has a waterfall and a large lake sheltering a green that doesn't seem to have any flat spots. Most golfers feel that a par on this hole is as big an achievement as a hole in one.

Bajamar has a putting green and a driving range. Both men's and women's locker rooms are huge and nicely outfitted. The clubhouse has a pro shop, a restaurant, and a bar in an observation tower with a 360-degree view. A luxury hotel and condos make up the balance of the resort, and special golf/accommodations packages and villa rentals are available. Greens fees include a mandatory cart and are $69 Monday through Thursday, $89 Friday, Saturday, and holidays, and $79 on Sunday. Reduced rates are offered for late afternoon play. Room rates start at $119 on weekdays, $145 on weekends.

Real Del Mar Golf Resort
Km-19.5, Ensenada Toll Road
(664) 631-3670, (800) 803-6038
www.realdelmar.com.mx

Just 12 miles beyond the border crossing, Real Del Mar is another outstanding resort and golf course down south. Like Bajamar, Real Del Mar overlooks the ocean and is a challenging course, with 5 lakes and 50 bunkers. Its looks are deceptive; it seems benign, but the course will reach out and bite you when you least expect it. Its fairways are narrow, and some of the greens are elevated on pedestals. If you miss one, you've got your work cut out for you. The par 3 18th consists of an immaculately appointed tee box and a beautiful green—and nothin' but agua in between. Making par on this one is cause for a post-round celebration.

Facilities include a putting green and driving range, luxury clubhouse with men's and women's locker rooms, sauna, and gym. Should you decide to stay for a few days, the on-site hotel offers a complete European-style spa, tennis courts, swimming pool, and Jacuzzi. Room prices begin at $119. Packages are available. The par 72 course is 6,403 yards of manicured fairways and greens, with a rating of 70.5/131 slope. Greens fees are $59 Monday through Thursday ($35 after 2:00 P.M.) and $79 ($40 twilight) Friday, Saturday, Sunday, and holidays.

NIGHTLIFE

Locals south of the border love their nightlife. So do the hordes of Americans who regularly cross the border just for a taste of something different. You'll find everything from rock bands to traditional Mexican mariachi music. Cover charge, if any, varies according to the day of the week, time, and if there's live entertainment. The drinking age in the border zone is 18. Remember that it's against the law to drink alcoholic beverages on public streets.

Tijuana

Catercorner from the Cultural Center, **Plaza Fiesta** (Avenida Paseo de los Heroes and Independencia, no phone) offers a range of musical styles from

For more information on Baja cities, contact: Baja California Tourism, (800) 962-2252, www.discoverbajacalifornia.com; Tijuana, (888) 775-2417, www.seetijuana.com, tijuana.com, and tijuanaonline.org; Rosarito, (800) 962-2252, www.rosarito.org; Ensenada, (800) 310-9687, www.enjoyensenada.com.

Cuban to jazz at a variety of clubs, which are sandwiched between equally popular restaurants.

Señor Frog
Pueblo Amigo, Via Oriente 60
011-52 (664) 682-4962
Above this superpopular restaurant is a happening bar, where roving waiters speak perfectly inflected English and DJs often broadcast from the dance floor. It's loud and open and seems to be equally popular with young Americans cruising for fun, Mexican couples on first dates, and groups of friends relaxing after work. Drinks are expensive and not particularly fine; you're paying for the ambience. Drink in the restaurant downstairs for a more relaxed but still lively evening.

Rosarito

Papas & Beer
Avenida Eucalipto and Avenida Mar Adriático
011-52 (661) 612-0444
Open daily from 11:00 A.M. to 3:00 A.M., and longer when there's serious partying to be done, this 47,000-square-foot venue is right on the sand and open to the stars. There are many different areas, from the ocean-view "lounge" to the underground "womb," where a Gothic mood prevails. Geared toward young people, it is an amazing site that most anyone can enjoy—at least for one quick drink.

Ensenada

Hussong's Cantina
113 Avenida Ruiz, Ensenada
011-52 (646) 178-3210
You cannot go to Ensenada without stopping in at the legendary Hussong's. It has been an institution in the seaside town since 1892, and even though its hype is bigger than its reality, it's still a great party bar. If you want a table, be sure to arrive by early afternoon, and be prepared to dodge a raucous crowd. It's fairly tranquil in the afternoon and early evening, but as the night heats up, both mariachi and ranchera music are played nonstop.

RESTAURANTS

Dining south of the border offers many pleasant surprises. Of course, it's easy to find eateries that offer the familiar combo plates of enchiladas, tacos, and burritos. Beyond that, we'll show you where to find traditional treats from all regions of Mexico, as well as some cosmopolitan venues offering both Mexican and international fare. You'll also be happy to find that a full gourmet meal can be enjoyed for a price that might bring you an appetizer and a cocktail in the States. Toss caution to the wind, and try something new and unusual.

PRICE CODE

Prices given indicate the cost of dinner entrees for two, excluding beverages, tax, and tip.

$	**Less than $15**
$$	**$16 to $25**
$$$	**$26 to $35**

Tijuana

El Potrero **$-$$**
Boulevard Salinas 4700 at Boulevard Agua Caliente, Tijuana
(664) 681-8082

Stained-glass windows with Mexican scenes entertain diners in this casual eatery with superb food. The menu describes each dish in detail, which is great because these are not the tacos and enchiladas foreigners are most accustomed to. In addition to steaks prepared in various styles and served with a baked potato, there are wonderful hearty soups, a variety of salads, and a wide range of appetizers. Mexican businesspeople come for power breakfasts, but it's great any time of day.

Rosarito Beach

Ortega's **$**
Boulevard Benito Juarez 200, Rosarito Beach
No phone

Open daily 8:00 A.M. to 10:00 P.M., Ortega's, at the north end of town, is most popular for the endless and delicious buffet. Try such Mexican specialties as *menudo* (tripe soup), cow's tongue in red sauce or grilled cactus pads, or more mainstream potato croquettes, quesadillas (tortillas grilled with cheese), pork chops, bacon, and other chicken and meat cuts and dishes. (Labels telling what's what would be helpful.) There's an omelet station and salad bar, candied fruit, typical breads and pastries, and plenty of desserts. You can order a la carte until 4:00 P.M. It's equally popular with local families, businesspeople, and tourists. No credit cards accepted.

Ensenada

El Rey Sol **$$–$$$**
1000 Avenida López Mateos at Calle Blancarte, Ensenada
011-52 (646) 178-1733, (888) 311-6871, ext. 100
www.elreysol.com

This family-run restaurant opened in 1947. The dining room is decorated in old European style, with stained-glass windows, massive drapes, and heavy oak furniture.

Originally serving French food and still excelling in French pastries, crepes, and other elaborate desserts and homemade breads, the restaurant also serves modern international dishes and outstanding Mexican plates. Breakfast, lunch, and dinner are served daily. Outside is a charming sidewalk cafe, and there's a coffee bar at the front of the restaurant.

SHOPPING

Shopping is the sport of choice for most visitors who cross the border. Shopping for Mexican arts and crafts, curios, and souvenirs in downtown Tijuana, Rosarito, and Ensenada is just plain fun. You'll find some unique objects from the heartland of Mexico as well as striped blankets; leather jackets, wallets, and purses; silver jewelry by the ton; and designer knockoffs. Vendors in shopping arcades and markets expect you to bargain, so sharpen up your negotiating skills and wrangle yourself a good deal. One does not normally negotiate the retail price in shopping malls and shops, but many folks are able to score discounts when purchasing several items or paying cash rather than using a credit card.

Most stores, both in the shopping centers and downtown areas, are open from 10:00 A.M. to 9:00 P.M. daily.

Tijuana

Avenida Revolución
Between Calles 1 and 8, downtown Tijuana

This is the oldest tourist shopping street in Tijuana and is usually a first stop for visitors. Both sides of the street are lined with shopping arcades, curio shops, and apparel stores. The street is crowded with bars and eateries in addition to shops and revelers of all ages.

Don't neglect the streets bisecting Avenida Revolución; you'll find more shops selling Mexican arts and crafts, home furnishings, and clothing.

Avenida Revolución can be reached on foot by following the pedestrian walkway starting just beyond the border crossing and leading straight to the downtown shopping area, where Revolución is the main street. It's a mile-long walk, and it's very common to see folks walking from the border rather than driving or taking public transportation.

Plaza Río Tijuana
Paseo de los Héroes 96, between Avenidas Cuauhtémoc and Independencia, Zona Río, Tijuana
011-52 (664) 684-0402
This is a shopping center located within the Río Tijuana area, near several nice hotels and the cultural center. Several major Mexican department stores anchor the center, and you'll find lots of specialty stores, informal restaurants, and a multiplex movie theater.

Rosarito

Rosarito's shopping is found along one street—Benito Juárez—which is the main street through town. Look for home accessories, rustic wood furnishings, wrought-iron and unglazed red clay pots, as well as handicrafts from throughout Mexico.

If you're looking for fine art, sculpture, and innovative jewelry, peruse the work of a myriad of artisans at **Galería Giorgio Santini** (Carretera 1, Free Road to Ensenada, Km 40; 661-614-1459). In April 2006 the original space was expanded to include a deli and tequila-, mezcal-, and wine-tasting room in addition to new galleries featuring fine art, specialty tiles, and the glasswork of L.A. artist Jorge Luna. Cooking classes and other events will also be held at the complex. Closed Wednesday, this gallery is located near Foxploration, just south of Rosarito.

Ensenada

Seventy-five miles south of the border you'll find yet another kind of shopping experience. Ensenada is a pretty port city with several classy boutiques hidden among the souvenir stands and shops selling T-shirts and silver jewelry. Though more diverse than Rosarito, most of Ensenada's shopping is along the main street—Boulevard López Mateos—and it's just a block from the waterfront. One of the town's nicest shops is located here: two-story **Bazár Casa Ramírez** (Calle López Mateos 496, 646-178-8209), which offers a wonderful collection of arty bric-a-brac as well as mirrors and larger items on the second floor.

Guadalupe (Avenida Lopez Mateos 850-A, 011-52-646-175-9122) sells monotypes and colorful etchings, some commemorative of events like the annual Newport Beach—Ensenada sailing regatta and the Rosarito—Ensenada Fun Bicycle Ride. **Artesanias Tonala** (Avenida Lopez Mateos 778, 011-52-646-178-1918) sells fine art and picture frames as well as stained glass off the shelf or made to order. **Sara** (Avenida Lopez Mateos at Calle Blancarte, 011-52-646-178-2965) sells duty-free perfume and a small line of clothing for men and women, including some European brands not always available in the United States.

RELOCATION

After a few days in San Diego, visitors and newcomers inevitably reach the same conclusion—San Diego is really just a big collection of small towns. Even with a population of nearly 2.9 million countywide, San Diego has somehow managed to hold on to its small-town flavor while enjoying the advantages of a major metropolitan city. Most everything you would look for in New York or San Francisco is here: theater, opera, museums, first-class restaurants, and vibrant nightlife. But the sense of community that you find in smaller cities is here, too. And nowhere is that sense of community stronger than in its varied neighborhoods.

San Diegans appreciate and enjoy all the cultural and entertainment opportunities available to them, but they place even more value on life within their neighborhoods. Community pride is fierce. Almost without exception, neighborhoods within both the city and county limits have planning groups to monitor growth and plan activities. Residents care very much about what happens down the street and around the block.

Over the decades each neighborhood within San Diego County has developed its own unique characteristics. Take Poway and Rancho Bernardo, for example. Both are located in North County Inland; in fact, they're very close to one another. But they could hardly be more different. Rancho Bernardo is an interesting combination of high-tech industry, golf courses, and family and retirement communities. Poway, on the other hand, has a strong working-class population that focuses its energy on local festivals, politics, and public-school issues.

Farther south, in Central San Diego, is the neighborhood of Mission Hills. With its stately mansions and high-ticket real estate values, it makes a strangely genteel neighbor for adjacent Hillcrest, a buzzing, active neighborhood with a highly concentrated gay population.

Then there are the neighborhoods that have cute quirks. For example, Burlingame, a tiny area in North Park, is distinguished by its red concrete sidewalks—the only community in the entire county to sport such a feature. Birdland has a quirk of a different sort. Tucked away between Linda Vista and Serra Mesa, all its streets are named after birds: Hummingbird Lane, Peacock Drive, and Nightingale Way, to name a few.

We'll take you through the individual neighborhoods, region by region, so you can get an idea of the variety of lifestyles, architectural styles, and just plain old standout features—and there are many. You'll surely find something that appeals to you. Just keep in mind that in the city of San Diego alone there are more than 100 separate, identifiable neighborhoods. So we'll group many of them together and give you an idea of the characteristics of the general area.

One of the best ways to get a good idea of what an individual neighborhood is like is to attend one of its annual festivals or celebrations. Check out the listings in our Annual Events chapter or pick up a community newspaper in a neighborhood library, coffeehouse, or convenience store. You'll undoubtedly find a parade, block party, or arts festival that will give you the feel for what the area is like. Chat with the locals—you're sure to get an earful.

REAL ESTATE—A TALE OF BOOM AND BUST

The history of the real estate market in San Diego is one of excess. Either the market is booming and houses are snapped up the day they reach the market, or housing prices have gone soft and homes linger on the listings for weeks, their owners intent on a profit of double digits. Prices, however, will never be cheap. Most buyers must put together some creative financing to purchase even the most modest property.

Here's the scary part: In 2005 the median price for a single-family resale home hit $550,000, more than half a million dollars. In February 2006, the average price of a *new* home reached $861,759—a 350 percent increase over 1996 prices.

Those are daunting figures, we know. The high cost of housing is one of the main reasons San Diego habitually makes the least-livable city lists that come out periodically. And prices aren't going to decrease in the foreseeable future. The increase has been steady for the past decade. Sellers are certainly happy, but most buyers have to work extra hard to afford a home.

Housing prices are driving San Diegans out of the county. During the last half of the 1990s, 16,000 more people left that county than moved in. Many are heading to neighboring Riverside County, Nevada, and Arizona, where new housing developments are filling up as quickly as they appear.

But affordable (barely) housing can still be found if you're willing to be a little flexible in terms of neighborhoods and amenities. Many young families are buying homes in some of the older neighborhoods in the county and restoring the dwellings to pristine condition. As more and more people catch on to the idea, revitalized neighborhoods are emerging from previously run-down ones, and whole communities are being reborn.

Outlying areas are growing rapidly, too, as folks move farther away from Central San Diego in search of more affordable housing. Traditionally housing costs in North County Inland, East County, and the South Bay have been easier on the wallet than those along the coast. This adds a bit of a commute to the mix, but city planners are committed to making that commute as easy as possible. Currently their main focus has been on North County routes into the city. Freeways are being widened, and special commuter lanes are being added.

Rental units also are at a premium. They also are on the expensive side. In early 2006, the *San Diego Transcript* reported the average monthly rent in San Diego to be $1,254. Some of the best units for the best value are listed in the classifieds by their owners. Just be prepared to make an immediate decision and have cash in hand for first and last months' rent, plus a security deposit.

As we introduce you to the various neighborhoods throughout the county, we'll also try to give you an idea of housing prices. Aside from a few communities like Rancho Santa Fe and La Jolla, where home prices always have more digits than you want to know about, most neighborhoods have a range of prices. Modest cottages can usually be found right around the corner from some pretty impressive houses in most neighborhoods.

We'll steer you toward some good resources that will help you find a house, condo, apartment, or whatever your heart desires. Real estate brokers are abundant, and we'll give you the heads-up on some of the best resources for finding an agent. We'll also list home buyers' and apartment guides to help make your search easier.

Central San Diego

BEACHES: PACIFIC BEACH, MISSION BEACH, OCEAN BEACH

Beach life is different. It's special. It requires forbearance—forbearance for the tourists in the summer, the inflated housing prices year-round, and the damp air that sometimes settles in, threatening to never leave. But as soon as the sun pokes its head through the clouds, all the challenges of beach life are forgotten, and the benefits are abundantly clear.

Coronado excepted, the three beach areas in Central San Diego are so different, they may as well be on different planets. Many of those who live in **Pacific Beach** are twenty-something career people in search of San Diego's fabled beach scene, and they have minimal housing requirements. Apartment complexes are seemingly everywhere and are the residences of choice for this crowd. Sprinkled among the younger set, however, are residents who have called PB home for years. They have the same pride of ownership and community spirit that you would find elsewhere, but they also have an affinity and tolerance for the exuberance of their youthful neighbors. Together they add up to more than 42,000 residents, making Pacific Beach by far the most densely populated beach community. A half mile or so inland, in Pacific Beach homeowners have the perfect mixture of beach proximity and tranquil residential neighborhoods at the base of upscale Mountain Soledad, just to the north.

Mission Beach is a tiny isthmus only 2 blocks wide between bay and beach, and it stretches south from PB to the jetty at the mouth of the San Diego River. The vast majority of cottages, apartments, and condos in Mission Beach are rentals. This is where the college crowd settles in during the winter and vacationers rent during the summer months. A few hardy souls have made Mission Beach their permanent home, but you'll find few families here. The median price for single-family resale homes in Mission and Pacific Beaches is $905,000; for resale condos it is $540,000.

Ocean Beach is another story. Its northern edge is the southern jetty across the channel from Mission Beach, and it continues south to Sunset Cliffs and Point Loma. Sometimes called the Haight-Ashbury of San Diego, OB was an enclave for hippies and flower children during the late '60s and early '70s. Many of the erstwhile hippies stayed on, bought houses, and raised their children here. Other beach lovers have been in Ocean Beach for several generations. Still more newcomers have found it to their liking and have settled in, resulting in a population of more than 13,000. Still, much of the flavor of the community is reminiscent of that interesting generation of 30 years ago, only these days in a much more refined sense. The wide, flat public beach in OB is popular with families as well as surfers, and the downtown neighborhood boasts dozens of excellent antiques stores, casual restaurants, and one-of-a-kind shops.

Housing prices in OB used to be among the best bargains for beach communities, mostly because much of the neighborhood is in the flight path for jets taking off from Lindbergh Field. But OB prices have risen dramatically in the past few years. The median price for resale houses is $799,000; for condos it's $436,684. New houses, which are mostly custom built, cost closer to a million dollars and change. A lot of quality lies in between, so those who crave the beach existence might find something that matches their expectations and their budget. Rental prices in all beach areas tend to be higher than in other parts of San Diego, averaging about $950 to $1,000 for a small studio. Houses with one or more bedrooms typically rent for $1,600 or more per month. College students don't seem to have a problem with a dearth of amenities, but the older crowd might find rental life too much like roughing it.

DOWNTOWN AND GOLDEN HILL

Twenty years ago few people lived **Downtown** except for the poor who couldn't find housing elsewhere, down-on-their-luck transients, and drug dealers who inhabited the streets and seedy flophouse hotels that populated the area. A lot has changed, and now Downtown boasts a number of ultramodern high-rise condominiums, town houses, and artists' lofts. Buyers are flocking to the Downtown area because massive redevelopment projects have resulted in several hip and trendy neighborhoods, fine restaurants, shopping, theaters, and clubs. Plus many appreciate the convenience of being able to walk to work or

CLOSE-UP

California and the Burn

The last week of October 2003 will forever stand out as one of the saddest weeks in San Diego history. For six long days, wildfires raged over 300,000 acres in the city and county. There were 2,200 homes destroyed. At least 14 people died, including one firefighter. The sky was black with smoke and soot from the desert to the ocean. Entire neighborhoods were decimated. Scripps Ranch, a community of upscale family homes, lost 340 houses. The tiny town of Crest was virtually destroyed; 100 homes were lost. The fires spread into the city at Tierrasanta and up to the mountain town of Julian. It was one of the worst natural disasters San Diego had ever seen.

Wildfires are always a concern in autumn, when trees and brush are especially dry and hot, fierce Santa Ana winds blow so hard that they topple power lines. In San Diego County the winds fed three separate fires ranging from the Cuyamaca Mountains all the way south across the Mexican border.

Thousands were evacuated from their homes and neighborhoods, waiting days to find out if everything they owned had been consumed by flames. The entire San Diego community was affected in one way or another. Air quality was horrid throughout the county for many days; the cleanup was horrendous even 20 miles from the fires. No one was spared from the effects.

San Diego has sprawled into areas that seemed utterly inhabitable a few decades ago. Homeowners who cherish their rural lifestyle are reassesing the wisdom of living amid dry brush and trees.

Today local fire departments in both rural and urban areas are increasingly diligent about requiring homeowners to keep the area around houses and outbuildings clear of brush and debris.

Although it takes more than brush control to prevent the spread of blazes as huge as the Cedar and Crest fires, there's some wisdom to studying plants that grow naturally or thrive in our area. Brightly colored and easy to grow, iceplant can actually deter the spread of a

take a quick trolley or bus ride to offices outside the Downtown area.

Downtown's boundaries now include eight neighborhoods. Residential units are mostly gathered together in Little Italy, one of the fastest-growing residential neighborhoods in the city, East Village by the new ballpark, and in the Marina District. In 2004, 486 apartments and 1,424 condos were added Downtown as well as almost 100,000 square feet of commercial space. More than 40 residential developments are in the planning or construction stages in Downtown. Purchase prices are estimated to range from $200,000 to $1,000,000 and above. Rents will range from $800 to $3,000 per month. The Centre City Development Company (CCDC) is supporting the construction of low-income housing in Downtown, and fire—or at least not encourage it. Drought-tolerant to boot, these species require much less irrigation, saving one of San Diego's most precious resources. And although most people favor showy plants and flowers in favor of natives, an endemic garden can recover from a devastating fire much more easily than one full of imported beauties.

The habitat native to most of San Diego is chaparral. Because fire is an inevitable result of lightning strikes in the dry western states, this ecosystem has evolved to protect the plants as well as the animals that depend on them for food and shelter. These natives have different mechanisms for surviving, and even thriving, after being consumed by fire.

Take *Heteromeles arbutifolia*, commonly called Christmas Berry or Toyon. A member of the rose family, this large plant with tiny white flowers resprouts from burls or underground root systems after being consumed by fire. Native perennials called geophytes respond to the increased light present after the landscape has been denuded of competing plants to produce a higher than usual number of flowers and thus promote repatriation. In addition, geophytes resprout from their fleshy, underground tubers. Another member of the rose family, the hardy yet lovely *Adenostoma fasciculatum* both germinates and resprouts after a burn.

Our many species of *Ceanothus* are reborn like phoenix from the flames. Many of these elegant natives, commonly called California lilac, actually depend on the fire, their seeds requiring heat or smoke to germinate. Conifers like the Tecate cypress have a special type of cone that opens up after a fire to release its seeds. (For more information about chaparral and native plantings, go to www.californiachaparral.com.)

Although most calamities soon recede into "ancient history," for many San Diegans the memories of the 2003 fires remain all too clear. Native plantings, brush control, fire-retardant rooftops, and other appropriate measures all help to prevent disasters of this magnitude in the future.

several projects are under way for senior housing as well. The CCDC predicts a Downtown population of 80,000 by 2030 as compared to 27,500 today.

Just east of Downtown is **Golden Hill,** a community of mostly single-family homes developed in the early days of San Diego. Many of the homes are stately Victorian gems from the early 20th century, and some have been beautifully refurbished. Like Downtown, Golden Hill has seen a period of blight but is rapidly recovering. Much of it borders Balboa Park and the park's golf course, so it features some outstanding scenic properties.

Housing prices are still very affordable in Golden Hill. The median price for houses is $440,000. The median price for condos is $310,000. Many of the houses are in need of some TLC, but smart buy-

Living downtown near their jobs saves commuters time and money. PHOTO: COURTESY OF JOANNE DIBONA, SAN DIEGO CONVENTION AND VISITORS BUREAU

ers are snapping them up, recognizing that Golden Hill is one of the up-and-coming communities in San Diego.

EASTERN: TIERRASANTA, ALLIED GARDENS, GRANTVILLE, DEL CERRO, SAN CARLOS

Tierrasanta's development began in the late '60s, and it is a glowing success story. Located across Interstate 15 from Kearny Mesa, it has matured into an eye-pleasing community that focuses on families. The schools are great, housing prices have stayed within reach, and an amazing number of first-time buyers have stayed in the area rather than moving to bigger houses elsewhere. Tierrasanta was one of the neighborhoods hit in the 2003 fires. Residents are more concerned now with rebuilding than selling. The median rate for single-family resale homes in this area goes for the high $500s to low $600s; resale condos have remained steady at around $350,000.

Southeast of Tierrasanta are **Allied Gardens, Grantville, Del Cerro,** and **San Carlos,** communities that share common characteristics. Del Cerro is slightly more upscale than the others, featuring more custom homes with more floor space. But the solidly built tract homes in Allied Gardens, Grantville, and San Carlos have held their value over the years. Grantville was one of the first neighborhoods in San Diego because of its proximity to Misión San Diego de Alcalá. It once consisted of dairy farms, but along with Allied Gardens and San Carlos was fully developed in the mid-'50s and '60s. Now the neighborhoods are welcoming back children of the original home buyers. These returnees are either buying their parents' homes or ones nearby, a testament to the appeal of the community and its affordability. The median price for houses is $656,000, and for condos it's $435,000.

KEARNY MESA, SERRA MESA, BIRDLAND

Though designated as three separate neighborhoods, Kearny Mesa, Serra Mesa, and Birdland are so similar that they often are thought of as one. They do have their distinctions, however. There's no mistaking when you're in **Birdland,** for all the streets have an ornithological designation. **Serra Mesa** overlooks Qualcomm Stadium and has a couple of brain-teasing street names: Unida Place and Haveteur Way (sound them out—you'll get it). And **Kearny Mesa** is the location of the first major business district in San Diego outside of Downtown. So they do have their distinguishing features, but the housing remains much the same from area to area: mostly modest tract houses that have nevertheless been well maintained and upgraded over the years to accommodate growing families. The median price for single-family resale homes in these areas is $525,000; for resale condos it is $380,000.

LA JOLLA AND TORREY PINES

It seems as though everyone has heard of **La Jolla.** From Omaha to Orlando, folks have heard tales about the beauty and opulence of the seaside village that some say is like Beverly Hills—only with a view. Some, however, are surprised to learn it is part of Central San Diego, and many La Jollans wish its location were an even better-kept secret. Residents are close-knit and protective, and they fiercely guard the natural beauty and mystique of their neighborhoods.

Although "jolla" is not a word found in the Spanish dictionary, the word "joya" means jewel, and the two words are pronounced the same. That's close enough for the 38,200 or so residents who inhabit the palm-tree-lined hills and shores of La Jolla village. The jewel by the sea it is, and a more appropriate description would be hard to find. La Jolla sits squarely on top of some of the most valuable real estate in the United States. Multimillion-dollar homes are the rule rather than the exception. And if a view of the blue Pacific comes with the house, the price tag goes way up. To lucky residents, no amount of money is too great to have the opportunity to settle in what inarguably is one of the most glorious spots on earth.

For visitors (and many residents, too) it's the downtown village that draws them to La Jolla. Prospect Street and Girard Avenue, the two main streets in the village, are crammed with art galleries, chichi boutiques, and trendy (but fabulous) restaurants. The beaches are the stuff dreams are made of and offer a little something for everyone. La Jolla Cove is a treasure trove for snorkelers and scuba divers, and the fun sands of La Jolla Shores are a favorite of families.

The hillsides around La Jolla have exploded with growth, and there's barely a bare spot of dirt anywhere. Still, newcomers manage to construct their dream homes on tiny parcels or by destroying the previous owner's idea of architectural excellence. About 20,000 people live on the outskirts of the village on quiet residential streets and in jam-packed clusters of condos or town houses.

Just to the north of La Jolla is **Torrey Pines.** The campus of the University of California at San Diego is in Torrey Pines, as are many of the high-tech and biotech companies that are becoming such a significant force in the local economy. Many professors and scientists spend their daylight hours in Torrey Pines and then take a short drive down the coast to their homes in La Jolla.

The two communities are inextricably linked. The "town and gown" atmosphere is an integral contributor to La Jolla's social scene, and the educational and scientific community in Torrey Pines is heavily dependent on the generosity of its La Jolla benefactors. Drive south along Torrey Pines Road, and you can almost feel the waves of brain power exuding from UCSD. Then, as soon as Torrey Pines Road turns into La Jolla Boulevard, you can sense the luxury and see the beauty of this stunning oceanfront community.

Housing prices in both neighborhoods will make most people wince. A simple, tiny condominium can go for $750,000. Start adding such amenities as bedrooms, and you'll be pushing the envelope. The median price for houses is a whopping $1,825,000.

Every neighborhood has its little secrets. One of the nicest in Hillcrest is the Spruce Street Pedestrian Bridge. A suspension bridge linking Front and Brant Streets, it was built in 1912, is 375 feet long, and rises 70 feet above the canyon floor.

LOGAN HEIGHTS, ENCANTO, PARADISE HILLS

The neighborhoods southeast of Downtown have long been overlooked in the race for redevelopment and new housing development. **Logan Heights, Encanto, Paradise Hills,** and ajacent neighborhoods are populated largely by middle- to low-income working families, many African American or Latino. It's the most ethnically diverse area in the city, and often the most maligned. Several projects, including shopping centers, schools, and libraries, are bringing new life to the region. The median income in Encanto, for example, is $37,868 as compared to $43,640 in Kensington and $87,173 in La Jolla.

Housing is far more affordable here than anywhere else in Central San Diego. The median price for a resale single-family house in Encanto is $445,000; in Logan Heights it's $390,000. Conversions from apartments to condos create homes accessible to more potential buyers, but deplete the supply of rental housing, making life even more difficult for low-income families.

MID-CITY EAST: KENSINGTON, TALMADGE, NORMAL HEIGHTS, NORTH PARK, COLLEGE AREA

Atop a long mesa overlooking Mission Valley lie the neighborhoods that make up the mid-city area of San Diego. Rich in history and even richer in modern-day personality, these communities are home to San Diegans who enjoy a sense of neighborhood but savor the proximity to urban amenities, too.

Kensington is one such neighborhood. Developed in 1910 by a Canadian expatriate, it was named for the famous London borough. A stroll down the sidewalks of today's Kensington reveals the developer's original intent: Stately English Tudor houses are plentiful. The twist is that they are intermixed with houses sporting San Diego's traditional Spanish architecture—white walls, red tile roofs, and all. Strangely enough, the result is an appealing combination of the two styles, and the well-manicured landscaping attests to current owners' neighborhood pride.

Across the canyon from Kensington is its sister community of **Talmadge.** Silent film stars and sisters Norma, Constance, and Natalie Talmadge lent their name to the subdivision and were further rewarded for their generosity by having individual streets named for them. Norma, Constance, and Natalie Drives are the main streets that take you through this well-kept, quiet area. Real estate agents know that people who live in Kensington and Talmadge are rigorous defenders of their neighborhoods and are vocally active in local politics. The median rate for single-family resale homes in Kensington is $558,000; for resale condos it is $310,000.

West of Kensington and Talmadge are the neighborhoods of **Normal Heights** and **North Park.** Housing tends to be more affordable in both areas, with a median price of $589,500 for houses and $339,000 for condos. Both neighborhoods have suffered periods of neglect. They are rebounding, though, and many of the houses are remarkable. Along with the standard array of Spanish styles are some of the best examples of Craftsman cottages in San Diego. Many have been refurbished, and many more are awaiting a dedicated owner to restore them to their original glory.

Finally, there is the **College Area** and adjoining **College Grove,** called so because of their proximity to San Diego State University. This area is also an older San Diego neighborhood but, like communities to the west, is seeing an influx of younger families seeking good quality, affordable housing. The median price of a resale home is in College Grove is $495,000; it's $285,00 for condos.

All the mid-city neighborhoods are good places for families. And community pride has generated a new wave of restaurants, local watering holes, coffeehouses, and retail shops.

MID-CITY WEST: MISSION VALLEY, HILLCREST, UNIVERSITY HEIGHTS, MISSION HILLS

Mission Valley, named for San Diego Mission de Alcalá, is a valley that runs east-west between two overlooking mesas. Following the contours of the valley is the San Diego River. The valley has very few single-family homes, but it does have plenty of apartments and condominiums that attract buyers who appreciate the central location. The San Diego Trolley runs through the valley, and the Mission Valley and Fashion Valley shopping centers are a stone's throw from one another and right on the trolley line. The median price of condos in the neighborhood is $530,000; $350,000 for condos.

Hillcrest and **University Heights** are similar in housing styles. The difference is that University Heights—east of Hillcrest on the other side of California Highway 163—is strictly residential, while Hillcrest is one of San Diego's hippest commercial districts. The village area of Hillcrest is almost a miniature Gaslamp Quarter, with fabulous restaurants, way-cool shops, and trendy clubs. Hillcrest also has a large gay population that has been instrumental in revitalizing the area. Pride of ownership is clear as you drive down the streets of both Hillcrest and University Heights. Immaculately maintained houses and yards show off their owners' efforts. Many Craftsman-style houses dot the streets of the two neighborhoods and can still be purchased without having to win the lottery. The median price of houses in this zip code, which includes Mission Hills, is $800,000; for condos, $485,000.

Mission Hills is an old neighborhood that has never endured a downturn. The beautiful houses, many of which were built at the turn of the 20th century, maintain their original elegance. Second- and third-generation families keep returning to Mission Hills, and they do so for a number of reasons. First is its beautiful location, of course, overlooking Mission Bay and Presidio Park, the site of the original mission founded by Father Serra. Second is its central location. Tucked above the intersection of Interstates 5 and 8, it's close to everywhere. Third is its proximity to Hillcrest. It may seem an odd juxtaposition to have a predominantly gay neighborhood right next to a stately, old-money community, but the two intermingle beautifully.

NORTHEASTERN: MIRA MESA AND SCRIPPS RANCH

Mira Mesa is a bedroom community of tract houses that began to develop in the late 1960s. It provided a much-needed source of affordable housing for young families, especially military families in search of off-base living quarters. The neighborhood has stood the test of time and is still a haven for families. Schools, shopping centers, and restaurants have all made their way into Mira Mesa. So much so that it is nearly a self-contained community. The median price for houses is $520,000, and most are built with families in mind: lots of bedrooms, baths, and family rooms. Mid-price condos go for $326,000.

Just to the southeast of Mira Mesa lies the newer and slightly more upscale neighborhood of **Scripps Ranch.** Nestled among eucalyptus trees, the community has a kind of country flavor, yet it's commuter-close to downtown San Diego. The houses are tract homes, as they are in Mira Mesa, but are bigger and have many more amenities. Plus the entire community is within walking distance of Lake Miramar, which has jogging and bike trails around the perimeter. Many Scripps Ranch homes have a view of the lake, too. It's a serene setting, and you can't help feeling you're someplace much farther away from the bustle of the city.

Unfortunately, Scripps Ranch was hit hard by the 2003 fires. In the older section of the development, 340 homes were destroyed. Most have been rebuilt, and the median detached home in this area sells for $710,000, with condos going for $436,000.

NORTHERN: LINDA VISTA, CLAIREMONT, UNIVERSITY CITY, SORRENTO VALLEY

To the east of I-5 are the long-established communities of **Linda Vista** and **Clairemont.** So long-entrenched is Linda Vista that it has the distinction of being the home of the first shopping mall in the United States. Small in comparison to the megamalls we're familiar with today, it nevertheless put the tiny community on the map. Today Linda Vista is known for its most prominent neighbor: the University of San Diego.

Surrounding much of Linda Vista is Clairemont, which comprises the neighborhoods of Bay Ho and Bay Park, too. Large in area and population (Clairemont is home to more than 80,000 residents), the area has a melting pot of inhabitants, from young families to retired folks who have been living in the same house for more than 50 years. Many Vietnamese, Laotian, and Hmong families who emigrated to the United States after the Vietnam War ended up in Linda Vista. The neighborhood is packed with Asian restaurants and markets.

Linda Vista and Clairemont can't be considered suburbs, because they're right in the heart of the city. But quiet streets and neighborhood block parties blend right in with the shopping centers, strip malls, and other businesses that all coexist in a wonderful mix of everything that's good about San Diego. Plus the beach is 10 minutes away. Clairemont and Linda Vista both border Tecolote Canyon Park, a nature reserve with oodles of hiking trails and a golf course. Housing prices are reasonable in both communities, unless you happen upon one of the Clairemont homes with a panoramic view of Mission Bay and the ocean. Then you're likely to pay upward of $800,000 for a three-bedroom house. The median price for a house is $558,000 in this area.

University City, a slightly more upscale version of Clairemont, is located just to the north. The community is a little newer, and the houses are a little bigger. Other than that, it has the same neighborhood feel that Clairemont boasts. The north end of University City has been taken over by apartment buildings because of its proximity to UCSD. Rental rates are quite high—$1,000-plus for a bare-bones apartment. The median price for houses is $775,000; for condos it's $412,000.

North of University City is the community of **Sorrento Valley.** Sorrento Valley itself isn't new—it has long been a center for San Diego's high-tech businesses and industries. But it's only recently that housing developments have begun to spring up. Like any new community, it will take time to develop a personality of its own. The median price for houses is $815,000; $448,000 for condos.

POINT LOMA AND CORONADO

At the tip of the Point Loma peninsula sits the Cabrillo Lighthouse, a monument to the explorer who claimed San Diego for Spain. From the base of the peninsula to its tip are located some of San Diego's prettiest houses and longest-established neighborhoods. One of the most prolific industries in days gone by was tuna fishing, an enterprise started by San Diego's Portuguese community. Most of that community remains ensconced in **Point Loma,** where Portuguese festivals, food, and culture are abundant.

Somewhere along the way others discovered Point Loma, too, and took advantage of the hillside properties on either side of the peninsula to build houses that command magnificent, unobstructed ocean or bay views. The biggest drawback to life in Point Loma is the nearby airport. Lindbergh Field's runway is aimed right at the Loma Portal area of the peninsula, and residents endure airplane noise all day long, from 7:00 A.M. to 11:00 P.M. With a little extra soundproofing insulation and the advent of newer, quieter planes, it has become more bearable of late, and most feel it's a small price to pay for the beautiful houses and views.

Across the bay is the neighboring island of **Coronado,** with some 26,500 residents. Technically it's not really an island—it's a narrow spit of land that reaches north from Imperial Beach, near the U.S.-Mexico border. But Coronado residents like the idea of it being an island, and few outsiders are ungenerous enough to disagree.

Coronado may have more retired military officers than any other location in the country among its residents. It is home to a large Navy Command Center, and many young enlistees vow to return to the island to raise their families. But it's not just military brass who have discovered the charm of the island. It's an ideal place to raise a family—good schools, low crime, and beautiful beaches are among its attributes. And the downtown village of Coronado is so picturesque, it looks like something out of a movie. One-of-a-kind shops, theaters, and restaurants line Orange Avenue, the main boulevard through town.

Coronado and Point Loma have one thing in common: exorbitant real estate. In Point Loma you can still find the occasional fixer-upper to fit your budget, say for $850,000. Houses can easily top $2 million, especially if they have one of those coveted views. The median price for a house in the area is $900,000. Condos are a little more affordable, with a median price of $575,000. Bargains are not to be found in Coronado, however. The median price for a resale house is a whopping $1.5 million. Condos cost nearly as much, and gorgeous mansions near Coronado Beach sell for as much as $9 million.

North County Coastal

CARLSBAD AND LA COSTA

Carlsbad and its La Costa district are like fraternal twins, forever joined with similar backgrounds. Yet there's a world of difference in the twins' approach to San Diego living.

Starting with **Carlsbad,** a city of about 73,000 that stretches from Oceanside way down the coast to Encinitas and inland to Vista, you'll find a family community blended with small stores and shops. There's a real downtown area in this town. In it you'll find city hall, the main branch of the library, great restaurants (and some beach hangouts and clubs), supermarkets, antiques shops, beauty salons, and all you'd expect in a small town. (If you love to shop for antiques, be sure to read about Carlsbad's antiques district in our Shopping chapter.) There are also the usual downtown office buildings—and the growing high-tech community here—and hotels and motels, from posh resorts to more thrifty establishments.

The neighborhoods are a mix of ethnic backgrounds, and their population is young. It's unlikely this 42-square-mile community will grow to more than 54,600 residential units or 135,000 residents, as voters approved a dwelling cap in 1986.

The beach property of Carlsbad includes million-dollar oceanfront homes. New homes in Carlsbad are in the $700,000 to $1.35 million range. Resale homes to the east of I-5 are less expensive, but don't count on a bargain. Apartments on that side cost an average of $1,500 a month for a one-bedroom. The median cost of a resale house is about $811,750.

Now let's look at **La Costa,** the area south of Carlsbad and adjacent to the La Costa Resort and Spa. In this upscale area there are condos, some apartments, and lots of family homes. There are multimillion-

North County Coastal suffers from horrendous traffic gridlock, something to keep in mind if you're planning to commute to work. The worst areas are at the junction of I-5 and I-805 just south of Del Mar and around Carlsbad and Oceanside. The coaster train, with two stations in Carlsbad, is a great option for those working in or around downtown San Diego.

dollar homes, too. As in Carlsbad, it's not unusual in today's booming real estate market for a house to be sold even before a broker can decide what to put in an advertisement.

DEL MAR AND CARMEL VALLEY

Del Mar has a laid-back beach-tourist feel that visitors expect to find when visiting San Diego. Regardless of the time of day, there are people outdoors. Some are walking, jogging, or playing beach sports. Others come out to mingle at the cafes and coffeehouses that are sprinkled through town. When that first group goes back to work or school, the next wave takes its place, and the cycle continues until late in the evening. Del Mar is an outdoor town and home to outdoor institutions including a polo club, racetrack, and the Del Mar Fairgrounds, where there's something happening outdoors nearly every weekend. (Be sure to read our Annual Events chapter for some of the great things that happen at the fairground.)

Del Mar is only 1.8 square miles, and the residents (a number that hovers at about 5,000) like it that way. While some of the county's communities have less desirable areas, Del Mar is Del Mar and that means charming, small—and monied. In the section of Del Mar that's found west of I-5, the custom homes are in older neighborhoods with established landscaping and shady twisting streets. East of I-5, past the multistory business offices seen from the freeway, are planned neighborhoods whose homes have red Spanish-tile roofs and perfectly green lawns.

Housing prices have soared in this coastal community. A good number of homes have ocean views, which can tack on a cool hundred grand or more to that price tag. Those homes on the beach may be smaller but, alas, still go for the big bucks. The median price for single-family resale homes in Del Mar is about $1.7 million; for resale condos it is $701,950.

East of I-5 and Del Mar is **Carmel Valley,** a fast-growing region with master-planned communities and plenty of housing developments. Houses in this area tend to be big, around 4,000 square feet. Young families abound, and most housing communities have recreation centers, pools, and plenty of neighborly interaction. The median price for a resale house in the valley is just more than a million dollars.

ENCINITAS

Encinitas, a city of about 65,000 residences with its official boundaries incorporating the towns of Cardiff and Leucadia, is half the size of Carlsbad and enjoys a youthful community spirit. At one time Encinitas, Leucadia, and Cardiff-by-the-Sea were three distinct locales, but in 1986 they grouped together to form the city of Encinitas. Yet each area strives to keeps its individuality.

Driving north along I-5 from San Diego, you'll first see **Cardiff,** with its older, established family homes set on rolling hills. Most homes in Cardiff have an ocean view (or at the very least relish breezes). There are schools, supermarkets, sidewalk cafes, and sandy beaches in this town. The overwhelming flavor of Cardiff is casual.

Encinitas, the hub of the community, is filled with the energy of its growing families. It's going somewhere—and just where that is concerns residents. This pristine city strives for a clean and wholesome image that sets it apart from many other beach towns. As with other coastal communities, Encinitas has a downtown with shops, cafes, restaurants, businesses, and specialty stores lining Pacific Coast Highway and along the few blocks on either side of it. Inland, on the east side of I-5, are most of the city's homes, typically in planned communities with shopping centers and strip malls.

If Insiders think that Cardiff is quiet, **Leucadia** could be accused of taking a full-time siesta. It has sleepy neighborhoods with architectural jewels mixed in with simpler homes. Leucadians are reluctant to promote growth and take an active part in the decisions that affect their part of Encinitas.

Resale homes in Encinitas, in all three areas of the city, have a median price of nearly $900,000.

OCEANSIDE

Oceanside, incorporated on July 3, 1888, was one of the first cities in North County Coastal. It's the largest in area of the cities, too, with more than 40 square miles within its boundaries and about 173,000 people. Housing prices vary in this ethnically diverse, working-class community.

Median house prices are around $532,333. There are more rental units in Oceanside than in other parts of North County Coastal due to the military presence in Camp Pendleton. Rent prices vary with location and are somewhat lower than those of Oceanside's neighboring cities.

Oceanside has well-established parks, a marina and big sandy beaches, a respected community college, and a recreation system that brings programs to kids, adults, and seniors.

RANCHO SANTA FE

The community that Insiders refer to as "the Ranch" doesn't come with a visible price tag. As the cliché goes: If you must ask the price of property in **Rancho Santa Fe,** you probably can't afford it.

The median price for a home here (we're talking a spacious home with plenty of prime property, perhaps a pool and a tennis court—the kind you see in better decorating magazines) in 2005 was $2,800,000, while the median price for a condo was $899,000. Rentals here are traditionally handled by agents and can be anything from a condo near the tiny downtown to oversize mansions on oversize lots with matching monthly rental fees.

Streets are tree-lined and inviting. As you drive through the Ranch, you can glimpse mansions tucked behind the lush landscaping. Traffic is regulated and slower than in other cities. Parking can be a challenge, especially during the lunch hours. People know each other, and those who work in the Ranch often walk to work and walk at lunch. People meet at the post office often since there is no home mail delivery in the Ranch.

Rancho Santa Fe feels safe and is rather old-fashioned. The downtown is small, with exclusive jewelry shops, clothing boutiques, the usual doctors' and dentists' offices, and a supermarket. You'll find the busy post office there, too.

SOLANA BEACH

Solana Beach is hugged by Del Mar and Encinitas. The city seems to have the best of its neighbors' best qualities, plus an added shot of adrenaline. There's energy everywhere. Check out the downtown area along the Pacific Coast Highway: You'll see early-morning, lunchtime, and evening walkers and runners; parents pushing kids in strollers; businesspeople on break and out for a browse; and shoppers claiming prizes in those famous Cedros Street home furnishing stores.

This is a family town, too, with good parks and schools and recreational activities. Residents in Solana Beach think about the environment—the ocean is their best neighbor—and recycling programs abound.

The town has an excellent blend of family homes, condos, and some apartment living. The median price for a resale house is nearly $1.2 million. Condos have a wider range since some are built overlooking the ocean and garner bigger price tags. Again, it's all in the location. Rentals, if you can find them, start at about $1,500 for an apartment or very small house.

North County Inland

ESCONDIDO

Escondido seems to have been transplanted from another time. It's a hometown, with a downtown and a civic pride rivaling that of any Midwestern community. People live and work in this town that's situated in North County Inland, about an hour's drive (in traffic) from downtown San Diego. That's not saying there aren't those who brave the rush and commute out of Escondido using I-15.

The drive can become a gridlock similar to that found on I-5 along the coastal communities, yet a lot of people who work in San Diego drive in from Escondido daily. While there are express buses that take commuters into San Diego and diamond lanes for car-poolers, there's no commuter train yet.

With the California Center for the Arts, a multipurpose facility with a multistory theater, culture is established in Escondido. (Be sure to read more about the center in our The Arts chapter.) The center draws big-time performers from around the world and audiences from around the county.

Obviously highbrow opportunities are not lacking, but people like the community fun in this town, too. There are parades, arts and crafts fairs, picnics, and historical tours of houses built in the late 1880s, which is about the time the city was incorporated. Back then it was a hub of agricultural activity. Fifteen years ago you could still visit avocado and citrus packinghouses and working orchards within the city limits.

Escondido has a blend of older and newer neighborhoods. You may find smaller houses, family homes at the low end of the real estate price range for around $180,000 and more posh family abodes netting close to $600,000. The median price for a detached home is $556,300.

Homeowners in the moderate-income range pay more than half their income for housing. The San Diego Association of Governments estimates that fewer than half of the San Diego families earn enough to afford a median-priced home. If you're moving to San Diego because of a job opportunity, see if your employer offers assistance in searching for a home that suits your needs and income.

FALLBROOK AND VALLEY CENTER

There's lots of fresh air in these communities situated about an hour and a half northeast of downtown San Diego. You'll also find working avocado and citrus orchards, people who love horses and dogs, and lots of families who've chosen **Fallbrook** and **Valley Center** for the elbowroom.

The cities provide a nice combination of stores, services, and eateries. In both towns there's a main street and neighbors who still stop and chat. The schools encourage civic pride, and there are lots of family activities, from Fallbrook's Avocado Festival to Valley Center's local art fairs.

Homes in this area are usually custom-built and situated on hillsides—both communities are known for the views of tree-studded mountains and miles of open backcountry. Most have at least an acre of ground, some quite a lot more. People who want to have horses and other farm critters often move to these communities for the land and the friendship of other animal lovers.

The average home is reselling for a median cost of $436,000. Condos and apartments are limited.

RANCHO BERNARDO

Rancho Bernardo is many things to many people. Seniors think of it as the perfect retirement community because of its lovely weather, great services, easy freeway access, and super golf courses. Families think of it as a family town. And large corporate entities such as Hewlett Packard see it as the perfect business site. Whatever you name this inland city, you'll find a bucketful of reasons why people live here.

Just off I-15, about 40 minutes north of San Diego, the community stretches out on both sides of the freeway. There are shopping centers, parks and golf courses, excellent medical facilities, and a number of colleges. The University of California, San Diego, has a satellite center in the area.

The range of housing prices is extreme and again depends on location. The median price is $751,250, for condos, it's $388,500, though there are not that many that go up for sale. You can figure that rental homes and apartments will begin at about $2,000 and skyrocket straight up if you're in the market for a six-bedroom, six-bath home on the ninth green with a back view of a private country club.

RANCHO PEÑASQUITOS AND POWAY

The communities of **Rancho Peñasquitos** and **Poway** are grouped because they are lively, family towns with a younger-than-average population. If you move to Peñasquitos or Poway, your neighbor might be a doctor who works at Scripps Hospital, a local landscaper with a thriving business, a computer genius who interfaces with colleagues over the Internet, or someone in public service or the military. People and professions blend well in these cities, which offer planned communities with tree-lined streets.

Homes in Poway and Peñasquitos are slightly more expensive than those in neighboring communities. Poway resale homes have a median cost of $615,000; Peñasquitos house price tags are about $665,000. New homes in both cities, in well-planned developments, are upwards of $800,000. There are a few apartments, but most people look for condos and homes in this family-oriented, newly developed area.

SAN MARCOS, VISTA, BONSALL

These "sisters" are happily connected by proximity. To the newcomer they seem to be very much alike, with planned developments, acres of roofs topping lowland and hillside alike, and clustered areas of shops and malls. They are all family towns, where younger people are beginning their lives. Each is unique, however, and that's where your choices enter the picture.

San Marcos is home to California State University, San Marcos. The campus graces one of the hills just off California Highway 78. Having CSUSM in San Marcos is slowly providing the city with that college feeling and cultural activities. Right now everyone in the community is still getting used to the new civic center, increased traffic, and the change from a rural to a suburban environment.

Home prices in San Marcos have a median cost of $635,000. Condos run a little less (about $440,000). You'll have to look for houses and condos if you want to rent in this community; apartments are scarce.

Vista is more established than San Marcos. It has older neighborhoods, and if you're a handy person, you might just find a fixer-upper here. The median for resale homes is $516,500. Condos may come with a price tag as low as $260,000, although the median is $335,000. This is still a deal for North County, which is within 20 minutes of the coast.

Bonsall, connected to Vista on the south and Oceanside on the east, is spread out amongst winding roads meandering through groups of custom- and owner-built homes. It has the feel of a backcountry town. People stable horses and farm animals, meet friends at the feed store, and then dash to work in their expensive 4x4 or foreign car. The median price for a resale home in this exclusive area is nearly doubled in 2005, to a cool million dollars. You won't find rental apartments or condos here; most dwellings in Bonsall are homes.

East County

ALPINE

Unlike the other communities in East County, **Alpine** was a planned community (we're talking the planner of the late 1800s). It started in life as Viejas Stage Stop. The town originated when drivers hauled supplies to the mines in the Cuyamacas and returned with gold destined for San Diego. Farther along, the Butterfield Stage line allowed passengers to get out at the stop and shake off some of the dust. As more people began passing through, more services came to the area.

Today an interstate highway, not a dusty trail, connects Alpine to the cities of San Diego County. There's a cozy downtown with cafes and stores. And if you're searching for the perfect glamorous outfit or a fine wine or want to do some serious shopping (as in a huge mall), Alpine now has the Viejas Shopping Outlets, a beautifully designed shopping center near the Viejas Casino.

Alpine became a desirable community in the 1980s as custom homes began rising on the outskirts of town. Today you can find older, rustic houses for under $400,000, but the median price is around $660,000. You may find a rental home in Alpine, but don't expect to find many condos or apartments.

DESERT COMMUNITIES, JAMUL, BORREGO SPRINGS

Like Palm Desert in the 1980s, the desert communities—including those of **Jamul** and **Borrego Springs**—are beginning to boom. The median price for resale houses rose 95 percent in 2005, to $783,250 in Jamul and $312,500 in Borrego Springs.

Tourists and snowbirds flock to the desert during the mild falls, wonderful winters, and delightful springs. Town people stay year-round and love that hot, dry desert air. Those who want to enjoy desert living normally purchase land and build their dream house.

EL CAJON, LAKESIDE, SANTEE

The cites of **El Cajon** and **Santee** are neighbors and have been linked since the founders of Misión San Diego de Alcalá chose this valley area to graze cattle. Sandwiched in between and heading east is the unincorporated area of **Lakeside,** still home to chickens, horses, cows, and even cowboys.

In more recent times they were thought of as bedroom communities to San Diego, but that's changing. Now that younger families select these cities to put down roots, there's a feeling of renewed vigor, excitement, and youthful energy. Plenty of folks still head to San Diego or North County for work, however.

The housing ranges from modest to elaborate; prices follow along that range. The median single-family dwelling in El Cajon goes for $530,000 as opposed to $505,000 in Lakeside and $475,000 in Santee.

You will find condos and rentals in these areas, and these are especially attractive to those needing a place (with an okay commute) close to SDSU. Condos average about $316,00 in El Cajon, and about $296,000 in Lakeside.

JULIAN AND RAMONA

Julian and Ramona are known for their quiet country, feel-good environments. While some folks live in Ramona and work in San Diego, few if any people commute "down the mountain" from Julian into the urban areas. In these towns you'll find sprawling ranches, quaint custom homes, and plenty of wide-open spaces. That makes the area especially attractive to people who like to spread their wings and add some horses, hiking trails, and natural habitats to their estates. Houses are normally custom-built.

Julian is known for the Western-town atmosphere and much-hyped apple pie. The town is tucked within Cleveland National Forest. It's a favorite community for artists, writers, craftspeople, and those who own the local establishments, from bed-and-breakfast inns to antiques stores. Folks are friendly in Julian and enjoy knowing they live in a desirable area. When houses come up for resale, the median cost is $379,000. New custom homes can easily exceed $600,000.

Think of a town in Wyoming, without the really big mountains and all that snow, and you have a romanticized idea of **Ramona.** With its annual dusting of snow and warm, dry summers, it's an ideal location for those who want to get just far enough away from it all. Within town are enough stores, services, and shops for more than the basics of life. Yet if you need something special, Escondido or San Diego are where you need to head. The city is over an hour from San Diego and about 30 minutes from Escondido. Resale homes range from rambling ranch styles. The median cost for detached dwellings is $555,000.

LA MESA AND SPRING VALLEY

La Mesa and Spring Valley were once considered backcountry by those cosmopolitan settlers of San Diego and people who made homes along the coast. Nowadays young families, retired people, students, and professionals continue to find their perfect homes in an area that suddenly seems close to it all.

La Mesa was originally known as Allison Springs. Early settler and rancher Robert Allison purchased a part of the area to graze sheep. Then it was renamed La Mesa Springs, and finally in 1912, when it was incorporated as a city, the name officially changed to what we call it today.

The Native American name for **Spring Valley** was Meti. For a while the mission padres called it the Spanish equivalent to "the springs of St. George." Finally, early farmer August Ensworth settled in the area. The story goes that he asked his young daughter for the perfect name, and Spring Valley was born.

The high cost of energy is a serious concern for San Diego's homeowners. For tips on cutting your energy costs, check out the energy conservation tips at the San Diego Regional Energy Office Web site at www.sdenergy.org. You'll learn about the state tax credits you can earn by using solar energy and find all sorts of tips for cutting your energy costs.

People continue to discover quality of life in East County, and there's a good mix of housing here. The median housing price is $515,000 in La Mesa (95 percent higher than in 2004) and $465,000 in Spring Valley, where prices also have nearly doubled.

South Bay

CHULA VISTA AND BONITA

Chula Vista is the second-largest city in San Diego County, with a population of around 217,000. It was originally part of El Rancho de la Nación, a huge area of land in the South Bay that was once part of Mexico—as was all of San Diego, and for that matter, California and the southwest United States. Nowadays it is a vital, bustling city.

Newcomers and longtime residents of San Diego are gravitating in increasing numbers to the developments in Chula Vista, and the master-planned communities offer grand amenities for families. The EastLake development, for example, has a man-made lake, complete with sandy beaches, and a first-rate public golf course. Another master-planned community, Otay Ranch, promises to rival the appeal of EastLake. Housing prices vary, but throughout the city they grew at least 96 percent. The median price for resale

One of the best sources for trivia about San Diego County neighborhoods is Evelyn Kooperman's **San Diego Trivia.**

homes ranges from $518,000 to $740,000; condos range from $375,000 to $440,000.

City leaders lobby hard to entice new industry to Chula Vista, and recent years have seen the opening of Soak City Water Park, the Coors Amphitheater, and an official Olympic Training Center. All are bringing greater recognition to Chula Vista, as well as an increase in tourism.

Neighboring **Bonita,** an unincorporated area, has a gentrified rural atmosphere complete with horses, stables, and an occasional farm animal. Residents of Bonita prize their detachment from city life and local politics, preferring the peace and quiet of country living. However, the benefits of the city are easily within reach. Houses are typically sprawling ranch style, with larger-than-average lots and swimming pools, and have a median cost of $750,000, half that for condos.

IMPERIAL BEACH

Imperial Beach is the most southwesterly city in the continental United States. Its motto in the 1940s was "Where the sun and the surf spend their continuous honeymoon." A little outdated today, the motto is still not too far off the mark. Imperial Beach was first settled in the 1880s by a developer who intended it to be a beach resort for residents of the Imperial Valley, a desert community east of San Diego. Though it achieved that status, other people soon discovered its charm, and it now draws visitors from all over.

Today Imperial Beach is home to one at the world's biggest sand castle contests (see our Annual Events chapter for details). Its proximity to Mexico is a big attraction, too. A self-contained, incorporated city, Imperial Beach has its own city council that attends to hot issues of the day. For the most part, though, the community tends to be unassuming and even unsophisticated a mecca for surfers.

Condos have a median price of $404,000. The median house price is $518,000. Real estate in IB (as residents call it) is appreciating rapidly. Prices increased about 97 percent in 2004.

NATIONAL CITY

National City was the second established city in the county after the city of San Diego. It was founded and developed by the Kimball brothers, Frank, Warren, Levi, and George. The brothers were the purchasers of El Rancho de la Nación, a 26,000-acre plot of land (of which Chula Vista was also a part). They laid out the town, founded a number of businesses, and helped establish the olive and citrus industries. Some of the lovely mansions later built by the Kimballs still stand today.

Today National City is a working-class town, with many of its residents employed by nearby National Steel and Shipbuilding Company. The city is also noted for its Mile of Cars, a large concentration of auto dealers.

Houses are modestly priced compared to the rest of San Diego County and have a median price of $430,000. Condominiums have a median price of $315,000.

SAN YSIDRO, OTAY MESA, NESTOR

San Ysidro and **Otay Mesa** are two southern communities that abut the U.S.-Mexico border. Thus their combined population of 59,000 includes a high proportion of Hispanic Americans and businesses that cater to shoppers who cross the border from Tijuana.

The history of San Ysidro is unconventional. It began as a utopian colony founded by William Smythe in the early 1900s. Smythe named the colony Little Landers to reflect his philosophy of life. He believed that his group of landowners needed only enough land to raise food for their families and have a little extra to sell. Their motto was "A little land and a living." The colony was fairly successful until a flood in 1916 wiped out the farms. All that remains of Little Landers today is Smythe Avenue.

Recent years have seen lots of development in San Ysidro and Otay Mesa, both of which boast relatively new housing projects. The median price of a resale house in San Ysidro is $520,000; for condos it's $290,791.

Nestor is a community of just under 17,000. It, too, began as a farming community, only its residents were mostly Japanese. The Japanese farmers pretty much disappeared, though, during World War II, when most were placed in internment camps. Today Nestor focuses on its schools. Its middle school and high school are invariably among the first to come up with new programs to stimulate young minds and encourage a love of learning. And community service is as deeply ingrained in residents of Nestor as is getting out of bed in the morning.

The median house price is $341,000, and the median condo price is $240,500.

SHOPPING FOR A HOME

By now you've probably figured out that real estate is of prime value in San Diego, so it should come as no surprise to learn that there are more than 8,000 Realtors, agents, and brokers doing business around town. Many companies are long established with excellent reputations. Others have a tendency to come and go.

If you're relocating to San Diego, we can suggest several ways to select a Realtor to best serve your needs. Probably the safest and most reliable route is to work with one of the national chains. They all have offices in every neighborhood, community, nook, and cranny in the county, and if you call one of the relocation numbers listed below, you'll be hooked up with a Realtor who is intimately familiar with the areas you might be considering.

Otherwise, a referral from a friend is usually reliable. With so many agents from which to choose, it's obviously a buyer's market, so we strongly suggest you interview potential agents. Ask questions—find out about their standard policies and what they can do for you. It doesn't hurt to ask if their commissions are negotiable, too.

Realtors tend to specialize in particular neighborhoods. If you already know what area you like, drive around and look at the for-sale signs. You'll soon find out which Realtor has the most properties listed and is most active in that area.

For further guidance, contact the San Diego Association of Realtors at (858) 715-8000 or (858) 592-7171 or see their Web site: www.sdar.com. Contact the San Diego Fair Housing Commission (619-544-9193; www.sdhc.net) for help finding a home to buy or to rent at less than astronomical prices.

i

Once you've chosen your home, you'll surely want to start redecorating. For tips on hiring an interior designer, contact the American Society of Interior Designer's San Diego chapter at (858) 274-3345; www.asidsandiego.com. To get a good overview of the traditions in local design, check out the San Diego Historical Society's showcase home, open for tours in May. Call (619) 533-7355 for information.

National Real Estate Offices

Century 21 National Referral Service
(800) 4-HOUSES
www.century21.com
Since the early 1970s Century 21 (then 20th Century) has saturated the country with its local offices with the intent of making home buying a happy and satisfying experience for its clients. With offices throughout the county, Century 21 has become a major force in the real estate industry here.

The Web site for SANDAG, the county's regional planning agency, at www.sandag.org lists links for its many member communities from Carlsbad to Vista. These local Web sites are loaded with info on community planning, issues, and events.

Century 21 is the world's largest franchiser of residential real estate brokerage offices, thus their agents and brokers receive the very best in training, management, and administrative and marketing support. If you call the number listed above, a representative will provide a referral to a San Diego Century 21 office. Alternatively, you can call any Century 21 office nationwide, and agents will be happy to help you find an office to suit your needs.

Coldwell Banker Residential Brokerage
(888) 912-2476
www.coldwellbanker.com
Colbert Coldwell founded his company in 1906 after the San Francisco earthquake, mainly as a result of his disapproval of agents who were taking advantage of vulnerable homeowners. His philosophy was to place the customer's interest above all, and that philosophy remains the driving force behind Coldwell Banker today.

Coldwell Banker has a long history of integrity, exceptional service, and customer satisfaction.

Prudential California Realty
(888) 888-7356
www.prudentialcal.com
With corporate offices in the North County Coastal community of Del Mar, Prudential California Realty is one of the main real estate players in San Diego. The company has more than 30 offices countywide.

By calling the relocation information number above, you can find the right agent to fit your special needs and one who speaks your personal language. You will also receive a free relocation packet that includes details about our region and average home prices. It also provides a good sketch of our neighborhoods.

RE/MAX Realtors
(800) 227-3629
www.remax.com
RE/MAX has more than a dozen offices in San Diego County. RE/MAX people are strong on community involvement and support volunteerism in the communities they serve. The type of involvement for a RE/MAX associate is as varied as the neighborhood he or she lives and serves. One might spend time with a scouting program and another provide expertise to Habitat for Humanity.

Apartment Hunting

Just as you can find magazines to help you buy a home, so can you find guides to help you rent an apartment. Located in the same places as home buyers guides—racks in supermarkets, drugstores, and convenience stores—these free guides will give you an idea of how the rental market stacks up in San Diego County.

Apartments for Rent
3883 Ruffin Road, Suite A, San Diego
(858) 279-2232
Serving all of San Diego County, *Apartments for Rent* is published every two weeks. It is broken down by region and features full-color photos of apartment complexes around the county. The guide also has a comprehensive list of amenities and restrictions of each complex (it will tell you, for instance, about pet policies). It also includes contact phone numbers and maps. When it comes to driving time, this guide can be a big time-saver.

SanDiegoApartments.Com
2878 Camino del Rio S.,
Central San Diego
(619) 209-4190
This excellent Web site lists up-to-date

rental units throughout the county. They can help you locate roommates and narrow your search to your specific needs. There's also a very informative section of background information on San Diego and links to the Metropolitan Transit District and other helpful Web sites.

Home-buying Magazine

Even if after digesting all our neighborhood descriptions you still feel in the dark about San Diego real estate, a good way to get a feel for what's out there is to pick up one of several free magazines or guides. They all have photos, descriptions, prices, and referrals to real estate agents. Look for these in racks at the front of most supermarkets and drugstores and some convenience stores, too.

Harmon Homes
9682 Via Excelencia, Suite 100
San Diego
(858) 874-2459
Broken down into several editions by region, this twice-monthly magazine features resale properties with descriptions and photos. Each property also has a referral to the listing agent.

EDUCATION AND CHILD CARE

Education is as essential to residents of San Diego County as a healthy dose of outdoor activity. While that might oversimplify our commitment to it, we're sincerely proud of the opportunities that exist for those in search of knowledge.

San Diego is nothing if not diverse. In fact nearly 42 percent of San Diego students are Hispanic, with about 37 percent white, 7 percent black, and the rest, a rainbow of other minorities. Twenty percent of the county's students speak Spanish. Of these, some are bilingual but many are English-learners, a fact that tends to lower standardized test scores compared to other parts of the country. Compared with students throughout the state of California, however, SAT scores of San Diego students are slightly higher: 511 on the verbal test and 527 for math. Our more than 600 public schools, hundreds of private schools, and scores of community colleges, colleges, and universities (described in the Higher Education chapter) teach children and adults from dozens of ethnic groups and economic backgrounds in settings as varied as mountains, deserts, farms, and urban areas. Subject areas taught in vocational and tech schools also reflect the diversity of San Diego's students and their varied interests: from computer sciences, interior design, and architectural drafting to the advanced massage and holistic health practitioner courses offered by the Pacific College of Oriental Medicine. It doesn't take much "book learning" to see the diversity of instruction, education, and training San Diego offers.

EDUCATION

Public Schools

Under the authority of the San Diego County Office of Education, 6401 Linda Vista Road, San Diego (858-292-3500; www.sdcoe.k12.ca.us), there are more than 600 public schools, kindergarten through 12th grade. Amazingly, San Diego County has 42 school districts within its boundaries. Throughout the county the average student to teacher ratio is 21:1; average class size is 20 in kindergarten and 28.6 in sixth grade. San Diego public schools enrollment went down by 20,000 students between 1999 and 2006, in part because the high cost of housing has squeezed out younger and lower-income families.

The breakdown of schools is impressive, too. There are independent study schools, special education schools (a selection that addresses special needs from learning challenges to hearing impairments), alternative schools, and continuation schools for students who learn best outside the traditional high school environment.

Another form of nontraditional schooling are charter shools, public schools that are independently run under the auspices of the school district. The charter school is freed from the obligation of complying with the state education code, for example, and given leeway to do things as it thinks best. Examples include High Tech High, whose name says it all, and Preuss School. Situated on the UCSD campus, Preuss School was formed to reach highly motivated students from lower-income areas in San Diego, where students often do not reach their potential.

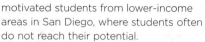

Although federal and state tax dollars and budgets are not what they should be, a large number of public and private organizations and businesses have thankfully stepped in to contribute both time and money to San Diego students through partnership programs. The San Diego Unified School District alone (San Diego's largest) has some 1,200 partnerships pairing students with such diverse entities as SeaWorld and the San Diego History Museum, Costco and Krispy Kreme donuts, public libraries, the army and navy, local banks, food co-ops, taekwondo studios and virtually every institution of higher learning in the county. Their contributions range from tutoring in basic math and reading skills to job shadowing, resume writing, and providing guest speakers and job fairs.

If you'd like to know more about the public schools in the area in which you're thinking of living, make an appointment with the school's principal or the district's superintendent.

Each year around two-thirds of all graduating seniors go on to higher education. The number is never exact, since some seniors take classes and work part-time or return to college after working for a year. For a complete look at the opportunities for higher education in San Diego County, be sure to read our Higher Education chapter. Many high school seniors attend our community colleges. Others focus on our excellent colleges and universities, often referred to as "alphabet soup," with school acronyms from CSUSM and USD to SDSU and UCSD.

Some kids need help to get into college. The American Center for Learning (www.americancenterforlearning.com) has centers in South Bay and San Diego where students can use their after-school time for studying for SATs, learning basic or remedial skills, taking classes beyond what's available at school, or learning Spanish or English as a second language. They have a location in the South Bay (Chula Vista, 619-656-6026) and in San Diego near Scripps Ranch (858-549-4250). In North County, Study Depot (760-632-0242; www.studydepot.com) tutors children individually or in small groups, after school or on weekends, in order for children to improve their grades and learn study skills like note-taking, concise writing, and speed reading.

Nearly one-fifth of San Diego County's high school seniors are taking advanced placement (college prep) courses.

Quite a number of San Diego's learners seek out other educational arenas, such as the no-cost programs offered by the Office of Education. Nontraditional students seem to be everywhere these days as they learn new skills or retrain in another career. Classes offered by the Regional Occupation Program (ROP) help these students pursue a myriad of educational choices. (For information call 858-292-3611, see www.sdcoe.k12.ca/rop.

ROP courses are diverse. They include the expected computer skills and welding, but you can also learn about media production, accounting, cabinet making, translation services, grocery operations, dog and cat grooming, international trade, and fashion design. With 500 current course offerings, ROP is perhaps the best educational bargain in San Diego. All classes are free, though some require a small materials fee. Some classes are held during the day; quite a few are evening classes. Lots of San Diego adults and high school students take ROP classes for the joy of learning new things.

Private Schools

In San Diego there are hundreds of private educational opportunities. The choices range from the tiny ones to those with large student bodies and worldwide pres-

Continuing education classes in a wide range of subjects are offered for California residents at locations throughout the county. Administered by the San Diego Community College District, the program offers free and inexpensive courses in everything from Mediterranean cooking to mobility skills and firefighting to floral design. For more information check the Web site at www.sandiegocet.net.

tige. As in many other larger cities and regions, the majority of San Diego's private schools focus on specific religious beliefs. For example, nearly every Catholic parish in San Diego has an elementary school, which in turn is affiliated with a Catholic high school. If you're interested in religious schooling for your kids, contact your pastor or the advisor for your church or synagogue. Tuition varies a great deal according to the size of the facility and its location, courses, and staff.

In addition to those schools with a religious affiliation, there are other well-respected private schools here in San Diego; most can only be described as expensive.

Most parents in San Diego County are comfortable sending their children off each day to one of our public schools. Because most of the private schools are out of financial reach for San Diego parents, we give you just a sampling. Check the yellow pages under "Schools" for other private schools.

Army-Navy Academy
2605 Carlsbad Boulevard, Carlsbad
(760) 729-2385, ext. 263,
(888) 762-2338
www.army-navyacademy.com

The Army-Navy Academy is a distinguished North County Coastal military school. It's located about 4 blocks north and east of the Coaster commuter train station in downtown Carlsbad, and, even more pleasing to students, it sits right on the beach. It is a year-round boarding school for boys in 7th through 12th grades. Students come from every corner of the globe and from San Diego, too. Instruction is diverse and intense, and, yes, students wear military-style uniforms. Four years in the junior ROTC program is mandatory; honors programs, an advanced English-as-a-second-language program, and full athletics are available. The student-to-faculty ratio is 9 to 1. More than 90 percent of Army-Navy Academy graduates go on to college; many attend military academies like West Point.

La Jolla Country Day School
9490 Genesee Avenue, La Jolla
(858) 453-3440
www.ljcds.org

A coed school, the respected La Jolla Country Day has an enrollment of about 1,000 students, nursery school through 12th grade. This is a college-prep school with an emphasis on traditional liberal arts. The average class size for K-12 classes is about 18. After graduation it's likely that its students will go on to notable universities like Harvard, MIT, and Stanford.

Montessori Schools

Montessori schools have the motto "The Child Comes First." There are some 30 schools throughout the county, from National City to Oceanside and Ramona to Coronado. The Montessori method emphasizes respect for the child and working at the pace and using methods that work best for the individual, highlighting hands-on experience. Each school is privately owned, so curriculum varies. Since the schools are independent, there's no central body. To find a school in your neighborhood, it's easiest to search the Web by entering into the search engine Montessori and the name of your community.

Vocational and Technical Schools

We'd be lax if we didn't point out some of the outstanding private vocational and technical schools in San Diego for specialized education. For a complete list, consult the yellow pages under "Schools." Remember, if you're looking for a technical or vocational program, review the cost-free possibilities with ROP mentioned above (and see the Close-up), ask plenty of questions, and, if possible, talk to graduates before enrolling.

The Art Institute of California–San Diego
7650 Mission Valley Road, San Diego
(858) 598–1200, (866) 275–2422
www.taac.edu

Devoted to advertising, animation, graphic and fashion design, interior design, culinary arts, and computer arts, The Art Institute of California offers both associate's and bachelor's degrees. Among the more than 60 courses in the curriculum are life drawing, typography, and multimedia design, as well as general education classes such as English, acting, and algebra.

Many students already have jobs in advertising and want to improve their skills, while others attend to develop a career in the field. Students' work is critiqued by other students and professors. Facilities include fully equipped classrooms, video cameras and monitors, still cameras, and audio recording equipment.

Student chefs in their final year of training run the on-site Palette restaurant, where both the menu and hours of operation are subject to change. (Call 858-598-1405 for a resservation.)

California Institute for Human Science
701 Garden View Court, Encinitas
(760) 634–1771
www.cihs.edu

The California Institute for Human Science, an accredited university, offers graduate and post-graduate degrees in the fields of life physics, comparative religion, and philosophy; human science; and clinical psychology. It also offers online courses and degrees.

Founded by Hiroshi Motoyama, Ph.D., the institute's unique curriculum is designed to prepare the mature student to contribute meaningfully as a professional and a scholar in the emerging global society.

The California Institute for Human Science has daytime, weekend, and evening courses and workshops.

Coleman College
8888 Balboa Avenue, San Diego
(858) 499–0202

1284 West San Marcos Boulevard, San Marcos
(760) 747–3990

Founded in 1963 to support the budding computer industry, Coleman College has established itself as a resource and cornerstone of private technical education in San Diego. Classes are small, typically about one instructor to 10 or 15 students, often less. The coursework is intensive. Classes are held in the day and evening, and start-up cycles occur often. Coleman's innovative curriculum gives career training first so students can become qualified for a computer-related position in as little as seven months. Longer programs include those for associate's, bachelor's, and master's degrees.

Oh-so-soulful mariachi tunes are played by students of 14 schools in South County's Sweetwater Union High School District. Classes teach students folkloric dancing as well as guitarrón, recinto, violin, and other traditional musical instruments played in Mexican mariachi music.

CLOSE-UP

A Star (Program) is Born

If the name Mary Catherine Swanson sounds like that of a famous star, it is. But if you're thinking a new Hollywood teen queen or perhaps a long-gone icon from the talkies, you're wrong. Mary Catherine Swanson is a well-known San Diego personality in the arena of education, not the silver screen.

The vivacious English teacher's claim to fame is the Advancement Via Individual Determination, or AVID program, created in 1980. The AVID program's goal is to give an emotional and intellectual push to poor students with potential. That's "poor" as in "underachieving"—but many of her students indeed come from families of lesser economic means as well as families of color.

Under a federal mandate to provide better education for all students, minority kids were being bused to white neighborhoods to improve their chances of success. Yet Ms. Swanson found that many were still failing. Despite a change of venue, the milieu of mediocrity and dearth of challenging, interesting classes meant that an unacceptably high percentage of bright students still struggled to achieve even passing scores. Remedial programs that should have helped them to conquer basic math and reading were almost as likely to bore them so badly that the kids would quit school instead.

Without any particular training or business background other than the desire to help her students succeed, Ms. Swanson designed the AVID program to offer poor and limited-English-speaking

Programs include computer information science, computer engineering technology, graphic design, and computer applications and networks. The college also has a placement service for graduates and those seeking part-time employment while studying.

Contractors Licensing Service
340 Vernon Way, Suite C, El Cajon
(619) 440-2122, (800) 454-2776
www.licenses4contractors.com
Contractors Licensing Service, established in 1965, provides exam preparation programs for would-be contractors. There are home-study programs and even a crash-course curriculum. In addition to the educational segment, their services include help in completing official forms and weekly progress checks with the state to ensure a timely issuance of licenses.

Design Institute of San Diego
8555 Commerce Avenue, San Diego
(858) 566-1200
www.disd.edu
This college is devoted exclusively to education in interior design and is accredited by the Foundation for Interior Design Education Research as well as the Accrediting Council for Independent Colleges and Schools. Founded in 1977, the institute teaches students creative and technical skills, sound business practices, and history of design. The four-year program leads to a B.A. in fine arts in interior design.

students more challenging material along with extra help. Results were almost immediate. Not only were her students passing basic courses and graduating from high school, many were excelling at college prep courses and applying for prestigious universities as well.

After several years' hard sell at her own Clairemont High School, within the San Diego Unified School District, Ms. Swanson broadened her scope by moving to the San Diego County Office of Education. As the years passed and successes mounted, detractors and skeptics became boosters. Since its inception, the AVID program is used in more than 20,000 schools in 16 countries. Worldwide, the year 2004 saw 98 percent of AVID students graduate from high school: an outstanding mark. In the same year, 81 percent of California's AVID pupils completed requirements for entrance to the prestigious University of California, as opposed to 34 percent of non-AVID students throughout the state.

For her efforts the innovative educator has received many awards and accolades, including in 2001 *Time* magazine's teacher of the year award and the Charles A. Dana Award for Pioneering Achievement in Education.

Poised to retire in 2006, the California native has had the satisfaction of preparing thousands of disadvantaged students for college and life beyond. She'll remain on the board of AVID, now a not-for-profit organization worth more than $20 million. And she'll no doubt continue teaching—teaching others to help students overcome the odds to succeed to the very best of their abilities.

Fashion Careers of California College
1923 Morena Boulevard, San Diego
(619) 275-4700, (888) 322-2999
www.fashioncareerscollege.com

Students interested in a career in the fashion industry can obtain a certificate or an associate of arts degree in either fashion merchandising or fashion design here. The curriculum includes internships and study tours to New York and Los Angeles, and as part of the program, students work on fashion shows and other activities in the San Diego fashion industry.

Certificates in either merchandising or design can be obtained in one academic year; associate of arts degrees take two years. Credits earned at the college are accepted at major colleges for the applied arts throughout the country.

Independence University
2423 Hoover Avenue, National City
(619) 477-4800, (800) 791-7353
www.cchs.edu

Although based in San Diego County, this is basically distance education for health and business professionals. It offers 10 different degree programs from AA to master's degrees, and is accredited by the Accrediting Commission of the Distance Education and Training Council. More than 10,000 students are enrolled nationwide, and independent study schedules are personalized for each student.

The Learning Annex (619-544-9700; www.learningannex.com) provides an eclectic assortment of classes. You'll find classes from the bold (Strip for Your Lover, Meet Your Guardian Angel) to the conventional (like Word for Windows™, Secrets of Internet Search Engines). Catalogs can be found at newsstands throughout the county or by calling the number above.

Pacific College of Oriental Medicine
7445 Mission Valley Road, Suite 105
San Diego
(619) 574-6909, (800) 729-0941
www.pacificcollege.edu

As interest in holistic medicine and practices becomes more widespread, people are pursuing academic knowledge to become practitioners themselves. Approved by the Accreditation Commission of Acupuncture and Oriental Medicine (ACAOM), this college offers a wide variety of degree and diploma programs at its San Diego campus. Students can earn a master's or doctoral degree in acupuncture and traditional Oriental medicine or become a holistic health practitioner, massage therapist, massage technician, Oriental body therapist, or Tui Na practitioner.

The college offers flexible scheduling for working adults, offering courses during the day, evenings, and weekends. It also offers discounted holistic health care to the public in its community clinic. Campus tours are welcomed, and financial aid is available to those who qualify.

Platt College
6250 El Cajon Boulevard, San Diego
(619) 265-0107, (866) 752-8826
www.platt.edu

Platt College offers an associate of applied science degree in computer graphic design and multimedia design, and a bachelor of science degree in media arts. Diplomas are awarded in the areas of multimedia/animation, Web design, graphic design, and digital video production. In the graphic-design program, students learn form, color, typography, and the development of design skills. Other curricula include digital editing and postproduction, Web-site animation, game animation, organic 3D animation, and motion graphics/special effects. One of the college's primary goals is to help students find careers related to their field of study, so they maintain an active placement-assistance program for their graduates. Coursework is normally completed within one to two and one-half years, depending on the field of study chosen.

CHILD CARE

Child care is an issue close to the hearts of San Diego residents, and we wish we could tell you we have answers to working parents' quandaries. Like our fellow workers in every part of the nation, we're faced with the fact that sometimes there are no perfect choices for the care of our kids. We've tried to provide resources to get you started, however, in your hunt for safe, happy day-care and after-school programs, which we assure you can be found in San Diego. We've included a couple of special camps for kids, too.

As you review the choices for child care, whether from the phone book or one of the giveaway magazines found at the grocery store, it's crucial to check references, make impromptu visits, and ask plenty of questions. If your child requires individualized attention or special medical care, you may want to ask your pediatrician, health-care provider, or school district for a referral. To read reports about specific day-care centers, call the **Community Licensing Board** at (619) 767-2200.

Religious and academic private schools often have extended day-care programs.

Within the city of San Diego, the "6-to-6" Extended School Day Program (www.sandiego.gov/6to6/schools/index.shtml) co-ordinates before- and after-school day care for students of San Diego City Unified Schools as well as private schools. The program currently serves some 22,000 kids a year. As part of the program, the Fern Street Circus (www.fernstreetcircus.com; 619-235-9756), located at the Roosevelt High campus near Balboa Park, teaches circus skills to children age six and older. After a long day at school, many children would prefer to study juggling, trapeze, and trampoline than more academic subjects. A number of YMCAs in San Diego (see our Kidstuff chapter) provide after-school activities for kids for a fee. You can reach the **YMCA Childcare Resources Service** at (800) 481-2151 or (619) 521-3055; www.ymcacrs.org, and this organization can also provide recommendations for day care in your area. Some school district elementary schools also provide this service.

For information about regional occupation programs throughout San Diego, visit www.sdcoe.k12.ca.us/rop/# or call (858) 292-3529.

Here on vacation or a business trip and need help caring for kids? If you're wondering how to keep the kids happy and safe while you're doing business and enjoying San Diego, the first step to the care issue may be a talk with the concierge or a reservations desk staff member. Often hotels, resorts, and spas have contacts with licensed and bonded babysitters and nannies (see our Spas and Resorts chapter). Some resorts have "camps" with special kid-style activities.

The Commodore Kids Club, at **Loews Coronado Bay,** 4000 Coronado Bay Road, Coronado, (619) 424-4000, has supervised programs for kids 4 to 12. Activities include arts and crafts, Ping-Pong, board games, outdoor adventures, and movies. The cost is $50 per child, including lunch; $30 for a half day. Evening care (Friday and Saturday night 6:00 to 10:00 P.M.) facilities are available for $60 per child. The resort's Generation G package provides mementos and special rates for people traveling with their grandchildren.

HIGHER EDUCATION

San Diegans took a look around one day and discovered that their recreation-oriented county had quietly turned into a remarkable enclave for higher education. Anchored by three major universities—San Diego State University (SDSU), the University of California at San Diego (UCSD), and the University of San Diego (USD)—the educational scene comprises more than 50 institutions for higher learning. Also multiplying in number are several well-respected business colleges. And finally, dozens of trade, technical, and vocational schools (which we cover in our Education and Child Care chapter) round out the higher education scene. It's really no wonder that so many fine institutions have sprung up in San Diego. After all, it's a piece of cake to draw students. The combination of excellent academics and the San Diego lifestyle is irresistible.

San Diego State University is the granddaddy of them all, established as the Normal School in 1897 by the California Legislature. It moved to its current site on Montezuma Mesa in 1931, where it evolved into the dominant liberal arts university it remains today. Opened in 1990, the San Marcos campus of the state university system serves North County students.

The university community is a crucial component of San Diego's industry. The majority of students stay put after they graduate, and they are the future of the county's business and industry. Working hand-in-hand with the local scientific community, UCSD produces the next generation of high-tech, biotech, and engineering talent so desperately needed. With its first-rate law school, USD provides the legal community with talented lawyers. All the universities are deeply involved in the surrounding community, and exchange ideas and resources among themselves. For example, the three majors established a library consortium to trade books among their students. When a student at one university requests a book from another, it is usually delivered the same day. This spirit of cooperation makes for a better educational experience for all.

In this chapter we'll give you an Insider's look at the major universities, the up-and-coming institutions, the colleges geared toward working adults, and the excellent community colleges. We'll also talk about extended-studies programs affiliated with the universities, where adult students with or without degrees can enhance their knowledge and skills or participate in certificate programs. Unless otherwise specified, all colleges are accredited by the Western Association of Schools and Colleges.

Keep in mind that we're giving you the best-known and most well-established colleges here. Plenty more await you, and if the ones described here don't fill your bill, there almost surely is an institution around town that will be perfectly tailored to your needs.

FOUR-YEAR UNIVERSITIES AND COLLEGES

Alliant International University
10455 Pomerado Road, Scripps Ranch
(858) 635-4772, (866) 825-5426
www.alliant.edu

The California School of Professional Psychology combined with U.S. International University in 2001 to form Alliant International University (AIU). The nonprofit university has six campuses in California, including one in San Diego County, as well as one in Mexico City and another in Toyko, Japan. The San Diego location serves more than 640 students and is the university's only residential campus.

Graduate and undergraduate degrees are available in a wide variety of fields, including liberal arts, education, communication, English, journalism, information systems, and business. There are post-graduate degrees in a variety of branches of psychology as well as in education, business, technology, and other fields. Distance, online, and evening courses are available for nontraditional students and those who work full time.

The Family Violence and Sexual Assault Institute, which trains individuals and institutions to understand and eliminate family violence, offers its services to the community while furthering research for the institution. The Virtual Reality Medical Center uses virtual reality therapy to treat specific neuroses, anxiety disorders, and phobias and also serves the community.

California State University at San Marcos
333 South Twin Oaks Valley Road
San Marcos
(760) 750-4000
www.csusm.edu

The new kid on the block in San Diego County, CSUSM first welcomed students in the fall of 1990 as the 20th campus in the California State University system. Nestled in the foothills of North County Inland, the 300-acre campus is home to some 7,500 students who attend one of three colleges: Arts and Sciences, Business Administration, and Education. The university is growing rapidly—by design. Enrollment is expected to surpass 18,000 by the year 2020.

CSUSM offers 20 bachelor's degrees, 13 teacher-credential programs, and 8 master's degree programs. Of the 210 faculty members (tenured and tenure-track), the vast majority have a Ph.D. The university is just starting to field some athletic teams, beginning with track and field, cross-country, and golf for men and women.

Chapman University College
7460 Mission Valley Road, San Diego
(619) 296-8660
www.chapman.edu

Chapman is the seventh-oldest university in California. An independent liberal arts college based in Orange, California, the San Diego campus offers degrees in liberal studies, criminal justice, psychology, social sciences, liberal studies, and computer information systems. There are more than two dozen campuses throughout California and Washington.

Chapman offers summer programs as well as online and evening classes. Chapman has long catered to the military population in San Diego and gives credit for military training and experience. About 1,000 students are enrolled in the school's San Diego locations.

National University
4141 Camino del Rio S., Mission Valley
(619) 563-7241
www.nu.edu

Headquartered in Mission Valley, National University has 27 campuses throughout California. There are 14 in San Diego County alone, including 6 on military bases. Its enrollment of 27,000 students makes it the second-largest private university in California. National offers a one-course-per-month format for both undergraduate and graduate programs, with most classes held in the evenings and on Saturday. The majority of students are graduate students.

Founded in 1971, the university is committed to adult learning in a convenient and practical way. Because new courses begin each month, students can enroll at any time during the year. Four schools—the School of Business and Management, the School of Education, the School of Engineering and Technology, and the School of Letters and Sciences—offer more than 45 undergraduate and graduate degree programs and 15 teaching-credential programs.

Point Loma Nazarene University
3900 Lomaland Drive, Point Loma
(619) 849-2200
www.ptloma.edu

Point Loma Nazarene University (PLNU), founded in 1902, sits on 90 acres atop the bluffs of Sunset Cliffs on the Point Loma

San Diego State University boasts modern mission-style architecture. PHOTO: COURTESY OF SAN DIEGO CONVENTION & VISITORS BUREAU

peninsula. Sponsored by the Church of the Nazarene, PLNU offers a liberal arts curriculum in an environment of Christianity in the evangelical and Wesleyan tradition. It has a small enrollment of just more than 3,000 undergraduate and graduate students. Ranked in the top tier in its category by the *U.S. News & World Report,* PLNU offers some 50 undergraduate degrees as well as graduate degrees in education, business, nursing, and religion, among other fields.

The university has satellite campuses at Mission Valley as well as two outside San Diego County, in Arcadia and Bakersfield. Nearly 80 percent of its faculty has a doctoral degree. Students participate in on-campus cultural events; extracurricular activities, including clubs and organizations, fraternities and sororities, and campus ministries; and programs abroad. Fourteen women's and men's intercollegiate sports are affiliated with the NAIA.

In 2003 Point Loma Nazarene University replaced its Crusader mascot with a snarling, African-type "sea" lion emerging from a churning ocean wave. Surfing magazine named PLNU's Young Residential Hall the "Best Surfing Dorm" in the nation.

San Diego Christian College
2100 Greenfield Drive, El Cajon
(619) 441-2200, (800) 676-2242
www.christianheritage.edu

Tucked away at the base of Shadow Mountain in East County's El Cajon, Christian Heritage College has a liberal arts curriculum. Founded in 1970 with a Christian-oriented mission, learning in all SDCC's academic programs is biblically focused.

In addition to its halls of learning, the 34-acre campus has playing fields and a swimming pool for intercollegiate and intramural sports for men and women students. Christian Heritage has 15 undergraduate academic programs, including aviation technology, sports medicine, and biblical studies to augment the more traditional disciplines. Because of its small student population of approximately 500, individualized attention is the norm. The student-teacher ratio is 15 to 1.

San Diego State University
5500 Campanile Drive, San Diego
(619) 594-5200
www.sdsu.edu

Part of the California State University system, SDSU celebrated its centennial in 1997. Since its humble beginning as a local teachers' college, it has grown into one of the nation's premiere universities, with recognized traditions of academic excellence and community service. Locals flock to the campus for concerts and lectures or to use the SDSU library, the largest library in San Diego. It is the largest institution of higher learning in San Diego, with a population of more than 26,000 undergrads and more than 5,500 graduate students.

Located atop Montezuma Mesa on the eastern edge of the city, the campus occupies more than 4.5 million square feet in 44 academic buildings, including the

106,000-square-foot Chemical Sciences Laboratory, which houses high-tech laser labs, DNA labs, and a nuclear magnetic resonance facility. Though SDSU is considered a teaching university, it has strong research programs, too. It ranks among the top universities conducting research nationwide.

Eighty-one undergraduate degrees are offered; there are also 59 master's and 13 joint doctoral programs. Complementing the academics are the extensive varsity athletic programs. Tony Gwynn Stadium opened for Aztec baseball in 1997, and Cox Arena seats 12,000 basketball fans. Inaugurated in 2001, the four-story, 130,000-square-foot Aztec Athletic Center houses the Aztec Hall of Fame, a state-of-the-art weight room, and an athletic training center for women's and men's varsity sports.

University of California, San Diego
9500 Gilman Drive, La Jolla
(858) 534-2230
www.ucsd.edu

San Diego State may be the biggest university in town, but UC San Diego is the most prestigious. Founded in 1959, UCSD incorporated the Scripps Institution of Oceanography, whose faculty is still ranked first in the nation in that field. Fifteen Nobel laureates and former astronaut Sally Ride have been enticed to teach at the university, which boasts state-of-the-art research facilities.

The San Diego Supercomputer Center, a research unit of UCSD, has a staff of 400 scientists and research personnel dedicated to developing new technology to advance science, including biosciences and environmental sciences for the national scientific community. Because of the university's close ties to San Diego's high-tech, wireless communication, and biomedical industries, its students have an advantage in securing internships, summer jobs, graduate school positions, and careers in the field. The neurosciences faculty is rated one of the best in the country.

If you're planning to attend a San Diego State University football game at Qualcomm Stadium, you can support the team by wearing the traditional Aztec colors: red and black.

Though best-known for its biotech and science programs, UCSD has plenty to offer students seeking liberal arts degrees, including theater arts, political science, and literature; its Eleanor Roosevelt College includes a mandatory two-year history program called "Making of the Modern World." Sixth College's curriculum is an amalgam of culture, art, and technology.

The undergraduate population is about 21,000, with some 3,600 in graduate programs. Despite its size and prestige, however, all six colleges offer a small-institution experience in the context of a major research university. Seventy-eight undergraduate majors are available along with more than 30 graduate programs. Seven joint doctoral programs are offered in conjunction with San Diego State University.

Though athletics are nowhere as important at UCSD as academia, Triton intercollegiate teams include men's and women's soccer, track and field, tennis, golf, and other sports. Social, athletic, and leadership opportunities include more than 300 student clubs and organizations.

Campus tours of UCSD are available Monday through Saturday (except holidays) promptly at 11:00 A.M. Stroll through the peaceful environment surrounded by eucalyptus trees, and be sure to see the extraordinary artwork, such as the mosaic snake pathway that leads to the library, an architectural wonder in itself. Call (858) 534-1935 for tour reservations and important information.

CLOSE-UP

University of San Diego

For decades the University of San Diego has been known around town as "that little Catholic college up on the hill." For a long while that was a relatively accurate assessment. It isn't any longer. That little Catholic college has grown up into a major university.

Officially chartered by the State of California in 1949, USD began as the vision of Bishop Charles Francis Buddy. Newly consecrated as Bishop of the Diocese of San Diego in 1937, the bishop visited his friend and colleague, Mother Rosalie Hill, superior vicar of the San Francisco College for Women. He shared with her his dream of inaugurating a Catholic college in his new diocese and hoped that she would join him in his quest.

Mother Hill eagerly accepted the challenge. By 1944 they were surveying sites, finally settling on a stunning piece of property in Linda Vista. The property, situated on a long mesa at the west entrance to Mission Valley, consisted of more than 100 acres overlooking Mission Bay, Old Town, and historic Presidio Hill, where Father Junipero Serra established his first mission in California. Bishop Buddy and Mother Hill named the site Alcalá Park, in honor of San Diego de Alcalá; the university had come one step closer to reality.

The two were committed to building separate colleges for men and women, but agreed that, to provide social interaction, the two should remain close to one another. Mother Hill decided that the architecture should be an adaptation of

University of San Diego
5998 Alcalá Park, Linda Vista
(619) 260-4600
www.sandiego.edu

A private Catholic institution, USD sits on a 180-acre hilltop campus overlooking Mission Bay. The university offers a liberal arts curriculum and is known for its commitment to teaching, values-oriented programs, and community involvement. The new Joan B. Kroc Institute for Peace and Justice hosts international symposia and conferences and promotes peace in the nation and the community.

More than 60 undergraduate and graduate degree programs are available to USD's 7,000 students, including doctoral programs in education and nursing. Six schools comprise the university: the College of Arts and Sciences, the School of Education, the School of Business Administration, the Hahn School of Nursing and Health Science, the Joan B. Kroc School of Peace Studies, and the School of Law (see School of Law entry that follows).

The university offers a master of arts program in international relations and has a strong international study program. ROTC and paralegal programs are increasingly popular among USD's students, who also avail themselves of more than a dozen intercollegiate sports along with dozens of club sports and intramurals. The vast majority of faculty members have a doctoral or terminal degree.

Spanish Renaissance because of its lasting appeal, its softness of line, and its quintessential California quality. Subsequent structures have remained true to that style, resulting in a campus of unparalleled beauty.

Ground was broken in 1948, and the first classes in the College for Women were held in 1950. The colleges remained separate for two decades but began allowing reciprocal course registration in the late 1960s. Finally, encouraged by Vatican II, they merged in 1972 to become the University of San Diego.

Today USD draws students from around the world who seek superior academics with a strong philosophy of values and ethics. Complementing the academic side of life at USD are intercollegiate and intramural athletic programs, campus ministry, fraternities and sororities, clubs and organizations, and a committed and wide-ranging community outreach program.

During the 1996 U.S. presidential campaign, USD received national exposure when it played host to one of the candidate debates. Those who watched the debate, which was televised live internationally, saw a beautiful campus and a flawless production. The preparations, however, were far from matter-of-fact. Shiley Theater, the venue for the debate, had to be gutted. New seats were added, air-conditioning installed, and, at the last minute, the stage was extended to accommodate the debate's town hall format. In the end all the preparations paid off, and USD got a gold star and national acclaim for its role as the perfect host.

Today the campus's buildings, the plaza, and the fountain are set off by the lush landscaping and a beautiful setting. The bishop's dream is realized; the little college on the hill has become a jewel in the crown of higher education in San Diego.

LAW SCHOOLS

All of the law schools listed here are accredited by the American Bar Association.

California Western School of Law
225 Cedar Street, downtown San Diego
(619) 239-0391
www.cwsl.edu

California Western School of Law, located in downtown San Diego, is one of just a few independent, nonprofit law schools in the country. Founded in 1924, it was admitted to the Association of American Law Schools in 1967. Dedicated to producing problem-solvers who will enhance the quality of justice in our society, Cal Western heads the California Innocence Project. In this unique program, students work with practicing criminal defense attorneys to seek the release of inmates in the state of California who maintain their factual innocence. The school runs on a trimester academic schedule, with options for full- or part-time study. The student population totals more than 900.

Thomas Jefferson School of Law
2121 San Diego Avenue, Old Town
(619) 297-9700
www.tjsl.edu

Founded in 1969, Thomas Jefferson School of Law is a private, nonprofit, independent law school whose mission is to provide legal education to a diverse array of students. The campus is located in Old

Town and consists of two Spanish-style buildings that overlook San Diego Harbor.

Dedicated to individualized instruction, class sizes at Thomas Jefferson average fewer than 30 students. Faculty and administration recognize that law school is a stressful experience, thus they provide maximum accessibility and many support services to help provide students with the necessary skills to successfully complete their course of study.

Special programs include a Judicial Internship Program that permits students to clerk for federal and state judges, and Field Placement Programs that provide opportunities for working with attorneys in public agencies such as the district attorney's office. Thomas Jefferson offers a three-year full-time or four-year part-time program.

University of San Diego School of Law
5998 Alcalá Park, Linda Vista
(619) 260-4528
www.sandiego.edu/usdlaw
Founded in 1954, USD School of Law is a member of the Association of American Law Schools and The Order of the Coif, the most distinguished rank of American law schools. The law school offers degrees of juris doctor and master of laws. In addition, joint degree programs are available in conjunction with USD's graduate schools: a master of business administration, a master of international business, and a master of arts in international relations.

The student population is approximately 365, and both full- and part-time programs are offered. The full-time program requires three years for completion; part-time students usually need four years of evening study plus one summer to complete the degree.

The Center for Public Interest Law at USD is an academic center for research, learning, and advocacy for the disadvantaged or underrepresented in state administrative proceedings. Likewise, the Children's Advocacy Institute is a legal advocacy and research center that promotes the health and well-being of California's children. The Patient Advocacy Center works to ensure the rights of the mentally disabled.

COMMUNITY COLLEGES

San Diego's eight community colleges often serve as an intermediate step between high school and university. They usually offer two-year associate's degree programs along with specialized certificate courses and vocational studies.

Grossmont-Cuyamaca Community College District
8800 Grossmont College Drive, El Cajon
(619) 644-7589
www.gcccd.net
The district includes both Cuyamaca College and Grossmont College, which offer a range of courses lasting from one day to a traditional full semester. Shorter, goal-specific courses of four to eight weeks are a great boon for working adults, as are telecourses, distance learning, weekend and afternoon-only courses, open entry/exit courses, and contract education. A bond passed by East County voters in 2002 is providing much-needed repairs and enhancements to existing structures at both colleges.

Cuyamaca Community College
900 Rancho San Diego Parkway, El Cajon
(619) 660-4000
www.cuyamaca.edu
Opened in 1978, Cuyamaca offers a comprehensive curriculum of lower division courses and academic preparation for transfer to any of the California State University or University of California campuses. In addition to general education courses, a variety of specialized disciplines are offered, ranging from anthropology and waste water management to engineering, drafting, and graphic design. Study abroad allows students to experience a foreign culture as they study the language; destinations vary but in the past have included Mexico, Central and South America, and Europe.

Cuyamaca College's 165-acre campus is located in East County. The college serves about 8,000 students in day, evening, and Saturday classes. Vocational and career education target working adults, while CISCO Academy trains students as network administrators. Entry-level and general-education requirement courses prepare other students for four-year schools. Community learning classes are free or inexpensive noncredit courses for adults, and there are summer programs for children.

Grossmont Community College
8800 Grossmont College Drive, El Cajon
(619) 644-7000
www.grossmont.net
Grossmont offers 81 associate's degrees and 68 certificates. In addition to a full range of courses in disciplines from theater arts to international business and computer systems management, students can take advantage of summer study-abroad programs. Academic and vocational counseling and resources support counseling and supplement instructional programs. Grossmont also has a community continuing education program and a Regional Occupation Program (ROP).

MiraCosta Community College
1 Barnard Drive, Oceanside
(760) 757-2121, (888) 201-8480

3333 Manchester Avenue, Cardiff
(760) 944-4449, (888) 201-8480
www.miracosta.cc.ca.us
Opened in 1964 to serve the educational needs of North County Coastal students, MiraCosta's Oceanside campus is located on a 121-acre hilltop site with panoramic views of the Pacific Ocean to the west and the mountains to the east. Seventeen miles south is the San Elijo campus, 42 acres above the San Elijo Lagoon reserve. The Oceanside campus has a student population of 6,500, and about 3,000 attend classes at the San Elijo campus. Approximately 1,000 students attend both.

General education courses prepare students for transfer to a four-year university, while associate's degrees in administration of justice, business, biotechnology, dance and dramatic arts, and many other areas are offered. Among dozens of certificate job-training courses is the CISCO certificate.

Palomar Community College
1140 West Mission Road, San Marcos
(760) 744-1150
www.palomar.edu
Serving North County Inland, Palomar's 200-acre San Marcos campus houses up-to-date classroom and laboratory facilities, the largest research library in North County, a planetarium, athletic playing fields, the Boehm Art Gallery, the 400-seat Brubeck Theatre, a wellness/fitness center, and a 45-acre arboretum. In addition to its phenomenal facilities, Palomar was named by the *Community College Journal* as one of three flagship community colleges in the United States for its emphasis on learning.

More than 26,200 students (mostly part-time) take classes at the main campus and at eight education centers throughout North County. Distance learning is available through Internet and TV courses. Students may choose from more than 250 associate's degree and certificate programs as a prelude to transfer or for vocational preparation. Palomar also offers foreign-language immersion programs and travel/study abroad.

San Diego Community College District
3375 Camino del Rio S., Mission Valley
(619) 388-6500
www.sdccd.net
All three of the colleges in the San Diego Community College District—City College, Mesa College, and Miramar College—have transfer agreements with the University of California, the California State Universities, and other universities and colleges as well.

San Diego City College
1313 Park Avenue, downtown San Diego
(619) 388-3400
www.communitycollege.net/city

Occupying 4 square blocks on the outskirts of downtown San Diego and next door to its namesake, San Diego High School, City College is the oldest community college in the San Diego District. Serving some 12,600 students, the urban campus offers an array of two-year associate's degrees and a large number of certificate programs. Associated with the college, continuing-education centers throughout the area offer both college and adult ed courses. It's perhaps the most ethnically diverse center of higher learning in the county.

The City Knights compete in intercollegiate baseball, basketball, cross-country, soccer, volleyball, tennis, and track for men and/or women. City College is distinguished by its on-campus radio station, KSDS-FM, San Diego's only 24-hour jazz station.

San Diego Mesa College
7250 Mesa College Drive, Kearney Mesa
(619) 388-2600
www.communitycollege.net/mesa
Among the largest of California's community colleges, 24,000-student Mesa College is situated in the geographic heart of San Diego, in Kearny Mesa. Sprawled across 104 acres, the college offers 70 degree and certificate programs, including a comprehensive array of health-care courses as well as those in animal health technology and biology. The $20 million Learning Resource Center—with a library, computer labs, and media facilities—opened in 1998, and the three-story Humanities and Multicultural Studies facility was inaugurated in 2003.

San Diego Miramar College
10440 Black Mountain Road, Mira Mesa
(858) 536-7800
www.communitycollege.net/miramar
Opened in 1969 on 140 acres of undeveloped land, Miramar College initially concentrated on law enforcement and fire science training. Part of a public-safety cluster of courses, these are still among the associate's degrees unique to Miramar, as are emergency medical technician (EMT) and advanced transportation (with an FAA-approved aviation program), as well as philosophy, music, and many other subjects. The college's 12,000 students avail themselves of general education and a variety of other courses for transfer to four-year colleges and universities. An athletic complex and $4 million aquatic center add to the campus's appeal.

Southwestern Community College
900 Otay Lakes Road, Chula Vista
(619) 421-6700
www.swc.cc.ca.us
The jewel of South Bay, Southwestern College was established in 1961, and construction was completed in 1964 on its 156-acre campus in eastern Chula Vista. Over the years the college has evolved into a facility that serves a diverse range of educational needs for its 19,000 students, including preparation for transfer, pursuit of two-year associate's degrees, courses for personal development and job enhancement, and acquisition of new occupational skills.

Specialized programs include hazardous material handling, emergency medical technology, and vocational nursing. Because of its proximity to the U.S.-Mexico border, Southwestern provides special focus on the maquiladora industry (binational manufacturing enterprises), importing/exporting regulations, international law, and foreign trade zones.

EXTENDED-STUDIES PROGRAMS

All three public universities in San Diego County offer outstanding extended-studies programs for individuals pursuing professional certificates, university course credits, professional development, or just general knowledge and information. The mission of extended-studies programs is to fulfill the lifelong knowledge and skill-development needs of the community at large. Classes are usually geared toward working adults and are held at flexible times during the day, evenings, and weekends.

California State University, San Marcos, Extended Studies
Foundation Classroom Building, CSUSM Campus, San Marcos
(760) 750-4020, (800) 500-9377
www.csusm.edu/es

Among the highlights of CSUSM's extended-studies program are community education courses, workshops, and seminars. At the Open University, students and community members can take regular university classes, when space is available, without going through the formal admission process. Cost per unit is the same as for matriculated students.

San Diego State University College of Extended Studies
Gateway Center, 5250 Campanile Drive San Diego
(619) 594-5152
www.ces.sdsu.edu

San Diego State's extended-studies program specializes in professional and executive development and training for some of San Diego's leading organizations. Certificate programs allow participants to become recognized specialists in a variety of fields. Most classes are held at the three-story Gateway Center, just a block off campus, which has its own parking structure. As at the CSU San Marcos campus, Open University permits students of any age to take regular university classes, space available, without formally matriculating.

Unique among extended-studies programs is SDSU's program for retired adults. This program offers not-for-credit classes such as Rival Queens of England and Harry Potter: Biblical Echoes, Kabbalah, and Mysticism. And its travel/study programs are a good way for seniors to see the world. Though geared toward older people, anyone older than age 18 can attend. The American Language Institute offers intensive a wide variety of courses, some to prepare non-native English speakers for University or work in the United States and others to prepare those people who want to teach English as a second language.

University of California, San Diego, Extended Studies and Public Programs
Extension Complex, UCSD Campus La Jolla
(858) 534-3400
www.extension.ucsd.edu

In addition to the main extension complex on the UCSD campus, the extended-studies program offers classes at several other locations. Programs at UCSD Extension focus on the telecommunications industry, information technologies, teacher education, applied health care, business management, and international languages. In addition to those specialized fields, a wide variety of general courses are available. All told, about 2,000 courses and 100 certificate programs are offered each year. Online courses are increasing in popularity, too.

HEALTH AND WELLNESS

Emergencies happen. Even the best-planned vacation or business trip can be interrupted by a visit to a doctor or hospital emergency room.

When relocating, it's always a challenge to find the right medical assistance. In this chapter we'll provide some help in locating the services you may need. Keep in mind that this chapter is not comprehensive. There are many health-care centers in San Diego, and additional satellite clinics open frequently. The ones we present are representative of the many options in this area.

San Diego has 26 accredited hospitals and several medical and scientific research organizations. Yet the demand for hospital beds is increasing, and some of the smaller institutions in outlying areas are struggling to keep up with growth and demand. We also have several specifically designated trauma centers. That means when serious trouble hits, you can be at a trauma center in minutes. In fact, San Diego is one of the nation's leaders when it comes to trauma care. San Diego is unique in that its trauma centers work together with the County Division of Emergency Medical Services to create an efficient system. That system, which coordinates the efforts of physicians, hospital staff, and county health officials, was put together in 1984 and was immediately successful: The county trauma death rate dropped by 55 percent in the first year. In 2006 San Diego's medical leaders proposed a similar system for cardiac care that would route patients to hospitals skilled in preventing heart attacks.

To say you're in good hands in San Diego is a truism. Insiders take wellness seriously, and the county has small, sophisticated wellness centers and state-of-the-art hospitals. ScrippsHealth and Sharp Healthcare are the largest providers of medical services, with branches throughout the county. Scripps includes some of San Diego's standard bearers, including Scripps Mercy Hospital, the oldest hospital in the county. Established in 1890, Mercy (as most locals call it) is San Diego's only Catholic hospital.

Our county also offers adequate mental health facilities, alternative medical care, walk-in facilities, and drug- and substance-abuse treatment centers. You'll want to check the yellow pages in the telephone directory under your specific need. The sections on home health care, mental health, physical therapists, nurses, and nursing registries, as well as clinics and care for the disabled, will help you find services. In this chapter we've included the major health-care facilities, including information on mental health, hospice programs, and alternative care. The hospitals are listed alphabetically by region. The sections on mental health, hospice, and alternative care are a countywide overview.

HOSPITALS

San Diego

Children's Hospital and Health Center
3020 Children's Way, Central San Diego
(858) 576-1700, (800) 788-9029
www.chsd.org

Opened in 1954, Children's Hospital's mission continues: to "restore, sustain, and enhance the health and development potential of children." It is now the region's only designated pediatric trauma center and the only area hospital dedicated exclusively to caring for kids, birth

Good Numbers to Keep Handy

For emergency or health-related questions and concerns, these phone numbers could help. Crisis lines are operated around the clock.

Throughout San Diego a call to 911 will bring police, ambulance, and paramedic services, most within five minutes.

Accessible San Diego (for travelers with disabilities)	(858) 279-0704
Airport Travelers Aid	(619) 231-7361
Alcohol Anonymous	(619) 265-8762
Customs, U.S.	(619) 690-8800
Dentist Referral	(800) 917-6453
Domestic Violence Services	(888) 272-1767
Harbor Police	(619) 686-6272
Highway Patrol (State Police)	(619) 220-5492
Mental Health Hot Line	(800) 479-3339
Poison Center	(800) 876-4766
Suicide Hotline	(800) 479-3339
Women's Resource Center, 24-hour help line	(760) 757-3500

through adolescence. The facility includes pediatric intensive care and neonatal intensive care. Roughly 125 trauma cases are seen per month.

From its 15 outpatient clinics to the hospital in Kearny Mesa, Children's Hospital serves all the communities in the area. It is also active in numerous outreach programs, including health education, early intervention and counseling for drug and alcohol abuse, childhood immunizations, child-abuse prevention, and child safety issues. Childrens' Chadwick Center offers programs focused on abused children and domestic violence. The center is staffed with professionals and para-professionals in the field of medicine, social work, psychology, psychiatry, child development, nursing, and education technology. The staff is committed to family-centered care and a multidisciplinary approach to child abuse and family violence. Services are provided in more than 14 satellite locations countywide, including offices in the San Diego Police Department, the County District Attorney's Office, and many family resource centers.

The elements of hope and beauty and life are represented in the main hospital's Leichtag Family Healing Garden, which is designed to provide a blend of integrative wonder and peaceful respite. The garden is available to patients, parents, and staff.

Kaiser Permanente Medical Care Center
4647 Zion Avenue, Central San Diego
(619) 528-5000, (619) 528-3290
(directions to county facilities)
www.kp.org

Centrally located in San Diego, this medical center serves those who belong to the Kaiser Permanente group. Here and at various other Kaiser facilities in the county, members can access outpatient treatments for anything from addictions to women's health problems. Most

U.S. Customs operates a phone line for information about immigration documents and making sure all your papers are in order. Visitors who are not U.S. citizens must be particularly careful about this issue if they decide to cross the border to Mexico even for a day. For information call (866) 474-4882.

patients go to the Zion Avenue facility for any care that requires a stay in the hospital. There are about 400 beds in this large medical center.

Other Kaiser facilities have pharmacies on campus; check the white pages of the phone book. The one at the Zion Avenue hospital, however, is open seven days a week. This hospital also features a well-staffed emergency facility where patients are treated for life-threatening and non-life-threatening needs.

Scripps Memorial Hospital, La Jolla
9888 Genesee Avenue, La Jolla
(858) 457-4123
www.scrippshealth.org

Scripps Hospital has been in its present location since 1964 and now includes a huge array of high-tech medical options and services. Many believe that the Scripps Health system is the finest in the country. It's by far the most extensive health provider in the county. Scripps is also part of the Trauma System. The Scripps Polster Breast Care Center provides comprehensive health care and educational services for women. The 293-bed acute-care facility is located on a 43-acre campus in the heart of the Golden Triangle area of Central San Diego. For doctor referrals call (800) 727-4777.

For general San Diego health-care information, contact the San Diego County Medical Society at (858) 565-8888, www.sdcms.org.

Sharp Coronado Hospital
250 Prospect Place Coronado
(619) 522-3600
www.sharp.com

This 204-bed acute-care hospital was established in 1942 and continues to serve the Coronado community. The hospital has four operating rooms, an intensive care unit, and a 24-hour emergency room. It provides obstetrical services, sub-acute and long-term care, and rehabilitation therapies.

The Motion Center, a state-of-the-art fitness facility, provides therapy and fitness programs for inpatients, outpatients, and the community. In addition to operating the Villa Coronado skilled nursing facility, the hospital also offers senior services such as skin cancer screening, mature drivers' courses, and health-education classes.

Sharp Mary Birch Hospital for Women
3003 Health Center Drive, San Diego
(858) 541-3400
www.sharp.com

Opened in 1992, this hospital provides services for women in all stages of life. In a single location and with more than 108 licensed acute beds and 61 neonatal intensive care beds, the hospital, which has its own pharmacy, focuses on complete care, including normal and high-risk obstetrics (delivering nearly 7,000 babies a year), diagnostic testing for women and infants, and in- and outpatient gynecological care. It is known for its Sharp Fertility Center and the services of the Sharp Perinatal Center, an ambulatory center for women experiencing high-risk pregnancy. It also provides a "mother's milk depot," which stores breast milk for babies in need. The hospital continues to be recognized nationally as one of few similar facilities dedicated to women's care.

Sharp Memorial Hospital
7901 Frost Street, Central San Diego
(858) 541-3400
www.sharp.com

With 340 beds, Sharp Memorial on Frost Street is Sharp HealthCare's largest hospital.

As one of San Diego's trauma centers, it handles more than 1,000 trauma cases annually. Also a provider of cardiac care, each year it performs thousands of cardiac cauterizations and hundreds of angioplasties and cardiac surgeries.

Opened in 1955 and staffed by more than 1,100 physicians, it is especially known for outstanding programs in cardiac care, trauma care, cancer treatment, pulmonary care services, rehabilitation, and multi-organ transplantation. The hospital is currently undergoing a major expansion, with a new hospital scheduled to open in 2007.

Memorial also offers extensive outpatient care and prevention programs. Its Sharp Senior Health Center offers health groups and services for seniors. Its Web site is an excellent source of health-care tips.

UCSD Medical Center - Hillcrest
200 West Arbor Drive, San Diego
(619) 543-6222
http://health.ucsd.edu
UCSD Medical Center, associated with the University of California system, is the only academic medical center in the region. It is also the only Level I Trauma Center in San Diego, admitting approximately 1,700 patients a year. Primary and specialized care are combined with education and research at this 386-bed hospital. Among the clinical specialties are the solid organ transplant and bone marrow transplant programs, the burn center, and high-risk pregnancy management and infant special care. In April 2006, UCSD Medical Center was designated as a Baby Friendly Hospital by the global program sponsored by WHO/UNICEF for its commitment to actively encouraging breastfeeding as the primary source of newborn nutrition. It is only one of 53 hospitals in the United States and only the second in San Diego County to receive this recognition.

The AIDS Foundation maintains a toll-free number for questions and assistance. They can be reached at (800) 367-2437.

North County Coastal

Scripps Memorial Hospital, Encinitas
354 Santa Fe Drive, Encinitas
(760) 753-6501
www.scrippshealth.org
This state-of-the-healing-arts hospital joined the Scripps Health system in 1978 with nearly 140 acute-care licensed beds available. The hospital's staff includes more than 700 trained professionals. You'll also find a caring team of volunteers. The facility provides 24-hour emergency services, intensive care, cancer/oncology, nuclear medicine, occupational medicine, orthopedics, neurology, and an ambulatory surgery center.

Tri-City Medical Center
4002 Vista Way, Oceanside
(760) 724-8411
www.tri-citymed.com
Tri-City Medical Center in North County Coastal has been ranked among the nation's top 100 hospitals four times. This 400-bed facility at the Oceanside center includes an around-the-clock emergency room (the second busiest in San Diego

Jonas Salk, the developer of the polio vaccine that bears his name, founded The Salk Institute for Biological Studies in La Jolla in the 1960s. Famed architect Louis Kahn designed the institute's campus at 10010 North Torrey Pines Road. Its simplicity and elegance make it a must-see for architecture buffs. The institute offers a weekly guided tour for the general public. For information and reservations contact the Institute Relations Office at (858) 453-4100, ext. 1287.

CLOSE-UP

Volunteer Doula Program

Unique to UCSD Medical Center at Hillcrest is the Hearts & Hands Volunteer Doula Program, offering a doula, free of charge, to any woman delivering her baby at this facility.

"Doula" is a Greek word originally meaning "woman's servant." The role of a birth doula is to provide continuous physical and emotional support to a woman during her labor. The doula is not part of the medical staff; she doesn't take blood pressures or temperatures and she doesn't give shots. Doulas "hold the space" for women as they labor, offering comfort and educating them and their families about the birth process.

To help laboring women with pain reduction and relaxation, doulas use massage, aromatherapy, acupressure, position changes, and music therapy. Numerous clinical studies have shown that birth outcomes for mother and baby are improved with the presence of a doula; labors are shorter with fewer complications and women report less negative feelings about their childbirth experience. Also, interventions such as epidurals, the use of forceps, and cesarean sections are substantially reduced.

The Hearts & Hands Volunteer Doula Program at UCSD Medical Center in Hillcrest is the only program of its kind in San Diego County. Women wanting to become volunteer doulas must attend a daylong introductory training course and a tour of the birthing facilities. New doulas then attend several births with mentors for actual "hands-on" experience. Volunteer doulas do not work in shifts; once a commitment is made to a woman

County) to provide on-the-spot care and dispense life-saving procedures. Services include a state-of-the-art cardiac care facility, family childbirth center, and neuroscience center for stroke victims. For physician referral call (760) 940-5781.

North County Inland

Fallbrook Hospital
624 East Elder Street, Fallbrook
(760) 728-1191, (800) 647-6464
www.fallbrookhospital.com

The Fallbrook Hospital, a 140-bed healthcare organization operated by Community Health Systems, Inc., has served the people of Fallbrook, Bonsall, Rainbow, De Luz, and Temecula Valley since 1950. It provides both high-tech care and loving high-quality caring to North County Inland residents.

The staff calls it "a hospital without walls," since it offers home-health nursing, a hospice program, private home services, and a nurse-monitored walking regimen (part of their Cardiac Rehabilitation program). At the hospital proper, you'll find a women's center and services, a skilled nursing facility, and emergency programs. You'll also find active volunteers who bring a pet-therapy program to patients.

to assist in her labor and delivery, the doula does not leave until the baby is born, no matter how long that may take. Statistically, the average time a volunteer doula attends a laboring woman is 14 hours, but that may vary considerably and can be much longer.

Ann Fulcher is the Hearts & Hands program manager and has been with the organization since its beginning. "UCSD Medical Center has highly trained experts in high-risk maternity care, but also a Birth Center with true midwifery care, plus one of the largest doula programs in the country. Doulas are still one of the best-kept secrets in some circles, but women who give birth with a doula by their side swear by the personal, one-on-one support."

Women giving birth at UCSD Medical Center may utilize the volunteer doula program whether they plan to deliver in the Birth Center or in the more traditional Labor and Delivery unit. The Birth Center handles low-risk pregnancies and is staffed by certified nurse-midwives. There are five birthing suites with comfy double or queen-size beds and rocking chairs. If a woman experiences complications or desires anesthesia during her labor, she is cared for in the Labor and Delivery unit.

Hope Renn, a nurse-midwife at UCSD Medical Center says, "For many of our clients, a doula is the difference between a medicated birth and an unmedicated one, a fearful experience and a peaceful one. I am continually awed by the great time commitment the volunteer doulas make to support our families."

—*Susan Humphrey*

Palomar Medical Center
555 East Valley Parkway, Escondido
(760) 739-3000
www.pphs.org

Located in the heart of Escondido, this 319-bed acute-care hospital boasts a well-respected trauma center. In addition, it has a 24-hour emergency department and the area's first state-of-the-art cardiac, oncology, and general medical/surgical center. The Birth Center offers mothers high-tech medical care in private suites.

This facility is part of the Palomar/Pomerado Health System and shares certain services with Pomerado Hospital. Among them are radiology services, a hospice, and an industrial medicine program. Palomar Medical Center is also a designated Kaiser Permanente emergency center. For doctor referrals for Palomar and Pomerado hospitals, call (800) 628-2880.

Pomerado Hospital
15615 Pomerado Road, Poway
(858) 613-4000
www.pphs.org

A 107-bed acute-care hospital located in the rapidly growing Poway area, this facility has a round-the-clock emergency center. Along with the fine medical and surgical care, the hospital provides the kind of caring atmosphere not found in some mechanized hospital settings. Pomerado shares a health-care board with Palomar Hospital;

the two facilities share radiology and hospice services, health-care boards, and an industrial medicine program. This facility is known for offering private rooms with a view of the surrounding countryside.

East County

Grossmont Hospital
5555 Grossmont Center Drive, La Mesa
(619) 465-0711
www.sharp.com

Affiliated with Sharp HealthCare, this is the largest and most comprehensive hospital in East County. Grossmont celebrated its 50th anniversary in 2006. In addition to acute-care services, it offers cardiac care, women's services, rehabilitation, orthopedics, cancer treatment, pediatric care, mental health services, a hospice program, and hyperbaric medicine. Also, the hospital has a comprehensive sleep-disorder program, unique in the area.

The hospital operates the David and Donna Long Center for Cancer Treatment and Cardiovascular Diagnosis, which was the first cancer center in San Diego County. In addition, there's a Senior Resource Center and Women's Health Center on-site.

South Bay

Paradise Valley Hospital
2400 East Fourth Street, National City
(619) 470-4321
www.paradisevalleyhospital.org

Along with fine general medical care, Paradise Valley offers outstanding service in the areas of cardiology and oncology. Here you'll also find 24-hour emergency and walk-in services and the New Life Family Center. Prospective parents come here for childbirth classes and then to have their babies in a comfortable, homelike atmosphere. The 237-bed campus also includes a center for health and well-being called the Body Works. The center offers low-cost massage and yoga classes. The hospital also offers pediatric services and a transitional-care skilled nursing service.

Scripps Memorial Hospital, Chula Vista
435 H Street, Chula Vista
(619) 691-7000
www.scrippshealth.com

Serving people throughout the South Bay, this is another in the string of Scripps Hospitals. Centrally located in Chula Vista on a 13.5-acre campus, the hospital has a 24-hour emergency department, intensive care unit, laboratory, and lobby. There are 138 acute-care-licensed beds and more than 700 employees. A Level II neonatal intensive care nursery provides short-stay care for low-birth-weight babies. The facility joined the Scripps Health system in 1986.

Sharp Chula Vista Medical Center
751 Medical Center Court, Chula Vista
(619) 482-5800
www.sharp.com

Sharp Chula Vista is a comprehensive medical center in South Bay. The hospital offers a variety of services, including outpatient surgery, cardiac-care programs and facilities, a certified cancer treatment program, and a full scope of programs for women in all stages of life. More than 2,000 cardiac procedures are performed every year, including 400 open-heart surgeries.

The hospital provides 24-hour emergency care and is equipped with a heliport. A women's and infants' pavilion provides obstetric and gynecological services.

MENTAL HEALTH SERVICES

Mental health facilities are often included in many of our county's hospitals. Some provide comprehensive care while others only offer emergency services. Some facilities specialize in substance-abuse problems. In the phone book's yellow pages, you'll find a listing for "Mental Health." When calling, you'll want to ask about the specific services offered and whether your health-care coverage provides for those services.

Sharp Mesa Vista Hospital
7850 Vista Hill Avenue, San Diego
(858) 694-8300
www.sharp.com
Sharp Mesa Vista is the largest freestanding psychiatric hospital in San Diego County. The 150-bed facility was opened in 1963 and became affiliated with Sharp HealthCare in 1998. It offers premier psychiatric services with a medical staff that includes 40 psychiatrists.

Treatment programs are designed for specific patient populations, including adults, children, and chemical dependents. It shares services with the U.S. Navy's adult psychiatric inpatient program, its child and adolescent psychiatry program, and the department of obstetrics.

IMMEDIATE-CARE FACILITIES

Walk-in clinics are found throughout the county, and they're an excellent resource for minor injuries and medical problems. Usually found in strip malls and the central areas of neighborhoods, these centers can treat non-life-threatening injuries and illnesses. They will treat anyone, but if you think you may want to use their services, check with your insurance carrier. If you have a life-threatening illness, some HMOs will pay for treatment at a hospital emergency room but will not pick up the tab for walk-in clinic treatment. The great advantage with these clinics is that you usually don't have to deal with the long waits that are often a necessary part of hospital emergency room treatment.

We do recommend that you visit a hospital's emergency room if you're in need of immediate, serious medical care. Our hospital emergency rooms provide excellent, state-of-the-art medical services on a round-the-clock basis. There is usually a hospital within 20 minutes of any place you might be in San Diego. No matter what your immediate need, you'll be directed to the level of care you require, often within minutes of your arrival.

Keep in mind that if you do not have insurance or your carrier cannot be billed for the services you require, you'll be required to pay when services are rendered, regardless of whether you go to a hospital emergency room or a walk-in clinic. You'll find listings for walk-in clinics and immediate-care facilities listed under "Clinics" in the phone book's yellow pages.

i

Before traveling anywhere, including south of the border, write down the prescription medications you're currently taking. Keep the list in your wallet. Should you need medical help, the list could be a lifesaver.

ALTERNATIVE CARE

Alternative health care isn't everyone's cup of java, yet for those who choose to seek health and wellness in some of the ancient traditions, the choices in San Diego are excellent.

Your best bet when seeking alternative medical care is to ask for referrals from people you know and trust. Remember, you can also call and ask questions about the practitioner's methods, background, and certification.

When making an appointment, discuss the expected treatment and costs in detail, along with possible side effects. It's fair, too, to ask for references.

Most alternative health-care facilities offer a full "menu" of services. These might include acupuncture, shiatsu, and acupressure techniques. The services may help you quit smoking or provide drug-free solutions to pain or alternative therapies for women's health problems. The yellow pages give a complete listing of practitioners in the areas of chiropractic, acupuncture, herbology, holistic medicine, Chinese herbal therapies, therapeutic massage, and other treatments. Swedish/circulatory massage, sports massage, and foot reflexology are additional health-wise options you may wish to explore.

The Chopra Center at La Costa Resort and Spa
2013 Costa del Mar Road, Carlsbad
(760) 931-7566, (888) 424-6772
www.chopra.com
Located at the La Costa Resort and Spa in Carlsbad, this wellness center was founded in 1995 by Deepak Chopra, M.D., one of the nation's most recognized specialists in alternative healing. The center offers single- and multiday programs on all aspects of wellness, medical consultations including the principles of Ayurveda, and a day spa. Dr. Chopra is a media celebrity, and his center attracts clients from throughout the world who want to improve the quality of their lives and their health.

HOSPICE CARE

Hospice care has long been a part of San Diego's health-care picture. Most hospice organizations have in-home services, and several are available for residential stays for terminal illness. The program is open to those whose disease prognosis is measured in months, not years, and who are seeking comfort, not cure. Patients may elect to stay at home or at a licensed facility. Most hospices include medical directors, registered nurses, social workers, the clergy, home health aides, and volunteers. Hospice is a model program, one that never forgets that patients are people.

San Diego Hospice & Palliative Care, 4311 Third Avenue, San Diego, (619) 688-1600, (866) 688-1600, is a county leader in hospice care and the oldest hospice in the area for persons facing a life-limiting illness. The organization is a nationally recognized leader in hospice care, education, and research.

In North County Coastal you can contact **Hospice of North Coast,** 5441 Avenida Encinitas, Carlsbad, (760) 431-4100, (877) 433-5591. This program reaches those who prefer care within their homes; however, the staff can coordinate licensed residential care, too.

In North County Inland hospice care can be coordinated by **Fallbrook Hospital District,** 624 East Elder Street, Fallbrook, (760) 728-1191, for both in-facility care and at-home hospice assistance.

Also in North County Inland is **Elizabeth Hospice,** 150 West Crest Street, Escondido, (760) 737-2050 or (800) 797-2050. The Elizabeth Hospice team is available to the general public and, as a nonprofit, mission-driven agency, provides services regardless of the patient's ability to pay.

Some of the county's hospitals also offer hospice programs, and, in addition, there are private hospice plans. The hospitals that provide hospice care include Grossmont Hospital, Fallbrook Hospital, and Tri-City Medical Center.

RETIREMENT

With San Diego's perfect weather, relaxed lifestyle, and great outdoor opportunities, most locals take leisure time as seriously as those who choose to retire from full-time employment. We believe that regardless of one's age, San Diego is easy on the body and soul.

Most who retire in San Diego immediately feel right at home; after all, seniors are a valued part of every neighborhood. Folks who call San Diego home try to stay here when retirement beckons, though it's tempting to take advantage of high real estate prices, sell our homes, and splurge on retirement fun. Others move from those places where the white stuff accumulates each winter—and we're not talking beach sand. The benefits include the weather and numerous outdoor activities. This is a water-sport and golf paradise (just check out our chapters on these topics). The downside of retirement in San Diego is the cost of living. The county is one of the more expensive areas in the United States, and fewer seniors are retiring here.

According to the U.S. Census Bureau, persons 65 years old or older made up 11.1 percent of the population of San Diego County. In some neighborhoods, such as Rancho Bernardo, San Marcos, and Rancho Santa Fe, that percentage is considerably higher. In nearly every community in our county there's a comfortable mix of families, singles, and retirees. See our Relocation chapter to get a feel for the area's communities.

Regardless of age, San Diegans love to sit at the marinas and watch the sailboats, picnic at Balboa Park on lazy summer days, and hike or bike in the wilderness areas with cameras slung around our necks. The only real difference is that some of us have to get back to work on Monday and others go out to find more fun.

In this chapter we've identified some opportunities for the 55-plus age group. We've included information on senior centers, senior programs, and organizations that offer senior advocacy. We've pointed out some senior publications and given information on how seniors can get any help they need. We have included a smattering of residential options that include multilevel care. These facilities abound in San Diego County, so we've tried to point out some ways you can compare the many choices before you sign on the dotted line.

SENIOR LIVING—HOUSING OPTIONS

Choosing the right retirement place can be tricky unless you do your homework. Location is, of course, a chief issue. If you prefer sea breezes to the inland area's dry summertime air, then a coastal home is best. However, as we've noted in the Relocation chapter, it's more expensive to live near the ocean. And many newcomers are surprised by how chilly the coast can be. If family, friends, church or synagogue, and community services are important, take these into consideration.

If your medical insurance plan limits the facilities you can use, you may want to live within a reasonable distance of your doctors' offices and hospitals. Beyond those considerations, you're free to live at the beach or in the desert, mountains, or city and still call yourself a San Diegan.

If you're interested in living in a retirement community or facility in San Diego County, give yourself plenty of time to examine your options and visit the places that sound interesting. San Diego County has several planned neighborhoods designed for older-than-age-55 residents. Buying a home in one of these requires many of the same conditions you would consider when choosing a family home, but there are some specific needs you'll want to take into account. As you tour

The **San Diego Eldercare Directory** ***is a must-have for anyone who is retiring in San Diego or caring for an elderly relative, spouse, or friend. The book lists everything from in-home solutions to caring for the disabled to choosing a hospice. The directory is published annually by the*** **San Diego Union-Tribune** ***and is available at public libraries and senor centers until their copies run out. Call (619) 718-5214 for a copy.***

various senior communities, think about ease of access for the future. Though it might be fun now to dash up a flight of stairs to your two-story condo with a view, five years from now those stairs may become tedious.

When buying a house, condo, town house, or apartment, consider how it might be outfitted for any special equipment needed later in life. Can a ramp be built by the front steps? Will the bathroom be big enough should a wheelchair be required? San Diegans constantly bemoan the amount of bureaucracy involved in acquiring building permits here. Several agencies, including the Coastal Commission, have strict regulations regarding residential construction. Ask about such issues before you buy—you'll save yourself considerable anguish.

If you're looking at a designated retirement home or community, there are other considerations. List the topics you'd like to discuss before visiting with the staff. Be sure to cover the options for ongoing medical care. Ask about activities, both at the facility and off grounds. If you are accustomed to urban living, find out if there are stores and libraries within walking distance and if there is a downtown business district nearby. If you prefer driving, make sure you have easy access to major freeways and shopping areas. Does the facility provide transportation to community programs, including church or synagogue services, along with trips to shopping malls and area attractions? If you'll be in a facility that provides meals, join the residents for a lunch or two. You'll want to know if you'll enjoy your dining companions. Ask for references, and try to talk with both residents and their families. Make a scheduled visit to talk with someone on the sales staff. Then stop by unannounced another time.

Some privately owned rental units throughout the county prefer to rent to seniors; some can help apartment dwellers arrange for rent reduction through HUD. To find senior rental housing, contact the senior centers in the communities you're considering.

As your selection of a retirement home or apartment narrows, think of security. Are you most comfortable in a gated community? Are you interested in having a security officer on-site at night? Is on-site medical staff essential? Will you want a multilevel facility (one that provides multiple levels of care) so that skilled nursing care is available when needed? Or do you prefer a community that caters to those interested in independent living?

Finally, consider how much of your current furniture will reasonably fit into your new home. Some communities listed below have furniture rentals available should you want to see what it's like to live in the area before having all your furnishings shipped.

The questions are endless, but they can all be answered. The salespeople at communities are accustomed to answering all sorts of inquiries. Keep going back and asking more questions until you're satisfied that you'll be happy in your new home. The entries below will give you a feel for the types of retirement-living options found in San Diego County. Take note: Many facilities have waiting lists.

Brookdale Place of San Marcos
1590 West San Marcos Boulevard
San Marcos
(760) 471-9904, (877) 977-3800
www.brookdaleplaceofsanmarcos.com

Senior Resources

AARP Information Center	**(619) 641-7020**
Access Center	**(619) 293-3500, (760) 435-9205**
Adult Protective Services	**(619) 283-5731**
Community Service Centers	**(619) 235-5202**
Elder Abuse Reporting	**(800) 501-2020**
Home Security Checks	**(858) 573-5043**
Library Services for Seniors	**(619) 236-5800**
Meals-on-Wheels	**(800) 573-6467**
Retired Senior Volunteer Patrol	**(619) 531-1503**
Senior Services Centers	**(619) 236-6905**

Beautifully landscaped grounds and the convenient North County Inland location draw seniors to this community. While most who live at Brookdale Place are independent, the facility also offers assisted-living options—meals, housekeeping, and transportation—as well as staff checks for medication and medical conditions. There is a heated swimming pool, a spa, walking paths, rose gardens, and a putting green. Beach walks, shopping, cultural events, and movies are favorite outings for the active crowd who live here. The complex, with studio, one-bedroom, and two-bedroom apartments (some facing the courtyard and rose garden), is close to grocery stores and other everyday shopping. Small pets are always welcome.

Fredericka Manor
183 Third Avenue, Chula Vista
(619) 422-9271, ext. 22
www.frederickamanor.com

There's no entrance fee or deposit for this senior complex that really is one of the nicest you'll find. To say that the individual cottages are cozy doesn't do them justice—they are downright darling and inviting. The grounds are pristine, and the people who choose to live at Fredericka Manor are typically active folks. In addition to the cottages, you'll find apartment-style living in an eight-story tower, assisted care, and skilled nursing. There's also an adult day-care center on-site.

The facility is located on 24 garden-like acres with paths and ponds and walkways and gardens. Living options range from a utility studio to a penthouse suite; prices go from about $1,845 (with an additional fee for a second person) a month and up. All of the units come with housekeeping services.

There are various meal options. You'll find 24-hour-a-day security and medical response, transportation, programs, and cultural events. And a friendly staff.

i

The Web site sandiegoeldercare.com is an invaluable resource. It contains recent news articles about eldercare issues and tips from legal and medical pros. There are even tips on how to make the letters you're reading larger so you can feel more comfortable using the Internet.

Volunteer opportunities abound for those with time to spare and talents to share. Libraries, schools, and neighborhood recreation centers all seek volunteers, and children seem to have an endless need for grown-up love and advice. Choose your cause—literacy, the arts, health care, child abuse—and get involved. More than 36,000 volunteers participate annually in Volunteer San Diego, a nonprofit organization that supports and manages volunteer operations throughout San Diego. For information call (858) 636-4131 or check www.volunteersandiego.org.

The White Sands of La Jolla
7450 Olivetas Avenue, La Jolla
(858) 454-4201, (800) 892-7817
www.whitesandslajolla.com
A Southern California Presbyterian Home, this exceptional community offers three levels of care, should you ever need the options. We're talking ocean close. This is understated luxury in the finest sense, with lovely rooms, some more pricey and spacious than others. Amenities include housekeeping, delicious meals, and transportation. At the end of Pearl Street in La Jolla, it is also blocks from excellent shops and restaurants.

White Sands began an extensive rebuilding effort in 2004, with completion and occupancy slated for summer 2007. The 45 units will all be larger than 1,000 square feet, and entrance fees for the community start at $335,000. This is definitely a high-end property, but those who can afford it will live in one of the most desirable neighborhoods in the county.

The Southern Caregivers Resource Center matches experienced caregivers with those who've just begun the process of caring for an aging or ill loved one. The encouragement and support is invaluable. Call (858) 268-4432, ext. 115.

SENIOR ORGANIZATIONS

You'll find a weekly listing of clubs, hobby groups, volunteer needs, and special activities in the *North County Times* and the *San Diego Union-Tribune*. Most organizations that help seniors always need dependable volunteers to deliver meals, visit shut-ins, and provide helping hands at activities. Volunteering is a great way to make new friends and learn new skills.

Alzheimer's Association
4950 Murphy Canyon Road, Suite 250
San Diego
(858) 492-4400
www.sanalz.org
This organization provides and coordinates a countywide effort to give information and referrals. They also offer respite programs, support groups, and education programs. The organization coordinates the Safe Return system, a wanderers alert program. The local helpline number is (800) 272-3900.

City of San Diego Senior Citizen Services
202 C Street, Downtown
Central San Diego
(619) 236-6905
www.sannet.gov/seniorservices/
The brochures, free newspapers, and general camaraderie of those working or visiting at this busy desk are all good reasons to visit. The office (actually a few cubicles and a counter) is located on the first floor in the city administration building along with several other agencies. Services include referrals for medical and psychological services and housing. This office also issues senior identification cards. Seniors who don't drive can use these cards to get discounts on bus fares, at restaurants, for accommodations, and for other services.

Information is available on discounts for special events and tours that help seniors get out to enjoy a play, for example, or a performance of the opera. The city of San Diego offers a variety of senior services that you can access through this office. There are liaisons with the city attorney's office, environmental services, the libraries, and the mayor's office. It's a good idea to become familiar with their programs no matter where you live. Stop by to pick up a copy of their free handbook. or download it at the Web site.

Jewish Family Service Senior Services
2930 Copley Avenue, San Diego
(619) 563-5232
www.jewishfamilyservicesd.org
This valuable organization has several offices in the county that are open to all seniors, and services are available on a sliding scale. Licensed clinical social workers give free consultations and provide information and recommendations on physical and mental health issues. You'll find people willing to help with issues of housing, managed care, adult day care, and counseling. There is even a hot meal delivery service available.

Meals-On-Wheels
Administration
(619) 260-6110, (800) 573-6467
www.meals-on-wheels.org

Central San Diego
(619) 295-9501

North County
(760) 736-9900

East County
(619) 447-8782

South Bay
(619) 420-2782
This agency provides two home-delivered meals per day to seniors who are ill or disabled, for a suggested fee based on a sliding scale. The association accommodates special and restricted diet choices, too. Dependable volunteers are always needed.

Meals-on-Wheels San Diego doesn't just provide meals for humans. Working with the Helen Woodward Animal Center, it also delivers pet food to clients who are unable to purchase food for their beloved dogs or cats. For information on obtaining animal meals or helping elderly people hold onto their pets, go to www.animalcenter.org/animeals/.

National Association of Hispanic Elderly
22 West 35th Street, Suite 127
National City
(619) 425-3734
This organization helps Hispanic seniors with social and economic concerns and provides programs to help with temporary employment and training.

SENIOR CENTERS

Most communities throughout the county have senior centers. The easiest way to find them is by calling each city's main phone number or its parks and recreation office. Senior centers and activities geared to the senior community are also available at religious centers. Many churches provide meal service, counseling, support groups, and housing referrals. Hospitals take an active part in helping seniors with a variety of programs, from those addressing substance and elder abuse to those offering respite and hospice assistance. Be sure to look at the Health and Wellness chapter for some tips to finding medical and wellness programs.

It's always best to call and find out what your neighborhood's center has available, as things do change. Most serve a well-balanced hot lunch one or more days a week for a suggested donation of about $2.00. A number of the centers can arrange for delivery of hot midday meals to the homebound. Many of the centers have bilingual staff members who serve as translators for elderly Spanish-speakers

In California senior drivers may be able to get a discount from their car insurance company by participating in the Mature Driver Improvement Program. Ask your insurance agent about this money-saving program.

needing assistance with medical care or housing.

The programs at the centers may include exercise and stretch classes, painting and craft activities, language arts and writing, bridge and poker, dance classes and performances, and discussions of current events. Most of the centers offer tax and financial information, senior advocacy programs, and medical checkups. Some centers have social workers on staff and weekly support groups that deal with many issues, from grief management to dealing with stress. Most of the services are free; however, it's always wise to ask.

A growing number of centers have classes coordinated with the YMCA program and local colleges.

There's no need to limit your activities to senior centers, however. Most community recreation centers offer exercise and arts and crafts classes that are open to students of all ages. San Diego's community colleges and universities have significant numbers of students older than age 50. Sign up for the class schedules and ponder all those things you always wanted to learn. Enjoy your endless opportunities.

SENIOR PUBLICATIONS

San Diego Eldercare Directory
P.O. Box 122512, San Diego 92112
(619) 718-5214
www.sandiegoeldercare.com
This annual publication lists senior services from health care to legal advice, along with living options such as assisted care and skilled nursing services. It's available at all *San Diego Union-Tribune* offices throughout the county, as well as city and county libraries. The publication is free if you pick it up yourself or $10 if you request that it be mailed to you.

New Lifestyles
414 North Central Expressway, Suite 100
Dallas, TX 75204
(800) 820-3013
www.newlifestyles.com
This national publisher puts out an excellent small magazine with information on retirement communities, assisted living facilities, home-care agencies, and nearly every type of facility you might require. The comprehensive listings will give you a great overview of what's available throughout the county.

MEDIA

Once San Diego was established as a full-fledged city, it wasn't long before journalists began surfacing, eager to report the daily news. Even though the city has only one major newspaper that covers the entire county, there's plenty of competition from community newspapers. More than 70 community and neighborhood newspapers are published, and though some may come and go, many have become old-timers in their respective neighborhoods.

Radio runs the gamut from adult contemporary to news/talk, and, of course, all three established television networks are represented. The city has a thriving film industry, and the San Diego Film Commission coordinates the various production companies wanting to take advantage of San Diego as a filming site. Among the feature-length movies shot in San Diego are *Charlie's Angels, Bruce Almighty, Top Gun, The Lost World, Mr. Wrong, Traffic,* and *Almost Famous.* Epsiodes of various television series have been filmed here, too, including *Silk Stalkings, Renegade, Cops,* and *Crime & Punishment.*

The following listings should give you a good idea of what's available to read, watch, and listen to locally.

NEWSPAPERS

Newspapers listed here are the major dailies and weeklies and those that cover a broad area of the county. For news and information specific to a neighborhood or community, look for weekly or biweekly publications that are easily found in neighborhood newsstands, coffeehouses, convenience stores, and restaurants.

Daily

North County Times
207 East Pennsylvania Avenue, Escondido
(760) 740-5456
www.nctimes.com
North County's only full-size daily newspaper has nine zoned editions covering Carlsbad, Oceanside, Vista, San Marcos, Escondido, Poway, Encinitas, Temecula, and Fallbrook. It features international, national, and local news and sports. Comparable to the *San Diego Union-Tribune,* the paper focuses on local news and editorials that pertain to North County. Its expanded Sunday edition features special sections on lifestyle, entertainment, and real estate. The paper has a circulation of 89,000.

San Diego Union-Tribune
350 Camino de la Reina, San Diego
(619) 299-3131, (800) 244-6397
www.uniontribune.com
Founded in 1868 by William Jeff Gatewood, the *San Diego Union-Tribune* is the oldest business in San Diego County and the second-oldest newspaper in Southern California. It began as a weekly and has been a daily since 1871. The *San Diego Union-Tribune* is the end product of a 1992 merger of the *San Diego Union* and the *Evening Tribune,* which was founded as an afternoon newspaper in 1895.

John D. Spreckels, a San Diego founding father, took over as publisher of

Looking for a job? How about an apartment or even a used surfboard? Your best bet is the Sunday edition of the* San Diego Union-Tribune *in its expanded classifieds section.

the *San Diego Union* in 1890 and subsequently founded the *Evening Tribune*. He remained publisher until 1926, and after his death the two newspapers were purchased by Colonel Ira C. Copley. The Copley family has remained at the helm since 1947, with David C. Copley as the newspaper's current publisher.

The original building occupied by the newspaper still stands in Old Town State Historic Park. Today the *Union-Tribune* is published from an editorial and administrative building and printing plant in Mission Valley, not far from its original location in Old Town.

Five separate editions are published daily: San Diego City, North Coastal, North Inland, East County, and South County. The *Union-Tribune* also publishes *Enlace*, a free weekly newspaper in Spanish.

Thursday editions have the tabloid "Night and Day" section, which has a wealth of information about nightlife, concerts, special events, performing arts, movies, restaurants, and leisure activities throughout San Diego County.

Sunday's edition features special sections on travel, the arts, and homes and has many feature-length articles to help pass the time on a lazy Sunday morning. Circulation is 312,457 Monday through Wednesday, 369,140 Thursday through Saturday, and 442,600 on Sunday. Circulation for *Enlace* is 85,000.

Almost Daily

San Diego Daily Transcript
2131 Third Avenue, San Diego
(619) 232-4381, (800) 697-6397
www.sddt.com

A broadsheet newspaper, the *Transcript* is published Monday through Friday and covers business, financial, legal, construction, real estate, and government news and includes legal notices as well. The *Transcript* is the only publication to provide listings of every publicly traded corporation based in San Diego. Its circulation is 15,000. The *Transcript* became the first online newspaper in San Diego in 1994.

Weekly and Semiweekly

CityBeat
3550 Camino del Rio, Suite 207, San Diego
(619) 281-7526

CityBeat is a free newspaper published every Wednesday. In addition to news editorials, many with an irreverent slant, *CityBeat* focuses on the local San Diego entertainment scene. There are music and movie reviews as well as movie showtimes, classifieds, museum listings, and calendars covering sports events, recreation events, theater openings, community meetings, alternative films, and the latest happenings at local clubs. *CityBeat* is distributed at more than 1,000 locations in San Diego, including Downtown, Mission Valley, Hillcrest, College Area, Pacific Beach, La Jolla, Ocean Beach, Mission Beach, Miramar, Del Mar, Leucadia, Encinitas, San Marcos, and Escondido.

The Coast News Group
828 North Coast Highway 101, Encinitas
(760) 436-9737
www.thecoastnews.com

This weekly newspaper group covers the North County from Carmel Valley to Camp Pendleton with a combined circulation of 165,000. The letters and opinion sections are very lively, and local issues get in-depth coverage. The *Coast News* is distributed throughout the area at some 650 markets and other locations; the *Village & Valley* and *Rancho Santa Fe News* are both found at public places and delivered to area residents.

East County Californian
119 North Magnolia Avenue, El Cajon
(619) 441-0400

Published every Thursday, the *East*

County Californian reports news affecting the East County cities of El Cajon, La Mesa, Spring Valley, Lemon Grove, Santee, Lakeside, Blossom Valley, Casa de Oro, Dulzura, Crest, and Rancho San Diego and the surrounding communities. It also covers issues dealt with by the various East County city councils and has a comprehensive editorial and commentary section. Also published each Thursday, its sister publication the *Alpine Sun* (619-445-3288; www.thealpinesun.com) serves Alpine and other more remote East County communities such as Potrero and Mount Laguna.

La Jolla Light
565 Pearl Street, Suite 300, La Jolla
(858) 459-4201
www.lajollalight.com
The *La Jolla Light* and its sister publications the *Del Mar Times, Carmel Valley Leader, Solana Beach Sun,* and *Rancho Santa Fe Recorder* cover these affluent areas of the coast and slightly inland empires. The first two have an online Web version of the paper. All have articles about local charitable and community events, business, the art scene, and other local news. These weekly publications cover a combined audience of some 66,000.

Pomerado Newspaper Group
13247 Poway Road, Poway
(858) 748-2311
www.mylocalnews.com
Published weekly on Thursday, the Pomerado Newspapers include the *Poway News Chieftan,* the *Corridor News,* and the *Rancho Bernardo News Journal.* In addition to the communities of Poway and Rancho Bernardo, coverage includes Rancho Peñasquitos, Carmel Mountain Ranch, Sabre Springs, and Scripps Ranch. Besides neighborhood news, the papers feature profiles of community leaders and in-depth features on issues affecting these North County cities, such as local politics and real estate development. Each week 42,000 readers are reached.

San Diego Business Journal
4909 Murphy Canyon Road
Suite 200, San Diego
(858) 277-6359
www.sdbj.com
The *Business Journal* provides weekly news and commentary on San Diego County businesses and industries to 18,500 readers. Each issue has news, features, and columns about San Diego's business environment. Its national award-winning weekly lists of businesses, agencies, and services and its annual *Book of Lists* keep readers in touch with San Diego's growing industries. It is part of a national chain of business journals in major cities. The *Business Journal* can be purchased at newsstands throughout the city of San Diego and is also available by subscription.

San Diego Community Newspaper Group
4645 Cass Street, San Diego
(858) 270-3103
www.sdnews.com
This community news group publishes five weekly newspapers that cover issues of interest to residents of coastal San Diego from Ocean Beach north to La Jolla. *The Beach and Bay Press,* the *Peninsula Beacon,* the *La Jolla Village News,* the *Downtown News,* and the *Golden Triangle News* together reach some 75,000 readers. Each paper has occasional features on local personalities and brings readers up to date on political issues affecting their neighborhood. Opinion polls are a common feature, too, giving readers the chance to have their voices heard.

The *San Diego Reader*
1703 India Street, San Diego
(619) 235-3000
www.sandiegoreader.com
This free weekly tabloid is noted for its comprehensive entertainment section. The section gives detailed information and reviews on the arts, dining, sports, and things to do around San Diego. Each issue also contains feature articles and columns about San Diego life and politics. The

Produced by the* San Diego Union-Tribune, *the weekly newspaper Enlace (Spanish for "ties") is written in Spanish, with a few articles summarized in English. It's distributed in predominately Spanish-speaking enclaves such as the South Bay, where a little more than half the population is Hispanic. Circulation is 85,000 readers.

Reader is distributed every Thursday to locations throughout San Diego County and reaches 169,500 readers. The Web site contains the weekly columns and reviews as well as the featured cover article, but not all of the additional articles or the ads.

Voice of San Diego
111 Elm Street, Suite 209, San Diego
(619) 325-0525
www.voiceofsandiego.org
Launched by Neil Morgan—writer and editor for the local San Diego newspaper (first the *San Diego Evening Tribune* and later the merged *San Diego Union-Tribune*) for more than half a century—*Voice of San Diego* is an excellent, independent online newspaper. There are a range of articles about San Diego culture, people, events, and topical local issues. The "This Just In" column gives the latest info about articles that have run previously in the *Voice*, the *San Diego Union-Tribune*, the *New York Times*, or elsewhere. The expansive calendar of events is updated daily.

MAGAZINES

San Diego Home/Garden Lifestyles
4577 Viewridge Avenue, San Diego
(858) 571-1818
www.sdhg.net
Local architecture, interior design, and gardening are the features of this monthly magazine. It also includes articles on remodeling, art, local personalities, and San Diego issues. The monthly guide to arts, culture, and entertainment is an excellent source for information about what's happening in San Diego. The magazine's circulation is about 53,000.

San Diego Magazine
1450 Front Street, San Diego
(619) 230-9292
www.sandiego-online.com
The first city magazine in the country, *San Diego Magazine* celebrated its 55th anniversary in 2003. This glossy monthly contains a selection of articles about San Diego, past and present, and its notable political, social, and business leaders. The magazine also has an extensive thumbnail-review section on arts, entertainment, and restaurants. It has a circulation of more than 54,000 and can be purchased at newsstands, supermarkets, and bookstores or by subscription.

San Diego Metropolitan Magazine
1250 Sixth Avenue, Suite 1200, San Diego
(619) 233-4060
www.sandiegometro.com
San Diego Metropolitan is a monthly news-print magazine that focuses on the downtown community. Its emphasis is on downtown businesses, arts, retail, and human-interest items. Downtown redevelopment, urban real estate, and political happenings are subjects that are frequently covered. It is distributed through chambers of commerce throughout the county, including the Hispanic Chamber and the Asian Business Association. It's sent free to homeowners throughout the county whose residences are valued at $1.5 million or more. Anyone can subscribe for $25 per month, but mainly it's a freebie distributed through the local chambers and other organizations to about 45,000 readers each month.

SPECIAL-INTEREST PUBLICATIONS

ComputorEdge Magazine
3655 Ruffin Road, San Diego
(858) 573-0315
www.computoredge.com
San Diego's free computer magazine is published weekly, and 85,000 copies are distributed to newsstands, computer stores, and libraries. It contains feature articles and columns with information on software and hardware for the computer buff. For true aficionados, *ComputorEdge* has a calendar of events to keep computer-heads entertained and up to date, as well as a listing of local Web sites and user-group lists. The magazine also has a classifieds section advertising computers and accessories for sale.

Gay & Lesbian Times
1730 Monroe Avenue, Suite A, San Diego
(619) 299-6397
www.gaylesbiantimes.com
With a print run of 15,200, the *Gay & Lesbian Times* is San Diego's largest publication specifically for the gay community. Heavy on guest commentaries, the newspaper also has news and articles of interest to gays and lesbians. Its extensive arts and entertainment section covers nightlife that often is neglected in mainstream publications. It's most easily found in libraries, bookstores, and coffeehouses in the Hillcrest and Downtown areas.

La Prensa San Diego
1950 Fifth Avenue, San Diego
(619) 231-2873
www.laprensa-sandiego.org
Bilingual *La Prensa* is published weekly and distributed throughout San Diego County, from San Ysidro in the South Bay to Oceanside in North County and east to El Cajon. It's available free of charge at libraries, government buildings, coffeehouses, and convenience stores throughout San Diego County but can also be delivered for a fee. In publication since 1976, *La Prensa* views the news and events through a Latino perspective. Their Web site has many links to San Diego businesses and events. The newspaper reaches 30,000 readers.

Check out* San Diego Magazine*'s January issue for its annual "50 San Diegans to Watch" article. It features profiles of the city's movers and shakers and up-and-coming leaders.

San Diego Family Magazine
1475 Sixth Avenue, San Diego
(619) 685-6970
www.sandiegofamily.com
Published monthly, this free magazine is full of articles, columns, advice and helpful hints to benefit families. Pick up a copy at libraries, grocery stores, and shops all over the county. In-depth articles discuss parenting, camps, teen issues, and safety, among other issues. It includes a comprehensive directory of private schools and a listing of classes for youngsters; the Web site has recipes, readers' movie reviews, a monthly calendar of local events, and various resource guides. The magazine is distributed to 120,000 readers.

San Diego Parent
3160 Camino del Rio S., Suite 313
San Diego
(619) 624-2770
San Diego Parent is a monthly magazine distributed free to 80,000 readers. It features monthly columns on parenting classes, health notes, and family fun, as well as feature-length articles on topics such as vacation options, summer camps,

The best lowdown on the club scene is found in the* San Diego Reader*. This weekly will help you decide what's happening at San Diego's numerous clubs as well as churches, restaurants, and more.

and exercising. Each issue also includes a calendar of events for parents and kids. It's usually located right next to *San Diego Family Magazine* in libraries, stores, and family-oriented restaurants.

San Diego Voice and Viewpoint
1729 North Euclid Avenue, San Diego
(619) 266-2233
Distributed weekly throughout San Diego County, the *Voice and Viewpoint* is a publication geared toward the local African-American community. The newspaper prints local and national news, editorial, and commentary, and it recognizes African Americans of distinction in special features. It includes a weekly calendar of events, and its circulation is 28.000. The newspaper can be purchased by subscription or at newsstands throughout the county.

TELEVISION

Like most other cities, San Diego's television stations have beloved anchorpeople and quirky personalities whose goal is to inform and entertain. With a good antenna, the major network stations can be pulled in without cable. But reception is iffy, and most San Diegans subscribe to cable. The three network affiliates, Channels 8, 10, and 39, and local Channels 6 and 51 all have news broadcasts throughout the day.

Local TV Stations and their Network Affiliates

KFMB Channel 8 (CBS)
www.kfmb.com

KGTV Channel 10 (ABC)
www.10news.com

KNSD Channels 7 and 39 (NBC)
www.nbcsandiego.com

KPBS Channels 11 and 15 (Public TV)
www.kpbs.org

KSWB Channels 5 and 69 (WB)
http://kswbtv.trb.com

KUSI Channel 51 (Independent)
www.kusi.com
News at 5:00, 6:00, 7:00, 8:00, and 10:00 A.M., and 6:00, 7:00, and 10:00 P.M.

XETV Channel 6 (Fox)
www.ketv.com
News at 5:30 A.M. and 10:00 P.M.

XEWT Channel 12 (TVA-Tijuana)

4SD Channel 4 (Independent)

T33 Telemundo Channel 33 (Spanish)

Cable Providers

Three main cable companies cover the majority of San Diego County. For the most part, each has exclusive rights to its area, and the area is divided roughly as follows: South of Interstate 8 and part of North County is Cox Communication's territory; north of I-8 and Coronado belong to Time Warner Cable. Confused? Obviously there's quite a bit of overlap, so if you have any doubt about which cable company controls your area, call any one of them. They'll be able to help you figure it out. Basic cable service can be purchased for around $15 per month, which will tune you in to the network stations as well as a few local independents. But if you wish to take advantage of the more than 200 premium and special-interest channels available in San Diego, expanded packages can be added, including digital cable.

Cox Communications (San Diego)
1535 Euclid Avenue, San Diego
(619) 262-1122
www.cox.com

Cox Communications (North County)
520 West Valley Parkway, Escondido
(760) 599-6060
www.cox.com

Time Warner Cable
8949 Ware Court, San Diego
(858) 695-3220
www.timewarnercable.com

RADIO

Whatever your favorite format, you're likely to find it somewhere on the dial. Some stations come in clear in some parts of the county and not so clear in others. If a station's signal originates in North County, for example, it'll be clear and strong in the northern regions, somewhat weaker in San Diego, and probably nonexistent in the South Bay. Don't give up, though. The old boom box has plenty of entertainment to please every taste.

CONTEMPORARY

90.3 FM Z90
93.3 FM KHTS
95.5 FM
96.5 FM KYXY
100.7 FM STAR
102.9 FM KLQV

ALTERNATIVE

102.1 FM KPRI
550 AM KCR
1320 AM KKSM
91.1 FM 91X
92.1 FM KSOQ
94.9 FM

ASIAN

1240 AM KSON

CLASSIC ROCK

92.5 FM XHRM
101.5 FM KGB
102.1 FM KPRI

CLASSICAL

1450 AM KFSD
90.7 FM XLNC

COUNTRY

95.5 FM XHA
97.3 FM KSON

JAZZ

88.3 FM KSDS
98.1 FM KIFM

NEWS/TALK/SPORTS

103.7 FM KCSF
600 AM KOGO (Talk/News/Padres Baseball)
620 AM ESPN
760 AM KFMB (Talk/News)
1000 AM KCEO (Business Talk)
1170 AM KCBQ (Conservative)
1360 AM KLSD
89.5 FM KPBS (National Public Radio)

OLDIES

94.1 FM
92.5 FM
1360 AM KPOP
95.7 FM KJQY
540 AM
690 AM

RELIGIOUS

620 AM KPLR
910 AM KECR
1040 KURS
1210 AM KPRZ
100.1 FM KLVW

ROCK & ROLL

100.7 FM
102.1 FM KPRI
105.3 FM KIOZ

SPANISH

860 AM XEMO (Regional Music)
1030 AM XESD
1040 AM KURS (Regional Music)
1130 AM KSDO
1420 AM XEXX (Spanish News/Sports)
1470 AM XERCN (Spanish News/Talk/Sports)
1550 AM XEBG (News/Talk/Sports in Spanish)
88.7 FM XHITT (Tijuana Public Radio)
91.7 FM XGLX (English/Spanish Contemporary)
97.7 FM XTIM (Regional Mexican)
98.9 FM XMOR (Rock Hits in Spanish)
102.5 FM XHUAN (Ranchera)
104.5 FM XLTN (Spanish Contemporary)
106.5 FM KLNV (Ranchera/Banda)
107.3 FM XHFG

WORSHIP

While driving around our easygoing communities from Pacific Beach and Alpine to Bonita and Fallbrook, it might seem that Insiders are too laid-back to care about spiritual beliefs and values. If you've already read the Attractions, Shopping, and Balboa Park chapters, you might be asking yourself: "How do they have time when there's so much to do?"

The answers are simple: Yes, we care, and yes, we make time.

San Diegans are diverse and run the gamut from conservative and orthodox to outrageous and unconventional. So you won't be surprised to learn that our places of worship also reflect a variety of spiritual preferences.

Whether we attend a nontraditional service or one that's steeped in ancient customs, religious beliefs are alive and active throughout the county.

But while our beliefs are both strong and diverse, we all still live the San Diego lifestyle, and so we hope you won't be shocked to learn that even at the most conservative services, the faithful may walk in with bare knees and toes. People in San Diego are comfortable in their breezy wardrobes as they mix with congregation members who might prefer to be dressed to the nines.

SERVICES

The choices of religious services available throughout the county are extensive. If you're here on a vacation, finding a worship center that's right for you might be as easy as looking in the yellow pages of your hotel's phone book. Someone on the staff at the front desk should be able to tell you which of the listings are closest. Many visitors, regardless of their faith, attend mass at one of our missions. The services are a way to touch San Diego's rich history and feel the past of our diverse community. (Be sure to read over our History chapter for more about religion's role in our past.)

Though some denominations' churches, including Protestant and Catholic, are ubiquitous, those of other faiths may require a bit of a drive to get to. The good news is that if you're attending a Sunday-morning service, the freeway traffic will usually be light. But as always, allow extra time for unplanned gridlock.

The Thursday edition of the *San Diego Union-Tribune* has a directory of religious services, which includes church addresses, phone numbers, and times of services. However, not every San Diego house of worship is included. So think of this resource as a starting point. Alternately, call the Ecumenical Council of San Diego (619-238-0649, Monday through Friday 8:30 A.M. to 12:30 P.M.; www.ecsd.org). If you have access to a computer, go to their Web site and type in one or more of the zip codes in your area to get a list of places of worship of various faiths.

If you're moving to San Diego, you may decide on specific neighborhoods or parts of our county that will be close to the house of worship of your choice. Some congregations have cultural events and groups for teens, singles, or seniors; others are focused around the young family unit, with everything from preschool programs and after-school programs to

Most religious services welcome visitors dressed in California casual; i.e., it's not necessary to wear suits or dresses and high heels. If you're in doubt, call first. On any first visit, slacks and a blazer are always appropriate.

The Church of Jesus Christ of Latter Day Saints, California Temple, is that huge white building you'll see on Interstate 5 in La Jolla. The golden figure on the top represents the angel Moroni, who, according to the Mormon faith, revealed the location of the plates on which the Book of Mormon was engraved to the teenage Joseph Smith.

family campouts and church camps. As throughout the country, a number of churches in our region specifically support the gay and lesbian community.

Those courting a new church might check out the *San Diego Reader*'s "Sheep and Goats" column, a weekly review of area churches. The column lists data such as congregation size and type of dress parishioners prefer, reviews the sermon, and describes the pastors and their ideology. Opinionated? Yes. But also informative, with plenty of direct quotes from the minister. You can see past reviews on their Web site, www.sdreader.com.

As you visit and consider where you'll put down your spiritual roots, remember it's okay to call and ask about the philosophies being shared or the programs in which the religious group is involved. If singles groups or senior day care are important, see if your needs are met as you connect with the congregation.

When you do decide on your new spiritual "home," you'll probably feel like you belong right away. People are friendly here in our county, and you won't feel like a stranger for long.

San Diego's largest mosque is the Islamic Center of San Diego (7050 Eckstrom Avenue, 858-278-5240), which holds a brief introduction to Islam Sunday at noon and a lecture series on various topics Friday at 7:00 P.M. The public is invited to attend. Be sure to wear modest clothing respectful of the culture: for women, long sleeves, loose-fitting trousers or a long skirt, and preferably a head scarf; for men, long pants.

HISTORY OF WORSHIP IN SAN DIEGO

The Misión Basílica San Diego de Alcalá, the first in the chain of 21 missions established in California, still holds services and celebrates christenings and weddings. It's been doing so since 1777, when the church was blessed by Father Junipero Serra. (The first was built at the site of today's Presidio Park; the second, at the present location, was burned by the Indians in 1774 and subsequently rebuilt.) Like the San Diego de Alcalá mission church, Oceanside's Misión San Luis Rey continues to hold services in Spanish as well as English. Tours of both missions are available, and the gardens and museums alone make them popular tourist attractions. (Be sure to read about the missions in our Attractions chapter.)

While *criollos* (people of Spanish descent born in Mexico), Spaniards, and other Europeans who settled San Diego were Catholic, many other religions came to San Diego with the farmers, cattle owners, and tradespeople that began to call our county home. (See the History chapter for more information on early settlers.)

As they cleared the land, established homesteads, and tried to figure out how to get water to make everything grow, these independent folks were determined to feed their souls, too. Just as it happens today, not everyone could decide on that spiritual "meal" or how it should be served, so diverse churches and houses of worship sprang up around the county.

If you stepped back in history 50 or 100 years, you'd find a spiritual scene much like today's. On any Sunday you could choose to attend a spiritualist church or a Baptist meeting or a Catholic Mass. The only difference between then and now is that today you'd have even more choices.

Founded in 1798, Mission San Luis Rey is probably the least known and one of the prettiest missions in the state. PHOTO: COURTESY OF ANDREW HUDSON

HUMANITARIAN ACTIVITIES

Our scores of religious institutions also happen to be a vital part of humanitarian activity in San Diego. At any one of them you may find a way to express your own faith by helping with these efforts. At **Saint Vincent De Paul's Village** in San Diego (see the Close-up in this chapter), volunteers and paid staff members assist those who need a helping hand emotionally, physically, and spiritually. If you volunteer here, you might be asked to read a book at the day-care center, help with distribution at the food bank, serve lunch, or work at a fund-raiser. The main center is located at 3350 E Street, San Diego (619-446-2100). **Interfaith Shelter Network** (1880 Third Avenue, #12, San Diego, 619-702-5399, www.interfaithshelter.org) works with area churches to provide refuge for homeless people during the winter months and transitional shelter year-round for battered women and children.

Talk with the pastor, rabbi, or head of your spiritual center to find out about volunteer opportunities sponsored by your group. While many religious groups cry out for financial support, it's often the priceless gift of willing hands that is the greatest contribution you can make.

CULTURAL ACTIVITIES

Our religious centers are more than sites where we join one another to worship. They're often places to enjoy the arts and cultural activities or centers where people can help themselves to a better life here on earth. **Deer Park Monastery** (2499 Melru Lane, Escondido, 760-291-1003, www.deerparkmonastery.org) is a Buddhist center. Visitors can come for a Sunday of Mindfulness or a weekend or weeklong retreat to practice the many tenets of Buddhism and listen to lectures on many subjects. **San Diego Buddhist Temple,** the

CLOSE-UP

Father Joe: God's Hustler

Born in New York City in 1941, the man who's been called both a hustler and a saint was raised in a close-knit neighborhood. One of eight Carroll kids, he was part of a family that never forgot to pray for the less fortunate, despite being a family of very modest means.

When he relocated to Southern California at age 22 with $50 in his pocket, Joe Carroll had a plan to become a millionaire. Instead, Joe's gregarious personality, coupled with the compassionate giving he'd learned as a child, led him to the priesthood. Following his ordination in 1974, Father Joe immersed himself in parish work, where he also found outlets for his businessman's instincts.

Under the direction of Bishop Leo T. Maher, who was appalled by the number of San Diegans sleeping outdoors, Father Joe and his colleagues devised a plan for a large urban shelter that would provide not only emergency care but also a free clinic, a public school, a children's library and play area, and a kitchen serving 2,000 meals daily. The cost of this plan? Eleven million and change.

Like dynamos of less lofty persuasions, Father Joe scrounged for money. The big break happened when a local television station aired his public-service spot. Viewers were captivated. "I'm a hustler," said the man in the clerical garb. Then he grinned and added, "And I want your money." Then as images of San Diego's homeless families were shown in the commercial, Father Joe explained the need for a residence where people could galvanize themselves and work toward another try.

Offers of help poured in from every corner of the county. With the help of many compassionate people, the millions were raised. The dream turned into reality.

Situated in what was once one of San Diego's seediest neighborhoods, the Joan Kroc Center has been a beacon of hope to the thousands of homeless people and families. The 350-room facility has been called the "Taj Mahal of homeless shelters." Since its opening day in 1987, the "Miracle of 15th Street" (actually at 1501 Imperial Avenue, San Diego)

Rev. Msg. Joseph Carroll is better known as Father Joe.

PHOTO: COURTESY OF SAINT VINCENT DE PAUL VILLAGE

has become just one of a half dozen structures making up Father Joe Villages. This and satellite sites provide medical programs, psychological and career counseling, chemical dependency help, computer training programs, and meals. The school teaches not only the three Rs but also techniques to bolster self-worth, social skills, and a sense of security.

An outspoken conservative, the good father doesn't believe in handouts. "Handouts are not the answer to today's volatile economy. People have to learn how to take care of themselves; that means learning how to spend, how to save, and how to maintain security for themselves and their families. We don't want to see our residents come back. If they do, then its time to reevaluate our methods."

After getting to know Father Joe, or about him, you won't be surprised that he's always looking for good volunteers—to serve meals, provide medical support, or teach someone how to read. To volunteer and be part of this successful mission, call (619) 233-8500, ext. 1575 or (619) 446-2100. Father Joe's Villages also accept donations of cars, boats, RVs, and motorcycles.

oldest in the county, (2929 Market Street, 619-239-0896, www.btsd.net.) offers Sunday meditation as well as lectures and a Buddhist book club.

The **Taoist Sanctuary of San Diego** (4229 Park Boulevard, San Diego; 619-692-1155, www.taoistsanctuary.org) offers meditation and exercise classes mingling Chinese medicine, martial arts, and spiritual discipline and often introduces newcomers to these practices during evening open houses in the summer months.

San Diego has two **Self-Realization Fellowships,** at 939 Second Street in Encinitas (760-436-7220) and in central San Diego at 3068 First Avenue, (619-295-0170, www.yogananda-srf.org). The church, brought to the United States in 1920 by Parmahansa Yogananda, teaches self-realization through meditation and prayer. It offers study lessons and group meditations in addition to weekly services. The larger temple in Encinitas has a particularly lovely meditation garden overlooking the beach, and both offer retreats for men and women.

For more mainstream activities the **First United Methodist Church of San Diego** (2111 Camino Del Rio South, San Diego; 619-297-4366, www.fumcsd.org) often hosts concerts ranging from piano or organ music to Renaissance, Baroque, classical, and romantic compositions played on brass instruments. Almost all feature well-known performers. This outgoing church also hosts a good number of singles and family events, including movies, discussion groups, and lunch dates.

Lawrence Family Jewish Community Centers (Mandell Weirs Eastgate City Park, 4126 Executive Drive, La Jolla; 858-457-3030, www.lfjcc.org) provides the community with an annual film festival, a

---

The week before Easter, the* San Diego Union-Tribune *prints a list of Easter services throughout the county. There are sunrise chants, outdoor services to release doves, and other special programs. If you're determined to wear a new spring outfit outdoors, bring a jacket.

For an energizing or meditative break from everyday stresses, visit the meditation garden of Encinitas's Self-Realization Fellowship temple. There are koi ponds and small waterfalls, lots of native plants, and a sweeping seascape to behold. Benches are dotted throughout the grounds.

music festival, and book fair. Affectionately known as "the J," this center also has a young people's theater group, and a performance venue and offers preschool classes and summer camp for kids age 10 months old to those in 11th grade, including programs for children with special needs. Like the summer camp, the excellent physical fitness center and Olympic-size swimming pool can be used by people of all faiths. There are a variety of other activities, including a dating service meant to help Jewish singles meet potential mates in a fun, safe setting.

The **First Spiritualist Church** (3777 42nd Street, San Diego; 619-284-4646, www.1st-spiritualistchurch.org) has been active in San Diego since the late 19th century. Very active in the community, it hosts psychic fairs, free healings, and classes on how to communicate more effectively with angels and spirit guides, herbology, and Tarot card reading. Healing sessions and church services are held Sunday mornings.

So if you're looking for a place to worship, to put your faith to work in social service, and to enjoy the companionship of others, San Diego's 12,000 congregations have much to offer. As with all of San Diego, just ask Insiders and you'll receive a cornucopia of choices.

INDEX

A

AARP Information Center, 361
Access Center, 361
Accessible San Diego, 351
accommodations
  bed-and-breakfast inns, 61–66
  hotels and motels, 34–60
  Mexico, 304–5
  spas/resorts, 67–74
  vacation rentals, 75–78
Ace Hardware, 136
Acura Tennis Classic, 195–96, 290
Adams Avenue Antique Row, 121, 133
Adams Avenue Business District, 121, 133
Adams Avenue Grill, 88
Adams Avenue Roots and Folk Festival, 189
Adelaide's, 136
Adult Protective Services, 361
aerospace industry, 31–32
Agua Caliente County Park, 234
Air California Adventures, 236
Airport Shuttle, 17
Airport Travelers Aid, 351
air travel, 15–19
Aladdin Parking Garage, 17
Alamo, 16
Alcazar Garden/Palm Canyon, 172
Alcoholics Anonymous, 351
All Golf, 279–80
Alliant International University, 340–41
Allied Gardens
  municipal pool, 266
  real estate, 316
Alpine real estate, 326
Al's Cafe, 90
alternative health care, 357–58
Always Fabulous, 127
Alzheimer's Association, 362
American Athletic Club, 242
American Cab, 22
America's Schooner Cup Charity Regatta, 187–88
AMF Eagle Bowl, 233
Amtrak, 19
Anderson's La Costa Nursery, 138
Angelo's Burgers, 90–91
annual events, 183–201
Annual Festival of Lights, 199
Annual Julian Weed Show and Art Mart, 196
Anthony's Fish Grotto, 100
Antique Gas and Steam Engine Museum, 153
Antique Row, 121, 133
antiques, 133–35
Antiques Shopping District (Temecula), 298
Antique Village, 134
Antique Warehouse, 134
Anza-Borrego Desert State Park, 227, 291–92
Anza-Borrego Desert Wildflowers Season, 185
apartments, 330–31
Apartments for Rent, 330
Aqua Adventures Kayak School, 257–58
ARCO U.S. Olympic Training Center, 157
area overview, 4–14
Army-Navy Academy, 334
Artesanias Tonala, 310
art film houses, 213–14
Art Institute of California–San Diego, The, 335
arts, 202–20
  classical music, 203–6
  dance, 206
  film festivals, 206–7
  galleries, 207–10
  museums, 210–13
  performance venues, 213–20
ArtWalk, 189
Art World–Western Heritage Gallery, 210
Asia-Vous, 96
Athens Market, 81
attractions, 141–58
  Central San Diego, 141–48
  East County, 155–56
  Mexico, 305–6
  North County Coastal, 148–53
  North County Inland, 153–55
  South Bay, 157–58
  transportational tours, 150–51
auto racing, 282
Avenida Revolución, 309–10
AVID program, 336–37
Avocado Festival, 189–90
avocados, 194

Avo Playhouse, 219
Azzura Point, 80

B

B. Dalton Bookseller, 128, 132–33
Back to the 50s Car Show, 155
Baily Vineyard & Winery, 298
Baja California Tours, 302
Bajamar Ocean Front Golf Resort, 307
Balboa Park, 141–42, 171–82
Balboa Park December Nights, 199
Balboa Park Inn, 62
Balboa Park Municipal Golf Course, 268
Balboa Park 9-Hole Course, 275
Balboa Tennis Club, 244
Bali Hai, 94
ballooning/biplanes, 230–31
Balloon or Biplane Adventures by California Dreamin', 230
B&L Bike and Sports, 231
Barbeque Pit, The, 98
Bar Dynamite, 109
Barnes & Noble, 128, 130, 131, 132
Barona Casino, 155–56
Barona Drag Strip, 282
Barona Valley Ranch Resort & Casino, 58
bars/brewpubs, 109–12
baseball, 282–83
Bates Nut Farm, 153, 166
Bay Books & Cafe, 129
Bazaar del Mundo, 122
Bazár Casa Ramírez, 310
  beaches, 248–56
  hotels and motels, 35–37
  restaurants, 86–87
Beachfront San Diego Rentals, 77
beach volleyball classes, 245
Beacon's Beach, 250
bed-and-breakfast inns, 61–66
  East County, 65–66
  North County Coastal, 64–65
  North County Inland, 65
  San Diego County, 62–64
Bella Luna, 81
Bellefleur Winery & Restaurant, 91
Belly Up Tavern, 107
Belmont Amusement Park, 142
belo, 102
Bertrand at Mr. A's, 82
Best Western Blue Sea Lodge, 35–36
Best Western Continental Inn, 58–59
Best Western Encinitas Inn and Suites, 52
Best Western Escondido, 56
Best Western Hacienda Suites, 51
Best Western Island Palms Hotel & Marina, 52
Best Western Stratford Inn Del Mar, 53
Best Western Suites Coronado, 37, 40
bicycle clubs, 232
bicycling/mountain biking, 231–32
Bikes and Beyond, 231
Bike Tour San Diego, 231
billiards, 232–33
biplanes/ballooning, 230–31
Birdland real estate, 317
Bird Rock, 253
Bitter End, The, 103–4
Black, The, 136–37
Black's Beach, 252
Blind Melons, 104
Blue Point Coastal Cuisine, 82
Blue Sky Ecological Reserve, 225
Boat Parades of Lights, 200
Bob's by the Bay, 94, 100
Bonita Golf Center, 280
Bonita Golf Club, 274
Bonita real estate, 328
Bonita Store, The, 100
Bonsall real estate, 325–26
Bookstar, 129
bookstores, 128–33
Book Works, 130–31
Boomer's, 142–43, 159–60
Boomer's El Cajon, 156, 168
border, Mexican, 25–26. *See also* Mexico
Borders Books, Music & Cafe, 129, 131–32
Border View YMCA, 169
Borrego Springs real estate, 326
Botanical Building/Lily Pond, 172–73
Boulevard, The, 107
bowling, 233–34
Branding Iron, 139
Breakfast Inn at La Jolla, The, 62
brewpubs/bars, 109–12
Britt Scripps Inn, 62–63
Brockton Villa, 86
Brookdale Place of San Marcos, 360–61
Brown Field Municipal Airport, 18
brunch, Sunday, 94
Brunswick Premier Lanes, 233
Budget (car rental agency), 17
Bud Kearns Memorial Municipal Pool, 266
Buick Invitational Golf Tournament, 185, 287

bullfighting, 283–84
Bully's, 91
Bureau of Tourism Palm Springs, 292–93
Burlington Coat Factory, 119
bus travel, 19
Butcher Shop, The, 100–101
Butterfield Bed & Breakfast, 65

C

Cabazon Outlet Stores, 292
cable providers, 370
Cabrillo National Monument, 143
Cafe Calypso, 107
Cafe on Park, 84–85
Cafe 222, 82
Cal-al-a-Vie, 67 -68
California Bistro, 91–92
California Center for the Arts, 213, 215
California Highway 52, 22
California Highway 54, 21
California Highway 56, 22
California Highway 67, 22
California Highway 78, 22
California Highway 94, 21
California Highway 125, 21–22
California Highway 163, 21
California Institute for Human Science, 335
California state highways, 21–22
California State Parks, 224
California State University at San Marcos, 341
California State University at San Marcos Extended Studies, 349
California Surf Museum, 148
California Water Sports, 258
California Western School of Law, 345
camping, 224, 234–35
Campland on the Bay, 234–35
Camp Pendleton Paintball Park, 241
Camp SeaWorld, 160
'Canes Bar and Grill, 104
canoeing/wave riding/kayaking, 257–59
Cardiff-by-the-Sea Lodge, The, 64
Cardiff real estate, 322
Carlsbad
 beaches, 249–50
 farmers' market, 125
 real estate, 321
Carlsbad Community Swim Complex, 266
Carlsbad Company Stores, 120
Carlsbad Danish Bakery, 138–39
Carlsbad Flower Fields, 148
Carlsbad Golf Center, 279
Carlsbad Inn Beach Resort, 53
Carlsbad Marathon, 183–84, 240
Carlsbad Paddle Sports, 258–59
Carlsbad Raceway, 288–89
Carlsbad Spring Faire, 191
Carlton Oaks Country Club, 273
Carmel Mountain Plaza, 126
Carmel Valley real estate, 322
Carolyn's Affordable Elegance, 127
Carousel and Miniature Railroad, 173
car rental agencies, 16–17
Carroll, Joe, 376–77
car travel, 19–20, 301–2
Casbah, The, 104
Cassius Carter Centre Stage, 214–15
Castle Creek Country Club, 272
Catamaran Resort Hotel, 36, 94
Cedros Avenue Shopping and Design Centers, 123–24
Cedros Design District Galleries, 209
Central San Diego
 area overview, 4–6
 art film houses, 213–14
 attractions, 141–48
 bars/brewpubs, 109–11
 classical music, 203–6
 coffeehouses, 112–13
 cultural centers, 214–15
 dance, 206
 film festivals, 206–7
 galleries, 207–9
 golf, 268–71, 275–76, 278
 hotels and motels. *See* Central San Diego hotels and motels
 kidstuff, 159–63
 museums, 211–13
 nightclubs/concert venues, 102–7
 parks, 221–24
 real estate, 312–21
 restaurants. *See* Central San Diego restaurants
 shopping. *See* Central San Diego shopping
 theaters, 215–19
Central San Diego hotels and motels, 35–52
 Beaches and Mission Bay, 35–37
Coronado, 37–41
 Downtown/Gaslamp Quarter, 41–47
 La Jolla/Golden Triangle, 47–49

Mission Valley, 49–51
Old Town, 51
Point Loma/Harbor and Shelter Islands, 52
Central San Diego restaurants, 80–90
Coronado, 80
Downtown/Gaslamp Quarter, 81–84
Hillcrest/Uptown, 84–86
La Jolla/Beaches, 86–87
Mission Valley/Inland, 88–89
Old Town/Point Loma, 89–90
Central San Diego shopping
antiques, 133
bookstores, 128–30
discount/outlet stores, 119–20
districts, 121–23
malls, 115–17
resale/consignment stores, 126–27
swap meets/flea markets, 135
unique/intriguing stores, 136–38
Centro Cultural de la Raza, 173–74, 214
Century 21 National Referral Service, 329–30
Chapman University College, 341
Cheap Rentals, 231–32
Chez Loma, 80
Chicano Perk, 114
Chieu-Anh, 96–97
Chilango's Mexico City Grill, 85
child care, 338–39
children's activities. *See* kidstuff
Children's Hospital and Health Center, 350–51
Children's Pool, 160, 253
Chinese New Year Faire, 186
Chin's Szechwan Restaurant, 92
Chopra Center at La Costa Resort, The, 358
Christian Community Theater, 220
Chuck E Cheese's, 160–61, 163–64, 166, 168, 169
Chuck Jones Studio Gallery, 207
Chula Vista
farmers' market, 125
real estate, 327–28
shopping, 126
Chula Vista Center, 118
Chula Vista Municipal Golf Course, 274–75
Chula Vista Nature Center, 157
Cinco de Mayo, 191
City Ballet School & Company, 206
CityBeat, 366
City Cab, 22
City of San Diego Senior Citizen Services, 362–63
Clairemont
farmers' market, 125
municipal pool, 266
real estate, 320
Clairemont Town Square Shopping Center, 115
Cleveland National Forest, 235
climbing, 235–36
Cloud 9 Shuttle, 17
Club Tropics, 107
Coaster, 23–24
Coast News Group, The, 366
coffeehouses, 112–14
Coffee Merchant, 114
Coldwell Banker Residential Brokerage, 330
Cole Library, 163
Coleman College, 335–36
College Area real estate, 318–19
College Grove real estate, 318–19
colleges. *See* higher education; *specific colleges*
college sports, 290
Comedy Store, The, 104
Comfort Inn, 56
community colleges, 346–48
Community Licensing Board, 338
Community Service Centers, 361
ComputorEdge, 369
Conceptions, 128
concert venues/nightclubs, 102–9
Confidential, 102
Consignment Classics, 126–27
consignment/resale stores, 126–28
Contactours, 150
Contractors Licensing Service, 336
Controversial Bookstore, 129
Coors Amphitheater, 108–9
Coronado
farmers' market, 125
hotels and motels, 37–41
real estate, 321
restaurants, 80
Coronado Brewing Co., 109
Coronado City Beach, 256
Coronado Flower Show Weekend, 189
Coronado Livery, 17
Coronado Municipal Golf Course, 269
Coronado Skate Park, 242–43

Coronado Tennis Association, 244
Corporate Helicopters of San Diego, 150
Cosmopolitan Fine Arts, 207
cost of living, 11–12
Courtyard Marriott San Diego Downtown, 41–42
Cox Communications (San Diego), 370–71
Coyote Bar & Grill, 111
crime, 14
Croce's Restaurant & Jazz Bar, 82–83, 104–5
Crown City Inn, 40
Crudo, 104
Cruisin' Night, 153–54
Crystal Pier Hotel & Cottages, 36
cultural centers, 214–15
Cupid's Carnival, 186
Customs, U.S., 351
Cuyamaca Community College, 346–47
Cuyamaca Rancho State Park, 168, 227–28, 237

D

Dana on Mission Bay, The, 36
dance, 206
Dave & Buster's, 143–44
day trips, 291–99
deserts, 291–93
    Orange County, 293–95
    Temecula, 295–98
    Temecula wine country, 298–99
D.D. Allen Antiques, 133
Deborah's, 128
Deer Park Monastery, 375
Del Cerro real estate, 316
Del Mar
    beaches, 251–52
    farmers' market, 125
    real estate, 322
Del Mar Fair, 165–66, 192
Del Mar Hilton, 53
Del Mar Plaza, 117
Del Mar Thoroughbred Horse Racing, 193, 195, 287–88
demographics, 9–10
Dentist Referral, 351
desert cities, 292–93
desert day trips, 291–93
Desert Walk (Balboa Park), 180
Design Institute of San Diego, 336
Día de la Independencia, 197
Dick's Last Resort, 105
Dirk's Niteclub, 108
Disabled American Veterans Thrift Store, 128
discount/outlet stores, 119–21
Disneyland and Disney's California Adventure, 293–94
Diving Locker, The, 261
Dizzy's, 103
D'lish, 101
Dobson's, 83
Dollar (car rental agency), 17
Domestic Violence Services, 351
Double-Take, 127
Doubletree Golf Resort, 56
Doubletree Hotel Del Mar, 53
Doubletree Hotel San Diego/Mission Valley, 49–50
doula program, 354–55
Downtown
    farmers' market, 125
    hotels and motels, 41–47
    real estate, 313–15
    restaurants, 81–84
Dress to Impress, 127
driving ranges, 278–80
DSW, 119
Dudley's Bakery and Cafe, 98, 139–40
Dussini, 102–3
D.Z. Akin's, 98

E

earthquakes, 14
East County
    area overview, 8
    attractions, 155–56
    bed-and-breakfast inns, 65–66
    coffeehouses, 114
    galleries, 210
    golf, 273–74
    hospitals, 356
    hotels and motels, 58–59
    kidstuff, 168–69
    nightclubs/concert venues, 108
    parks, 227–29
    real estate, 326–27
    restaurants, 98–99
    shopping. *See* East County shopping
    South Bay, 229
    swimming, 266
    theaters, 220
East County Californian, 366–67
East County Family YMCA, 168

East County Performing Arts Center, 220
East County shopping
    bookstores, 132
    discount/outlet stores, 121
    districts, 126
    malls, 118
    resale/consignment stores, 128
    swap meets/flea markets, 136
    unique/intriguing stores, 139–40
Easter egg hunts, 188
Eastlake Country Club, 275
Edelweiss, 101, 112
education, 332–38
    private schools, 333–34
    public schools, 332–33
    vocational/technical schools, 335–38
El Agave, 89
Elario's Bistro & Sky Lounge, 105
El Bizcocho, 94, 97
El Cajon Art Association, 210
El Cajon real estate, 326
elder abuse reporting, 361
Elizabeth Hospice, 358
El Paseo, 293
El Potrero, 308–9
El Rey Sol, 309
Elsbree House, 63
El Toreo de Tijuana, 283–84, 305–6
Embassy Suites Hotel, 42, 47
Emerald City Surf Shop, 263
Emerald Isle Golf Course, 276
emergency phone numbers, 351
Encanto real estate, 318
Enchanted Gallery, 209
Encinitas
    farmers' market, 125
    real estate, 322–23
Encinitas Ranch Golf Course, 271
Encore of La Jolla, 127
Ensenada, Mexico
    accommodations, 305
    nightlife, 308
    restaurants, 309
    shopping, 310
Enterprise Rent-a-Car, 17
ERA Coastal Properties, 77
Escondido
    farmers' market, 125
    real estate, 324
Escondido Drive-In Swap Meet, 135
Escondido Historical Society's Heritage Walk and Grape Day Park, 154
Escondido Municipal Gallery, 209–10
Escondido Sports Center, 243
Estate Sale Warehouse, 134
Estero Beach Resort Hotel, 305
E Street Cafe, 113
Expressions of Mexico, 208

F

Fallbrook Country Inn, 65
Fallbrook Hospital, 354
Fallbrook Hospital District, 358
Fallbrook real estate, 324
Family Christian Store, 129, 133
farmers' markets, 124–25, 298
Fashion Careers of California College, 337
Fashion Valley, 116
Father Joe, 376–77
Ferry Landing Marketplace, 122
Festival Del Mar, 196
Fidel's, 92
Field, The, 83
film
    art film houses, 213–14
    festivals, 206–7
First Night Escondido, 200–201
First Spiritualist Church, 378
First United Methodist Church of San Diego, 377
Fisherman's Landing, 262, 306
Fish House Vera Cruz, 92–93
fishing
    freshwater, 256–57
    Mexico, 306
    sportfishing, 262–63
5 Star Shuttle, 17
Five Star Tours, 302–3
flea markets/swap meets, 135–36
Fletcher Cove, 251
Fletcher Hills Pool, 266
Flower Fields of Carlsbad, 188
football, 284–86
Forum, The, 117
Four Seasons Resort Aviara, 53–54, 68–69, 70–71, 94
Four Seasons Resort Aviara Golf Club, 271–72
4th & B, 105
Fourth of July fireworks/parades, 193
Fredericka Manor, 361
Fred Hall's Fishing, Boat and RV Show, 187
freshwater fishing, 256–57
Fun-4-All, 169

G

galleries, 207-10
Galley at the Marina, The, 112
Gaslamp Books, Prints, & Wyatt Earp Museum, 129-30
Gaslamp Quarter
  attractions, 144
  hotels and motels, 41-47
  nightlife, 102-3
  restaurants, 81-84
shopping, 122
Gaslamp Quarter Easter Bonnet Parade, 188-89
Gaslamp Quarter Walking Tours, 246
Gay & Lesbian Times, 369
General Bead, 140
geographic regions, 4-9. *See also specific regions*
George E. Barnes Tennis Center, 244
George's Cafe & Ocean Terrace, 86
Gibson & Gibson Antique Lighting, 134-35
Gillespie Field, 18
Golden Door, 69
Golden Hill real estate, 315-16
Golden Triangle hotels and motels, 47-49
golf, 268-80
  Central San Diego, 268-71, 275-76
  courses, 268-75
  driving ranges, 278-80
  East County, 273-74
  executive/9-hole courses, 275-78
  Mexico, 306-7
  North County Coastal, 271-72, 276-77
  North County Inland, 272-73, 277-78
  South Bay, 274-75, 278
  spectator sports, 287
government, 9
Grade's Book Nook, 133
Grande Colonial, The, 47
Grantville real estate, 316
Grape Day Festival and Parade, 197
Grape Escape Balloon Adventure, A, 295
Greek Corner Cafe, 93
Greek Festival, 192
Greyhound Bus, 19, 302
Grossmont Center, 118
Grossmont Community College, 347
Grossmont-Cuyamaca Community College District, 346
Grossmont Hospital, 356
GTM Discount General Store, 121
Guadalupe, 310
Guajome County Park, 224, 257

H

Halloween festivals/haunted houses, 198
Handlery Hotel & Resort, 50
H&M Sportfishing, 263
hang gliding, 236
Hansen's Surf & Ski, 263-64
Happy Trails, 238
Harbor Island hotels and motels, 52
Harbor Police, 351
Harbor Sailboats, 260
Harbor Tours, 150-51
Harmon Homes, 331
Harrah's Rincon Casino & Resort, 154
Hart Winery, 298
health and wellness, 350-58
  alternative care, 357-58
  hospice care, 358
  hospitals, 350-56
  immediate-care facilities, 357
  mental health services, 356-57
Hearts & Hands Volunteer Doula Program, 354-55
Heritage of the Americas Museum, 156
Heritage Park Bed & Breakfast Inn, 63
Heritage Park Village and Museum, 149
Hertz, 17
Hidden Valley Antique Emporium, 134
higher education, 340-49
  community colleges, 346-48
  extended-studies programs, 348-49
  four-year universities/colleges, 340-44
  law schools, 345-46
high school sports, 290
Highway Patrol (State Police), 351
highways, 20-22
Hike Bike Kayak San Diego, 232, 259
hiking/walking, 236-38, 246
Hillcrest
  farmers' market, 124-25
  real estate, 319
  restaurants, 84-86
  shopping, 122
Hillcrest Cinemas, 213
Hilton San Diego Airport, 52
Hilton San Diego Gaslamp Quarter, 42
Hilton San Diego Resort, 36
history, 27-33
History Walk (Balboa Park), 180
Holiday Inn Carlsbad-by-the-Sea, 54

Holiday Inn Express, 51, 56, 60
Holiday Inn on the Bay, 42
holiday parades/celebrations, 200
homes. *See* real estate
Home Security Checks, 361
Hornblower Cruises & Events, 148, 1 50–51
horseback riding, 238
horse racing, 287–88
Horton Grand Hotel, 42–43
Horton Grand Theatre, 215, 218
Horton Square farmers' market, 125
hospice care, 358
Hospice of North Coast, 358
hospitals, 350–56
Hostelling International Point Loma, 36–37
Hostelling International-USA, San Diego, 43
Hotel del Coronado, 38–41, 94
Hotel Lucerna, 304
Hotel Parisi, 47
hotels and motels, 34–60
  Central San Diego, 35–52
  East County, 58–59
  North County Coastal, 52–56
  North County Inland, 56–58
  South Bay, 60
Hotel Solamar, 43
House of Blues, 105
House of Heirlooms, 133
House of Pacific Relations, 174
Humphrey's, 94, 105–6
Humphrey's Half Moon Inn, 52
Hungry Stick, The, 232
Hussong's Cantina, 308
Hyatt Regency La Jolla, 47–48
hydroplane/powerboat racing, 288

I

Iceoplex, 238–39
ice-skating, 238–39
Ice Town, 238
IKEA, 137
Imperial Beach, 256
Imperial Beach real estate, 328
In Cahoots, 106
Independence University, 337
Indian Fair, 191–92
industry/jobs, 10–11
Inez Grant Parker Memorial Rose Garden/Desert Garden, 174
Inn at Sunset Cliffs, 37
insurance, Mexican auto, 301–2
Interfaith Shelter Network, 375
International Dance Festival, 185
International Teddy Bear, Doll, and Toy Festival, 184
Interstate 5, 20
Interstate 8, 20
Interstate 15, 21
Interstate 805, 21
Islandia Sportfishing, 148

J

Jake's Del Mar, 93
Jamboree by the Sea, 185–86
Jamul real estate, 326
Japanese Friendship Garden, 174
jet skiing/windsurfing/waterskiing, 266–67
Jewish Family Service Senior Services, 363
jobs/industry, 10–11
Joe, Father, 376–77
Joe and Mary Mottino YMCA, 164
Joltin' Joes, 232
J Street Inn, 44
Julian Fall Apple Harvest, 196
Julian Grille, 98
Julian Main Street Shopping District, 126
Julian real estate, 327
J.W. Tumbles, 161, 164, 167, 168–69

K

Kaiser Permanente Medical Care Center, 351–52
Karen Krasne's Extraordinary Desserts, 85
Karl Strauss Brewery & Grill, 93, 109
Kate O. Sessions Memorial Park, 222
kayaking/canoeing/wave riding, 257–59
Kearny Mesa Bowl, 233
Kearny Mesa real estate, 317
Keating House, 63–64
Kemo Sabe, 85–86
Ken Cinema, 213–14
Kensington Club, 109
Kensington Grill, 88
Kensington real estate, 318
kidstuff, 159–70
  Central San Diego, 159–63
  East County, 168–69
  North County Coastal, 163–66

North County Inland, 166–68
South Bay, 169–70
Knott's Soak City USA, 157–58, 169–70
Kobey's Swap Meet, 135
Krause Family Skate Park, 243

L

L.A. Cetto Winery, 306
La Casa del Zorro Desert Resort, 59
La Costa Coffee Roasting, 113
La Costa real estate, 321–22
La Costa Resort and Spa, 54–55, 71–73, 358
Laguna Campground (Cleveland National Forest), 235
Laguna Mountain Recreation Area, 228
La Jolla
farmers' market, 124
hotels and motels, 47–49
real estate, 317
restaurants, 86–87
shopping, 122–23
La Jolla Beach & Tennis Club, 48
La Jolla Beach Travelodge, 48
La Jolla Children's Pool, 160, 253
La Jolla Country Day School, 334
La Jolla Cove, 252–53
La Jolla Light, 367
La Jolla Music Society, 203
La Jolla Playhouse, 216–17, 218
La Jolla Shores Beach, 252
La Jolla Tennis Club, 244
La Jolla Village Square, 119
La Jolla YMCA Day Camps, 161–62
Lake Cuyamaca, 257
Lake Hodges, 225
Lake Miramar, 257
Lake Morena County Park, 228, 257
Lake Murray, 257
Lake Murray Tennis Club, 244
Lake Poway Recreation Area, 225, 257
Lake San Marcos Resort & Country Club, 56–57
Lakeside real estate, 326
Lake Wohlford Cafe, 97
Lamb's Players Theatre, 218
La Mesa Ocean Grill, 98
La Mesa Racquetball, 242
La Mesa real estate, 327
La Mesa Shopping District, 126
La Mesa Village farmers' market, 125
Lamplighter, The, 110
La Paloma (film house), 214
La Paloma Restaurante, 97
La Pensione Hotel, 44
La Prensa San Diego, 369
La Quinta Inn Chula Vista, 60
La Quinta Inn San Diego Old Town, 51
Las Cuatro Milpas, 83
Laser Storm, 241
laser tag, 239, 241
Las Rocas Hotel, 304
L'Auberge Resort and Spa, 54–55, 69–71
Laurel Travel Center, 17
La Valencia, 49
Lavender Fields, The, 189
Lawrence Family Jewish Community Centers, 377–78
law schools, 345–46
LEGOLAND California, 149–50, 164–65
Lesbian and Gay Celebration, 195
Lestat's Coffeehouse, 112
Leucadia
farmers' market, 125
real estate, 323
library services for seniors, 361
Linda Vista real estate, 320
Lindbergh Field, 15–16
Living Desert Zoo and Gardens, 293
Living Room, The, 112–13
Local Authors Exhibit, 184
Lodge at Torrey Pines, The, 49
Loehmann's, 119
Loews Coronado Bay Resort, 41, 73, 94, 339
Logan Heights real estate, 318
Longboard Grotto Surf Shop, 264
Los Peñasquitos Canyon Preserve, 225–26, 237
Lowell Davies Festival Theatre, 214–15

M

Maderas Golf Club, 272
magazines, 331, 368
Magdalena Ecke YMCA, 165
Magdalena Ecke YMCA Skatepark, 243
Mainly Mozart Festival, 192–93, 203
Malashock Dance & Co., 206
malls, 115–18
Manchester Grand Hyatt San Diego, 44–45
Mardi Gras in the Gaslamp, 186
Marian Bear Memorial Park, 222
Marie Callender's, 94

Marie Hitchcock Puppet Theater, 162, 175
Marine Corps Air Station Miramar Air Show, 198
Marine Gear Swap Meet, 187
Marine Room, 86-87
Marine Street Beach, 253
Mario's de La Mesa, 99
Marriott Mission Valley, 50
Marshalls Department Store, 120
Martin Luther King Jr. Day Parade, 184
Mary's Tack & Feed, 139
McClellan-Palomar Airport, 18-19
McNally Company Antiques, 134
McP's Irish Pub and Grill, 110
Meadows Del Mar, The, 272
Meals-on-Wheels, 361, 363
media, 365-72
- magazines, 368
- newspapers, 365-68
- radio, 371-72
- special-interest publications, 369-70
- television, 370-71

Medieval Times, 294-95
Mental Health Hot Line, 351
mental health services, 356-57
Meritage Restaurant & Bar, 93
Metropolitan Transit System, 22-23
Mexico, 300-310
- accommodations, 304-5
- attractions, 305-6
- auto insurance, 301-2
- fishing, 306
- golf, 306-7
- nightlife, 307-8
- restaurants, 308-9
- transportation, 301-3

Mexicoach, 302
Michael J. Wolf Fine Arts, 208
Midnight Madness Spring Bicycle Ride, 196
Mille Fleurs Restaurant, 93, 95
Mingei International Museum, 175, 211, 213
MiraCosta Community College, 347
Miramar Reservoir, 222
Mira Mesa Lanes, 233-34
Mira Mesa real estate, 319
Misión San Luis Rey de Francia, 150-52
Mission Bay Golf Course, 276
Mission Bay hotels and motels, 35-37
Mission Bay Park, 222-23
Mission Bay Park beaches, 255
Mission Beach, 254-55
Mission Beach real estate, 313
Mission Hills real estate, 319
Mission San Juan Capistrano, 294
Mission Trails Golf Course, 269
Mission Trails Regional Park, 223, 237
Mission Valley
- hotels and motels, 49-51
- restaurants, 88-89

Mission Valley Resort, 50
Mission Valley YMCA, 162
Model Railroad Museum, 175
Monster Bash, 198
Montessori schools, 334
Montgomery Field, 18
Moonlight Amphitheater, 219
Moonlight State Beach, 250
Morrison Hotel, 208
Motel 6, 59
motels. *See* hotels and motels
Mother Goose Parade, 169, 199
motocross racing, 288-89
mountain biking/bicycling, 231-32
Mr. Paintball, 241-42
MS Walk, 188
Museum of Contemporary Art, 211
Museum of Photographic Arts, 175-76, 211-12
Museum of San Diego History, 176
museums, 210-13
Museum Shops of Balboa Park, 137
music, classical, 203-6
My Bridal Gown, 140
My Own Space, 137
Mystery Cafe, 218

N

National Association of Hispanic Elderly, 363
National (car rental agency), 17
National City Golf Course, 278
National City Mile of Cars, 140
National City real estate, 328
National City Swap Meet, 136
National Park Service, 224
National University, 341
Nestor real estate, 329
New Lifestyles, 364
newspapers, 365-68
nightclubs/concert venues, 102-9
nightlife, 102-14
- bars/brewpubs, 109-12
- coffeehouses, 112-14

Mexico, 307–8
nightclubs/concert venues, 102–9
94th Aero Squadron, 94
99 Ranch Market, 137
Nordstrom Rack, 119
Normal Heights real estate, 318
North Beach, 251
North Coast Repertory Theatre, 219
North County Coastal
area overview, 6–8
art film houses, 213–14
attractions, 148–53
bars/brewpubs, 111
bed-and-breakfast inns, 64–65
coffeehouses, 113
cultural centers, 215
galleries, 209
golf, 271–72, 276–77, 279
hospitals, 353–54
hotels and motels, 52–56
kidstuff, 163–66
museums, 213
nightclubs/concert venues, 107
parks, 224–25
real estate, 321–24
restaurants, 90–93, 95–96
shopping. *See* North County Coastal shopping
swimming, 266
theaters, 219
North County Coastal shopping
antiques, 134
bookstores, 130–31
discount/outlet stores, 120
districts, 123–26
malls, 117–18
resale/consignment stores, 127–28
swap meets/flea markets, 135
unique/intriguing stores, 138–39
North County Cycle Club, 232
North County Inland
area overview, 8
attractions, 153–55
bars/brewpubs, 111–12
bed-and-breakfast inns, 65
coffeehouses, 113
cultural centers, 215
galleries, 209–10
golf, 272–73, 277–78, 279
hospitals, 354–56
hotels and motels, 56–58
kidstuff, 166–68
museums, 213
nightclubs/concert venues, 107–8
parks, 225–26
real estate, 324–26
restaurants, 96–97
shopping. *See* North County Inland shopping
swimming, 266
theaters, 219–20
North County Inland shopping
antiques, 134
bookstores, 131–32
discount/outlet stores, 120
districts, 126
malls, 118
resale/consignment stores, 128
swap meets/flea markets, 135
unique/intriguing stores, 139
North County Times, 365
North County Transit District, 23
North Pacific Beach, 254
North Park real estate, 318

N

Oaks North Golf Course, 277
Obon Summer Festival, 195
Ocean Beach, 255
farmers' market, 125
real estate, 313
Ocean Beach Antique Mall, 133
Ocean Beach Kite Festival, 187
Ocean Beach Shopping, 123
Ocean Enterprises, 261
Oceanside
beaches, 249
farmers' market, 125
real estate, 323
Oceanside Drive-In Swap Meet, 135
Oceanside Harbor, 152
Oceanside Marina Suites, 55
Oceanside Municipal Airport, 18
Oceanside Museum of Art, 152, 215
Oceanside Pier, 152
O.E. Express, 262
OE Express Dive & Kayak Center, 261
Offshore Surf Shop, 264
Oktoberfests, 198
Old California Coffee House, 113
Old Globe Theatres, The, 176, 214–15
Old Town
hotels and motels, 51
restaurants, 89–90

Old Town Holiday in the Park and Candlelight Tours, 200
Old Town Mexican Cafe, 89–90
Old Town State Historic Park, 144–45
Old Town Trolley Tours, 151
Olympic Resort Hotel & Spa, 279
Omni San Diego, 45
On Broadway, 106
101 Artists' Colony, 209
Onstage Playhouse, 220
Onyx/Thin, 106
Orange County day trips, 293–95
Orchard Hill Country Inn, 65
Orchid Source, 139
Ortega's, 309
Otay Mesa real estate, 328–29
outlet/discount stores, 119–21
Over the Border, 109
Over-the-Line World Championships, 195, 289

P

Pace Realty, 77
Pacific Beach, 254–55
  farmers' market, 125
  real estate, 313
Pacific College of Oriental Medicine, 338
Pacific Life Holiday Bowl, 200, 284–85
Pacific Q Billiards Club, 233
paintball, 241–42
Pala Casino Resort & Spa, 57
Pala Mesa Resort, 57, 272–73
Pala Mission Fiesta, 193
Palm Canyon, 172
Palm Canyon Resort, 59
Palm Springs, 292–93
Palm Springs Aerial Tramway, 292
Palm Springs Art Museum, 293
Palm Springs Celebrity Tours, 292
Palm Walk (Balboa Park), 180
Palomar Community College, 347
Palomar Medical Center, 355
Palomar Mountain State Park, 226
Palomar Observatory, 154
Pannikin, The, 113
Papas & Beer, 308
Paperback Book Exchange, 131
Paradise Hills real estate, 318
Paradise Point Resort & Spa, 37
Paradise Valley Hospital, 356
Park and Ride Co., 17
parks, 221–29
  Central San Diego, 221–24
  East County, 227–29
  North County Coastal, 224–25
  North County Inland, 225–26
  South Bay, 229
Parkway Bowl, 234
Parkway Pool, 266
Patio Playhouse Community Theater, 219–20
Patrick's II, 106
Pegleg Smith Liars Contest, 189
Pelican Cove Bed and Breakfast Inn, 64–65
Penguin Day Ski Fest, 183
Pennant, The, 110
Penny Property Management, 77–78
Pepper Grove, 176
performance venues, 213–20
  art film houses, 213–14
  cultural centers, 214–15
  theaters, 215–20
Petco Park, 284–85
Pine Hills Lodge, 59
Pinnacle Peak Steak House, 99
Pizza Nova, 90
Pizza Port, 95, 111
Platt College, 338
Play It Again Sports, 262
Plaza del Pasado, 123
Plaza Fiesta, 307–8
Plaza Rio Tijuana, 310
Point Loma
  farmers' market, 125
  hotels and motels, 52
  real estate, 320–21
  restaurants, 89–90
Point Loma Nazarene University, 341–42
Point Loma Seafoods, 90
Point Loma Sportfishing, 263
Poison Center, 351
polo, 289
Pomerado Hospital, 355–56
Pomerado Newspaper Group, 367
pools, municipal, 266
Portuguese Festa, 191
Posada El Rey Sol, 305
Poway
  farmers' market, 125
  real estate, 325
Poway Center for the Performing Arts, 210, 215

powerboating/sailing, 259-60
powerboat racing, 288
Prego, 88
Presidio Park, 223
private schools, 333-34
Prontos' Gourmet Market, 95
Prudential California Realty, 330
publications
  home-buying magazine, 331
  magazines, 368
  newspapers, 365-68
  senior, 364
  special-interest, 369-70
public schools, 332-33
public transportation, 22-25

Q

Quail Botanical Gardens, 152-53
Quails Inn, 94
Qualcomm Stadium, 281-82

R

racquetball, 242
radio, 371-72
Radisson Knott's Berry Farm and Knott's Soak City USA, 295
Radisson Suite Hotel, 57
railroad history, 29-30. *See also* trains
Ramona real estate, 327
Rancho Bernardo
  farmers' market, 125
  real estate, 325
Rancho Bernardo Inn, 57-58, 94
Rancho California Sports Park, 296-97
Rancho Carlsbad, 276-77
Rancho La Puerta, 73-75
Rancho Peñasquitos real estate, 325
Rancho Santa Fe Garden Club Rummage Sale, 190
Rancho Santa Fe real estate, 323
Rancho Valencia Resort, 55-56, 74
Real Del Mar Golf Resort, 307
real estate, 311-31
  apartments, 330-31
  Central San Diego, 312-21
  East County, 326-27
  home-buying magazine, 331
  national offices, 329-30
  North County Coastal, 321-24
  North County Inland, 324-26
  South Bay, 327-29
  wildfires, 314-15
recreation, 230-46
  ballooning/biplanes, 230-31
  bicycle clubs, 232
  bicycling/mountain biking, 231-32
  billiards, 232-33
  bowling, 233-34
  camping, 234-35
  climbing, 235-36
  hang gliding, 236
  hiking, 236-38
  horseback riding, 238
  ice-skating, 238-39
  laser tag, 239, 241
  paintball, 241-42
  racquetball, 242
  skating/skateboarding, 242-44
  tennis, 244-45
  volleyball, 245-46
  walking/hiking, 246
Red Fox Room, 110
Red Lion Hanalei Hotel, 51
Red Lion National City, 60
Red Pearl Kitchen, 83-84
regions, 4-9. *See also specific regions*
Reidy Creek Golf Course, 277-78
REI (Recreational Equipment, Inc.), 259
relocation. *See* real estate
RE/MAX Realtors, 330
rental car agencies, 16-17
rentals, vacation, 75-78
resale/consignment stores, 126-28
resorts/spas, 67-74
Resort Watersports, 259, 260
Restaurant Row, 108
restaurants, 79-101
  Central San Diego, 80-90
  East County, 98-99
  Mexico, 308-9
  North County Coastal, 90-93, 95-96
  North County Inland, 96-97
  South Bay, 100-101
Retired Senior Volunteer Patrol, 361
retirement, 359-64
housing options, 359-62
resources, 361
  senior centers, 363-64
  senior organizations, 362-63
  senior publications, 364
Reuben H. Fleet Space Theater and Science Center, 176-77
Reuben's, 94
Rhinoceros Cafe, 80

Riverwalk Golf Club, 269
roadways, 20–22
Roar and Snore Sleepovers, 167
Robb Field Skate Park, 243–44
Robert Burns Supper, 184
Romance World, 132
Romano's Dodge House, 99
Ronald Reagan Sports Park, 296–97
Rosarito, Mexico
  accommodations, 304–5
  nightlife, 308
  shopping, 310
Rosarito Beach, Mexico restaurant, 309
Rosarito Beach Hotel & Spa, 304–5
Rosarito-Ensenada 50-Mile Fun, 197
Rose Pruning Demonstration, 184
Rose Society Annual Show, 190

S

Sacred Pathway, 131
safety, personal, 14
Saffron Noodles and Saté/Saffron Thai Chicken, 86
Saffron Thai Chicken, 86
sailing/powerboating, 259–60
Saint Patrick's Day Parade, 187
San Carlos real estate, 316
SANDAG (San Diego Association of Governments), 12–13
San Diego Aerospace Museum, 177
San Diego Aircraft Carrier Museum, 145–46
SanDiegoApartments.com, 330–31
San Diego Art Institute, 208, 212
San Diego Association of Governments (SANDAG), 12–13
San Diego Automotive Museum, 177–78
San Diego Bicycle Club, 232
San Diego Bicycle Touring Society, 232
San Diego Brewing Co., 110
San Diego Buddhist Temple, 375, 377
San Diego Business Journal, 367
San Diego Cab, 22
San Diego Chamber Orchestra, 203–4
San Diego Chargers, 285–86
San Diego Christian College, 342
San Diego City College, 347–48
San Diego Civic Youth Orchestra, 204
San Diego Community College District, 347
San Diego Community Newspaper Group, 367
San Diego Concourse Convention and Performing Arts Center, 214
San Diego-Coronado Bay Bridge, 24
San Diego-Coronado Ferry, 24–25
San Diego County bed-and-breakfast inns, 62–64
San Diego County Fair, 165–66, 192
San Diego County Parks, 224
San Diego County Routes, 22
San Diego Crew Classic, 188
San Diego Daily Transcript, 366
San Diego de Alcalá Mission, 146
San Diego Eldercare Directory, 364
San Diego Family Magazine, 369
San Diego Hall of Champions Sports Museum, 178
San Diego Harbor Excursion, 150–51
San Diego Home/Garden Lifestyles, 368
San Diego Hospice & Palliative Care, 358
San Diego Ice Arena, 239
San Diego International Airport/Lindbergh Field, 15–16
San Diego International Auto Show, 200
San Diego International Film Festival, 206
San Diego Jewish Film Festival, 206–7
San Diego Junior Theatre, 162–63
San Diego Latino Film Festival, 207
San Diego Magazine, 368
San Diego Maritime Museum, 146
San Diego Marriott Del Mar, 56
San Diego Master Chorale, 204
San Diego Mesa College, 348
San Diego Metropolitan Magazine, 368
San Diego Miramar College, 348
San Diego Museum of Art, 178, 212
San Diego Museum of Man, 178
San Diego Natural History Museum, 179
San Diego Opera, 204
San Diego Padres, 282–83
San Diego Parent, 369–70
San Diego Polo Club, 289
San Diego Reader, The, 367–68
San Diego Repertory Theatre, 218
San Diego Scenic Tours, 303
San Diego State University, 286, 342–43
San Diego State University College of Extended Studies, 349
San Diego Symphony, 204–5
San Diego Trolley, 24
San Diego Union-Tribune, 365–66
San Diego Vacation Cottages, 78
San Diego Vacation Rentals, 78

San Diego Voice and Viewpoint, 370
San Diego Water Taxi, 25
San Diego Wild Animal Park, 154–55, 163
San Diego Workout, 242
San Diego Youth Symphony, 205
San Diego Zoo, 154–55, 163, 179–81
San Dieguito Half Marathon, 185
sand softball, 289
San Elijo Lagoon Ecological Reserve, 224, 237–38
San Elijo State Beach, 250–51
San Luis Rey Downs, 273
San Marcos Brewery & Grill, 111–12
San Marcos real estate, 325
San Onofre State Beach, 248–49
San Pasqual Battlefield State Historic Park and Museum, 226
Santee Lakes Regional Park, 228–29
Santee real estate, 326
San Ysidro real estate, 328–29
Sara, 310
Saska's, 87
schools, 332–38
  private, 333–34
  public, 332–33
  vocational/technical, 335–38
Scott White Contemporary Art, 208
Scream Zone, The, 198
Scripps Inn, 64
Scripps Memorial Hospital, Chula Vista, 356
Scripps Memorial Hospital, Encinitas, 353
Scripps Memorial Hospital, La Jolla, 352
Scripps Ranch
  farmers' market, 125
  real estate, 319–20
scuba diving, 260–61
Sea Breeze Shuttle, 17
Seaforth Boat Rental, 267
Seaforth Sportfishing, 148, 263
SEAL: Sea and Land Adventure, 151
Sea Lodge, 49
Seaport Village, 123, 147
Seaside Bazaar, 135
Seau's: The Restaurant, 88–89
SeaWorld, 146–47
Self-Realization Fellowships, 377
senior centers, 363–64
senior housing options, 359–62
senior organizations, 362–63
senior publications, 364
senior resources, 361
Senior Services Centers, 361
Señor Frog, 308
Sergio's Sportfishing Center, 306
Serra Mesa real estate, 317
Sevilla, 84, 106–7
Shades, 87
Sharp Chula Vista Medical Center, 356
Sharp Coronado Hospital, 352
Sharp Mary Birch Hospital for Women, 352
Sharp Memorial Hospital, 352–53
Sharp Mesa Vista Hospital, 357
Shelter Island hotels and motels, 52
Shoe Pavilion, 119–20, 121
shopping, 115–40
  antiques, 133–35
  bookstores, 128–33
  discount/outlet stores, 119–21
  districts, 121–26
  farmers' markets, 124–25
  malls, 115–18
  resale/consignment stores, 126–28
  swap meets/flea markets, 135–36
  unique/intriguing stores, 136–40
Sierra Club, 246
Silver Bay Kennel Club Dog Show, 166, 186
Silver Cab, 22
Silver Strand State Beach, 256
Simon Edison Centre for the Performing Arts, 214–15
skating/skateboarding, 242–44, 296–97
Skysurfer Balloon Co., 230–31
snorkeling, 261–62
Society Billiard Cafe, 233
softball, sand, 289
Solana Beach
  farmers' market, 124
  real estate, 323–24
Solid Rock, 236
Sorrento Valley real estate, 320
Soulscape, 131
South Bay
  area overview, 8–9
  attractions, 157–58
  bars/brewpubs, 112
  golf, 274–75, 278, 279–80
  hospitals, 356
  hotels and motels, 60
  kidstuff, 169–70
  nightclubs/concert venues, 108–9
  parks, 229
  real estate, 327–29
  restaurants, 100–101

shopping. *See* South Bay shopping
swimming, 266
theaters, 220
South Bay shopping
antiques, 134–35
bookstores, 132–33
discount/outlet stores, 121
districts, 126
malls, 118
resale/consignment stores, 128
swap meets/flea markets, 136
unique/intriguing stores, 140
South Carlsbad State Beach, 235, 250
South Coast Surf Shop, 264
South Mission Beach, 254–55
south of the border. *See* Mexico
Southwestern College Tennis Center, 244–45
Southwestern Community College, 348
Spanish Village Art Center, 181, 208
spas/resorts, 67–74
spectator sports, 281–90
auto racing, 282
baseball, 282–83
bullfighting, 283–84
college/high school, 290
football, 284–86
golf, 287
horse racing, 287–88
hydroplane/powerboat racing, 288
motocross racing, 288–89
polo, 289
sand softball, 289
tennis, 290
Spike & Mike's Sick and Twisted Festival of Animation, 207
sportfishing, 262–63
Spreckels, John D., 30
Spreckels Organ Pavilion, 181–82
Spring Harvest Gift and Food Festival, 187
Spring Valley real estate, 327
Spring Valley Swap Meet, 136
St. Germain's Cafe, 95
St. Vincent De Paul's Village, 375
Stadium Golf Center, 278
Starlings, 245–46
Starlite Theatre, 205–6
State Police, 351
State Street Stores, 125–26
statistics, 6–7
Steele Canyon Golf and Country Club, 274
Stephen Birch Aquarium-Museum, 147
Stephen Clayton Galleries, 208–9
Stingaree, 103
Street Scene, 196–97
Suicide Hotline, 351
Summers Past Farms, 140
Summer Sports Camps, 163
Sun Diego Surf & Sport, 264–65
Sunset Cliffs Park, 255–56
Super 8 Motel, 58
surfing, 263–65
surfing contests, 191
Surf Ride Board Shop, 265
Surf & Turf Driving Range, 279
Sushi Deli 2, 84
Sushi Performance Gallery, 218–19
Swami's, 250
Swanson, Mary Catherine, 336–37
Swanson municipal pool, 266
swap meets/flea markets, 135–36
Sweetwater Regional Park, 229, 235
swimming, 265–66
Sycuan Resort and Casino, 108, 156
Sycuan Resort Golf Courses, 273–74

T

Talmadge real estate, 318
Taoist Sanctuary of San Diego, 377
Taste of Gaslamp, A, 192
taxis, 22
Tecate Score Baja 1000, 198–99
technical/vocational schools, 335–38
Tecolote Canyon Golf Course, 276
Tecolote Canyon Natural Park, 223–24
television, 370–71
Temecula Creek Inn, 298
Temecula day trips, 295–98
Temecula Valley Balloon & Wine Festival, 295
Temecula Valley Winegrower's Association, 298
Temecula wine country day trips, 298–99
tennis, 244–45, 290
That Pizza Place, 95–96
theaters, 215–20
Theatre in Old Town, 219
Thee Bungalow, 87
Thomas Jefferson School of Law, 345–46
Thornton Winery, 298–99

Thunderbird Driving Range & Training Center, 279
Thunderboats Unlimited, 288
Tide Beach, 251
Tierrasanta
- municipal pool, 266
- real estate, 316

Tijuana, Mexico
- accommodations, 304
- nightlife, 307–8
- restaurants, 308–9
- shopping, 309–10

Tijuana Cultural Center, 306
Tijuana River National Estuary Research Reserve, 229
Time Warner Cable, 371
Timken Museum of Art, 182, 212–13
Tomatoes, 94
Top of the Hyatt Lounge, 110
Torrey Pines Gliderport (Air California Adventures), 236
Torrey Pines Golf Course, 270–71
Torrey Pines real estate, 317
Torrey Pines State Beach, 252
Torrey Pines State Reserve, 224–25
Torrey Pines Transfer, 17
Tour del Dia (Balboa Park), 180
Tourmaline Surfing Park, 254
tours
- Balboa Park, 180
- Mexico, 302–3
- transportational, 150–51

Tower 23, 37
Town & Country Hotel, 51
trains, 19
transportation, 15–26
- air travel, 15–19
- bus travel, 19
- car travel, 19–22
- Mexico, 25–26, 301–3
- public transportation, 22–25
- taxis, 22
- tours, 150–51
- trains, 19

Trattoria Positano, 96
Travelodge El Cajon, 59
Tree Walk (Balboa Park), 180
Tri-City Medical Center, 353–54
Trophy's Sports Grill, 89, 110
Twiggs Green Room, 113
Two Sisters Consignment Home Furnishing, 128

U

UCSD Medical Center at Hillcrest, 353, 354–55
UFO-Upholstery Fabric Outlet, 120, 121
Ultrazone, 241
Union-Tribune Run/Walk for Literacy, 190
universities. *See* higher education; *specific universities*
University City real estate, 320
University Heights real estate, 319
University of California, San Diego, 125, 343
University of California, San Diego, Extended Studies and Public Programs, 349
University of San Diego, 344–45
University of San Diego School of Law, 346
Upstart Crow Bookstore & Coffee House, 130
Uptown restaurants, 84–86
U.S. Customs, 351
U.S. Grant Hotel, 45–46
U.S. interstate highways, 20–21
U.S. Open Sand Castle Competition, 195
USDA Forest Service, 224

V

vacation rentals, 75–78
Vagabond Inn Point Loma, 52
Valley Center real estate, 324
Van Roekel Vineyards & Winery, 299
Vertical Hold Climbing Center, 236
Victoria Rock Bed and Breakfast Inn, 65–66
Viejas Casino & Turf Club, 99, 108, 156
Viejas Outlet Center, 121
Vietnamese Tet Festival, 186
Village Garden Restaurant & Bakery, 99
Vincent's Sirinos Restaurant, 97
Vinge Antiques, 134
Vista
- farmers' market, 125
- real estate, 325

Vista Terrace municipal pool, 266
Visual Arts at the California Center for the Arts, The, 213
vital statistics, 6–7
Vivace, 96
vocational/technical schools, 335–38
Voice of San Diego, 368
volleyball, 245–46

W

Wahrenbrock's Book House, 130
Waldenbooks, 132
Walkabout International, 246
walking/hiking, 236–38, 246
Walter Andersen's Nursery, 137–38
Warwick's, 130
Waterfront, The, 111
waterskiing/jet skiing/windsurfing, 266–67
water sports, 256–67
  freshwater fishing, 256–57
  kayaking/canoeing/wave riding, 257–59
  sailing/powerboating, 259–60
  scuba diving, 260–61
  snorkeling, 261–62
  sportfishing, 262–63
  surfing, 263–65
  swimming, 265–66
waterskiing/jet skiing/windsurfing, 266–67
wave riding/kayaking/canoeing, 257–59
Wave Waterpark, The, 155, 167
Wax Museum, 306
Wear It Again Sam, 127
weather, 12–14
Weidners' Gardens, 139
Welk Resort Center, 58, 220, 278
wellness. *See* health and wellness
Wentworth Gallery, 209
Westfield Shoppingtown Horton Plaza, 116
Westfield Shoppingtown Mission Valley, 116–17
Westfield Shoppingtown Mission Valley Center West, 120
Westfield Shoppingtown North County, 118
Westfield Shoppingtown Parkway Plaza, 118
Westfield Shoppingtown Plaza Bonita, 118
Westfield Shoppingtown Plaza Camino Real, 117–18
Westfield Shoppingtown University Towne Center, 117
Westgate Hotel, 46–47, 94
whale watching, 148
Whale Watch Weekend, 184
Whaling Bar, 111
White House Black Market, The, 138
White Sands of La Jolla, The, 362
Whole Foods, 138
wildfires, 314–15
Windansea Beach, 253
Windsport, 259
windsurfing/waterskiing/jet skiing, 266–67
Winston's Beach Club, 107
Witt's Carlsbad Pipelines, 265
Women's Resource Center, 24-hour help line, 351
Woodland Park Aquatic Complex, 266
World Body Surfing Championships, 196
worship, 373–78
  cultural activities, 375, 377–78
  history, 374
  humanitarian activities, 375
  services, 373–74
W San Diego, 45

X

Xpress Shuttle, 17

Y

Yellow Book Road, 132
Yellow Cab, 22
YMCA, 167–68
YMCA Childcare Resources Service, 339

Z

Zoro Gardens, 182

ABOUT THE AUTHORS

MARIBETH MELLIN

Maribeth Mellin is an award-winning journalist who has been covering San Diego for more than two decades. Like many San Diegans, she is a transplant from the East Coast, having moved to San Diego from Washington D.C., in 1976. She's most definitely content to be called a Southern Californian. Maribeth developed her knowledge of the inner workings and far-flung regions of the county as senior editor at *San Diego Magazine.* In the role of travel editor, she covered vacation destinations around the globe and was always delighted to return to her home in San Diego. Her articles on social, legal, and medical issues have garnered her more than two dozen awards from journalism organizations. Her travel books on California, Mexico, and other Latin American countries have also received commendations, and she is the recipient of the prestigious Pluma de Plata award for her coverage of Mexico.

JANE ONSTOTT

Jane Onstott is a professional editor, travel writer, and translator. She moved to San Diego in 1976 to attend San Diego State University, where she received a B.A. in Spanish language and literature. She tempers her adulation for America's Finest City with frequent forays to Spanish-speaking countries and has worked in Oaxaca, Mexico, where she studied fine art as well. Previously, she worked as public relations director for the Charles Darwin Research Station on the Galapagos Islands, off the coast of Ecuador.

She's written for many years about Mexico and South America for Fodor's Travel Publications and worked with coauthor Maribeth Mellin on *Travelers Companion to Mexico, The Unofficial Guide to Mexico's Beach Resorts,* and *Access Mexico.* Jane's travel guide, *National Geographic Traveler Mexico,* was published in 2006 by the National Geographic Society. She has contributed her knowledge of San Diego to various guidebooks.

HELP US KEEP THIS GUIDE UP TO DATE

Every effort has been made by the authors and editors to make this guide as accurate and useful as possible. However, many things can change after a guide is published—establishments close, phone numbers change, hiking trails are rerouted, facilities come under new management, etc.

We would love to hear from you concerning your experiences with this guide and how you feel it could be improved and be kept up to date. While we may not be able to respond to all comments and suggestions, we'll take them to heart, and we'll also make certain to share them with the authors. Please send your comments and suggestions to the following address:

The Globe Pequot Press
Reader Response/Editorial Department
P. O. Box 480
Guilford, CT 06437

Or you may e-mail us at:

editorial@GlobePequot.com

Thanks for your input, and happy travels!